And Did Those Feet

The Story and Character of the
English Church AD 200–2020

— PATRICK WHITWORTH —

Sacristy
Press

Sacristy Press
PO Box 612, Durham, DH1 9HT

www.sacristy.co.uk

First published in 2021 by Sacristy Press, Durham

Sacristy Limited, registered in England & Wales, number 7565667

British Library Cataloguing-in-Publication Data
A catalogue record for the book is available from the British Library

ISBN 978-1-78959-151-4

To our grandchildren—at present Rory, Eliza, James, George, Molly and Lauren—that they too might appreciate this story.

Contents

Preface

It is forty years since a previous history of the church in England was published by David Edwards, in three volumes. This is a book about the development of the church *in* England, *not* the Church of England. The Church of England is a comparatively recent invention, not quite 500 years old in a history of nearly nineteen hundred years of Christianity in these shores.

Broadly speaking there are three streams of Christianity in this country. They are in chronological sequence: the Roman Catholic Church, the Church of England and the Independent Churches. The third stream (the Independent Churches) has been variously categorized as Non-Conformist, Dissenting or Free Churches (free of the state). In each of those nomenclatures they are described in contradistinction to the Established Church (or Church of England) of 1660. Many of the Independent Churches have their origin in the Commonwealth, or the period of Oliver Cromwell. These include Independents, Presbyterians, Quakers and Baptists. Methodists were added in the 1780s and Pentecostals in the 1920s. The Roman Catholics were proscribed in England for nearly three hundred years from 1558–1829. The hierarchies of the Church of England and the Roman Catholic Church did not pray together until the Blitz of 1940. By 1960 other new churches were beginning but at the same time a further cultural shift was underway in England.

What must be true is that you cannot understand our nation's story without understanding the impact of Christianity. Christianity provided cohesion and common values to the various Anglo-Saxon kingdoms. Christianity absorbed and, in the end, moulded the effects of the Viking invasions and was the common bond with the Norman French. Christianity provided the social and spiritual framework to medieval England. Its struggles were the state's struggles. Its divisions split the nation and since Parliament was used to negotiate a new church settlement from 1534, politics and faith became completely intertwined. (In fact, arguably politics and faith have been more intertwined than in any other nation.) Parliament proscribed Catholicism, as the Pope had excommunicated or dethroned Elizabeth I: so one spiritual and political entity took on another, using all the weapons to hand. Parliament established a national church: The Church of England, with its liturgy, doctrine and hierarchy, and it punished those who were not a part of it. Christianity continued in the eighteenth and nineteenth centuries to provide inspiration to many for the abolition of the slave trade and slavery and social reform in the nineteenth and twentieth centuries.

As with other volumes of church history that I have written on the Early Church, I have included the political, social and cultural context in which the church bore witness, however poorly, to her Lord. As no individual is an island, nor is the church. The church is in permanent interaction with the political, social and cultural context in which it finds itself. In fact, so tethered was the Church to the political context by virtue of church and state being joined at the hip by the Emperor Constantine, and then by subsequent European governments, that it often used secular methods to further spiritual aims. Never was this more seen than when force was used to gain spiritual objectives. Jesus said put away the sword (Matthew 26:52) but again and again Christians sought to establish the kingdom of God by force.

The poet and mystic William Blake asked the question in a romantic and metaphorical way, when England was being industrialized, whether "those feet" of Jesus walked England's green and pleasant land. Obviously, Jesus himself did not literally walk England's green and pleasant land. Indeed, so often church institutions shrouded those metaphorical feet: but in a mystic here or a social reformer there, in a scholar here or a politician there, in a missionary here, a pastor there and a spiritual writer here the gait of Jesus may nonetheless be discerned.

Although in many ways I have been reading and working towards this book for fifty years, there are very many who have helped its gestation and birth. They are Gos Home, Tom Peryer, Charles Marnham, Roger Salisbury, John Collins, Tricia Murdoch, Tim Wood, Professor Mark Edwards of Christ Church Oxford, Abbot Geoffrey of Douai College, Dr Anne McLaughlin of the Parker Library, Corpus Christi College Cambridge, Richard Ward, Parliamentary Archivist Westminster, Lance Pierson of the Gerard Manley Hopkins Society, Dr Robin Gwyn on the Huguenots, Dr Jill Barber and the Primitive Methodist Museum, Dr Andrew Atherstone, Michael Fowler and Nigel Rawlinson who travelled with me around the WWI Cemeteries and Toc H at Poperinge, Gladstone's Library, the Bodleian Library and the British Library.

I would like to thank Douglas Dales, Abbot Geoffrey of Douai College and Russ Parker for reading all or part of the manuscript and offering many helpful observations. I would like to thank Benedict Books, the team at Sacristy Press especially Natalie Watson my editor, Kevin Sheehan for the maps, including the cover illustration, and Marian Aird for the index.

I am well aware that in such a large undertaking as the English Church over eighteen centuries there are bound to be omissions. I will have to leave it to another to rectify such failings.

Finally, I would like to thank my wife Olivia for all her support in what has been a three-year commitment of travel to the four corners of England and writing what has been my most challenging task to date. I hope it will be useful, possibly in places inspiring.

For further material relating to this book, including an extensive bibliography and a full index, see the author's website <https://www.patrickwhitworth.co.uk>.

PART I

The Conversion of England

ROMAN BRITAIN
circa 300 AD
Showing the major towns, forts & roads

CALEDONIA

Vallum Antonini

Bodotria Aest.

OCEANUS GERMANICUS

Vindolanda

Luguvalium (Carlisle) Vallum Hadriani

HIBERNIA

Ituna Aest.

MONABIA

Eboracum (York)

Seteia Aest.

Abus Fl.

Lindum (Lincoln)

Metaris Aest.

MONA

Deva (Chester)

Ryknild Street

Ermine Street

Ratae (Leicester)

Via Devana

BRITANNIA

Sarn Helen

Fosse Street

Watling Street

Icknield Way

Camulodunum (Colchester)

Glevum (Gloucester)

Corinium (Cirencester)

Verulamium (St. Albans)

Isca Augusta (Caerleon)

Ermin Way

Londinium (London)

Tamesis Aest.

Aquae Sulis (Bath)

Sabrina Aest.

Venta Belgarum (Winchester)

Duroverum (Canterbury)

Dubris (Dover)

Noviomagnus (Chichester)

Isca Dumnoniorum (Exeter)

Fosse Way

Portway

VECTIS

OCEANUS BRITANNICUS

Fifty Miles

CHAPTER 1

Christianity in Roman Britain

Christianity came to Britain with the Romans, either with the army or through the administration of the province. It is uncertain when Christians first arrived; what we do know is that the earliest Christian martyr, St Alban, was traditionally believed to have been killed at the very beginning of the fourth century, quite possibly in the Great Persecution of Emperor Diocletian (AD 284–305).

There could well have been Christians in England much earlier than the fourth century, however, since the Roman occupation dated from AD 43, when a campaign, led by the Emperor Claudius (AD 41–54) for publicity purposes, succeeded in occupying the country. From then on thousands of soldiers and auxiliaries were stationed in Britain, with the likelihood that by the third century at least some officials or soldiers may well have been Christians. Christians appear to have arrived in Rome from Palestine—without any Apostolic mission—in the AD 40s. Suetonius records their expulsion from Rome in c. AD 49 by Emperor Claudius, who complained of riots caused by one *Chrestus* (Christ) in the Jewish community. It is thus not unreasonable to suppose that some Christians may have found their way to Britain during the next 150 years, some arriving through the activities of Jewish traders.[1] The movement of Christians to this new northern province of the Empire by the third century seems quite possible, or even probable. Indeed, by the early third century, both Origen in Alexandria, and later in Caesarea, and Tertullian (see *Against the Jews* 7.4) in Carthage, wrote of Christians living in Britain.[2]

Invasion

It was Gaius Julius Caesar who put Britain on the Roman map. The reasons for invading Britain were part military, in that he maintained that Britons were helping his Gallic enemies, but mostly political. Caesar needed a quick victory to further advance his popularity and prestige in Rome. To this end a successful invasion of Britain would only add to his *kudos*. So, after relatively scanty planning, Caesar decided to invade Britain. Pompey and Crassus were informed at a meeting in Lucca in 56 BC.[3] An envoy, Commius, king of the Gaulish Atrebates tribe, was sent to Britain from France to win hearts and minds. Caesar then prepared to invade Britain, having concluded a ruthless campaign on the Rhine. At midnight in late August 55 BC, his fleet crossed to Dover, but found that "enemy forces were lined up on the cliff tops and that the cliffs came straight down to the sea to the narrowest of beaches".[4] The legionaries had to disembark directly into the sea as they were unable to get the ships to dry land. The soldiers were encumbered by their armour and immediately opposed by British fighters. Caesar wrote in his history of the Gallic War: "All this struck terror into the hearts of our men, who were completely unfamiliar with this type of warfare, so that they did not demonstrate that alacrity and zeal that was usually their hallmark in infantry battles."[5]

The unwilling troops were eventually galvanized by the sight of the standard-bearer of the Eagle of the Ninth Legion in the waves, whereupon they entered the sea and made for the shore, but worse was to follow. The transport and cavalry ships were delayed by a storm in the Channel and forced to turn back to Gaul. Caesar found himself marooned on a beach. His soldiers were attacked on the shoreline and barely survived. They soon re-embarked for Gaul. To use his famous saying: Caesar had certainly *come* to Britain, he had *seen* it, with its inclement weather of storms and heavy rain—and the difficulties of turning a bridgehead into an occupation—but he had not, as yet, *conquered*. Being Caesar, as soon as he reached Boulogne, he planned a much larger expedition for the following year.

Caesar was determined that his invasion would succeed. In 54 BC, he gathered a huge force: five legions (approximately 27,000 troops), a further 2,000 cavalry and an armada of over 200 ships. It was an invasion force of shock and awe proportions; in fact, it would not be equalled until William of Orange brought an army with him to take the English throne in 1688. On 7 July 54 BC, after sixteen hours crossing the Channel, the armada made landfall between Deal and Walmer. They were opposed by a coalition of tribes led by Cassivellanus, a powerful chief of the Catuvellauni in his own right who was determined to put up a fight. After securing the fleet and leaving a garrison to guard it, Caesar marched north again to attack Cassivellanus's main fortress, which he took after a pitched battle. Then, with the coming of the autumn equinox and sharp storms in the Channel, and having taken slaves and booty, Caesar decided to return to Gaul and eventually to Rome.

Back in Rome, news of the British expedition received a muted response. Cicero, Caesar's political foe and foil to his populist stance and dictatorial ambitions, wrote to Atticus about the expedition in these terms: "We await the outcome of the British war; it is well known that the approach to the island is ringed round with rigid ramparts; it's already clear that there is not an ounce of silver on the island nor any hope of booty except slaves; and I imagine you're not expecting much in the way of literary or musical accomplishments from them."[6] Cicero held out scant hope of British culture.

Apart from the pursuit of military glory, what was it that commended Britain to the Romans, necessitating this risky and expensive invasion and subsequent occupation? As Cicero pointed out, Britain was certainly *not* a sophisticated culture of art, music and literature. Britain in 54 BC was illiterate, with neither written language nor literature. To a Roman bathed in the Greek and Roman classics, as Cicero was, Britain's attractions were limited. The great historian Bede, to whom we will return at much greater length later, said the island of Britain had much to commend it agriculturally, but not culturally:

> Britain excels for grain and trees, and is well adapted for feeding cattle and beasts of burden. It also produces vines in some places, and has plenty of land and waterfowls of several sorts; it is remarkable also for rivers abounding in fish, and plentiful springs. It has the greatest plenty of salmon and eels; seals are frequently taken, and dolphins, as also whales; besides many sorts of shell fish, such as mussels, in which are often found excellent pearls of all colours, red, purple, violet, and green, but mostly white. There is also a great abundance of cockles, of which the scarlet dye is made.[7]

Britain was culturally primitive compared with Rome but blessed with natural agricultural prosperity and minerals. It was, however, occupied by many competing and at times belligerent tribes. Caesar divided these tribes into two main groups: those on the south coast, who he said were Gallic or Belgic immigrants like the Atrebates and Cantiaci, while further north, the Catuvellauni (whom Caesar attacked) and the Iceni were more autochthonous and aggressive. Tacitus noted the large limbs and red hair of the Caledonians (in Scotland) were similar to the

Germans, while the Silures of South Wales reminded him of the Spaniards.[8] These tribes were Celtic and drawn from the people groups that were spread over the Atlantic seaboard of Europe, from Britain in the north to Portugal in the south. Over preceding centuries forests had been cleared, such that by 1000 BC, Iron Age Britain had a patchwork of open fields of grain and beans. Trade existed between tribes, many of them of Celtic extraction that had moved across northern Europe and the Channel around 500 BC. The population appears to have numbered about two million. Minerals were plentiful and soon to be exploited by Roman surveyors and engineers: lead from the Mendips; copper from Anglesey; tin from Cornwall; iron from the Forest of Dean and the East Midlands; stone and marble from Bath and the south coast; and some silver and gold. Such metals were essential for arming the 30,000 Roman soldiers based in Britain and for providing a coinage minted in the province.

Worship, which had once been centred on innumerable stone circles from the Orkneys in Scotland to Stonehenge and Avebury in Wiltshire, was now based upon the worship of trees, stones and special places of ancient significance, and was conducted by Druids, who were anathema to the Romans. According to Caesar, Druids were "in charge of religion. They have control over public and private sacrifices and give rulings on all religious questions. Large numbers of young men go to them for instruction, and they are greatly honoured by the people."[9] Caesar went on to record their practice of sacrifice, in which humans and animals were bundled into giant wicker frames in the shape of humans to be killed and burnt. Pliny recorded their use of mistletoe in the oak groves where sacrifices were conducted. The Romans stamped out these practices and their presence wherever they found them, not least in Anglesey, where Tacitus describes their role in supporting the Ordovices tribe.[10]

Occupation and possession

Despite Caesar's invasion in 54 BC, it would be another ninety years before another invasion with the intention of occupying Britain occurred. In 44 BC, Caesar was assassinated, and a further civil war was conducted against Caesar's assassins by his heir Octavian. This war ended with a final campaign against Mark Antony and Cleopatra in Egypt after the Battle of Actium in 31 BC.

Augustus, as he became in 27 BC, had little opportunity for a further invasion of Britain, and little appetite for the exertion and expense required. In 34 BC, he had intended to invade Britain, but instead had to quell an invasion in Dalmatia. An invasion was again considered in 27 BC, but this time unrest in Gaul intervened. Strabo repeated what was probably the official line of Augustus's administration in explaining the failure to invade: the cost of direct rule, including an army and an administration in Britain, would not be recouped. It was not until the reign of Caligula (AD 37–41), properly known as Gaius Julius Caesar Germanicus, whose father was the brilliant Germanicus (grandson of Livia, Augustus's wife), that the idea of an invasion of Britain was reinstated. At the invitation of Adminius, the son of a British chief of the Catuvellauni, Caligula reassembled an invasion force with the support of the Senate. But his army refused to obey orders and embark for Britain because they feared the Channel crossing! They thus humiliated Caligula and he sought to humiliate them in turn by ordering them to gather seashells from the beach in their helmets and by erecting a lighthouse to commemorate their revolt. Before any further invasion could take place, Caligula was assassinated. In his place the much-maligned member of the imperial family, the absent-minded, historically obsessed, short-sighted, limping and drooling Claudius, succeeded as Emperor. He was to be more effective than anyone could have guessed. With the support of the Senate, and a political situation in Britain that provided an opportunity to ally with a client king, a full-scale invasion and occupation was planned.

The invasion force was led by the experienced commander Aulus Plautius, a former governor of Pannonia and well connected to the imperial family. He led 40,000 troops, roughly five times the size of William the Conqueror's invasion force of 1066 and one of the largest invasion forces to cross the Channel until the D-Day landings in 1944. The crossing of the Roman army, as on previous occasions, was delayed by bad weather, but also, once again, by their own reluctance. For the Roman soldiers, crossing to Britain was like falling off the edge of the earth. Once again, they refused to embark, but Plautius, having executed the ringleaders, cajoled the legionaries to cross the Channel. Eventually a beachhead was made, most probably at Richborough, and after the landings a full-scale campaign of occupation ensued.

Cassius Dio, the Roman historian, records that the British army of resistance under Togodumnus and Caratacus was nowhere to be seen. Eventually they were found and engaged near the Medway. Vespasian, later Emperor and the suppressor with his son Titus of the Jewish revolt in AD 70, and Gnaeus Geta, were given command by Plautius; and over a two-day engagement they defeated the Catuvellauni tribe. At a subsequent engagement near Westminster on the Thames, Togodumnus was killed. With victory assured, Claudius was invited to take command of his troops at what would be a mixture of a *durbar* and formal surrender of defeated British rulers. As Josephus says of Vespasian in his *Jewish War*: "It was Vespasian who acquired Britannia for the empire through armed struggle (until then it had been unknown); thus he enabled Nero's father, Claudius, to be awarded a triumph, which had cost him no sweat of his own."[11]

Claudius journeyed by boat from Ostia, the port of Rome, to Massilia (Marseilles), up the River Rhone, and across Gaul to Boulogne, arriving in Britain in August AD 43. He eventually came to Colchester. It was there, as if in some Roman pageant lifted from the Coliseum, that Claudius received the surrender of Camulodunum (Colchester) and the homage of various British kings, one from as far away as Orkney. Other obeisant rulers came to do homage to Claudius: Togidubnus, king of the Regini, later to be given a fabulous palace at Fishbourne, near Chichester, and who took the names Tiberius Claudius in faithful homage, as well as rulers from the Iceni tribe of East Anglia and the queen of the Brigantes from Yorkshire. However banal this occasion may have been, with Claudius accompanied by elephants, never before seen in Britain, it changed the course of British history for the next 400 years, and arguably forever. Claudius remained in the cold and damp climes of Britain for sixteen days before returning to Rome, no doubt purring over this climax to his military career, having achieved what the great Julius Caesar had not been able to do. In recognition, he was given the title Britannic Majesty by the Senate. Thereafter he was commonly called Britannicus, after his greatest victory! Coins were minted, the Senate awarded him a triumph, victory arches were erected, and an annual festival was declared. Claudius was assured of his place in history. But it would be wrong to suppose that in this contrived piece of imperial theatre at Colchester *Pax Romana* came to Britain. In fact, for the next forty years Britain would only be won by Rome after a great spilling of blood.

The conquest period, which included the revolt of Boudicca, continued from AD 43–83, and it was bloody indeed. At first, four legions were stationed in Britain, a number that was later reduced to a permanent deployment of three. There were about 5,500 soldiers in each legion, with a large number of supporting troops as well, making a permanent garrison in Britain of around 30,000 soldiers, one of the largest in any province of the Empire. This was a formidable force, and it shaped both the economy and many landholdings, especially for retired soldiers. The governor Scapula (AD 47–52) took on the task of mopping up the opposition. Caratacus, the famous British leader who escaped from the earliest battles against the Romans, continued resistance from Wales until he was defeated and captured by Scapula. Deported to Rome as a captive, he was given his freedom for his spirited defence and martial bearing. He was to remain in Rome for the rest of his life. Others were not so well treated. The Iceni tribe from East Anglia had long been a client kingdom of the Romans and was based in Norfolk, around Thetford. By AD 60, the relationship had turned sour: traditional places of worship had been closed, and very large loans made to the tribe through Seneca, Nero's tutor, were being recalled. Dio writes that the loans made to British rulers by Seneca totalled as much as 40 million sesterces. The Empire, under the tyrannical and rapacious rule of Nero, needed money. The treatment of the king of the Iceni, Prasutagus, was high-handed, with attempts by Nero's finance office in Britain to forcibly take all the Iceni's assets. When King Prasutagus suddenly died, his wife Boudicca raised a revolt against the Romans. Of Boudicca, Dio writes: "She was very tall and stern; her look was penetrating; her voice harsh; her auburn hair fell to her waist and around her neck was a heavy golden torc; she wore a patterned cloak with a thick cape over it fastened with a brooch."[12]

Standing on a platform, she addressed 120,000 troops, Dio says. The size of the army was in fact greatly exaggerated by Dio. It was probably much closer to a third of this size. Boudicca's appeal was to liberty, and the idea that Britons should never be subservient to Rome. Ever since then, deep in the psychology of the British has been the notion, which, apart from Winston Churchill, has often been expressed most sharply by female leaders, that "Britons never, never shall be slaves".[13]

A small force of 2,000 legionaries from the Ninth Legion stationed at Peterborough managed to engage Boudicca, but they were easily cut down. Their commander, Petilius Cerealis, escaped with his life back to Peterborough. Boudicca drove on to London, which Paulinus decided to sacrifice rather than defend with inadequate forces, and the city was destroyed. Around 70,000–80,000 had lost their lives in the campaign to that point.

Paulinus mustered 10,000 troops against what Dio describes as 230,000 Britons. However much this figure might be exaggerated, it does show that the Romans were significantly outnumbered. Boudicca once again raised the blood of her troops with a speech reported by Tacitus as follows: "It is not as the daughter of a noble family that I fight now, avenging my lost kingdom and my wealth; but rather as a woman of the people avenging our lost liberty, my own scourged body, and my daughter's rape."[14] The battle was engaged, but this time it was a massacre of the Britons: 80,000 are said to have died, with just 400 Romans killed. Boudicca herself died, possibly by her own hand with poison, fleeing the battlefield, according to Tacitus.

Severe reprisals followed: many were executed, many others sold into slavery as whole families, and a reign of terror cowed the population. Much later, in AD 83, a campaign against the Caledonian Scots ensued, resulting in the Battle of Mons

Graupius, near Aberdeen. Agricola, the father-in-law of Tacitus, conducted this campaign of conquest, killing 10,000 Caledonians. It is estimated that over this whole period of conflict from AD 60–83 some 100,000–250,000 Britons lost their lives. No wonder a subdued peace followed.

By AD 68, Roman power had undergone dramatic change and the Church was facing the full scale of persecution unleashed by Nero in Rome. The apostles Peter and Paul were executed there a little after the Boudiccan revolt, around AD 64. Mark's Gospel was probably first published in Rome about that time. After a reign of capricious terror and limitless self-indulgence, Nero was assassinated in AD 68. This was followed by the year of the four emperors referred to in the Book of Revelation (see Revelation 13:3). The Jewish revolt began in AD 66 and continued until the army commander Vespasian brought Palestine back under Roman control. He had moved from Britain to Palestine and was later chosen Emperor by the army. In AD 70, Jerusalem and the Temple were destroyed. A period of relative calm followed in the Empire. Likewise, in Britain, after huge bloodletting, the province acquired a more settled, if repressed, existence as the full panoply of Roman imperial power and structure was rolled out. It is quite possible that individual Christians arrived quietly in Britain during the second century, wary of attracting attention and so being ostracized or persecuted.

The limits of Roman power in Britain

Britain would always have three legions based in the province, which in AD 197 became two provinces: Britannia Superior in the South and Wales and Britannia Inferior in the North—terms hardly likely to commend themselves nowadays. There were legionary fortresses in Chester, Caerlon in South Wales and York. Other cities like Wroxeter (near Shrewsbury), Gloucester, Alchester and Colchester could host legions with sufficient enclosed space. Colchester, Gloucester and Lincoln were the main centres or *coloniae* for retired soldiers. Scattered across England and Wales were innumerable garrisons and forts, or camps. Linking them was the famous Roman road system: the Fosse Way from Exeter to Leicester; Watling Street from London to Wroxeter on the Welsh border; Ermine Street from London to Lincoln and York; Portway from Dorchester to London; and Dere Street from York to the Antonine Wall between Glasgow and Edinburgh.

The army was increasingly diverse in its racial background, with more and more barbarian Germans being enlisted, along with others from North Africa and Syria. Indeed, the Praetorian Guard that surrounded Caligula, and was responsible for his assassination, was mostly German. It would be wrong to think that the occupation force and the administration were from Italy: the commanders may have been, but the ranks were drawn from across the Empire. Famously, a soldier from Palmyra erected a monument in South Shields to commemorate his British wife Regina, depicting her as a Roman matron.

The army and its auxiliary forces and administration drove the economy. Minerals were required for its armour and equipment, and mints for the coin to pay the soldiers' wages. Food and clothing came from local sources and not from Gaul. Delicacies arrived from near and far: the elite officers and commanders required a diet of olives, oil and fish sauce, transported from the continent in hundreds of thousands of pottery amphorae. Even snails, still found close to Chedworth Villa in the Cotswolds, had their origins in Italy. A Roman army, especially its officers, marched on its stomach. Each year 25,000 troops required approximately 10,000 tonnes of wheat, 9,000 tonnes of barley for cavalry horses and approximately 12,000 cattle, sheep and pigs.

The borders of the Empire were set more or less by Hadrian, the ever-travelling, aesthete Emperor who was capable of sleeping on the ground with his soldiers or reciting Greek poetry. He fixed the borders of the Empire in the east in Syria, the south in North Africa, and in the north at Hadrian's Wall—the Atlantic being the barrier in the west. The wall, forever associated with Hadrian, was begun in his reign. Hadrian himself came to Britain in AD 122 and initiated the project, with construction taken on by the governor of the province, Platorius Nepos. He may have addressed his troops on the banks of the Tyne where a new bridge, Pons Aelius, was built in his honour. The construction of the wall was on the scale of the Egyptian pyramids. The materials required ran into hundreds of thousands of tonnes of masonry, roof tiles and even twelve tonnes of nails.

Not content with one wall, a further barrier was built between the Forth and the Clyde during the reign of the Antonine Emperors in AD 140, but was relinquished around AD 160. Other Emperors, like Severus and Caracalla, campaigned in Scotland to subdue the land, but in the end Hadrian's Wall became the northern border of the Empire.

Hadrian's Wall was to yield the most important Roman archaeological find in Britain: the writing tablets at Vindolanda. They add greatly to our understanding of Roman life in Britain. Vindolanda was a fort that pre-dated the construction of the wall but was to form part of its defensive system. The writing tablets are slight wooden slips with messages written in ink on the surface that survived 2,000 years of lying sealed against oxygen and bacteria in the clay ground of Northumberland. In these sealed conditions, they survived to tell their tale. They form a collection of 2,000 letters, records and other documents dating from AD 90 to 130. Their brilliance is that they give a mundane, everyday account of life on the wall among settled Roman communities at the edge of the Empire. In the most precarious of situations, normal life continues—food and clothing are discussed, birthdays and feast days are kept, pleasantries are exchanged. In one touching and famous letter, an invitation is made by the fort commander's wife, Claudia Severa, to Sulpicia Lepidina, the wife of Flavius Cerealis, the prefect of the Ninth Cohort of Batavians (from Holland). In c. AD 97–107, she wrote: "Claudia Severa to her Lepidina, Greetings. My birthday is on 11 September, sister. Please accept my warm invitation to spend it with us, to make the day more enjoyable for me if you are there. Give my greetings to your Cerealis. My Aelius and my little son send their greetings. Farewell my sister, my dearest soul, and may you prosper."[15] It is signed by Claudia and is the only extant feminine signature of the Empire.

Vindolanda shows the effect of the coming of Christianity by the fourth century, if not on writing tablets then on a stone. Such a stone was used as a table for the sacraments. It bears both an engraved cross and the *Chi-Rho* symbol, the first two letters of *Christos* in the Greek alphabet. A leather belt-end decorated with a bishop and his staff, which fastens to a buckle, has also been found in Vindolanda. Likewise, in the commander's house at Vindolanda there is an apsidal-ended building, which could very well have been used as a church. Two hundred years after Claudia Severa wrote her birthday invitation, the commander's family might well have been worshipping in a church.

Britain: A home for usurpers

The northern part of the Empire, including Germany, Gaul and Britain (and sometimes more southerly Spain), was prone to secession and rebellion, and this was especially true of Britain. The first usurper was the governor of Britain, Clodius Albinus, who declared himself Emperor in AD 196 after the murder of Pertinax and the "Year of the Five Emperors". He marched into Gaul, but was defeated by a rival, Septimus Severus.

Septimus Severus (AD 193–211), an African Emperor from Leptis Magna (present-day Libya), proved to be one of the most powerful Emperors. He sought to re-establish Roman power. During his reign, a fierce persecution of Christians resumed, accounting for a wave of arrests in North Africa, including the sensational martyrdom of Perpetua and Felicity in Carthage. Determined to subdue the Scots and Picts, he conducted a campaign in Caledonia in 201 as recorded by Cassius Dio, but the terrain and guerrilla opposition wore down his attack. He retreated and died in York, after first rebuilding cities and reviving the fortunes of the province.[16]

The busiest time for usurpers in Britain was during the fourth and fifth centuries. Indeed Jerome, always good for a sharp one-liner, remarked that Britain was "fertile in usurpers".[17] In 286, Carausius seized power in Britain, only thirteen years after Aurelian's re-assertion of Roman power across the region. He was an able military commander who had the support of the legions. He rebuffed an attempt to depose him by the Emperor-in-the-west, Maximian. (Under Diocletian [284–305], the Empire was divided into East and West. Both the eastern and western parts of the Empire had an Augustus or Emperor, and a Caesar.) Carausius went on to effectively establish his own rule in Britain. His coinage speaks of the stability of his reign. However, in 293 Carausius was murdered by Allectus, and only with the arrival of Constantius Chlorus, the father of Constantine I, was a renewed attempt made to overthrow the renegade regime. With great military planning and skill, Chlorus secured the Channel ports and then invaded Britain to recapture the country for the Empire, and defeat Allectus.

Constantius Chlorus had restored Britain to the Empire in 296—an empire governed overall by Diocletian from Nicomedia in the East and by Constantius in the West, from the cities of Trier and York. His son, Constantine I, would soon come to rule over the Empire in its entirety, and would at the same time establish Christianity as the religion of the Empire through the Edict of Milan in 313. This edict officially granted toleration to Christianity soon after its sharpest and most prolonged phase of persecution under Diocletian and his colleagues. That usurpers were spawned in Britain so repeatedly must in part be due to its distance from the centre of the Empire and the militarized nature of the province providing a ready force for rebellion. But before the eventual downfall of the Empire in the West, Constantine I brought a renewed period of prosperity to Britain, and with it, for the first time, free worship of Christ in the province, as throughout the Empire.

Constantine and fourth-century Britain

It is well to remember that Constantine I was declared Emperor in the western part of the Empire by his father's troops in York. A bronze sculpture outside York Minster of a relaxed Constantine seated in his chair records this truly historic event. Hitherto, Constantine had been held a virtual captive at the court of Galerius in Thessalonica and Nicomedia, where Galerius was the eastern

Augustus. Galerius sought to destroy his potential rival by exposing Constantine to great danger during campaigns against barbarians on the Danube.[18] Hearing of his father's plans to embark on another campaign against the Picts beyond Hadrian's Wall, Constantine escaped to meet him at Boulogne. They crossed the Channel together and defeated the Picts, but Constantius died soon after in York on 25 July 306. On the same day Constantine was proclaimed Constantius's heir and Augustus of Britain, Gaul and Spain: the western part of the Empire. It was a date that changed the course of history.[19] Constantine was either thirty-four or thirty-five years of age. In six years, he had taken Rome, after defeating Maxentius at the Battle of Milvian Bridge on 28 October 312, and was soon to be master of the whole Empire in 324.

Constantine acted quickly to show his sympathy and support for Christianity. In 307, he restored property taken from the Church under the edict of Diocletian, which had started what became known as the Great Persecution. Galerius was to do likewise in a fit of remorse on his death bed in April 311. Then, on the eve of the Battle of Milvian Bridge, Constantine had his famous—and much debated—vision of Christ. His soldiers fought under the *labarum*, an avowedly Christian banner, incorporating the *Chi-Rho* symbol. Constantine's vision and victory signalled a radical change from a Roman general's usual dependence on Jupiter or Mars.

From 312, Constantine supported churches and worshipped Christ. He gave freely from the imperial treasury to build, decorate or endow churches. Clergy were exempted from taxes and were freed from having to take part in public (pagan) liturgies; slaves could find their freedom in church and become Roman citizens; gladiatorial combat was ended in 325; church courts were set up, with bishops hearing cases; and punishments like crucifixions or the disfiguring of the face were abolished. A new age had been ushered in, and its effects extended to Britain.

Up until 307, Christianity in Britain had existed underground. During the Great Persecution of Diocletian's reign any known Christians, such as Alban, would have been persecuted to the point of torture, confiscation of property or even loss of life. Alban was arrested for sheltering a priest who had brought him to faith in Christ, whereupon he was tortured and executed, Bede says, in 305. But if Tertullian and Origen were right in saying that Christians existed in Britain from the third century, then the Church may have already existed in a fragile way for many years. This seems likely, since Christian communities and leaders sprang up in Britain quite quickly in Constantine's reign from 307 onwards, principally in the main cities. Bishoprics emerged in London, York and Lincoln, with bishops from these communities attending the Council of Arles in 313.

The Council of Arles was probably the second church council that the new Emperor Constantine called to deal with the Donatist controversy in North Africa in particular, but also with other less pressing matters, such as the date of Easter. The first council, held in Rome, had amounted to an unsatisfactory failure to deal with the same issues. In brief, the Donatist church had split from the Catholic or Orthodox church in North Africa because of the way members of the Catholic church known as *traditores*—from which we get the word traitor—had compromised the faith in times of persecution, either by handing over Bibles or prayer books to the authorities, or worse, by burning incense to, and hence worshipping, the Emperor. The Donatist church, led by Donatus, alleged that the Bishop of Carthage, Caecilian, was himself a *traditor* because of his association with another *traditor*, Felix of Abthungi, who had ordained him. Constantine called the Council of Arles in August 314 to settle this dispute and himself sat in the assembly as a layman. The Donatists did not have the necessary documentary support to prove their case against Caecilian. The council found in favour of Caecilian, and informed Constantine formally, although he was present, to which he replied that he found the Donatists "abhorrent even to the heavenly dispensation".[20] It would have been the first taste of church controversy at the highest level for these three British bishops: Eborius from York, Restitutus of London and Adelphius, probably of Lincoln.[21] Later British bishops were known to have attended church councils at Nicea in 325, Sardicia in 347 and Rimini in 359.[22] In the future, the Church, even in Roman Britain, would be no stranger to controversy.

Roman Britain was to last only a further ninety years before the withdrawal of the legions in 409, but during this time the Christian community developed considerably. Some churches or even cathedrals were built, including, possibly, one in London. A unique and very early collection of church plate has been found at Water Newton; and a Christian mosaic at Hinton St Mary, Dorset, including the *Chi-Rho* symbol. The first half of the fourth century was certainly prosperous, with many villas built and expensively decorated at places like Chedworth and at a new find at Boxford in Berkshire. An older palace at Fishbourne, dating from the first century and provided originally for the British king Togidubinus, was probably extended.

Amidst signs of prosperity in the British provinces and growth of the Church, important church leaders emerged. Principal among them were a heretic, a visiting bishop, an evangelist and a monk. Between them they had a significant impact during the final years of Roman Britain, and in one case soon afterwards. They were Pelagius, Bishop Germanus, Patrick and Gildas.

Pelagius

Pelagius, whose name and teaching gave rise to the Pelagian controversy that so exercised Augustine of Hippo and Jerome, was by nature an ascetic and a moralist.[23] He was a native of the British Isles, a well-educated man with a profound knowledge of the Bible, although not a correct one. He was born sometime between 350 and 380. Although sometimes called a monk, he was a layman, and there is no evidence that he belonged to a religious community.[24] He left Britain for Italy, North Africa and Palestine. In 405, Pelagius was in Rome and heard Augustine's famous dictum from the *Confessions*, "Give what thou commandest and command what thou wilt."[25] The notion behind this statement is that we can make no contribution to our salvation; it is all of grace and God must create in us the response of faith he is looking for. These words of Augustine created a furious reaction in Pelagius. He is reported to have cried out, "I cannot bear it". Pelagius believed that with discipline and training, a person can win God's approval. Human beings are not guilty from birth, nor have they fallen morally or spiritually with Adam; instead people can live morally acceptable lives through discipline and effort. Later, Pelagius and his colleague Caelestius were accused of teaching that Adam was created mortal and would have died even if he had not sinned; that Adam's sin only injured himself and not the whole human race, and that infants at the time of their birth *are* thus in the same state that Adam was in *before the fall*. It is possible to be sinless and there were sinless people before Christ, and the law as well as the gospel can bring someone to salvation.[26]

While Pelagius was in Palestine, Caelestius was brought before the Bishop of Carthage to give an account of his views. Caelestius was condemned, and Augustine picked up his pen and wrote a veritable broadside of works: *De Peccatorum et Remissione et de Baptismo Parvulorum*, *De Spiritu et Littera*, *De Natura et Gratia* and *De Peccato Originali*. In effect Augustine wrote on all the issues raised by the controversy: the nature of original sin, the limits of nature and the need for grace, and the need for baptism of infants. Augustine made it clear that "the vice which darkens and disables these good natural qualities, so that nature has need of enlightenment and healing, did not come from the blameless maker but from Original Sin, which was committed by free will".[27]

In Palestine, Pelagius found many who sympathized with his views, not least Bishop John of Jerusalem, but he was implacably opposed by Jerome, now living in Bethlehem in a community he and his devoted admirer Paula had founded. After various brushes with Jerome and a Spanish priest, Orosius, Pelagius was charged with seven counts of heresy at Diospolis (Lydda) by the Bishop of Caesarea, the

Primate of Palestine. Asked to condemn his colleague Caelestius and uphold the Synod of Carthage, Pelagius in fact did so and was found to be orthodox. Nevertheless, Pope Innocent, at the request of sixty-seven African bishops, excommunicated Pelagius, although Innocent's successor sought to soften the order. In 417, Augustine preached against Pelagius in Carthage, and other treatises on predestination and the gift of perseverance soon followed. A middle position was found between Augustine and Pelagius that was taken up by Cassian, the distinguished monk from Dobruja on the Black Sea who founded a monastery at Marseilles, and by Faustus, Abbot of Lérins, off the French Riviera. Although the unrefined form of Pelagianism was condemned, its milder form was continually to erupt in church debates, not least between Calvinists and Arminians in the seventeenth and eighteenth centuries and between Wesley and Whitfield in the eighteenth century in England. Pelagius died around 420, either in Palestine or Egypt, a long way from home.

Germanus

Back in Britain, Bishop Germanus of Auxerre made it his business to squash any vestiges of Pelagianism. According to Prosper of Aquitaine, Germanus was sent by Pope Celestine to counter heresy and restore orthodoxy to the British Church.[28] Bede also tells us that he came over to Britain from Gaul in 429, proving his effectiveness by first quelling a storm in the Channel after pouring holy water on the waves.[29] This was but a prelude to Germanus and his colleague Lupus, Bishop of Troyes, quelling theological turbulence at a gathering at which the Pelagian leaders in Britain debated with him. The "venerable prelates", Bishops Germanus and Lupus, Bede tells us, "poured forth a torrent of their apostolical and evangelical eloquence" so that the crowd could scarcely be restrained from assaulting the Pelagians. Having silenced his opponents, Germanus, armed with relics of all the Apostles and several martyrs, visited the shrine of St Alban. He called for the opening of St Alban's tomb, wherein he laid relics of the martyrs he had brought with him. He then gathered dust from where St Alban's blood had fallen to add to his own collection of relics. At the same time, Bede records that the visit of Germanus enabled "an innumerable multitude of people" to be converted to the Lord that day. Germanus returned home following a fall in which he broke his leg and was miraculously rescued from a fire whilst convalescing in a house close to the outbreak. It was from here that he helped to secure a bloodless victory over the Saxons and Picts.

Germanus returned to Britain in 447 to silence other Pelagians and then went to Ravenna. There he met Galla Placida, daughter of Theodosius I and mother of the Emperor Valentinian III. She was one of the most notable women of the late Roman Empire in the West. Germanus's visit demonstrated the close connection between the Gaulish Church and the Romano-British Church, both in Britain and Ireland. In 430, Pope Celestine sent the first mission to Ireland. Palladius, quite possibly a deacon of Germanus, went to the Irish, according to the chronicler Prosper of Aquitaine,[30] but his mission was short-lived. Instead, shortly after Palladius's visit, Patrick undertook the first effective mission to Ireland around 432.

Patrick

Patrick is the third figure to consider in the Romano-British Church after the heresiarch Pelagius and Germanus, the visiting bishop from Gaul. Patrick's own mission to Ireland was not sponsored by a pope but arose out of the circumstances of his life and the prompting of the Spirit. He grew up in Britain, probably in Somerset or Wales. The only clue we have to his birthplace is his own admission in his *Confessio*, a kind of personal testimony to his calling, that his family owned "a small estate near the village of Bannavem Taburniae".[31] Patrick's father Calporinus was a deacon and his grandfather a priest. When he was sixteen, Patrick was captured by pirates and taken to Ireland. He was not a practising Christian at that time, but the terror of his capture, which he later regarded as punishment for his unbelief, together with his own Christian background, served to bring him back to his family's faith. Patrick himself says in the *Confessio* that whilst in Ireland "the Lord opened my understanding to my unbelief" and "I turned with all my heart to the Lord my God".[32] Having declared his faith in the Trinity, as expressed by the Council of Nicaea,—incidentally only a hundred years old then—Patrick recalls his escape from the pirates. He managed to escape, although it seems at one point he was recaptured. He reached home to hear the call of God on a number of occasions, and, not being given a position in the British Church on account of some previous misdemeanour, decided to return to Ireland to preach the gospel at about the age of forty-five. He may well have had access to the Old Latin Bible, or parts of it, the *Vetus Latina*, before it was re-translated by Jerome and others and known as the Vulgate. Despite, or maybe because of, his acknowledged lack of education and training, he had frequent revelations, the result of which was a compulsion to undertake his mission to Ireland. The mission was successful, and its fruits took root from c. 430. Literally thousands were baptized, monasteries flourished free of episcopal oversight and under the leadership of abbots, who resembled the clan leaders of Irish culture. Although dioceses and parishes were strange to the Irish mentality, Patrick founded one in Armagh, of which he was bishop. In spite of the lack of support, even criticism and mockery, from the British Church, a lasting legacy to his labours was established in Ireland, and this would later provide a springboard for the evangelization of England.

As we shall see, Patrick's initiative was to be richly repaid in terms of a reciprocal mission to England, and in particular to Northumberland, beginning in the late sixth century, a hundred years later. That mission was monastically based and driven by prayer, Patrick being a man of deep prayer. Indeed, his example was an inspiration for many other ascetics in Ireland subsequently. Given the extremely rural nature of Irish society in Patrick's time, with family-bonded communities or clan ties resulting in a myriad of small kingdoms, a Roman-styled church of parishes and diocese was not appropriate, nor would it have been so mission-minded. Instead, with the support of Gaulish monasticism, a fertile, faithful and missionary form of monasticism emerged in Ireland by the time of Columbanus (543–621) and was the antecedent to Columba of Iona and Aidan. Patrick's Spirit-inspired mission had lasting effects and sometimes in the teeth of fierce opposition. His letter to the soldiers of Coroticus, who had slaughtered a group of Christian neophytes still in their white gowns, and who had only just been baptized, demonstrates the vulnerability in a lawless society of Christians who had broken with worship previously led by Druids or from other ancestral forms of worship. It also demonstrates Patrick's willingness to challenge the powerful. To the neophytes, Patrick wrote, "And so my dearest friends, I grieve, grieve deeply for you, but at the same time I rejoice within myself that 'I did not labour in vain' and my journeying has not been useless. For while such an indescribably awful crime has occurred, still, thanks be to God, it is as faithful baptized people that you have left this world to go to Paradise."[33]

Gildas

If Patrick was the Spirit-inspired, untutored, but effective evangelist in the late Roman world of the British Church, the final leader whose writings have survived is a monk called Gildas. Gildas belonged to the sub-Roman period of the early sixth century, when the western Empire had collapsed, the impact of which we shall consider in the next chapter. He was a product of a powerful vein of the

Romano-Celtic Church. By tradition, he was a member of a royal family from northern Britain with Irish connections, possibly from the Clyde region, where he may well have trained for the priesthood and become a monk.[34] He later emigrated to Brittany, where he ended life as a hermit at Rhuys. He is famous most of all for his extant work, *Excidio Britanniae* or the *Ruin of Britain*, which charts the failures of the British nation after the Roman period and the consequent divine judgement that the nation suffered. Gildas is a representative of the indigenous Celtic Church left behind at the departure of the Romans, with its deep-seated love of scripture, knowledge of the Church Fathers and strong monastic or ascetic tendencies. He is one of very few commentators on the post-Roman world upon whose information we depend.

The end of Roman Britain in terms of the presence of the legions and imperial administration was sudden. The legions were withdrawn around 407 by the usurper Constantius III. His abortive mission came to an end in 411 when he was deserted by the army and executed. From that time onwards, the legions did not return, and only a trace of Roman administration was left behind. As the historian Procopius wrote: "From that time onwards it [Britain] remained under the rule of tyrants."[35] The end of the Roman period brought sudden change and lasting impact. Some urban communities founded by the Romans survived after the withdrawal of the legions, with only walls, streets and gates surviving, later to be revitalized by the Anglo-Saxons, but neither the names nor the places of British Roman life would be extinguished. Among them were Lincoln, Colchester, Chester, Winchester, London, St Albans, Leicester, Exeter, Chichester, Gloucester, Wroxeter, York and Carlisle. Many would become cathedral cities in the future, even if their populations and prestige declined in the post-Roman period. Rome had effected huge changes in the landscape of the nation, from roads to architecture, materials, markets, coinage, literacy, bathing, diet, farming and social habits. The development of the Roman model in Britain had been slow. Initially resented and rebelled against, that model was probably never fully embraced by the indigenous population. Warring tribes, especially the Picts, gave rise to a large military presence. This in turn led to higher taxation and less enthusiasm for Rome from the population. "The insular position of Britain, beyond the limits of the continental empire, contributed to this difference and its end-of-the-line location further weakened its integration."[36] This was a theme to be repeated in England's history. And a theme of this book must be the influence of continental Europe on England and vice versa, and particularly of Christian continental Europe on the English Church.

One of the greatest legacies of this Roman period is the existence of a local British Church, but in the end, because of subsequent migrations, these churches or communities lasted precisely in those regions least Romanized: among the Picts in Scotland; among the Dummonii and Cornovii in Devon and Cornwall; in Dyfed in south-west Wales and Gwynnedd in north-west Wales. Whithorn, Tintagel, Glastonbury and St David's became centres of Celtic Christianity and a legacy of the Celtic-Roman Church, with a monastic rule originating from as far away as Wadi Natrun and Thebaid in Egypt, Palestine and Syria but mediated to Britain by the Gaulish Church.

Resistance to Roman authority did not prevent attachment to Christianity, based on the Latin Scriptures and the Latin Church Fathers. It was a faith no doubt preached in Celtic, but expressed more formally in Latin, whose political Roman associations were for the most part rejected by the indigenous British and Celtic Church, despite there being Christian Emperors from Constantine onwards. This would become an important fissure in English Christianity in the future. Continental influence was to come next in an entirely new form, not with Roman legions and well-tested administration, but with German migration, as Saxons, Angles and Jutes began their piecemeal annexation of Britain. Over time a new name would be added to mainland Britain, that is, England. The English came from Germany and they intermingled, or did not intermingle, with the Romano-British Celts and other incomers from the Empire who had arrived over the previous 400 years.

ANGLO-SAXON
BRITAIN
CIRCA 600 AD
Showing the HEPTARCHY
& other minor kingdoms

CHAPTER 2

The Anglo-Saxons: Migration and Conversion

The period immediately following the withdrawal of the Roman legions and administration can justifiably be called the "dark ages", if only because of the extremely limited knowledge we have of this time. The years covered in this chapter can be divided into two: the period immediately following the departure of the Roman legions until 600—a span of about one hundred and ninety years—and then a further one hundred and ninety years from the arrival of Christianity in the newly formed Anglo-Saxon kingdoms until the first Danish invasions in 793-5. These 400 years equal the amount of time Britain was part of the Roman Empire. And in many ways the eight centuries combined laid the foundation for English life. (A more detailed explanation of the term "English" will follow, differentiating it from the earlier term "British".) Further invasions by the Danes and the Normans added to the mix but did not supplant what had gone before.

The initial years following the departure of the Romans were characterized by dislocation and disruption. Towns emptied and were left desolate, and the four hundred or so villas were soon overrun by the encroaching countryside, as there was no longer the infrastructure to maintain them. But there was still continuity of functioning landholdings in the post-Roman period. From the scant records that remain, we know that plague, warfare, famine and German immigration—not to mention invasions—dominated the coming years. Furthermore, disease and plague struck often. Bede wrote among other things of "a severe plague falling upon a corrupt generation" in the fifth century.[1] Above all, in the fifth century there seems to have been a sense of political uncertainty and anarchy following the four centuries of Roman rule. Although Roman rule in Britain was bloody at first, the fourth century was marked by general prosperity and, for Christians, the sweet prize of freedom of worship.

Our main source for the period immediately following the Romans is Gildas, the monk who had a Jeremiah-like tendency to see God's judgement in the difficulties facing Britain. Another principal source is Bede, who wrote from the joint monastic foundation of Monkwearmouth-Jarrow in Northumberland during the eighth century. Lastly there is Procopius, writing from distant Constantinople, whose history of the Empire included a section on Britain. Procopius's account of Britain veered from the accurate to the completely fanciful, and included a passage on "the ferrying of disembodied souls from Gaul to Britain".[2] Nevertheless, Procopius rightly maintained that from the sixth century *Angiloi*, *Frissones* and Britons inhabited the land, to which we must add Saxons. If we include some more specific archaeological evidence from cemeteries and the occasional headstone, such as the one dedicated to Vortipor, King of Dyfed, who Gildas also mentions in his *Ruin of Britain*, then this work more or less completes the evidence for this murky period of England's past.[3]

What appears to have happened after the withdrawal of the legions is that various local rulers or kings came to the fore and had to face the increasing threat of the Picts from Scotland and the Scots from Ireland. The British found themselves unable to defeat these groups, so King Vortigern invited the Saxons to help combat them. For a time, this worked well, until the Saxons saw an opportunity to rebel against their paymasters. While at one point there was a British recovery with the defeat of the Saxons by Britons at the Battle of Mons Badonicus, gradually the Saxons and other tribes from north Germany and Scandinavia settled in the south and east of England. Saxons such as these defeated a British king at Deorham (Dyrham) outside Bath, effectively pushing the Britons west into Wales, with the Saxons forming the territory called Hwicce. Gildas has depicted Saxons as fierce and cruel fighters, gradually wearing down the indigenous British, who were eventually pushed to the west, i.e. the West Country and north-west Britain around Strathclyde, and Wales.

Bede famously described the arrival of these German immigrants in these terms:

> Those who came over were the three most powerful nations of Germany—Saxons, Angles and Jutes. From the Jutes are the people of Kent, and of the Island of Wight, and also the province of the West Saxons who are to this day called Jutes, seated opposite the Island of Wight. From the Saxons, that is the country, which is now called Old Saxony, came the East-Saxons and the South-Saxons. From the Angles, that is, the country which is called Anglia, and which is said, from that time, to remain desert to this day, between the provinces of the Jutes and the Saxons, are descended the East Angles, the Midland-Angles, Mercians, all the race of the Northumbrians,

that is, of those nations that dwell on the north side of the Humber, and the other nations of the English. The two first commanders are said to have been Hengist and Horsa.[4]

This is probably the first time the word *English* appears in English literature. It is used as a generic term describing the coming of these mostly German tribes to British shores. Gildas considered these Saxons cruel invaders, who, like the Assyrians or Babylonians in the Old Testament, were used to punish the British for their sins, and in particular for the failure of leadership by the princes and the judges. He says of the Saxons:

> First they fixed their talons in the eastern part of the country, as men intending to fight for the country, but more truly to assail it. To these the mother of the brood, finding that success had attended the first contingent, sends out also a larger raft-full of accomplices and curs, which sails over and joins itself to their bastard comrades.[5]

Few could resist them, but one king, Ambrosius Aurelianus, organized British defences against the Saxons, and may have been the king who gave the British respite for about forty years around 500, after the Battle of Mons Badonicus, even while the Saxon immigration in the East continued. It was around this time that a Welsh poet fleetingly said of someone that "he is not King Arthur", but in doing so started a legend that has run and run.[6] Nennius, a Welsh chronicler of the ninth century, gave further legs to the Arthurian legend by listing twelve battles Arthur won against the Saxons. The legend was centred on Glastonbury, a place rich in legends, including one about Joseph of Arimathea burying the Holy Grail—the Chalice of the Last Supper—on Glastonbury Tor. (This was an invention of the monks of the twelfth century to raise funds for the rebuilding of the abbey after a disastrous fire there!)

The romance of a group of chivalric knights, with the few fighting the many, was further embellished by Geoffrey of Monmouth's account (1100–55) until it flowered finally and fully into the chivalric age of Edward III and the Knights of the Garter. The narrative of glorious resistance against an invader by a chivalric few, bound in close fellowship, has been part of British or English mythology ever since, right up to the Second World War. It is worth noting that the original context was the Celtic British resisting the Anglo-Saxon invaders, but after that the legend lost its ethnic moorings and became an inspiration to the English in resisting further continental invaders. As F. M. Stenton writes, "the silence of

Gildas may suggest that the Arthur of History was a less imposing figure than the Arthur of Legend."[7] Nevertheless, the legend, with its flimsy historical base, has had lasting influence on the English story, not least in the chivalry of Edward III, the founder of the Knights of the Garter.

Between 470 and 520, the trickle of immigration became more frequent, as more Saxons followed the conquest of land by elite Saxon bands. The vast majority of migration sites came into existence sometime between 470 and 520.[8] They weren't all pagan sites: a significant number of coins, found in burial sites, were inscribed with the *Chi-Rho* monogram signalling Christ. For the most part, pagan customs predominated: cremation reappeared as the funeral rite most favoured by the Angles, and pagan worship of Woden was common. In East Anglia, the Sutton Hoo treasure reveals the level of power, sophistication and wealth reached by a leader, quite possibly from Scandinavia, in these early kingdoms of the seventh century. Jewellery found in graves in Sarre, Kent, the great gold buckle of Sutton Hoo weighing 414.6 grams, the Byzantine Anastasius dish also found at Sutton Hoo, and the treasures found at Finglesham in Kent, all exemplify the confidence and culture of these emerging kingdoms. Likewise, the Staffordshire Hoard (found in 2009), with its intricate working and profusion of gold coin and jewellery, demonstrates the sophistication and prosperity of sixth-century Saxon society, belying any notion of the "Dark Ages" at the turn of pagan Saxon kingdoms to Christianity.

By 600, the political landscape of Britain had changed forever. In less than two hundred years since the departure of the Roman legions, a permanent change had occurred: the English (i.e. the German races) were added to the Romano-British. The story of the next century would be the conversion of these pagan Saxon kingdoms to Christianity through the Roman or papal missions of Augustine, as well as through the Celtic missions from Iona and Lindisfarne.

The Saxon kingdoms

Anglo-Saxon kingdoms were established in what came to be England during the sixth century. Ethnically a mixture of Germans and Scandinavians, they pushed the indigenous British Celts to the fringes of western Britain, especially to Cornwall, Wales, the North-West and Strathclyde. These Saxon kingdoms were more or less established by 570, by which time many of the British had been defeated and shifted west. Underlining this trend, and as we have noted, the

Anglo-Saxon Chronicle tells of a significant defeat of British forces by the Saxons at Dyrham, six miles north of Bath, in 577. In the south, the Saxon kingdoms consisted of the kingdoms of Kent and those of the South Saxons (Sussex), the East Saxons (Essex) and the West Saxons (Wessex). In the central part of England was the kingdom of Mercia or the Middle Angles, based in present-day Leicestershire and Derbyshire. The East Angles populated Lincolnshire and Norfolk and the Hwicce occupied Gloucestershire and Worcestershire. Lastly, to the north of the Humber, there was Northumbria, which consisted of two kingdoms: Bernicia to the north and Deira to the south. Sometimes these two northern kingdoms were ruled together and sometimes independently.[9] Over time, three Saxon kingdoms would gain ascendency over the others successively: Northumberland in the early seventh century; Mercia from 628 until 870, with the emergence of the Danelaw; and thirdly, Wessex under King Alfred and his successors from 871 onwards, until its final demise at the time of Edward the Confessor.

The character of these Saxon kingdoms was built around strong loyalty to a leader. The rule of these leaders, kings or, in some cases, *bretwaldas* (overlords) was the defining feature of the kingdom. The claim of a king's rule rested on his *virtus* or *nobilitas*. *Virtus* meant success in war and wisdom in ruling; *nobilitas* meant aristocratic descent from the gods, and in particular from Woden. Later on, genealogies would be written up to trace this noble line. The nature of this rule attracted warriors, who would become the king's stout companions on the battlefield and his fellow revellers in the hall. One such warrior, Beowulf, gives us the name of the oldest and longest poem in Old English.

Beowulf was a warrior who fought for Hrothgar, a Danish king. He defeated the monster Grendel, who attacked Hrothgar's hall and kingdom. For this service Beowulf was rewarded: "Thus the Danish Prince, descendent of Ing, handed over arms and horses, urging Beowulf to use them well."[10] Rewards were the prerogative of the king and a necessary payment for faithful service. The boundaries of kingdoms were thus not defined by hard and fast borders, but by confederations of peoples tied together by feelings of loyalty to a king or *bretwalda*. Early exemplars of this style of kingship were Redwald of the East Angles and Edwin of the Northumbrians. Given the nature of allegiances among these Saxon kingdoms, in order to convert the people, it was first necessary to convert the king.

The paganism of the Saxon kingdoms is clear from the names given to the days of the week in English, which arise from a mixture of classical and German deities: Sunday and Monday are ascribed to the sun and the moon respectively; Tuesday is derived from Tiw, the Norse god of war; Wednesday is Woden's day; Thursday Thor's day; Friday is Frigg, the goddess of love's day; and Saturday is named after Saturn. The pagan naming of weekdays is clear, and despite the later conversion of the Anglo-Saxons to Christianity no changes were made to the names of each weekday. Likewise, many place names in Saxon England betray their pagan origins. Harrow-on-the-Hill in Middlesex is derived from the Anglo-Saxon word *hearh*, meaning a sanctuary. This dominating hill was a "high-place" of pagan worship. The Saxon word *leah* means grove or shrine, so Thursley means the shrine of Thor. The names of pagan gods, such as Tiw, Woden and Thor, recur in place names throughout England. New ones would come with the Danes from the eighth century onwards, but the Saxon, Jute and Angle immigrations of the fifth and sixth centuries provided a new bedrock of pagan place names, indicating their original pagan worship. It was into this pagan England of the late sixth century that two new Christian missions came: one from Rome, the other from Ireland. Their coming was to transform England forever and bring a new Christian basis to the previously disparate and pagan peoples.

The Roman mission to England

By England I mean the Anglo-Saxon kingdoms of the south, east and north-east, as opposed to the Roman-Celtic communities of the south-west, Wales and the north-west around Carlisle and Whithorn, where there were Romano-Celtic churches, even with their own dioceses, in the fifth century. The story of these churches and their relationship with the Roman mission and the newly converted Saxon kingdoms forms part of the narrative of the Church in Britain and should not be overlooked or ignored, but they are not specifically English or Saxon.

The Roman mission to England stems from the extraordinary personality and ministry of Gregory the Great, the Pope from 590–604, some thirty years after the great Byzantine partnership of Emperor Justinian and Empress Theodora had briefly revived the Empire in both East and West.[11] Too soon the Lombards under King Alboin invaded Italy, capturing most of the north of the country, but falling short of Rome. Despite the pressure he was under, Gregory pushed on with the mission of the Church.

Gregory came from a rich and well-established Roman family with strong connections to the papacy. Like Ambrose of Milan in the fourth century, he was initially a civil administrator who rose to be the Prefect of the City of Rome in his thirties. Then, on coming into a considerable inheritance from his father, he turned the family palace on the Caelian Hill into a Benedictine monastery and became a simple brother.[12] He might have remained a monk for the rest of his life, but his diplomatic and administrative gifts were not allowed to lie dormant. He was sent to the Byzantine court of Constantinople for five years by Pope Pelagius, who had ordained him (no link to the aforementioned heresiarch Pelagius). His task was to persuade the Emperor to attack the Lombards who were threatening Rome, but in this he had little success. When Pelagius died from the plague, Gregory succeeded reluctantly to the papacy, the first monk to do so.

Gregory interpreted his life in terms of an allegory about Leah and Rachel, the two wives of the patriarch Jacob (Genesis 29–30:24). Rachel represented the contemplative life, beautiful but for the most part sterile, while Leah was ugly, but fertile. What Gregory came to advocate was a life of contemplation that leads to action: of prayer that leads to transformation. His contemplative experience was to be harnessed to action. With this objective in mind, he continued the life of a Benedictine monk as far as practicable but used it as the basis for action. "It is hard to name another occupant of the see of Peter who is at once so great a ruler and so sensitive to the spiritual possibilities of his position."[13] He reorganized the administration of the vast papal estates in Italy, Sicily and North Africa, and administered an energetic secretariat, leaving behind some 850 letters. He supported attempts to convert pagan monarchs in northern Europe, including Queen Brunhilde of Metz, who shockingly employed very dubious tactics of baptism at spear-point. Gregory advocated brotherly love and mutual dependence, calling himself the servant of the servants, and it was his mission to England, for which he is justly famous, that was to become the jewel in his missionary crown.

An anonymous author from Whitby tells the famous story of Gregory coming across Angles, either in the slave market of Rome or sent by a priestly envoy in Gaul, with the name of Candidus. Asked from which race these people came: "They answered, 'The people we belong to are called Angles'. 'Angels of God', he [Gregory] famously replied. Then he asked further 'what is the name of the King of that people?' They said 'Aelli', whereupon he said 'Alleluia, God's praise must be heard there."[14] Gregory chose the abbot of his own monastery to lead the mission to England: a man who would be known as Augustine of Canterbury.

Augustine was not an especially charismatic or imaginative character. He little resembled his more famous namesake, Augustine of Hippo. The reason for Gregory's choice of Augustine was that he was not so much looking for a single individual but was instead sending a whole community to England—a monastic plant you might say, numbering some forty monks. Augustine was the prefect of Gregory's personal monastery in Rome, committed to the Benedictine rule and presumably well known to Gregory. He was sent to Britain via Arles in Gaul, equipped with several letters of recommendation from Gregory for sees or monasteries along the way. These communities were found in Lèrins, Marseilles, Vienne, Autun and then the Loire, with the contingent probably pausing to pray at the shrine of St Martin of Tours. Martin's life as a monk bishop in Gaul, with all its profound influence on Gallic Christianity, was told by his biographer Sulpicius Severus. After one false start, which necessitated returning to Rome from southern France, Augustine's party eventually reached Etaples, from where they crossed to Kent to meet King Ethelbert of the Southern Saxons on the Isle of Thanet.

The choice of Kent and Ethelbert was not only due to their location on the south coast, but also to Ethelbert's Frankish Christian wife, Bertha, who had a bishop as a chaplain. Although the King was not immediately persuaded by Augustine's presentation of the faith, wanting him to perform the liturgy outside for fear of evil spirits, he was sufficiently impressed to give Augustine Canterbury to reside in. It was there that Augustine set up a more permanent community and ordered the lives of the monks on the Rule of Benedict. Bede tells us that several believed and were baptized. Augustine then wrote a lengthy letter to Gregory asking many questions about pastoral discipline, not least when women could enter the church after childbirth; whether men could enter the church without washing after intercourse or a nocturnal emission of semen; or how long a woman should wait after childbirth before "being approached by her husband".[15] Such were the concerns of Latin pastoral theologians from Augustine of Hippo onwards. What is clear is that the mission was the establishment of a community in Canterbury which was to express the Christian life in every detail, sexual and practical, and which was itself missional or evangelistic.

It was an incremental approach to mission, as advised by Gregory, and one that built on previous sites and ceremonies, and bore fruit gradually. Nevertheless, Gregory wrote to Eulogius, the Patriarch in Alexandria, on 29 July 598, saying that at Christmas 597, "more than 10,000 Englishmen are reported to have been baptized by our brother and fellow-bishop".[16] We need not take these figures literally, but they do demonstrate that an impact was being felt in Kent. The gains were hard to hold onto, however. Ethelbert's sons did not convert, and after the King's death, Kent reverted to paganism. Redwald, the overlord King of East Anglia and therefore *bretwalda*, also converted, but later relapsed. The magnificent memorial and burial site at Sutton Hoo was quite likely his. Redwald's main influence on English Christianity was in supporting Edwin as King of Bernicia or Northumberland; and to Edwin's memorable story of conversion we will return soon.

Augustine began a community in Canterbury, made some inroads for Christ into Kent, saw the King of Kent baptized before his death in 616, and appointed two assistant bishops: Mellitus, who became Bishop of London, and Justus of Rochester. His relationship with the Romano-Celtic Church was parlous, however. Bede tells how Augustine alienated the British church leaders and shows sympathy for Augustine—the appointee of his hero Gregory the Great—in the telling. The Celtic Church had been driven to the extremities of Britain. Although some doubtless intermingled with the pagan Saxon kingdoms, the bulk of their support was in Wales, the extreme west of England, particularly Cornwall, and in the north-west of England up to Whithorn in the Pictish kingdom of Strathclyde. Gregory had laid down that the British bishops and church should be subject to Augustine, so Augustine approached them with this objective in mind. For their part, the British leaders of the Church, mindful of the vicissitudes they had passed through and the way they had suffered at the hands of the pagan Saxons, now being evangelized by Augustine, were not about to easily yield their customs to his authority. A hermit advised the British church leaders that "if [Augustine] rises on your approach, you will know that he is a servant of Christ and will listen to him obediently; but if he despises you, and is not willing to rise in your presence, even though your numbers are greater, you should despise him in return".[17] Augustine did not rise. What is more, he asked them to fall in line with the Roman method of calculating Easter. They refused and Augustine pronounced a curse upon them, that they be defeated in battle: hardly a good start to ecumenical relations. Bede recalls that the British Christians later fought alongside a pagan king against their old enemies, the Saxons, and gleefully recounts that the British were defeated at the Battle of Chester by Ethelfrid, the King of Northumbria. Even the monks of Bangor, 1,200 of them according to Bede, who were praying for a British victory, were a legitimate target for Ethelfrid's forces. It was a defeat that would linger long in the minds of the British Christians, creating a rift between them, Rome and Canterbury.

Augustine died on 26 May 604, and it would be some years before a new Roman initiative of evangelization was effectively underway. The next mission was conducted by the more sensitive and subtle evangelist, Paulinus, who planted the seeds for an extraordinary flourishing of the Northumbrian Church.

The Northumbrian Church and the Irish connection

Soon after the death of King Ethelbert of Kent in 616 and the succession of his pagan sons, the Augustinian mission in Canterbury was interrupted. Augustine had died in 604. Laurentius succeeded him with the assistance of Mellitus of London and Justus of Rochester. Their efforts at evangelization were frustrated, however, and Mellitus and Justus returned to Rome, occasioning a lull in their work. Laurentius was even severely reproved by the Apostle Peter in a dream for not pressing on with the work and for considering flight to Gaul.[18]

Bede's attention then moves from Kent and Canterbury to the North of England, and the lands of the two kingdoms north of the Humber, called Deira and Bernicia. The former is roughly present-day Yorkshire and the latter Durham, Northumberland and eventually Cumberland. Sometimes separately ruled, and often at war with each other, these two kingdoms of Deira and Bernicia were combined by the military successes of Aethelfrith. Edwin, Aethelfrith's heir, was in exile in Kent, where he met his wife, the Christian Ethelberga. Kent had reverted to Christianity under Eadbald and Edwin was now under pressure to convert from Eadbald, Pope Boniface and his new wife, Ethelberga. After Edwin was saved from death in 626—when one of his *thegns* interposed himself between Edwin and an assassin's knife—a sense of God's providence increased. In addition, Edwin defeated the West Saxons, who had planned his demise, and had his daughter baptized a Christian. Paulinus, an Italian member of the community at Canterbury, was then assigned to Edwin's court as bishop.

The story of Edwin's conversion is worth telling, as it marks the first stage in this extraordinary period of Northumbrian Christianity, which lasted until the sack of Lindisfarne by the Danes in 793. It is also a story told vividly and movingly by Bede himself.

Edwin was born in 586 and was ejected from the kingdom of Deira by his neighbour, Aethelfrith of Bernicia. He then lived in exile at the court of Redwald of East Anglia, the Saxon overlord king or *bretwalda*. Edwin was reinstated by Redwald in 616, at the age of thirty, and ruled until 633, when he was killed in battle by pagan Mercians, who were in an unholy alliance with the Romano-Christian kingdom of Gwynedd under Cadwalla.

Edwin proceeded cautiously to faith despite the pressure of the court in Kent, the Pope and his wife. He held a council of leading men in 627, at which the pagan high priest Coifi opined: "O King, consider what this is which is now preached to us; for I verily declare to you, that the religion which we have hitherto professed has, as far as I can learn, no virtue in it."[19] Then, in a memorable passage, a leading member of the court said:

> The present life of man, O king, seems to me, in comparison of that time which is unknown to us, like to the swift flight of a sparrow through the room wherein you sit at supper in winter, with your commanders and ministers, and a good fire in the midst, whilst the storms of rain and snow prevail abroad; the sparrow, I say, flying in at one door, and immediately out another, whilst he is within, is safe from the wintry storm; but after a short space of fair weather, he immediately vanishes out of sight, into the dark winter from which he emerged. So this life of man appears for a short space, but of what went before, or what is to follow, we are utterly ignorant. If, therefore, this new doctrine contains something more certain, it seems justly to deserve to be followed.[20]

Paulinus also movingly recalled how the King's life had been spared when he was an exile in the court of Redwald and brought this to Edwin's attention.

In response to all this encouragement, Edwin embraced the faith and, on Easter Day in York in 627, was baptized. Edwin was only to live for another six years before he was killed in battle, but the seed had been sown in Northumbria and Deira. It was 180 years, says Bede, since "the English" came to Britain.[21] Many nobles and ordinary folk were baptized at the same time. Paulinus was occupied for thirty-six days, baptizing people in the River Swale near Catterick. Other kingdoms followed, such as that of the East Angles, now ruled by the son of Redwald, and the province of Lindsey around Lincoln. It reached the point where all of eastern England was Christian, apart from the East Saxons in Essex, who succumbed to the preaching of Cedd, some thirty years later. The bright light of Northumberland's Christian profession was all too soon extinguished by Edwin's defeat and death at the hands of Penda of Mercia and the British king Cadwalla at Hatfield Chase in 633.

Both Deira and Bernicia were subject to devastation by Cadwalla, who ruled "like a rapacious and bloody tyrant".[22] The light was to re-emerge when Oswald, heir to the kingdom of Northumberland, having been exiled to Iona in 633, returned in 634 to defeat Cadwalla at Heavenfield near Hexham. It was a turning point. Before the battle, Oswald, like Constantine before Milvian Bridge in 312, had a vision of victory. Straight after the victory his nobles were baptized, and Oswald sent to Iona for a bishop to come and evangelize Northumberland. After an initial mismatch, Aidan was sent, and took up residence at Lindisfarne. The

Irish mission to Northumberland had begun. Where Augustine had failed to include the Celtic or British Church in the south, Oswald now did in the north.

The period from 540 to 615 was the great age of Irish monasticism. The Irish took to monasticism like a hermit to his cell. Monasticism had steadily spread west from its origins in Egypt, Syria and Cappadocia. Pachomius (292–348), a former soldier, had begun a large community of hundreds of monks at Tabbenesi in Upper Egypt, for whom he wrote a rule of life. Basil of Caesarea (330–79) likewise wrote a rule for a more urban community around his hospice in Caesarea, Cappadocia. Athanasius (296–373) published the seminal work on the ascetic hermit, Antony the Great, which was to be highly influential. The Desert Fathers and Mothers made the wastes of Egypt to be like a city, it was said. There was a flight to the desert in the fourth century, and ascetic practices knew no bounds, whether these were minimal diet, sleep deprivation, posture (some quite literally stood upright for days on end), or poverty and chastity.

When Abba Serenus entertained Cassian and his friend for a meal, they ate table salt, three olives each, five grains of parched vetches, two prunes and a fig. Virginity was an elemental first step in the ascetic or monastic life. Cassian (360–435), the chronicler of monasticism in its various forms, be these solitary or communal, was a conduit of ascetic practices to the West. His *Institutes* and *Conferences* (discussions with a number of Desert Fathers, ranging over whole areas of monastic life, from humility to sex) became handbooks for the eremitic way of life.

Benedict of Nursia (480–547) pioneered a new monastic rule at Monte Casino in Italy: spare, simple, but humane, and which eventually became the gold standard of monasticism in the West. Monasticism spread to Gaul, to the south with Cassian at Marseilles and Lérins, and to the Loire basin with Gregory and St Martin of Tours (336–97). It is probable that the Irish first connected with the Gaulish ascetics on the Loire through trade—being well-known purveyors of good quality shoes—and then through more religious contacts. The Irish were also open to the Coptic and Italian traditions.

The monastic life had a ready appeal for the Irish. It resonated with their close kinship groups and family law, whereby a monastery could stay within a family. In this way, aristocratic families could found monasteries and retain certain rights over them. The monastic movement appealed to the more dynamic and less structured model of authority in Ireland: dioceses and the Roman system were relatively untested as the country had not been colonized by Rome. Monastic life was also compatible with Ireland's wild and windswept landscape, emerging from the spiritual discipline of pilgrimage, as new shorelines and remote islands were discovered through prayerful journeys. Thus, Skellig Michael provided the perfect setting for a community: it was as remote as a cave in the Egyptian desert but set among the Atlantic rollers and sea birds. Skellig Michael hung on the side of a 600ft cliff, with six stone beehive cells clustered around an oratory that housed a small community. It was out of this context that the golden age of Irish monasticism sprang, with its love of learning, of the Trinity, prayer, and the natural landscape. These communities were both prayerful and missionary. From among these monks Columbanus and Columba came to give new missionary vistas to their free movement, the former to Gaul and then Italy at Bobbio, the latter to Iona.

Columbanus trained for a time under Comgall at Bangor after earlier schooling in Leinster. He went to Gaul in about 590, around the same time Augustine arrived in Canterbury. He left Ireland, as his biographer makes clear, because he too wanted to set out on pilgrimage, much like Abraham leaving Haran (Genesis 12). He was not so much seeking to establish a new evangelistic thrust in fresh territory as looking to see where the Spirit led him. The Spirit led him to Gaul, where he asked King Theuderic for a wilderness in which to settle, and was given wasteland at Annegray in Burgundy. An extant record reveals that his monastic rule was severe and his penances were strict. It would be wrong to imply that because he was Celtic in ethnic origin, he, and Columba after him, were anti-Roman; far from it. In 613, Columbanus wrote to Pope Boniface IV, having founded monasteries in Gaul and Italy at Luxeuil and Bobbio, saying, "For all we Irish, inhabitants of the edge of the world, are disciples of saints Peter and Paul . . . none has been a heretic. The Catholic faith (*fides catholica*) as it were delivered by you first, who are successors of the Holy Apostles, *is maintained unbroken*."[23] For a time he lived as a solitary in a cave, expelling a bear to do so, thereby demonstrating that characteristic Irish connection with the natural world. But his allegiance, despite his solitary existence, was to the See of St Peter.

What Columbanus did in the heart of France, his contemporary Columba did on the north-west coast of Scotland, in a community that survives to this day on Iona. Columba was a member of the kingly O'Niall family and was born around 521. The village of Gratan in County Donegal is celebrated as the place of his birth.[24] Fostered by a priest called Cruithnechan, he was then taught in Leinster. Like others, such as Guthlac from Mercia, St Francis Assisi and Ignatius Loyola, he may have been a soldier undertaking this voyage of pilgrimage to Britain out of a sense of penance. In 563 he left Ireland, "choosing to be a pilgrim for Christ". By 574, the community was well-established. The Picts, Bede tells us, were converted by Columba's preaching.[25] Columba's life, according to his biographer Adomnan, the eighth-century ninth Abbot of Iona (679–704), was characterized by three things: the gift of prophecy, the performance of miracles and the presence of angels. Together these made for a powerful ministry and were typical of Irish monastic spirituality. Adomnan's first book begins:

> When countless hosts of horrible devils remained making war against him (Columba), visible to his bodily eyes, and beginning to inflict deadly diseases in his monastic community, he, one man alone, with God's help repelled them and drove them out of this our principal island. With Christ's help, he curbed the raging fury of wild beasts sometimes killing them and sometimes driving them away.[26]

The *Life* continues at the same pace, showing the holiness and power of St Columba's life. He died on Sunday, 9 June 597. The monastery continued strongly, and in 633 arguably had its greatest opportunity when Oswald, the successor to Edwin of Northumberland, sought sanctuary on the island from Cadwalla, and began an association with Iona and Irish monasticism that was to change England.

Oswald returned to Northumberland when the time was right, rallied his nobles and army and defeated Cadwalla, but not before erecting a holy cross and, with his nobles, praying before it and promising to fight for the glory of God.[27] The place of battle was called Heavenly Field. Following his victory, Oswald requested that a bishop be sent from Iona to begin a community in Northumberland. After a false start, when an unsuitable man was despatched, Aidan was sent to Oswald. Aidan, Bede wrote, was a man "of singular meekness, piety and moderation; zealous in the cause of God, though not altogether according to knowledge: for he was wont to keep Easter Sunday according to the custom of his country, which we have before so often mentioned from the fourteenth to the twentieth moon".[28] Of that lack of "knowledge" we shall hear more later in connection with the Synod of Whitby, but there was to be no short-changing the power and humility of Aidan's ministry. He was given Lindisfarne as a place for his monastery, and so was founded one of the seminal influences on English Christianity. Separated from the mainland by a causeway that was and is covered with sea water at high tide, and thus both isolated and connected, Lindisfarne provided a suitable springboard for this Irish mission to the North. Aidan gave himself to monastic prayer, studying the scriptures, learning the psalms, building a wooden monastery—later rebuilt in stone—and travelling by foot to evangelize in the countryside or visit the King at Bamburgh Castle on the mainland. When given a horse by the King, Aidan refused to ride it and gave it away, believing it inappropriate for an evangelist, whereupon he was upbraided by Oswald—who later repented of his attitude and earnestly sought

Aidan's forgiveness. This special and mutually respectful relationship between a king and his bishop was cut short by Oswald's untimely death at the age of thirty-eight in battle against the Mercians in 642, after only nine years' rule.[29] He was considered a martyr king: light shone round his body and bones, devils were exorcised in his now mortal presence.[30] Aidan was to live for nine more years before being succeeded by Finan—an Irish monk who held to the same "knowledge" about Easter. He was buried in the chapel at Bamburgh.

Amidst the continuous fighting between Anglo-Saxon kings, not least in Northumberland between the two main areas of Deira and Bernicia, and between Mercia and the Britons, the conversion of the other kingdoms went forward. Bede tells us that in Kent, Earconbert ordered the destruction of the idols.[31] Likewise, the West Saxons received the word of God through the preaching of Birinius in 635.[32] Oswald stood godfather at the baptism of the West Saxon king, Cynegils. Fursey, another Irish monk, baptized by St Brendan the traveller, was honourably received by the East Angles and built a monastery there.[33] Oswy of Northumberland persuaded Sigbert of the East Saxons to become a Christian, and Cedd, an Anglo-Saxon monk from Lindisfarne, was sent to teach and evangelize the East Saxons. He established a monastery at Bradwell-on-Sea. Perhaps most significant of all, Prince Paeda of the Mercians received the faith in 653 on the occasion of his marriage into the Northumberland royal family of Oswy. Chad was sent as bishop to the Mercians and Oswald's brother, who ruled Northumberland from 642–70, was the effective overlord king or *bretwalda* of the English. Chad's mission was most effective in bringing Christianity to the Mercian kingdom. He was buried in Lichfield, and the Lichfield Angel may well have been part of Chad's tomb there.

It was not long before a resolution was needed between the so-called lack of "knowledge" of the Irish monks about the date of Easter and the existing Roman practice. To this end a synod was called at the Abbey of Whitby, which was to define the future direction of the English Church in terms of its main association with either Rome or Ireland. The Abbey of Whitby was founded by Abbess Hilda, who had been trained by Aidan at a foundation in Hartlepool begun by Oswy for his infant daughter, a member of the Deiran royal family. She was admirably qualified to host this landmark conference: energetic, capable, intelligent and sought out by kings on account of her wisdom. The Synod of Whitby was to herald the decline of Irish influence in the English Church and the ascendency of Rome.

The Synod of Whitby

Whitby was one of the east coast monasteries and convents that determined the shape of Northumbrian Christianity in the seventh and eighth centuries, along with Lindisfarne and Monkwearmouth-Jarrow. Just as Emperor Constantine summoned the bishops of the East to the imperial palace at Nicaea to determine the Church's response to the Arian heresy—then a dagger to the heart of Christianity—here King Oswy, in much humbler circumstances, provoked by his son Alfrith, summoned the main protagonists in the debate over the observance of Easter to Whitby. The issues were not as great as those of 325, but Whitby would determine the nature of the English Church thereafter: whether it would be Celtic or Roman.

The date of the celebration of Easter was an ecclesial issue with powerful symbolic overtones, and it had come to the surface both in the court of Oswy and in the practice of the Church. In short, two methods of calculating the date were in use. The issue was over whether Easter should be celebrated on Nisan 14, which was the fourteenth day of the first lunar month of the Jewish year and the first day of Passover. Part of the anti-Jewishness of the Early Church led Nicaea to condemn as heretics all who celebrated Easter on Nisan 14, regardless of whether or not that day was a Sunday. It was of paramount importance for them that Easter was celebrated on a Sunday, the first day of the week. In order to avoid any celebration of Easter on Nisan 14, the Roman Church celebrated between Nisan 15 and 21. Yet the Irish monks from Iona celebrated Easter according to an earlier tradition, which followed Anatolius, Bishop of Laodicea, and which ran from Nisan 14–20. This meant that sometimes the two celebrations of Easter could be a week apart. The issue was further complicated by the need to compute the Roman calendar into the lunar cycles used to establish the month of Nisan. The intricate business of matching or intercalating Roman calendars with lunar cycles provoked Victorius of Aquitaine to work out, with great diligence, a 532-year cycle (19x28) in the mid-fifth century. Although both the Alexandrian system and Victorius's system adopted a nineteen-year cycle, they varied over the prediction of the vernal equinox, thereby creating a further divergence over the date of Easter. The Irish made things even more complicated by using an older eighty-four-year cycle wrongly attributed to Bishop Anatolius. You can see that calculating the date of Easter was no easy matter, and the world-wide Church is still at variance today.

The complexity of the Easter calculation might have muddled along were it not for the fact that King Oswy (following Iona) and his Queen Eanfled (following Kent or Rome) celebrated Easter on different dates.[34] To have a court so split was complicated and confusing. And Oswy's son, the ever-busy Alfrith, who had come under the influence of Wilfrid—about whom we will hear more—wanted the discrepancy sorted out. A synod was thus called at Whitby.

The proceedings of Whitby and the speeches of the main protagonists are vividly recorded by Bede.[35] On the Celtic side were Bishop Colman of Lindisfarne, the successor to Finan and Aidan, supported by Abbess Hilda and Cedd. On the Roman side were Bishop Agilbert, the Frankish bishop of the West Saxons, Agatho and Wilfrid. Colman spoke for the Irish, basing his preferred observance of Easter on Anatolius, while Wilfrid was put forward by Agilbert as the advocate for the Roman practice. Wilfrid, aged thirty-three, in the full flush of manhood, and already extensively travelled (having been to Gaul and Rome), deployed powerful, sophisticated arguments against the simple tradition of the Irish, concluding as follows:

> We found the same (Roman observance) practised in Africa, Asia, Egypt, Greece, and all the world, wherever the church of Christ is spread abroad, through several nations and tongues, at one and the same time: except only these and their accomplices in obstinacy. I mean the Picts and the Britons, who foolishly, in these remote islands of the world, and only in part even of them, oppose all the rest of the universe.[36]

It was an uncompromising argument. Wilfrid was the type of man to win an argument and lose an audience. When Wilfrid appealed to Rome's supremacy, which he based on the authority of Peter, the old King Oswy gave his assent. "Whom should we obey," Oswy asked, "St Columba or St Peter?" Put like that, there was only one answer. The English Church would follow the Roman practice. Colman, disappointed and cast down, left for Scotland and eventually founded a community in Inishboffin, off the west coast of Ireland. Cedd decided to comply and Wilfrid was soon made a bishop.

Although the decision was ostensibly about Easter and adopting the Roman tonsure, it was about much more. It was a submission to Roman authority advocated by a forthright English ascetic nobleman rather than to the Irish missionaries. It was a decision to follow the Catholic Church vested in Rome rather than a specific type of Irish Catholicism with its distinctive love of the environment, its prayerful devotion to the Trinity, simplicity, asceticism, penitence and scholarship. Whitby decided the direction the English Church would travel for almost a thousand years, until the Reformation.

Theodore, Wilfrid and Cuthbert

The later part of the seventh century, after the conversion of most of the Anglo-Saxon kingdoms, belonged to the influence of three men very different in their outlook and their priorities. Two of them, Wilfrid and Cuthbert, were Northumbrians; both had roots in Lindisfarne, but their priorities in ministry were quite different. The third, with whose story we will begin, was completely different in background, outlook and talents; but had an unexpected and powerful influence on the English Church.

Theodore was from Tarsus in present-day southern Turkey, twelve miles from the Mediterranean and close to the Syrian border. The Apostle Paul had made the city of Tarsus famous by being its citizen. In 602, the date of Theodore's birth, it was part of the Byzantine Empire, but was to be invaded by the Sassanid Persians and later, from 637, by the rampant Muslim forces, which most probably drove Theodore west to Rome. Greek-speaking, Theodore was educated in nearby Antioch, with its distinctive theology and literal rather than allegorical interpretation of the Bible, and also in Constantinople. At some point before 660 he travelled to Rome as a monk, where with his evident theological and linguistic skills—having added Latin to his native Greek—he came to the attention of the Pope.

When the Archbishop of Canterbury, Deusdedit, died in 664—the same year as the Synod of Whitby—his successor Wighard was sent to Rome to take up his *pallium*. On arriving in Rome, he died from the plague, whereupon Bede tells us Pope Vitalian looked for a successor. At first the Pope chose Hadrian, an African "well versed in holy writ, experienced in monastic and ecclesiastical discipline, and excellently skilled both in the Greek and Latin tongues".[37] Hadrian declined and recommended Theodore in his place. Theodore was well-qualified as a teacher and holy man and was then sixty-six years old. Accompanied by Hadrian on the route to Britain, he took the now well-tried journey by ship from the port of Rome to Marseilles, then up the Rhone, across country to the Loire, and thence to the Channel ports and Canterbury. The journey took approximately two years from the time of his consecration in Rome. Amazingly, this sixty-six-year-old man would hold the office of archbishop for twenty-one years. For Bede these were golden years. He writes:

> For as much as both of them (Hadrian and Theodore) were well read both
> in sacred and secular literature, they gathered a crowd of disciples and there
> flowed from them rivers of knowledge to water their hearers; and, together

with books of holy writ, they also taught them the arts of ecclesiastical poetry, astronomy, and arithmetic. A testimony of which is that there are still living at this day some of their scholars who are well versed in the Greek and Latin tongues as their own.[38]

Theodore toured the country, appointing bishops to dioceses, which he established by paying scrupulous attention to where their boundaries should be in relation to tribal lands. He appointed Chad as Bishop of Lichfield among the Mercians at the request of King Wulfhere. During his archiepiscopacy he also held two councils, one at Hertford in 672/3 and another at Heathfield ten years later. At Hertford, Theodore sought to limit bishops' authority to their own diocese (surely a warning shot across Wilfrid's bows), forbade all second marriages, and ruled that no priest should "wander about" performing ministry wherever he wished. It was the beginning of structure in diocesan ministry, to which would be added new dioceses over time, and the eventual internal sub-divisions of parishes.[39] One man who would test these rules to the limit, however, particularly concerning bishops, was Wilfrid.

Wilfrid, unlike the Greek-speaking Theodore, was a Northumbrian nobleman who, as a young man, was assigned to care for a paralysed *thegn* and was himself pursuing a monastic vocation on Lindisfarne. After this time Wilfrid appears to have gone south to Canterbury at the invitation of Queen Eanfled of Northumbria, from where he went on his first visit to Rome in 653, aged twenty, along with Biscop Baducing, the founder of Monkwearmouth-Jarrow.[40] Wilfrid stayed a long time en route with Archbishop Dalfinus of Lyons, was welcomed into his home and even offered the hand of his niece in marriage. Wilfrid remained true to his original purpose, however, and proceeded to Rome, where Eddius, his devoted biographer, tells us "he spent many months in daily visits to the shrines of the saints" and made a close friend of Boniface, Archdeacon of Rome. On his return journey he received the Roman tonsure from Dalfinus at Lyons, denoting his monastic calling and commitment to all things Roman.

Back in Northumberland, his patron, King Alhfrith, gave him a site for a monastery at Ripon, consisting of ten hides of land (approximately three hundred acres), which was to be the first in a whole line of monasteries that Wilfrid would establish nationwide. Following the Synod of Whitby, where Wilfrid energetically upheld Roman customs, Colman, the Irish bishop and Prior of Lindisfarne, had withdrawn to work amongst the Picts and later returned to Ireland. Tuda was appointed in Colman's place, and then, on the sudden death of Tuda from the plague, Wilfrid was appointed Bishop of Northumbria in York, whereupon he went back to Gaul for his consecration "to avoid any question of the validity of his orders".[41] Wilfrid was by now a persuasive leader. Eddius enthusiastically says of him:

> He was always pure and open, tempering scrupulous regard for truth and solemnity of manner with persuasive charm. His main topics of conversation were the mysteries of the law, the teachings of the faith, the virtue of continence, and the practice of right living. He knew before ever he opened his mouth, exactly what to say and when and how to say it. He laid special emphasis on prayer, fasting, and vigils, and was forever searching the scriptures and studying the canons of the Church.[42]

Wilfrid's consecration as Bishop of Northumbria must have happened while Theodore was travelling to Canterbury. Eschewing an English consecration because of its rudimentary liturgy and perfunctory buildings (York was then just a wooden church), Wilfrid opted for the full panoply of Gaul and its more elaborate liturgy, its more ancient institutions, and its untainted Easter practices. The trouble was that he was away so long that Chad, a Celt, was consecrated Bishop of York in his place by King Oswy, "in complete defiance of canon law".[43]

When Wilfrid returned from Gaul and found Chad in his place as Bishop of York, Theodore "upbraided" Chad and reinstated Wilfrid in 669.[44] Wilfrid set about rebuilding the church in York with stone and "acquiring vast tracts of land" for its endowment.[45] New stone churches were also built in Ripon and Hexham. Despite Theodore's support of Wilfrid in re-appointing him Bishop of York, a quarrel broke out between them about the size of the diocese of York, resulting in Wilfrid's dismissal and his appeal to the Pope for arbitration. Theodore wanted to divide the enormous diocese that ran from South Yorkshire to the borders, but characteristically Wilfrid would have none of it—for him biggest was best.

A further journey to Rome ensued in 679, with a fruitful mission in Frisia en route. In Rome, Wilfrid laid his case for unfair dismissal from York in person before Pope Agatho. The synod that heard Wilfrid's case proceeded to find against Archbishop Theodore and thundered, "We decree and lay down that Bishop Wilfrid, God's beloved, to take possession of the see which until recent times was his. According to the terms previously defined."[46]

Wilfrid returned triumphant to Northumberland with this bull of vindication, signed and sealed by the Pope, only to find that King Ecgfrith refused to recognize it. Earlier, Wilfrid had persuaded Ecgfrith's first queen, Etheldreda, to refuse intercourse with her husband, thus preserving her virginity, and instead found a convent in Ely, which she did. Humiliated and resentful, not surprisingly, the King was no friend of Wilfrid's. Wilfrid was imprisoned for nine months and then exiled, and the Queen, to biographer Eddius's horror, wore Wilfrid's reliquary as a necklace "both at home and in her chamber".[47]

Wilfrid's exile took him to Mercia, then on a further visit to Rome, and on his return through a storm in the Channel to the South Saxons at Selsey in Sussex, where he conducted a successful mission amongst the pagan court "baptizing the principal generals and soldiers of that country"[48] and, inevitably, founding a monastery on eighty-seven hides (2,500 acres) of land very generously granted by King Ethelwalch.[49]

In 686, a further attempt at reconciliation between Theodore and Wilfrid was attempted. Wilfirid's biographer sees this as very much the result of Theodore's uneasy conscience, since Theodore reached the end of his life in 690. By now King Ecgfrith had been killed in battle against the Picts and his successor, King Aldfrith of Northumberland, was willing to invite Wilfrid back, although peace between the two did not last long. A synod at Austerfield, near Bawtry in Yorkshire, decided that far from restoring Wilfrid's position, they would instead "strip Wilfrid of all he possessed". Wilfrid was typically uncowed by their actions, remonstrating with the synod that he alone had stood up for Catholic orthodoxy in Northumberland:

> After the death of those elders whom Pope Gregory sent to us, was I not the first to root out from the church the foul weeds planted by the Scots (i.e. the Irish)? Did I not convert the whole of the Northumbrian nation to celebrating Easter at the proper time as the Holy See demanded, and to having the proper Roman tonsure in the form of the crown instead of your old way of shaving the back of the head from the top down? Did I not teach you to chant according to the practice of the early church, with two choirs singing alternately, but simultaneously for responsories and antiphons and doing the responses and chants together antiphonally? Did I not bring the monastic life into line with the rule of St Benedict never before introduced into these parts?[50]

None of these Roman achievements persuaded the synod of English bishops, brought together by the new Archbishop Berhtwald, to endorse him. Instead Wilfrid was stripped of all his offices and excommunicated. His uncompromising Roman ways and papal support availed him nothing. Despite his powerful gifts of oratory and persuasion, his single-minded purpose, his ascetic lifestyle, his undoubted courage and tenacity, he was unable to gain the support of his peers and the affection of his fellow countrymen. He might have been able to win an argument, but he lost the constituency he sought to gain.

He appealed to the papacy once more, travelling again to Rome in 703. Pope John was the new man in office. A long enquiry followed, lasting months, until the Pope, in line with his predecessors, exonerated Wilfrid. The English bishops were requested to be reconciled with him. Wilfrid returned home, but another synod of bishops found it hard to be reconciled with him. It was agreed that Wilfrid be given back Ripon and Hexham, but on his way to Hexham he became ill again, and died eighteen months later in 709, having settled the future of the monasteries. How different was the course of Wilfrid's life from that of his fellow countryman, Cuthbert!

Cuthbert

Cuthbert was also a Northumbrian, probably born in the lowlands of present-day Scotland, although trained by the Irish at the monastery at Melrose, founded by Aidan of Lindisfarne, in turn a product of Iona. When Cuthbert was about seventeen, around the time of the death of Aidan in 651, he was called to the monastic life. He served in Ripon, Melrose and finally at Lindisfarne, from around 665. He became Prior of Lindisfarne, implementing the decisions of Whitby in the monastic life there, seemingly without difficulty, although for many years he would give himself to the life of a hermit and become the very epitome of Celtic sainthood.

Two *Lives* of Cuthbert exist: one by Bede, as well as a previous anonymous *Life* and a poem about Cuthbert's life also composed by Bede. As with other biographies or histories of the period, there are accounts of the appearances of angels and many healings. Bede has a famous account of Cuthbert praying all night in the sea whilst a monk at Melrose:

> Down he went towards the beach beneath the monastery and out into the sea until he was up to his arms and neck in deep water. The splash of the waves accompanied his vigil throughout the dark hours of the night. At daybreak he came out, knelt down in the sand and prayed. Then two otters bounded out of the water, stretched themselves out before him, warmed his feet with their breath, and tried to dry him on their fur. They finished, received his blessing, and slipped back to their watery home.[51]

Cuthbert was, it seems, the St Francis of the North Sea, albeit in a far more inhospitable climate than that of Umbria.

After Melrose he was then transferred to Lindisfarne, where he became prior. He preferred the life of a hermit, however, and so built a hermitage on Farne Island, a little distant from Lindisfarne—having first experimented with the solitary life on a rock close to Lindisfarne, which is still visible today. There he remained, and in the best tradition of the Desert Fathers, Bede tells us, "was delighted after a long and spotless active life that he should be thought worthy to ascend to the stillness of divine contemplation".[52] Like Simeon Stylites, he gave spiritual advice to all who sought him over the next twenty years: "There he gained victory over our invisible enemy by solitary prayer and fasting."[53] From this eremitic life he was called by King Ecgfrith to be a bishop in 684 (reluctantly from Cuthbert's point of view). His episcopal ministry was literally exemplary:

> He protected the flock committed to him by constant prayer on their behalf, by wholesome admonition and—which is the real way to teach—by example first and precept later. He took care to comfort the sad and faint-hearted and to bring back those that delighted in evil to godly sorrow. He fed the hungry, clothed the destitute, and had all the other marks of a perfect bishop.[54]

A three-year ministry of teaching, healing and evangelization followed. Bede tells us that Cuthbert "brought down the grace of the Holy Ghost by the imposition of hands on those newly regenerated in Christ".[55] Aware of his impending death, Cuthbert returned to his hermitage for his final two months of life. His death was to be as powerful as his life. After eleven years, his body was disinterred and found to be free of corruption. A century later, when the Vikings invaded and destroyed Lindisfarne, his body was once more disinterred and carried as a moving symbol of Christian resistance to the Vikings around the North. Like the Ark in the Old Testament, Cuthbert's body traversed the region until an eventual resting place was found in Durham Cathedral, where it remains to this day. (This was after having reposed for years in Chester-le-Street.) A Gospel of St John was buried with him (being the oldest book in the West in its original binding and now in the British Library) along with vestments made from Byzantine silk.

Theodore, Wilfrid and Cuthbert can be seen as three "types" to occur and re-occur in English church history: one being the scholarly church administrator of foreign extraction, another the forceful Romanized church leader, and the third the hermit saint: humble, self-effacing, but tough and self-disciplined. Of the three, Cuthbert was taken most to the hearts of the English, particularly in the North, although he was to be a powerful influence on King Alfred in his resistance to the Vikings. Irish or Celtic in missionary manner, but faithful to the Roman hierarchy and devoted to mission inspired by contemplation, Cuthbert became the unnamed patron saint of the Anglo-Saxon kingdoms, especially in the coming days of resistance to the Vikings.

Edward the Confessor was to be the idol of Norman and later kings, followed by St George, who would be the emblem of the crusading and military kings of the later medieval period, but Cuthbert remained the patron saint of the North of England, and was arguably closest to the genuine centre of English spirituality. Add to these three figures the fair-minded and scrupulous teacher, Bede, the Christian King Alfred, and the missionary martyr Boniface, and by the ninth century most of the key "types" in the English Church had been laid down. Much of the spiritual fertilizer for their flowering came from Northumbrian monasticism, which was to flourish especially in the first half of the eighth century, and to which we now turn.

Bede and Northumbrian monasticism

Northumbrian monasticism was the result of three principal influences: the missionary zeal of the Irish monks who founded Lindisfarne, Coldingham,[56] Melrose and Ripon; the northern Gaulish monasteries that influenced aristocratic Anglo-Saxon women; and the introduction of the Rule of Benedict, mostly by Wilfrid. In terms of spiritual formation and mission, the monastic life was well-suited to the customs of the Anglo-Saxons and the Irish, for both valued strong family ties and close identification with a leader (in the case of monasticism, with an abbot or abbess). The chief Northumbrian monasteries were on the east coast: Whitby, which was a foundation of men and women; Monkwearmouth-Jarrow, Hartlepool; and of course, Lindisfarne. Inland, Ripon and Hexham were influential houses. Of all these foundations, the most influential in the eighth century were Lindisfarne and Monkwearmouth-Jarrow, and that largely because of Bede.

Monkwearmouth-Jarrow was founded by Benedict Biscop (originally Biscop Baducing, until he added the Christian name Benedict whilst in France). It was a double monastery in the sense of being based in two places: Monkwearmouth (founded in 674) is in present-day Sunderland on the north side of the Wear, and Jarrow (founded in 681) on the south side of the Tyne. By 716, they had some 600 monks and were indeed large—in fact there never was, probably, a larger monastic community in England. Biscop was a member of the Northumbrian aristocracy, who, after spending time at Canterbury where he was temporarily abbot, travelled extensively on the continent. He went to Rome, and to the famous monastery at Lérins in the south of France, where he stayed for two years, as well as to Ravenna. During his travels—a kind of monastic Grand Tour of the seventh century—he observed monastic and church practices of both Roman and Byzantine kinds. He even included Coptic artefacts in his collections of art and books. His wealth enabled him to procure stonemasons, glaziers, pictures of both Old and New Testament scenes, icons and chalices. He also acquired the customs of Latin chanting, and in 679 took John, the arch chanter of St Peter's in Rome, back to the windswept Northumbrian coast.

The most important addition to the life at Monkwearmouth-Jarrow, however, was the arrival of Bede, aged seven, in 680, dedicated by his parents to lifelong service in the community. Bede would eventually carry the reputation of the monastery throughout Europe. He became a Doctor of the Catholic Church, recognized for his biblical theology, which had a wide impact on the medieval Church. It was the combination of Bede and the *scriptoria* (writing rooms) in the monasteries that made for such a profound and lasting influence on European Christianity.

Bede was like the sharp arrowhead at the end of a well-crafted shaft. As with all really great advances in science or the arts or scholarship, the achievement was the result of various factors *simultaneously and providentially* coming together: the patronage of King Ecgfrith, who gave land for the establishment of the monastery; the presence of the cultured and enlightened founder, Biscop, endowing the monastery and giving it its spiritual resources; and the steady and holy hand of Celofrith, first Prior of Jarrow and then abbot of the joint foundation, so much loved and revered by the community and by Bede (who wrote a delightful *Life* of this humble and holy man). In this context, Bede offered his own unique gifts as historian, exegete of the biblical text, faithful guardian of a spiritual tradition combining Roman with Celtic spirituality, and vigilant intercessor for the Saxon Church.

He was not without his blind spots: his dislike of the indigenous Romano-Celtic Church for instance, but his merits far outweighed these flaws. He was a grammarian, a shrewd observer of nature—having the makings of a scientist—, a diligent and honest historian, a counsellor and teacher of many pupils. He died as he lived. He was working with urgency on a translation of John's Gospel into Anglo-Saxon before he died. On the day before he died, he said to his pupil,

"Learn speedily, I know not how long I will be with you, or whether my Maker will remove me shortly":

> On the afternoon of the day Bede died, his scribe and boy Wilbert said, "There is still one sentence dear Master, which is not written down." And he said, "Well, then, write it." And after little space the boy said, "Now it is finished." And he answered, "Well thou hast spoken truth; it is finished. Take my head in thy hands, for it much delights me to sit opposite my holy place where I used to pray, that so sitting I may call upon my Father." And thus upon the floor of the cell singing "Glory be to the Father, and to the Son, and to the Holy Ghost" and the rest, he breathed his last.[57]

Bede's many biblical commentaries all survived him, along with his *History of the English Nation*, and were all copied many hundreds of times. Eventually, they were included in the great Victorian publications of Migne's *Patrologia Latina*[58] and in Giles's *Patres Ecclesiae Anglicanae.*[59] For translation and exegesis, he was the Jerome of the North, but a good deal less quarrelsome. As historian, he was to the English what Livy or Tacitus or Varro were to Rome.

Bede hardly moved from Monkwearmouth-Jarrow—his scholarship was made possible by the *scriptoria* and library there. Biscop had stocked the library from his travels, doubling its contents. He brought back works of the Latin Fathers and, from Rome, a copy of the complete Bible from Vivarium in southern Italy, a monastery founded by the great exegete and scholar Cassiodorus, made famous by his *Institutiones*. This Bible, probably the *Codex Grandior*, a pandect, i.e. a complete Bible, was one of three complete texts held in the library in Vivarium, which, along with other books, were dispersed following the death of Cassiodorus in c. 580 and the monastery's probable destruction by the Lombards. Italy's loss was Northumbria's gain, and it was this *Codex* that most probably served Bede as the sumptuously illustrated biblical text from which other famous copies were made. The most celebrated of these was the *Codex Amiatinus*, which was made with two other copies. These were vellum manuscripts requiring an estimated 1,550 calves' hides. The cost of production, the skill needed, and the time spent on each *Codex* was more than a labour of love; indeed, it was a lifetime's work. Of the three *Codices*, the Vikings destroyed two, and the third was taken by Abbot Ceolfrid to Rome. In fact, Ceolfrid had resigned the abbacy in 716, knowing himself to be near the end of life. He left the monastery for good, to the consternation of the monks, who, Bede tells us, "(fell) to their knees and repeatedly imploring him with sobs and tears [to stay], but in the end he had his wish".[60]

Ceolfrid died en route to Rome at Langres in Burgundy, but his fellow monks delivered the *Codex* to the Pope, who in turn gave it to a monastery. It now resides in the Laurenziana Library in Florence, as the earliest complete *Codex* of the Latin Bible in the world, and the most accurate rendering of Jerome's original text, produced in Monkwearmouth-Jarrow. If Ceolfrid had not decided to resign the abbacy and go to Rome, it would almost certainly have been lost in Viking raids.

The skill of the scribes in Northumbria, the accuracy of their work, and the beauty of their illustrations, were demonstrated in this *Codex* and in the Lindisfarne Gospels. Using Insular or Hiberno-Saxon script as opposed to the Italian script of *Codex Amiatinus*, the Lindisfarne Gospels were the work of Eadfrith, later Bishop of Lindisfarne. He was a master of Irish calligraphy, a tradition that stretched back to the first century. Written in honour of Cuthbert around 715, the Lindisfarne Gospels were rescued by the monks during the Viking invasions and resided in Chester-le-Street until the dissolution of the monasteries. (They were later collected by Sir Henry Cotton and passed to the British Library.) The calligraphy of the Gospels, the decoration of Northumbrian crosses—used to mark graves and gathering places for worship and memorials—are lasting monuments to the vitality of Northumbrian Christianity in the seventh and eighth centuries.

The most famous cross at Ruthwell in Dumfriesshire has fragments of the famous Old English poem the *Dream of the Rood* inscribed upon it.[61] Such spiritual and artistic vitality was not confined to the North of England, although it found its apogee there.

Elsewhere in England

Centres of worship, prayer and training grew in number throughout England from the late seventh century. Canterbury flourished as one such centre under Theodore and Hadrian, Pope Vitalian's first choice for archbishop. In Canterbury, the schools there taught biblical studies, Greek and Latin, and the preferred—by Greek-speaking Theodore—Antiochene style of exegesis, which was more literal in style than the allegorical Latin style favoured by Ambrose, Augustine and others.

Teaching about penance was commonplace, with Theodore writing a book on the subject. To accompany the penitential season of Lent, a Gallic blessing of simplicity and power may well have been used: "Protect your people, O Lord, and mercifully clean them of all sins, for no adversity will harm them if no wickedness has hold of them."[62]

The spiritual logic was impeccable, the language sparse, but profound. Like Gregory the Great's "Epiphany Collect", rendered in Old English, it said all that was needed in a few insightful words:

> O God, whiche by the leadying of a starre didest manyfeste thy onely begotten sonne to the Gentiles: mercifully grant that we which know thee nowe by faythe, maye after this lyfe have the fruicion by thy glorious Godhead.

It was to stand the test of time: Cranmer incorporated Gregory's collects into the Prayer Book almost ten centuries later. Further west in Malmesbury and Cerne, Dorset, other traditions and spiritualities emerged. In Cerne, Irish features combined with Byzantine ones, mediated through Spain in the early seventh century. They were stark, unmistakeable and realistic. Thus, one prayer ran: "By your loins which were always filled with divine virtue, renew in my loins the spirit of holiness. By your most chaste head, O Christ, have mercy on my wicked head. By your blessed eyes, spare my polluted eyes . . . "[63] The drift of the prayer is clear, the realism unsparing.

Elsewhere, in Malmesbury, another formidable teacher emerged in the person of Aldhelm (639–709). A member of the Wessex royal family, he was educated at Malmesbury, the most prestigious monastery in the West, then under the leadership of an Irish abbot, Mailduph, from whom the monastery and town get their name. From there he went to Canterbury to train under Hadrian and Theodore.

Aldhelm was as circuitous in his Latin prose as Bede was direct, preferring rhetoric to plain writing.[64] He frequently wrote in both prose and metric verse, as in his treatise on virginity for Cuthburga, the sister of the famous King Ine of Wessex. He was deeply influenced by Isidore of Seville (560–636), often thought to be one of the last of the Church Fathers, and also by the Archbishop of Seville, a century before the Moors invaded Spain in the eighth century.[65] Isidore's *Etymologies*, a compendium of teaching demonstrating the influence of Byzantine and Italian thought from the Mediterranean, was an encyclopaedia of grammar and instruction: a veritable treasury of phrases and philosophy. Aldhelm was to use it liberally in his teaching in Sherborne, where he became bishop, and in the schools at Malmesbury. What these characteristics of devotional writing and liturgy show is the interconnectedness of European and Eastern Christianity.

Alongside this important teacher in Wessex was the evangelist and later martyr Boniface (c. 675–754), who followed the example of Willibrord. Willibrord

(658–738) was a Northumbrian monk trained by Egbert who went as a missionary to the Frisians and founded a community with papal support at Echternach in Germany. It is a sign of the energy and vitality of the Church in Wessex that it produced a great missionary to the Frisians in Boniface. A man of aristocratic birth, Boniface trained as a monk under Winbert, the scholarly Abbot of Nursling in Hampshire. Born in 675, he would spend thirty-five years on the continent until his martyrdom in 754, working among the pagan tribes of northern and eastern Germany.

He was a complex character: at once pedantic and compassionate; fastidious in dealing with boorish Franks, yet magnetic in drawing people from England to work with him. He was outspoken in his attacks on paganism, as in his diatribe against pagan shrines, but tender in his nurture of those in his care. He founded churches in Erfurt, the city where centuries later Luther would present himself in the Augustinian friary for training as a monk. Later he became Archbishop of Mainz and sought to reconcile the papacy and the Carolingian monarchs. He gave oversight to Erfurt in Thuringia and Würzburg, an association that still exists today. When in his seventies, and on a final mission to Frisia, which was uncharted territory north-east of the Zuiderzee, he and his companions were murdered for their inconsequential possessions; his body was taken to Utrecht and then rowed for a month down the Rhine to Mainz. He was buried in the great monastery in Fulda, later patronized by Charlemagne, and is now remembered as the Apostle to Germania. Nearby, the Abbess Leoba is also buried. Originally from a community at Wimborne and a close friend of Boniface, she started the convent at Bischofsheim. Near Boniface's tomb today is the book he was reading at the time of his death, about which Willibald, his biographer, tells us in his *Life*.[66]

If Wessex was showing increasing signs of spiritual vitality, the east of England was also deepening in the faith. Cedd (620–64), the founder of Lastingham in Northumbria, conducted a mission to the East Saxons from c. 660, following a mission to Mercia. He became Bishop of London after Mellitus and founded the monastery at Bradwell-on-Sea, the kind of remote and lonely spot beloved of Irish and Coptic monasticism. Trained by Aidan, he brought that sense of pilgrimage and freedom that was so typical of Irish missionaries. A little later, in 673 or thereabouts, Etheldreda, an East Anglian princess who had been married to King Ecgfrith of Northumbria, and one of four sisters, all of whom became abbesses, founded the dual monastery in Ely. She had, under Wilfrid's influence, chosen a life of virginity. Etheldreda's devotion was to make Ely a place of pilgrimage for centuries to come, and her shrine is still in Ely Cathedral today. Other monasteries were founded in the east, as on the Isle of Sheppey, another natural spot for a monastery, since it is cut off from the mainland like Lindisfarne, and for the most part surrounded by the sea. Although not at the forefront of spiritual developments as Northumbria was, East Anglia was somewhat ahead of Mercia.

Mercia

Mercia was essentially middle England, located south of Northumbria around Repton (the burial place of several kings). The region included Tamworth, Lichfield and what would come to be known as the Midlands. Lindsey, situated around Lincoln and an old Roman colony, was a satellite state of Mercia. Following the death of one of her leading kings, Penda, at the Battle of Winwaed against Oswy of Northumberland, the pagan tradition of Mercia came to an end.[67]

A mission led by Chad began from Northumbria. Chad was sent by Theodore after his retirement from York (because of the objection of Wilfrid, as we have seen). Chad was given land by the King of the Mercians, Wulfhere, and he established a monastic community at Lichfield that would later become the cathedral of a new diocese for the Mercians.[68]

Mercia's growing influence and power, as both a Christian and military kingdom, occurred under the rule of Athelbald, who took the crown of Mercia in 716.[69] His long reign, lasting to 756, made Mercia the dominant kingdom in England. Although he was ostensibly Christian, it was not until he received a stinging rebuke in the form of a letter from St Boniface, accusing him of violating church privileges by imposing forced labour on the clergy and fornicating with nuns, that Athelbald restrained his excesses. He supported and helped Mercia's Council of Clovesho (746/7), which gave uniformity of worship to the English Church and affirmed its privileges and exemption from taxation. (An account of the council is given by William of Malmesbury.) However much Athelbald reformed himself, he was nevertheless ignominiously murdered by his bodyguards near Tamworth in 757, and was buried in Repton. He was succeeded after a period of civil war by the greatest of the Mercian kings, his cousin Offa.

Under Offa, Mercia was the virtual overlord of all Saxon kingdoms, although not formally over Northumbria or Wessex. Known as one of the greatest Anglo-Saxon kings, Offa ruled for forty years, from 757 to 796. He took every opportunity to strengthen Mercia: building the famous Offa's Dyke to contain the Welsh, making Lichfield an archdiocese to the consternation of Canterbury, absorbing Kent, Sussex, Hwicce (the Welsh border kingdom of Worcestershire, Herefordshire, parts of Gloucestershire and Shropshire) and for a while East

Anglia, and corresponding with Charlemagne's court through Alcuin, as if they were equals.[70] Art flourished; the Lichfield Gospels were produced; a sophisticated coinage was created; ornate jewellery was traded; and intricate metalwork was crafted. Together, all these endeavours spoke of a prosperous and confident kingdom.

Despite the seeming strength of the Anglo-Saxon kingdoms and their professed faith, they were in fact on the brink of their greatest test, which would last all of two centuries. Perhaps with a premonition of disaster because of weakness in the Church, Bede wrote to his pupil Egbert, then Archbishop of York, in 734 about church abuses: episcopal greed, exploitation of monasteries by noblemen as tax-free havens, and inadequate training of the clergy. Only sixty years later, disaster would strike with the first assaults of the pagan Vikings.

The period from the withdrawal of the Roman legions to the first Viking invasions lasted almost 400 years, but perhaps more than any other period it would establish the nation. Indeed, purely secular historians often quickly pass over this formative period.[71]

England would emerge from these Anglo-Saxon kingdoms. Christianity, which had arrived afresh with Augustine and Aidan, gave cohesion and perspective to these new disparate Anglo-Saxon entities. Every Anglo-Saxon court would accept the faith, and in time Irish, Gaulish and Roman Christianity would be re-expressed in an Anglo-Saxon model. The most enlightened monks like Bede or Cuthbert would accept the best from each: the humility of Irish evangelism, the catholicity of Roman teaching, the simplicity and scholarship of the Irish monastic community and the colour and visual images of Roman and continental expression. At best they blended together into what we might call English Christianity.

These qualities would be demonstrated by Aidan or Chad eschewing ever to ride a horse, by Benedict Biscop bringing back a pandect Bible for copying in Monkwearmouth-Jarrow and by Cuthbert preferring the ascetic life of Irish spirituality. While some combined the best of both worlds, others forced conformity to a single style: Augustine, sure of his commission, failed to rise to meet the British bishops, Wilfrid enforced his Roman ways on others, Colman found it hard to agree with Rome's method of calculating Easter. Divisions were the result. The Romano-Celtic Church in Wales was at best overlooked, and at worst treated as no better than pagan. At Whitby, Celtic spirituality was subsumed into Roman ways. And the glories of that Celtic expression of the faith—the devotional delight in the Trinity, the expectation of prophecy, miracle and risky pilgrimage, and the celebration of the environment—became minor keys in a growing institutionalizing of Christianity from the continent.

Unfortunately, Welsh or Celtic kings like Cadwalla brought deep suspicion upon themselves in the eyes of the Saxons by fighting with the pagan Penda against King Edwin and defeating and killing the saintly Oswald at Maserfield in c. 642. (Although it is disputed whether Cadwalla was still alive at the time of this battle.) In the case of the British (as opposed to the Anglo-Saxons), ethnic dislike trumped a common faith. Nevertheless, the achievements of these missionaries—whether it was Aidan from Ireland or Theodore from Tarsus—were deeply impressive. The faith that had been sown since 590 among these new Anglo-Saxon kingdoms was now to be tested, literally by fire—a crucible that was to have a profound result before a further, this time Christian, onslaught from Normandy.

CHAPTER 3

The Vikings: Invasion and Absorption

For Alcuin, the scholar statesman from York serving at the court of Charlemagne, the year 796 was an *annus horribilis*, marked by the murder of Ethelred of Northumbria, an event which capped the many tumultuous years of crisis in that kingdom since 759.[1] That year also saw the death of Offa of Mercia and his son Ecgfrith, just six months later, as well as the death of Archbishop Eanbald I of York.[2] Alcuin's feelings of insecurity were only increased by his move from the court of Charlemagne to become Abbot of Tours that same year. All this followed just a few years after the first ominous incursions of the Vikings along the Northumbrian coast at Lindisfarne, and also on the south coast near Dorchester, which were accompanied by burning and looting and killing. The *Anglo-Saxon Chronicle* records these first raids near Dorchester as follows:

> In this year Beorthric (king of Wessex) took to wife Eadburh, daughter of King Offa. And in his days came first three ships of Norwegians from Horthaland: and then the reeve rode thither and tried to compel them to go to the royal manor, for he did not know what they were: and then they slew him. These were the first ships of Danes to come to England.[3]

On 8 June 793, the Vikings destroyed the monastery at Lindisfarne. For many years, there had been intermittent raids in Northumbria, East Anglia and along the south coast, until in 865 the great army of Danes led by Halfdan and Ivar the Boneless landed in East Anglia with the intention of staying. It was one thing to deal with indiscriminate raiding and looting parties that came for quick gain and booty, but quite another to face a full-scale invasion of Vikings who had every intention of settling.

The English kingdoms and Church were hardly ready to combat such aggression. The prolonged pagan Viking assault could not be met without extreme courage, resilience and recourse to the strength provided both by Christian faith and by well-honed Saxon fighting qualities. Since it was pagan Viking fighting Christian resistance, it also became an age of martyrdom. In Wessex a kingdom was found capable of resistance. In Alfred a king of such exceptional qualities was found that he was able to turn the tide from near disaster to eventual victory, as well as begin a renaissance of learning and nation-building. To accomplish one would have been a triumph, but to accomplish both required a unique vision allied to sterling qualities of character not often found. Hence Alfred's epithet: The Great.

England and Europe in the eighth and ninth centuries

The eighth century had been dominated by the ascendancy of Mercia under its great king Offa.[4] Little is known about the process of that ascendancy, or Mercia's treaty or charter relations with other kingdoms. Equally little remains of Offa's powerful rule except the formidable earthworks that bear his name, and which acted as his border with Wales, in the same way that Hadrian's Wall defended Roman Britain against the Picts. Only by degrees did Wessex begin to assert its independence from Mercian hegemony. This process occurred under Egbert, who ruled Wessex from 802–39, and who ended Mercia's overlordship by defeating Wiglaf, King of the Mercians, in 825 at Ellandum, near Swindon. Egbert even invaded Northumbria to assert his overlordship, but in so doing weakened his position and allowed Wiglaf to retake London for Mercia.

Egbert's son, Aethelwulf, succeeded him unopposed: the first smooth succession in Wessex for forty years. Aethelwulf was the father of Alfred the Great. However, the Anglo-Saxon kingdoms were, as so often, divided, and indulged in intermittent warfare to see which was the greatest. They were not in a position to repel easily a powerful and determined invader.

In the first half of the ninth century, the Church reflected some of these cracks in its own life and needed strengthening. We have seen how Bede was anxious about the corruption in the Church towards the end of his life, writing to Egbert, Archbishop of York, about the fake monasteries in Northumbria, started by noblemen in order to avoid military service and to gain exemptions for their property from tax and other feudal obligations—an early form of tax evasion. There appears also to have been a weakening of the link with Rome and some decline in church administration during the final years of the eighth century. Perhaps it was with this in mind, and an awareness of Offa's desire to have an archdiocese in Lichfield, that Pope Hadrian I sent a delegation to England to strengthen church life and links with the papacy. Ever a long way from Rome geographically, the temptation was to pursue church life independently of papal oversight. No papal legate had been to England since Augustine, although many archbishops had been appointed with the *pallium* from Rome.

Hadrian (772–95) was a resourceful and powerful pope who sought to re-establish Rome's authority in Italy over and against the Byzantine East and the Lombards. To this end, Hadrian forged a close relationship with Charlemagne and sought a similar relationship with the chief English king, Offa. He therefore sent two legates to England: George, Cardinal-Bishop of Ostia, and Theophylact, Cardinal-Bishop of Todi. The canons (church rules) that they brought, some twenty in all, were aimed at strengthening the authority of the Church in England: kings were called to obey their bishops, illegitimate children were to be excluded from succession, tithes were to be paid, irregular marriages and heathen practices were to be forbidden and penitential discipline was to be enjoined on all. In other words, canon law was to be enforced.

The canons of the legates matched the earlier ones of the Synod of Clovesho (747), which called for the proper reading of scripture, simplicity of dress and lifestyle, abstention from alcohol, and sobriety of life by monks and nuns alike. Both sets of rules demonstrate that Christianity in England was still only skin deep, often limited to the ruling classes, while paganism, occult practices and disorderly conduct went on beneath the surface. The legates insisted on reform and the canons were accepted in Canterbury (Kent), Mercia, Wessex and Northumbria. The acceptance of these canons demonstrates the deference with which English rulers accepted the authority of the Pope, which was not something that would last into the later Angevin and Plantagenet periods of the monarchy. Offa hoped that his compliance would result in an archdiocese in Lichfield, which he longed for, to give him status. And this happened in 788, but it was not to last because of long-term objections from Canterbury. Quite apart from rivalries, three archdioceses in a relatively small country, excluding Wales, was ecclesiastically overcrowded.

Meanwhile, in the seventh and eighth centuries, the continent of Europe and the Near East were undergoing enormous and seemingly irreversible changes. Nations that had first come to prominence at the end of the Roman Empire were establishing themselves in Europe, notably the Lombards in Italy, the Franks in northern France and Germany, and the Visigoths in Spain. The new power to mesmerize Europe and Constantinople, however, was that of the Muslim Arabs, following the death of Muhammad in 632.

As Christianity was being established in England, Islam was about to begin its world-changing advance in the Levant, North Africa and Spain. In 618,

Constantinople had been cut off from Egypt by Persian conquerors, soon to be followed by Arabs. In 636, at the Battle of Yarmuk, near the Sea of Galilee, the Arabs comprehensively defeated Byzantine forces, despite earlier victories against the Avars and Persians by the Emperor Heraclius (610–41). Byzantium and Constantinople were thereafter under threat from Islam until the eventual fall of Constantinople in 1453. The Arabs took Syria in 636, Palestine in 638, and Egypt from 639–42.[5] Constantinople's population fell from 500,000 to between 50–70,000 in 650. Its grain supply from Egypt had been cut off in 618.

The Arabs began to sweep through North Africa in the 690s, taking Carthage in 698. The Bulgars arrived in Bulgaria in 680, later to be effectively evangelized from Constantinople in the ninth century by the extraordinary missionary brothers Cyril and Methodius. Their conversion gave the Slavs the Cyrillic script and the Orthodox Church. Around the same time, a great Viking army landed in East Anglia in 861. While much of the Arab conquest of North Africa, Sicily and Baghdad took place under the Abbasid Caliphate (750–1258), which succeeded the Umayyads (661–750), the Byzantine emperors, Leo III (717–41) and Constantine V (741–75), saw the veneration of icons as a cause of Byzantium's military defeat. Thus, Byzantium became absorbed in iconoclasm in the middle years of the eighth century.

The advance of Islam also affected Europe. Tariq ibn Ziyad, the Berber leader of a largely Berber army, invaded Spain for the Umayyad caliphs of Damascus and defeated and killed the Visigoth ruler Roderic in 711. The Iberian Peninsula— al-Andalus as it is called in Arabic—was quickly taken. Seville, Córdoba, Mérida, Toledo and Zaragoza were all captured. The Arab advance went almost to Tours, where just a little further south near Poitiers, Charles Martel defeated the Arab invasion of Gaul in 732. His grandson, Charlemagne, would become the bastion of Christian resistance, albeit of a powerful military kind (and which, much to Alcuin's dislike, did not baulk at baptisms or mass conversions at the point of a sword). The effects of Arab incursion into Spain and Gaul would have been known and felt in England, especially in the years of Offa. Offa himself was not averse to trading with the Arabs using gold coins minted as though issued from the Caliphate. They were in fact produced in England, with Offa's name and title misspelt in Arabic. The Mercians were nothing if not enterprising in their quest for trade.

The link between Charlemagne and Offa was forged directly between the two monarchs, but also through the statesman, writer and monk, Alcuin. Alcuin was educated in York, where, as librarian, he gained his appetite for learning and travelled extensively on the continent: to Rome, Pavia and Murbach.

In 781, he met Charlemagne at Pavia and was invited to join his court. His presence there was to be a link between York, King Offa and Charlemagne. It was from there that Alcuin wrote letters in 793 warning Northumbria of impending doom unless corruption was rooted out. He wrote similarly to the Archbishop of Canterbury, calling the Viking attack on Lindisfarne a *flagellum* or chastisement from God.

For Alcuin, the loss of the monastery at Lindisfarne was like the fall of Rome to Augustine: a goad to seek the eternal City of God, to seek God's kingdom in this present life, and to re-arm morally as a nation. Alcuin corresponded with Offa's court: with Ethelburh, one of Offa's daughters, an abbess upholding the call to virginity; with Speratus, the Bishop of Leicester, whom he warned in 796 of coming judgement; and with Osbert, a Mercian nobleman, to whom he similarly stated that the mayhem following Offa's death was due to immorality on the part of their leaders.

Alcuin concluded that, "the happiness of the English is coming to an end".[6] In this he was right, for just as the Muslim Arabs came to dominate the Levant, North Africa and Spain, fighting their way into the heartlands of Europe before being checked at Tours, so now pagan Vikings began their 200-year assault on northern Europe. They did, however, show a marked ability to assimilate the Christian culture around them, both in France and England, but for a time it looked as though Christendom was being squeezed in the south by the Arabs and in the north by the Vikings—a powerful pagan pincer movement.

The Vikings

The term "Viking" was first used in Old English and simply means "robbers". It is not a marker of ethnicity, but rather a collective term to describe those bandits who came by ship to destroy, plunder and make captives of men, women and children. The Irish called them *gaill*, meaning simply "foreigners".[7] To others they were *Northmanni* or *Dani*. If Viking was the nickname given by the English, their origin nonetheless was Scandinavian.

The Scandinavians were basically made up of three peoples: the Swedes, who had by the eighth century absorbed the house of Geatas, i.e. Beowulf's people; the Norwegians, who were the farthest from any political unity of the three groups; and the Danes, the most southerly. The Swedes, whose capital was at Upsala, had not yet begun their incursion into present-day Russia down the Volkhov river from Lake Lagoda to Novgorod, where Prince Rurik was to establish the state of Rus. The reason for these attacks on northern Europe by one or other of the Scandinavian peoples, whether against France, the Low Countries, England or Ireland, was rivalry in the Baltic. Not only that, but the expansion of Charlemagne's kingdom into Frisia and Saxony brought him face to face with the Danes, who considered themselves his equal and wanted to prove it. With Frisian sea-power reduced to insignificance and neither Charlemagne nor the Saxon kingdoms in England regarding themselves as sea-faring powers, the North Sea and the surrounding landfalls were vulnerable to Danish or Scandinavian attack. With the end of Charlemagne's rule, and with it the tactic of playing Danish lords off against each other, the North Sea coast became more vulnerable.

The largest attacks occurred after Charlemagne's death in 814. Apart from some marauding Vikings, the Danes were held in check by their principled king, Horik, who welcomed the missionary St Anskar, a Saxon Benedictine. Horik also respected the Frankish kingdom. But internal divisions brought about Horik's fall to his nephew Guthrum. By this point, the concept of a full-scale invasion of England was fully formed. The sporadic, but frightening, small-scale assaults— aimed at looting moveable wealth from the British coast, seeking ransom of high-value individuals, and taking any moveable treasure, especially ornate books that had been assembled lovingly and expensively in monasteries—now turned into something like a full-scale invasion. Initially these incursions were like testing probes, as in 850 and 854, when the Vikings quartered over the winter in Thanet and Sheppey. Then, in 865, the whole fabric of English society was threatened by the landing of a great army transported in over two hundred ships. Furthermore, in 893, another great army numbering thousands of men landed in 300 ships.

It was then that the full testing of the English Saxon kingdoms occurred: the only kingdom capable of answering the challenge was Wessex; and the only leader capable of marshalling effective resistance was Alfred.

Alfred the Great

Alfred's succession to the Wessex crown was circuitous. Born in Wantage, Berkshire,[8] in 849 to King Athelwulf of Wessex, he was the youngest of five sons. Like King David, who was the youngest of Jesse's sons, he was the least who became the greatest.[9] And like Jacob's son Joseph, of the coat of many colours fame, he was, according to his biographer Asser, the favourite of his parents. Alfred was brought up exclusively in the royal court by his parents and tutors. Although he never learnt to read Latin, he enjoyed hearing English poetry and rose to the challenge when his mother Osburh said she would give a book of poetry to whomever of her children could learn its contents by heart. Alfred won the prize. He was not simply bookish; he was also an accomplished huntsman. Asser wrote that "no one else could approach him in the skill and success in that activity".[10]

Athelwulf took Alfred on a second visit to Rome (the first having occurred when Alfred had been sent there by his father at the age of four). This second visit took place in 855, after nearly sixteen years of his father's reign and when Alfred was six. Athelwulf died in 858.

Wessex had been re-united under Aethelberht, the third son of Athelwulf, but in 865 he too died without issue. It was in this year that the great Viking invasion occurred and another of Alfred's brothers, Ethelred, succeeded. Alfred became fully engaged in supporting his brother the king in checking the advance of the Vikings.

The Vikings were led by Ivar the Boneless—possibly named thus because of a condition that involved recurrent bone dislocations—and his brother Halfdan. Taking Northumbria and York first, they then re-invaded East Anglia in 869, basing themselves at Thetford and killing King Edmund with a firing squad of arrows. Edmund's place in the first rank of English patron saints and martyrs was promoted by Alfred the Great and his successors as part of their claim to represent English Christianity.[11] (A great shrine was later built to his memory in the monastery of Bury St Edmunds.) Having secured the north and east of the country, the Viking forces now turned west to Wessex. In the autumn of 870, the Viking army moved to Reading and was located between the Thames and Kennet. After two initial inconclusive engagements at Englefield and Reading, the Viking forces were checked at Ashdown on the Berkshire Downs. Ethelred did not enter the battle until he had completed his act of worship. Ashdown resulted in heavy Viking casualties; five earls and King Bagsecg were killed. But in 871, Ethelred died, and although he had infant children, such were the times that Alfred succeeded. Even while he was burying his brother, the Vikings attacked again, defeating Alfred at Wilton and forcing him to come to terms, including payment for peace. The Vikings returned to London, while Viking control of Northumbria, East Anglia and large parts of Mercia continued. Monasteries were denuded, libraries with precious books and charters destroyed. Vikings settled as peasants in what came to be the Danelaw, and new landlords moved in.

The Vikings had by now taken four of the Anglo-Saxon kingdoms: Northumbria, East Anglia, Mercia, which they had divided, and the kingdom of the East Saxons. Only Wessex remained. In 878, a new assault on Wessex from Exeter and Gloucester was led by Guthrum. A surprise attack on Alfred and his court whilst they were observing Christmas at Chippenham meant that Alfred was forced to flee to Somerset, where in the bogs or the "levels" around Athelney he reached the nadir of his fortunes. From this low point of seeming hopelessness, where Asser tells us Alfred and his companions had neither food nor resources, and where, through a distracted mind, he famously allowed the cakes to burn, Alfred managed one of the greatest *volte-faces* in English history. It is indeed an extraordinary moment in English history. The Battle of Edington was a turning point for England, and it meant the survival of Christian Wessex.

Alfred was able to call the Saxon field army (*fyrd*) from Somerset, Wiltshire and Hampshire, west of Southampton Water, and defeated the Vikings emphatically and unexpectedly at Edington on the edge of Salisbury Plain. Guthrum, the leader of the Vikings, agreed to terms in which he consented to leave Wessex and also to be baptized. Guthrum was baptized at Wedmore by Alfred himself, who stood as godfather. Guthrum stayed with Alfred for twelve nights after his baptism and eventually the Viking army left Wessex and retreated to East Anglia, where Guthrum was a virtual king. Guthrum had concluded a treaty with Alfred that set the boundaries of his territory, giving him East Anglia and an area north of London along the Lea Valley and then along Watling Street, the Roman road that joined London to Chester. This agreement defined, as it happens, the future Danelaw—the area of England colonized by the Vikings. But now a more confident Alfred ranged further afield, defending Rochester in 884 and taking London in 886. Guthrum died in 888, whereupon new Viking leaders sought to renew the attack against Alfred and Wessex. Alfred returned London to Mercia and its king Aethelred. Aethelred then married Alfred's resourceful and feisty daughter Aethelflaed, who would prove to be the hammer of the Vikings in Mercia in the years ahead.

By the 880s, Alfred was both defending Wessex and initiating a renaissance of learning and faith there. To defend his territory, Alfred began establishing a line of defensive towns called *burhs*, set his militia on a more disciplined footing which involved conscription, and built a fleet, thus making him the father of the English navy. The fortress towns or *burhs*, such as Bath, Winchester, Chichester and Exeter, were garrisoned by free men who were given "hides" of land. A hide was the Anglo-Saxon term for a family, and amounted to about thirty acres, enough to sustain an extended family. In exchange for a hide, a family built and defended the walls of the city in question, in much the same way as the Israelites rebuilt and defended the walls of Jerusalem in the days of Nehemiah. Indeed, the idea may have come from the Old Testament and from imitating a strategy adopted by Charles the Bald on the continent. A register called the *Burghal Hidage* was drawn up, a kind of precursor to the Domesday Book, but with a specifically military purpose. Alongside this well-worked-out defensive posture against the Viking threat, Alfred's genius was such that he also sought a long-term improvement in education.

Asser tells us in his *Life of King Alfred* that there came a day, probably after 885, when he was reading aloud to Alfred, who then commanded him to write down in a separate book what he was reading.[12] Asser was struck by Alfred's evident enthusiasm to read and understand, for which, "I stretched out my palms to the heavens and gave mighty (albeit silent) thanks to Almighty God, who had sown such great enthusiasm for the pursuit of learning in the King's heart."[13] Asser thus began to create a new commonplace book, which was quickly filled and which Alfred kept beside him wherever he went. Alfred was not only keen to rectify his lack of learning, but also to train his people. Above all, he wanted them to read in their own language. To this end he assembled a group of scholars from far and near and set about translating a set of influential texts from the Church Fathers and others into English. He persuaded a reluctant Archbishop of Rheims to part with two eminent scholars, Grimald and John. And from St David's, he secured Asser for six months each year. He also pressed into his service talented bishops in England, such as Aethelstan of Mercia, Werferth of Worcester and Archbishop Plegmund (who had previously demonstrated vision by dividing the See of Winchester into four dioceses: Crediton, Wells, Ramsbury and Sherborne).[14]

The books Alfred decided to translate with the help of these men were eclectic, but indicative of what appealed to him and to the Saxon frame of mind. Whenever possible he had books read to him by one of his appointed clergy. Asser tells us how earnest and diligent Alfred was in worship, hearing mass every day and listening avidly to the reading of the Psalms. He suffered from an unknown illness from the time of his marriage, which Asser calls "a sudden severe pain that was quite unknown to all physicians".[15] This illness, his flight to Athelney to escape the Viking threat, and his hiding in marshy land there must have meant he readily identified with King David of the Psalms. David too had felt himself abandoned and pursued, yet trusted in God. Little wonder then that Alfred translated the first fifty Psalms into English himself, and was only prevented by death from translating the rest of the Psalter.

Besides scripture, Alfred and his assistants translated works of pastoral theology and philosophy: Gregory the Great's *Pastoral Care* and *Dialogues*, Boethius's *Consolation of Philosophy*, Augustine's *Soliloquies*, and Bede's *Ecclesiastical History*. It was a catholic mix of philosophy, pastoral direction and history of England's Christianity. Alfred's overriding ambition, as expressed in his preface to the translation of Gregory's *Pastoral Care*, was that his people should read these works in their own language.[16] He was, therefore, a devoted advocate of Old English and a firm believer in people understanding spiritual truth in their own tongue. It was an ambition that was to reappear powerfully down the ages in English church history.

The choice of Gregory's *Pastoral Care* or *Rule* is indicative of a particular style of pastoral theology developing in English church life: i.e. not doctrinaire, but practical; insightful without being speculative. It was a style that struck a chord in English church life that was to be repeated over the years. Boethius's *Consolation of Philosophy*, the reflections of a Roman nobleman and imperial administrator who was sentenced to death by the Ostrogoth King of Italy Theodoric (475–526), was also very popular in the Middle Ages. Boethius, although not a Christian and despite the difficulties of his own life, upheld the role of fate and providence in the universe. Not only did Alfred translate these works with the help of others, but he also formed a school in the royal household to teach these principles of living and ruling to a new cadre of leaders drawn from both Anglo-Saxon and Danish backgrounds. In this, too, he was prescient, allowing a new generation of leaders to emerge who were not bound by ethnic restrictions. Alfred believed in the power of education to transform a nation through the raising up of widely educated, well-taught and motivated men, and, more indirectly, women. It was an inspiring legacy and a time-honoured policy.

Added to all his other achievements, Alfred was a lawgiver, and promulgated a new law-code that bears his name. Beginning with quotations from the Mosaic Law, it goes on to lay great stress on the performance of oaths, the payment of *wergild* (the fixed value for a life) to the family of someone killed, the observation of church rules, fines for forcible entry, and on being permitted to fight with someone who is found with your wife, "behind closed doors or under the same blanket," without incurring a feud.[17] The code even prescribed specific fines should a man place his hand on the breast of a nun or layperson. Restraining sexual abuse was part of law, even then.

Given his life as a successful defender of Wessex against the Vikings, a founder of a new defensive system of navy, standing army and defended towns, a translator, an educationalist and lawgiver, and a devoted Christian, it is no wonder Alfred is regarded as the father of a nation. Patrick Wormald writes, "If Alfred may have owed his initial survival to his family's efforts as much as his own, there is no doubt that what happened after 878 was all his own work; and it amounted to the most sustained programme of military, administrative, diplomatic and cultural change in the West since Charlemagne."[18] More than all this, his children and family gave expression to these ideals through succeeding generations.

The rise of the House of Wessex and kingship

Alfred died in Winchester on 26 October 899 and was buried in the Old Minster there, before being transferred to Hyde Abbey. His grave was subsequently dug up at the time of the dissolution of the monasteries and his remains were lost! The remains of the greatest of English kings were thus scattered to the four winds because of the vagaries of the most tyrannical of all English rulers, Henry VIII. Alfred's legacy lived on in his heirs, however, and his son, Edward the Elder, succeeded him.

The next seventy-five years, until the coronation of Edgar as King of England in Bath Abbey in 973, saw the almost uninterrupted ascendancy of the House of Wessex. It was a golden age: a Pericles moment for the English nation. Three kings in particular accounted for this: Edward the Elder, Athelstan and Edgar the Peaceful. Lesser monarchs, Edmund (939–56), Eadred (946–55) and, least of all, Edwy (955–9), accounted for the intervening years between the reigns of Athelstan and Edgar.

The fabric of English life was set by the ninth and tenth centuries. The village became the basic unit of English life with about five to ten hides of land attached to each, corresponding to approximately 150–300 acres. Villagers who were freemen or landowners or tenants were called *sokemen* (in the Danelaw) and *villeins* (from Villanus) in Saxon territory. If land was owned it was deemed *bookland*, that is, granted by charter with certain exemptions sometimes attached. Otherwise much land was *folkland*, held in common by the community by virtue of common law or because of use over time. Alfred gave burghs, which were often based on old Roman communities, new meaning and purpose. Later, in the eleventh century, new administrative districts called *hundreds* emerged, comprising anything from twenty to 200 hides. In time, these *hundreds* were annexed to manors or estates, which in turn were often owned by monasteries or bishops, ealdormen or *thegns*—if not by the king and his family. Extensive forest (often royal hunting grounds), woodland on the edge of pasture, arable land ploughed by oxen and swine pasture were all common features of the countryside and made up the landholdings belonging to king or subjects.

With the accession of Edward the Elder, a new phase of re-conquest of Viking-held territory in the five kingdoms began in Northumbria and Lindsey, Mercia, East Anglia and some of Kent. It is hard to be exact about the extent of the Danelaw, which was a term that was *not used* until the reign of King Aethelred II from 978, but much of northern and eastern England was under Viking control from Watling Street northwards. In the early part of his reign, Edward had to deal with a rebellion within his own borders, led by his cousin Aethelwold, son of Aethelred I. Aethelwold combined with Danish forces to fight Edward, and in a campaign that ranged from Wimborne in the west to Cambridge and the Fens in the east, Edward was hard pushed. Eventually he defeated the Danes and Aethelwold at Holme, an unidentified site in East Anglia, in 902.[19]

While Edward's forces ranged over England, his sister, Aethelflaed, who came to be known as the "Lady of the Mercians", followed in her father's footsteps. She reinforced towns as her father had done, kept the devotion of her military household and planned and led successful campaigns against the Danes, taking Derby in July 917 and Leicester in 918. She was, as Henry of Huntington later wrote, "A queen by title, but in deed a king". She was a foreshadowing of Elizabeth I, and had the courage of Boudicca. She was buried next to her husband at St Oswald's Priory in Gloucester, but her legacy lived on in Athelstan, her nephew, whom she had effectively raised in Mercia.[20]

With Athelstan came a further advance of kingship and government. His father Edward had been the very epitome of a warrior king; his grandfather Alfred a warrior and a statesman, a survivor and a victor. If Alfred never forgot his abject state in the marshes of Athelney, founding a monastery there in gratitude for his deliverance, Athelstan was, by contrast, born in the purple: ready to enforce, extend and apply his kingly power in a way not seen since Offa. His kingship was even more in keeping with Christendom than Offa's had been, his rule more enlightened. Whereas the Frankish monarchy in Gaul was imploding and the Carolingian model of kingship appeared vulnerable, Athelstan would enforce a greater uniformity of governance than had been seen before in England: military, financial, legal and religious.

First, Athelstan had to stamp his military authority in England. He went north to take on Guthfrith, king of the Dublin Norsemen who had joined forces with the young King Olaf of York, successor to Sihtric. In a swift campaign, Athelstan defeated them and was acknowledged overlord at Penrith on 12 July 937. In the next four years, his supremacy was extended over Wales and into Cornwall. The Welsh princes were paying yearly tribute of an unspecified number of hounds and hawks, 25,000 oxen, 300 pounds of silver and thirty pounds of gold, an incredible sum! The greatest threat was to come in 937, when Olaf, son of Guthfrith of Dublin, together with the kings of Scotland and Strathclyde, and Constantine of Alba, amalgamated their forces to break Athelstan in the north of England and hand Northumbria and York to Olaf. But combined armies from Mercia and Wessex led by Athelstan defeated these kings at the Battle of Brunanburh, an iconic victory for the English forces and for the future unity of England. Athelstan left behind carrion or dead bodies for the scavengers, and in a victory that made him supreme had raised up the possibility of a united England.

He only had two more years to build his kingdom. In his many charters he would call himself King of the English and ruler of Britain. His court remained mostly in Wessex, only occasionally going north to Tamworth or York, or east to London and Colchester. Provincial rulers attended him, and continental alliances were strengthened, as with the King of the West Franks, Charles the Simple, a descendant of Charlemagne, who married Athelstan's sister, Eadgifu; and with Otto, the son of Henry the Fowler, who married another of Athelstan's sisters, Edith. Otto would become Holy Roman Emperor in 962. Athelstan aided other rulers in France in their struggles with the Vikings.

Athelstan was both a lawgiver and an unusually generous benefactor of the Church. He promulgated many laws, especially against thieves, but struggled with the harshness of the code. Free women who harboured thieves could be thrown from a cliff, delinquent slaves might be stoned by fellow slaves.[21] Although punishments remained very severe, he did lift the death penalty from those under fifteen. He sought to care for the poor. He went to Chester-le-Street himself and revived the shrine of Cuthbert. He restored dioceses in Northumberland and began new ones, as at St Germans in Cornwall. He endowed monasteries with books and relics, especially Malmesbury, where he would be buried and to which he had a special attachment, as well as the great Wessex Abbey of Glastonbury. During his reign, the beginnings of a revival in monasticism began, as we shall see. Furthermore, like his grandfather Alfred, he made his court a centre for education and the training of future leaders.

A vision of a united England had been given by Edward the Elder and Athelstan, but as soon as Athelstan died the flood tide of Viking assault returned. In reality, the English nation was still "an artificial piece of statecraft".[22] As soon as Edmund, aged eighteen, succeeded his brother Athelstan, a new wave of Viking assaults occurred, once again led by Olaf, King of Dublin. Olaf invaded, took York, and attacked Mercia. Then he died suddenly, and his successors made peace with Edmund in 942. But in May 946, Edmund himself was killed defending his steward from a violent attack and was succeeded by Eadred, who was the brother of Edmund and Athelstan. Once again, there was a new Viking threat, this time from Norway, led by a renegade son of the royal house, Eric Bloodaxe. In the end, Eric was defeated by Eadred, although little is known of the circumstances of the campaign. Eadred died a year later in 955 on St Clement's Day, in Frome, Somerset. The two young sons of Edmund, Eadwig and Edgar, succeeded to the West Saxon and Mercian thrones respectively. Eadwig used his coronation banquet to cavort with two women, about which the *Anglo-Saxon Chronicle* says, "a certain foolish woman, noble by birth, with a daughter ripe and alluring, attached herself to him. She pursued him and enticed him into intimate relationships, clearly in order to ally either herself or her daughter with him in marriage."[23] Dunstan, the Abbot of Glastonbury and later Archbishop of Canterbury, left the coronation banquet in disgust to recall the King to his duties, whereupon he was sent into exile in Flanders for his pains. Edwy (or Eadwig) continued in the same vein, was ill advised, and was soon deserted by the Northumbrian and Mercian people. His reign lasted four years and in 959 Edgar came to the throne.

Edgar's long reign from 959–75 was a time of flourishing for the cultural and religious life in England. It ended with an evocation of kingship at his coronation in Bath Abbey in 973, which would stand as a marker for English monarchy thereafter. It was also a time free of Viking invasion, and thus Edgar ushered in a new period of peace which lasted until 980.

The Church in the tenth century

One of the notable features of English existence in the tenth century was that church life in *parts* of England carried on normally despite the continual harrying, looting and full-scale invasions by the Vikings during most of the ninth and tenth centuries. In the latter part of the tenth century, the Church would flourish in Saxon-held territory. Undoubtedly there were losses and gains and there is no doubt that church life in the north and east of England suffered deeply from Viking attacks. The great monasteries of Northumbria were either destroyed in the fighting or severely dislocated. The 400 monks in Monkwearmouth-Jarrow were no more. Ripon and Hexham were destroyed. Heathenism and pagan practices returned, as indicated by Viking place names. For instance, Ellough in Suffolk probably means "heathen temple". Although the Danes were not necessarily implacably opposed to Christianity *per se*, they saw monasteries as centres of moveable treasure. There can be little doubt that the loss of monasteries, centres of worship, diocesan structures and clergy in the north and east was little short of a disaster. The dioceses of Lindisfarne, York, Lincoln or Lindsey, Leicester, Lichfield, Elmham in East Anglia and Dunwich either disintegrated or, for a time in the ninth and tenth centuries, ceased to exist. London, Rochester and Canterbury survived, particularly once Edward the Elder (899–924) began his process of reclamation of territory from the Vikings in the east. Elsewhere, in

Wessex and on the borders of Mercia around Oxford, there was a new dawn of Christian communities and institutions.

We have already seen Alfred's desire to revive learning and spiritual life in Wessex, and, if possible, further afield in England. He had reinvigorated learning by himself translating several spiritual and philosophical works into English. He founded a monastery at Shaftesbury that flourished, and at Athelney, which never took root. Indeed, there was an attempted murder there of the Abbot John, who was left half-dead in the marshes.[24] A start was nevertheless made in reviving learning and community, which would be continued later by Alfred's successors. New monasteries and dioceses began in the tenth century, and these shaped the development of English Christianity.

At the end of the ninth century, Pope Formosus wrote to King Edward and Archbishop Plegmund (890–923), encouraging them to evangelize the Danish settlers and strengthen the institutions of the Church by appointing bishops. Whether in response to this letter or not, new dioceses were founded: Wells, Sherborne, Ramsbury (which later moved to Salisbury) and Crediton were all formed out of Winchester, with the centre of gravity of English Christianity moving from Northumbria to Wessex. The founding of dioceses required patronage from the King: at least three hundred hides were needed to pay for a bishop and his household, the maintenance of the diocese, and to initiate new ministries there. Likewise, new monasteries, which in turn became influential institutions, were founded or greatly enhanced at Glastonbury, Abingdon, Cerne Abbas, Wilton, Ramsey, Pershore, Winchcombe and several other places.

Some form of community already existed in Glastonbury before its regal upgrade by Edmund in 940. In fact, charters can be traced back to West Saxon kings like Cenwealh (641–72), Centwine (676–85) and the famous lawgiver King Ine (688–726), making it an immensely old foundation. A new charter was issued in 940, making Dunstan abbot and increasing its built footprint. Before Dunstan, there had been a community following an ascetic way of life there, quite possibly made up of Irish monks. Dunstan, who was to become the leading figure in the Saxon Church from this time, and later Archbishop of Canterbury between 960 and 988, was determined that the rule at Glastonbury should become a pattern for all English monastic life. In time he established the Benedictine Rule and an Order of Life based on the *Regularis Concordia*, which was promulgated around 870 with the full support of the King. The *Regularis* was nothing less than a codification of monastic discipline to be rolled out throughout England. It owed much to continental practice and, in particular, to Fleury and Ghent, and to the administrative strength and spiritual commitment of Dunstan himself. Like

Cuthbert in the North, Dunstan learnt from the Irish a form of Christianity which was both austere and contemplative. This was to shape his own life. Emphasis on prayer, resisting evil, angelic support, prophetic insight and bold mission would be marks of his life, as they had been of the Celtic mission in the North of England. After difficult beginnings, in which he felt the opposition from courtiers and his own family,[25] Dunstan, now aged thirty-one, had a work he could throw himself into. For twenty years he laboured at Glastonbury. One swallow does not make a summer, however. Dunstan could not have reformed and revived English Christianity after the intensity of Viking aggression and the dislocation it produced on his own. Admittedly, there was strong, coherent leadership from a series of Saxon kings: Alfred, Edward, Athelstan, Edmund and Edgar. But there were other outstanding church leaders of the same period emanating from Winchester and Wessex. Winchester had itself undergone considerable renewal and expansion. A new minster and nunnaminster (convent) were founded. Winchester became the seat of government at a time when London was too exposed to Danish attack, and the site of St Swithun's remains became a popular place of pilgrimage. The King and the *Witan* (the King's Council) met there regularly.

Just as in Northumbria, where a succession of Christian kings and spiritual leaders had led to an explosion of Christian activity in the seventh and eighth centuries, so the same occurred in Wessex in the ninth and tenth centuries. Wessex church leaders included the saintly Oswald, of Danish descent, who was Bishop of Worcester and Archbishop of York (972–92); Aelfric, the scholar and homilist; Ethelwold, Bishop of Winchester and the Abbot of Abingdon; and his biographer, Wulfstan of Winchester.

Somewhat later, Wulfstan II (c. 956–1023), who was Bishop of London and Worcester and Archbishop of York, and also a jurist and preacher, became a powerful voice when the Viking attack resumed at the end of the tenth and start of the eleventh century. (The bishoprics of Worcester and York were often held together, with the strong diocese of Worcester helping the weaker York during the years of Danish occupation.) In his famous sermon, *The Wolf to the English*, and like Gildas before him, Wulfstan II explained, in arresting and powerful Old English, that fresh attacks by the Vikings on the English were caused by the moral and spiritual failure of the nation. "Too many are sorely blemished by the stains of sin," he declared.[26]

It was Dunstan who encouraged King Eadred (946–55) to enlarge and endow the monastery at Abingdon and to appoint his protégé Ethelwold as abbot. Ethelwold, already tutor to the young Prince Edgar (later king from 959–75), was a man of singular gifts. Following the Benedictine community at Fleury, Ethelwold instigated a Rule at Abingdon that was both strict and rigorous. He attracted a large number of vocations, but in 963 was appointed to the see of Winchester. As with Chrysostom's arrival in Constantinople in 397, Ethelwold brought a strong new broom to many of the communities in the city, sweeping away bad practices and earning himself the animosity of the clergy he expelled. In other words, he was a disciplinarian, and a backlash followed. They tried to poison him. But Ethelwold, remembering the words of Jesus that "you shall drink any deadly poison and it shall not hurt you" (Mark 16:18), survived.[27] Many other stories of Ethelwold emphasizing his holiness are recorded by Aelfric: a workman who fell from the roof of the Old Minster was healed; an ampulla of holy oil which had gone missing was quickly found; young people were instructed in the faith with kindness and encouragement and many themselves became bishops and abbots.[28]

Along with the founding of monasteries, the creation of dioceses, and the emergence of new leaders for the Church, a new stability and confidence was seen in the beginnings of parish churches and the renewed art of creating illuminated manuscripts. Eadmer, the English historian of the twelfth century and biographer of Anselm, records the faint beginnings of a parish system.

As long ago as the seventh century, in the reign of King Ine of Wessex (688–726), revenue in kind was being raised for the local church. In Ine's laws, *church-scot* (a church levy) was to be paid by Martinmas (11 November), and failure to do so resulted in a fine of sixty shillings and a payment of twelve times the original sum.[29] The levy was to be paid by all free men and was normally paid in kind: a horse-load of grain, hens or some stock. A further source of revenue, *soul-scot*, which was a voluntary gift to the Church and may have had a heathen origin, existed in parallel to the *church-scot*. All these methods of raising revenue for the Church would have initially been assigned to a minster church, then to a village church—generally built by the local landlord—but funds would have been raised unevenly before being slowly replaced with the *tithe* by the tenth century.

What is clear is that over the whole Anglo-Saxon period there was a mixed economy of organized Christian communities: minsters, some cathedrals— although only on a small scale until the coming of the Normans—monasteries, either independent or patronized by kings, and parish churches—e.g. Brixworth in Northamptonshire, c. 680—that sprang up in an unplanned fashion according to the patronage of local landlords and the provision of clergy. In the north and east of the country especially, their life or existence was frequently interrupted by war. The means of support was there, and in times of infrequent peace, further advances were made in the provision of Christian communities.

In the tenth century, after the dislocation of the Viking invasions, artistic work in the form of illuminated manuscripts resumed. We have already seen the extraordinary blossoming of Christian art in Northumbria in the early eighth century, exemplified in the Lindisfarne Gospels, the *Codex Amiatinus* (now held in Florence) and the Lichfield Gospels. The Viking invasions led to the ransacking of monastic libraries and the destruction of many illuminated manuscripts of the Gospels, Psalms and, in a few cases, of the whole Bible. The highly skilled production of such books or codices moved south to more peaceful parts of England, where monastery *scriptoria* could exist. Dunstan sought to build up the library at Christ Church, Canterbury, for example. He "would correct erroneous books [himself] and erase false writings as soon as he could study them by the first light of dawn".[30]

Dunstan's efforts were once again thwarted following further invasion by the Danes in 1011 and a fire in 1067 destroyed much of his library in Canterbury. Indeed, only some thirty-seven volumes were preserved from the library.[31] At the same time, codices were being produced, notably the *Codex Aureus* (now in Sweden's Stockholm Royal Library) and the *Royal Bible* (British Library), both produced in the ninth century, and probably in Canterbury. The *Codex Aureus* was so named because of the generous use of gilt in the illumination. These manuscripts built upon earlier work produced in southern England, such as the *Book of Cerne* (Cambridge University Library) and the *Nunnaminster Prayer Book*, that contains the Passion narrative of the four Gospels and some liturgical prayers. This was probably part of the royal collection belonging to the House of Wessex, and then given to the Nunnaminster, a convent in Winchester.[32] Again, at Cerne Abbas, and later at Eynsham, Aelfric, the greatest scholar of the Benedictine reformation of monasteries in the late ninth and tenth centuries in England, spent a lifetime of study and exposition. At Ramsey in Cambridgeshire, Byrhtferth (c. 970–1020) wrote, among other works, a diverse mathematical and scientific miscellany: *Enchiridion*.

The tenth century was a period of establishing the House of Wessex as the premier kingdom in England through a succession of—for the most part— brilliant and able rulers, beginning with Alfred the Great. It saw the revival of learning and of the spiritual fabric of the nation through a succession of able and committed church leaders. In many ways, the high point of these developments was Edgar's coronation in Bath in 973. This service of coronation would be a model for later coronations, such as Edward the Confessor's and William the Conqueror's, and was influenced by the Carolingian tradition on the continent mediated by Alcuin to England. Indeed, many of its features remain unchanged.

By 973, Edgar had ruled for fifteen years, but he was thirty years of age, the age for ordination, and now also of his almost priestly consecration or coronation. The day for the coronation was Pentecost. Archbishop Dunstan, then sixty-four, led it. Edgar was portrayed as the shepherd of his flock. The *ordo* (order of service) of the coronation may have owed much to Rheims and the coronation of Carolingian kings such as Charles the Bald, a grandson of Charlemagne. Edgar's crown was removed, and the *Te Deum* intoned. Edgar made the threefold promise of obedience to Christ, to support the Church, and to uphold the laws of the land. He was anointed with oil by Archbishop Dunstan of Canterbury and Oswald of York. Words from the Old Testament were read out: "Zadok the priest and Nathan the prophet anointed Solomon king" (1 Kings 1:39ff.). Dunstan then gave Edgar a ring, a sword, the crown, the sceptre and a rod, each symbol redolent with meaning: the ring symbolizing orthodox faith; the sword, power to defend; the crown, the authority to rule; the sceptre, a sign of the king's government; and the rod, a sign of justice. Together they made Christian kingship: a kingship that was to be expressed and tempered in England in coming generations. At the end of the service Dunstan pronounced "a solemn and prolonged" blessing. The coronation expressed his authority in powerful symbolic language. The following year eight kings from Cumbria, North Wales and Scotland gave Edgar their allegiance on a royal barge near Chester on the River Dee. It was the apogee of West Saxon power; it was also the beginning of a decline.

The decline of the House of Wessex

Within two years of his coronation and receipt of the allegiance of eight kings on the River Dee, the peace-loving, Church-supporting Edgar suddenly died. The only blemish on his record in the *Anglo-Saxon Chronicle* is in these, now contemporary-sounding, words:

> Yet he did one ill-deed too greatly: he loved foreign customs and brought firmly heathen manners within this land, attracted hither foreigners and enticed harmful people to this country. But may God grant him that his good deeds prove greater than his ill-deeds, for the protection of his soul on its everlasting journey.[33]

To consort too closely with continentals was a blemish then and was part of the insularity and character of the English who, ironically, were themselves immigrants from Germany only a few centuries before.

The sudden death of King Edgar on 8 July 975 was followed by a serious crisis over the succession. Edgar had two sons by two marriages. From his first marriage to Aethelflaed (which was discounted by some nobles) he had a son, Edward, later called Edward the Martyr because of his untimely death. From his second marriage to the daughter of an ealdorman, Ordgar of Devon, he had a second son called Aethelred, later known as "Aethelred *the Unready*", which in Old English meant "ill advised". Edward had already offended significant leaders with his violent temper and his uncertain legitimacy, while Aethelred, still only a boy, was well liked. During Edward's reign there was disorder and the growth of an anti-monastic movement, since monasteries were perceived to have taken away too much land from the nobility.[34] However, on 18 March 978, Edward was murdered at Corfe in Dorset whilst visiting his half-brother, Aethelred, and his stepmother. He was hastily buried without a service at Wareham, and later transferred to a convent at Shaftesbury. The murder was not pinned on anyone, but within a month Aethelred was ruling in an atmosphere of suspicion. Miracles were reported at the tomb of Edward, by then called a martyr.

While the twelve-year-old Aethelred succeeded to the English crown (978) in an atmosphere of suspicion, the Scandinavian kingdoms were united under a powerful Danish ruler, Harold Gormsson or Blue Tooth. Just as Scandinavia looked powerful, England looked vulnerable. Harold was then overthrown by his son, Swein, who together with many Viking nobles, despised Harold's attempts to convert them to Christianity. Viking raids began on the English coast again, giving us place names like Scarborough, which, derived from a Viking named Thorgils "Skarthi", means the "hare-lipped".[35] The attacks escalated and in 991 an attack at Maldon saw the defeat of ealdorman Byrthnoth, and the heroic action of his *thegns*, who fought to the death in his memory. The battle was later immortalized in a poem. Byrthnoth's courage—he paid in blood rather than buy security through gold—was proclaimed in the epic poem, which closes with the lines: "Thought must be more resolute, heart the more fierce, courage the greater, as our strength diminishes."[36]

What Byrthnoth and his *thegns* refused to countenance was the ignominious price of peace. The Viking leader, Olaf Tryggvason, made a treaty with the rulers of Kent, West Hampshire and Wessex in which large sums were to be paid in return for peace. It was the beginning of Danegeld: a tax to buy off the Danes or to provide protection. The treaty of 992 specified that 22,000 pounds of gold and silver must be paid. It was a huge sum.

Worse was to come. In 994, Olaf of Norway and Swein of Denmark joined their fleets and forces: "It was the most formidable invasion England had experienced in half a century."[37] The outcome was not as dire as expected: Olaf and Swein fell out; London resisted stubbornly; and Olaf sought a treaty with Aethelred which was confirmed at Andover. Olaf returned to consolidate Norway, but Viking attacks resumed in 999 in Wessex, Dorset and Hampshire. A further truce was only secured with the payment of 24,000 pounds of tribute money. The cost of Danegeld was now impoverishing the nation.

By 1002, Aethelred was about thirty-four years old. Two events that year were to affect his reign greatly: his marriage to Emma of Normandy and the massacre of St Brice's Day. Emma was the daughter of Duke Richard I of Normandy and Gunnora, herself of Danish descent. In time Emma would become the great-aunt of William the Conqueror. Richard I, Emma's father, was the grandson of the founder of the Norman dynasty, the Viking Rollo. Normans were therefore Scandinavian in origin and had settled in Normandy in the same way Vikings settled in northern and eastern England. Emma married Aethelred at the age of seventeen in 1002. By then, Aethelred had already fathered ten children with other wives and concubines. Emma was to have two sons and a daughter with Aethelred: Edward (the Confessor), Alfred and Goda. From a book in praise of Emma's life entitled *The Encomium of Queen Emma* (an eleventh-century work produced by a monk from Saint-Omer), the marriage appears to have been little more than a diplomatic alliance, although with important dynastic repercussions.

The occasion for this new Viking invasion of England by the Danes was, in part, the massacre of Danes on St Brice's Day, 13 November 1002, in southern England, on the orders of Aethelred himself. Many Danes in Oxford were slaughtered, quite possibly in St Frideswide's Church. New raids on eastern England then took place, led by Swein Forkbeard, who now ruled the greater part of Norway. In 1004, Norwich was sacked. Tribute money was demanded and raised. In 1009, a much larger invasion materialized, led by Thorkell the Tall and his brother. Periodic invasions continued and yet more sums of tribute money or Danegeld were raised. English resistance was weak. The defection of Thorkell the Tall to Aethelred in 1012 only provoked more serious revenge attacks from Denmark. Swein once more attacked, taking northern England, and entered English Mercia. The royal family fled to Normandy, where Edward the Confessor would be raised as an exile. Swein died on the campaign in 1014, only to be replaced by Cnut, the younger of his sons, who in 1015 invaded England.

Once again it was a period of great testing and confusion for the Church, and it produced the first martyred archbishop: Alphege. Born in Weston outside Bath, Alphege was for a time a hermit. He then became a monk at Deerhurst, a monastery by the River Severn, then Abbot of Bath, and in 984, in his thirties, Bishop of Winchester. In 1006, he became Archbishop of Canterbury. Alphege was captured by the Danes in 1011 and put up for ransom. He requested that no money be paid for him, and at a drunken feast his captors began to stone him and then beat him to death with jawbones taken from their feast.

In 1016, during Cnut's invasion and during the defence of London with his son Edmund, Aethelred died. His reign had been one of the longest of any English monarch (thirty-seven years), and one of the most ignominious. The realm had effectively been lost by an Anglo-Saxon king some forty years or so after the coronation of Edgar in Bath. If his reign was remembered for anything, it was for payment of huge sums of Danegeld. The fact that such huge sums could be raised and paid to the Danes was a tribute to the coinage and taxation system in England.

With the death of Aethelred and his son Edmund, the first Danish king, Cnut, began his reign in England. Still only in his twenties when he defeated Aethelred's son, Edmund Ironside, Cnut was to rule a north European empire that included England, Denmark, Norway and parts of Sweden. He was the first Viking leader to be overtly Christian. Although Cnut had an earlier relationship with Aelfgifu, the daughter of the Earl of Northumberland, with whom he had a son, Harold I Harefoot, his second marriage was to the ubiquitous Emma of Normandy, the widow of Aethelred. Now in her early thirties, she nevertheless gave Cnut a son, Harthacnut, who would briefly reign for two years from 1040. Emma, with her Norman and Danish pedigree (through her mother), appears as one of the great survivors in the final years of the Saxon monarchy. Like Galla Placidia, the daughter of the final Roman Emperor of east and west, Theodosius I, she married two opposing rulers, Aethelred and Cnut.[38] Emma typified the complex relationship between Viking, Norman and Anglo-Saxon in eleventh-century England, a relationship which was to dominate the final years of the Anglo-Saxon kingdom before the Norman Conquest.

Cnut's rule of England was firm, enlightened and progressive. In 1018, he raised a huge tax of £72,000 to sustain his navy and army.[39] He personally attended to appointments in the Church, going to Rome for the institution of the Holy Roman Emperor, Conrad II, in 1027. He appointed earls to govern the whole country, with Thorkell the Tall acting as regent when he was in Scandinavia. He personally defended the northern border against the Picts and Scots. He buried the body of the martyr-archbishop Alphege in Canterbury, with great solemnity and pageantry.[40] It must have been a deeply symbolic event: a Christian Danish king of England burying an archbishop martyred by the Vikings, attended by Queen Emma and her infant son Harthacnut, with large crowds and a large body of bishops and clergy following, including the current archbishop, Aethelnoth.

Cnut is presented by the *Chronicle* as the willing pupil of the church hierarchy, and a conscientious protector of Anglo-Saxon law. He himself decreed a substantial addition to the already well-developed legal codes of Anglo-Saxon kings. Ethelbert of Kent, Ine, Alfred, Athelstan, Edgar and Aethelred of Wessex all promulgated laws supported by their respective *witans* (king's councils). Cnut was strongly guided by Archbishop Wulfstan of York, who, as already noted, famously preached the *"Sermo Lupi ad Anglos"* ("Sermon of the Wolf to the English"), with its play on the first part of his own name. These laws followed a by now familiar pattern: penalty fines were updated and often imposed in the court of the Hundred, the village court; children over twelve must swear publicly that they would not steal; people must raise "a hue and cry" when witness to a theft or otherwise be fined; defendants must undergo trial by ordeal; adultery, fornication and incest must be punished by payment of the *wergild* (the set value of the person offended). Eighty-three laws in all were decreed in this code, together with rules on the conduct of marriage.[41]

These laws were introduced in a "Letter to England" in 1019, and a further letter in 1027. Cnut began his second letter in 1027, saying, "I make known to you that I have recently been to Rome, to pray for the remission of my sins and for the safety of the kingdoms and of the people which are subject to my rule."[42] He goes on to say that he commands no unjust force "be used against any man, neither rich, nor poor, but that all men, of noble or humble birth, rich or poor shall have the right to enjoy just law".[43] In many ways these sentiments anticipate the Magna Carta by 200 years.

When Cnut died, his two senior sons succeeded in turn to the English throne: Harold I Harefoot (1035–40, son of Aelfgifu of Northampton) and Harold Harthacnut (1040–2, Emma of Normandy's son). Yet the dynasty was greatly weakened by rivalry between the factions of these two heirs and the necessity of ruling an empire that included Demark, Sweden and parts of Norway. Try as he had to ensure a smooth succession for Harthacnut in Denmark and Norway, by 1035 "Cnut's great empire was in ruins".[44] The Norwegians were now zealous supporters of St Olaf, a Christian Norwegian prince who drove out the Danes, and with them Harefoot and his mother Aelfgifu. At the same time Cnut had raised up a powerful earldom in Wessex, which was granted to the Godwine family to help him in his Scandinavian wars. The Godwines would become major players in the succession to the English throne after Edward the Confessor.

Edward himself had been an exile in Normandy during his stepfather Cnut's reign. He was hosted for twenty-five years as an exile by the Norman court—then ruled by Richard II, Emma's brother, called either the "Magnificent" or "the Devil", whichever one preferred! Edward's court was a mixture of English, Scandinavian and Norman French. Edward himself remains an enigma: beneath a benign exterior, he was a shrewd and calculating man. Later generations knew him as the Confessor, meaning that he was a saint who had not suffered martyrdom. He was canonized in 1161 by Pope Alexander III. Also, because he had no heir, medieval minds were quick to credit him with holy abstinence with his beloved queen Edith, the daughter of Earl Godwine, rather than suspect them of infertility. Furthermore, his generous endowment and rebuilding of Westminster Abbey, where he was eventually buried, created a perfect setting for a Confessor's shrine. It was also to be the place of all future English coronations.

Edward was crowned on Easter Day 1043 in Winchester, at the New Minster. The coronation followed the pattern of coronations laid down by Dunstan's *ordo* in Bath Abbey in 973. As was traditional, Edward promised in the service to protect the rights of the Church in the *Promissio Regis*. Like Cnut's laws the *Promissio Regis* was a forerunner to Magna Carta two centuries later.

His appointments of church leaders drew on his connections with France, not just from Normandy, but also from Alsace-Lorraine. His rule had to balance the different sectional interests that made up the kingdom. The Saxon/Danish interest was powerfully represented by the Godwine family. Earl Godwine was the King's most exalted subject. His daughter Edith married the King; his disreputable son Swein (who later kidnapped an abbess) became Earl of Mercia and of parts of Wessex; and Harold became Earl of Essex. The other earls—Leofric of northern Mercia and Siward of Northumbria—were suspicious of the Godwines, and Edward could not forgive them for the murder of his brother Alfred.

It was in this period that Duke William, a teenager of fifteen and a great-nephew of Edward's mother Emma, came on a visit to the court in 1052, no doubt eyeing up the English crown. The triangulation of succession, Danish, Norman and English, was revived in 1052 by the restoration of the Godwines, who had effectively invaded the south coast and marched to Southwark with an army. An agreement was brokered by Bishop Stigand of Winchester, hostages were exchanged, and the *witan* met with Godwine, Edward's father-in-law, present. "Friendship" was established between Godwine and the King, and the Norman French were outlawed. Civil war had been averted. Godwine had shown his hand

and Edward had stepped back. Godwine died the following year in 1053, and his son Harold was made Earl of Wessex.

The remaining years of Edward's rule were taken up with war against the Welsh, a rebellion in Northumbria against the taxation imposed in 1065 by Earl Tostig Godwinson (Harold's brother), who was then driven from England, and the mysterious reappearance in 1057 of the King's nephew and *aetheling* (Saxon heir) Edward from his exile in Hungary. By December 1065, the King had become too ill to attend the consecration of his beloved Westminster Abbey. On 5 January, Edward died at Westminster with no clear heir. By Christmas Day that year a new ruler of England was crowned in the same abbey: the Norman Duke William, who by force of arms had conquered England, and who was now busy with its subjugation.

PART II

The Late Middle Ages

CHAPTER 4

The Church after the Norman Conquest

The next discernible stage in the development of the Church in England was from the Norman Conquest to the arrival of the Tudors (1485), a period of 400 years. If England's main weakness at the beginning of 1066 was the lack of a clear line of succession to Edward the Confessor, it was a weakness that did not mask the country's many strengths. As we have seen, the crown now had an efficient system of minting coins and raising large sums of money in taxation. Indeed, by the eleventh century, English coinage had been accepted as a model by all the Scandinavian peoples.[1] It may have been that the English currency was also acceptable tender in Scandinavia. England also had a strong administrative and legal system.

The population of England was still around the two million mark, and mostly distributed through the countryside in village communities fast becoming known as *mansiones*, or what Norman clerks in the Domesday Book would call *manoirs*. Beneath the local landowning lord or *thegn*, there appear to have been at least four types of peasantry. At the bottom were slaves with no rights at all, making up ten per cent of the population. (Slavery was later phased out by the Normans.) Then—according to a contemporary treatise on estate management entitled *Rectitudines Singularum Personarum*—there were *kotsela*, best translated by our word "cottager", who gave three or four days' service a week to their lord in exchange for about five acres. A sign of their relative independence was that they had to pay *church-scot*, which was a church due. Above them were *geneat*, virtually freemen, who gave limited service to their lord in exchange for land. Lastly, there were *geburas*, who held up to thirty acres and worked two or three days a week for the lord, depending on the time of year. An interesting variation of these peasant classes can be found in the Danelaw, where it seems there were larger numbers of freemen or sokemen (*soke* meaning a jurisdiction or tenancy). This was probably due to the fact that these freemen may have been soldiers first, and their tenure, which may have included some judicial responsibility, was a reward for military service. Overall, this variegated peasant class came to be known as *villeins*, simply meaning "villagers". Lay and ecclesial manors were administered in a similar way and those of the peasant classes who were not enslaved paid *church-scot*. What is clear about this period, even before the Conquest, was that "the lord was beginning to supersede the influence of communal association as the controlling force in rural life".[2] There was a great degree of dependency on the local lord or *thegn*.

Alongside the rural peasantry serving their local lord was a growing number of successful market towns or boroughs. By the time of the Conquest, the populations of these towns were as follows: York 8,000; Thetford 4,750; Ipswich 3,000; and Norwich 6,600. We have no figures for London or Winchester, but they are likely to have been home to tens of thousands. Boroughs had at first been defensive units in the fight against the Danes or Vikings; now they were trade centres or market towns authorized by royal charter. Local lords and burgesses were expected to fulfil the customs laid on them by the charter. Boroughs were also the sites of shire and borough courts. A mixture of king and local lords owned this borough land. What is clear is that boroughs were prosperous centres of trade and town life and complemented the rural economy.

A well-developed system of justice operated in conjunction with the rural and borough economies. Several Anglo-Saxon kings had codified and issued laws over the preceding 200 years. Courts now sat in the hundred, shire and borough. *Thegns* were granted land with the rights of "sake and soke", meaning that they had a right to administer the law in the hundred. In the shire courts, the king's reeve (later sheriff) sat, along with the bishop and possibly other recognizable local figures. In addition, the beginning of a jury system is discernible in the Wantage Code of Aethelred the Unready (978–1013). It states therein that twelve leading *thegns* in each *wapentake* (a division of the country in the Danelaw corresponding to the hundred in Wessex) should swear on relics that they would only apprehend those who were guilty, bringing them to court for judgement by ordeal. Later, these *thegns* would give judgement in legal cases. The agreement of eight of these twelve "jurors" was sufficient for a verdict and thus the principle of jury service, as we now know it, was not far away.

At the Conquest, England was a society with strong local traditions of order, justice, administration and land tenure, and was capable of providing considerable revenue for the crown. Its coinage was dependable and lent stability to the economy. The Anglo-Saxon kings had ruled with the consent of the *witan*, the king's council of leading nobles and churchmen. Charters, the preferred style of Anglo-Saxon government, were agreed and witnessed by the *witan*, whose names were affixed thereto. This then was the method of government in England, about to undergo a huge shock and profound change. England's customs and obligations of local government would nevertheless survive.

International relations around the first millennium

Substantial changes in international relations made the Norman Conquest more likely, and those changes need to be appreciated if the Conquest is to be understood. The ninth century saw the gradual decline of the Carolingian dynasty, made up of descendants of the Franks, after it had reached its zenith under Charlemagne (who was consecrated Holy Roman Emperor on Christmas Day 800). On his death, his great empire was split between his sons, and never again reached such prominence. In 888, the death of the Carolingian king Charles the Fat saw the final years of the dynasty: a demise that was brought about in part by the Viking attacks in northern France. In 911, Charles the Simple, a Carolingian king of West Francia and Lotharingia, ceded land around Rouen to Rollo, the Viking leader and ancestor of William Duke of Normandy. By this arrangement Normandy was established. The Normans, in origin Viking, intermarried with native Franks and Bretons and became a major military, cultural and eventually Catholic force in both northern and southern Europe. They were the "attack dogs" of Europe and their Viking spirit drove them as far south as southern Italy, and then Sicily, making inroads into the Byzantine Empire.

The papacy could not ignore the Normans as they had made substantial incursions into the bailiwick of the popes. Pope Leo IX (1049–54) led an army against the Normans, whose power in Italy had been growing since the early eleventh century. Pope Leo and his Swabian mercenaries were defeated at the Battle of Civitate near Foggia in 1053, however, and Leo was held "honourably captive" for a year but died in Rome soon after his release. The Normans now held considerable territory in Puglia and Calabria and would soon begin to wrest Sicily from the Muslims from 1072, after taking Palermo. Normans were now powerful players in both northern and southern Europe. The Byzantine Empire was growing again under Basil II, taking land in Georgia and Armenia. The Muslim advance was temporarily checked until the arrival of Saladin and the Ottoman Turks a century later. The Pope was looking for new allies with military ability. In 1054, there was a schism between Rome and Constantinople when Cardinal Humbert, sent by Leo IX, and Patriarch Keroularios mutually excommunicated each other.[3]

It was indeed time for a change in papal policy on several fronts and especially towards the Normans.

It was a period of growing papal aspirations too. Before long Gregory VII, previously the powerful Archdeacon of Rome, was acclaimed Pope (1073–85) by the people, who cried out at the Lateran: "Let Hildebrand be pope." Gregory soon began an all-out campaign against lay involvement in appointments (investitures) of clergy. He even famously brought Henry IV, the Holy Roman Emperor, to his knees in penance at Canossa in 1077 for lack of obedience. The policy also provoked a running battle between church and state, not least in England.

A little time before, when Pope Nicholas II (1059–61) was elected, a change in policy towards the Normans began. Nicholas was determined to cultivate the Normans, and in particular Duke William and the Italian Abbot of Bec, Lanfranc: perhaps the greatest churchman in Europe and soon to be Archbishop of Canterbury (1070–89). Lanfranc was an Italian from Lombardy, and a trained lawyer. By temper he was a politician and a teacher of persuasive magnetism. Nicholas II wrote to him, asking him to educate two chaplains in the skills of grammar, dialectic and the study of the Bible. He also told Lanfranc to instruct the Duke, "so that he may flourish in this world and in Christ. I have great confidence in him and in the counsel and companionship which he has with you."[4] In 1059, Nicholas II and Lanfranc met in Rome at a council that had been called to iron out doctrine on the Eucharist raised by Berengar, but opposed by Lanfranc. A problem of consanguinity over Duke William's marriage to Matilda of Flanders was also sorted out during the council and William was assured of more than a sympathetic ear to plans he might make for the future. The papacy was now a friend of the Normans' duke, and when the time came, the duke was not disappointed.

Contenders for the throne of England

When Edward the Confessor died on 5 January 1066 and was buried with full honour in his beloved Westminster Abbey, there was deep uncertainty about the future. It is hard to know his mind concerning his successor. He and his wife Edith—the sister of Harold Godwinson—had no children, probably the result of infertility rather than the explanation put about of Edward's unwillingness to consummate the marriage because of a vow of celibacy. The myth of celibacy was circulated in *Vita Edwardi Regis*, which was largely the creation of Queen Edith, who wanted to promote the Godwinson family and Harold, rather than her husband.[5] Edward seems to have made no clear, unassailable written or proclaimed will.[6] Whoever Edward had in mind, he failed to communicate it. There were, in fact, four potential heirs: William of Normandy, Edward's second cousin; Harold Godwinson, his brother-in-law; the *aethling* (meaning the Anglo-Saxon next-in-line) Edgar; and Harald Hardrada, the Norwegian king. Four more varied claimants could scarcely be imagined, and the paths they each represented for England were momentous and determinative for the future of the nation.

The Norman claim was further boosted in their eyes by two things: a supposed promise made by Edward the Confessor to William that he would succeed to the English throne on Edward's death and an oath made by Harold Godwinson to Duke William when he fell by chance into William's hands, possibly through a shipwreck off the Normandy coast, about which the Bayeux Tapestry makes much in its telling of the story of the Conquest from the Norman point of view.

The struggle for England

When Edward the Confessor died, three of the claimants saw their moment and activated their plans to take the English crown. Harold, who was on the spot, quickly declared himself King of England with the support of the council or *witan*, which had met during the King's final illness. He was crowned the following day, 6 January, in Westminster Abbey, but was king for only nine hectic months, dying on the battlefield of Hastings on 14 October of that year.[7] Harald Hardrada (whose name means "the ruthless") landed with a Norwegian army in the Humber. Initially successful in taking York, the Norwegians prepared to march south. At the same time, Harold Godwinson of England marched north, confronted the invader at Stamford Bridge near York on 25 September, and more or less wiped out the army of Hardrada and Tostig—an earl and the brother of Harold Godwinson who confusingly had sided with Hadrada—both of whom were killed.

No sooner had the dead been counted than news of William's arrival with an army on the south coast at Pevensey filtered through to Harold. He marched south, raising fresh levies of troops near London, and made ready to engage the third and most pressing claimant, the thirty-eight-year-old William of Normandy.

William had persuaded the Norman barons to join him in his very risky plan of invasion with some difficulty. By now, William was secure in France. A child had come to the throne of France, and his regent was Baldwin of Flanders, a relative of William. His old foe, the Count of Anjou, had died. With the eventual support of his barons, gained through promises of large-scale booty, William assembled a fleet of some 700 ships and an army of 7,000 men, plus horses and provisions, at

Dives-Sur-Mer on the estuary of the Somme. At the same time, William sought divine assistance through the consecration of a new abbey at Caen, and received the blessing of the Pope, who promised William's soldiers "indulgences" for their action. The papal legate, Ermenfrod of Sion in Normandy, called this invasion "a public war" (that is, a just war). With the papal blessing, the belief that this was a "just war" against a usurper, the thought that the invasion would earn participants "merit" towards their eternal salvation, and the promise of very large gains, all that was needed was a fair wind. Eventually it came, and according to his chaplain and chronicler, William of Poitiers, William crossed the Channel in a calm mood, "eating a hearty breakfast with spiced wine".[8] They landed on 28 September, three days after Stamford Bridge, and, a little over a fortnight later, the battle that changed English history began.

If the Battle of Stamford Bridge had finally seen off the possibility of England becoming part of the Scandinavian system, and therefore becoming part of a Viking empire, the victory of William over Harold at Hastings tied England emphatically to a continental future politically, culturally and spiritually. This became the inescapable conclusion of Hastings once the victory was extended nationwide by the Conqueror. The battle itself was hard-fought, costly and close, but in the end, with the death of Harold Godwinson, the Saxon-Dane, it was conclusive.

The two armies met on 14 October 1066 at "the grey apple tree", as the Anglo-Saxon chronicler called it, but which later was simply called Battle.[9] Harold assembled his army on high ground above the Normans, taking the traditional Saxon formation of a "shield wall". The Normans, replete with archers and cavalry, were below. William's high-risk strategy from the outset had been to place his forces in three divisions: archers, infantry and cavalry. The battle began with salvos of arrows fired at Harold's troops, but they held their formation. The Normans advanced and were soon engaged in hand-to-hand fighting of the fiercest kind. Still the English line held, and casualties were mounting. The Norman cavalry failed to make an impression. When it seemed as though the English army was winning and the Normans were retreating, either in fear or as a deliberate ruse, only then did Harold's army break rank and lose their positions. The Normans thought that William had been wounded in the chase, but when he lifted his helmet and showed his face to his troops, encouraging them to fight back, the Normans rallied and their cavalry turned from flight to advance. The English, having broken line, were cut down. It is estimated that altogether the losses were around six thousand: 3,500 English and 2,500 Normans.

It was a great slaughter, so much so that William required his soldiers to do penance for it and later he founded an abbey on the spot, not so much to thank God for the victory as to atone for the bloodshed incurred there. It was typical of the medieval mind that if on the one hand he resorted to violence, necessary and just as William believed it to be, on the other hand he nevertheless felt culpable for the bloodshed, for which an act of penance was required—hence the abbey. William had won a battle on which the fate of a nation turned.

William did not go directly to London from Hastings, nor did England cease all resistance. Edgar the *atheling*, the final claimant of 1066, was now proclaimed king, as the last male in the line of Cerdic (467–534), the founder of Anglo-Saxon Wessex, and great grandson of Aethelred the Unready. William first traversed the south coast from Dover to Canterbury, remaining there for a month. Winchester offered terms of surrender through the influence of Edith, the Confessor's widow and sister of Harold. However, when William approached London, he met resistance from Edgar's troops in Southwark at London Bridge, so he decided to cross the Thames much further west at Wallingford. From there, he went along the Chilterns, reaching Berkhamstead, where he received the submission of Edgar, Wulfstan the Bishop of Worcester, Edwin of Mercia, Morcar of Northumbria and the remaining earls. It seems that William's slow advance had given his enemies time to make a realistic assessment of their chances, and they had come to the conclusion that resistance would be useless. William was now virtually King of all England. He received the surrender of London, and assured citizens that he would respect their customs and laws. Then, on Christmas Day 1066, a year after the death of the Confessor, he was crowned in Westminster Abbey. His troops burnt and pillaged the area outside the abbey, while William was crowned within. A bid for legitimacy inside the abbey was matched by unrestrained violence outside.

During the following years William would ruthlessly apply his victory across the country. He faced continuing opposition in the Fens around Ely, where vestiges of Harold's family joined with the citizens of the city, but mostly in the North. There were two uprisings in Northumbria in 1067 and 1069, where the *aethling*'s party was active. William's forces were defeated and a renewed invasion by Danish forces led by Swein Estrithson threatened Yorkshire in an alliance with the recalcitrant English. William himself marched north and began his "Harrying of the North", a scorched earth policy that saw the death by starvation or from fighting of some 100,000 people, according to the chronicler, Vitalis Orderic. The rebellions elsewhere in England were also repressed. In 1071, the Abbot of Ely and Hereward the Wake, together with other English lords, Morcar and Edwin, and various exiles, took up arms against William. They too were eventually defeated.

Morcar and Edwin were put in prison for the rest of their lives, but Hereward the Wake escaped into the fens, and into the legend of English resistance. By 1072, William had conquered most of the country, and his gains seemed irreversible. The *aethling* Edgar had fled to Flanders and his sister Margaret had married Malcolm III of Scotland. Their daughter Matilda would marry Henry I, William's youngest son, thus forging an alliance between Saxon and Norman.

The effects of the Norman Conquest

The issue of how much the Norman Conquest changed England is often debated, and a famous question for the history student. It was the last of four invasions of England over the preceding thousand years. These invasions were by the Romans, the Anglo-Saxons, the Vikings and then the Normans. Apart from occasional incursions of forces from France, as in the minority of Henry III, it was to be the last invasion of size and significance in the history of England. The Normans, over time, created a new ethnic mix in England with the now indigenous Anglo-Saxon population, but left, for the time being, the Celtic population to hold sway in Wales and the South-West.

The Norman invasion and settlement of England was a revolution of a particular kind. The Norman Conquest saw the replacement of one ruling class with another. Almost all of the English leaders were swept away. "Some 4,000–5,000 *thegns* (English lords) were eliminated by battle, exile or dispossession in the biggest transfer of property in English history."[10] Similarly, almost all the church leaders of abbeys, of dioceses and in government were removed, with only two or three exceptions. At the root of this transfer of power to a new ruling elite was a feudal commitment to William, who now owned all the land *de jure* and *de facto*, and who granted tenancies in exchange for an oath of feudal loyalty and service, be it from a churchman or a layman. In this way a new French-speaking and Latin-using elite class came into existence, building on the English or Saxon base. This base provided continuity of administration in terms of taxation and the courts, which was probably the most extensive and well-managed system in Europe, and which gave the king and his chief magnates immense power. Finally, the Norman kings and their successors added a twist to English policy. Whereas the Anglo-Saxons had looked no further than the shores of Britain for territory, now the Norman, Angevin or Plantagenet kings were preoccupied with two things: gaining territory in France and fighting among themselves for what Shakespeare called "the hollow crown".[11]

This revolution, begun by the conquest of England, was essentially a vast transfer of power, which rested on the redistribution of land. Sometimes this land redistribution maintained the *status quo*, as with many of the monasteries. The land was entailed (let) by the King as "fiefs or fees" to his tenants, and with this came the obligation of military service, thereby providing knights for William's army. The national landholding was split up as follows: the crown held 20 per cent of all land, mostly in the form of royal hunting forests, each with their own strict legal code, such as the New Forest; the Church held 25 per cent; and about a dozen magnates, mostly situated on the perimeters of England, the Marches and the North, held a further 25 per cent. Some two thousand foreign knights held the remaining land. Some of these landlords still have vast landholdings today, as in the case of the Percys of Northumberland. (In Alnwick Castle, a charter from William granting these landholdings—initially in Yorkshire—to the Percys may be viewed today, and is the basis of the family's current ownership.)

By contrast, out of the two million English population, only four Englishmen held large landholdings and only twenty Englishmen had incomes of more than £20 a year. The revolution in ownership could not have been more complete, and the Domesday Book recorded it.

The Domesday Book came late on in William's reign. "Domesday" sounds like an ironic nickname given by the English when accounting for this great transfer of land. It was a survey of the assets of the realm and who tenanted each recorded holding. Following a council meeting at Gloucester, where there was "much thought and deep discussion", this extraordinary audit of England got underway.[12] This was held at the Christmas Court of 1085, almost twenty years after the Conquest. The project was masterminded by the Bishop of Durham, William de St Calais, and, extraordinarily, was completed in seven months. Admittedly, there had been a pilot project in the West called the *Liber Exoniensis*, which had honed the procedure of collecting the information and then writing it up in Exeter Cathedral's *scriptorium*, but nonetheless it was a remarkable demonstration of Norman administrative power based on English procedure. Commissioners toured the shire and hundred courts taking testimony from local people about the assets of the countryside: landholdings were registered, mills listed, and fisheries, slaves (28,000), villeins and plough teams recorded. The document listed 13,000 places and 30,000 lordly estates. A jury of six Normans and six Englishmen corroborated the facts. It transpires that there was as much land under the plough then as there was in 1900, and most of the villages that exist now existed then! By August 1086, the Domesday Book was complete, minus certain parts of England that were assessed separately, such as the Palatinate of Durham. On 1 August at Old Sarum near Salisbury, this book formed the basis of a great ceremony of homage to William for the land vested in his tenants, both lay and ecclesiastical. At Old Sarum, where William had built a cathedral (before Salisbury Cathedral was built) and a castle, the bishops, abbots, barons and sheriffs all paid him homage for land received, and in turn promised to supply military service. The feudal system was in place and would, in theory at least, last until 1660 and the Restoration of Charles II, when the crown's feudal revenue from land was replaced by an excise on alcohol, as enacted by the Tenures Abolition Act of that year.

If part of the Norman revolution had to do with land tenure and the replacement of the old English ruling class, another part was the straightforward replacement of the old Saxon ruling royal family with a Norman one. The line of Cerdic, which went back to the Anglo-Saxon invasion of Britain in the fifth century, was replaced by the descendants of Rollo, the Viking Northman, known simply now as Norman. William, who had been plagued with issues of legitimacy all his life, now set about establishing his claim to the English crown. We have already seen the reasoning for this claim, special or otherwise, bolstered as it was by the Pope and by Lanfranc, his archbishop. Now William made it the cardinal principle of his government "to be accepted by Englishmen as King Edward's legitimate successor".[13] As far as possible William airbrushed the usurper Harold from the record of royal government and built the continuity of his government on the writs of Edward the Confessor. Again and again he referred back to "the time of King Edward" or *tempore regis Edwardi*, abbreviated in the Domesday Book as T. R. E. He made it clear to all who could read or hear that he was the successor who preserved the English state, however much he handed the reins of power to new men.

The Normans and the English Church: Lanfranc and Anselm

Another part of the realm in which William made a clean sweep of leadership was the Church: the most influential part of the nation, whose teaching, life and presence permeated all of society. As with the lay tenure, in which almost all of the English *thegns* or lords were swept aside, when it came to abbots and bishops, almost all the senior English clergy were likewise evicted. Only Wulfstan II of Worcester, Giso of Wells and Aethelwig, the Abbot of Evesham, remained. All new appointments were Norman. Because the Church held up to 25 per cent of the land, its leaders also had to pay homage to the King for those holdings, and similarly provide knights for military service. For instance, Peterborough Abbey was assessed at sixty knights, Glastonbury and Bury at forty, and Abingdon at twenty.

Whereas in the old English system, abbeys held land by royal charter, agreed by the *witan* and signed and witnessed by its members, now the abbot himself had to pay homage to the King for the land that supported the abbey he led. As Eadmer, the perceptive observer and English monk from Canterbury, wrote in his *History of Novelties*, "everything, divine and human alike, waited on the King's nod", another typical piece of English irony at this new all-powerful system.[14] On the one hand, the right of appointment and the investiture of a bishop or abbot with his temporal or worldly demesne was an important matter for the King in strengthening the "feudal system". On the other hand, however, Gregory VII made the abolition of lay investiture (that is, the king appointing clergy) the central plank of his papal reforms. Inevitably, there would be clashes between kings and popes, and between the church and the state. In Germany, this came to a head between Gregory VII and the Emperor Henry IV, resulting in Henry's penance at Canossa. In England, it would have its tragic but defining moment in the murder of Becket in Canterbury Cathedral. That drama lay some way ahead, but the seeds of the dispute were sown in William's system.

This new rigid and personal feudal system made senior churchmen vassals of the king, but churchmen believed as a point of faith that the temporal rights and expectations of the laity, including the king, must be subservient to the spiritual authority of the Church. What Ambrose had demonstrated in the fourth century, when he all but excommunicated the Emperor Theodosius for the behaviour of his troops in Thessalonica, was soon to occur in England. It was only a matter of time, and of having protagonists with the necessary convictions, before the breach between church and state would open up.

William came to England with the blessing of the papacy and the counsel of Lanfranc, the Abbot of Bec and St Étienne, Caen. Lanfranc became the premier teaching abbot throughout Europe, and as we have seen, was entrusted by Pope Nicholas with the training of his chaplains. Nicholas wrote in a letter: "We have heard that you are now fully occupied in the study of the Bible. If this is the case, we order you in the name of St Peter and ourselves, to give us your obedience in teaching the two chaplains those subjects for which we have sent them."[15]

Lanfranc was also a supreme church lawyer, and he wrote a book on the canons of the Church. He was at ease in the corridors of power, in Rome as in Westminster or Caen. He was a scholar, a student of the Bible, a teacher of grammar, rhetoric and logic, and the counsellor of aspiring and able monks. For twenty years as Abbot of Bec, and like Benedict Biscop in Monkwearmouth, he increased the scale of the monastery with new buildings, a greatly enhanced library and a more elaborate way of life and monastic rule. Known throughout Europe, he became the spiritual director of Anselm, who like Lanfranc, travelled from Italy to develop his calling at Bec.

The English Archbishop Stigand was deposed by papal legates in 1070 for his disloyalty to the papacy and to Lanfranc, an Italian with a Norman career behind him, who was then appointed Archbishop of Canterbury in Stigand's stead. Lanfranc had effectively become the second man in the realm. He was the primate of all England, even though there was a continuing dispute with York about the supremacy of Canterbury. He was the Abbot of Christ Church, Canterbury and, beyond that, a statesman of international repute. What Lanfranc found in England did not fill him with delight. He thought that monastic observance was primitive or lax; he considered English saints weak in their claim for sainthood; church buildings were small and poky; and the libraries sadly lacking in books. No wonder Eadmer, an English monk and writer at Canterbury, took a wry look at Lanfranc's reforming zeal. Within fifty years of 1066, every English cathedral and most major abbeys, apart from Westminster, had been razed to the ground and new stone buildings begun in the Romanesque style. Saints, such as Swithun, Alphege and Dunstan, were exhumed, their credentials assessed, and their remains reburied in new cathedrals. Anselm had to persuade Lanfranc of the sanctity of Alphege, and insist that his martyrdom was for justice and that he was therefore worthy of the martyr's crown.[16] Norman cathedrals were started in Canterbury, Winchester, Worcester, Durham, Ely, Old Sarum, Lincoln, Rochester, St Albans and elsewhere. New diocesan centres or sees replaced old ones: Lincoln in place of Dorchester, Old Sarum instead of Ramsbury and Norwich in place of Elmham. The Normans transformed the landscape with stone castles at Windsor, Durham, Chepstow, London and many other places besides. So swift was the building and the workmanship sometimes so poor that cathedral towers fell down in Ely, Lincoln and Winchester. Cathedrals that were begun a little later show that lessons were learnt, and these remarkable buildings have achieved an extraordinary permanency. Never again were so many breathtaking worship buildings erected in so short a time.

If the monarchy and leadership of England changed from English to Norman or continental almost overnight, and the built landscape changed with the appearance of stone castles and soaring cathedrals, so also did the language. The official language of administration continued to be Latin, while the language of power was Norman French, and English became the spoken language of ordinary people. To get on you needed Latin and French. Indeed, Robert of Gloucester wrote: "Unless a man knows French he is little thought of, but low born men keep to English and to their own speech still."[17] Kings would speak French until the reign of Edward III, and English literature did not flower until Richard II's reign, with the coming of Chaucer and Julian of Norwich. For the best part of 300 years, French would be the language of the court.

Lanfranc's was a reforming archiepiscopacy: dioceses and cathedrals were reformed and begun; synods were held at Winchester and London in 1072 and 1075 respectively, providing fresh discipline in church life;[18] monastic life was reinvigorated; scholarship was stimulated and resourced by better equipped libraries, especially at Christ Church, Canterbury; and, fatefully, lay and church courts were separated. Previously, earl and bishop had administered justice in the shire courts together, but now ecclesiastical courts were to administer justice over clergy, monks and church business separately. What started as a sensible administrative provision was to become the deepest bone of contention between church and state.

For nineteen years, Lanfranc laboured as Archbishop in England (1070–89), providing substantial reform and stability for the Church through his good relations with the King. He sought to bring, as he would see it, a "central normality to a barbarous land".[19] He managed to deal with the King's enemies on a number of occasions, trying Odo of Bayeaux and William de St Calais for defrauding the crown, and persecuting them in lay courts for a feudal breach of duty. He also unearthed a conspiracy against the King by the Earls of Norfolk and Hereford in 1075.

In two areas Lanfranc unwittingly sowed seeds of division for the future: through the separation of justice into lay and church courts, which would form the centre of Henry II's dispute with Becket, and by his clear espousal of the eucharistic doctrine of transubstantiation, which became a central objection of the Reformers. Each policy stored up huge difficulty, dissension and indeed bloodshed for the future, and both took on a life of their own in the practice of the Church. At the Council of Rome in 1059, and at Pope Nicholas's request, Lanfranc defended the position of a *substantial* change taking place in the elements (the bread and wine) of the Eucharist against Berengar of Tours, who taught otherwise. Lanfranc's position was based on the Aristotelian understanding of *categories*, in which the *accident* (the outer character of something) might stay the same, but the inner *substance* changes. Lanfranc was successful from the point of view of the papacy, but both ecclesiastical courts and the doctrine of transubstantiation stored up fury for the future. He died in office when almost eighty, having been a powerful, resolute and loyal reformer, and was succeeded by his pupil and friend, Anselm.

Anselm could not have been more different from Lanfranc in personality, temperament and intellectual method, although they both came from the same monastic stable. Anselm was born and brought up in Aosta beneath the Great St Bernard Pass through the Alps, before its descent into Lombardy, which was then still just within the kingdom of Burgundy. Anselm's family had distant connections with the Counts of Savoy, particularly on his mother's side, but he could not rely on any prospects from this faint connection. His thoughtful, introspective nature and intellectual ability marked him down for a career as a monk or teacher. Anselm had little interest in temporal advancement or in the schools of rhetoric or law. He had a faltering start as an oblate in Aosta, so when his mother died and he quarrelled with his father, he decided at the age of twenty-three to leave Aosta and seek his future in France. His character and aspirations were already forming: the simplicity of his objectives and thought, the otherworldliness of his ambitions, his unquestioning literalness of outlook, his horror of sin and his desire for a deeper communion with God. He left Aosta with the haziest of plans, going west through the Mt Cenis Pass into the Rhone Valley, seeking only to move on from the small-town oppressiveness of Aosta. It was a journey that would eventually lead him to becoming the Abbot of Bec and the Archbishop of Canterbury and would also result in some of the most enduring theological writing of the Middle Ages.

In 1059, just a few years before the Norman Conquest of England, Anselm arrived at Bec, which was a little south of Rouen. He was drawn there by the presence and reputation of Lanfranc, who had already been there for twenty years. On arrival, Anselm was in a state of nervous and physical exhaustion and was uncertain about the direction his vocation might take. He made friends with another monk, Gundulf, who would later become Bishop of Rochester. Friendship was essential to Anselm's well-being. Though introverted in theological reflection, the great Benedictine virtues of friendship and stability were essential to his peace of mind and fecundity of spirit. In time he took the step of becoming a monk, and more especially, a pupil of Lanfranc, who drew him on in his vocation. Bec provided the essential setting for Anselm's development, while Lanfranc gave purpose and confidence through which Anselm could progress. The library was well stocked with many of Augustine's works, especially his commentaries on the Psalms and St John's Gospel, his *Confessions*, the *City of God*, *On the Trinity*, his *Enchiridion* and some more polemical works. There were also Bede's commentaries, Cassian's *Collations* and Eusebius's *History of the Church*. For someone with Anselm's enquiring mind and thirst for knowledge, this proved a spiritual feast. Augustine's reflective method of theologizing would prove pivotal in Anselm's own development. In addition, there were Lanfranc's own commentaries on Paul's

Epistles, which were a model of acute attention to the words and arguments of the text. While Lanfranc was most influenced in his theology by Aristotle, and his view of reality as expressed in the *categories* (which we will come to later in chapter 7), Anselm had the same point of departure—a close attention to the text—but his reflective method, which was a mixture of meditation and contemplation, would lead him to a different presentation of truth. Lanfranc based his arguments on the authority of the Church Fathers, as he understood them, whereas a reflective process of prayer and contemplation guided Anselm to arrive at first principles. As a lawyer, Lanfranc proceeded from one quoted authority to another, whereas Anselm, a man of prayer driven by an acute intellect, sought "a first principle" from spiritual intuition.

With the intellectual stimulus of Lanfranc and a library of works mostly from Augustine, Anselm had all that he needed for the next stage of his spiritual development. For seven years, from 1063–70, Anselm lived the life of a monk at Bec and "pondered all these things" in his heart (Luke 2:19). He wrote an initial work called *De Grammatico*, which, as one might expect from the title, details the tools of criticism: the role of nouns and adjectives, of subjects and predicates, and of substances and their attributes—all of which served to get beneath the meaning of words in order to establish their purpose and intent. This, together with his *Prayers and Meditations* so well translated by Benedicta Ward, constituted Anselm's *aperitif*, before the main course of his *Monologion* and *Proslogion*, which we shall come to later. During these seven years of theological gestation, Anselm gave himself to the rhythm of offices in the monastery, to building deep-seated friendships, to studying the Bible and the Church Fathers, and to times of almost visionary or ecstatic prayer.

Meditation lay at the heart of Anselm's spiritual discipline. For Anselm, meditation was solely concerned "with pure reflection on the essence of things".[20] As with Augustine, meditation meant self-knowledge leading to self-rejection and complete dependence on God. The process was driven by the principle of "faith seeking understanding" or "*fides quaerens intellectum*", which was itself Augustinian. Self-examination turned to meditation, and meditation led to contemplation, which might in turn be rewarded by revelation. This essentially introspective process was in tune with the Platonic notion of the ascent of the soul, which had been well known to some of the Church Fathers. It had been employed by Origen, the Cappadocian Fathers and Augustine especially. More than any others, these individuals used introspection as a tool of sanctification. Other principles that guided Anselm were the necessity for obedience, framed by the monastic vow, and flight from the sin for which he had a horror.

The period from 1070 until 1093 would be the most productive and rewarding of Anselm's life. In 1093 he would become Archbishop of Canterbury, once again following Lanfranc. He was appointed by William Rufus, William the Conqueror's third son and his successor as King of England. (William's eldest son, Robert, became Duke of Normandy, because Normandy was still regarded as the jewel in William's crown of inheritance.) Yet Anselm's appointment as archbishop would launch him into the struggles of church and state, and into the political sphere of the Church, for which, unlike his predecessor, he had no liking and was ill-prepared. Until 1093, Anselm therefore relished his life at Bec. In 1078, he became Abbot of Bec, having been prior since 1063. The years spent in the monastic round of prayer, teaching younger pupils, fulfilling his vows of obedience, and writing his prayers and meditations were the high point of his life, and the life to which he was best suited.

For Anselm, friendship was the "central experience" of his life. It was expressed in his letters and in emotional and intimate language. Familiar with the early monastic writer, Cassian, he knew that there were three general types of friendship: those of family association, husbands and wives, parents and children and brothers and sisters; those of groups with common purpose such as merchants, soldiers and household servants; and finally those united in a common noble purpose in which souls are bound together in divine love. The eternal nature of this last form of friendship irradiated Anselm's life and sustained his journey. He expressed the emotion of that bond with what sounds to our ears extravagant and intimate language, influenced by the romantic ideal that was so much a part of the new French *troubadour* expression of chivalry and courtly love. Anselm therefore introduced into friendship a new expression of passionate regard and affection, not to be confused with homosexuality: "So here, as everywhere, he stands uneasily between two worlds, the world of rational friendship and the new world of romance, between this world and the kingdom of heaven, between tradition and innovation."[21] Thus, in a letter to Gundulf, soon to be Bishop of Rochester, he wrote:

> When I sit down to write to you, oh soul most dear to my soul . . . I am uncertain how best to begin what I have to say. Everything I feel about you is sweet and pleasant to my heart; whatever I desire for you is the best that my mind can conceive. For such as I have seen you to be, I have loved, as you well know; and such as I now hear you to be, I desire, as God well knows. And so wherever you go, my love follows you; and wherever I may be, my desire embraces you.[22]

This is one of 400 letters, of which 140 were written in the period 1070–93 before Anselm became Archbishop of Canterbury. These letters are full of emotional intensity, joy at anticipated meetings, and longing for the other's physical presence. They are not private letters, but precursors to a demand for greater spiritual dedication. Friendship was a spur to deeper devotion and the expression of love was an emotional charge to enable that to happen. Physical expressions of that love, whether a kiss, hug or embrace, were symbols of solidarity in the quest for complete submission to God. Kisses were used as the completion of penance, in the profession of new monks, in reconciling penitents, in the election of new abbots, in dedicating altars and in a farewell to the dying. The scriptural injunction comes from 1 Thessalonians 5:26: "Greet one another with a holy kiss."

If friendship was a God-given gift in the context of working out and pursuing a vocation, meditation and prayer were the essential channels of connection with God himself. Anselm would make himself a teacher on prayer and meditation, and also demonstrate how faith allied to intellectual enquiry in the context of meditation can bring clarity to faith. The *Monologion* and the *Proslogion*, which we will look at in chapter 7, were the fruits of this process. Anselm also became a teacher of prayer for many of his correspondents. He wrote a number of prayers: to God, to Christ, before receiving the body and blood of Christ, to the Holy Cross, to Mary, to St John the Baptist, to St Peter, to St John, and to Stephen. Many of these prayers were sent to the nobility of France. One example from his *Prayer to Christ* demonstrates the intensity and clarity of his devotion:

> Most kind lover of men
> "The poor commits himself to you,
> For you are the helper of the orphan",
> My most safe helper,
> Have mercy upon the orphan left to you.
> I am become a child without a father;
> My soul is like a widow.
> Turn your gaze and behold my tears
> Which I offer to you till you return
> Come now, Lord, appear to me and I will be consoled;
> Show me your face and I shall be saved;
> Display your presence and I have obtained my desire;
> Reveal your glory and my joy will be full.
> My soul thirsts for you, my flesh longs after you,
> My soul thirsts for God, the fountain of life:

When shall I appear before the presence of God?

My consoler, for whom I wait, when will you come?

O that I might be satisfied with the appearing of your glory for which I hunger;

That I might be satisfied with the riches of your house for which I sigh;

That I might drink of the torrent of your pleasures for which I thirst.[23]

Anselm shows here that, like Augustine and the Cappadocian Fathers before him, he had richly meditated on the Psalms, and the Song of Songs. In many ways his writings and prayers are closer to theirs than to anyone in the intervening years, and in that sense, he was a bridge to the fourth and fifth-century Church Fathers.

Anselm's creative and productive years at the Abbey of Bec came to an end when he was drawn into the affairs of the Norman and English state. In 1089, William the Conqueror died and was buried in Abbaye-aux-Hommes in Caen. He suffered two interruptions and indignities at his funeral: firstly when a protester remonstrated during the funeral service that his land had been illegally sequestered to build the abbey, and secondly when William's body, now very corpulent, could not fit into the coffin and was punctured in the process, letting off an evil smell that drove all but the officiants from the church!

William's third son, William Rufus, succeeded as King of England. He was a man at home in warfare and on the hunting field, unlettered and uncouth, whose statecraft was severely limited, but whose prowess in battle was unquestioned. Lanfranc also died in 1089 at the end of almost twenty years of oversight, and his death represented the passing of an era. For over three years William Rufus kept the archbishopric empty, enjoying its revenues, until in 1093 he appointed Anselm. Once again Anselm stepped into Lanfranc's shoes, and would remain Archbishop until 1109, when he died aged seventy-nine.

Anselm would serve as Archbishop during the reigns of William Rufus and Henry I: the most ambitious, able and demanding of William the Conqueror's sons. Apart from writing his important work *Cur Deus Homo* (reviewed in chapter 7), Anselm's tenure as Archbishop was quickly dominated by matters of church and state at a time when these were being hammered out between a reforming papacy and ambitious kings. Anselm was to find himself in a dilemma similar to the one Thomas Becket would face seventy years later, i.e. how to reconcile the Church's new insistence on liberty (meaning freedom from interference by lay rulers) and separate jurisdiction, while at the same time remaining a faithful liegeman of the King, from whom very extensive lands were leased. In Becket's case the dilemma would be resolved by death; in Anselm's case it would mean exile and a threat to excommunicate Henry I.

Only a few years before Anselm's appointment, Gregory VII, the most reforming and zealous of popes, had undertaken a root and branch reform of the Church in order to enhance its standing and to delineate the boundaries between lay and papal power. It was Gregory, more than any other, who laid the groundwork for the medieval Roman Catholic Church, with its celibacy of the priesthood, doctrine of transubstantiation of the bread and wine, its use of excommunication against the most powerful lay rulers, such as Henry IV and the Holy Roman Emperor, and its upholding of ecclesiastical liberty (i.e. freedom to act sovereignly). This last point gave the Church its own jurisdiction (i.e. there was to be no lay involvement in the appointment or discipline of its clergy, monks or clerks by rulers or courts). This effectively made the Church "a state within a state", giving bishops right of appeal to the pope for arbitration in disputes between church and state. It was against this background of "the liberty of the Church" that Anselm was consecrated Archbishop of Canterbury, swearing an oath of allegiance to William for landholdings in 1093, and receiving the *pallium* of his appointment from the Pope in 1095. Anselm's consecration was made more complicated by a dispute over the succession to Gregory VII, following the brief papacy of Victor II. In time, the Frenchman Urban II established himself as Pope, and made himself notorious by calling for the First Crusade.

The hallmark of Anselm's archiepiscopacy was his simple and profound obedience to the Pope. Obedience had always been an essential part of his *credo*, worked out during his time as a monk and abbot. What he expected of himself he expected of others too. He defended the rights of the Church to its temporal resources, which were granted by the King, and over this he had his first acrimonious dispute with William Rufus.[24] Anselm's instincts were, if possible, to resign his office, but the Pope would have none of it, calling him instead to defend the Latin doctrine of the Procession of the Holy Spirit. He did this in Italy in 1098, and thereafter wrote on the doctrine. By 1099, the papacy had hardened its position on lay investiture, instructing clergy not to pay homage of any kind to lay rulers for land or offices held. Anselm stayed in France, mostly at Lyons, with his friend Bishop Hugh, until Henry I called him back to England. Henry had succeeded his brother William as king after William had been (most probably) accidentally killed by an arrow shot by Walter Tirel while out hunting. A new chapter in Anselm's life was about to open up which would see him become an ecclesiastical administrator to a new, demanding and ambitious king.

CHAPTER 5

Becket: Murder in the Cathedral

Henry I was a masterful king and quickly seized the throne after William's unexpected death. He was thirty-two years old and would govern England and Normandy for thirty-three years. In November 1100, he married Matilda (or Edith), who was daughter of Margaret and Malcolm III of Scotland, but more significantly, granddaughter of the *aethling* Edgar, the prince who had returned from Hungary during the reign of Edward the Confessor as the Anglo-Saxon claimant for the English throne. In marrying Matilda, Henry strategically grafted the Norman succession on the old Saxon root. He furthermore curried favour with the English barons by imprisoning in the Tower the rapacious Bishop Flambard of Durham, previously Rufus's Chancellor. Henry had every intention of making a positive new beginning to his rule, healing old wounds, but also increasing his territory by ousting his brother Robert from Normandy. For this he needed moral support, military knights and revenues of the Church.

Anselm would not easily oblige the new King, however. He returned to England, took the King's marriage in Westminster Abbey, but outlined his principles on "the liberty of the Church". Anselm dug his heels in: he refused to do homage to Henry for his lands at Canterbury and he refused to consecrate the bishops and abbots Henry had chosen. He believed this "was a personal act of obedience to decrees [from the papacy] which he had heard".[1] Anselm had moved in his spirit from flight from the King to obedience to the Pope, from seeking retirement when opposed to disputation, but he was still, intrinsically, more pastor than prophet. When he sensed that the strong papal line on lay investiture was weakening under Urban II's successor, Paschal II, he simply did not open the Pope's letter, believing that with time the Pope's stance would change further. In 1103, Anselm went once more to Rome to seek papal guidance and was gone for the best part of two years, also spending time in Lyons with his friend, Bishop Hugh.

Anselm now began to prepare to excommunicate the King for withholding revenue from the Church, especially in connection with the Canterbury lands. In the end, the two met in 1105 on the borders of Normandy at L'Aigle. An agreement was reached in which revenues were returned to the Church. Furthermore, an exchange of letters with the Pope yielded a compromise with Henry, who renounced the rights of investiture but retained the expectation of homage for all lands held. The King now had larger matters on his mind, such as the invasion of Normandy. Anselm stayed a further year at Bec, returning to England in 1106. By now his health was failing. A second church council was held at Westminster in 1108, and the following year he died. He had been archbishop for sixteen years and out of the country for nearly seven of them. As a man of prayer and a theologian—much like Archbishops Michael Ramsey and Rowan Williams in the modern era—he disliked the politics of his office, caught as he was between the decrees of the papacy and the King's need for revenue and feudal service. He was spared the anarchy that was to follow.

The great tragedy that beset Henry was the drowning of his son and heir William the *Aethling*, aged seventeen, in the sinking of the *White Ship* just off the coast of Normandy at Barfleur on 25 November 1120. A drunken steersman of this royal vessel failed to notice a rock—the Raz de Barfleur—close to the shore.[2] When the news was eventually given to Henry by terrified courtiers, he went into a dead faint, and, it is said, never smiled again. The succession to the crown was thrown into question, and in the end civil war overtook the land from 1139 to 1153. Before Henry's death in 1135, on 1 January 1127, he had made his barons and bishops swear to uphold his daughter Matilda's claim to the throne. Matilda had been previously married to the Holy Roman Emperor, Henry V, hence her title of Empress. She was next married to the teenage and unpredictable Count of Anjou.

Yet after Henry's death another claimant came forward: Stephen of Blois, the grandson of William the Conqueror through William's daughter Adela. He was also the greatest baron in the Anglo-Norman world. His brother Henry was Bishop of Winchester. On hearing of King Henry's death, Stephen crossed the Channel, seized the royal treasury at Winchester and on 22 December was crowned in Westminster Abbey. What followed, according to one chronicler, was "nothing but disturbance, wickedness and robbery".[3] The Church increased its landholdings, playing one side against the other, a game often conducted by Bishop Henry of Winchester—one of the great prince-bishops of the age and responsible for the sumptuous Winchester Bible. During Stephen's reign, the new Cistercian order, championed by the charismatic and legendary figure Bernard of Clairvaux, rapidly increased the number of its houses in England to fifty, including those at Fountains and Tintern. In time, there would be nearly a hundred such foundations. The age was effectively a free-for-all for Church and barons alike: anarchy would follow and, finally, full-scale civil war.

During the 1140s, England descended into civil war, misery and starvation. By 1140, Matilda was in England, having crossed from Normandy. The civil war ebbed and flowed. At first militarily successful in Lincoln and Winchester, Matilda was soon forced into occupying only the South-West, and waiting for her son, the future Henry II, to come of age and take up the struggle. In time he did, and if her tempestuous marriage to Geoffrey of Anjou achieved nothing else, it provided England with one of its most energetic kings. It also provided the sharpest struggle with the Church before the Reformation, a dispute largely centred on the characters and ambitions of two men: Henry and Thomas Becket.

Thomas Becket

On 21 December 1119, Thomas was born into a middle-class Norman family who were living in London. His parents, Gilbert and Matilda Becket, were from Rouen, and had been attracted to London by opportunities for trade. "Becket" usually means "little beak" or "beak-face", and Thomas was known to have inherited a fine aquiline nose. His father, Gilbert, was a successful businessman, who owned property and rose to become one of the four sheriffs of London, which was at that time a largely autonomous and self-governing city, with some 40,000 inhabitants. The city had a commercial centre with a mint, moneylenders and goldsmiths, and a sizeable Jewish community resident in Cheapside and Lombard Street. St Paul's Cathedral was still being rebuilt in Romanesque style, with Westminster Abbey two miles upstream. Otherwise, parish churches and the Norman Tower of London remained the most significant buildings on the emerging cityscape.

A Londoner through and through, Thomas was educated at one of the three London grammar schools. There he learnt and polished his Latin and English, grammar, logic and rhetoric. As in a classical education, the art of speaking eloquently in public was highly prized. Whether or not he learnt to write is debatable, but he would have been used to the practice of "composition" or of dictating "pieces" to a scribe. Tools for writing, such as parchment, ink, stylus or quill, knife and razor were expensive, so dictation was the normal means of composition. Outside school, water sports took place on the Thames, there were tournaments at Smithfield, and informal "football" in the streets. Thomas was athletic and tall. He loved sport and often went out hawking at Pevensey with an aristocratic friend called Richer.

Thomas completed his education in Paris at the city's new university located on the south bank, which would later be the Sorbonne. The city numbered about 100,000 inhabitants and the student population was between two and three thousand. By the mid-thirteenth century, this would be the premier university in Europe. One of its most famous teachers was Abelard (1079–1142), who attracted literally thousands of students. Apart from his theology (which we will look at in chapter 7), he became famous for his love affair with his pupil Heloise. And for this affair he suffered castration at the hands of her angry guardian and uncle, Fulbert, followed by seclusion in the Abbey of St Denis from the age of forty. If Thomas ever attended Abelard's lectures, it would only have been for a year before the latter's withdrawal to St Denis. Little is known of Becket's studies in Paris, although he did make one important long-term friend of John of Salisbury, a notable scholar and one of Becket's later biographers. John was more easy-going than Thomas but was nevertheless candid in his assessment of his friend's strengths and weaknesses. After two years in Paris, where Thomas revealed his love of fashion as much as a love of learning, he was recalled to London at the sudden death of his mother. He was then twenty-one with an ageing father and three sisters to look after, and in need of a career.

Thomas was by then well-educated, charming and athletic. He was not a great scholar, but had a retentive memory, excellent negotiating and communication skills, and winning ways. Although showy, he was personally self-disciplined. He could be stubborn and impulsive. His break came when he was offered a position as a clerk in Archbishop Theobald's household. Theobald, a relatively unknown Norman monk, had been appointed archbishop in 1139 in succession to William de Corbeil, after a three-year vacancy. Like two of his predecessors, Lanfranc and Anselm, Theobald had been Abbot of Bec, then a well-known *alma mater* to the higher echelons of the English clergy. Becket was set to work as a clerk in his household while the civil war between Stephen and Matilda raged on. Theobald did not side with either of the protagonists but sought in the midst of the turmoil to protect the Church's interests. Becket was soon followed by his colleague from Paris, John of Salisbury, who had been recommended by no less a man than Bernard of Clairvaux. The two of them were to become invaluable to Theobald: John drafting stylish and well-crafted letters and Thomas acting as the chief negotiator. Soon Thomas would become Theobald's favourite. He gained an education in ecclesiastical law, becoming familiar with Gratian's *Decretum*, the most up-to-date work on the subject from Bologna. Indeed, so keen was Theobald to train Thomas that he sent him to Bologna to study for a year.

Because of his pre-eminent position in Theobald's household and administration, it was only a matter of time before Henry noticed Becket during the final years of the civil war. By that time Henry was prosecuting the interests of his mother, Matilda, and of his own future inheritance. On 6 November 1153, Theobald brought Henry, then only twenty years old, together with Stephen to Winchester to negotiate the future of the realm. In the resulting Treaty of Westminster, it was agreed that Stephen would reign until his death, and Henry would succeed him. Theobald and Becket were at the forefront of this negotiation. In fact, Henry did not have long to wait before his accession, for Stephen died in 1154 of a "bloody flux", and the twenty-one-year-old Henry succeeded to the throne and embarked upon what would be one of the most influential and eventful reigns of any English monarch.

Becket was by now Archdeacon of Canterbury, Dean of Hastings and Provost of Beverley, all rich livings. He was still a deacon, not yet a priest, and committed thereby to celibacy. Within a few months of his accession and coronation, Becket was transferred to the King's household. He was then almost thirty-four, a seasoned negotiator, and an athletic man who, like his sovereign, loved hunting. He was also a brilliant chess player with a compendious memory for detail and possessed a brave but impulsive nature. He became an intimate of the King, and within six years he was Chancellor of England. As such he established his own flamboyant and showy household. His table glittered with silver and gold; he ate the most expensive and luxurious delicacies. If Becket excelled in style, glamour and *realpolitik*, his master Henry was a man of incessant and crude energy and ambition. Henry's chronicler, Walter Map, tells us he rarely stood still, keeping his courtiers literally on their toes.[4] He made his plans at the last moment, often changing his mind and catching his courtiers out. His voice would become harsh and cracked, as he barked out orders from horseback. Much restless energy was needed to traverse an empire that had doubled in size as a result of his marriage to Eleanor of Aquitaine in 1152. Eleanor (1122–1204) was the divorced wife of Louis VII of France, to whom she had been married for nearly sixteen years, and with whom she had two daughters. Now divorced from Louis on the specious grounds of consanguinity, she sought greater prizes and more passionate love in her thirties.

Henry and Eleanor were a kind of Anthony and Cleopatra of northern Europe—less well proven in war and diplomacy, but equally ambitious. Eleanor was a woman of truly exceptional intelligence and personality, with flashing dark eyes, courtly ways and an inheritance that stretched from La Rochelle to the Pyrenees. The marriage made Henry one of the greatest monarchs in Europe at the age of twenty-two, reigning over an area that included all of western France and all England. No wonder his court moved ceaselessly between Westminster, Bordeaux, Caen, Poitiers, Chinon, Argentan, Winchester and Windsor, to name but a few of around thirty different locations.[5] Eleanor would give Henry seven children: four sons, including Richard I and John, and three daughters. Their marriage was both passionate and tempestuous, with Eleanor siding in the end with her son Richard against her husband.

For seven years of this whirlwind court, Becket was Chancellor. Although close to the King, he was also thoroughly dependent upon him. He had been raised from obscurity as a middle-ranking official in the character of a Tudor statesman, for he was no baron in his own right. The bosom friendship of king and chancellor may have been overstated by the court chronicler William Fitzstephen, for, in the end, Henry demanded his way with energy and fierce anger. In one fit of anger, the nature of which only increased as time went on, he is described as having flown "into his usual temper, flung his cap from his head, pulled off his belt, threw off his cloak and clothes, grabbed the silken coverlet off the couch, and sitting as it might be on a dung heap started chewing pieces of straw".[6]

Henry's aim was to restore to England the ways of his grandfather Henry I after the anarchy of the civil war. He sought to reform the laws of the land, centralize the government in his court, impress royal power upon the realm, and suppress revolt in his extensive empire. For these ends, he employed Becket, who took embassies and a retinue of 200 knights to France to contract a marriage alliance with the French king, Louis. Later, Becket actively took part in the King's campaign in Quercy, France, personally leading 700 knights in battle out of the city of Cahors. He prosecuted the King's business in the courts, sometimes to the detriment of the Church, as in the case over Battle Abbey, which sought exemption from the Bishop of Chichester's interference. Not respecting the bishop's authority, both Henry and Becket sided with Battle Abbey, ensuring its independence of the bishop and indirectly also of papal power. It was a decision Becket would later come to rue.

After Becket had been Chancellor for seven years, Theobald, who had been largely neglected by Becket, died. Seeing an opportunity to impress his will on the Church, Henry appointed Becket archbishop after a year's vacancy. So began a relationship of king and archbishop that would in time shake the foundations of church and state, and, because of the spilling of the archbishop's blood in his own cathedral church, shock Christendom. Although welcomed by the monks of Christ Church, Canterbury, and duly elected archbishop and their abbot, Becket was opposed by some jealous bishops, notably Gilbert Foliot, soon to be Bishop of London, and Roger of Pont l'Évêque, Archbishop of York. Like Ambrose of Milan, Becket was ordained priest and consecrated archbishop on the same day. For four months, Becket retained the Chancellorship as Henry desired, but then resigned without consulting Henry, in order to be his own man. Hearing this, Henry flew into a fury, which was an indication of what was to follow.

Henry's overall desire was to return the realm "to the customs of his grandfather", and this meant restoring the unity of church and state that had existed in the late Anglo-Saxon kingdom and at the time of the Conquest, a unity which rested on the authority of the King. Such an aim took little account of the papal reforms of Gregory VII, who had established "the liberty of the Church" and its freedom from lay (i.e. monarchical) control. The Church was to be answerable only to the Pope, its privileges kept intact, and its systems of administration and justice separate from those of the crown. The problem was that the Church was immensely powerful, owning about a quarter of all the land of the kingdom, with its tax contribution vital to the Exchequer. Worse still, it had its own courts, which meant that since approximately one in six of the adult population was connected by service to the Church, the King's writ could not touch them. Criminous clerks, as they were called, were subject to church courts and given more lenient sentences: the church courts would let a clerk off with a penance for theft, but the civil courts exacted either death or mutilation. In a word, the Church was a state within a state. Henry would have none of it, and Becket would yield no privilege or church custom to the crown. They were on a collision course.

Becket implacably opposed the King's wish to humble the Church. At the Council of Woodstock in 1163, Becket objected to a new method of taxation on church lands. In July of the same year, he preached the Pope's supremacy in all matters spiritual, as well as his supremacy over the Church. Again, in the same year, Becket defended the interests of a priest, Philip de Broi, who had been accused of murder, but was acquitted in the Bishop of Lincoln's court. Henry wanted a re-trial. Becket refused. Furthermore, Becket excommunicated a tenant-in-chief of the crown, William of Eynsford, for refusing his appointment in a parish within William's lands, thereby breaking a convention that an archbishop would consult the king before taking such action. Henry then sought to reassert his authority over the reburial of Edward the Confessor in Westminster Abbey in October 1163.

The stage was set for a showdown when the King summoned all the senior clergy of the Church for a council at the Palace of Clarendon near Salisbury. The council at Clarendon was in many ways the defining moment in Becket and

Henry's relationship and struggle. Henry, who had failed to impose his will on the Church at an earlier council at Westminster, came with a clear aim in mind. It was to get Becket and the Church to "concede publicly" Henry's right to govern the Church in accordance with "ancestral customs" of England. In an important meeting between the King and Archbishop at Woodstock, Becket had already agreed "to observe the customs of the realm in all good faith and to obey the King in what is right (*in bono*)". Yet despite the appearance of subservience to the King, much resided in the little phrase "in what is right". Indeed, if the King could sum up his aim of wanting the re-establishment of these "ancestral customs", Becket would only do so whilst "saving our order". In those three words, "saving our order", lay the whole idea of the liberty of the Church (i.e. freedom from lay interference) and the preservation of its inalienable rights conferred by God. Having started the custom of travelling royal judges (eyres) who sat at "assizes" to hear cases involving the crown based on "writs", which in turn led to the accumulation of common law, Henry wanted this process to cover all his subjects. Becket, on the other hand, wanted to "save the order" of ecclesiastical courts on the principle that lay courts could not adjudicate over those who administered the sacraments, or were in some way involved with the ministry of the Church.

The Council of Clarendon began on 25 January 1164. Henry, with his son Prince Henry—aged nine and hitherto educated in Becket's household—beside him, immediately demanded that Becket redeem the promise made at Woodstock. Becket could not persuade the bishops to give up the phrase "saving our order" previously agreed at Westminster in 1163. They refused and Henry fell into a rage, threatening to castrate any who opposed him! The crown brought forward the Constitutions of Clarendon. These included a ban on travel for clergy without royal licence, restrictions on church courts, and appeals to the pope being severely curtailed. Becket vacillated, wanting to fulfil his earlier promise to the King, but not wanting to denude the authority of the Church over the heads of his bishops. The King's scribes wrote out the Constitutions in the form of a *chirograph* (a hand-written document, written out three times, then cut horizontally with a ragged edge, then vertically, before being shared). This method demonstrated authenticity and prevented forgery, but Becket did not sign it. He took it, however, thereby giving the King's party the impression that he had accepted it. When he rode away from the meeting, Becket was strangely silent. It was to be the lowest point of his career. He blamed himself for his lack of preparation. He confessed his mistakes to Pope Alexander III, the great international statesman of his day, who was navigating between wanting Henry's support and not wishing to water down the Church's liberty. He was also having to contend with a rival or anti-pope supported by the German Emperor Frederick Barbarossa (Emperor from 1155–90).

If Becket regretted the implication of compliance given to the King at Clarendon, he was determined to reverse it at a subsequent council at Northampton in October 1164. Henry saw this council as the final opportunity to obtain Becket's unequivocal submission, as well as that of the Church to the crown. If he failed, Becket was to be arraigned for treason. It was a bad omen for the meeting when Becket found that his lodgings were not his usual rooms in the castle, and that he had been evicted to a nearby priory. The business of the council was designed to impugn Becket. He was charged with corruption, perverting justice in the case of John Marshal, and of false accounting. He was accused of stealing from the crown while Chancellor and asked to return the money. Some of the bishops, like Foliot, advised Becket to ask for the King's mercy, else catastrophe would follow. On hearing that he was to be tried for treason, Becket refused to submit to the King's jurisdiction and said he would appeal to the Pope. The next day Becket rode into the castle, dismounted in the yard, and taking the Archbishop's processional cross, strode boldly into the main hall like a Crusader. "The king's sword is an instrument of war, but my cross is a sign of peace for myself and the English Church," Becket exclaimed. Henry, wary of the threat of excommunication, refused to confront him. For his part, Becket refused to be tried by the court and appealed again to the Pope. The bishops were divided in their support. Becket left the council and the castle, said vespers in the priory with his clergy, and with no assurance from the King of a safe journey to Canterbury, left the country immediately. He made for France and went into exile as a fugitive. When he returned, just six years later, he would be murdered.

The next five years were marked by Henry's vengeance on Becket's family and friends, including his sisters, nephews and nieces, who were either deported or thrown into debtors' prisons; and by Becket's appeal to the Pope, who was still walking gingerly between not alienating Henry further because of his open quarrel with Frederick Barbarossa, and his failed attempts at reconciliation. This may have been the time, more than any other, when the once showy courtier and powerbroker Becket, now in a hair shirt, read deeply in the scriptures and the Church Fathers. On his appointment as Archbishop, he had begun acquiring seventy books, including copies of the Vulgate Bible and works by Cyprian of Carthage (himself martyred), by Gregory of Nazianzus, a felicitous defender of the Trinity, and by Isidore of Seville. Now in exile in the Burgundian monastery at Pontigny, Becket was encouraged by his chaplain, Herbert of Bosham, to read the Psalms and the Pauline Epistles, a commentary on Job by Gregory the Great and Ambrose's work *On the duties of Ministers*. If Becket's inner conversion had been slow in coming, his extensive fasting at Pontigny and his rigorous study and prayer support the idea that, whilst in exile, he became in Christ what he had not been before.

With increased backing from Pope Alexander, who had returned to Rome more confident of his position, Becket was appointed legate in 1166. Thus fortified by the Pope's support, Becket stood his ground against Henry. When the King was in France and sent for him, he reminded Henry that although he was the King's subject, he was still the King's pastor and the King his spiritual son. As such, Becket had the right to reprove and restrain Henry. If anything, Becket's sense of spiritual authority was increasing. On 3 June 1166, in Vezelay Abbey in northern Burgundy, Becket released his bombshell: he condemned the Council of Clarendon and its provisions, he excommunicated some bishops and barons, and he called on the King to repent. The breach had become a chasm. Further excommunications of Foliot of London and Jocelin of Salisbury were made at Clairvaux, although these were later rescinded by the Pope, to Becket's deep consternation. Eventually Louis, King of France, and Eleanor of Aquitaine's former husband, brought the Archbishop and Henry together for what was intended to be a great reconciliation. All appeared to go well, with Becket agreeing that the King might rule according to "ancestral customs", until Becket fatefully added, "saving God's honour", which was medieval code for the complete liberty of the Church.

Henry was humiliated and angered beyond words. He called Becket a traitor. In November 1169, a further opportunity to reconcile the two was engineered by Louis at Montmartre, but this too failed when it came to agreeing how much to compensate Becket for loss of income from the crown's seizure of church land.

Further humiliation was loaded on Becket when Henry engineered the coronation of his eldest son, Henry (who died before his father), without Becket being present. It was highly unusual to crown an heir while a king was still living, but Henry wanted to avoid another civil war. It was still more unusual to do so without the participation of the Archbishop himself. The coronation went ahead, and was performed by the Archbishop of York, Roger of Pont l'Évêque, assisted by Foliot and Jocelin of Salisbury. For such a breach of convention, an interdict followed, firstly on Henry's French territories, which meant that no church services could be held there, including marriages or funerals, until a settlement was made. A conference was called at Fréteval and once more reconciliation was attempted between Henry and Becket. All seemed to go well until Becket ranted for well over an hour about the King's traducing of his rights in the coronation of Henry. There was no insistence on "ancestral customs" by Henry, but this was a tactical retreat to lift the interdict and prevent a further one being placed on England. This time it was Becket who was unwilling to be reconciled. He nevertheless thought it was time to return to Canterbury, so in October 1170, at a frosty meeting with the King at Tours, arrangements were made for Becket's return. On 24 November, Becket left Rouen to return to Canterbury. In London, a 3,000-strong crowd welcomed him back, bells were peeled and *Te Deums* sung, but the newly-crowned King Henry (Henry II's son) refused to see him, even though he had been raised in Becket's household.

Across the Channel, Henry was keeping his Christmas Court at Bur-le-Roi, ranting against his Archbishop who would not come to heel. "What miserable drones and traitors have I nourished and promoted in my realm, who let their lord be treated with such shameful contempt by a low-born clerk!"[7] Four knights slipped from Henry's court intent on proving to the King that he had men who would fulfil his desires. They crossed the Channel independently on 26 December and by Tuesday 29 December were at Canterbury, asking for Becket. John of Salisbury was with Thomas and records the men called on Becket to "depart this realm". An argument ensued. The knights left and returned in full armour and with swords. Thomas entered the cathedral for vespers; the monks sought to restrain him, but Thomas ordered that the door be left open. After a further verbal altercation about Becket's authority, he was attacked. Kneeling and committing himself to God, Mary, St Denis and St Alphege, he was cut down, one blow slicing his skull and spilling his blood and brains on the cathedral floor.

Within two years, Becket was made a martyr of the Church. His tomb was more visited by pilgrims than any other in Europe; his blood became a holy relic, performing, it was said, many miracles. By 1220, a sumptuous shrine had been built, covered with precious stones and magnificent stained glass, and is still there today (although much reduced since the Reformation), recording Thomas's life and posthumous miracles. Later, Henry VIII, aided by Reformation doctrine, and having no time for a recalcitrant archbishop who opposed his king, had Becket's bones scattered, the shrine looted, and every memory of Becket destroyed in the parish churches of England. For 350 years, Thomas Becket thus dominated Canterbury, with the "liberty of the Church" secured by his death until the Reformation. From the Reformation to T. S. Eliot's *Murder in the Cathedral*, with its object lesson in resisting evil—and in this case the power of Nazi Germany— Becket's martyrdom took a back seat in Protestant England.

After Becket's murder in Canterbury Cathedral, Henry II did penance for the death of his Archbishop in July 1174. He walked in penitential clothes from an out-of-town lepers' colony, discarded his shoes at St Dunstan's Chapel and proceeded barefoot to Becket's tomb in Canterbury Cathedral. Kneeling at the tomb he confessed the "incautious words" that precipitated Becket's death and was scourged by the monks, albeit lightly. Henry would live a further fifteen years, and his final days were marked by the rebellion of his sons: first Henry the younger, like a latter-day Absalom against his father, then Richard, and finally John. Eleanor was estranged from her husband and used her sons, especially Richard, to damage him. By then, Henry was the elder statesman of Europe, and was even offered the throne of Jerusalem by the Patriarch, together with the keys to the Holy Sepulchre, in a bizarre ceremony at Reading in 1185. Though flattered, Henry refused. Although lauded in Europe, his immediate family despised him. Richard, on the death of his older brother, Henry the younger, sought affirmation from Henry II that he would inherit Aquitaine, Anjou, Normandy and England. No such affirmation was forthcoming from the ageing king, so Richard, along with the new King Philip Augustus of France, son of Louis VII, made war on Henry, who died in Chinon during this campaign and was buried in borrowed clothes in nearby Fontevraud Abbey. His sons Richard and John succeeded him in turn. One immersed England in the Crusades, the other, through his nefarious rule, provoked Magna Carta.

The Crusades

Both the Crusades and Magna Carta had their origins in the teachings of the Church. When Henry did penance for the murder of Becket, he sent 2,000 silver marks a year to the Templars and Hospitallers in Jerusalem, the two principal orders of crusading knights. Over the years this grant amounted to £11 million in today's money but had infinitely more purchasing power then. By the time of Becket's murder in 1170, the Crusades had been going in their present form for eighty years. Two Crusades had been despatched to the Holy Land to secure the sacred places there for Christian pilgrimage from 1096–9 and 1145–9. The story of the Crusades, from the best-known ones in the Holy Land to those in Egypt, Spain and the Baltic States, not to mention wars against heretics like the Albigensians or Cathars in south-west France, cannot be fully told here. What we can note is how they arose, the thinking behind them, their course and significance, and their effects today.

Christian thinking about holy war has a long history, however uncomfortable we may find it. Augustine wrote about a just or holy war in his works against the Manichees and also in the *City of God*.[8] Both Augustine of Hippo and Chrysostom considered Emperor Theodosius to be God's instrument against pagan incursions into the Roman Empire. His defeat of the usurper Maximus in AD 388 in the Battle of the Save in modern-day Croatia was also seen as a God-given victory. Charlemagne's campaigns against the pagan Saxons were construed as holy wars, although they were criticized by Alcuin for their brutality. Alfred the Great saw his campaigns against the pagan Vikings as battles for the survival of the Christian faith in England. Later, in the thirteenth century, and in the teaching of Thomas Aquinas, clearer reasons for a just war were delineated. War could be justified ethically—most commonly for self-defence or to combat something plainly evil and aggressive—so long as it was prosecuted without hope of gain and in a proportionate manner. Furthermore, scholars pointed to the idea of struggle and the legitimate use of force in the Bible, whether it was the Old Testament battles against immoral nations like the Amorites, or the more personal New Testament struggles, not against flesh and blood, but against "the rulers, against the authorities, against the powers of this dark world and against spiritual forces of evil in the heavenly realms" (Ephesians 6:12 NIV). Christian holy war therefore derived its essential elements from the Bible: i.e. a sense of divine command; identification of God's people with Israel (as happened in the English Civil War by the Parliamentarians); and a sense of participating in and hastening the apocalypse.[9]

Although the term "Crusade" is largely an eighteenth-century invention, those who went on the Crusades saw themselves pre-eminently as taking up the Cross, *crucesignati*, or more euphemistically, as going on *peregrinatio*. It was a short, but fateful, step by the preachers of the Crusades to identify this struggle as one between the Muslims, who had taken over the holy sites in Palestine, and the Christians, whose faith rested on the significance of these sites. Since Jerusalem had fallen to the Islamic Arab army in 638, what was it that triggered the First Crusade in 1095, over 400 years later? The answer is that it was a combination of politics and preaching.

The Crusades to the Holy Land in 1095 were politically motivated by a specific request for help from the Emperor of Byzantium, who resided in Constantinople, and also by matters of timing. In the 1090s, Alexius I Comnenus was battling against the encroachments of the Seljuk Turks in Anatolia, led first by Malik Shah and then his successors.[10] Pilgrim traffic to the holy sites began to dry up. Relations between Constantinople and Rome had reached their nadir during the papacy of Gregory VII because of Latin insistence on the *filioque* clause in the Creed, but with the accession of Urban II there was a marked improvement in relations. Urban was an impressive man, a good communicator and diplomat, with a courteous, but commanding presence.[11] He was keen to improve relations with the Eastern Church. At a Church council held at Piacenza in 1095, Emperor Alexis's messengers asked for help to further diminish Seljuk power. Alexis already had mercenaries composed of Pechenegs and even some Anglo-Saxon exiles from Norman England, but he hoped for more support. His request fell on receptive ears. Urban also sought a cause that would unite the quarrelsome knights of the West, and he therefore expanded the request to include the regaining of control of the holy sites of Palestine, and most of all, Jerusalem. A cause had been found that suited the papacy, but more importantly, it was one that resonated deeply with the military and aristocratic classes of Europe. Not only did it appeal to those groups, but also to some of the most influential church leaders in the West. It was a cause that could divert the warring factions in Europe into what seemed like a holy war, capable of bringing spiritual rewards to its participants. At least, that is how it was preached.

The Crusade was not just authorized by the Pope, he also preached it. Urban sought to place the renewed papacy square and centre in the spiritual aspirations of Europe, and later in the reign of Richard I and England. For now, Urban would preach the Crusade or, more exactly, the call to take up the cross in a holy war. The notion of taking up the cross was central to the message and became the defining theme of a Crusade. Urban had been handed a propaganda coup. On Tuesday 27 November, at the Council of Clermont and in the presence of 300 clerics, Urban painted a sombre picture of the need for a Crusade: pilgrims were being molested, holy sites desecrated, Jerusalem was being ransacked, and what is more, the fraternal Emperor of Byzantium had asked for help. Urban pleaded with knight and peasant alike to take up the cross in a holy war and liberate the Holy Land. Penitent participants would have their sins forgiven, and those who died would be received with alacrity into heaven. At the end of his sermon, there were immediate cries of "God wills it" ("*Deus vult illud*"), and the Bishop of Le Puy knelt and begged leave to go. Thousands followed. The Crusade was preached throughout Europe and the movement spread like wildfire. Peter the Hermit, a wizened peasant figure with singular gifts of communication, joined the Pope in preaching the Crusade with the same huge effect: as many as 15,000 ordinary peasants swelled the train. In a subsequent generation, the Cistercian reformer and passionate theologian, Bernard of Clairvaux (1090–1153), would do likewise.

Of all the Crusades, the first of 1095–9 had the greatest impact on those who were contemporaneous. Forces recruited from eastern France, the Rhineland, southern Germany and Lombardy agreed to rendezvous at Constantinople. The Byzantine Emperor had hoped for well-trained mercenaries; instead he got a rag-tag army of knights and peasants with several commanders who had recruited them, little discipline and even less military skill. The Turks annihilated these advancing but uncoordinated armies in October 1096. Other troops led by Raymond of Toulouse and Bohemund of Taranto were more effective. Some troops took Edessa, beyond the Euphrates. Antioch in Syria was taken and defended (1098), and it was there that the Holy Lance—said to have pierced Christ's side at the Crucifixion—was discovered and subsequently became a famous Crusader relic. The final siege of Jerusalem took place between June and July 1099, but the ensuing massacre after the capture of the city on 15 July shocked both Jews and Muslims. Streets were literally turned to rivers of blood. When Raymond of Aguilers visited the Temple area he had to pick his way through corpses and blood up to his knees. It was an orgy of killing. The holy sites were retaken, but any reputation for chivalric warfare had been lost. The massacre would forever besmirch the Crusade, and a long shadow was subsequently cast over Christian actions in Palestine and the Levant ever since.

Whereas the First Crusade had left England fairly untouched, as that country was in the process of responding to its new Norman management, the Third Crusade of 1188–92 deeply affected England because of Richard I's involvement. Richard was very much his father's son, but also the favourite of Eleanor, his mother. He "was dominating in the Council chamber and supreme in the field of war".[12] He was a master of strategy, battlefield tactics and logistics; and never more content than when planning and executing war. He spent less than six months of his ten-year reign in England, which was simply a treasury for his campaigns.

Following the First Crusade, the territories conquered by the Crusaders in Syria and Palestine were divided into four kingdoms: Jerusalem (1099–1291), Antioch (1098–1268), Edessa (1098–1144) and Tripoli (1102–1289). Together they formed the territories known as *"Outremer"*, meaning the land overseas. In the mid-twelfth century, these lands suffered losses and faced renewed attack: Edessa was lost to a Turkish warlord, the Atabeg Zengi.

The Second Crusade, made up of French and German armies under Conrad III and Louis VII, proved unsuccessful, and included a failure to take Damascus. Forty years later, in 1188, it was evident that the Crusader kingdoms were under renewed threat. On 4 July 1187, Saladin won a crushing victory over the Kingdom of Jerusalem at the Horns of Hattin in Galilee, leading to the fall of Jerusalem on 2 October 1187, followed by most of the Frankish ports and castles. News of these defeats galvanized Europe.

The Pope called a new Crusade, with the Kings of France, England and Germany taking up the cross. Frederick Barbarossa, the German Emperor, assembled a vast army of 100,000, only to be drowned when crossing a river in Cilicia. His army lost morale and disintegrated, barely reaching Acre. By contrast, Richard I came by sea from Sicily, taking Cyprus, where he was married *en route*, and arrived at Acre in 1191. Cyprus was the first of the Mediterranean islands taken for crusading purposes; Malta, Crete and Rhodes would follow. Richard managed to check Saladin's forces, but was unable to take Jerusalem, nor could he dislodge Saladin from his power base in Egypt. A kind of stalemate obtained in which the Crusaders held on to the coastal strip from Acre to Jaffa and their most impregnable castles, such as Krak des Chevaliers (in modern-day Syria), while Saladin held on to the interior. Richard had shown himself a violent and bold enemy, beheading 3,000 prisoners at Acre. Saladin died six months after the Treaty of Jaffa (1192), but his Muslim forces held on to Damascus, Jerusalem, Aleppo and Mosul.

Richard and England paid dearly for the Crusade. Richard's fleet alone cost £14,000, which represented half a year's income in the Exchequer. A "Saladin Tithe" was levied on England in 1188. Richard's capture outside Vienna by Leopold of Austria and Emperor Henry VI in 1192 led to a ransom of £100,000, which was a vast sum for England to find, representing four years of royal or exchequer income. It was left to Hubert Walter, the Chief Justiciar, Archbishop of Canterbury, Chancellor and fellow Crusader at Acre, to help raise the money with the support of Richard's indefatigable and devoted mother, Eleanor. Undoubtedly the Crusade affected the Church and England: it turned bishops like William Longchamps, a low-born Norman, into a despised enforcer and sole agent of the crown with little or no pastoral interest. In 1199, Richard died from an arrow wound whilst campaigning in France, in "friendly fire". He died in his mother's arms and parts of his body were buried in Rouen, Chalus and Fontevraud. The Crusades staggered on, culminating in the disastrous Fourth Crusade, called by the hawkish Innocent III. The Crusade got mixed up with Byzantine politics and ended up with the Crusaders sacking Constantinople for three days in April 1204. Other Crusades followed, for by now they had become a common method of prosecuting papal policy in the Holy Land, Spain and the Baltic States, and against heretics like the Cathars in south-west France. For the best part of two hundred years, Europe gave itself in blood and treasure to the Crusades. It was a violent cul-de-sac for the Christian faith, and an episode of history that has lingered long in the mind of Islam ever since. The Knights Hospitallers and Templars were founded to prosecute the Crusades. The Templars were closed down in 1307 by Pope Clement V, accused of idolatry, abuse and fraud. The Crusades, whilst providing fascinating history, are an aberration of Christian mission.

Magna Carta

After the death of Richard, his youngest brother John succeeded in 1199. Already a cruel chancer, John's rule was to be as cynically capricious as Richard's was romantic and brutal. Where Richard was generous, John was mean. Where Richard was a remarkable soldier, John was unimpressive. Where Richard was admired, John was loathed. The only mitigating factor in John's reign is that it precipitated Magna Carta. The political narrative of John's reign is both straightforward and tragic. Matthew Paris, the contemporary chronicler, hardly had a good word to say about him. He seems to have had the ability to antagonize all those on whom he depended. He angered Hugh de Lusignan by taking Hugh's fiancée, Isabella of Angoulême. He angered William de Roches, a great Angevin magnate, and crucially, Philip King of France also. He murdered Prince Arthur of Brittany in a fit of rage, thereby provoking war with the King of France, Philip Augustus, who proceeded to take Normandy—by storming Chateau Gaillard, whose "saucy walls"[13] defied all comers—Chinon and Poitiers. With the death of his mother in 1204, John had lost most of his French possessions. He was thrown back on England and the support of his barons for a supply of knights and soldiers adequate to match a greatly enriched France. The Capetian (the French royal house) conquest of Normandy was a turning point in European history.

In little over a century, the Anglo-Norman state had come to an end. Furthermore, John had alienated the papacy, which was then led by the most powerful pope in recent times, Innocent III. For refusing the Pope's choice of archbishop, Stephen Langton, and for seizing church property, John was excommunicated and an interdict (a ban on services for lay people and the last time this happened until COVID-19 in March 2020) was imposed on England. This was the final sanction in the armoury of the Pope. Churches were sealed, the dead received no Christian burial, and the sacrament was banned. In the meantime, John sought to raise money from England by any means, foul or fair, in order to launch a campaign to win back his French territories. After turning his relationship with Innocent III around by installing Stephen Langton as the Archbishop of Canterbury and also seeking the Pope's protection, he proceeded to wage war against Philip Augustus of France, but his troops were catastrophically defeated at Bouvines in 1214. A dispirited baronetage seeking renewed protection of their rights and a weak king needing to be restrained from causing further harm were now the backcloth to the events of Runnymede, and the sealing of Magna Carta.

It is hard to exaggerate the importance of Magna Carta, a single sheet of parchment containing sixty-three clauses. It was almost certainly the work of Stephen Langton, who coordinated the barons' demands, a work which must have been done over several months before being sealed by John. Affixing the royal seal would give the document royal authority, the only real authority in the land. By then, in 1215, the King had no alternative but to agree unless he wanted civil war and probable defeat.

Magna Carta is framed as a Christian document, so John declares, "We have, in the first place, granted to God and by this our present charter confirmed for ourselves and our heirs in perpetuity that the English Church is to be free and have its rights in whole and its liberties unimpaired."[14] The sixty-three clauses cover a variety of issues: a widow has the right to inherit her dower and stay in her deceased husband's home for forty days (7); debts to Jews are to be paid out of the deceased's residue (11); the city of London is to have all its ancient liberties and free customs, both by land and water (13); no vill (villein) or man will be forced to build bridges at river banks (23); all fish-weirs will be completely removed from the Thames and the Medway and throughout all England (33); and there will be one measure for wine, ale and corn throughout the realm (35). If these are lesser-known clauses, the seminal ones for the future constitution of England were that "no free man will be taken or imprisoned or disseised or outlawed or exiled or in any way ruined . . . save by the lawful judgement of his peers and by the law of the land",[15] and if a new tax (aid) is to be raised then it can only be done after consultation with the Council, consisting of senior clergy and barons (14).

In a real sense, Magna Carta was a peace treaty between king and lords, both spiritual and lay. It would be enforced by the provision of Clause 61, in terms of which a group of twenty-five barons would "observe, maintain and cause to be observed the peace and liberties that we have granted and confirmed to them by this our present charter".[16] As with all else with John, he got out of it as soon as the ink was dry. He refused to comply with the agreement to get rid of alien constables, who were mostly French. Stephen Langton lost the confidence of barons and king alike. John then appealed to the Pope, who annulled the oaths John had taken to uphold Magna Carta, for reasons of papal *realpolitik*. By September 1215, the King ordered the seizure of the lands of the barons who had forced Magna Carta on him. They in turn invited Louis, the Dauphin, to become King of England. A French army occupied London and John was restricted to the south-west of the country. A year later, having lost most of his treasure while crossing the Wash from north Norfolk, John died at Newark and was buried in Worcester Cathedral. England was then a divided and occupied nation, in hock to the highly successful

French king, Philip Augustus. The only fragile sign of hope was the accession of a nine-year-old, King Henry III—John's son—in Bristol.

Magna Carta was then simplified and reissued as a coronation charter for Henry III at Bristol, sealed by his chief minister William Marshal and the papal legate Guala Bicchieri. Thus "England's liberties were won from a nine-year-old Angevin king, provoked by a French Invasion, and conformed under the seal of an Italian cardinal. So much for the idea of the English constitution as something isolated from continental politics, immunized against European influence."[17]

Magna Carta was to have a life of its own. It would be issued and reissued in 1216, 1217, 1225, 1234, 1265, 1297 and 1300. In 1300, under Edward I, it was distributed to the counties and cathedrals of England. In some cases, as in Durham, the monks carefully guarded their Magna Cartas of 1216, 1225 and 1300. The charter's influence increased even as its original context diminished. It became absorbed into the very genesis of Parliament from its embryonic form in Henry III's reign until today. It became part of statute law. It was published in 1508, once the printing press was in use, and was translated into English in 1534. Some of its more arcane or feudal elements were repealed as the years went by. Yet whatever else Magna Carta may have been, it was the faint outline of a birth certificate of freedom, and at the same time the death certificate of despotism. Dig beneath its clauses, which oscillated from the practical—e.g. the removal of fish-weirs from the Thames and Medway (33)—to the substantial—e.g. that no one should be denied justice (40)—and we find a fundamental worldview, which is both legal and religious. With regard to law, Magna Carta could no longer be seen as the whim of the monarch but was an expression of inalienable natural law with an independent power in its own right to which all are answerable, king and subject alike. Behind that was a religious principle, indeed a Judeo-Christian one, that God himself holds all to account and it was in his name that the charter was drawn up and promulgated. The charter was drawn up by "the prompting of God and for the salvation of our [John's] soul . . . for the exaltation of holy church and the repair of our realm, through the counsel of our venerable fathers".[18] The simple truth is that a document like this would not even have been possible without the underlying belief that both king and subject alike are accountable to a God whose own laws are inviolable and binding. This had been previously expressed in the *Promissio Regis*, and the promises made to God on behalf of the Church, the people and the law by the later Saxon kings at their coronations.

CHAPTER 6

The Church during the Plantagenets

The next 150 years of political government in England represented the triumph of English customs over Norman and French practices. Only four kings ruled during the period from 1215 until the accession of Richard II in 1377. These four kings, Henry III and Edward I, II and III, saw the development of an English parliament, almost continuous warfare in France, the subjugation of Wales, war with Scotland, the increasing prosperity of the English nation (particularly from wool), a more indigenously led Church, and the proliferation of medieval guilds and trades. The main smear on the face of those years was the treatment of the Jews.

After the death of King John, and with England once again riven by civil war, a new beginning was made with the accession of the nine-year-old King Henry III and the reissuing of Magna Carta in Bristol. At the time, the French Dauphin was harrying the south of England and government was all but paralysed. Bit by bit stability returned, mostly due to the power and wisdom of Henry's regent, William Marshal, who was quite probably the greatest tournament knight in Europe. Of relatively humble origins, Marshal, who had an unequalled reputation for valiance and probity, was married to a great heiress, Isabel de Clare, the daughter of Strongbow. At the start of Henry's reign, Marshal was in his seventies, but was completely and touchingly loyal to the young Henry, for whom he was regent. His aim was to re-establish Henry's rule and eject Louis of France from England in the process. After the Battle of Lincoln (1217) in which Marshal, aged seventy-two, successfully fought on horseback beneath the towers of Lincoln Cathedral, the tide of resistance to the infant king began to turn. A further defeat of Louis' navy off Sandwich (1217), when the French fleet's admiral, Eustace the Monk, was captured and beheaded, further secured the kingdom for Henry.[1]

The years of Henry's personal rule began fully in 1234, and it was one marked by both piety and partiality. Despite his lionizing of Edward the Confessor, and his devotion to Edward's shrine at Westminster Abbey, Henry became too dependent on French courtiers (never popular in England!) and neglected to develop the principles of Magna Carta. His reign of fifty-six years was markedly inconsistent. His father, King John, having died when Henry was a boy, had given him no steady example of kingship. Henry married Eleanor of Provence, whose sister Margaret married the French king. Eleanor was a talented, artistic woman, but brought with her Savoyard relatives who were soon resented by the English. Henry's mother, Isabella of Angoulême, another powerful matriarch in the tradition of Eleanor of Aquitaine and Blanche of Castile, had given King John five children, including Henry, but after John's death she married the son of her first suitor and fiancé, Hugh of Lusignan, with whom she had a further nine children! The French relatives of Henry's mother, like those of his wife, became a running sore for the increasingly English-orientated nobility.

Isabella and her Lusignan children were to become a source of deep resentment amongst Henry's English subjects, and one of the chief causes of complaint against him. Unlike his predecessors, Henry always appeared to prefer overseas support, such as from the Pope, to the support of any English baron. He sought to project his own image as a pious king through an increasing number of elaborate church services and rituals. He made the rebuilding and extension of Westminster Abbey his chief national project, while spending many months residing at the Palace of Westminster. Over time he appeared too remote and too continental for many of his subjects, and in this opposition to his policies an opportunity was created for a wider consultation with representatives of his people, through what would become known as Parliament. As one Poitevin satirist put it, "White bread, chambers and tapestries . . . to ride like a dean on a docile mount. The king likes better all that, than to put on a coat of mail."[2] In other words, to the English barony he seemed a wuss.

What Henry lacked in military appetite he looked for in others, but in doing so he gave those others a visibility and influence that would prove dangerous. When Henry's continental policy proved ineffective, he increasingly relied on Simon de Montfort. Simon's efforts in France were unsuccessful, however, and in 1259 Henry came to terms with Louis, resigning all claims to Normandy, Anjou and Poitou and doing feudal homage for Gascony and Aquitaine, which he retained. This Treaty of Paris would remain intact for twenty-five years. To compensate for these continental losses, Henry took other dubious honours: notably the kingdom of Sicily granted by the Pope, which he accepted at great cost on behalf of his son Edmund. The Church in England raised £40,000 towards the cost of Sicily. The crown had to find a further £90,000 to secure Sicily from another claimant, Manfred, an illegitimate son of Frederick II of Germany. These were prodigious sums for a far-off island with only a crusading use, and that had been acquired by money and not military victory.

Costs mounted and questionable titles accrued. Having paid handsomely for the rather spurious claim to Sicily, Henry's brother, Richard of Cornwall, now took on the role of Holy Roman Emperor or King of the Romans by bribing the Electors of Germany in 1257. All this expensive dalliance in faraway places was exacerbated by a policy of promoting foreigners at home. Henry's wife, Eleanor of Provence, gradually increased her household, managed her own finances, and had her uncles Peter and Boniface made Lord of Richmond and Archbishop of Canterbury (1249–70) respectively. Of Boniface, the monk and chronicler from the Benedictine abbey at St Albans, Matthew Paris wrote sardonically, "He was noted more for his birth than his brains." The Lusignans and the Savoyards, Henry's mother and wife's families, came to dominate the court. English money paid their pensions and what with the continental accretions of Sicily and the title King of the Romans, it seemed as if hard-earned English money was paying for foreign baubles. It was an argument with resonance both then and now. Again, Matthew Paris wrote of Henry, "He loved aliens above all (more than) the English"—a telling charge.[3]

By 1258, the balloon was about to go up. Henry was arraigned by his barons, not for cruelty or despotism, but for his disregard of true national interest. Throughout Henry's reign, Magna Carta had been reissued, and it was this sense of a contract between king and subjects that was put in jeopardy by Henry's foreign ventures and foreign personnel. In 1238, there had been a request for a standing council, a successor to the Anglo-Saxon *witan*. This council insisted on the public appointment of officials. From 1253, and during the Gascon campaign, money grants were refused.[4] The council gradually exercised control over the King's appointments and the use of the King's income. The hated Poitevins were ejected, the money paid for Sicily was stopped, a settlement was made with Scotland, and peace was made with France.[5]

By 1258, a party led by Simon de Montfort, Earl of Leicester, sought to impose more restrictions on the King's expenditure, on the accountability of the royal administration, and on foreign policy. Simon was the son of the equally implacable Catholic Crusader, Simon de Montfort (senior), who had led the brutal Crusade against the Cathars or Albigensians in south-west France. (He was married to King Henry III's sister Eleanor, who had previously been married to William Marshal II. After Marshal's death she had taken a vow of chastity, but at Simon's insistence she later reneged on this.) Simon had been the governor of Gascony at the request of the King until he was relieved of the post against his will, creating more bad blood between this austere Catholic reformer and a more dilettante but still pious king.

Simon now led the opposition to the King in England, seeking to restrict his powers. He swore an oath with seven leading barons to bring the King under control. In 1258, there was a meeting between the King and these barons in Westminster Hall, and an agreement to have a *parlemenz*, literally a conversation, in Oxford. An oath was taken in the name of *le commun de Engleterre*, endorsed by most of the bishops of England, a clear case of the Church being on the side of reform.

The Provisions of Oxford were agreed between king and barons. They provided for regular future public *parlemenz* and for elected committees to supervise the royal government. In 1259, the Provisions of Westminster sought to impose restrictions on baronial courts, passing on the concessions given by the King to those who appeared in those courts.

The King did not accept these restrictions to his power without a fight. He renounced the agreement in 1261 with the support of the Pope. De Montfort then returned to England to lead the barons against the King. At the Battle of Lewes (14 May 1264), the King was defeated and captured, together with his son, the Lord Edward, leaving De Montfort in control. Matthew Paris put the numbers killed at 5,000.[6] The battle was celebrated by the *Song of Lewes* in which the "community of the realm" was heralded and in which "what everyone feels should be taken into account and the customs of the realm respected".[7] Henry and Edward were taken into custody, although fatefully Edward would escape and, supported by the Marcher Lords, take up arms against Simon.

In 1265, De Montfort summoned his great parliament, which included twenty-three barons, 120 clerics and representatives from selected boroughs. It was not the first such parliament in England, for Queen Isabella had summoned one at the instigation of Henry III, then in France, in 1254. It was, however, the most memorable. In Isabella's parliament, knights from the shires were summoned to grant money for the campaign in France that was being led by her husband Henry. The decisions of De Montfort's parliament were more far-reaching: not simply raising money, but also appointing new sheriffs for the shires, taking a tithe from the Church, commandeering the wool supply, and enabling Simon himself to take charge of various castles. But by August 1265, Simon was dead, killed and dismembered by Prince Edward's troops at Evesham.

Simon was in the tradition of the crusader knight, pious and powerful, unyielding in his Catholic devotion, austere and ambitious. There is no doubt that for the most part he had the support of the Church, as Matthew Paris shows.

For some he was even a saint, with some two hundred cures ascribed to him in a record at Evesham Abbey. His legacy in calling the Great Parliament is unassailable. Yet his religious and reforming zeal was in conflict with his own strong personal ambition. He could be hard and acquisitive, and was determined to carve out a position of power for his family. Credited as the convenor of the first true parliament, he is therefore regarded as the father of the English constitution.

Henry III lived for four more years. His son, the Lord Edward, took part in his own Crusade in 1271, but hearing of his father's death while in Sicily in 1272, returned home slowly, recovering on the way from a wound suffered in Palestine. He was crowned, aged thirty-three, on 19 August 1274. Already a hardened soldier, he was six feet, six inches tall, earning him the sobriquet Longshanks. If Henry III left a legacy consisting of Westminster Abbey, the shrine of Edward the Confessor, of foreign advisers and a number of ineffective military campaigns, Edward, by contrast, would leave a legacy of martial triumphs, castles, the ascendancy of England in the British Isles, further reform of the law and important developments in the constitution of government. His would be a seminal rule in the development of England, but at the cost of relations with Wales, Scotland and the Jews.

Edward I

Edward made it his business to subjugate Wales, and in particular the mountain fastnesses of Snowdonia in Gwynedd, with its noble prince, Llewellyn ap Gruffyd, the grandson of the great Llewellyn ap Iorweth, who had been the bane of the Angevin kings. After several campaigns, Llewellyn was killed near Builth, and his brother, Daffydd, was ignominiously dragged through the streets and hung, drawn and quartered in Shrewsbury after his fateful attack on the English garrison at Hawarden in 1282. It was a humiliating end to a great line of Welsh princes. In 1284, in the Statute of Rhuddlan, the Principality of Wales was incorporated into England. Castles of occupation modelled on those in *Outremer* were to follow. Conwy was built between 1283 and 1287 with no less than 2,000 workmen overseen by master builder James of St George, a Savoyard whom Edward had met on the way back from the Holy Land. Harlech, Caernarfon and Beaumaris were to follow, although in some cases never completed. A ring of stone surrounded Wales and Edward's younger son, later Edward II, was proclaimed Prince of Wales. Thereafter, every first-born son of the English monarch was entitled Prince of Wales.

Having dealt with Wales, Longshanks turned his attention to Scotland. Scotland had long prospered under Alexander III, who was married to Edward's sister Margaret. Disaster would swiftly overtake the royal house of Scotland: Margaret died in 1283, and her children likewise by 1284. In his haste to be with his new queen, Yolanda of Dreux, Alexander fell from his horse on a stormy night and broke his neck. His death brought to an end almost three centuries of royal success. Alexander's granddaughter had been promised to Edward II, but when she, the so-called Maid of Norway, died in 1290, Edward Longshanks determined to press his own case of feudal overlordship on Scotland. When Edward's exertion of his overlordship met with resistance from John Balliol, Edward invaded and annexed Scotland to the English crown. Sixty years of age, with a mane of white hair, Edward Longshanks was still very much the warrior king. The size of Edward's armies was immense: 25,700 infantry and 3,000 cavalry. In three weeks, Edward had overrun Scotland. The Stone of Destiny at Scone was taken to Westminster to form part of the Coronation Chair of Edward the Confessor. (It remained there until 1996, when it was returned to Scotland, except for coronations.) Yet the strength of the Scottish state, the distance from its administration in London, and the inhospitable terrain, made the project unworkable from the beginning. When the Chancery was moved to York while the King was on campaign in Scotland, a procession of carts from London was required to transport the necessary documents. Then, when Robert Bruce was crowned king at Scone in 1306, the process of liberation from English rule grew strong, especially after the guerrilla tactics of William Wallace (of *Braveheart* fame) in the 1290s. Wallace, like his Welsh counterpart Daffydd, was handed over to Edward and hideously disembowelled for his "treason", but he remained thereafter a romantic rallying point for resistance against the English. By 23 June 1314, Bruce was to have his way in defeating the army of Edward II at Bannockburn, thereby ensuring Scotland's independence.

The Jews in England

If the Welsh and the Scots were to suffer invasion and defeat by a warrior king at the head of an increasingly prosperous state, the Jews faced persecution and, in the end, deportation from England during Edward I's reign. This was a series of events that followed almost a thousand years of persecution of Jews by Christians. The history of theological diatribe against the Jews by the early Church is both long and, at times, hard to understand. The scriptures made it clear that in God's wisdom, the Jews were to be a light to the nations, a chosen race. They had been privileged with the Law, the Oracles of God, a divine destiny (Romans 9:4–5), the covenants and many promises. Because they had failed to live up to these expectations, being mired in idolatry and corruption, they were sent into exile in Babylon, and this was the consistent message of the prophets. In Babylon, Ezekiel explained their guilt and the cause of their exile. Their eventual return to Israel and Jerusalem was planned by Cyrus and executed under Nehemiah and Ezra. Yet Israel's independence was far from assured. It was to suffer occupation, first by the Greek Seleucid kings, and then by the Romans, who occupied Judea from 63 BC as part of the province of Syria. In AD 70, after the Jewish revolt, which began in AD 66, the Roman legions under Vespasian and then Titus destroyed Jerusalem. Jerusalem was to be once more, and finally, crushed and renamed *Aelia Capitolina* by the Emperor Hadrian in AD 136 after the rebellion of Simon bar Kokhba.

Jesus had been rejected as the Messiah by the greater part of the Jewish establishment, and the Gospels of Matthew and John made this plain. Both Matthew and John were Christian Jews who sought to show that Jesus fulfilled all the predictions of the Messiah in the Old Testament. The rejection of Jesus by the Jews was to become one of the causes of their persecution by Christians. Although Paul the Apostle asked for Jews to be treated as an older brother (see Romans 9–11) and be regarded as the root upon which the Church was grafted, there was little sign of this in the writings of the Church Fathers.

Almost all of the Church Fathers (the leaders of the Early Church in both the Greek East and the Latin West) took a judgemental and sometimes very aggressive stance towards the Jewish people. There seem to be two reasons for this: first because of the perceived responsibility of the Jews for the crucifixion of the Messiah, although this was clearly the plan of God (see Peter's address at Pentecost in Acts 2:23—an important view on the apostolic understanding of the Crucifixion), and second because the Jews posed a threat to the Christian community while in its infancy. This second reason, of being a threat to the Church, resulted from the fact that the Jews were given space in the Roman Empire to worship and develop and were not persecuted as the Christians were. Their community therefore offered a temptation to Jewish Christians to revert to Judaism in order to escape persecution.

Among the Church Fathers who particularly excoriated the Jews were Ambrose, Chrysostom and Jerome. Ambrose sought to prevent the rebuilding of a synagogue that had been torched by Christians in religious riots in Callinicum on the Euphrates, and also wanted to prevent punishment of the bishop who had encouraged the action.[8] In 386, before his appointment as Bishop of Constantinople,

Chrysostom delivered a visceral attack on the Jews in Antioch in the form of a *psogos*, which was a Greek style of speech amounting to a vilification of an opponent, and the very opposite of an *encomium*, a tribute of praise. Chrysostom preached in his typically uncompromising way, "Don't be surprised if I've called the Jews wretched, for truly they are wretched and miserable since they spurned the numerous blessings which came into their hands from heaven, and took great pains to throw them away."[9] Chrysostom went on to say that a synagogue is no better than a theatre, as its members indulge in effeminacy and even prostitution. Tertullian, like Justin Martyr, in his *Answer to the Jews* gave a more reasoned account of their failure to recognize their Messiah—as described in their own Law and the prophetic writings—without castigation.[10] Augustine of Hippo likewise took a more mellow approach to the Jews. Whilst condemning the Jews' failure to recognize their Messiah because of an incorrect reading of the Law and the prophets, Augustine concluded that they were to be approached with respect, saying, "Let us proclaim them [their Scriptures] with great love for the Jews."[11]

If, at the very least, mixed messages came from the teaching of the Church Fathers on how to treat the Jews, the construct that generally reached the medieval European mind was that the Jews were at best to be ostracized and at worst vilified and persecuted for their blasphemy. The issue of money further complicated their welfare.

As elsewhere in Europe, the Jews in England had become creditors to a Christian society, lending money at interest, which Christians, by reason of their doctrine, believed they were unable to do. William the Conqueror had brought Jews from Rouen and established them in London, their first known settlement in England. These Jews acted as moneylenders and dealers in coin, plate and bullion. They were the medieval *bureau de change*, exchanging continental silver, paid for with English wool, into English money.

Jews also acted as bankers, facilitating the money supply. By 1086, there were thought to be about nine million pennies in existence, with a penny being the cost of a day's labour. By 1300, money circulation had risen to 216 million pennies, or 54d per head of population. The value of money may have reduced by a factor of three or four due to inflation, but the money supply had increased twenty-four-fold. At the heart of this currency circulation were the Jews. They did not mint coins, but they helped circulate them by the provision of credit and the payment of interest. By Henry II's reign, they were the main source of credit. They had become the bankers for the nation. In Magna Carta, two clauses concern the Jews and payment of debts or interest after death. In the event of a debt to a Jew being outstanding at death, it was to be paid last of all, after all other debts (clause 11) and no interest was to be paid on a debt to a Jew by a minor or a wife on the occasion of a father or husband's death (10). On that count and according to those clauses, Magna Carta is antisemitic. Jews were very much at the centre of society's financial web and the crown regulated payments of debt and interest without consideration for their wishes.

By 1190, Jews numbered fewer than 5,000, but there were significant communities in seventeen English towns. Most of the money loaned was to great lay and ecclesiastical lords. One William Cade, a Christian financier, had lent at least £5,000 to clients, including some of the most influential men in the realm. One leading Jew in Lincoln, Aaron, was owed £18,466 at his death, almost the entire annual revenue of the crown. Rates of interest could be as much as 44 per cent per annum, which is two pence per pound per week. Not surprisingly there was envy of Jewish wealth, which was exacerbated by their isolation from medieval Christian society. Insult was added to injury when the Lateran Council of 1179 stressed the "dangers of spiritual contamination by association with them".[12] English bishops were often implacably opposed to the Jews, and thus Grosseteste of Lincoln, fine scholar and Christian though he was, expelled Jews from Lincoln when he was Archdeacon of Leicester in 1231. Furthermore, malicious rumours were spread, including, for example, that Jews murdered children. These pernicious rumours—or fake news, we would say—such as the one about little St William of Norwich being murdered by Jews in a parody of the execution of Christ, swept through the country, with many wanting to believe them true. Such child murders were also attributed to Jews in Gloucester (1168), Bury St Edmunds (1181) and Bristol (1183), creating sentiment that was increasingly fuelled by the effects of the Crusades (which had provoked antisemitism in Germany along the Rhine and elsewhere).

Those who "took the Cross" believed they could legitimately pay for their expeditions by despoiling the Jews. It was only a short step from this to violence against the Jews, given the heady mix of rumour, the heightened religious fervour from the Crusades, and the ostentatious wealth of richer Jews. Violence broke out in King's Lynn, Bury St Edmunds, Norwich and Lincoln, finally climaxing in York in 1189, when anger erupted against a small but important community of about 150 Jews who lived there. Local barons, by then significantly in debt to Jewish lenders such as Benedict and Josce, led the attack, which was further fuelled by hermits or monks with extreme views about the Jews, and by Crusaders who had returned from Palestine. The Jews took refuge in York Castle, where they were besieged. So savage was the attack that Rabbi Yom Tov sanctioned a mass suicide rather than fall into the hands of the mob: fathers cut the throats of their wives and children, and Rabbi Yom Tov took his own life. It was Masada all over again, but in York. Longchamp, Richard I's Chancellor, eventually restored order. The chronicler William of Newburgh condemned the violence. Jews returned to York and were placed under royal protection. A kind of royal protection racket then developed, through which the King sought to encourage the payment of debts to the Jews, whilst at the same time taxing them for his administration and protection of their loans and livelihood, and for placing royal castles at their disposal for security. In that way credit was still available, debts were paid, and the crown gained from taxing the Jews. In 1186 and 1194, the total demanded of the Jews was well over £13,000, that is, half the King's revenue. Taxation of the Jews by the crown increased further thereafter, with Henry III taxing them the sum of £66,000 between 1241 and 1255, whilst at the same time heightening religious intolerance against them. In 1255, nineteen Jews were executed in Lincoln for supposedly kidnapping and crucifying a small Christian boy called St Hugh.

By 1290, over-taxation, persistent persecution and declining numbers left Jewish communities decidedly broken. The heavy taxation of the Jews between 1240 and 1260 had destroyed their wealth and thus their value to the crown as a source of revenue was much diminished. Their numbers had also declined by about 4,000, down to less than 2,000. The total value of debts owed to the Jews in 1290 was around £20,000, whereas in the 1240s it had been closer to £80,000. The value of taxation of the Jews to the crown likewise dropped proportionately. Whereas the crown had gained about £73,333 in taxation on the Jews between 1241 and 1256, by 1290 this sum was down to only £9,300. It was still a large sum, but when the tide of religious feelings against the Jews increased, Edward saw his moment to increase pressure. First, he forced Jews to wear a badge (or *tabula*) identifying them in the community, and then partially expelled them from certain lands and cities (e.g. Lincoln and Leicester). Lastly, when Edward I was sure of receiving a tax in lieu of their dismissal, in 1290 the Jews were finally expelled from England, not to return until the time of Cromwell. The expulsion was in keeping with edicts of other continental rulers, such as in Maine, Anjou and France. Like his successors, Edward I would then turn to Italian bankers. The Frescobaldi of Florence lent Edward I and II £150,000 before their ruin by the Barons' War of 1311 against Edward II and their ejection by the nobility. In the time of Edward III, when he was prosecuting almost continuous warfare in France, the Riccardi family lent him £392,000 over twenty-two years between 1272 and 1294.[13] These were huge sums, secured for the most part against the wool trade, but despite that, northern Europe would be the graveyard of many an Italian loan. English kings were not reliable borrowers.

The reign of the three Edwards

It is almost a truism to say that the leadership of the king was the cornerstone of the welfare of the nation, and the reign of the three Edwards in the fourteenth century was an object lesson of this maxim. Any politically astute continental visitor to England during that period (1272–1377) would have noticed a state of affairs that was a paradox: on the one hand there were strong ties of community in the nation underpinned by the strength of the king's administration, and on the other, chronic political instability that would reach boiling point in the Wars of the Roses. The legacy of the Anglo-Saxon system, harnessed to the power of the crown after the Norman Conquest and linked to an efficient legal and taxation framework, gave a strong sense of cohesion to the country. This cohesion was expressed through the royal administration of the Chancery and the Exchequer. The Chancery was the administrative secretariat, staffed for the most part by clergy, while the Exchequer was "the audit department of the state to which all spending and collecting officials were eventually called to account".[14] This central power and these organs of government gave cohesion and great revenue-raising ability to the crown, especially from taxes on the wool trade and levies granted by Parliament that by and large gave the kings what they wanted. In fact, a radical tract at the end of the thirteenth century, called the *Mirror of Justices*, complained "that the powers of Parliament in matters of taxation have made it a tool of oppression", enabling the King to exact taxes and hoard money.[15]

The flip side to this exceptional royal power of government and its ability to tax a wealthy country was the crown's dependency on the nobility. The crown could only effectively govern with the support of the nobility. On three occasions in the previous hundred years the crown had lost the support of the nobility: in the reigns of John, Henry III and Edward II. In each case the King was more or less overthrown by the nobility. William Marshal and the young Henry III had to regain the government of the nation after John's failure. Edward I had to defeat De Montfort and regain his inheritance by arms. Likewise, Edward III had to regain his inheritance after Mortimer and his own mother Isabella had taken over the reins of government from Edward II.

The nobility of England was small but very powerful. In 1331, there were nine earldoms, which were purely honorific titles carrying no political power in themselves. Edward III created the first English duke in 1337. Beyond that, the parliamentary peerage comprised another forty of fifty laymen who received personal writs of summons.[16] By the fourteenth century, about 20,000 individuals and 1,000 institutions, mainly ecclesiastical, owned the land. The crown owned 3 per cent of the land directly, compared with the 25 per cent owned by William the Conqueror. The seventy or so magnate families had incomes of between £1,000 and £4,000 a year. The most powerful magnates in the reign of Edward II were Thomas, Earl of Lancaster, a descendant of the youngest son of Henry III, Edmund Crouchback, who enjoyed annual income from land of £11,000, and the Earl of Warwick, who held 50,000 acres in 100 manors. Below the great magnates and lesser nobility were the knights, who were given many duties by the crown. These duties went beyond fighting to include chasing bandits, and acting as sheriffs, members of parliament, coroners and jurors. Their average income was £40. Below them were esquires and gentlemen. The king's most important duty was to keep his great magnates on side; failure to do so was fatal to good government. Whereas Edward I and Edward III were able to achieve this, Edward II notoriously failed.

The reason for the failure of Edward II's government was that he ignored the nobility; worse still, he chose favourites who exasperated them. Piers Gaveston, a Gascon and son of one of his household knights, became Edward's chief favourite.

Edward's rule foundered on a number of issues: the choosing of favourites who became arrogant, in particular Piers Gaveston and later Hugh Despenser, his defeat by the Scots at Bannockburn in 1314 and the subsequent Harrying of the North by the Scots and, worst of all, his wife Isabella's affair with Mortimer and the virtual imprisonment of his heir Edward III by them. In the end, Edward II was forced to abdicate and was murdered in a very unsavoury way in Berkeley Castle in 1337, with a red-hot poker being thrust up his anus.

Edward III, having overcome his capture by his mother and her lover Mortimer, secured his throne, with Mortimer being hung at Tyburn. In brief, Edward's reign would become shaped by chivalry and war on a grand scale. The Scots would be defeated at Halidon Hill in 1333. But then, in 1337, Edward III renewed the English claim to the French throne, and the Hundred Years' War followed. Notable victories over the French were secured at sea at Sluys in 1340 and on land at Crecy in 1346, Calais was taken—with the burghers of Calais being hung—and the French king was captured at Poitiers in 1356 and held hostage, pending a large ransom, in the Savoy Palace in the Strand, London. Edward revived the Arthurian legend with the Knights of the Order of the Garter, and the St George's Garter Chapel being founded at Windsor. But the reign was to be deeply marred by the appearance of the Black Death in 1348, with the terrible loss of life that ensued. Nor did Edward, despite all the fighting and destruction of French countryside, end up with any more territory in France than he had begun with. The reign continued until 1377 with Edward's heir, the Black Prince, dying just before his father, and with a nation decimated by the plague and growing uneasy with a Church caught up in increasingly corrupt ways and looking for a new, more evident spirituality.

PART III

Medieval Religion

CHAPTER 7

The Medieval Quad

As the nation's chaplain, the Church had more than enough to contend with in the late fourteenth century. It is hard to imagine the trauma and the effects of the Black Death. Those infected by the bacillus *Yersinia pestis*, carried in the guts of black-rat fleas, did not have long to live.[1] The symptoms were terrifying, the outcome fatal. At the very least, the Church had to bury the dead, but often this was too overwhelming a task since most of the clergy had perished too, and great burial pits were used instead.

The plague first appeared in Melcombe in Weymouth in June 1348 and spread throughout the British Isles. Days after the appearance of buboes in the armpits and groin, the infected person died. The ordered society of the medieval world was overwhelmed and, in consequence, only 28 per cent of children had surviving parents.[2] The routines of agriculture, whether on a peasant's smallholding or on choice seigniorial lands, were brutally affected. Travelling officials of the crown died disproportionately. Cities and nucleated villages were rife with infection and death. The interlocking community of the medieval village or town, as illustrated in the exquisite *Luttrell Psalter*, with its delightful rural images, was sundered by the plague.[3]

With so much grief and loss, the institutions of the Church took up, as best they could, the burden of prayer and solace for the nation. Christian groups were on hand in almost every community, to help, aid and succour, although frequently the effects of the plague overwhelmed them too.

The disease killed two archbishops, London was halved in size from 100,000 to 50,000; in Bristol it seemed as though the city was annihilated, priests could not be found for love or money to visit the sick or administer the last rites. At least a third of the population died, with huge social and economic consequences. Medieval institutions barely survived.

The monastic orders

As we have seen, England was evangelized by monastic communities. The residual Romano-Celtic Church, strong in Cornwall, Wales and the North-West, had not been in a position to undertake this mission, in part because of the antipathy between the Celtic and Anglo-Saxon kingdoms. The north of England was evangelized by Celtic missionaries from Iona, and previously from Ireland, who inspired other indigenous leaders. After a slow start, the south-east of England was evangelized from Canterbury. Monastic communities were the engine rooms of mission to England, there being little residual church left in sixth-century England.

Monasticism, originating from the Greek word *monos* meaning "alone", began in the Egyptian desert in the third century, partly precipitated by the persecution of the Church. The Nile Delta, Nitria and the Thebaid became filled with ascetics, either in community or as solitaries. Monastic rules were written, among others, by Pachomius (286–346), Basil of Caesarea (330–79) and Evagrius of Pontus (345–99). In turn, Western monasticism was initiated by the transference of Eastern ideas by Cassian to Lérins and by a new Rule written by Benedict.

Cassian, a native of Scythia and a disciple of John Chrysostom and Pope Leo the Great, lived for fifteen years among the hermits of Egypt and presented their wisdom and life to the monks of Lérins and Provence in two seminal works, the *Institutes* and the *Conferences*. The former is more a rule of life, while the latter are reported conversations with the Desert Fathers on various themes. From Lérins, monasticism would spread north to Tours, Bangor, Iona, Melrose and Lindisfarne, and later be replanted on the continent by Columbanus of Ireland, and Willibrord and Boniface of York. The *Conferences* was destined to be read in early medieval monasteries every night before Compline—the night office of prayer. The Rule that came out of this tradition—the Rule of St Benedict—would sweep all before it in the West until the coming of the friars in the thirteenth century.

Benedict (c. 480–547) was an Italian who was an abbot at a time when the Church was entering the dark ages, following the collapse of the Roman Empire in the West. His brilliance was to simplify and codify the rules by which an effective monastic community could be run, building on a now lost Rule written by an anonymous Master. The Benedictine Rule is remarkable for its brevity and succinctness. It is just a small booklet that can be read in an hour, and that can easily be slipped into the pocket of a habit, even in manuscript form. It held sway in European monasteries for a thousand years and is still used as a guide today. Mostly based on Scripture, it is "unique among monastic rules in containing in a few pregnant paragraphs a fund of spiritual and human wisdom that can guide abbot and monks in all the vicissitudes of life".[4]

Its seventy-three brief chapters range from the spiritual to the practical. Some overall themes emerge, in particular obedience to the authority of the abbot (the word comes from the Aramaic *abba*), who is the father of the community. In a telling phrase, the abbot must study to be loved and not feared. The whole community will choose him in an election. The abbot is to hold the place of Christ in the community, and must therefore "never teach or decree or command anything that would deviate from the Lord's instructions".[5] He must lead by example, not words, and must not have favourites. He must not threaten, but "use argument, appeal and reproof".[6] He must accommodate himself to the character and intelligence of each member of the flock. For their part, monks must follow their vows of obedience, poverty and chastity, and grow in humility. Indeed, humility is firstly to be expressed in obedience. Humility and growing or ascending in the quality of humility is the longest of the chapters in the Rule. Humility covers everything from gentle speech to not being given to uproarious laughter. Humility begins with turning away from one's own desires and submitting one's will to the abbot, to whom must be confessed any evil secret thoughts.

If the relationship between abbot and monk is critical for the well-being of the monastery, it is to be conducted in an environment of prayer, stability and balance.[7] Chapters 8–20 cover the saying of the offices of prayer, which are seven in number—Lauds, Prime, Terce, Sext, None, Vespers and Compline—generally said at three-hourly intervals during the day after a night time vigil at 2am. Furthermore, the Rule specifies which Psalms are to be used at each service. Between the offices of prayer there was time for manual work, reading scripture (*lectio divina*) and the copying of manuscripts in the *scriptorium* by skilled calligraphers. Meals were held in silence with readings from the scriptures or Church Fathers. Other rules cover the times of meals, working in the kitchen, the reception of guests, sleeping arrangements, the care of the sick, the discipline of monks, the use of silence, the appointments of cellarers and a porter for the gate. With creditable clarity and brevity, the whole life of the community is covered in a disciplined, humane and spiritual way by the Rule. The object of the Rule was to help the monastic community be a family and be devoted to prayer, work and spiritual disciplines. It was exacting, but in a fragile world it offered stability and the resources to bring hope to the wider community. It was a point of reference in the frequent life-storms of the Middle Ages, not least in times of plague and hunger.

English Benedictine monasticism was to be the subject of several waves of reform from the continent before the coming of the friars in the thirteenth century, and before the beginning of university education—as distinct from monastic education—first at Oxford, and a little later in Cambridge. These waves of reform from the eleventh century onwards came from Normandy and Cluny, from the Augustinians, and from the Cistercians of Citeaux and Clairvaux. This period, which extends from 1066 until the mid-thirteenth century, in many ways saw the high-water mark of monasticism in England in terms of spirituality, and the fulfilment of its purpose of prayer, study, scholarship and service. In fact, from 1060–1120 there were more new foundations and a higher rate of recruitment of novices than in any previous period of similar length.[8] It could be termed the golden age of monasticism, before the coming of the friars (Dominicans and Franciscans).

With these new monastic movements, places were created for aspiring monks from the families of the land-owning classes. This was an ongoing need for "at no time in the Middle Ages were the resources of society expanding fast enough to provide honourable positions in secular life for all the children of noble families".[9] In time, the function of the monastery would be challenged by the growth of a more articulate artisan class, by the activities of the parish, and by people obtaining an education in grammar schools and then at a university. This trend left monasteries functioning increasingly as administrative centres of large estates and open to the temptations of corruption. By the time of *The Canterbury Tales*, written by Geoffrey Chaucer between 1387 and 1400, the only religious character among the pilgrims to get a good press was the country parish parson.

The first movement to reform English monasteries came from Normandy through the revival of monastic life there, centred on Bec and Caen. We have already seen how Lanfranc and Anselm, both Abbots of Bec, one of the premier monasteries in Europe, revived monasticism in England. They brought scholarship, discipline and impetus to the artistic, liturgical and administrative life of the earlier Anglo-Saxon monasteries. New monasteries, like the one at Battle, were founded, and many were reinvigorated. Most of the abbots, apart from at Evesham, were Norman.

The influence of Bec was soon to be surpassed by a monastery more famous than any other: Cluny. Cluny in Burgundy and Gorze in Lorraine held the palm during the tenth and early eleventh centuries. What Cluny offered was a further step in the Carolingian style of worship, which was more elaborate than what had gone before. Over two hundred priories and abbeys would look to Cluny for leadership, submitting themselves to its oversight. New monasteries or priories (a lesser monastery) were founded along the pilgrim routes in France, to Compostela in Spain, and in south-west Germany and Italy. A succession of able, holy and long-lived monks brought Cluny to its point of greatest influence. Hugh the Great (1049–1109) expanded the monastery to well over three hundred monks and created a string of new foundations, including one at Lewes that was subject to Cluny's control. The last of this run of influential abbots was Peter the Venerable (1122–57), who was noted for his diplomatic skills, his gifts of reconciliation—particularly in relation to Abelard—and his study of Islam. However great this monastic reformation emanating from Cluny was, it would be overtaken by two other movements in the years following 1075: those of the Augustinians and the Cistercians.

The Augustinians represented the first proper break from the Benedictine monopoly of monasticism since the sixth century. Six hundred years was a long time to dominate the field, and it is a credit to both the strength and portability of the Benedictine Rule that it survived unchallenged for so long. The Augustinian life was based on a letter of spiritual advice written in the fifth century by Augustine of Hippo to a woman seeking to establish a new religious community.

It was a flexible rule, if we can call it that, requiring common ownership of property, communal prayer at set times, dressing without distinction and obedience to an acknowledged superior.[10] Little more was specified. Between 1075 and 1125, new communities following this rule appeared all over Western Europe.

The other great movement of reform emanated from Cîteaux in France in 1098. Some years earlier, a group of hermits sought to follow a strict observance of the Benedictine Rule at Molesme. "Their aim was to combine solitude and poverty with a severity of life lived in the exact observance of the rule."[11] Theirs was a movement that took monasticism from relaxation to discipline, from failure to strict observance, and from indulgence to unsullied purity. They came to be called Cistercians, with their new foundation at Cîteaux becoming the mother house of the movement. Their greatest proponent was Bernard of Clairvaux, who was probably the most powerful voice in Christendom in the first half of the twelfth century.

The marks of the Cistercians were a stricter observance of the Benedictine Rule; a greater enforcement of discipline, including an annual inspection; a break with the more elaborate style of Cluny; the restoration of hard manual labour, incorporating to that end a lay-order who helped with ground clearance (which enabled the cultivation of land and sites on the margins of habitation); and an annual synod or conference of abbots at Cîteaux. They wore a distinctive white habit and hood, unlike other Benedictines, who wore black. The result of this new spiritual energy was an explosive foundation of Cistercian monasteries. By the time of Bernard's death in 1153, there were 339 Cistercian abbeys, of which Bernard of Clairvaux himself founded sixty-eight, and of which 122 were in Britain. They were the flavour of the twelfth century. Typifying their remote locations were Tintern in the Wye Valley, and Fountains Abbey and Rievaulx in North Yorkshire. Even the ruins of these buildings remain inspiring and deeply suggestive today.

In many ways, we have in the Venerable Peter of Cluny and St Bernard of Clairvaux two counterpoints of Christian leadership. In Peter we find a man who was conciliatory, moderate, gentle, conservative, considerate and open to new ideas. He was willing to house Abelard, the controversial teacher from Paris, and to study Islam thoroughly. In Bernard, we have someone ardent, violent, provocative, a champion of the Crusades, uncompromising and revolutionary. He was an exegete of the Bible, and even John Calvin, presumably no friend of the monastic life, approved of him on account of his views on faith and devotion and his inveighing against all luxury, whether at Cluny or St Denis outside Paris. Yet despite all the evangelical purity of the Cistercian movement, it too was susceptible to the same corruption as others. At first the leaders were the harbingers of a new monastic orthodoxy, as shown by Aelred of Rievaulx and Stephen Harding of Sherborne, but this ambitious aspiration turned to a lacklustre imitation within fifty years. This surely underlines the point that spiritual vision must be renewed in every generation, whatever the form.

The Cistercians were bitterly criticized by Gerald of Wales (1146–1223), a monk and Archdeacon of Brecon. They ceased to keep their statutes, turned away the poor, and became greedy landlords and wealthy landowners whose flocks and land attracted the attention of King John and the bankers. By 1215, the movement had passed its religious peak. In that year, not only was there a new charter, Magna Carta, sealed at Runnymede, giving new rights to the King's subjects in England, but also, far away in Italy, a new religious genius, Francis of Assisi, was about to change the monastic landscape for good. Dominic, a fellow monk from Spain, likewise began a new teaching order the following year. The Franciscans and Dominicans, as they came to be known, were to fill the religious landscape for the next 250 years.

Just as some of the monastic movements of the past century were passing their peak in the early thirteenth century, these two new religious orders came on the scene well matched to the new social conditions of the time. An increase of population in the towns and a plethora of urban guilds and associations had sprung up on the back of greater commercial activity. The guilds became one of the main economic and social features of the twelfth century. One of the new monastic orders, the Franciscans, had at its heart a winsome dependence on Jesus, linked to a vow of complete poverty, while the other, the Dominicans, was a teaching order that plugged the teaching gap in the ministry of the Church.

Francis was the son of a prosperous merchant from Assisi. Romantically minded, he espoused the chivalric code, taking part in local warfare as a minor knight until he was challenged to give up this way of life in a series of dreams. He resolved to help the poor and to join piety to mercy. He contemplated a life of poverty alongside repairing a nearby chapel at San Damiano for the purpose of contemplation and prayer. Following a rift with his father, he laid aside even his clothing and committed himself to a life of poverty, preaching and prayer.

The Little Brothers, or Franciscans, wore brown habits and sought alms for their support. Soon they met with Pope Innocent III, who had the insight and good sense to accept Francis and his brothers as a new missionary order within the Church. The Poor Clares, a sister order from Assisi, were to follow soon after, and were given papal approval in 1253 by Innocent IV. Both communities were committed to simplicity and desired to stay within the Church. Dependent on little gifts from ordinary people and seeking to live in small houses in towns, the movement spread like wildfire across Europe. It coincided with the gradual urbanization of medieval Europe and the beginnings of university education. The Franciscans were to capitalize on both, staying in the towns and forming close ties with the fledgling universities of Europe. In England, having been introduced by Peter de Roches and welcomed by Archbishop Stephen Langton, they quickly moved to London and Oxford.

The Dominicans had a different origin, but a clear mandate also: to teach and to instruct. Dominic was a young Augustinian monk of Castilian Spanish background. Following a commission to combat heresy in the Languedoc region of France, which he received from Innocent III in 1206, Dominic saw the need for a new flexible, well-schooled, vigorous teaching order to direct the burgeoning intellectual life of Europe and to counteract heresy in an area of France that had recently produced the Albigensians or Cathars. In 1216, this order of friars, who were dependent on alms, was started with Pope Innocent's blessing. Dominic began his first house in Toulouse. Thus, as King John sealed Magna Carta, the two new influential orders quickly spread to England. By 1223, there were 120 Dominicans in Paris, and nine of the fifteen Doctors of Divinity at the university were Dominicans. Soon both orders came to Oxford, including teachers like Roger Bacon (a Franciscan) and Richard Rufus. Henry III openly sought to entice a brain drain of scholars from Paris. By 1251, the much less organized Franciscans had thirty lecturers holding formal theological disputations in Oxford and Cambridge.[12]

By the early fourteenth century, a century after their inception, there were 1,400 Franciscan houses across Europe with 28,000 friars and 12,000 Dominicans in 600 houses. Taken with the Cistercians, the Premonstratensians and the Augustinians, we can see that in the first three centuries of the millennium monasticism had become a boom industry. The Franciscans were especially popular, probably because of their closeness to the middle and lower middle classes of the towns. In the last half of the fourteenth century, after the Black Death, it is estimated that one third of the wills of the citizens of Oxford contained bequests to the Franciscans. The gifts ranged from those of the King, who gave £33 6s 8d, to the parishioners of St Ebbe's parish where the friars' house stood, to a group of bakers who together gave 6d a year. One Oxford butcher, Richard Bampton, left the following in his will:

> Two shillings for the repair of the porch of all Saints Church where he hoped to be buried;
>
> Six shillings and eight pence for the payment of any tithes or offerings, which he had neglected to pay;
>
> Ten shillings for the distribution to the poor on the day of his funeral;
>
> Ten shillings for the distribution among the mendicant friars of Oxford;
>
> Three pounds, six shillings and eight pence for a chaplain to say a daily mass for his soul for a year;
>
> And his house property in Oxford to the Augustinian canons of Osney Abbey after his wife's death.[13]

It seems Richard had no children to inherit his property, and his will appears to touch all the religious sectors: previous omission of payment of the tithe, legacies to reward the town's religious and, most strikingly, daily masses for a year in order to commend his soul to God—an aspect of medieval theology and practice to which we shall return.

Monasteries or friaries filled the landscape of the Middle Ages. The sight of monks or friars in the street would have been commonplace both in the towns (the Augustinians and Friars) and in the countryside (the Friars and Benedictine or Cistercian institutions). Their influence during the period from the Conquest until the fourteenth century cannot be overestimated. Thereafter this influence declined as other institutions gained ground. England had been evangelized from monasteries in the sixth century and the resulting church life supported minsters, priories and not a few cathedrals. It was in the monasteries that scholarship, history and elementary science were nurtured. It was in the *scriptoria* that manuscripts were produced in the centuries before the printing press. We have seen how the oldest Vulgate edition of the Bible, *Codex Amiatinus*, was produced at Monkwearmouth-Jarrow. Hundreds more manuscripts of infinite skill and extraordinary patience were to follow: The *Codex Aureus* at Canterbury, the Lichfield Gospels and the Winchester Bible, commissioned probably by Bishop Henry of Blois (1098–1171), with its extraordinary illuminations by one called the Amalekite Master, which took thirty-five years to complete. Then there were countless psalters, such as the fourteenth-century Luttrell Psalter, which is so wonderfully illuminated, and the many books of hours, such as the one belonging to Margaret Beaufort (1441–1509), in which she annotated key political events in her life.[14] It was in monasteries that the chroniclers of English history were found: Bede, Eadmer of Canterbury, Anselm's biographer, William of Malmesbury, William of Newburgh (c. 1136–98), an Augustinian canon from Bridlington, and Matthew Paris in St Albans. These chroniclers ranged from the gossipy to the devout and provided almost our only source of history in the Middle Ages. Before the arrival of the grammar and cathedral schools, the monasteries were places of education for oblates, the young aspiring monks. Church music also developed in monasteries: not only through the well-known plainsong of monastic offices, but also through the introduction of primitive organs—as evidenced in Glastonbury—and manuscripts of notation that were in circulation by the eleventh century.

Finally, monasteries were hotels and hostels for pilgrims en route to Canterbury, Glastonbury or further afield to Compostela or Jerusalem. They also functioned as hospitals or hospices of care for the sick and dying. All of these functions had at their root the care of the stranger (*hospes*) by a host, in this case a community. The twelfth-century St John's Hospital for pilgrims in Bruges may have provided an inspiration for St Bartholomew's, which was founded in 1123 in London. Once a medieval monastery caring for the poor, it is now a thriving hospital at the centre of the City of London. If monasteries, priories, and later friaries, formed part of the givens of medieval society, forming one side of the "quad", another was the diocese and cathedral.

The diocese and cathedral

When Gregory the Great sent Augustine of Canterbury to England in 597, it is clear that he envisaged that the Church would be set up as a province in England. In response to Augustine's enquiries about the morals of clergy and laity, particularly in relation to marriage, sex (including "wet dreams"), sex after childbirth, the churching of women and an enquiry about the establishment of the Church in England, Gregory was characteristically comprehensive. Despite severe illness delaying his response, he wrote a careful and lengthy reply to these questions, as recorded by Bede.[15] Augustine was to consecrate bishops with the help of two or three other bishops from England or France. There seems to have been the implication (although not an explicit statement) that Augustine should remove his see from Canterbury to London in due course. Canterbury was to have metropolitan authority over twelve sees in southern England and a separate province of York was to be established with a further twelve bishops. This made for a continuing rivalry between Canterbury and York, which flared up through the early Middle Ages. From these provinces, England was to be evangelized and the Church governed and administered, reflecting the divisions of political power in the country, especially in the earliest years between Northumberland and the South.

Much of what Gregory the Great hoped for in terms of dioceses for England did not come about, either quickly or at all. The province of Canterbury only gained its twelve suffragans (sub-divisions) or sees with the establishment of Leicester in 737. An archbishopric was not permanently established in York until 735. Hexham, Lindisfarne and Whithorn were its only suffragan sees, and even this meagre number was reduced with the decline of Northumberland during the Viking invasions. With the establishment of the diocese of Carlisle in 1133, there were seventeen dioceses in England (and four in Wales). They varied greatly in size: Lincoln covered eight counties, including Oxford, a state of affairs that would not change until after the Dissolution of the Monasteries in the reign of Henry VIII.

The administration of a diocese was generally well-established by the time of the Normans. Dioceses were divided into archdeaconries and their archdeacons were often powerful administrators and judges in the ecclesiastical courts. Their offices were well-endowed, as Becket discovered when he was made Archdeacon of Canterbury by Archbishop Theobald in 1154. Rural deaneries were a further administrative sub-division, with the rural dean exercising pastoral care of parish clergy. Cathedral staff consisted of a dean—the leader of the cathedral community—who had responsibility for the worship, mission and fabric of the cathedral; a precentor, who was in charge of music and the choir; a chancellor, who was a theologian and in charge of education; and a treasurer, who was in charge of the finances. Besides these, the cathedral community was made up of canons or prebends (honorary appointments to the cathedral with a stipend or prebend attached) and often a monastic order. Prebends or canons who were absent had a priest-vicar or vicar-choral living in the close (the area surrounding the cathedral, i.e. close by) ministering on their behalf. The chapter comprised the clergy of the cathedral foundation who advised the bishop and oversaw the running of the cathedral. Several cathedrals had monastic foundations attached. The bishop, although principally a pastor, increasingly became an executive or legal officer concerned with implementing canon (church) law, rather than being a pastoral shepherd. He would be engaged in resolving disputes, managing large tracts of lands and walking a tightrope between resisting or complying with papal demands and appointments, and following the crown's wishes and impositions. Often bishops not only supervised dioceses, but also ran great departments of state; and many held important crown appointments.

Not surprisingly, bishops themselves varied greatly, from the saintly scholar to the knight in "ecclesiastical armour", from the placeman of the crown to the appointee of the Pope. Some went on Crusades, taking part in fighting; others preferred the library and cloister. In general, a bishop's rule was marked more by severity and correction than by compassion and care. The military kind of bishop included Henry le Despenser, Bishop of Norwich, who led a "Crusade" to the Low Countries in 1383, purely in English political and economic interests. He was later impeached by Parliament, but he stood by Richard II, fighting in his armies against Scotland and Bolingbroke. By contrast, but no less bold, Robert Grosseteste (1175–1253) was a scientist, theologian, tutor of Roger Bacon, lecturer at Oxford University and Bishop of Lincoln (1235–53). Revered as a scholar saint, he was nonetheless a committed pastor. He was a great scholar and educationalist, as we shall see. He had strong convictions. He called for the expulsion of the Jews when he was Archdeacon of Leicester. He opposed the appointment by the Pope of his (the Pope's) nephew, Frederick Lavagna, to a canonry in Lincoln in 1253 and also the payment of some papal taxes. He opposed the right of the Pope to make appointments in England through a papal system called Provisions (which was eventually overturned in 1351). He wanted an English Church run by the English, even though he was Norman French by descent.

Of the seventeen dioceses in existence in England during the Middle Ages and before Tudor additions, at least eight had monastic orders attached to their cathedrals. That there were relatively few bishops covering the whole of England meant larger dioceses, and at the same time increased the influence of the bishop. The great medieval cathedrals were built between the Norman Conquest and the fifteenth century. One of the last to be completed during this period was York Minster in the late fifteenth century. Most of the cathedrals were built over hundreds of years, with parts being added at different stages. In Canterbury, for example, the great crossing bell tower, standing 235 feet high, was not added until 1433. The result of this construction effort is a collection of buildings unsurpassed anywhere in the world. Their scale and presence—the glass in Canterbury and York, the stonework, apses and arches (including the scissor arch at Wells), the roofs and bosses (with one at Norwich even including Noah, complete with ark and animals), and the wooden screens and stalls, chapter houses, towers and chapels—all display a breath-taking combination of imagination, engineering and craftsmanship. They truly fulfil the view of William of Malmesbury, who wrote, "And certainly the more grandly constructed a church is the more likely to entice the dullest minds to prayer and to bend the most stubborn wills to supplication."[16] Prayer and worship, in said and sung form, has over the centuries been inspired by the majesty of these buildings.

Cathedrals became a locus of national and local significance. Kings and queens were buried in them, not least in Westminster Abbey, which, though not a cathedral, was the sanctuary of the English nation and monarchy. Other cathedrals did have monarchs buried in them, giving them national significance: King John in Worcester, Edward II in Gloucester, Henry IV and the Black Prince in Canterbury, and latterly Richard III in Leicester. Following its construction by Edward III, St George's Chapel in Windsor became both the chapel of the Knights of the Garter and also the burial place of many monarchs, including Henry VIII and Charles I. Queen Eleanor of Castile, the beloved wife of Edward I, was in part buried in Lincoln Cathedral. Married to Edward from the age of thirteen, she bore him sixteen children between the ages of fourteen and forty-four, although many died in infancy. When she herself died near Lincoln in 1290, her viscera (internal organs) less her heart were buried in Lincoln and her embalmed body was moved in stages to London. At every stage, Edward commissioned a stone cross, to be built in her honour; the last of the twelve was at Charing Cross—a memorial to this much-loved queen. She was then buried in Westminster Abbey. If cathedrals were places where bishops had their seat (*cathedra*), from which the church got its name "cathedral", and resting places for the royal family, they were also a focus for the local populace and the diocesan clergy.

The parish church and clergy

Alongside the monastic communities and the dioceses with their powerful bishops were the parish clergy. Parishes or parish churches began in Saxon times, mostly in the tenth century, but some much earlier. There is evidence of the endowment or support of "lesser churches" by soul-scot, a voluntary contribution by Anglo-Saxon people to support a priest; by plough alms, a penny paid within a fortnight of Easter for each plough in the parish; and by church-scot, an offering generally in kind, for example grain or hens, paid by a member of the parish, sometimes on their death, to maintain the priest. All these church levies were well-established by the time of the Conquest and kept parishes and local clergy in business. Such levies are also referred to in the Laws of Ine and Athelstan.

Monasteries and minsters (larger local monastic churches) by and large gave birth to parish churches. The term "parish" comes from the Greek word *parochoi*, meaning an exile and stranger (see 1 Peter 1:1). This usage reflects the early Christian notion, so well expressed in the *Epistle to Diognetus*, that Christians are strangers in the world, gathered into a community or parish.[17] Ironically, the word "parochial" came to mean something supremely settled; yet its true meaning is of a pilgrim or stranger, residing only temporarily in this world. Thus, the original meaning is the exact opposite of the accepted meaning, since parish means a group of pilgrims in a locality, not a community of the immovable!

As self-contained manors proliferated in the tenth and eleventh centuries, presided over first by *thegns* and then by new Norman lords, and as villages developed as new social units, so the demand for local places of worship increased. The only persons capable of providing such buildings were the local landlords, who in turn controlled them and used them as burial places for their families. Likewise, religious guilds developed ways of both burying the dead and remembering the departed, and their influence was also soon found in the parish church. Saxon churches were built frequently during this period and many survive, such as Brixworth in Northamptonshire, dating from the seventh century, which "for age and size . . . has few rivals in Northern Europe"[18], and Earls Barton, where many of my Whitworth ancestors are buried, and which boasts a fine Saxon tower. Bradford-on-Avon in Wiltshire and Bosham in Sussex, as well as many others, are also later Norman churches either in entirety or in part.

The architecture of the parish church followed a similar pattern, though it varied greatly in terms of local materials and craftsmanship. From 1050 to 1150, in what is called the "Great Rebuilding", many parish churches were built or rebuilt along Romanesque lines.[19] This particular church construction followed the pattern or style of the Carolingian architecture on the continent, which in turn followed the design of the earliest Christian basilicas. Gradually, the apse disappeared in favour of a rectangular chancel; a transept was added instead of porticos, giving the distinct cruciform shape with a nave for the body of the church. There were no seats in the nave, and the congregation either stood or knelt. Decorative sculpture proliferated, with a zigzag chancel arch separating nave from chancel and a retained apse being a favourite (see the exquisite Langridge parish church near Lansdown, Bath). Baptismal fonts were set at the west end, while further decorative features and porches took on greater significance than simply providing shelter.

Porches were places for village meetings and where weddings were conducted, as the Wife of Bath memorably recounts in Chaucer's *Canterbury Tales*.[20] Memorials, tombstones and brasses (inlaid brass effigies) soon appeared inside churches, connecting the parish to local families or guilds. Rood screens depicting the Crucifixion, with Mary, Jesus's mother, and the Apostle John, became familiar decorations at the crossing by the chancel. The parish church was the hub of the community's faith, a reassuring presence in a turbulent world and the focus of local skills and generosity. The church also represented a sense of continuity, celebrating within its walls birth, through the "churching of women" (the custom that mothers present themselves following childbirth), infant baptism, marriage at the church door, and death. Life indeed was encapsulated in the stones of the parish churches. Its offices (services) became a familiar accompaniment to the great moments of a person's life.

The parish church was also increasingly the place where local people gained understanding of the Christian faith. Christian festivals divided up the year, giving it structure and rhythm. Prayer and worship were linked to seasonal agricultural cycles. Thus, Rogation Sunday in May was set aside to ask for God's blessing on the harvest, in a pre-eminently rural society. (The term rogation comes from the Latin *rogare*, to ask.) The decorations in the church provided generally illiterate villagers with some knowledge of the faith, especially of the Crucifixion. John Mirk, the Prior of the canons (Augustinian monks) of Lilleshall in Shropshire, wrote in 1400, "I say boldly that there are many thousands of people that could not imagine in their hearts how Christ was crucified if they did not learn it by looking at sculpture and painting."[21] Relics of either English or continental saints—brought back from the continent or Holy Land by travelling clergy, pilgrims or crusading knights— were kept in reliquary caskets in parish, minster or cathedral churches. What started as a celebration of the martyr's faith from the fourth century onwards, and was endorsed by the Second Council of Nicaea in 787, then became a kind of superstitious insurance policy from the king's court downwards. Relics made real the cost of discipleship, even martyrdom, and the demands of the Gospel at the outset. Later they became sources for superstition, and a supposed insurance policy against accident, disease and death.

The main liturgical rite used in worship was the communion service or mass, which took its name from the final words of the Lord's Supper, "*ite missa est*", meaning "go, the dismissal is made". The original Roman rite or service of the mass was plain enough, but was influenced by a more elaborate Gallican rite from the time of Charlemagne. In time, it was this Gallican rite (meaning liturgical service) that was incorporated into the Church and introduced into England by the Norman Bishop of Salisbury, Osmund (c. 1045–99), a contemporary of Anselm, Chancellor of England (c. 1070–8). This rite became known as the Sarum Rite and was common throughout England by 1200. It would hold sway until the introduction of the Prayer Book in 1549 by Cranmer and Henry VIII.

The parish church was to take a central role in village life, providing coherence in a turbulent world. The seasons were marked off by the Church's year: Lent, Easter, saints' days, Advent and Christmas. There were services or offices for each stage of life: birth, marriage and death. Church buildings illustrated something of the narrative of Christ's life, or even the Trinity, through paintings and carvings. The kind of faith, its strengths and weaknesses, that this "system" gave rise to we will discuss further in chapter 8. In many ways the coherence of the Church's structure reflected the coherence and stratification of feudal society. Over the centuries, the parish church would be the laboratory and/or the theatre of Christian faith, through which either contemporary religious movements or the state itself would seek to influence and control the faith and expectations of individual worshippers. The parish church would be both purified and politicized, stripped of suspect accretions and subject to state-controlled preaching. It would have used in it all the range of theatre: drama, tragedy, comedy and musical. The main participants would be the parish clergy, an extraordinarily influential body of people in English national life during that period.

Numbers of parish clergy increased greatly with the explosion of parish churches between 1150 and 1250. This growth happened alongside the increase in population of the same period. The population had grown to around 2.5 million by 1250 and would continue to grow until the famine of 1315–22 and the Black Death. It was during this period that our ancestors came to be known by their occupations: smiths, cooks, masons, millers, shepherds, potters, skinners, tailors, thatchers, tylers, etc. Occupations became surnames, e.g. Paul Shepherd, Martha

Potter or Margaret Thatcher. England began to be covered by a myriad of parish churches.

In London, there were over a hundred parishes for a population of 40,000 and likewise in Norwich and York, which were important regional centres, there were at least twenty-five churches for 10,000 people in each city.[22] In 1291, over eight thousand parishes were registered in a survey entitled *Taxatio Papae Nicholai*, which was a survey for ecclesiastical taxation administered by the papacy. There were some 23,000 priests, with possibly another 10,000 junior clergy. Add to this some 20,000 monks and friars by the mid-thirteenth century, and that meant one religious person per every fifty head of population, including women and children. The level of full-time ministers or religious per head of population has probably never been higher. (There are approximately 12,500 Anglican parishes today and in 2016 there were approximately 7,500 stipendiary clergy in the Church of England for a population more than twenty times greater, although of course there are other denominations.)

Levels of education, literacy and understanding were minimal, considering kings could not read or write until the twelfth century. Bible reading and reflection on the scriptures played a very limited role. Complete Bibles were scarce. The well-to-do had their own prayer books or books of hours copied for personal use in their homes or private chapels and some bishops provided their clergy with books on pastoral care. The practice of Christianity was undoubtedly a community affair: pilgrimages, processions, feast or holy days, mystery plays, and vigils over Christ's tomb were taken up by all. Understanding of the faith was gleaned not so much by reading and listening, but by taking part in events and by doing. Wall paintings and screens provided elements of understanding, and the priest, depending on his level of education, provided instruction and catechism. A parish might have part of the Bible in Latin, some psalters, prayer books or missals (a name for a prayer book) and an antiphonary (which contained music to be used in worship).

Celibacy was a burden to clergy, with the consequence that many had secret wives or concubines. Women and priests would regularly confess their failure before ecclesiastical courts and be punished. If the moral and intellectual life of the Church was patchy, its connection with the community was strong: not least because the parish was the place of local civil administration. Its officers, like church wardens, had civic duties in the community. Its services of baptism, marriage and funerals marked off the course of most people's lives. The Church provided the whole setting for life: its calendar, its feast days, its rhythms, its buildings and its personnel. An irony was to emerge from this: when the Church's ministry was at its least literate, it was arguably closest to the ordinary people, and at its most literate it seemingly became more distant from the bulk of the population. The evidence for this trend will be clearer the other side of the Reformation. At the same time, learning in England was going through a revolution: moving from the monastery to the grammar school, and from the private house of the wealthy to newly founded universities.

The universities of Oxford and Cambridge

Universities were founded in the twelfth and thirteenth centuries. There were no schools of higher learning before the end of the eleventh century and the existence of the university at Oxford cannot be established before 1214.[23] There is evidence of a university in Bologna in north Italy in 1189, and in 1194 some formal recognition was given by the papacy to schools in Paris, initially begun as cathedral schools but which soon developed into a university, which Becket attended in 1140. Paris University was already a thriving concern, and by 1215 had its first statutes. By 1378, there were sixteen more *Studia Generalia* scattered across Europe in Italy, Germany and Spain, and in England at Oxford and Cambridge. The constitution of each of these various universities was dictated by local customs and arrangements: in Bologna the students elected the rector, and in Paris the rector was appointed. A form of examination or testing evolved which licensed a student to teach either in his own university or in another *studia*. Broadly speaking the courses were the *Trivium*—grammar, logic and rhetoric—and the *Quadrivium*, which consisted of arithmetic, geometry, music and astronomy. These courses, with their strong classical influence, imitated the schools of grammar and rhetoric of the ancient world, and were based on the works of Boethius and Cassiodorus, philosophers and teachers of late antiquity. Once mastered, these subjects in the *Trivium* and *Quadrivium* were the gateway to the study of philosophy and theology, the latter moderated or even "intellectually policed" by the papacy.

Oxford is credited as being one of the oldest universities in Europe. Like many universities, it had informal beginnings, with teachers gravitating to the city as one of several centres of education. There were other schools at York, Exeter, Lincoln and Hereford, but Oxford flourished. The reason for national interest in Oxford was pure serendipity. In 1209, a student murdered a woman, probably his mistress, and fled, whereupon local townspeople, at odds with the "gown" party in the city, hung two of the students. At this point, the remaining teachers and students left, and the city realized the loss to its economy. King John was petitioned, but he was preoccupied with greater problems, since the country then lay under an interdict.

The papal legate was petitioned and, on 20 June 1214, Nicholas de Romanis, Cardinal Bishop of Tusculm, gave a judgement in which student rents were established for twenty years; the city was fined fifty-two shillings a year, to be paid for twenty years to support poor students; food was to be available to students at a fair price; and lastly, students were to be given immunity from lay jurisdiction and tried in church courts and later the courts of the Chancellor's Court. This charter remains in Oxford University's archive, and by it the university was founded. In 1215, the year of Magna Carta, a scholar's chancellor was appointed, first by the Bishop of Lincoln, within whose diocese Oxford was situated, and thereafter elected by the Congregation, the senior governing body of the university. The chancellor settled disputes and issues between town and gown, had responsibility for the welfare of the students, tried cases in his court, and moderated the academic life of the university. The Congregation that elected him became the governing body of the university. It had its own officers, called proctors; enrolled teaching masters, who granted degrees; moderated the syllabuses of the five faculties of arts, theology, civil and canon law, and medicine; admitted colleges; and generally oversaw the conduct of the university. Although it is hard to establish the size of the student body or the number of clerks, it is generally thought that there were about 1,500 by the time of the Black Death, when the numbers fell back to a thousand during most of the fifteenth century. Early colleges were Merton College (1274), University College (1280), Balliol (1282), Exeter (c. 1314) and New College (1379). Founded on a monastic pattern, they had a principal (like an abbot), a chapel, a hall for dining, an enclosed quad, a porter's lodge (as described in Benedict's Rule), a teaching and student body, and accommodation inside the college or in lodgings in the town.

In what could have been no more than a small fenland town, the sister university to Oxford was founded at Cambridge. It may have been that a riot in Oxford, or at least a general disturbance in 1209, which closed the university, was the signal to begin another institution in a more peaceable place. They were unstable times: King John was still under a papal interdict banning all services in the realm, and the antagonism towards the King is well known. Roger Wendover, a monk in St Albans, recalls that some of the Oxford masters moved to Cambridge in 1209 following these disturbances. Locating themselves around the already existing church of St Mary the Great, they began to teach students. At the time, there was no Bishop of Ely, as its bishop Eustace was in exile.[24] Early masters at Cambridge were John Grim and John Blunt, both of whom may have had previous associations with Ely and already knew Cambridge. Henry III would personally support the university's inception. Soon, houses of Friars were founded in Cambridge by the Franciscans and Dominicans: the two great teaching orders, whose powerful imprint was now present all over Europe, from Italy and Spain to England. In 1284, Peterhouse was founded and was followed by fifteen other colleges between 1284 and 1596. The oldest colleges after Peterhouse are Clare (1326), Pembroke (1347), Conville and Caius (1348) and Trinity Hall (1350). A manuscript of the earliest constitution of Cambridge University was found in the Angelica Library in Rome and can be dated to 1250 in the reign of Henry III. It calls for the election of a chancellor by the masters, the regulation of dress, a court to hear disputes, and the appointment of bedells to order the schools, serve writs and announce times of lectures. In 1570, Elizabeth I revised these statutes, giving more authority to heads of houses and less to regent masters. The university was by then well-established and protected for its foreseeable future.

These medieval institutions of monastery and later convent friary, diocese, parish church and university, along with their functionaries, gave context to life in the Middle Ages alongside the king's officers, the courts and the feudal land ownership. Up until the Dissolution of the Monasteries and the coming of the Industrial Revolution, these institutions together shaped most of life. The Dissolution of the Monasteries would see the strengthening of a greater landowning and mercantile class. But in the fourteenth century there were still only sixty great baronial families owning at least a third of the land. Much was concentrated in the hands of a few. Parish life, with, for instance, the administration of the Poor Law from Elizabeth I's time, and new grammar schools from the time of Edward VI (1547), would supplant the monasteries and become the great units of Tudor society. The universities would grow powerfully. But for the moment they gave, between them, a kind of safe and sustaining space among the fierce currents of disease, hunger, war, labour and taxation which constantly faced the great bulk of the population. The nature of intellectual life, the range of ideas circulating, the content of this religious life and its perspective are what we must consider.

C H A P T E R 8

Theology and the Universities

Ideas are the stuff of human progress, whether they are scientific, spiritual, medical, mathematical or philosophical. Like seeds or spores in the wind, they have a way of traversing human boundaries and borders, and this was certainly the case in the Middle Ages when communication took time. When it comes to concepts, borders are in the end porous. This was true in the thirteenth century when ideas travelled across the borders of Italy, France and England (although nation states did not exist as they do today). Many of these ideas were to come from the universities that were founded from the twelfth century onwards. It was in these universities of Europe—Bologna, Paris, Salamanca, Oxford, Cambridge, Heidelberg and later Wittenberg in Saxony—that many ground-breaking ideas or revolutionary thoughts germinated. What was a steady flow of ideas in the eleventh to fourteenth centuries would become a torrent from the sixteenth century onwards. New universities were founded. Printing transmitted knowledge across cultures and languages in a new and powerful way from the early sixteenth century onwards.

Looking back over the centuries, the development of thought or ideas in Europe has various discernible phases. The origin of Western thought in science, mathematics and philosophy lies with the Greeks. Pythagoras from Samos (c. 570–495 BC), Euclid of Alexandria (died c. 285 BC) and Archimedes from Syracuse in Sicily (died c. 212 BC) provided the foundation for mathematics and astronomy. What they did for physics, Plato and Aristotle would do for philosophy and metaphysics. Plato (428–347 BC), the pupil of Socrates, founded the Academy in Athens in c. 387 BC, and his pupil, Aristotle, studied and taught there from c. 367–46 BC. Those forty years in which Plato and Aristotle learnt and taught in the Academy in the fourth century BC were to become seminal for the development of Western thought thereafter. A thousand years later, these two thinkers still provided the philosophic prism through which much of Christian theology would be viewed, and the basis, with the aforementioned mathematicians, for the development of what became an arts degree in the universities. These Greek thinkers laid the foundations of Western thought and science.

The Romans took over from the Greeks, but their contribution was mostly in literature. Their skills were demonstrated much more in the rolling out, administratively and militarily, of a way of life or culture across the Empire than in making further philosophical or scientific advances. Their Empire was to come to an end in the West in AD 476, but it would survive in Byzantium for a further millennium. At the end of the first century AD, the Church's Patristic period began, in which the Church Fathers of both East and West explained, defended and proclaimed the Christian faith against persecuting Roman authorities and contended with numerous heresies, not least Gnosticism to Arianism. The Church Father who was to have the greatest influence on later centuries of Christian thought and teaching was Augustine, himself deeply influenced by Plato. The period following the Church Fathers, which began in about AD 451, can justifiably be called the Dark Ages, especially in the West. During this period, it was the monastic movement, first in Egypt and Palestine and then in Italy, Gaul and Ireland, that kept the flame of Christian faith alive. And by the seventh century, Christianity was taking root in the Anglo-Saxon kingdoms in England.

Following the Patristic Age, the Dark Ages and the monastic missionary movement of Ireland, Gaul and Italy, the next phase of the Christian tradition was the Carolingian Age in Europe. This period, which gave new energy to Christian intellectual life, arose in the Frankish kingdom in central Europe under the Emperor Charlemagne and was encouraged by his mentor Alcuin, from York, both of whom directed fresh educational reforms. Following Alcuin, John Scottus Eriugena (800–77) led the Palace School at Aachen, the capital of Charlemagne's administration. John was an idiosyncratic Irish teacher with great linguistic ability and strong Neo-Platonist leanings. Today he would be considered as having a new age or pantheist view of nature, investing it with almost divine significance. His main work, *Periphyseon*, drew heavily on Greek sources, as he sought a synthesis between Greek philosophic thinking and Christian doctrine.[1] His work was widely condemned by later church leaders at the Council of Sens in 1224, notably by Pope Honorius III, the successor of Innocent III, who was known as the hammer of the Cathars. But even if wayward, John kept learning alive during a time of struggle against the Viking invasions of France.

By the late eleventh century, new teaching schools were started which were successors of the cathedral schools in Rheims and Chartres and the great teaching monasteries of Bec and Cluny: first in Bologna, then Paris, and then Oxford. The curriculum for the best part of four centuries revolved around an arts course, based on classical works of philosophy, rhetoric and mathematics; a theology course based on the Bible, and then the *Sentences* of Peter Lombard; two law courses on civil and ecclesiastical law; and finally, a course on medicine. The classical and the scriptural, the legal and the medical, the philosophical and theological would dominate for centuries to come, at least until the Copernican revolution (early sixteenth century).

Plato and Aristotle

The foundations of Western thought, and the reference grid through which Christian theology was frequently understood, were, in the Middle Ages, the works of Plato and Aristotle. When the great Renaissance artist Raphael was asked to decorate the library of Pope Julius II (1503–13) he included a fresco entitled *The School of Athens*. It is a picture heavily influenced by later humanist learning and the Renaissance. But it also demonstrates the profound effect that Plato and Aristotle were to have on the understanding of both the Church Fathers and the university schoolmen of the twelfth to fourteenth centuries. In the fresco, Plato is holding *Timaeus*, the work that has perhaps been most influential for theology, and is pointing *upwards* towards the heavens, while Aristotle holds his book *Ethics*, looks at Plato's raised hand, and in contrast gestures *outwards* to that which is around him. It is a visual illustration of the main driver in each man's philosophy.[2] Plato draws conclusions from intuitive reflective thought about the nature of eternal ideals, while Aristotle looks around him to prove truth and reality from empirical study. The two look at each other in an attitude of serious argument or dialogue. Thus, Raphael makes the point that Plato is more interested in understanding the world through contemplation of abstract principles of the higher or divine life, whereas Aristotle understands the world by observation of what is around him, setting out to interpret its significance.

To understand Plato's work, we must grasp the way in which he presents his ideas, which are usually in the form of a dialogue. Often the dialogue is between a character and Plato's erstwhile master Socrates, who wrote nothing himself and died by being forced to drink hemlock in 399 BC, charged with corrupting the youth of Athens. Socrates invented the Socratic method, which aimed to arrive at understanding of a matter through questioning and dialogue. This was to be highly influential in the schools (i.e. the new universities) where theology was thereafter taught according to this method, although the fluid conversation of a Platonic dialogue hardened into a sclerotic question and answer framework called a disputation. Few philosophers were more passionate in the beliefs they held than Plato, but for all that he never simply foisted his ideas directly on the reader or listener; he believed that people must arrive at their own conclusions having worked them out for themselves, if they are to learn properly. Socrates saw himself as a midwife through whom people "have discovered within themselves many fine things, and brought them to birth".[3] This was the merit of the Platonic dialogue. It was essentially a liberal method of education and did not sit well with the authoritarian methods of the Middle Ages, where an ever-vigilant papacy sought to enforce doctrines that ensured its position of supremacy.

Plato's ideas were highly influential for the Church Fathers, especially Augustine, Origen and the Cappadocian Fathers, above all Gregory Nyssen. In the first instance, Plato rejected the plethora of gods that was part of the background belief of his culture. He rejected the indifferent, hostile or human-style gods who continually interfered in human affairs and were in constant need of placating.[4] Instead, he held to a single divine being who was responsible for all that is good. Evil was for Plato, as for Augustine, the absence of good. God himself was entirely good, as was his creation. But any deficiency in creation for Plato was to be accounted for by the fact that God did not create *ex nihilo* (out of nothing) but used materials already available, which were in part faulty.

The ancient world and its teachers were consistently preoccupied with the origin of evil. For Plato, as for the Church Fathers, evil was not an equal and opposite force at work in the world, but followed a rejection of the good and the fact that God, or the One as Plato calls him, used defective material at the outset. The Bible illustrates this rejection of God and the resulting occurrence of evil in the Fall of Adam and Eve in Genesis 3, but in Plato's thought the occasion for evil occurs wherever good or virtue is rejected. Furthermore, all *entities* that were created had an ideal and universal *Form* as their pattern, from which they took their existence. The result of this doctrine is that humans and other beings are in a process of *becoming what they were created to be*. This process involves the ascent of the human soul through conquest of the body and its inherent downward drag, to greater contemplative oneness with God.

The soul for Plato was the essence of a human being. Souls were attributed to all creatures, for example animals, and even planets. Hence, when Socrates is dying, he jokingly says that his friends will be burying only his body, as his true self or soul will continue. Sometimes the soul is the seat of reason for Plato, while at other times it is the motivator of action, the master of the body, or the prisoner waiting to be released. As Plato describes it in the *Republic*, the soul may be driven by desire, reason or ideals.

Alongside Plato's views on God, creation, the soul, the Forms, and good and evil, he has influential ideas about knowledge and the good life. For Plato, knowledge is best attained by abstract thought. But it can be illustrated by mathematics, in particular through geometry, as expressed by Pythagoras. This combination of abstract thought validated by mathematics may lead us close to truth. Our life will therefore be good and fulfilling in as much as we attain the truth about reality. Ethics becomes a quest to live a good and virtuous life. Fulfilment will not come through unrestrained satisfaction of our own desires, especially if they come from the body. Rather it will come from living out a life of virtue, just as Socrates gave himself to philosophy and its consequences. Fulfilment is not produced by the things you possess, or the success you have attained, but by a life put to *good* use. Virtues are called the *Laws*, which dictate how to make good. "So the value for us of health, wealth, and the like depends on our possession of virtues like wisdom, courage and justice."[5]

We can see why Plato was so influential among the early Church Fathers. Sometimes Platonism was overplayed in theology, as in the case of the erring and erratic Origen, leading to the rejection of his exaggerated Platonic theology, which included the reconciliation of all things at the end, even the devil. But for Augustine, who would become the doyen of Western medieval theology, Platonism was a handmaid to theology. In Plato could be found a spur to contemplation, and an explanation of creation, with God as the craftsman of earthly substance. Even mathematics could be put to theological use. And Plato expressed the struggle of soul and body which the Apostle Paul appeared to endorse in passages in Romans 6–8. As Lane Fox says, "the Platonists stand out from all other pagan philosophers because they have grasped two crucial truths: there is one supreme God and there is a higher spiritual world."[6] Augustine's works were to be among the most widely followed in the monasteries and universities of Europe and England, whether by Anselm in Bec and then in Canterbury, or by Bonaventure in Paris and Duns Scotus in Oxford (all of whom will be discussed). Plato's influence on Augustine is always apparent. Plato was like a concealed Greek soldier inside the Christian Trojan horse.

While Plato was especially channelled through Augustine to the teachers and scholars of the Middle Ages, Aristotle's influence came by another route, as we shall see. Of the two, Aristotle would probably be the most influential in the Middle Ages, not least because of his full-scale adoption by Thomas Aquinas. As we have seen, although Aristotle was Plato's pupil and a member of the Academy in Athens, his philosophy followed a very different method.

Aristotle lived from 384–22 BC. He came from a wealthy family and was a lucid and persuasive speaker. After his first period of learning and teaching in Athens from 367–47 BC, he prepared Alexander the Great for what became a life of conquest and rule. Aristotle's second period of teaching in Athens was from 335–23 BC, after which he died in Chalcis, to the north, in 322 BC. His philosophical writings are extensive in range and impersonal in tone. There are over fifty volumes covering what we call the biological sciences: zoology (including the classification of animals and fish), physics, conceptual categories, logic, metaphysics, ethics and politics. Of all his writings barely a fifth have survived. He does not write in the form of a dialogue as Plato did, but in concise and terse prose. His method could not be more different from Plato's. For Aristotle, the primary tool for discovering reality is perception, which is filtered by reason. Observation of life and the environment is therefore the source of knowledge, rather than metaphysical contemplation as with Plato.[7] Perception of something leads to memory, and memory leads to experience, and experience leads to true knowledge of what exists in the universe. Through such a process we come to understand. Particular species are thus understood on their own terms, rather than through the notion of a universal form, as Plato taught, to which particular entities are being conformed.

Beyond the new method of study and classification that Aristotle brought to science, which we would call empirical, his main ideas, which were to become highly influential in theology of the Middle Ages, were his writings on logic and knowledge, his teaching about the particularity of forms, his distinction between potentiality and actuality, his theory of causation and change, and his ethics. Broadly speaking, and for ease of understanding, his works can be divided into his metaphysical works, his logical works, his scientific or biological works, and his ethical or political works. We can only skim the surface here.

In the age when universities began, theory of knowledge and the classification of knowledge was a matter of primary interest. One of the questions, which was to provoke considerable debate, was whether theology could be truly called a science or a discipline, dependent as it was on the narrative theology and revelation found in the Bible, rather than on evidence drawn from the world and the working of human reason. This issue was acutely raised by the developing universities moving from a course based on the *sacra pagina* (the sacred page or scripture, which was and had been the foundation of theology) to one which was *scientia divina*, meaning divine science or theology. In other words, could theology ever be regarded as a science in the Aristotelian sense of gathering evidence and knowledge to prove God's existence and purpose? Whether theology could be admitted as a scientific discipline depended on whether reason and logic had a function in determining the existence and activity of God. Aristotle's works on *Logic*, *Categories*, and *Prior* and *Posterior Analytics* provided ways of formalizing logic and reason. Aristotle laid down the principle that if we are to understand something, we must understand both its cause and its purpose. We must distinguish its *substance* (its inner being or essence) from its *accidents* (its secondary expressions), or its "being" from its secondary properties. Furthermore, Aristotle affirmed that there were no *universal* forms as such, as Plato had suggested, but only *particular* things, which may have universally understood qualities. In other words, there was no such thing as a universal form of man that existed as such, although the identical form of humanity existed in various individual men. Similarly, the health in a healthy person could be understood as a universal. Such axioms, once in the public sphere, were inevitably used to describe the existence, being, purpose and activity of God and humankind, and no more so than by the Dominican Thomas Aquinas.

Other areas of Aristotelian thought which were to have influence during this period were the distinction between actual and potential, his understanding of the relationship of the soul to human beings, and his ethics setting out the means to flourishing and happiness. The relationship of potential to actual is part of Aristotle's theory of change in which God is seen as the prime mover for all of creation. For Aristotle, actuality is the result of potentiality. If a person has the potential to be a great sprinter, the actuality in the form of an Olympic gold is its realization. This was given a twist in the theology of the Franciscan Duns Scotus (1266–1308) and others who distinguished the *potentia absoluta* of God from his *potentia ordinate*, in which God restricts his absolute power or potentiality by the covenants he has freely entered into, thereby confining the *actuality* of his power in reality. When it comes to the soul, Aristotle differs from Plato. Whereas Plato posited a pre-existent soul cleaving to a human body, for Aristotle the soul is the form of a person, thereby coming into being only with the individual, rather than pre-existing.

Aquinas's legacy got into difficulties with the church authorities for wholeheartedly adopting this Aristotelian idea, positing a single unified essence of the human rather than the traditional tripartite division into mind, spirit and soul. Robert Kilwardby, the Archbishop of Canterbury (1272–8) who had previously taught in Paris and had lectured on Aristotle, condemned Aquinas in 1277 for his "philosophical theory of the unicity of substantial form in human beings".[8] It was a condemnation that was renewed by the Franciscan John Pecham (c.

1225–92), who succeeded Kilwardby as archbishop. The nature of man was the topic of a continuing debate. Finally, Aristotle's *Ethics* (especially his *Nicomachean Ethics*) were a powerful influence on Aquinas, who adopted Aristotle's ethical views pretty much in their entirety. Ethics as a Greek term meant "matters to do with character". The ethics commended by Aristotle are focussed on the concept of virtue *(arete)* and the result of acting virtuously is human "flourishing" *(eudaimonia)* rather than, as it is often translated, "happiness". Again, Aquinas adds to the specifically Christian and Pauline (after St Paul) virtues of faith, hope and love the Greek "cardinal" virtues that may be acquired by the operation of the will, though for the Christian they might also require the infusion of grace. They are prudence, temperance, fortitude and justice. The notion of justice occupies the greatest amount of space in Aquinas's Second Part of Part II of the *Summa Theologiae*. Thus, Aristotle serves as the foundation of much of Aquinas's ethical work, as he was the foundation of the scientific work done in thirteenth-century Oxford and Paris.

Knowledge of Plato in medieval times was mediated by the Church Fathers, especially by Augustine, the most Platonic of all the Western Church Fathers, as well as through translated works of Plato held in monasteries in the West. By contrast, the first reception of most of Aristotle came through translations of his works made by Muslim Arab scholars, notably Averroes. Averroes, or Ibn Rushd (1126–98), was an extraordinary Arab polymath from Andalusia in Spain, teaching in Cordoba, Seville and Morocco. It was his commentaries on Plato and Aristotle that revived classical studies of these philosophers in Western Europe. Translations of his works into Latin were made in the kingdom of Sicily and in Naples, after it was conquered by the Normans of Sicily, with the rise to power of Roger II of Sicily from 1112. Roger, both a soldier and scholar, and the builder of the remarkable *Cappella Palatina* with its astonishing Byzantine mosaics, encouraged the dissemination of Averroes's work through the university in Naples, which Aquinas attended as a student in 1242/3, when he was aged nineteen. Later, in 1270, Thomas would condemn some of Averroes's interpretations of Aristotle, but Averroes had the merit of making him aware of the great philosopher. Aristotle and his interpreters were to set the cat among theological pigeons in the late thirteenth century. Before investigating the course of that dispute, we must discuss the passing of one way of doing theology, and the rise of another.

Anselm and Peter Lombard

In many ways, Anselm was the last of the great monastic teachers, the end of a tradition that went back to the early Church Fathers, including Basil of Caesarea, Chrysostom and Augustine of Hippo. Like all of these, Anselm would go on to be a bishop, indeed Archbishop of Canterbury, but as we have seen, he was more a theologian and a monk than an administrator of a great province with all the political repercussions that were associated with such an office in the medieval world.

The high point of Anselm's theological output, mainly the result of extended meditation before he became Abbot of Bec, appeared in 1075–8 with the *Monologion* and the *Proslogion*. His next great work, *Cur Deus Homo*, would arrive some twenty years later when he was Archbishop of Canterbury (1095–8).[9] The method by which Anselm arrived at his theological conclusions did not conform to that of the secular schools or the universities of the future. They delighted in disputation, arranging theological confrontations both to sharpen the wits of the student body and enable them to think on their feet, as well as to reconcile divergent tenets of theology. Anselm, on the other hand, came to his conclusions through study and prayerful contemplation and humiliation of the self. This was much more the way of the great Augustine of Hippo. Anselm did not employ the structure of *pro* and *contra* (i.e. on the one hand and on the other hand), the dialectic so beloved of the schools. Nor did he quote authorities in his works as did his predecessor at Bec, Lanfranc. His conclusions were rather the result of prayerful reflection on works he had read, ingested, digested and then re-expressed, without making reference to chapter and verse of the authority understood. Anselm did sometimes use dialogue rather in the manner of Plato, though he was no Platonist. But Anselm, like Plato, valued the discipline of introspection, of faith seeking understanding through prayer and inner intellectual searching, his great principle of *fides quaerens intellectum*, meaning that only through faith can we truly understand.

This process of reflection or meditation, based on years of biblical study and reading of the Church Fathers, is a part of worship, and leads to a sense of revelation, which pervades his works *Monologion* and *Proslogion*. Indeed, the *Proslogion* was the result of the inspiration received in Matins.

The *Monologion* is closely dependent on Augustine's *De Trinitate* (*On the Trinity*). The *Proslogion* is more concerned with the being or existence of God and contains the famous ontological argument for the existence of God. The *Monologion* is concerned with the process of creation by the Creator or Supreme

Being, who is changeless. It explores the nature of the Trinity, the relationship of Word and Spirit to the Father or, as Anselm puts it, to the Supreme Being.[10] The meditation moves on to a description of humans as having immortal souls capable of either supreme joy or misery. The soul must believe in the Supreme Being in such a way as to reach out for it. In many ways, the *Monologion* is surprisingly Deist in tone, with little of the biblical warmth of the Fatherhood of God, the redemptive love of the saviour or the experiential love of the Spirit. It is a meditation on the Trinity in distinctly rational terms. But as Southern says, "Faith and reason each add something to each other. Faith adds the glory of self-abandonment to the statements of reason; reason adds the glory of systematic understanding to the statements of faith."[11]

The *Proslogion* is also a meditation, written under the impulse of a philosophical impetus gained in worship as Eadmer described, and as Anselm confided to him. In it he sets out his famous ontological argument. He sought to show that the attributes given to God in the *Monologion* of goodness, justice, truth etc must necessarily cohere in a single being and this being cannot be thought of as non-existent. At this point, Anselm introduces a phrase first used by Seneca in answer to the question "what is God?", stating that God is "something than which nothing greater can be thought".[12] This is the heart of Anselm's argument for the existence of God, which came to be called the ontological argument. The argument recalls the much later arguments of the philosopher Descartes. In the final analysis, our own internal conception of God corresponds to a reality that exists because we think its existence; just as Descartes will later say "*cogito ergo sum*", "I think therefore I exist", to prove our own existence. In this sense it is an essentially Platonic argument using internal thought rather than external proofs as the ground for believing in God. It was Anselm's greatest insight, ranking him as a philosopher with an enduring place in the chain of Western thought. It was not his last work. *Cur Deus Homo* was to follow, answering the question as to why God became human in Christ. But the *Proslogion* was probably his defining work.

Cur Deus Homo was written in the form of a dialogue between Anselm and Boso, a later Abbot of Bec. It explores the central question as to why Christ became man. Written between 1095 and 1098, it was composed in response to questions from the Jews about the incarnation and the honour and dignity of God, who would mix his divinity with human flesh. At a time when Christian art was more explicit about the sufferings and indignity of Christ's death, it was necessary to explain his "honour" and divinity whilst suffering, especially when the notion of honour in feudalism was becoming more prominent. Anselm sets out in *Cur Deus Homo* to show the fittingness of God's incarnation in Christ. Like Athanasius,

Bishop of Alexandria, defending Christ's divinity in his *De Incarnatione*, Anselm set out to show why it was necessary for Christ to suffer voluntarily for human redemption. Only God, Anselm argues, can make an offering which transcends the whole unpaid debt of past offences. But God should not have to make it, because it is man's debt. Since only man ought to, and only God can, make this offering, it must be made by the one who is both man and God. Therefore, only a God-Man can achieve the redemption required for the whole of creation. This alone, for Anselm, was a harmonious and beautiful solution, which also reflected the feudal categories of vassal and lord in which Anselm was steeped. It was an argument that would lie at the basis of future atonement theories concerning the death of Jesus. It supplanted the view that the atonement was essentially a payment to the devil. Anselm thought that notion an affront to the honour of God. It was a diminution of divine majesty that any payment should be made to the chief usurper, the devil. *Cur Deus Homo* established Anselm's standing as a theologian of the first rank, in the same way as the *Proslogion* argument established him as a philosopher. But he was to be largely overlooked. The schools largely disregarded him, although not Bonaventure (1221–74) nor Albert the Great (c. 1193–1280) who both taught in Paris. But scholastic theological teachers preferred a man made in their own image, Peter Lombard.

Like Anselm, Peter Lombard (c. 1095–1160) came from Italy. He was from Piedmont and received his early training in Novara and Lucca. He came from a poor family and was sponsored by Odo, Bishop of Lucca, and was sent to further his studies at Rheims and Paris. In France, he was exposed to the *Glossa ordinaria* created by Anselm of Laon (not of course Archbishop Anselm of Bec, but one of his pupils) which consisted in excerpts from the Fathers and medieval authorities. It was the most advanced biblical tool of its time and continued to be used until the eighteenth century. In 1136, Peter moved to Paris, attracted by the Parisian masters and the teaching of Peter Abelard (1079–1142) and Hugh of St Victor (c. 1097–1141). Hugh of St Victor had written an influential manual of theology entitled *De sacramentis christianae fidei* (*On the Sacraments of the Christian faith*). Abelard was a controversial teacher who wrote *Sic et Non* (*Yes and No*), a codification of a set of rules for the reconciliation of conflicting sentences of the Fathers. So, for instance, if Augustine contradicted Jerome, how should the two be reconciled? This reconciliation lay at the heart of *Sic et Non*. Abelard, known for his passionate love affair with Heloise, had been castrated, as we noted earlier, on the orders of Heloise's guardian, Master Fulbert. He was a celebrity in Paris with his controversial views, his love of disputation, and the aura of one who kicks against religious and moral traces of the day, an aura which is so appealing to students.

By 1140, Lombard had become affiliated to the Cathedral School at Notre Dame. He was to remain there for twenty years until his death. His *Book of Sentences* was the result of his long years of teaching at the School of Notre Dame. By 1200, the various schools were consolidated into Paris University and the *Sentences*, after Lombard's death, became a standard text for theological study at the university. It would quickly migrate to Oxford, and then Cambridge. It would become central to university study for 300 years, until the Reformation. The full title of the book is *The Sentences Divided into Four Books*. Lombard follows a scheme suggested by Augustine in his *De doctrina christiana* (*On Christian Doctrine*) of dividing everything into the category of either a *thing* or a *sign*. Each had a corresponding purpose: a thing (God) was to be enjoyed and a sign (creation) was to be used. In effect, the only *thing* or uncreated being is God, the Trinity, and the *signs* are everything that proceeds from him in creation, redemption and the Church. The former is to be enjoyed; the latter has an ordained function or use. *Book I* is therefore about God; *Book II* is about Creation; *Book III* is about Christ, who combines the *enjoyment* pertaining to the godhead and the *use* pertaining to humankind; *Book IV* concludes with the sacraments. Each of the four books falls into chapters: 210 in the first, 269 in the second, 164 in the third and 290 in the fourth book. There are therefore 1,100 pages in all, giving a collection of quotations from the Church Fathers on the subject concerned. It made a formidable book and, in a pre-printing age, a huge undertaking to replicate. The text was therefore very expensive and rare, leading to further abbreviations of, or commentaries on, the original work. Lombard provided a table of contents, and the colour red was used to highlight headings. These were then called *rubrics* from the Latin word for "red". But despite these novel additions, more digestible editions of the *Sentences* were needed, and some emerged which altered some of Lombard's original conclusions. In fact, there was a veritable academic industry in producing variations of the *Sentences*. It served as a Trojan horse for smuggling all kinds of ideas into university life.

From the twelfth to the fifteenth century, the *Sentences* spawned a new industry of producing many abridged editions and glosses or *ordinationes*, as they came to be called. The greatest names in theological education and biblical studies were to try their hand at commenting on the *Sentences*, from Bonaventure to Duns Scotus and from Aquinas to Wyclif (and later even Luther). All wrote their own glosses, summaries or equivalent *Sentences*. The first began with the *Figlia Magistri* (*Daughter of the Master*) in 1232, an anonymous work which in turn used a summary of the *Sentences* prepared by William of Auxerre. One copy surfaced in the library of a George Dunn of Maidenhead, from whom it was purchased by the John Rylands University Library in Manchester. This work was an interlinear text consisting of the *Sentences* in large characters with space for comments between the lines and in the margins. New headings were given to the *Sentences*, reflecting the four rivers that water the earth (Genesis 2:10–14) and consisting of The Creator, Creation, Re-creation and Retribution. Re-creation was further sub-divided into the person of Christ and the sacraments of the Church. This was a further elucidation of a systematic theology to be used in the schools and elsewhere.

Glosses were a frequent occurrence in medieval teaching. Even Peter Lombard, after originally publishing his *Sentences* in 1156/7, was adding glosses from his subsequent lectures in 1157/8. Thus it was a dynamic text, with no copyright attached to confine it to a single form. Eventually the glosses migrated into a separate text. In the end the text itself was displaced in the lecture room by its own margins, separately composed and separately used from the original text of which it was a gloss. Elaborate glosses resulted in works like the *Pseudo-Poitiers Gloss*. In the prologue to this work, we are told the *Sentences* were written for the lazy, the faint-hearted and blasphemers. The Master's (i.e. Lombard's) intention was to call back the faint-hearted, to spur on the lazy, and to refute the blasphemers. The Scriptures and the Church Fathers, grouped under the respective headings being discussed, are the chief sources Lombard uses to achieve this aim in the *Sentences*.

By the thirteenth century, the *Sentences* became a staple for teaching in the newly emerging universities. In Paris, the future Archbishop of Canterbury, Stephen Langton, who drafted the Magna Carta, lectured on the *Sentences* from 1180–1206. His glosses on the *Sentences* were separately copied, and often discussed theological difficulties. It was also Langton who first established a standard division of chapters in the text of scripture, giving a new rigour to the study of the Bible. Langton was followed in Paris by Alexander of Hales (1184–1245), another Englishman from Hales in Shropshire, who lectured from 1220–45 for the first time almost exclusively on the *Sentences*, making it the standard theological textbook, and not solely on the text of scripture. He was regarded more than any other as the yardstick for theological studies, perhaps more so than Albert the Great (Thomas Aquinas's great teacher), Bonaventure, or Aquinas himself. Hales further systematized the *Sentences* by dividing them into *distinctions*, which grouped existing chapters into new sections with new headings. This illustrates the scholars' love of classification, another effect of Aristotle, the great classifier of all that was around him.

This movement from scripture to the *Sentences* marked the move from *sacra pagina* (scripture) to *scientia divina* (theology), which occurred in the thirteenth century. A further boost to this process was given when the Fourth Lateran Council of 1215 named Lombard's *Sentences* as teaching orthodox Trinitarian doctrine. In Oxford, this move was to be vigorously protested by Robert Grosseteste, the Bishop of Lincoln, whose influence will be discussed shortly. But both universities in the end endorsed the teaching of the *Sentences*.

Later in the thirteenth century, the *Sentences* were to be commented on by the Seraphic Doctor, Bonaventure (1217–74), the leader of the Franciscan teachers (the Grey Friars) in Paris, and by Aquinas (c. 1224–74), the leader of the Dominicans (the Black Friars). Bonaventure, more personal in tone in his glosses than his predecessors, was not above criticizing Lombard, especially for his equating the Holy Spirit entirely with charity or love. Bonaventure used allusion and allegory in his style, taking the four rivers metaphor (as above) and further elaborating it by pointing out that a river is of perennial duration, is broad, is circular (see Ecclesiastes 1:7) and is purifying. He thought the *Sentences* could be understood in these categories. Furthermore, Bonaventure believed that by identifying principles in the narrative of scripture, it was possible better to understand creation and hence science. Like a true Franciscan he would hold together insights from the created order and scripture and weave them into a unified whole. If Bonaventure was mellifluous and metaphorical in his interpretation of the *Sentences*, Aquinas, nicknamed "the Angelic Doctor", was highly didactic and methodical. He taught on the *Sentences* from 1254–6. Aquinas's aim, as would be more fully shown in his *Summa Theologiae*, was to place the *Sentences* in an overarching system of knowledge, but at the same time to distinguish theology from philosophy. His teaching on the *Sentences* would not last long, because he was seeking this wider synthesis of philosophy and theology, bringing together Aristotle and scripture, which would make up his *Summa*.

The Dominican mentioned above, Robert Kilwardby (1215–79), who was to become Archbishop of Canterbury (1272–8), studied in Paris and was a master in Oxford from 1256. He was a further example of the influence of Paris on Oxford and on the English Church. He was an indexer and tabulator *par excellence*. He composed *intentiones*, *conclusiones* and *capitula* and created alphabetical indices of these various summaries, having meticulously trawled through the Church Fathers, and especially Augustine. His study aids on the *Sentences* were likewise exhaustive and have survived because of their popularity, however arcane they might seem to the modern reader.[13] Classification systems were still novel and agreed systems of classification had yet to emerge fully.

The thirteenth century was extraordinarily fertile as regards intellectual activity and has given us some of the greatest names in medieval theology and biblical studies. It was a time of integration and classification, and this was very much a mark of the Schoolmen's method. The effect of this intellectual movement in the fourteenth century was the establishment of the *scientia divina* in the universities. This had the result of setting rather rigid parameters for the reception of revelation through the scriptures, and provided what Aquinas calls an "order of discipline" in the prologue to his *Summa theologiae*. In other words, there was a movement towards systematizing theology through Lombard's work, as well as extending the system by further comment.

By the fourteenth century, commentators on Lombard in university theology faculties were using the Master as a springboard for their own ideas, rather than simply adding glosses. This was true of the Englishman John Duns Scotus, called "the Subtle Doctor". Another Franciscan, he was considered one of the most important theologian-philosophers of the late Middle Ages and was well-known for his metaphysical arguments for the existence of God, like Anselm and Plato, but unlike Aquinas and Aristotle. On three occasions Scotus "read" or lectured on the *Sentences* in Oxford (1300–1), Paris (1302–3) and again in Oxford (1304–5). He produced his *ordinatio* or dissertation on the *Sentences*. By now the *Sentences* had been reduced to a convenient cover for a teacher's own ideas. The result was effectively just a kind of disputation, with a question like, "Does the human being need supernatural teaching?", followed by answers for and against, leading to a conclusion. The method of disputation remained the stuff of academic study for the next 200 years. Scotus became known as the "Subtle Doctor" because he had so many intricate and sub-divided syllogisms. He explored the relationship between natural and revelatory theology and the contrasting validity of each, as well as questions to do with human free will and divine foreknowledge, and God's absolute and self-restricted power.

The final great Doctor of the Church to comment on the *Sentences* in this period before the emergence of John Wyclif in the late fourteenth century was William of Ockham (1285–1347), called the "Venerable Inceptor", also of Oxford. In Ockham, to whom we will later return, we find a yet greater disassociation of speculative theology from the moorings of either scripture or of Lombard's use of it in the *Sentences*. Although in theory he sought to base his theology on both scripture and the dogmatic decisions of the Church, in practice he was caught up with questions about evidence and knowledge (epistemology). In the prologue to Ockham's *ordinatio*, or commentary, on Lombard's *Sentences*, which runs to 370 pages in the modern critical edition, he has only one quotation from scripture.

Theology in the Schoolmen's hands had strayed far from the style of Augustine's works, which the Schoolmen professed to follow, including Augustine's copious use of scripture. Dry questions of logic and epistemology replaced the heart cry of Augustine as expressed in the *Confessions*, which was often in turn linked to Platonic introspection. Classification and disputation had by degrees reduced revelation and inspiration to a desiccated system. By 1370, the murmurings for change in church and state were to be heard.

Oxford

The thirteenth and fourteenth centuries saw great changes in Europe, which would continue through the successive centuries. The peoples of Europe were in a continual state of flux. In 1241, the Mongols defeated a combined force of Polish conscripts and Bavarian miners at Liegnitz in Silesia. Fortunately, issues over the succession to Genghis Khan at home meant that they did not press their military advantage. In 1254, a Flemish Franciscan missionary, William van Ruysbroeck, reached the court of the Great Khan in Karakorum, where he debated with Muslim and Buddhist scholars. When Pope Innocent IV opened the Council of Lyons in 1245 after the papacy had been ejected from its papal lands by the Emperor Frederick II, he chose as his text: "According to the multitude of my sorrows in my heart, thy comforts have given joy to my soul" (Psalm 94:19). He enumerated the five wounds to his heart: corruption in the Church, the possession of the Holy Land by the Saracens, the division of the Church in the East and West (Orthodox and Roman Catholic), the invasion of Europe by the Mongols or Tartars, and the persecution of the Pope by the Holy Roman Emperor Frederick II, nicknamed *stupor mundi*, the "Wonder of the World", who sought to subjugate the Pope's rule to his own. Thirty years earlier, in 1215, at the Fourth Lateran Council, summoned by Innocent III, the position of the Church looked more hopeful.[14] The Franciscan and Dominican orders, recently begun, brought the hope of renewal to church and society, while the founding of the new universities brought new intellectual vigour to the Church.

Present at the First Council of Lyons was one of the great figures of English intellectual and spiritual life, Robert Grosseteste (1168–1253), by then Bishop of Lincoln. Almost certainly his early years, although poorly chronicled, were spent teaching at Oxford, with a probable earlier stint in Paris. The university at Paris had been granted a royal charter in 1200, bringing together various cathedral and monastic schools under one roof. Just fourteen years later, as we have seen,

Oxford was likewise given a royal charter, followed soon after by Cambridge, which was to draw large numbers of students, mostly from the North and East of England.[15] Grosseteste was one of Oxford's early masters, and quite possibly its first chancellor. His intellectual energy, great integrity of spirit and statesmanlike qualities helped to fashion the early days of the University of Oxford.

Students were generally drawn from the middle or upper sections of society. In an age when a labourer was paid anything between 2d–5d a day, the cost of a year's board, often in a convent (a male community) or friary, plus tuition, was £2–£3 a year (there being 240d in a pound). The penny was the most basic coin in the realm and was in fact a small silver coin. Many of the sons of the very wealthy, as well as sons of noble families, did not attend, preferring a life of courtly and chivalric arms to study. Most of the students were the sons of prosperous yeoman and were clerics, either secular (i.e. non-monastic) or regulars (in a monastic order). Students lived in rented accommodation overseen by graduate students until the advent of halls, friaries, convents (by which is understood not houses for nuns, but for those who literally journeyed together, i.e. members of the mendicant orders) or colleges. By the middle of the thirteenth century, many of these "regulars" belonged either to the Dominican, Franciscan or Augustinian orders (also called the Austin canons). Between 1200 and 1400, some 15,000 students passed through the University of Oxford, of which 17 per cent were monks. Secular clerics went up to the university in their late teens and were ordained after they graduated with a bachelor's degree. Graduation lists are not extant until 1449. It is thought that before the Black Death, the student body was around 400–700, but greatly increased to 1,700 by 1450. However, in Paris the student body was four times the size and far more international.

The schools were divided, as we have seen, into arts, medicine, law (ecclesiastical and civil) and theology. The arts were divided into the *trivium* (philosophy, logic and dialectic) and *quadrivium* (geometry, arithmetic, astronomy and music), which was based on classical education. Set texts for the arts course in 1268 in Oxford included Aristotle's *Topics*, *Elenchi*, the *Prior* and *Posterior Analytics* as well as three of his works on science, including *Physics* and *De Anima*. Priscian's grammar and Donatus's rhetorical work, together with Boethius's *Topics*, were also included. Having studied arts for four years, including the *trivium* and *quadrivium*, the student would go on to specialize in one of the other courses: theology, law or medicine. It was a pattern followed all over Europe for at least 400 years, although the content would vary. A graduate, ready to practise in any of these areas, would emerge in his early twenties.

A suitable method of teaching was soon devised, which was broadly accepted. In a world before the printing press, the set text would be read in Latin by a lector and then commented on by either a graduate teacher or by one of the regent masters. Students not having their own copies of the text would have to copy it down as best they could. Few students would have many books, although Chaucer in his "Miller's Tale" tells of the sweet-smelling Nicholas, seducer of the Miller's wife, having "Twenty books clad in blak or reed, of Aristotle and his philosophye".[16] But perhaps these books were more for show than study! The commentary by the lecturer would revolve around a series of *quaestiones* in which the lecturer would comment on a word or phrase from the text, and then propose a number of meanings. This was further debated between students in public disputations, overseen by a master. Reading, explanation and disputation were the standard method of teaching, with ordinary or common texts dealt with in the morning and extraordinary, or more unusual, texts in the afternoon.

Such was the basis of university teaching. However, tensions in the emphases of teaching theology soon emerged. These could be between the authority of the Church and the desire to experiment and push new boundaries, between the classical philosophers of Greece and Rome and biblical teaching, between the metaphysical insights of Plato as opposed to the deductive ones of Aristotle, between the science of the ancients and biblical descriptions (e.g. of creation), between the interests and rivalries of different orders of monks and friars, and between accepted norms of theology and newer methods.

Grosseteste was at the forefront of many of these disputes in his years of teaching in Oxford from c. 1215–35. Born of humble Anglo-Norman stock in Stradbroke in Suffolk, he was a Norman French speaker. His early education was in Hereford, influenced by Gerald of Wales and patronized by the Bishop of Hereford, William de Vere. Hereford Cathedral's small but well-stocked library would have been available to him, given it was used by the cathedral school. It contained works by Jerome, Augustine, the Cappadocian Fathers, Origen, Eusebius and others. Roger of Hereford and Alfred Sareshal taught Greek and Arabic science. Learning flourished in this remote corner of England near the Marches with Wales.[17] From 1214, at the very beginning of the newly chartered Oxford University, Grosseteste began to teach at the university. He was to remain there until 1235, when he was made Bishop of Lincoln, although for a few years he had been Archdeacon of Leicester.

Grosseteste was a polymath, both in his interests and his teaching, but was driven by an overwhelming pastoral concern for the Church and his pupils. "There is a sense in which almost all that Grosseteste wrote, whether as a Regent Master (that is as a teaching professor appointed by the Friars to instruct in the university) or as a bishop, was pastorally motivated."[18] As a bishop, he famously resisted the attempt by the papacy to appoint Italians to pastoral positions in the Church in England, in particular the appointment of a nephew of Pope Innocent IV (Sinibaldo Fieschi) to a benefice in Lincoln diocese in 1253. Grosseteste saw this as the abandonment by the papacy of an earlier agreement not to ride roughshod over local needs through use of papal provisions, made in 1239 by Pope Gregory IX. In a strongly worded letter in 1253, Grosseteste rebuked the Pope for such an unwarranted appointment of his nephew. In Grosseteste's mind, the fact that a proposed Italian would not be able to speak or understand English, and hence could not hear or understand confessions, was reason enough to refuse such an appointment. Furthermore, in pursuance of his pastoral objective, Grosseteste told the Pope that on his appointment as Bishop of Lincoln by his colleague from Oxford, now Archbishop Edmund of Abingdon, he made it his practice to visit every deanery (a grouping of clergy in a given area) in his huge diocese, instructing them in their responsibilities. And during this time, friars from his visitation team taught the lay people.

Matthew Paris, part-chronicler and part-gossip of St Albans Abbey, stoked the fires of Grosseteste's quarrel with the papacy by telling the story that, after Grosseteste's death, he appeared to Innocent IV as a spectre in the night, attacking him with his episcopal staff, bringing on pleurisy from which the Pope later died! This was a clear example of medieval "fake news" that built up Paris's narrative of unwelcome interference by the papacy in the English Church, but did not reflect Grosseteste's more statesmanlike and principled approach to pastoral appointments. However, with this boost to his English credentials (although he was a French-speaking Anglo-Norman by background), it is not surprising that Grosseteste was a darling of the Reformers and cast thereafter as a Proto-Protestant.

Regarding Grosseteste's earlier teaching career in the newly formed Oxford University, before he became a bishop in 1235, scholars are uncertain as to when he arrived. It seems quite probable that he was a teacher in Oxford from 1214. He may have gone to Paris University after his time in Hereford, and before his teaching career in Oxford, but there is no documentary evidence of this. He joined Edmund of Abingdon (or Edmund Rich), later Archbishop of Canterbury, a revered scholar and saintly man who was teaching at Oxford. Edmund was well known for his spiritual exegesis of the Bible, often accompanied by contemplation, leading to strong moral lessons. The distinct quality that Grosseteste brought to his teaching and writing was that, like Edmund, he was "undogmatic" in character. He did not set out to build a *summa theologiae* of his own like Peter Lombard in Paris fifty years before him. He was less systematic than his continental counterparts, but had a deep love of the scriptures and the Greek Church Fathers, along with an appreciation of both the physical sciences and Greek philosophy. His extensive knowledge and study ranged over a huge field, but he responded to the new wave of knowledge sweeping over the universities in a more piecemeal and pastoral way, which could be described as both insular and English in character. He was neither an Aquinas nor a Bonaventure. He had no desire to give a comprehensive structure to knowledge and revelation.

But he gave the scriptures and the Church Fathers pride of place in his teaching at Oxford and was deeply committed in his lectures to the daily exegesis of the Bible. A regent master was expected to take his pupils through the Gospels and Pauline Epistles. A portion would be read by a lector, possibly a graduate, or by the master himself, and then he would comment on it in the form of a gloss. Church Fathers who had commented on the text previously would be referred to, for example Jerome, Augustine of Hippo, Ambrose and Greek Fathers like Basil of Caesarea, Chrysostom and Origen. His work on Galatians and the Acts of the Apostles exhibits a fascination with the relationship between Jew and Gentile in the Early Church. Much more of his Old Testament teaching is extant than his teaching on the New Testament. His most impressive Old Testament works are his commentary on the Psalms 1–100, his *Hexaemeron*—a study of the first six days of Creation from Genesis, in which there is a crossover to his scientific studies on light—his work on the Ten Commandments (*De Decem Mandatis*) and his work *On the Cessation of the Ritual Torah* (*De Cessatione legalium*). Once again, his evaluation of the Old Testament in the light of the New is to the fore. On more doctrinal issues—and like many others before and after—he taught on the question of human free will, divine foreknowledge and predestination. This is exemplified in his work on the freedom of the will (*de libero arbitrio*)—a topic well suited to that other great part of university education, disputation. On the highly speculative question of whether the Word *(logos)* would have become incarnate if Adam had not fallen, Grosseteste took the view that he would have.

Turning to his study of the Church Fathers, we see that he was proficient in Greek and this proved a powerful tool for his biblical teaching with its aim of forming young students for a preaching and pastoral ministry. His experience of reading the Greek Church Fathers made him bewail the split between the Western and Eastern part of the Church all the more, since they seemingly shared so much in common. His conclusion on studying Basil of Caesarea, Gregory the Theologian (Nazianzen), Gregory Nyssen, Cyril of Alexandria and John of Damascus, Jerome, Augustine and Hilary was that, "if this wide expression were more subtly understood and analysed, it would emerge clearly that the doctrine which finds opposing expressions is in fact the same".[19] His was a generous orthodoxy linked to a pastoral heart.

Allied to his study of the scriptures was his work on Greek philosophy, especially Aristotle, and his scientific work. Grosseteste's work fitted the English translation of his French name, "Big Head" (Grosseteste). His knowledge was vast and diverse, and although it is hard to date the chronology of his works, most of them were completed during his teaching years at Oxford and possibly Paris (1215–35). This work covered the liberal arts (*trivium* and *quadrivium*, as discussed above), philosophy, and what we would call the physical and biological sciences. Both these disciplines fell within the range of Aristotle's published work. All these areas of research and thought belonged to the liberal arts course at Oxford and preceded further specialization in theology, medicine and law. However, it would be wrong to make the curriculum too neat or too cut and dried, since there is little surviving documentary evidence as to what exactly it was.

Some of his works were clearly intended for more advanced study than the basic liberal arts course, for example the intriguingly titled *Computus correctorius*, a late work on mathematics possibly written after 1230. Grosseteste came to an intuitive conclusion that mathematics makes up the "very internal texture of the natural world and presides over its functioning".[20] It is this conclusion that lies at the root of Newton and Einstein's work. He wrote about comets in *De cometis*, and about astrology in *De impressionibus aeris*, even going so far as predicting the state of the weather on 15 April 1249.

Grosseteste's most profound interest was in the nature of light, which he wrote about in *Tractatus de Luce* and in *De impressionibus elementorum*. The Greek philosophers and Church Fathers most influential for Grosseteste were undoubtedly Plato, Aristotle, Basil—who wrote his own *hexaemeron*—and above all Augustine, in particular his *De Trinitate* (*On the Trinity*).

Grosseteste's translations of, and glosses on, Aristotle's work were used long after his death. His glosses on Aristotle's *Physics* remained influential, likewise his annotated commentary on Aristotle's *Nicomachean Ethics*. Unlike his Parisian contemporaries, to whom we shall return, Grosseteste's work was not systematized in the way that earlier authors attempted, like Lombard, Aquinas and Bonaventure. It was scattered through numerous works, many still unedited. It required his foremost pupil Roger Bacon (1219–92), and Adam Marsh, to carry them forward.

Bacon, like Grosseteste a polymath, continued the blend of Aristotelian science, mathematics and astronomy which he combined in his major work *Opus Majus*, a work presented to the Pope in 1267. But he combined his scientific studies with liberal amounts of alchemy and astrology. Like Grosseteste, he preferred to concentrate on scriptural teaching rather than follow the growing fashion of lectures on the *Sentences*. Tempestuous in nature, critical in style and impatient with inaccuracy, Bacon soon made many enemies and was often in trouble with church and academic authorities in England and Paris, where he was closely monitored by the church hierarchy. In a conservative backlash in Paris and Oxford after 1270, Bacon appears to have been cautioned or worse. Oxford was destined to take a further step forward in its reputation with the advent of Duns Scotus and William of Ockham, both of whom responded to what was going on in Paris.

Paris and Oxford in the thirteenth and fourteenth centuries

There is no doubt that the founding of universities in the thirteenth century had a great effect on the development of learning, especially in Paris and Oxford. As also did the two teaching orders of Dominicans and Franciscans whose presence grew quickly at the universities. They attracted to their schools a number of remarkable teachers. Chief among them in Paris was Albert the Great, a German Dominican, who had become one of the regent masters in Paris from 1245, and Alexander Hales, a Franciscan regent master who taught in Paris and among whose pupils was Bonaventure. Albert the Great was a polymath: theologian, philosopher and scientist, and among his pupils was Thomas Aquinas. Hales came from Shropshire and was called the "Irrefutable Doctor", so great was his standing in the university at Paris. Their respective pupils, the Dominican Aquinas and the Franciscan Bonaventure, developed two important streams of theology.

Aquinas, who was called the "Angelic Doctor", was the great synthesizer of divinity and Aristotelian philosophy, and this was amply displayed in his unfinished *Summa Theologica*. This, in part, was an answer to the papacy's distaste for, and persecution of, the teaching of Aristotle in the universities, which had led to some burnings.

In Part I, Aquinas sets about proving the existence of God by answering 190 questions, using reason and philosophy, which Aquinas calls *sacra doctrina*. Having "proven his (God's) existence", he sets about describing his being: as Trinity, his attributes, his creation of the world, the creation of angels and humanity, and finally his manner of governing the world or his providence.

In Part II, Aquinas describes how we may flourish according to biblical teaching and Aristotelian precepts and how *desiring and willing* can be virtuous as humans cooperate with the working of God's grace in our lives. He brings forward the Thomist axiom that God "does not destroy nature but perfects it".[21]

Finally, in Part III, he uses the metaphor of *exile and return* to show how Christ's incarnation (or exile from heaven) enables our return. The goal of Christ's coming is our inclusion in divinity, or as Athanasius put it, "God became man that we might become God". This is affirmed in the sacraments, especially through Christ's presence in the bread and wine.

If Aquinas reflected in his work a synthesis between Aristotelian method and ethics and a scriptural understanding of Christ's coming, Bonaventure (the "Seraphic Doctor", 1221–74) attempted no such overarching presentation of theology. If Aquinas was deeply influenced by Aristotle, Bonaventure was more Platonic, that is he looked within, guided by the Spirit, to understand God's call to man. There was no need to annunciate philosophical reasons for the existence of God, his presence in Creation was self-evident (a true Franciscan). His theology was deeply Christ-centred, his use and knowledge of the scriptures immense, and he was mystical in the sense that the transforming love of God is at the heart of all God's dealing with humankind. Thus "God has made us for himself and nothing else but divine love can fulfil a human person."[22] Bonaventure reflected the long tradition of contemplative theology going back to Augustine of Hippo, Gregory the Great, Dionysius the Areopagite and Anselm. He was a friend and foil to Aquinas.

Meanwhile, in Oxford there was another distinctive approach. As in Paris, the method of teaching and the course of study was similar; and Lombard's *Sentences* was the set text in theology. In 1300, Duns Scotus (the "Subtle Doctor", 1266–1308) began teaching at Oxford, although he too went between Paris and Oxford. Primarily a philosopher, he emphasized the uniqueness of being, its *haecceity* (a word of his own invention). Unlike Aquinas, he made no distinction between the essence and existence of a thing. He recognized the distinctiveness of a quality but also its universality; hence, in appraising philosophers such as Socrates, Plato and Plutarch, he recognized their distinctiveness but also their common universal quality of humanity. One could say he stood halfway between Plato and Aristotle.

He was followed by William of Ockham (1285–1347), a Franciscan and pupil of Scotus in Paris, but who moved away from any metaphysical understanding of universals to something much more empirical and materialist. Known for Occam's Razor, he looked for the simplest explanation of a thing, demonstrating the most efficient cause through reason, but this more scientific method was tethered still to the starting point of faith. One could say that in Oxford there was a little more latitude for exploration and invention than in Paris, and this was to become all the clearer with the arrival of Wyclif. Twin emphases of pioneering philosophical thought and a willingness to test political conventions were beginning to shape the future. And in the end what could not be pursued at Oxford, as it was too close to the conventions of the establishment, would be taken up in Cambridge.

By 1347, at the death of William of Ockham, the Black Death was taking a hold. The victories of Sluys and Crecy in the Hundred Years' War were already in the past. A new era was opening up, brought on by war and plague. Fault lines had been exposed between the enquiring minds of the universities and the establishment of the Church, between the scientific impetus stimulated by Aristotle and the metaphysics of Plato, between tying down theology in systems as in Lombard's *Sentences* or exploring new vistas as envisaged by Ockham, or between traditional approaches and the new possibilities expounded by Aquinas in his *Summa*, between biblical scholarship and philosophical enquiry. In Oxford, and then in Cambridge, new learning would challenge old ways, and not least when John Wyclif determined to translate the Bible into English at a time of social unrest after the Peasants' Revolt. By then many of the building blocks of the future were to hand: the search for what could be truly termed fundamental, the critique of the association of Aristotelian method with scriptural interpretation, the questioning of the Church's right to determine individual conscience and its right to wield power in the secular sphere. The whole edifice of medieval religion was about to be challenged. But first the shape of that religion must be described and its essential medieval construction uncovered, to show that it was tethered to a particular order, which was beginning to pass.

CHAPTER 9

The Practice of Medieval Religion

In medieval England, Christianity revolved around the parish, the diocese, the monastery, the university and the King. At the universities of Oxford and Cambridge, teachers and thinkers explored Christianity in relation to changing ideas, especially those from the Greek philosophers and their interpreters, along with other concepts emanating from the continent. The worlds of most people operated at a more down-to-earth level, however. Their concerns, as in any age, were with birth, marriage, succession, disease, food, death, war and taxes. Medieval religion, which had been built up over a period of almost a thousand years, provided a way of coping with the exigencies of life. It was a birth-to-grave presence firmly woven into the pattern of life. That way of life was often violent, always intrusive, and closely connected to the presence of the Church, with its beliefs and expectations. This was as true for the King as for the peasant, and in that sense medieval England was religious in a way we can scarcely conceive in today's contemporary secular society.

At the centre of this way of life were a cluster of beliefs and practices that formed a social pattern and culture, and that determined the mindset of the people. It is a coincidence that most of these beliefs and practices appear to begin with the letter P: purgatory, penance, the passion of Christ, pictures, plays, pilgrimages, processions, piety, primers, prayers, paternosters and even *Piers Plowman*, the poem! Only relics, saints and the mass fell outside the P remit of the religious practices of the people of England, as was true of most of medieval Europe. To get a flavour of this cultural, religious and social construct, which in essence constituted medieval England, we shall deal briefly with all of these.[1] For when the time comes to consider the gains and losses of the Reformation in England, an appreciation of the religious and cultural cohesion created by medieval religion is important in making that assessment.

Ever-present death, purgatory, penance and indulgences

We shall begin with the end of life, rather than its beginning, and consider the doctrine of purgatory and "the last things" and the effect these beliefs had on the medieval mind. The concept of purgatory had slight beginnings in scripture, but massive endings in the medieval system of religion, where in many ways it was the driver of faith or, many would argue, superstition. This is not surprising in view of the unremitting prevalence of death, especially during the Black Death itself. Unlike our age—where looking upon death, even upon the coffin of a loved one, is avoided—in the medieval world the permanent reminders of death's presence called for a very different perspective. We try not to think about death; medieval people were forced to think about it almost all the time. The medieval view was that purgatory was a period of *being* after death in which people were refined through fire in preparation for heaven. For Bonaventure, for example, there were three categories of people in the afterlife: those with no possibility of heaven and in everlasting torment, those in limbo or purgatory who were being refined, and those who were enjoying the beatific vision and were therefore in bliss. And Dante's great poem the *Divine Comedy* revolves around these three tiers: hell, purgatory and paradise.

Belief in purgatory has a very slight basis in the Bible. In the Old Testament there is mention of a shadowy place of existence called Sheol, of which the Psalmist says: "If I make my bed in Sheol, you are there" (Psalm 139:8, NIV). The Jews disputed about the existence of heaven and hell and the certainty of resurrection. The Pharisees believed there was a resurrection, whilst the Sadducees did not (see Acts 23:8). One of Jesus's New Testament parables about the afterlife tells of Dives, who is in hell, and in torment, looking up and seeing Abraham far away, with Lazarus by his side: "So he called to him, 'Father Abraham have mercy on me and send Lazarus to dip the tip of his finger in water and cool my tongue, because I am in agony in this fire'" (Luke 16:23,24). While for most interpreters, Dives's situation suggests hell, others have taken it to mean purgatory. This parable, with its vivid language and images, was used in dramatic illustrative displays, such as those found in the *Codex Aureus Echternach*, an illuminated gospel from Nuremberg created between 1030 and 1050, which shows a roasting Dives, bound and beset by devils. In this vein, Paul speaks of a minister or disciple's spiritual work for God being tested by fire, to see whether it is like gold, silver, costly stones, wood, hay or straw. The quality of a person's work "will be shown for what it is, because the Day will bring it to light. It will be revealed with fire, and the fire will test the quality of each man's work. If [his work] is burned up, he will suffer loss; he himself will be saved, but only as one escaping through flames" (1 Corinthians 3:10–15, NIV). Purging was a reality, and fire gives credence to an idea of purgatory. Finally, in his first epistle, Peter writes of Jesus preaching to the prisoners in *hades* after his crucifixion and before the Resurrection (1 Peter 3:18–21). It appears from this that there is a belief in a shadowy place beyond death from which people who have not yet heard the gospel can respond.

On these slender foundations a great edifice was built. Death, judgement, purgatory, hell and heaven were at the forefront of the medieval mind. The medieval obsession with death and an afterlife, in whatever form, was widely depicted in church art—and most morbidly in the *Danse Macabre*, an illustration found in the Sarum Primer (the earliest of the English prayer books). The "dance" is represented as death accosting a nun, a labourer and a monk with the intention of taking their lives. Similar illustrations are found in the cadaver tombs of the fifteenth century, such as that of John Baret, a wealthy cloth merchant, in St Mary's, Bury St Edmunds, or in the still more macabre cadaver tomb of Baylham in Suffolk. Preparation for dying was part of living, so in the *Ars Moriendi* (*The Art of Dying*) it was considered normal practice to bring a dying Christian to the knowledge of their impending death so that they might prepare for it with acts of repentance, confession and faith. The *Ars Moriendi*, which became immensely popular throughout Europe, depicted in graphic line drawings eleven deathbed temptations that might beset the dying person and which must be overcome with the help of priest and family. The priest would administer the sacrament and anoint the patient with oil while the family encouraged repentance and faith. Jesus would be called upon in one of four English (not Latin) prayers found in the Sarum and York Primers. It was thought better if friends confronted the patient with the imminence of death, and did not hesitate to trouble them with "a holsom fere and dred", rather than allowing them to be damned with "flaterynge and false dissimilacioun". The deathbed was a hallowed place where patience was learned, despair overcome, repentance made and faith reasserted. Such deathbed scenes were even recorded in stone, as in the parish church of Gresham, Norfolk. It was tough love indeed, yet at the same time, "the hour of death" was embraced with deep devotion and seriousness.

Art, whether in stone, wood, wall paintings or literature, was frequently employed to warn the living of the tortures of hell and the improving pains of purgatory, and to remind congregations of the Day of Doom, or Judgement. There were plenty of Doom carvings in parish churches up and down the land, reminding parishioners of the Day of Judgement. The realities of death and judgement were inescapable, their reach unavoidable. Every time a medieval person attended the

parish church there would be reminders, in one way or another. This rhyme by
Sir William Basterfeld gives vivid warning of the sufferings and torments of hell:

> Therefore I byde here in this cage
> This cage is everlasting fire
> I am ordeynde ther-in to duelle
> It is me given for myne hyre
> Ever ti bryne in the pittye of helle.[2]

Just as Basterfeld's rhyme warns worldly sinners of everlasting torment in hell,
there were many descriptions, whether in letters or stone, describing the reforming
pains of purgatory. Purgatory was deeply etched in the medieval mind as a reality.
After all, as we have recalled, the greatest of all medieval poems, Dante's *Divine
Comedy*—written between c. 1308 and the year before Dante's death in 1321—
follows his imaginary journey through hell (*inferno*) and purgatory (*purgatorio*) to
heaven (*paradisio*). Purgatory was, in Dante's view, a tool of divine love, by which
the soul was prepared for heaven. Its activity and "staff" (devils) made it an outpost
of hell rather than an antechamber of heaven. One medieval Christian handbook,
The Ordynare of Crysten Men, published by Wynkyn de Worde in 1502, described
purgatory as being "one part of hell and the place of right mervvaylous payne".[3]
According to Thomas More, the ministers of reform in purgatory were "cruel
damned spirits, odious, envious and hateful, despitous enemies".[4] Others were
less certain, believing angels accompanied souls to and through purgatory. The
difference between hell and purgatory was that in hell punishments were eternal,
while in purgatory they were reformative in aim and limited in extent, even if the
length of time to be served there was unknown. It is against the backdrop of this
commonly accepted medieval view of purgatory that a whole industry of piety,
a whole department of art, and a whole theology of merit or mitigation built
up. At the centre of it all was a church whose teaching underpinned the belief
in purgatory and whose services mitigated the effects of it. The Church had the
power, as it preached, to hasten the springing of souls from purgatory through
penance, masses, indulgences, good works and prayer. The Church was effectively
a very considerable, multi-national business. In a world plagued by death and its
consequences, the Church alone claimed the power to influence outcomes. It was
an extraordinarily powerful position; its servants thereby were open to corruption
and abuse, and were able to hold the minds of men in subservient fear.

While the realities of judgement, hell and purgatory were ever before the
congregations of England in the Middle Ages, the Church also taught that the

living and the dying were not entirely powerless. They could at least shorten the time spent in purgatory, even if they could not reverse or ameliorate the punishments of hell. Much piety was therefore focussed on accruing merit so as to release relatives from the grip of purgatory. It was hoped that such meritorious acts would be placed on the scales of judgement and effect someone's early release from purgatory. Merit was acquired through almsgiving, works of mercy, penance, the purchase of indulgences, prayer and the saying of masses in churches, chapels or chantries.

In the first instance, merit could be accrued through almsgiving, works of mercy, prayer and the saying of masses. Alms may be given either in person in life or through a will after death. In fact, a will was often seen as a final proof of the spiritual condition of the deceased and might contain, in its preamble, a statement of faith, followed by dispositions to charities.

It is no surprise, then, to discover the vast extent of almsgiving, in life, but mostly in death. "Common doles" were distributed to mourners (a dole was a small amount of money, now used in common parlance in the phrase "on the dole": meaning one is in receipt of benefit). To receive the "dole", mourners were expected to pray for the soul of the deceased. By the sixteenth century, and to counteract abuses, the dole was increasingly restricted to gifts to particular charities. Thus in 1521, Richard Clerke of Lincoln forbade the distribution of the penny dole, leaving instead a groat piece (a silver coin worth 4d) to 100 persons "that be in poverty and age, dwellers in the town ether as I shal departe".[5] Gifts to the parish church for a particular piece of upkeep were also common. These gifts and the names of their donors were entered into the painstakingly kept bede rolls. So, in Morebath on Exmoor, the incumbent Sir Christopher Trychay entered every gift on his roll with the sums ranging from 26s 8d to 2d. The bede roll was regularly read out from the pulpit, reminding parishioners of who in the congregation, either living or dead, had contributed to the community.

Works of mercy as enjoined in Jesus's parable of the Sheep and Goats (Matthew 25:31–46) were also considered meritorious. Again, these might be acts performed during the deceased's lifetime or those made possible through the financial provisions of a will. Such acts of compassion, which were foundational throughout the Church in Europe, were feeding the hungry, giving water to the thirsty, clothing the naked, visiting the sick, relieving the prisoner, welcoming the stranger and burying the dead; and all came from Jesus's parable of the Sheep and the Goats. Together, they constituted the "seven acts of mercy". Thus in 1502, Elizabeth Greystock from Yorkshire made provision in her will for the relief of prisoners and the burial of the poor, and in particular for the payment for candles around the coffin. "The burning of candles around the corpse was an act with profound resonances."[6] In addition, some people provided in their wills for the building of roads and the repairing of bridges, which were also seen as acts of mercy, since bridges and roads created the living conditions of a community, granting safety and a sense of neighbourliness.

If almsgiving and acts of mercy were considered meritorious in medieval religion, so too were prayers and the saying of masses for the dead. Prayers for the dead were highly regulated and highly formalized in the medieval world. They involved saying or singing a liturgy of the Office for the Dead called the *placebo*, from its opening words in Latin, which meant "may I be pleasing", and also the *dirige* (taken from the words in the Vulgate of Psalm 5:8, "direct me in your righteousness"). Together, the *placebo* and the *dirige* formed one office.

The *dirige* was also derived from the opening word of the liturgies of Matins and Lauds. From the *dirige* comes the word "dirge", which literally means a lament for the dead. These services were often led by choir members, or by guild members, if the deceased was a member of a guild. In addition, the seven penitential psalms would be read, including the *De Profundis* (Psalm 130), which begins with the words, "Out of the depths I cried to you Lord." This pattern made up the unvarying form of prayers or obsequies for the dead.

Masses were also said for the deceased, paid for either by the person or by his or her family. It was commonly believed that masses reduced time in purgatory and those who could afford them employed mass priests to perform various cycles of masses for their souls. For instance, after conspiring to murder Richard II, Henry IV paid for 1,000 masses for Richard's soul. One such cycle of obsequies, called the Trental of St Gregory, involved three masses being said on all the ten major feasts of Christ and Mary. The mass, which takes its name from the final words of the Latin *mass*—"*ite, missa est*" or "you are dismissed"—was understood by the medieval Church to involve the transubstantiation (or changing) of the bread and wine into the actual body and blood of Christ. The mass was also thought to have efficacy or spiritual merit simply by virtue of being said. Saying prayers and masses was a liturgical means of shortening time in purgatory. Other ways by which purgatory might be shortened, either for oneself or one's relatives, included penance and indulgences.

Penance, which was linked to confession, was part of church life from the earliest centuries. It was familiar to the Church Fathers, and in an age when the Church suffered persecution, leading to the presence of the "lapsed" (i.e. those who complied with magistrates), penance was the accepted means by which the lapsed might be readmitted to the Church. They had to perform a penance demonstrating their repentance and their desire for readmission into the fellowship. Basil of Caesarea laid down specific tariffs for the repentance of those who had fallen. In a letter to a younger bishop, Amphilochius of Iconium, Basil spelt out the precise penances for such sins as theft, fornication and murder. In severe cases, this could involve being excommunicated from the sacrament for twenty years and having to stand outside the house of prayer.[7] While penance started out as a necessary part of church discipline, over time the practice became more functional. Bonaventure, along with the medieval Church in general, regarded penance as "a life-saving plank after a shipwreck. It is specifically a plank for the human drowning in mortal sin."[8]

There were three aspects to penance: contrition of soul, confession in words and satisfaction in deed. In other words, evidence of contrition was confession, which was then followed by action. By the Middle Ages, the practice of confession and penance had become entrenched. Canon 21 of the Fourth Lateran Council of 1215 commands all church members to confess their sins to their parish priest or his appointee once a year. Failure to do so could result in excommunication and exclusion from Christian burial. Margery Kempe, a remarkable mystic from Kings Lynn, made it her business to regularly confess her sins to a Confessor and do penances throughout the year. She enjoined the same on some widows that they might shorten the time spent by their deceased husbands in purgatory.[9] Penances might involve saying prayers, abstaining from meat or fish or from all food, performing acts of mercy and almsgiving, or going on a pilgrimage or a Crusade. Through these acts, not only was the penitent showing contrition, but was also possibly reducing the time they would have to spend in purgatory.

Finally, indulgences could be purchased with a similar aim. The sale of indulgences on the continent by the Dominican Tetzel, the Papal Grand Commissioner for Indulgences in Germany, sparked a broadside from Luther and the commencement of the Reformation in 1517 with the posting of his famous 95 Theses. Indulgences were the most venial of all means of reducing time in purgatory, but were commonplace in continental Europe and England. Self-respecting relatives would buy indulgences to mitigate the effects of purgatory on deceased family members. It would be embarrassing to arrive in purgatory (partly because of miserliness) only to find your disappointed relatives enduring a prolonged stay there, simply because you had failed to purchase them indulgences. Anchorites or friars sometimes conveyed "messages" from those in purgatory, urging relatives on earth to hasten payment for their speedier release. Indulgences, which were essentially a certificate issued by the Church on behalf of a named relative, specified the number of days or years by which the torment had been reduced. It was a racket. In *The Canterbury Tales*, Chaucer writes of a Pardoner, who has just returned from Rome:

> His knapsack, which he carried on his lap, was filled with papal pardons smoking hot from Rome. "If any man full penitent come to me and pay for his sin", he said to me, "I will absolve him. If anyone gives seven shillings to Saint Anthony's, I will bestow on him an indulgence of seven hundred years" [the time spans were huge]. I told him that I had scarcely enough to pay my way. He had a voice as high as a goat. He had no beard at all, nor was he likely to grow one. His chin was as smooth as a girl's arse. He was a eunuch or a homosexual, a nurrit or a will-jack, as the common people put it. I did not wish to investigate further. Yet, as pardoners go, he was effective enough.[10]

Stirring emotions of fear, loyalty or guilt, the Pardoner would always make a sale, whatever he looked like, or however he acted. With the whole Church seemingly behind this theology of purgatory and standing to gain from the sale of indulgences, it would require a sweeping movement to effect change.

Death and the Last Things: Judgement, Heaven, Hell and Purgatory, thus dominated the landscape of medieval life. Around their too frequent and intrusive reality a whole edifice of church practice had been built. It was not the only aspect to medieval piety, but it was the most emotive force behind it.

Medieval piety

While death and its consequences were ever present in the medieval mind, this was far from the only aspect of a vast religious system enveloping men, women and children. In an age when even the King could barely write or read (William the Conqueror simply affixed the sign of a cross to documents, rather than his signature), the population lived in an oral rather than a written culture. It was a culture of visual displays rather than one of the written word, and of community events rather than individual reflection or writing. Over the period, literacy would increase, and by the fourteenth century there were a number of English devotional authors outside the universities. By the fifteenth century, literacy was becoming more common. Medieval spirituality thus depended, as we shall see, on a combination of feasting and fasting, on the visual more than the written, and on the corporate rather than the individual. Spirituality resided in the interaction of these partnerships. It was a world that was about to change drastically with the advent of the printing press and the rise of the written word in the late fifteenth century. It was a spirituality that was about to change and, for many, to be superseded.

Judaism recognizes that great theological events are accompanied by the very human need to celebrate in company. God himself provided for festivals three times a year in Jerusalem. These festivals of Passover, Pentecost (Weeks) and Tabernacles recalled God's acts of salvation, such as the Jews' deliverance from Egypt, their wanderings in the desert, and the provision of harvest blessings in the promised land, as in the Festival of Weeks. The Christian Church then created a new series of festivals for the Christian calendar. While there is no doubt that there was a building upon, and indeed use of, previous pagan festivals in the assembling of these new Christian festivals, their significance was entirely new. Pope Gregory had advised Augustine of Canterbury to make use of the religious fabric he found in England, and not to ignore or destroy it. Frequently in Christian mission, fresh significance has been given to previous religious understanding and expressions.

Feasting and fasting offer a good perspective on the Christian liturgical calendar. The Christian calendar is not set out in the Bible as such, but the main events are to be found there: the Incarnation (Christmas), our redemption (Easter), and the Gift of the Spirit (Pentecost). Christian festivals, like Jewish festivals before them, recall God's acts of salvation, only now these are fulfilled through Christ.

In northern Europe, such festivals coincided with the changes of the seasons, thereby tapping into the primal energies of winter and spring, harvest and winter. There were in fact four church festivals through the year to coincide with the four seasonal divisions of the year: Christmas, the Annunciation on 25 March, the birth of John the Baptist on 24 June, and St Michael and All Angels on 29 September.

By the Middle Ages, the Church, being centuries old in Europe, especially in Greece and Italy, had already created many liturgical traditions. Lent had become the main fast, coinciding with the preparation of candidates for baptism, and going back to the earliest days of the Church. Advent was used to reflect on the Last Things, and preceded Christmas, which celebrated the Nativity. Epiphany recalled the coming of the Wise Men or Magi and signified the revelation of Christ to the nations. It was also associated with the Baptism of Christ and his first miracle at Cana. Candlemas was celebrated on 2 February and was added to commemorate the presentation of Christ in the Temple and his reception by Simeon and Anna. Candlemas was the last of the incarnational cycle of services, emphasizing the appearance of light in the darkness of human sin, and the reception of the hope of the Christ child in the bleakness of the world, symbolized by winter. After Easter, there followed the feasts of Ascension, Pentecost, Trinity Sunday and Corpus Christi (the Thanksgiving for the Institution of the Eucharist). These completed the cycle of festivals. Most were feasts. Others, like Lent, were fasts. At a stroke, definition had been given to the whole year. A rhythm to life had been granted; and that was only the start of it.

In addition to the major festivals, there were hosts of saints from far and near celebrated in various parts of England, and there were also days of prayer devoted to the blessing of crops and agriculture. Furthermore, city guilds often adopted a particular saint and celebrated that saint's day in their town or city. Geographical and historical traditions often lie behind the celebration of saints, particularly in Cornwall, where saints were frequently "locally beatified" or informally recognized. To this day St Piran remains the patron saint of Cornwall. He was a sixth-century Irish missionary credited with the rediscovery of tin (the Romans had mined tin) and the saying "as drunk as a perraner" indicates his was a feast day and definitely not a fast! Elsewhere, regional saints abound: Richard of Chichester, Cantilupe of Hereford, Our Lady of Walsingham, Etheldreda of Ely, Swithun of Winchester, Cuthbert of Durham, etc. All had, and still have, strong local followings of those who celebrate their lives. Some observances travelled, such as those of St Faith of Conques from the Aveyron in France, who is also warmly remembered at Horsham St Faith near Norwich, through a shrine established by Robert Fitzwalter and his wife. Later, Catherine of Siena and Bridget of Sweden, both notable mystics, were added by William Wulcy to the screen in that church. The writings of these two mystics were in circulation among devout laity in the early sixteenth century in England. Specific communities therefore remembered and celebrated particular local saints, or saints who had come to have a connection to that community, sometimes brought back to a country village by an enthusiastic travelling landlord, quite possibly on a Crusade.

Likewise, the church was at the centre of services of blessing for agriculture. In a world where there was no separation between worshipping and working life, and where working life was mostly agricultural, it is no surprise to find that praying for crops was a regular part of church life. There were plough ceremonies held on the first working day after Christmas when hopes for the new year were shared.

May had Rogation days when the congregation prayed for the fields by "beating the bounds", which meant going around the perimeter of the parish on a prayer walk. Sometimes there would be special prayers for protection from crop diseases or for rain, and these found their way into later prayer books, such as the Book of Common Prayer of 1662. There were other ceremonies or prayers for community life: on St Agnes Eve, young women sought to discover through prayer the identity of future spouses or lovers; on St Nicholas Day, 6 December, boys were made bishops to exalt children and give them the opportunity to exercise priestly functions, such as leading services or prayers. In these various ways, reasons were found for feasting and for ceremonies that gave life, colour and expression to the community, while still locating them in the prayers of the Church and the teaching of scripture. After all, in connection with children and the making of boy bishops, it was Isaiah who said that on God's holy mountain "a little child shall lead them" (Isaiah 11:16) and Jesus said, "Unless you change and become like little children, you will never enter the kingdom of heaven" (Matthew 18:3).

The Church and its life gave texture to the annual remembering of the great events of Christ's life. It did this most of all by *preparation for* and *celebration of* these salvation events: incarnation, redemption, resurrection and ascension: themselves the preparation for Pentecost. Mostly this was done through visual means. This was a glory but was also seen as a snare. In a culture where few could read, and where books were written by hand and were thus both rare and expensive, visual presentation of the faith grew up spontaneously. In many ways, one might say that seeing was believing, rather than faith being brought about by hearing or reading.

Future radical changes effected by the Reformation would signify a movement from seeing and sensing to hearing and reading, from experiencing corporately to understanding individually: for faith indeed comes from hearing (Romans 10:17). But the danger was that the corporate was lost to the individual. This is a simplification, but there is more than a grain of truth to it. The question (which will seem like a tautology) remains: how much of a place for *seeing* is there in the process of *hearing*? This in turn takes us back to a more fundamental, indeed a philosophical and psychological, question: how do we experience and understand truth, or indeed God himself?

Leaving aside any prescriptive answer to these questions, the Middle Ages greatly depended on the visual representation of Christian truth and some popular accretions to those basic truths, which gathered over time. Thus pictures, symbols, dramatic liturgical events, mystery plays and the mass itself all had a part to play in the visual representations of Christianity. Some of these were overplayed, some did slip into plain superstition, some even into idolatry—that is, when the things themselves were worshipped rather than what they were intended to signify. The whole framework could be used to maintain a dependency on the clergy that prevented personal spiritual growth. Yet without this visual display how much would be grasped by a non-book culture? For all its spiritual risks, visual representation kept the story of Christ alive and the meaning of the great salvation events present at the heart of society.

There are several aspects to this visual representation. We shall begin by looking at the liturgical aspect: that is, what the Church does together in a service of worship to God. From earliest times, Christians had come together for a shared meal, sometimes called an *agape*, to remember the Lord's death. Paul himself wrote to the Corinthian church about the practice of sharing bread and wine in remembrance of the Lord's death, and how to do this correctly (1 Corinthians 11:17–34).

Pliny the Younger, the Roman governor of Bithynia in c. AD 110, drew the Emperor's attention to this practice of the Christians, and sought his advice on how to treat such gatherings for worship and Eucharist. The *agape* and then the Eucharist became central to the life of the Church. Over time, liturgies were written for these communal services. In the East, John Chrysostom, Bishop of Antioch and then of Constantinople, wrote a liturgy that is still in use today in the Orthodox Church. In Armenia, the first Christian kingdom, a liturgy that has remained pretty much unchanged since the fourth century, and whose founder was Gregory the Illuminator, kept a nation together for millennia in the face of profound persecution.

In the West, the main liturgy, called the Roman Rite, dated from the sixth century and was developed during the time of Pope Leo. In England, St Osmund, Bishop of Salisbury, established the Sarum Rite in the eleventh century. There were many local variations, with dioceses publishing their own prayer books and variant liturgies in manuscript form, but this formed the essential basis. There were four essential parts to the liturgy: in the first section the priest vested himself (put on his liturgical robes and prepared himself to celebrate), recited the confession, led an opening prayer or collect, and read the Epistle and Gospel, sometimes followed by a homily. The second section was the offertory, the collection of mass pennies (the basic silver coin of the realm) and preparation of the bread and wine for consecration (at a requiem mass, prayers for the deceased were invited). The third section comprised the *Pax* or Peace, the prayer of consecration and the elevation of the host and chalice for adoration by the people. In the fourth section, the Lord's Prayer was recited, the people received communion (generally only the bread) and were blessed and dismissed. The elevation of the host was the climax of the service, not least because of teaching about transubstantiation, in which it was believed that the bread and wine *became* the body and blood of Christ. (It was believed, at least in the Aristotelian sense, that the interior *substance* of bread and wine changed, even if the *accidents*, or the external properties, remained the same.)

The host (the bread) and the chalice (the wine) were reverenced by the people at their elevation: a bell was rung, a taper or candle lit, and the congregation bowed towards the raised host. It was pure liturgical theatre and was also to become a point of fierce contention in the future.

If the mass or Eucharist was at the centre of the visual liturgy, the parish church was full of other demonstrations of the Christian message. Each church was a visual reminder of the main teachings of Christianity. In St Mary's, Chalgrove, Oxfordshire, wall paintings survive that tell the whole Christian story. Church buildings were mostly built in the form of a cross, or cruciform, with the baptismal font placed near the west end, a symbol that baptism was the entrance to the community of the saved. The altar was placed at the east end, where the mass was re-enacted and offered as a kind of sacrifice (i.e. the *anamnesis*: the recalling in real time of the one sacrifice of Christ). Often the chancel at the east end was divided from the nave (where the people stood) by a rood screen that took its name from the standard depiction of the Passion of Christ, i.e. a crucifix with Mary the mother of Jesus on one side and John the Apostle on the other. (*Rood* was an Anglo-Saxon word for a rod—hence cross.) An Easter sepulchre was erected during Holy Week. People took part in a ceremony of penitence on Good Friday called "creeping to the cross" and the story of the Passion was sung from the gallery. Besides images of saints or Mary there would frequently be a Doom painting, i.e. a representation of the Day of Judgement. Such a painting survives at St Peter and St Paul, Chaldon, Surrey. Churches thus decorated abounded in the fourteenth to early sixteenth centuries. In fact, of the 10,000 or so medieval churches still standing, "between a third and a half were wholly or partly re-built during these two and a half centuries".[11]

Undoubtedly, and more so than Christmas, the centre of the medieval church year was Holy Week and the remembrance of the Passion. At the start of the week, Palm Sunday was given over to an elaborate procession. Palm branches made of yew, willow and box were sprinkled with holy water and blessed in the church by the priest. The Gospel account was read from St John, and the people, following a painted wooden cross without a figure, processed into the churchyard, where there was a palm cross on the north side of the church. Any relics belonging to the church were added to the procession, carried under a silken canopy. The choir would sing anthems recapitulating the biblical story. During the week, *Tenebrae* services were held from Wednesday to Friday, in which candles were snuffed out one by one to symbolize the abandonment of Jesus. On Maundy Thursday, a solemn mass was held in which three hosts were consecrated: one for that day, one for Good Friday, and one to be laid in the Easter sepulchre. The Good Friday liturgy included the veneration of the cross or "creeping to the cross", and often this liturgy concluded with the wrapped host (the bread) and a crucifix being buried in the Easter sepulchre. In all, it was a strongly visual, community-based remembrance of the Passion of Christ, although the symbolism and ceremonies would be seen as highly contentious come the Reformation.

There is no doubt that the significance of the Passion was seared in the medieval mind, and inevitably there were different levels of understanding of its meaning. Evidence of this is found in the literature we have from the fourteenth century. Margery Kempe (1373–c. 1440), the mystic and pilgrim from Kings Lynn, a spiritual *tour de force* as we shall see, wrote movingly of the effect a vision of the dying Christ had upon her:

> Another time, as the creature [the way Margery refers to herself throughout the book] lay in her contemplation in a chapel to our Lady, her mind was occupied in the Passion of our Lord Jesus Christ, and she truly thought that she saw our Lord appear in His manhood to her spiritual sight, with his wounds bleeding as freshly as though He had been scourged in front of her. And then she wept and cried with all her bodily might, for if her sorrow had been great before this spiritual vision, it was even greater after than it had been before, and her love increased towards our Lord. And then she was really amazed that our Lord had wished to become a man and suffer such grievous pains for her, who was such an unkind creature to Him.[12]

Such was the sensitizing of her soul by the Passion that she wrote that she could not see a leper (in Norfolk) without crying and weeping (a frequent occurrence for Margery) "as if she had seen our Lord Jesus Christ with his wounds bleeding". She would have seen many Palm Sunday processions, Holy Week ceremonies, creepings to the cross on Good Fridays, sermons given by friars and many others, and there is no doubt she understood the significance of the Passion. One Palm Sunday, having heard a sermon entitled "Our Lord Jesus languishes for love", she wrote:

> These words [from the sermon] worked so in her mind when she heard talk of the perfect love that Our Lord Jesus Christ had for mankind, and how dearly He redeemed us with his bitter Passion, shedding his heart-blood for our redemption, and he suffered such a shameful death for our salvation, then she might no longer keep the fire of love enclosed within her breast but, whether she wanted to or no, such things which were enclosed within

would appear outwardly. And so she cried very loudly and wept and sobbed really bitterly, as though she would burst out of pity and compassion that she had for the Lord's Passion. And sometimes she was all soaked with the effort of crying, it was so loud and violent, and many people were amazed by her and cursed her bluntly, supposing that she had pretended.[13]

A more restrained, but no less influential, account of the Passion and its significance is given by the great devotional writer Walter Hilton (c. 1345–96). Hilton was an older contemporary of Margery, an Augustinian canon who later became a hermit. In his *Ladder of Perfection*, written as advice to an anchoress (a female solitary hermit), he states: "For the Passion and precious death of our Lord Jesus are the means whereby the soul of man is re-formed, and without them we could never have been restored to His likeness nor come to the joys of heaven."[14] Even Chaucer puts into the mouth of the Wife of Bath, his most colourful and ribald character, who had five husbands at the church ("Five of them trooping up to the church door"), that "only Jesus could save us when he purchased our redemption with Holy Blood". Not even John Calvin would have quibbled at that, although he might have looked for more changes of life in the Wife of Bath as a consequence of her understanding, and more submissive speech towards men! Chaucer, who used Boccaccio's (1313–75) *Decameron* as a chief source for his *Canterbury Tales* (written c. 1387–1400), may have read Boccaccio's summary of the Gospel in his little classic, *The Life of Dante*, where he wrote:

> Divine Scripture, which we call theology, sometimes under the guise of history, sometimes as if by a vision, sometimes in the form of a lament, or in many other ways, endeavours to show us the high mystery of the incarnation of the Divine Word. It shows us his Life, the events which occurred at his death, his victorious resurrection, and his wonderful ascension, and all his other acts, through which we, taught by him, may attain to that glory which he by his death and resurrection opened for us, after it had long been closed to us by the sin of the first man.[15]

In summary, although the life of Christ was represented by visual images, whether through pictures, plays or processions, and through which means most medieval people came to know about his life and the significance of his death and resurrection, and although the mass was a piece of visual theatre centring on the controversial doctrine of transubstantiation, there was nonetheless widespread understanding of the significance of the Passion. Furthermore, as the fourteenth century proceeded, there was greater evidence of literacy and more people were using books to supplement and instruct their faith. Among these were books of hours or primers, which were summaries of offices used in monasteries or churches, but now also used by literate laity in their homes. These books of hours contained the fifteen gradual psalms (120–134), the seven penitential psalms (6, 32, 38, 51, 102, 130, 143), the Office for the Dead and the Psalms of Commendation (119, 139). Famous scripture readings were also included, as in *In Principio* (the Prologue of St John's Gospel). There were also various prayers, including those for exorcism, as well as a liturgy devoted to Mary called the Little Office. By the end of the fifteenth century, these books were being mass-produced by teams of copyists and illuminators. In fact, they were an early form of what came later to be called the prayer book. Their retention after the Henrician Reformation was virtually proscribed, however, and although many are referred to in the wills of the gentry and the urban middle class, very few have survived. They smacked too much of heterodoxy, or heresy.

The final significant aspect of religious life of the late medieval period was its community outworkings. As Eamon Duffy writes, "the overwhelming impression left by the sources for late medieval religion in England is that of a Christianity resolutely and enthusiastically orientated towards the public and corporate, and of a continuing sense of the value of cooperation and mutuality in seeking salvation".[16] Although there was a growth of individual piety in the fifteenth century among the better off who could afford primers, the great majority were corporate Christians. In fact, the secular-sacred divide that came into being with the Enlightenment, and which was encouraged by the individualism of the Protestant Reformation, did not exist. There was instead a complete identification of society with the Church.

The corporate nature of medieval religion can be seen on many different levels. There was an extraordinary upsurge in the building of parish churches in the late medieval period of the fifteenth century. About a third to half of the 10,000 parish churches in England were built during this period. If people were putting their money where their hearts were, then the hearts of these patrons were definitely in their parish churches. Pious laity built many of the great wool churches in East Anglia and the Cotswolds, from Southwold to Chipping Campden. They were also kitted out and decorated with donations from the local community. Not until the Victorian era would there be anything like such a comparable build. No doubt some of this generosity was hastened by the fear of death, and the desire to mitigate the length of time spent in purgatory, but it still amounted to extraordinary generosity by local communities.

Processions and feast days were another aspect of corporate Christianity; hardly a month would go by without the celebration of a significant day in the Church calendar. Palm Sunday, Rogation Days, Corpus Christi and local saints' days were all celebrated with processions and feasts, where the church ale flowed, providing a consistent source of revenue to pay for church maintenance.

The great links between society—a mercantile society at that—and the parish churches were the guilds. Guilds were highly influential associations of craftsmen who supported their trade in a given place but were also based at and supported their parish churches. In the City of London these guilds would come to be known as the City livery companies. There are 110 such livery companies; to this day, thirty-seven have premises in the City of London. The oldest, like the Goldsmiths, received a royal charter in 1327. There was a mutual arrangement of support with the local parish church; indeed, the guild became part of the fabric of the parish. The guild would support parishes and their clergy and would maintain a guild light in the church (literally the provision of a candle each week to burn in the church on Sunday and during mass). For its part, the parish church would have prayers said or masses performed in church or chantry for present and past guild members. There would be an annual feast day for each guild, with a procession to the church, the welcoming of new members with "love, charity and peace" and distributions to the poor. The guilds founded charities and schools (the Skinners Company still have several schools in Tonbridge Wells and east London, for example; the Merchant Taylors in north London). The guilds chained the commercial world to the parish church, linking business with prayer.

In short, medieval Christianity dominated people's lives. For every thirty head of population there was a priest, a monk or a parish assistant. For every 250 people, there was a parish church. The population of England in 1400, still recovering from the Black Death, was about 2.5 million. There were 10,000 parish churches with chantry chapels and monasteries beside. With such a monopoly of religious institutions, the practice of Christianity was open to abuse. The *Canterbury Tales* illustrates popular feeling about the Church and the extent of its corruption. "The Friar's Tale" tells of the venality of the Summoner (an ecclesiastical court's official), who used his position to extract a bribe from an old woman terrified of being excommunicated for some indeterminate charge or summons. The Summoner was "as full of gossip as a carrion crow is of worms",[17] for "there is nothing good to be said about that profession".[18] For moral equivalence, "The Summoner's Tale" has nothing good to say about the Friar, either. Wherever Friar John went he would cry, "Donate arms for the sake of masses for the dead."[19] When he visited a certain bedridden Thomas in "The Summoner's Tale", he set about getting more money: "I need your charity, Thomas! For God's sake charity! And at that he fell on his knees, and crossed himself."[20] But all he got, in true Chaucerian tradition, was a fart![21] The Pardoner, who had a bag of indulgences (certificates for time off purgatory for penances done or alms given) brought straight from Rome, with relics as well, sought to sell them widely. He boasted:

> I am used to preaching in churches . . . I show them my papal indulgences. I mutter a few words of Latin to spice up my sermon . . . I get out of my sack the glass cases that hold the relics of the holy saints—a collarbone here and a wrist bone there . . . Wash this bone in any well and it will cure your cattle of any murrain or blight.[22]

Money once again exchanged hands, but it was the Church that generally took it. Only the parish priest received a good press:

> He stayed at home, and protected his flock from the wolves of sin and greed that threatened it. He was a true shepherd and not a religious mercenary. He wanted to draw people to God with kind words and good deeds.[23]

In a Church much tempted by corruption because of its powerful position, with a sulphurous teaching on the afterlife that preyed on the anxieties of the living, few in its professional echelons were untainted. Yet just as Elijah in the Old Testament complained to YAHWEH that only he was righteous in all Israel, to be at once told there were 7,000 who had not bowed the knee to Baal (1 Kings 19:18), so among the English it was not only parish priests who remained faithful up and down the land, but there was also a group of mystics who showed genuine devotion and whose writings continue to inspire today.

The English Mystics

The extraordinary flowering of mystical writing in the fourteenth and early fifteenth centuries is one of the marvels of English Christianity. Such activity existed within the Christian construct of the age and did not seek to destroy it. The tradition of mysticism, which seeks an intense spiritual relationship with the Trinity, has a long pedigree. In the Old Testament, the lives of Abraham, Moses and Elijah were ever an inspiration to the Church Fathers, speaking of the possibility of a close, intimate and transformative relationship with God. Gregory of Nyssa wrote an important mystical work called the *Life of Moses*.[24] Mount Carmel, strongly associated with Elijah, would inspire the Carmelite movement and also the later mystic, John of the Cross, in sixteenth-century Spain. Augustine's *Confessions*, particularly Book IX, and Dionysius the Areopagite, a sixth-century writer, would both be powerful influences on the mystical tradition. Mystical authors are, in the first instance, practitioners of contemplation and prayer. They write from an undeniable and sometimes overwhelming experience of the love of God in their own lives. This is the kernel of their spirituality and they often speak of the wound of love in their souls.[25] Thus they experience theology, are given to revelation, their *modus operandi* is contemplation, and they are not frightened to speak of their emotions and feelings. Their writings gathered influence in the twentieth century, in fact, and have a profound influence on many today.

For the most part, the English Mystics lived in the fourteenth century, and most famous among them are three men and two women, who together offer a fine balance of spiritual insight from both sexes. Richard Rolle (c. 1300–49), a hermit from Yorkshire, is most famous for his work *The Fire of Love*, but he also wrote widely on the scriptures, translating some of the Bible, notably the Psalms, into English. The Lollards were to read and cherish his biblical works. His later contemporary, Walter Hilton (c. 1345–96), was an Augustinian and an influential writer on prayer, mysticism and spiritual development. Both men wrote to anchoresses advising them on their spiritual lives: Richard Rolle wrote to Margaret Kirby, who later collected and publicized his works, and Walter Hilton wrote his famous *Ladder of Perfection* to an unknown "ghostly sister in Christ". Later in the same century, Julian of Norwich (c. 1342–1416) began her life as an anchoress in a cell in a small church in Norwich, and this is still a place of counsel and prayer today. Julian's *Revelations of Divine Love* remains a classic of mystical English spirituality and is quite possibly the first book written by a woman in English. Not far away in Kings Lynn, her redoubtable contemporary, Margery Kempe (c. 1373–1439), began dictation of her own very different life, also suffused with an unusual presence of God, and rich in mystical experience. Finally, the century gave us a fifth major mystic: the unknown author of *The Cloud of Unknowing*.

That the works of each of these mystics have survived and are in print today is thanks to a combination of their original popularity, their extraordinary preservation due to providence, and the serendipity of life. As the manuscript of the exquisite second-century *Epistle to Diognetus* was discovered by a Dominican monk amongst the packing cases of a fish shop in Constantinople in 1436, and the Dead Sea Scrolls were discovered by shepherd boys throwing stones into caves near the Dead Sea in 1948, so Margery Kempe's book was discovered by a group of young people playing table tennis in the hallway of Southgate House, Derbyshire, in the early 1930s. While searching for a new ball in a cupboard in the hallway, the players found "a clutter of smallish brown books".[26] It was Margery Kempe's life, which would have remained unknown to the world but for the need of a ping-pong ball to continue a game! By contrast, Richard Rolle's works were very popular in his own day, with over 400 manuscripts surviving. Likewise, Walter Hilton's works were well-known, while the manuscript of Julian of Norwich's *Revelations of Divine Love* had a much more fragile line of transmission. Passed from hand to hand, and convent to convent, suppressed for years, manuscripts of her work were eventually found in a Benedictine convent in Rue des Anglais, Cambrai, in Stanbrook Abbey near Thirsk in North Yorkshire, and in the Sloane Collection of papers in the British Library, where one was tracked down by Grace Warwick. By such "mysterious" means the writings of the fourteenth-century mystics have been preserved.

Richard Rolle came from an educated family in Thornton-le-Dale near Pickering in North Yorkshire. Following his education at Balliol, Oxford (which he did not seem to complete by taking his degree, and where he was supported by the Archdeacon of Durham, Thomas Neville), he was granted a site for a hermitage on the estate of John de Dalton in Yorkshire. He later moved to Hampole, where he lived as a solitary near a Cistercian monastery. He pursued the life of a hermit, but was also popular in local houses with young people and women.[27] He had a wide circle of affectionate admirers, drawn no doubt by the sense of joy and love he had about him. In many ways he remained an outsider to the institution of the Church. The friendlessness of the poor, the oppression and worldliness of the rich, the destructiveness of sin and the hypocrisy of those who filled the Church distressed him too much to allow him to be part of its institutions. His was a purer path, if also a greater struggle. His most popular mystical work was *The Fire of Love* (*Incendium Amoris*), which stood in the tradition of earlier medieval mystics, such as Bernard of Clairvaux, Richard of Victor and St Bonaventure. Like all the mystics, he espoused the way of contemplation. Rolle spoke of a three-stage journey of contemplation involving an experience of heat, followed by sweetness, and finally by song: each stage was an expression of God's love in the soul. To find this love was to find the essence of all mystical experience. It was what St Paul means in his letter to the Ephesians about knowing the love of God "that surpasses knowledge" (Ephesians 3:19) and grasping "how wide and long and high and deep is the love of Christ" (3:18).

Like the Egyptian Desert Fathers, who were his spiritual forbears, Rolle suffered many privations and fierce struggles. He mortified his flesh with many fasts, with frequent vigils, and repeated sobs and sighings, "quitting all soft bedding and having a hard bench for a bed and for a house a small cell".[28] He fixed his mind continually on heaven, and his desire was to depart and be with Christ. His struggles with the devil were at times intense: on one occasion the devil came to him in the form of a beautiful woman who pinned him to his bed. He made the sign of the cross, invoked the Trinity and escaped. He wrote most passionately of the joys of contemplation and its sweetness, for "the memory of Jesu be to him as a melody of music at a feast and is sweeter in his mouth than honey or the honeycomb".[29] His aim is summed up as becoming God's lover, one who seeks "nothing in this world but that he may be in the wilderness, only taking heed to the likings of his Maker".[30] Knowing and communicating to others the burning heat of God's presence was the sole purpose of his life.

Another mystic who lived only a little after Richard Rolle was Walter Hilton. It seems he was born just two years before Richard's death. While Rolle's *Fire of Love* is an account of the experience of ecstasy or the profound work of the Holy Spirit that may follow contemplation, Hilton's *Ladder of Perfection* is a thorough treatise on how a person may be restored and then embark on the path of contemplation. Halfway through this book Hilton affirms his purpose in writing it is to show "how man's soul may be, and is, reformed in the likeness of Him who first created it".[31] In many ways Hilton reflects Irenaeus's (c. AD 130–202) great dictum in his seminal third-century work *Against Heresies*, that "the glory of God is a man fully alive".

Hilton carefully charts how this might occur. The second part of *The Ladder of Perfection* concentrates on the foundation that Christ has laid to make this possible. Only God can restore the human soul: "for the passion and precious death of our Lord are the means whereby the soul of man is re-formed, and without them we could never have been restored to His likeness nor come to the joys of heaven."[32] Anticipating Luther, he goes on to say, "the reformation comes about in two ways: one is by faith alone, the other is by faith and experience. The first—reformation by faith alone—is sufficient for salvation, but the second earns a high reward in heaven."[33] The second type of reformation is what would later be called "sanctification": a process Hilton says involves "the eradication from the soul of all carnal impulses and worldly desires, and allows no imperfections to survive".[34] He acknowledges the necessity of grace; he endorses the concept of spiritual struggle, as explained by Paul in Romans 7; he presses for the need for humility and self-discipline. He is, like Rolle, utterly Jesus-centred, writing, "you must realize that whatever you may have or achieve is of no value or satisfaction without the love of Jesus".[35]

As the title of his book indicates, Hilton was a proponent of staged spiritual development, hence the analogy of the ladder—a popular spiritual image for Christian progress. Like Pope Gregory before him, he divides the Christian life into the contemplative and the active, the breathing in and out of Christian living. He talks about the three degrees of spiritual progress: the first stage consisting of the knowledge of God, but without strong feelings of devotion; the second consisting in principally loving God and experiencing the fire of his love; and the third, the highest attainable in this life, consisting of true knowledge and love of God. Likewise, when it comes to prayer, there are three degrees of prayer: firstly, vocal prayer as in church services when someone joins in the corporate prayer; secondly, vocal but extempore prayer—employing no fixed form; and thirdly, prayer in the heart alone "accompanied by great peace and tranquillity of body. One who wishes to pray in this way must have a pure heart, for the gift comes only to those who, either through long bodily and spiritual effort, or through such visitations of love as I have described, have attained quietness of soul."[36] Alongside this framework, Hilton emphasizes the need for humility and charity; a struggle against the devil and carnal thoughts if progress is to be made; and the dismantling of the image of sin in the life of a contemplative. His instruction is clear, well-illustrated and from genuine personal experience: no wonder it was so popular in his own day. It would not be until the Puritans that such a systematic description of the journey of a soul would be attempted in England again, although elsewhere in Norwich an anchoress called Julian would also have the sort of remarkable "visitations of love" described by Hilton.

Mother Julian almost certainly came from East Anglia and became an anchoress (a recluse) living in a cell in a church off Norwich's Rouen Street, which is now named after her and open for all to visit. Although she spent much of her time in prayer and reflection, she also gave spiritual advice to those in need, rather like Simeon Stylites (c. 390–459), the hermit who did much the same from his more unusual location on top of a pillar outside Aleppo in Syria. During her sojourn in her cell, Julian pursued her own spiritual quest, or in her words, her desire that she might receive the wound of Christ's love in her soul. The wound of Christ's love is a common theme among mystics from earliest times and can be found in the writings of both Augustine and Gregory of Nyssa. At the age of "thirty and a half years old" Julian was on the verge of death.[37] A priest was summoned and showed her a crucifix. She suffered shortness of breath and felt she was dying. She seemed to welcome death so that she might "receive all the rights of the church",[38] but "at this moment all my suffering suddenly left me, and I was as completely well in my upper body, as ever was before or after. I marvelled at this change, for it seemed to me a mysterious work of God, not a natural one."[39] She then made it her prayer to experience three gifts in her life: the gift of a "deeper perception of Christ's passion"; bodily sickness that she might know Christ's sufferings; and the sacrament of the church and the three wounds of contrition, compassion and longing. On 8 May, Julian received fifteen "showings" (her word), or revelations of divine love, relating to God's purpose in allowing her to be so close to death. The first revelation began early in the morning of 8 May around 4 a.m. and continued "until it was well past the middle of the day".[40] Another revelation came the following morning, confirming the revelations of the previous day, and one final revelation came fifteen years later, which prompted her to write her *Revelations of Divine Love* for wider circulation. The work was written up in two versions, a shorter and a longer text. Neither were widely circulated in her lifetime—nor in the medieval period generally—but, after fresh translations were made at the beginning of the twentieth century, these became spiritual classics and have become deeply influential.

Julian's revelations, which came to her in a cascade of understanding—and the greater part in a single day—are the bedrock of her theology and the substance of her message. There are sixteen in all. The principal themes of the revelations are the Passion of Christ, the love and courtesy of God, the call to prayer, and the assurance of his goodness. Most of the revelations are to do with understanding the Passion of Christ, for example, numbers one, two, four, five, eight, nine and ten, in which Julian saw different aspects, very often accompanied by visions of Christ's shed blood: "Then I saw red blood trickling down from under the crown of thorns, hot and fresh and very plentiful."[41] The Passion is the greatest proof of his love, for "he is our clothing, wrapping and enveloping us for love, embracing us and guiding us in all things, hanging about us in tender love, so that he can never leave us".[42] Eternity is granted by being an object of that love, like the hazelnut that Julian sees. Indeed, Julian understood that "he made everything that is made for love".[43] Courtesy is the quality of that love, and this gave Julian great happiness and joy, even contagious laughter. Only when we understand this love will we pray aright. The outcome of Christ's love is that "he does not only concern himself with great and noble things, but also with small, humble things, with both one and the other; and this is what he means when he says, 'All manner of things shall be well'".[44] Indeed, a little earlier Julian had affirmed: "The good Lord answered all the questions and doubts I could put forward, saying most comfortingly, 'I may make all things well and I can make all things well and I will make all these well:

and you shall see for yourself that all manner of things shall be well.'"[45] In the final revelation, given fifteen years after the healing of her acute illness, everything is summarized with these words which God speaks to her and her own conclusion:

> "Do you want to know what your Lord meant [that is, by the illness and the revelations]? Know well that love was what he meant. Who showed you this love? Love. What did he show? Love. Why did he show it to you? For love. Hold fast to this and you will know and understand more of the same: but you will never understand or know from it anything else for all eternity". This is how I was taught that our Lord's meaning was Love.[46]

Whilst Julian reflected and prayed about these revelations in her cell in Norwich and spoke to the many enquirers who came to her window, one particular woman who was to have a considerable influence came to her from Kings Lynn. Her name was Margery Kempe (c. 1379–c. 1439). Julian's advice to Margery, who had been instructed by God to go and see her, was "to be obedient to the wishes of our Lord God and to fulfil with all her might whatever he put into her soul, if it were not against the worship of God or the profit of fellow Christians, nor against charity".[47] She encouraged Margery to look for signs of the Holy Ghost in her life: contrition, chastity, devotion, compassion, groaning prayer, lament and weeping and not to be afraid of spite, shame or rebuking from the world—for this must be so with those in whom God makes his seat. Finally, she advised: "Patience is necessary for you, because in that you shall preserve your soul."[48]

Margery Kempe's life was not that of an ordinary mystic. She was far from enclosed: more a wandering spiritual Catherine wheel than a closeted, quiet contemplative. Shunned as much as admired, she was from the merchant class of prosperous Kings Lynn. Her father, John Burnham, was a successful merchant in one of the richest wool ports of the country. At the age of about twenty, she married John Kempe, also a merchant. She had fourteen children by him and then determined to live a life of chastity, but her husband was not willing to give up sex without a contest. After eight weeks of abstinence, he asked her if she would rather see him killed than renew sexual relations. When she said she would, he replied: "You are not a good wife."[49] After she prayed, her husband said: "May your body be as freely available to God as it had been to me."[50] So began a life of pilgrimage, journeys, preaching, mockery, near misses with the authorities, visions, sermons, several confessors and copious weeping when moved by a service, an account of the Passion or an address. She had the energy of the Wife of Bath and the devotion of a Poor Clare. All her adventures, both spiritual and physical, were dictated to several priests she employed as writers, being herself semi-illiterate. She could understand Latin and read somewhat, but to write a good text she needed support, and being of considerable means, she was able to hire clerks to write her memoirs.

Her book has a number of distinguishing features. There are the many conversations with Jesus she records from her life, the revelations she receives, the account of two pilgrimages to Jerusalem and Rome, her brushes with ecclesiastical law almost resulting in punishment, as she was often mistaken for a Lollard (for a description of a Lollard, see chapter 9), her courage, her self-designation as "this creature" throughout the book and her mystical experiences as a contemplative.

Called to go on pilgrimage to Jerusalem, she first settled her husband's debts in the town, with her offer of settlement announced from the pulpit of her parish church in Kings Lynn. She then took leave of the town and sailed from Yarmouth. She was not a popular member of the party because she refused to eat meat and "they were most displeased because she wept so much and was always talking about the love and goodness of the Lord, at table as well as in other places".[51] In other words her burning love of God was a challenge or an embarrassment to those who were merely seeking an extended holiday.

Her spiritual diet was crafted by confessors familiar with Bonaventure and his *Prick of Love*, with Richard Hampole and his *Incendio Amoris*, with Elizabeth of Hungary, a celebrated mystic, and Bridget of Sweden. This widespread knowledge demonstrates the degree to which mystical theology was current among the clergy and religious of the time. Margery frequently confessed her faith and failures to confessors. Thus to one priest, the Prior of Lynn, "she disclosed all her life, as accurately as she could, from her youth: both her sins, her labours, her vexations, her contemplations, and also her revelations and such grace as God performed in her through his mercy, and so that priest trusted well that God performed very great grace in her".[52] The centre of her devotions were long and intimate conversations with Christ himself, in which she experienced "high contemplation".[53] Christ assured her: "You can never say a word more to my liking than 'as certainly as I love you'—for I then fulfil my grace in you and give you many a holy thought, it would be impossible to describe them all."[54] She loved to reflect on Christ's Passion, which frequently moved her to tears, and to join in the parish processions. When she did, "she could not stop herself weeping and sobbing, she really had to weep, to cry, and to sob, when she saw her saviour suffer such great pains for her love."[55] Hers was a remarkable spiritual journey, right in the midst of unreformed medieval religion, full of passion: an ordinary person with an extraordinary heart and insight.

The final great mystical work to come from this period is the anonymous *Cloud of Unknowing*.[56] It appeared at the time of the Black Death. Influenced by the mystic Dionysius the Areopagite, *The Cloud of Unknowing* was written for a solitary hermit, possibly like the author himself. The author is in the tradition of a mystic like Gregory of Nyssa who sought the otherness of God, and a transcendence that goes beyond mere reason. They both stress the apophatic qualities of God (his so-called negative—in a grammatical sense—qualities): his invisibility, his immortality, his inscrutability and his incomprehensibility. The author of *The Cloud* takes up the idea that a cloud is a symbol of the unknowable presence of God and that "thick darkness [is] where God is" (Exodus 20:21). This darkness can only be breached by the dart or wound of God's love, conveyed by his words and presence, and by which the soul may have an impression of his being and thus be granted an inner vision of God. The author, like so many others before, speaks of a journey in faith, overcoming sin, growing in humility, following the disciplines of reading, thinking or reflecting and praying, and preferring the way of Mary, or of contemplative prayer, over Martha's activity. This theme comes from the story in Luke's Gospel where Jesus commends Mary for choosing the better *way*, and for sitting at his feet rather than being caught up in anxious activity like her sister Martha (Luke 10:42). Following this path, the contemplative may come to the "cloud of unknowing" and be ravished in their soul:

> Then will He sometimes peradventure send out a beam of ghostly light, piercing the cloud of unknowing that is betwixt thee and Him; and shew thee some of his privity, the which man may not, nor cannot speak. Then shalt thou feel thine affection inflamed with fire of his love, far more than I can tell thee, or may or will at this time.[57]

In the fourteenth and early fifteenth centuries, there was a flowering of devotional and mystical literature, which reflects a healthy desire to know and follow God in the midst of the full panoply of medieval religion. Other works, like William Langland's moral allegory *Piers Plowman* (c. 1370–90) and Robert Manning's *Handling Synne* of 1303—a series of moral tales to invite contrition and reformation of life—were also very popular. Indeed, a work which contained such riveting stories as "The adulterous wife whose skeleton split in two" or "The Cambridgeshire miser-parson who stuft his moth with gold" was bound to attract a readership. John Mirc wrote *Instructions for Parish Priests* and Dan Jeremy *The Lay Folks Mass Book*, a commentary on the mass. Both were widely used.

Although the Reformation would demonstrate the deep shortcomings of medieval religion, with the Reformers taking exception to the medieval emphasis on the visible (e.g. the theatre and doctrine of the mass and the depicting in art of the Gospel narrative) and the communal (for instance, processions and public penance) over the verbal and the individual, and would drive out the more obvious rackets, like indulgences based on the notion of purgatory, there is no denying that, despite a corrupt and poorly educated clergy, the late medieval Church nonetheless flourished as a popular institution. In fact, it was arguably never more popular and closer to the people at any other time, having accompanied them through their greatest trauma, the Black Death. Yet by 1370, there was the beginning of change in the realm, both politically and spiritually. But it would take a further hundred years of political, dynastic struggle and spiritual controversy before cracks in the old ways began truly to emerge.

CHAPTER 10

The Rumblings of Revolt

With the death of Edward III in 1377, one epoch of English history had ended and a new, unstable one was about to begin. Edward's reign closed with a long sunset on his earlier achievements. He drifted into senility in the end, which created a vacuum of power. By 1377, the nation was exhausted: from the Black Death, from long years of warfare, from high taxation to fund these campaigns in France, and from the demands of feudalism on a shrinking population and labour market. At the same time, Parliament had become more powerful, electing its own speaker for the Commons in 1343, one William Trussell. When Edward III died, his grandson, Richard II, succeeded. Richard's father, the Black Prince, the hammer of the French, had died a year before in 1376.

As happened on several other occasions in medieval England, a minority rule by a young prince followed (Henry III was nine when he succeeded his father King John in 1216; Richard II was ten when he succeeded his grandfather Edward III in 1377; and Henry VI was nine months when he succeeded his father Henry V in 1422). Minorities make for instability and rivalry between noble families, only some of whom are included in the regency. Henry III's rule was increasingly resented by his subjects because of the influence of his continental relations on both church and state. Henry Bolingbroke (later Henry IV), the son of John of Gaunt, deposed Richard II, and Henry VI was unable to emerge from his very long minority as a commanding figure. It is no surprise that William Shakespeare found more than enough material in the hundred years from 1377 to 1485 to support eight historical plays—*Richard II, Henry IV Parts I & II, Henry V, Henry VI Parts I, II, III,* and *Richard III.* The Bard provided from these plays legends about England and a vocabulary of defiance that would inspire England in its greatest struggle in the twentieth century, echoing previous defiance and patriotism.

This final hundred-year period before the emergence of the Tudors, and which we consider in this chapter, would be marked by almost constant instability, eventual defeat in France, the end of continental ambitions and descent into dynastic civil war—the Wars of the Roses—among the descendants of Edward III. It was also a time when the first cracks appeared in the structure of medieval religion, which, under the Tudors, would later expand into a complete breach.

Richard II and the Peasants' Revolt

When Richard II succeeded, aged ten, the nation was restless and also exhausted by disease, war and taxation. The government had sought—on pain of imprisonment—artificially to hold down wages to pre-Black Death levels through an Ordinance of Labourers, even though labour was scarce. Slavery was still practised in some places. John of Gaunt, the new King's uncle and regent, was continuing to campaign in France. In November 1380, Parliament imposed a flat-rate poll tax of one shilling a head, three times the poll tax of 1377. The tax, with its intimidating collection methods, was the trigger for a revolt, which became the Great Revolt (commonly called the "Peasants' Revolt") of 1381. It was hardly a Peasants' Revolt, however, since it was led by educated people including businessmen, office holders and individuals of some power and wealth. If the poll tax was the spark that set the commons of England alight in Kent and the South-East, the attitudes of ordinary men were tinder dry towards the hierarchy, both lay and spiritual. In letters circulating at the time and collected by chroniclers of the day, there is more than an echo of Langland's great poem *Piers Plowman*. One such letter puts these words into the mouth of that most English of characters, John Ball:

> John Ball greets you well all and gives you to understand he has rung our bell. Now right and might, will and skill. God speed every single one. Now is the time. . . . Now reigns pride on high, and covetousness is held wise, and lechery without shame, and gluttony without blame, Envy reigns with treason, and sloth is taken in great season.[1]

In other words, there was a deep sense of grievance and outrage that the commons of England should foot the bill for endless chivalric wars that gave the English nothing except temporary glory in the face of grinding poverty. In May 1381, therefore, villagers in Essex set upon a tax collector. From there they marched through Kent to London, led by Wat Tyler. The young King took flight to the Tower. They were not against the King; indeed they believed him to be on the side of the commons of England, for their watchword was: "With King Richard and with the true commons."[2] They arrived in London, sacked Lambeth Palace, released the prisoners in the Marshalsea and Fleet prisons, destroyed the lawyers' records at the Temple, and burnt down the Savoy Palace of John of Gaunt. Eventually the King bravely decided to meet them at Mile End on 14 June. He conceded to all their demands. That same evening some rebels broke into the Tower and summarily executed the Archbishop of Canterbury, Simon Sudbury, and the King's Treasurer, Sir Robert Hales. Richard called them to a further meeting at Smithfield on 15 June. It was then that the Mayor of London killed Wat Tyler in a scuffle. When Tyler's followers raised their bows to press their attack, Richard rode out to meet them, calling out he was *their* King. He promised an amnesty and said that all their grievances would be looked into. The following day they dispersed, the Mayor of London raised a militia, and the rebels were attacked on 25 and 26 June at North Walsham. Their leaders were arrested, and over 1,500 killed. The rebellion was repressed, and all promises rescinded. In many ways it was the young King's finest hour. Richard had met the rebellion courageously with his own personal authority, even though he and his officials were heavily outnumbered, and he had provided the breathing space for the rebels to be confronted later.

Richard soon exhibited impatience with the old ways and with the courtiers of his grandfather, Edward III. Like many a young aspiring king, he wanted to be rid of them and their suffocating restrictions or presence at court, even as the war in France descended into a series of losses and unsatisfactory treaties. He focussed instead on a court more in keeping with his personality: full of younger knights "more valiant in bed than on the battle field".[3] Richard showed a marked preference for ceremony, deference and luxury, accompanied by escalating costs. Chroniclers had long observed his "lust for glory and his eagerness to have from everybody the deference properly due to kingship".[4] In 1387, when he was twenty, the old guard reasserted their power as the Lords Appellant in the persons of the King's uncle Thomas, Duke of Gloucester, Henry Bolingbroke, the son of John of Gaunt, Richard Earl of Arundel, Thomas Earl of Warwick and Thomas Earl Marshal.

The Lords Appellant effectively removed power from the King and exiled his friends and advisers. In response Richard began a slow march towards re-establishing his authority. In 1389, aged twenty-two, he announced his intention of taking back power as King. His first wife, Anne of Bohemia, died childless and in 1396 he contracted an influential dynastic marriage with Isabella Valois, the daughter of King Charles VI of France. She was seven years old at the time of her marriage, so there would be no possibility of an heir for at least six years, but her dowry was £130,000 and a truce with France was agreed. (Her sister Katherine or Kate would later marry Henry V and then become the wife of Owen Tudor, after Henry's early death.)

Richard was now emboldened to act. In September 1397 he called what came to be known as the "Revenge Parliament", executing or exiling the Lords Appellant. Two of the Appellants, Henry Bolingbroke and Thomas of Norfolk, each calling the other a traitor, were called to judicial combat until Richard hastily abandoned the joust. Henry Bolingbroke, the future Henry IV, was exiled to France for ten years and, on the death of Henry's father, John of Gaunt, in 1399, Richard seized all his extensive lands. The seeds of rebellion by Bolingbroke were now sown.

With a change of policy in France, brought on by the madness of Charles VI, and discontent in England at the rule of Richard II, Bolingbroke, the chivalric Crusader knight who had fought in a Crusade in the Baltic States, returned to wrest the crown from Richard. In June 1399 he landed at Ravenspur in Yorkshire (now eroded by the North Sea), not far from Kingston upon Hull. Richard was in Ireland at the time. In Shakespeare's words, on arriving on the coast of Wales and hearing of Bolingbroke's arrival, Richard wonders and hopes that,

> Not all the waters of the rough rude sea
> Can wash the balm from an anointed king:
> The breath of worldly men cannot depose
> The deputy elected by the Lord.[5]

It was a sentiment with which Richard would have wholeheartedly agreed, but it could not save him. While the anointed of the Lord was too easily overcome, commanding legitimacy in his place was not easily achieved by his successor, Henry IV. Bereft of support, Richard surrendered to Henry's messengers at Flint Castle on 19 August 1399. He was arraigned before Parliament and formally deposed on 1 October. By 19 February of the following year, he had died in Pontefract Castle, quite possibly of starvation—a pathetic and deserted figure captured with great bathos by Shakespeare.

Richard's reign, his end and his concept of kingship became a tragic refrain through English history. Charles I was not so dissimilar in his ideas about kingship or in his fate. Richard, like Charles I, lived by an image of kingship that made him both remote and unpredictable to his subjects. It is an image burnished brilliantly in the Wilton Diptych, which hangs in the National Gallery and is a European vision of royalty captured in courtly gothic style.[6] Edmund the Martyr, Edward the Confessor and John the Baptist surround a kneeling King Richard, but the projections of such "holiness" and such exalted company did not exempt Richard from the more mundane tasks of kingship of which his subjects were increasingly critical. To neglect them was to court disaster, and for him such neglect led to a terrible death. Buried hastily at the priory at King's Langley, Richard's body was transferred by Henry V with great ceremony to Westminster Abbey, where it rests in a kind of Plantagenet mausoleum at the centre of which is Edward the Confessor's tomb. Near the door of the abbey is the iconic and familiar picture of Richard II, at once elegant and vulnerable. His successor and usurper, Henry IV, would discover that "uneasy is the head that wears the crown"[7] and that to talk of kingship was to talk "of graves, of worms, and epitaphs" for "within the hollow crown, that rounds the mortal temples of a king, keeps death his court".[8] If there was alarm and change in the highest echelons of English society with the usurpation of Richard II, there was also a murmuring and revolt that threatened the *status quo* of medieval religion, put forward by an erstwhile royal servant and Oxford don, John Wyclif.

John Wyclif

Wyclif, a member of the minor nobility in Yorkshire, was born in the North Riding in c. 1328 at either Hipswell or Wycliff-on-Tees. He was ordained priest in York Minster on 24 September 1351.[9] He was educated at Oxford, most probably as an undergraduate at Queen's College, graduating in 1356 in the Faculty of Arts. He went on to become a probationary fellow at Merton before pursuing a master's degree at Balliol, which had a strong connection with the North of England. He was elected the third master at Balliol, but in 1361 left to become rector of Fillingham in Lincolnshire and prebend of Aust at Westbury-on-Trym, near Bristol. In 1363, Wyclif began his theological training at Oxford (as opposed to his earlier general arts degree), which involved a further four years of lectures, followed by years of formal disputation. He achieved his bachelor's degree in theology in 1369 and his doctorate in 1372. By all accounts Wyclif was of bird-like physique with a frail but charismatic aura, an acerbic manner, and a scowling demeanour. He had a quicksilver donnish wit, but over time left more academic pursuits and became devoted to the pastoral responsibilities of preaching and teaching.

Wyclif's most influential period was between 1372 and 1382. After the long years of training at Oxford, he became a prolific author on a whole host of subjects, not least the organization of the Church and its clergy, of which he was deeply critical. Because of his critique of the Church and his opinion that, as a considerable landowner, it should pay tax to the realm and not be given privileged exemption, he came to the notice of John of Gaunt, one of the most powerful men in government and the second son of Edward III. For different reasons, John of Gaunt also believed the Church should be cut down to size and should make a significant contribution to the nation's resources. If on the one hand John of Gaunt used Wyclif as ammunition for his own attack on the structure of the Church, on the other he gave political cover and support for Wyclif's own increasingly radical ideas about church reform. In November 1372, Wyclif entered into some form of royal service in the retinue or court of John of Gaunt.

Wyclif came to the attention of John of Gaunt because of his academic prominence in Oxford. One of his earliest works was *De Logica* (1360), an exploration of the fundamentals of scholastic logic. Further treatises on logic followed, such as *Tractatus de Logica*, a compendium of earlier tracts on the subject, and a commentary on the eight books of Aristotle's *Physics*.

Like most of his contemporaries, Wyclif entered the debate about "universals". He made clear in his *De Actibus Anime* (concerning *The Action of the Mind)* that he did not hold to the Platonic concept of "universals" existing independently of God, but rather he believed that they proceeded from, and existed originally in, the mind of God. In this he was closer to Grosseteste than Ockham. At Oxford, Grosseteste had argued for the existence of universals, albeit not in the Platonic sense of a perfect form existing by itself, but as existing only in the mind of God. By contrast, Ockham argued for knowledge based entirely on particulars. It was in this debate that Wyclif sharpened his academic thought and made his own major contribution, his *Summa de Ente* (*A Summary of Being*), written between 1365 and 1372.

The *Summa de Ente* is made up of two books: the first has seven treatises on being and how being relates to human beings, and the second has six on formal theology: e.g. the divine nature, its attributes and the Trinity. The first part deals with philosophical subjects that address our understanding of created reality and therefore broaches the divide between Plato and Aristotle. The second part treats six aspects of divine reality. Thus, in a lesser way, it seeks to do what Aquinas did with his *Summa*. Yet while Aquinas comes out in support of Aristotle's perceptions of reality and how we may know that, Wyclif is very much in support of Plato. He has what is called a "realist" ontology regarding universals, which sets him apart from the views of Ockham, Aquinas and Duns Scotus. If the first book of *de Ente* is controversial, rejecting the fusion of Aristotle and the Bible that was so prevalent in Aquinas and others, the second book is much more conventional and is a re-statement of Augustinian theology, and is also quite possibly Wyclif's own commentary on Lombard—still an academic staging post in the fourteenth and fifteenth centuries.

If we ask why Wyclif preferred the reality of a universal being prior to its actual existence, the answer seems to be that everything must first exist in the mind of God as an idea, from which the nature and purpose of its existence takes shape. Thus, humanity exists originally in divine thought (which is a universal) and later comes into existence in reality. Humanity is thus defined, not by a scientific survey of what is common to all human beings, but by what God reveals to us as the essence of humanity. Since theologically the essence of humanity is what God conceives to be human, namely the pre-fallen Adam who corresponds perfectly to God's idea of humanity and the incarnate Jesus Christ, they (Adam and Christ) alone demonstrate what it is to be fully human, and Adam only before his Fall. These are universal examples of humanity. What we may be sure of is that "in each body of work, [Wyclif's] analytic rigour and his tendency to return to specific issues suggest a mind determined to resolve error by using remorseless reason".[10] Having employed reason in this fashion in his academic disputes at Oxford, Wyclif now applied the same logic to the Church and the predestination that underlay its call. There were four areas on which Wyclif shone the beam of his reasoning, and these were in turn anchored in scripture. They were the teaching about transubstantiation, the purpose or logic of scripture, the rightful lordship or dominium of the Church, and the predestination of the elect.

Wyclif's teaching on the sacrament of communion or the Eucharist was an arrow shot at the heart of the medieval Church. The doctrine of the change in the bread and wine at the time of consecration in the mass was first promulgated by Paschasius Radbertus (c. 790–865) in the Carolingian church of Charlemagne. Radbertus was an abbot of Corbie in Picardy and published his influential *De corpore et sanguine Domini* between 831 and 833, putting forward the idea of transubstantiation, which gained wide acceptance in the Roman Catholic Church. Radbertus was canonized in 1073 by Pope Gregory VII (Hildebrand), the great reformist pope who implacably opposed lay investiture (the right of laypeople to make church appointments). In particular, he opposed the Holy Roman Emperor, Henry IV, whom he excommunicated and famously forced to come in penance to the castle at Canossa.

At the heart of the doctrine of transubstantiation was the idea that although the bread and wine may not have changed in *appearance*, they were *really* changed, becoming Christ's actual body and blood. However, Ratramnus, another monk at Corbie during the same period, objected to this formulation, saying that Christ could not be really or empirically present in the bread and wine, but was present in figure only. From 1140 onwards, the word transubstantiation occurs, becoming the touchstone of Roman Catholic theology of the Eucharist. This theology was further bolstered by Thomas Aquinas's Aristotelianism and by the Franciscan Duns Scotus, who held the variant view of consubstantiation, which allowed for Jesus's bodily presence in heaven and his real presence in the bread and wine.

If these Aristotelian theories had become generally current in Paris and received in different ways by both Scotus and Ockham in Oxford, not all of the academic body in Oxford were convinced. The so-called "Merton Calculators", a group of academics who subjected theological theories to rigorous mathematical testing, set to work scrutinizing the doctrine of transubstantiation and how it might work. The argument now moved to the mathematical, physical and logical possibility of transubstantiation. While Ockham took the view that the previously physical structure of the bread and wine was annihilated and restructured through consecration, Wyclif disagreed. By a process of scientific analysis—bearing in mind the existence of particles and atoms composing the elements of bread and wine—Wyclif decided that this was not a likely or consistent use of divine power. He rejected the possibility that Christ could at the same time be in heaven and in the bread or wine, arguing that this teaching depended on the possibility of infinite divisibility. On these grounds, Wyclif opposed transubstantiation, and made this the central part of his *Confessio* and also expressed it in his work, *De Eucharistia*. In holding this view, he assailed the heart of Roman Catholic sacramental theology, but his assault did not stop there.

Wyclif's unquestioning espousal of scripture led to him being called "Doctor Evangelicus". It is not difficult to find the chief influences on Wyclif when it comes to his appreciation and interpretation of scripture. Foremost was Augustine of Hippo, who provided a fourfold interpretation of scripture: the allegorical, tropological, moral and analogical. More recent, and in Oxford, the clearest influence was Grosseteste, and in particular his *De Decem Mandatis* on the Ten Commandments, and his *De Cessatione Legalium* on the evolution of divine law from the Old Testament to Christ. Both these works were critical influences, seeing Christ as the supreme lawgiver to all humanity and believing his call was to love God and neighbour. Unlike some of the medieval theologians, Wyclif would place scripture rather than the works of philosophy as central to human experience. In 1376, and like Grosseteste before him, Wyclif wrote his own work, *De Mandatis Divinis*, in which he demonstrated that Christ's loving command is the basis for all lawgiving and has its fulfilment in the Beatitudes and the Sermon on the Mount. The means whereby we may comprehend the character and purpose of God is meditation with the expectation of *illuminatio*, as in the case of Anselm's

Proslogion. This emphasis represented a clear shift from Aristotelian-influenced arguments for the existence of God from creation to a scripture-centred theology.

It is thus no surprise that Wyclif gave himself to commentaries on the scriptures after the fashion of early Church Fathers such as Origen, Augustine and Jerome. Following the example of the Franciscan Nicholas of Lyra (1270–1349), whom Wyclif regarded as "a copious and gifted postillator of Scripture",[11] he lectured on the scriptures from 1372–4 and later published his *postilla* on the Bible in eight parts, five of which survive. One of Wyclif's final works, the *Opus Evangelicum*, is more sharply focussed, in that it does not cover scripture in its entirety, but concentrates on key passages that serve to illuminate the whole. These are the teachings of Christ (as found in the Sermon on the Mount especially), which can be grasped through a right metaphysical understanding of universal concepts and a sense that only in God can there be true eternal knowledge. What we see here is a pulling back to scripture, although without the complete clarity of understanding about grace and faith that will come through Luther.

Given this renewed emphasis on a biblical theology, it is not surprising that Wyclif gave himself to the work of translating the Bible into English and to the task of preaching from it in a more systematic way and teaching others to do the same. It is extraordinary to think that *the entire Bible* had not been translated into English since the arrival of the Christian faith in Anglo-Saxon England in the sixth century. Individual parts of the Bible, in particular the Gospels (e.g. the *West Saxon Gospels* of Aelfric of Keynsham, c. 955–1010) and the Psalms (e.g. the *Suttees Psalter*), did exist in translation, but the entire Bible may well have only been translated into English in the first part of the fourteenth century. The Franciscans were opposed to translation, however, and the Dominicans or parish clergy did not take the task forward either. Only a few contemplatives, such as Richard Rolle and some Augustinian canons, took the project forward, albeit in a piecemeal way. Wyclif and his colleagues were to make the first known full translation of the Bible into English.[12]

In his later years, while he lived in Lutterworth after his banishment from Oxford, Wyclif and a band of scholars continued this great project of Bible translation, an endeavour which did not receive the support of the hierarchy. Indeed, the very reverse was the case, with Archbishop Arundel writing in 1411 in the following terms to Pope John XXIII (a corrupt antipope well known for his debauchery):

> This pestilent and wretched John Wyclif, of cursed memory, that son of
> the old serpent endeavoured by every means to attack the very faith and

sacred doctrine of the Holy Church, devising—to fill up the measure of his malice—the expedient of a new translation of the Scriptures into the mother tongue.[13]

By 1384, the English Bible was more or less complete. Wyclif was responsible for the New Testament and in particular the Gospels and Epistles. Nicholas of Hereford, a Fellow of Queens, Oxford and later chancellor of the university in 1382, was responsible for much of the Old Testament, along with John Purvey, who revised the whole work after Wyclif's death. Over two hundred manuscripts of the Wyclif Bible exist. Although widely condemned by the Church, it was a benchmark of translation, upon which Tyndale would build over a century later. Not only did Wyclif inspire the translation of the Latin Vulgate into English, he also encouraged preaching from it.

Preaching in late medieval England was in Latin or English, depending on the occasion and venue. There were, broadly speaking, four venues for preaching: parish churches, cathedrals and family chapels during the liturgy; market places and festivals which were used by the friars for open air preaching; universities where theological competence was demonstrated; and lastly, on some occasions, preaching was used to stir up the populace on a particular issue. There had been notable preachers in the past, in particular Robert Holcot and Robert Grosseteste. Wyclif was especially influenced by Grosseteste, quoting whole chunks of his teaching in his own sermons.

Wyclif's collected sermons fall into several categories: the polemical, which are against corruption in the Church; the academic, preached at Oxford to elucidate his favourite themes; the elucidation of his *Summa Theologiae* and scriptural exegesis. Johannes Loserth has gathered these sermons into four volumes. The sermons had a wider purpose than simply teaching in themselves, however: they were to train a body of preachers well after his death. Wyclif's aim was to remind others that preaching the Word lies at the heart of the priest's life, more so than the celebration of the sacraments. Preaching requires not only understanding of scripture, but exemplary demeanour. His was a call to preach, overcoming laziness or intimidation, and in so doing face down both social and mortal danger. This call was taken up by the Lollards, a pejorative Flemish term literally meaning "mumblers". Wyclif either trained or inspired an educated corps of preachers who championed his ideas throughout England from the 1380s onwards.

If translating scripture into the vernacular and disseminating its meaning through a body of preachers lay at the heart of Wyclif's mission to England, it went hand-in-hand with deep criticism of the Church and new awareness of what the Church was called to be. From 1370, Wyclif began to write a whole series of treatises on jurisdiction and lordship. At first, in *De Dominio Divino, De Mandatis Divinis* and *De Civili Dominio*, he began to look at the whole nature of power, and then later he looked more critically at the way in which the Church used its power in his *De Ecclesia, De Potestate Pape* and *De Officio Regis*. In essence, Wyclif argued that all power was held by God and since human beings are responsible to God alone (and not to the Church) there can be no need for a church hierarchy and there should be no distinction between priest and layperson.

This was revolutionary teaching, and when Wyclif took it further by arguing that anyone found to be exerting power corruptly or holding onto property unjustly should be relieved of office or purged of their responsibilities, he was striking at the heart of medieval church structure. He called for a complete divestment by the Church of all temporal or civil power. The Catholic Church had already demonstrated its suspicion of the Franciscan ideal, soon abandoned, that the Church should never own property, and the Waldensian ideal (a Swiss sect deemed heretical) that only the community, and not individual office-holders, could own property. Furthermore, writers like Giles of Rome (c. 1243–1316) had argued that the papacy and the Church were the chosen vice-regents of God in all things temporal and spiritual. Against this, Wyclif argued that church authorities should only administer power or possession of property on the basis of grace, in which he believed that every human lord is a steward or bailiff of God, dependent on his grace to exercise this *potestas* correctly. The aim of the Church should be to live in apostolic poverty without property and with a purity exceeding any human-made institution. In other words, it should be above reproach and should aspire to this poverty. Wyclif's harshest invective was against the Church's inability "even to desire to return to this apostolic state".[14]

Finally, Wyclif had a strong sense of the predestination of the Church. He thought that *for God to be God*, he must logically determine all things and that everything that occurs, occurs of necessity. This was one of Wyclif's axioms. Only those predestined by God would know salvation. In this, Wyclif was not as extreme as Thomas Bradwardine (1300–49), one of the Oxford Calculators who wrote strongly against the Pelagians for believing that humans *could* contribute from their own free will to salvation. Bradwardine believed there was nothing human beings could do to alter the divine destiny of their lives. Wyclif believed that God's grace could find a response in the human heart. In this Wyclif was following Augustine, who argued strongly against the Pelagians for the sovereignty of God's grace in enabling the response of humanity to grace, although he too fell into fatalism at times.

For Wyclif, the Church was therefore the congregation of the elect or the chosen. It was not a structure or a visible cohort of people, but rather an invisible body known only to God himself and which would become clear at the end time, hence the apocalyptic side to Wyclif's teaching.

The combination of Wyclif's view on scripture and preaching, his deep criticism of the hierarchy of the Church and the abuses of monasticism, and his rejection of transubstantiation, made him too hard to protect, even for someone as powerful as John of Gaunt. Faced by an increasingly conservative church hierarchy following the Peasants' Revolt of 1381, it was not long before Wyclif was called to answer for his teaching. In 1377, the Pope had issued five bulls condemning the teaching of Wyclif. In 1381, he was banished from teaching at Oxford and took refuge as rector at Lutterworth. In 1382, Wyclif was summoned to London to what became known as the Earthquake Council, since an earthquake interrupted the proceedings. The new archbishop, William Courtenay, was determined to stamp out Wyclifism at Oxford and in the country. He summoned seven other bishops, sixteen masters of theology, fourteen doctors of civil and canon law, and six bachelors of theology to this council, held at Blackfriars, the chapter house of the Dominicans. Wyclif was arraigned on several counts, but not before an earthquake in London had frightened some members of the council, and was presumably seen by Wyclif as a divine warning to the establishment of the Church that they should tread carefully.

A process was nevertheless begun whereby those associated with Wyclif—e.g. Philip Repingdon and John Aston from Oxford—were called to recant. They refused to do so and were immediately excommunicated. It was the end of their careers as teachers. By 1401 and the arrival of Henry IV, who had displaced Richard II and was seeking the support of the Church, a harsher measure of ecclesiastical control was introduced. The 1401 Act of Parliament *De heretico comburendo* decreed that anyone adjudged to be a Lollard by ecclesiastical courts was to be handed over to the sheriff and burnt on a high place. William Sawtrey was one of the first to be burnt. It was the beginning of outright persecution of those who questioned church orthodoxy in England, and it paved the way for a century and more of religious violence.

This new severity, used to bolster the Church, was more than matched by the rise of competing factions within the Plantagenet dynasty, which sought the crown. This bitter quarrel in the royal family eventually came to be known as the Wars of the Roses, coined as such by the great Victorian historian Thomas Carlyle. The "hollow crown" for which Lancastrians and Yorkists fought was ever enthralling, and was the object of almost continuous rebellions, intrigues, murders and short-lived triumphs to obtain its gilded power. We must briefly follow its course to understand the development of the nation and Church.

A divided house: Civil War

Effective and successful medieval rulers needed a number of characteristics: an engaging personality full of energy and judicious statesmanship; the ability to lead the sixty senior barons of the realm in a way that both dignified and occupied them; an inspiring presence; and the aura of a successful general. A combination of these qualities with a reasonable length of life was a rarity, and of the seven kings who ruled England from 1377–1485 only one manifested all these gifts. He was Henry V. But his reign was cut short by sickness—victory and health *together* eluded him—and he was succeeded by the weakest of all these kings, Henry VI, who was barely nine months old.

Over this one-hundred-year period, two kings were usurped: Richard II by Henry IV, and Henry VI by Edward IV; three kings were murdered: Richard II, Henry VI and Edward V (one of the Princes in the Tower); and one king who was himself a usurper, Richard III, was killed in battle on Bosworth Field in 1485 by another Henry Tudor, Earl of Richmond. The political history of this century was dominated by intrigue and dynastic struggle that culminated in the Wars of the Roses (1455–85). Only Henry V, the victor of Agincourt (1415), died having united his country in military success and in the chivalric ideal; but his death was premature, he was only thirty-five. Despite this almost permanent state of political dislocation, so strong was the basic economy of the realm that the late fourteenth century produced an Indian summer of economic and artistic flowering.

Henry IV or Bolingbroke, the son of John of Gaunt and Blanche of Lancaster, had seized the crown with the support of nobles alienated by Richard II's high-handed ways. Nobility who did not recognize his legitimacy and who rebelled against him permanently plagued Henry's rule.

In the early part of his reign Henry was faced by rebellions led by Owen Glendower, who called himself the Prince of Wales, Harry Hotspur, the heir to the Earl of Northumberland, and even by the Archbishop of York, Richard le Scrope, who would be executed. At other times Henry faced rebellion led by the Earl of Northumberland, together with the Scots. Although each were defeated—as Hotspur was at Shrewsbury in 1403, where he was killed—Henry's tenure as monarch was often precarious; his legitimacy as king, having usurped Richard II, was repeatedly challenged. The sense we get of Henry's reign was of a serious-minded man called upon, as he saw it, to reverse the aggrandizing reign of Richard II as well as his own personal punishment of exile. Never a popular character, Henry was nevertheless an effective military commander, a pious churchman, and a solid if unimaginative ruler.

His relationship with his heir, Prince Henry of Monmouth, later Henry V, was strained, as Shakespeare vividly depicts. In company with the comic figure of Falstaff, who amusingly lived out his own words, "the better part of valour is discretion in the which better part I have saved my life",[15] Prince Henry, according to Shakespeare, sowed his wild oats of youthful rebellion, but when it came to it, solidly backed his father's cause and proved a loyal son. If Henry IV's reign had been one of dogged persistence in retaining power, his son's was to be the very apogee of Lancastrian power: a bright comet that burned with uncommon intensity, but came to a swift end.

There is no doubt that of the six kings who followed Richard II before the accession of Henry VII, the youthful Henry V was Shakespeare's hero, and England's most charismatic king. The cornerstone of his government was to be the renewal of the English claim to the French throne, not simply for the purpose of extending his rule, but to provide a solution to the continual warring in France itself, which had broken out again in 1407 between the Burgundians and the Armagnacs.[16] Henry succeeded to the throne in 1413, aged twenty-six. He pressed his claim to the French throne on Charles VI of France, reasserting the terms of an earlier Treaty of Bretigny and requesting the hand of Catherine of Valois, the daughter of Charles VI, in marriage. When these overtures were inevitably rebuffed, Henry prepared for war. His method was not the scorched-earth policy implicit in the style of war called the *chevauchee* which Edward III and the Black Prince had followed, but rather to take towns and territory and then defeat France in the field. Money was granted by Parliament; troops were raised.

On 16 June 1415, Henry rode out of London on his way to Southampton.[17] Surprisingly, much of Henry's army was raised through the clergy. The Diocese of Lincoln found 4,500 suitable men, of whom 4,000 were archers, and the Diocese of Bath and Wells produced sixty men-at-arms, 830 archers and ten mounted archers. This once again shows how the Church remained a fundamental part of the feudal system and rendered martial obligations in exchange for holding land from the crown. What William the Conqueror had initiated nearly 400 years earlier still obtained. The total army numbered over 12,000 fighting men. It sailed in 1,500 ships from Southampton on Sunday 11 August 1415. On arrival, Henry besieged the town of Harfleur (present-day Le Havre) at the mouth of the Seine, which, after a siege of a few weeks, surrendered on 22 September. The population was expelled, the standard of St George raised, and the surrender of this well-fortified town sent shock waves through France.

The siege of Harfleur was costly to the English. Disease invaded their camp and only half the army could take on the march north to Calais. On their way, tired, wet, demoralized and less than a sixth of the size of the French host of 35,000, the English faced an army well supplied in their own country and fresh in the field. The battle took place on 25 October, which was St Crispin's and St Crispinian's Day, the patron saints of cobblers, both of whom were executed in the Great Persecution of Diocletian. On the eve of the day, Henry rode up and down the lines encouraging his troops and proclaiming the justice of his cause. And so, in Shakespeare's verse, the legend was born:

> We few, we happy few, we band of brothers;
> For he today that sheds his blood with me
> Shall be my brother; be he ne'er so vile
> This day shall gentle his condition;
> And gentlemen in England, now a-bed,
> Shall think themselves accursed that were not here
> And hold their manhoods cheap, whiles any speaks
> That fought with us upon St Crispin's day.[18]

There was doubtless more than an echo of these words in 1940 in Winston Churchill's speeches, when the few once again took on the many on behalf of the nation with a similar result: leadership, defiance and skill won the day. At Agincourt, the slaughter was great. As at Crécy and Poitiers, the English archers proved irresistible. Thousands of French lay dead, with bodies piled high in great mounds, among them the flower of the French nobility. Thomas Walsingham said 3,069 knights and esquires were killed and a hundred barons. English losses were a few hundred at most and, with news of a group of French stragglers breaking into the King's tent at the rear of the field, Henry gave the merciless order to kill the prisoners and a further thousand died.

The immediate fruits of victory were that Henry's claim on the French crown was upheld. Normandy was occupied and France continued in a civil war. At the Treaty of Troyes in 1420, Catherine of Valois was given to Henry as his queen. But despite "the witchcraft in her lips", as Shakespeare put it (*Henry V*, Act V) and the birth of a son to Henry and Kate, Henry V succumbed to dysentery and died at Vincennes in 1422. His son, barely nine months old, succeeded, and the result is summarized again by the Bard:

> Henry sixth, in infant bands crown'd King
> Of France and England, did this king succeed;
> Whose state so many had the managing,
> That they lost France, and made his England bleed.[19]

It was an unhappy summary of his reign.

The Wars of the Roses

All the gains made by Henry V were to be wiped out under his son: the acquisitions in France, the stability of the House of Lancaster, and the very future of the monarchy. England would indeed bleed. Henry VI's reign can be divided into at least three parts: his minority lasted until his sixteenth birthday when he assumed the reins of power in 1437; he then ruled until 1461 when the Yorkists took power; finally, he was readepted or restored for a year from 1470–1. His broken reign is accounted for by his character: he was pious, shy and uninterested in warfare or affairs of state. His mental state gave way to a kind of collapse in 1453 and he increasingly became the target of the ambition of his cousin Richard, Duke of York: his Protector during the period of his mental collapse. The ingredients of an uncertain character, mental weakness and pious indifference to worldly affairs created a vacuum at the heart of kingship that unruly, powerful and ambitious nobles—all descendants of Edward III—were quick to fill. The result was civil war, the Wars of the Roses, a title once suggested by Shakespeare, but made popular by Walter Scott in his novel *Anne of Geierstein*.

An example of Henry's indifference to ruling is demonstrated in Blacman's anecdote that once, when Henry was sitting with his chaplain, "a mighty duke of the realm knocked at the door, [and] the King complained 'they do so interrupt me that by day or night I can hardly snatch a moment to be refreshed by reading of any holy teaching without disturbance'".[20]

During his minority, Henry's uncles, John, Duke of Bedford and Humphrey, Duke of Gloucester, governed with the Council when not squabbling with each other, supported by the Earl of Warwick as Henry's tutor. The uncles would both be dead by Henry's mid-twenties and Warwick resigned his charge in May 1436. Initially the war in France was prosecuted effectively, but gradually reaped only successive failures. In 1429, Orleans was lost and Joan of Arc inspired a French military resurgence. Rheims, Troyes, Châlons, Laon, Sens, Provins and Beauvais were lost.[21] Henry VI was crowned King of France in Paris, not in Rheims, the traditional place for coronations, on 16 December 1431, but his rule looked increasingly precarious.

From 1437, when Henry assumed personal power, it would be sixteen years before he would have a mental breakdown in his early thirties in 1453. It appears that he suddenly entered a kind of catatonic state and was unable to remember anything or respond appropriately. Whether or not this was the result of news of the loss of France, we cannot be sure. Yet his rule was not without ambition, if only of a religious and scholastic kind. The main projects in the early years of Henry's reign were the building of Eton College and King's College Cambridge from 1441. The foundation of these colleges was to be the greatest achievement of his reign, although they would both be completed by later monarchs. Finances were greatly depleted by the war in France and finding £15–16,000 for each foundation was a huge commitment. Henry gave considerable personal attention to each: laying the foundation stones, drawing up plans and frequently visiting the sites. He visited Cambridge ten times between 1441 and 1461.

The increasing failure of the war in France had deep repercussions at home. Normandy was lost by the incompetent Duke of Somerset, followed by Gascony and Bordeaux in 1451—the latter being one of the greatest of English possessions in France. In 1444, Henry married Margaret of Anjou, who was as ambitious as Henry was weak, and was characterized as such by Shakespeare. She would come to dominate Henry's court, prompting Paston, a contemporary East Anglian chronicler, to say: "The Queen is a great and strong labour'd woman, for she spareth no pain to sue her things to an intent and conclusion of her power."[22] Margaret showed ample resolution in easing out the Duke and Duchess of Gloucester, the King's uncle and aunt, from their premier place at court and government.

By 1450, finances were in a parlous shape. Royal debts were at £370,000, a mammoth amount. France was lost and, as Hamlet said, "When sorrows come, they come not in single spies, but in battalions."[23] Henry lost his principal minister, the Duke of Suffolk, who was impeached by the House of Commons for French losses, while one Cade from Kent fomented a rebellion. In 1453, the King suffered his first nervous mental collapse while still only thirty-one years old. His wife gave birth to a son, Edward, after eight years of marriage, but when brought to the King with the Duke of Buckingham and the Queen he gave "no answer or [change of] countenance, saving only that once he looked on the Prince and caste his eyes down again".[24] Richard of York, the father of Richard III, was then appointed Protector on 27 March 1454. Relations between Richard of York, the Neville family—the Earls of Warwick and Salisbury—and the Dukes of Somerset and Northumberland and the King deteriorated, and on 22 May 1455 the first battle of the Wars of the Roses was fought at St Albans. The King was wounded; the Earl of Northumberland and the Duke of Somerset were killed. Richard was once more appointed Protector and the King's illness re-emerged. But Richard of York, although Protector, could not reverse the King's policies: his ennobling of his half-brothers Jasper and Edmund Tudor (their father Owen had married Henry V's widow Catherine Valois, and Edmund was the father of Henry VII); his grants of land to religious institutions; and the costly royal foundations at Eton and Cambridge. Henry retreated more and more from government and Queen Margaret effectively ruled in his stead. War was once more sparked between Richard of York and the Lancastrians. This time Richard of York was defeated by Margaret's forces at Wakefield, where Richard was killed, while his son Edward, soon to be Edward IV, took on the Lancastrians at Towton and severely defeated them.

The Battle of Towton is often described as the bloodiest battle in English history. Over 50,000 soldiers fought on Palm Sunday, 29 March 1461, in a snowstorm near this small Yorkshire village near Selby, and 28,000 were killed.[25] The battle ended Lancastrian rule, apart from the short readeption of Henry VI in 1470. Edward IV became king, aged nineteen, with Richard Neville, Earl of Warwick, "The Kingmaker", by his side. Warwick was a savvy political fixer allied with a young and able new king: they formed a formidable combination of experience and flair. Henry VI fled with Margaret to Scotland and soon thereafter Margaret left for France. After another failed engagement at Hexham in 1464, Henry was captured and imprisoned in the Tower of London in relative comfort, where he remained until 1470 and the sudden and unexpected reversal of his fortunes. In the meantime, Edward reigned for ten years from June 1461—the so-called Summer King.

Edward was everything Henry VI was not. While Henry never led his troops in battle except to be defeated at St Albans in 1455, Edward convincingly won the bloodiest of the battles of the civil war at Towton six years later. While Henry fathered a child after eight years with Margaret of Anjou and averted his eyes when confronted "by a show of ladies with bared bosoms who were to dance in that guise before the King, perhaps to prove him or to entice his youthful mind",[26] Edward had no such aversion. He was well known for his promiscuous ways and fathered many children.

Edward together with Warwick, the greatest nobleman in England and a most adept politician, proved a formidable combination. Edward elicited a mixed response from an anonymous contemporary chronicler called the Crowland author, probably a monk from Crowland Abbey, Lincolnshire, who praised

Edward's prudent, far-seeing rule, but disapproved of his dissipated lifestyle, his gargantuan appetite for food and sex.[27] Edward's rule was nonetheless forceful: he subjugated rivals; he enforced the law against criminals; he used the common law court of King's Bench and the civil law court of Common Pleas extensively; and he effectively raised revenue for the crown, which was facing bankruptcy. Yet all these gains were risked by his clandestine marriage to a widow of a minor nobleman called Elizabeth Woodville, previously married to Lancastrian Sir John Grey. When Warwick heard of this marriage while on an embassy to the French court to secure Edward's marriage to Lady Bona, the sister of King Louis XI, he was enraged. The young king had married for passion and not for politics behind his back. Warwick, piqued and in a fit of anger, switched sides, supporting his enemy Margaret Anjou and the reinstatement of Henry VI as king. The penultimate convulsion of the Wars of the Roses now began.

Warwick arrived with an army supported by the French crown to avenge the slight on himself and France, and London welcomed him. Henry was released from the Tower and "readepted" as king. Edward fled via Kings Lynn to Holland, where he found Charles the Bold of Burgundy, his brother-in-law, under attack from Louis XI. With Burgundy's support Edward mustered a force and, like Henry IV before him, landed at Ravenspur in Yorkshire. The two armies of Warwick and Edward met at Barnet on Easter Day, 14 April 1471. It would prove a resurrection of Edward's fortunes. Warwick was killed, as well as his brother, the Marquess of Montague. Elsewhere in Weymouth, Margaret of Anjou and her son, Prince Edward of Lancaster, landed with an army to restore Lancastrian fortunes, but Edward, with new forces raised, caught up with them at Tewkesbury and defeated the Lancastrians. Edward of Lancaster, son of Henry VI, notionally Prince of Wales, was summarily executed on 4 May, the day of the battle, while just over two weeks later on 21 May, his father Henry VI was murdered in the Tower in a brutal end to the Lancastrian dynasty.

Edward would reign for a further twelve years, but despite being master of all his foes, his reign did not prove as fruitful as it might have done.

These years of Edward's rule provided an Indian summer for the Church, which defended its privileges and was supported by a succession of kings from Henry IV to Edward IV. Years of unbeknown turbulence lay ahead, but for the moment the Church defended its authority diligently and built its presence visibly. A series of conventional and traditionalist archbishops hunted down "heresy" in the early part of the century. Among them were Thomas Arundel (1399–1414) and Henry Chichele (1414–43), the founder of All Souls, Oxford, both of whom strongly opposed the Lollards and John Wyclif. The unsuccessful Lollard rebellion led by

Sir John Oldcastle in 1417 (the historical figure for Shakespeare's Sir John Falstaff)
was not repeated. Then, despite Wyclif's earlier protestations that senior clergy like
John Kemp and Thomas Bourchier, as Archbishops of Canterbury (1452–4 and
1454–86 respectively), should not hold secular office, both were wholly engaged
in government. Edward had at least four senior bishops on his Council. The tie
between Church and government was as strong as ever. Along with such senior
appointments in government, the Church flourished visibly. It was the high-water
mark of English perpendicular architecture: Eton and King's College chapels were
started, likewise St George's Windsor and Bath Abbey were built. Half the parish
churches of England were repaired or extended during this period, almost all
being in East Anglia and the West Country.[28] Oxford and Cambridge colleges were
founded, including New College, Oxford, by William of Wykeham in 1379, while
in the fifteenth century, Lady Margaret Beaufort founded Christ's College and St
John's, Cambridge, and endowed the Lady Margaret Professorship of Divinity.
There were few greater patrons of scholarship than Lady Margaret, mother of
Henry VII and descendant of John of Gaunt, and few more influential personages
in the realm. Indeed, Margaret of Anjou, Anne Neville, Margaret Beaufort and
Elizabeth Woodville made an extraordinarily influential group of women in the
fifteenth century. On the face of it, the Church and its many institutions never
looked stronger than in 1485, but within two generations it would have undergone
profound change.

The final and ultimate twist to the Yorkist hold on power would come at the
death of Edward IV. Another usurper came to the fore, Richard of Gloucester, the
dead king's youngest brother. He followed a by now familiar pattern: Henry IV had
usurped Richard II, having him either starved to death or killed outright; Edward
IV had usurped the pious and mentally incapacitated Henry VI, having him killed
in the Tower; and now Richard usurped Edward V and entertained the motive
(if never proved) to kill the two sons of Edward IV in the Tower. Richard may
have been more of an opportunist than the darkly conspiratorial figure presented
by Shakespeare in his *Richard III*, but others, such as the Crowland chronicler,
Polydore Vergil (also proxy Bishop of Bath and Wells and Archdeacon of Wells),
Dominic Mancini (both Italian writers and diplomats in England) and Sir Thomas
More, all wrote darkly of Richard. Despite his *Titulus Regius*—his Parliamentary
claim to legitimacy—Richard never took the country with him. His harsh rule,
which included his summary execution of Lord Hastings, provoked renewed
dissent, and the alienated nobility fled to the court of Henry Tudor, the son of
Margaret Beaufort and Edmund Tudor, the half-brother of Henry VI, who was
waiting for his moment in France.[29] Against the odds Henry Tudor would end

Richard's rule at the Battle of Bosworth Field. Richard was then carried dead and naked from the battlefield, his body draped over an ordinary horse, his scoliosis clear for all to see. He was hastily buried in Greyfriars Priory in Leicester; to be discovered and exhumed in 2012, and finally reburied with ceremony in Leicester Cathedral.

The English Church at the end of the fifteenth century

The accession of the Tudor dynasty in 1485—a minor branch of the House of Lancaster—marked, at least in retrospect, as great a turning point in English history as the Battle of Hastings had been some four hundred years before. As such it provides an opportunity to appraise the nature of the English Church—all the more so because in a matter of years the Church in England would undergo its greatest change since its inception.

Resulting from the geography of Britain, the Church in England was the product of Christian mission from the south and from the west: from the continent of Europe, in particular Italy, France or Gaul, and from Ireland. At the fateful Synod of Whitby (AD 664), and because of the way that synod was persuaded by Wilfrid, the English Church turned away from its Irish origins in the north and west of England and aligned itself more fully with Rome, and with the mission sent by Pope Gregory to Canterbury with Augustine. From this point in AD 664, and for almost four hundred years, the Saxon Church would develop until the coming of the Normans in 1066.

The more informal arrangements of Saxon kings and Saxon church leadership, whether monastic or diocesan, would give way with the Normans to a much more formal feudal system in which the Church was expected to play an important part. With one or two rare exceptions, the Normans despised the Saxon leaders they found, and replaced them with Norman continental appointees. They likewise began a systematic programme of replacing the more meagre Saxon buildings with Romanesque cathedrals that survive to this day. Leaders of the Church were now ecclesiastical feudal barons, tied into the system of land tenure and inevitably drawn into politics and power play, in a way the Saxon church leader had not been (except in the matter of giving advice on the *witan*, the king's council). Many prelates were the monarch's officers of state and they were taken up more with statecraft than leading the flock of God. However, with the controversy over lay investiture of bishops, which reached its peak under Gregory VII (1073–85), and the intransigence of Becket in preserving the jurisdiction of the Church over against the crown, an uneasy truce developed between monarch and Church. The Church rendered its feudal dues in military service and taxation when called upon (finding both money and knights for Henry V's campaign in France in 1415, resulting in the victory at Agincourt), but preserved its ecclesiastical autonomy wherever it could.

The English Church shared fully in the medieval theological and pastoral system that spread across Europe, at least in western Europe, because by 1054 the split between the Orthodox Church in the East and the Roman Catholic Church in the West had come to a head. Wave upon wave of monastic orders that had sprung up on the continent took root in England: the Benedictines, the slightly more ascetic Carthusians, the Cistercians, the Augustinians, and then the Friars—Dominicans and Franciscans—all flourished in England. By 1485, there were some 900 religious communities, made up of about 12,000 monks and nuns.[30] By the beginning of the fourteenth century, there were 8,000 parishes in England. In 1485, London was a city of 50,000, a quarter of the size of Paris, but it had a hundred parishes, one for every 500 souls. At the centre of religious life nationwide were parishes, religious guilds, continual celebrations of the mass for the living and the dead, the doctrine of transubstantiation, the fear of death, purgatory, penance, pilgrimages, Crusades, processions (especially at Palm Sunday and Corpus Christi), the saying of the Psalms and the Pater Noster, the memorial of the Passion of Christ with pictures, and the presence of the rood screen and other images in churches great and small.

The life of Christ was made real to the population through pictures, carvings, plays and ceremonies. Spiritual practice gave rise to architecture, so that in the village church of Bishops Canning in Wiltshire a penitential bench for sinners can still be seen. No part of the community was untouched by the Church, and the community was in many respects coterminous with the Church. Church courts tried cases of heresy, adultery and fornication, generally supervising the morals of the nation and punishing immorality. The guilty were made to carry a candle to the altar at Sunday worship for all to see and were forced to declare their guilt and request forgiveness. Neighbour accused neighbour of immorality in the church courts and officials like the summoner were given ample opportunity to take bribes to spare the guilty or the framed, while the pardoner could sell his wares to alleviate guilt and provide indulgences. What was true of the continental Church was true of the English Church in this regard. But what of the discernible distinguishing features of the English Church, characteristics that carried in them the seeds of its future? Some such features can be identified.

By 1480, there were several characteristics of English Christianity. Organizationally it had melded together its Saxon roots with its Norman showcase, the parish system and the cathedrals, to create a new entity. In its spiritual life it followed much of the pattern of medieval religion, which had a consoling presence in times of national emergency like the Black Death, but increasingly its venial side was there for all to see, as *The Canterbury Tales* make clear. Its intellectual life was growing in significance with the establishment of the universities, but the diet of Lombard's *Sentences* was growing thin. Other minds, whether Scotus, Ockham or Wyclif, were questioning the traditions of the past and the rights of papal power and the secular power and jurisdiction of the Church. It was a powder keg ready to be lit by a fuse. This would soon come through the liberating of the scriptures from their Latin straitjacket and allowing everyone to interact with what they found there, in his or her own language. This was enabled by those with the linguistic gifts to do this, and by the printing press—still the greatest revolution in information technology in history.

PART IV

Reformation and Revolution

CHAPTER 11

The Break with Rome

In 1485, Richard III was carried dead and naked from the Battle of Bosworth Field and his body was displayed in public for days. His death marked the end of the Middle Ages in England: it was not that everything was different the day after Henry's victory in August of that year, but the Tudors as a dynasty would make, in time, a clear break with the past. And the next 200 years, until the restoration of the monarchy after the Civil War, were the crucible in which a new England was cast. Up until then England had been part of the European system: for almost 400 years it was part of the Roman Empire—albeit often a semi-detached part. Thereafter it became part of the continental Roman Catholic hegemony which dominated Europe for nearly a thousand years, but which by the sixteenth century showed signs of corruption and decline.

By the beginning of the sixteenth century, two great European movements were underway. The first was the Renaissance, which at its foundation saw the revival of the classical ideal, albeit in a Christian setting. It was marked by the pursuit of ancient classical languages, including Hebrew, and a consequent rediscovery through biblical exposition of the true source and meaning of faith. The Renaissance was personified by the Florentine literary humanists, Pico della Mirandola (1463–94) and Erasmus (1466–1536). Under Lorenzo de Medici (1449–92), fifteenth-century Florence became the richest city in Europe and humanism, as the pursuit of classical learning and languages, was first fully followed there. The latter movement came to be called the Reformation, and found its epitome in the teaching of Martin Luther (1483–1546) with his translation of the New Testament into German and his challenge to the Roman Catholic world in the form of the *95 Theses*, which he published on the door of the Castle Church in Wittenberg in October 1517. But the desire for reformation of the Church had come earlier in Bohemia with the writings and preaching of Jan Hus, burnt in 1415. The Reformation had had a long fuse.

The man who founded the Tudor dynasty and unwittingly set the scene for all that was to follow was Henry Tudor: a Welshman (although he never made much of that), an exile, an opportunist, and a conservative at heart. Henry was intent on founding the Tudor dynasty and accruing wealth, albeit at the cost of impoverishing all who might oppose him. As his chronicler, the Italian Polydore Vergil—who came to England to collect Peter's Pence and became Bishop of Bath and Wells—wrote in his *Historia Anglicana*, Henry was chiefly remembered for his rapaciousness and greed, and few mourned his passing. Yet he established a dynasty that forever shaped the nation.

England under Henry VII

Henry Tudor had anything but a secure childhood. He was the only son of one of the most extraordinary late medieval women, Margaret Beaufort, a formidable disciplinarian and founder of colleges. Henry was born when his mother was just fourteen, and he was to be her only child. Margaret's ambition for Henry was matched only by her piety, strength of purpose and commitment to education, which led to the founding of two Cambridge colleges, Christ's College and St John's, and her resolution to be the matriarch of her family. A Lancastrian of royal descent, she gave substance to Henry's otherwise tenuous claim to the monarchy. She also gave strength to Henry at several points of crisis in his life: such as after the death of Elizabeth,[1] Henry's wife, and the death of his two sons, Arthur and Edmund.

The Tudors were Lancastrian, like Margaret herself. Henry's grandfather, Owen Tudor—a courtier to Henry V—had married the widow of Henry V, Catherine Valois. Thus the Tudors were related to the House of Lancaster by marriage. Henry's father Owen Tudor, Earl of Richmond, died before Henry's birth, and it was his uncle Jasper who gave oversight to his early life, along with his mother Margaret whenever she could.

While the Yorkists ruled England in the persons of Edward IV and Richard III, Henry remained in exile in Brittany. But the disaffected nation at the seizure of power by Richard III gave Henry his chance. With French help and soldiers, and his mother's steely encouragement, he invaded Britain, arriving at Mill Bay in Pembrokeshire and going on to gather more troops and defeat Richard III at Bosworth Field, with the help of Lord Stanley (now married to the ubiquitous Margaret Beaufort), who dramatically and fatefully changed sides during the battle.

Henry's rule was characterized by shrewd leadership, miserly tendencies and cunning use of the courts. He married Elizabeth of York, the daughter of Edward

IV, to reconcile the Yorkists and strengthen his legitimacy. He saw off two Yorkist rebellions led by Lambert Simnel and more seriously by Perkin Warbeck, posing as Edward IV's youngest son, Richard of Shrewsbury, Duke of York. He repressed the nobility of England, who still numbered only fifty to sixty families, by imposing heavy fines on them for trumped up charges in the courts. He used officials like Edmund Dudley and Sir Richard Empson to manage this policy. In short, he was effective but despised. His was a style of rule out of kilter with the martial and chivalric expectations of the barony. And his court had none of the attractions of those of Edward IV, Richard II or, most of all, his son, Henry VIII.

The Church was also ruled by the King. On the one hand, Henry needed papal support to legitimize his kingship; on the other hand, he wanted to reduce papal power and influence in the realm wherever he could. His lawyers used the statute of *praemunire*, which restricted the rights of foreign jurisdictions—usually the papacy—in the interests of the crown. Fees and claims upon English churches could be restricted.

The fifteenth century had been a period of consolidation for the Church and a final flourishing of late perpendicular constructions, such as at Eton College, King's College, Cambridge, St George's Chapel, Windsor, and Bath Abbey, all within a period of religious conformity. This outward show matched a period of stability and conservatism. As far as the crown was concerned, orthodoxy was to be maintained in the Church. Lollardy was to be resisted as a sign of "true piety", foreign power was to be restricted, and the Church was to pay its dues for the privileges gained. In keeping with these aims, of the twenty-seven bishops appointed, six were theologians, but sixteen were lawyers! Archbishop Morton was a Lancastrian lawyer and churchman appointed by Henry as Archbishop in 1486, and then Chancellor in 1487. He remained in his post until his death in 1500. He was succeeded by William Warham after the brief archiepiscopacy of Henry Deane. Warham was to be a conservative archbishop between 1503 and 1530, a time of unprecedented change. Born in Hampshire, where his father Robert was a farmer at Malshanger near Basingstoke, Warham was educated at Winchester College and New College, Oxford, and went down the route of law, becoming Master of the Rolls. He and Bishop Foxe of Winchester were instrumental in negotiating the marriage of Catherine of Aragon and Prince Arthur. Foxe, a friend of the redoubtable Margaret Beaufort, founded Corpus Christi, Oxford, the college that was to prove so important in the establishment of the King James Bible. In the meantime, they were both priests determined to serve the King, but also determined to preserve the Church and its "liberties", as they knew them. Little could prepare them for the roller-coaster of serving the new king, while at the same time preserving what they considered to be the interests of the Church.

England was a more ordered society. The population remained at about 2.5 million, barely increasing over hundreds of years because of plagues, poor harvests, war and the inhospitable climate. It was a predominantly agricultural society, with the chief export being wool to cities in the Low Countries, especially Antwerp, Ghent and Bruges. Some cloth was manufactured in England with large quantities of alum—a mineral that fixed dye to cloth—imported under licence from the Papal States in Italy. Trade with Italy, France, the Low Countries and the Hanseatic League grew, though disrupted too frequently by war. The merchant adventurers operating out of London—now a city of 50,000—sought new markets. In Bristol, the Genoese sailor and navigator, John Cabot, successfully petitioned Henry that he might explore on his behalf. On 24 June 1497, his ship *Matthew* made landfall in either Maine or Newfoundland, although no colonies would be founded for generations. Cabot was given a pension of £20 a year from Bristol customs by the King, but on a further voyage in 1497 he disappeared, and nothing more was heard of him or the *Matthew*. The New World had yet to be explored, but it would have to wait until the reign of Henry's granddaughter, Elizabeth I.

Henry had succeeded in his ambition of establishing the House of Tudor on the throne of England. He passed his throne on to an adult heir, the first king since Henry IV to achieve this, and, as it turned out, it was the first time since 1399 that a usurper had seemingly made secure his house's hold upon the throne. The years of war between the successors of Edward III were over, but a new and more unfamiliar revolution was about to begin.

Henry VIII: His style, his court and his servant Wolsey

Henry began as he meant to go on: his father's loathed councillors, Edmund Dudley and Sir Richard Empson, the enforcers of Henry VII's policies of financial asperity and extortion, were sent to the Tower and executed. It was a popular move, commending Henry to his nobility. At the time no one knew that it would become a well-trodden path for his closest advisers in the future. What they did quickly see was that Henry VIII could not have been more different from his father. Only seventeen years of age, he was over six feet tall, and agile of mind and limb (measured from suits of armour, his girth grew from thirty-four to fifty-five inches over the course of his reign). Projecting the image of a contemporary prince and with a sense of entitlement to the crown, which his father had laboured to gain, he was the harbinger of a bright, new, confident age. While his father had spent all his waking hours devising schemes for obtaining wealth at his subjects' expense, Henry had no trouble in finding ways of lavishly spending it on entertainment for himself and his beloved companions. His was to be the new Arthurian court and Henry V was his hero. Courtly love and chivalry, jousting and pageants, were all back to stay. It was the Middle Ages celebrated with all the texture and perspective of the Renaissance. It was back to the future. Wordsworth's famous words during the upheavals of the Europe of his youth could also be applied to this new Tudor beginning: "Bliss was it in that dawn to be alive, but to be young was very heaven."[2] The early years were carefree: lived out in the court and made possible by an unusual and brilliant counsellor, Thomas Wolsey.

Henry's court was developing into both a centre of entertainment and the basis of government. In his early years, Wolsey more or less administered the state. The court was an arena of entertainment with continual jousts and tournaments, masques and feasts, with plenty of opportunity for lovemaking and showing off. At the same time, its officers were beginning to change from personal support of the King, like the Groom of the Stool, to being state advisers. Thus, during his reign, the Privy Chamber would become the Privy Council: the domestic becoming the public, the personal becoming the official. And amidst this court life was the Chapel Royal, costing £20,000 a year with its chaplains, singers and musicians.[3]

At the centre of the court was the King himself: literally the sun at the centre of the galaxy. On his right stood eight Knights of the Garter and on his left a number of prelates. It was a vision of glory bound to impress and intimidate. Despite this projection of majesty, the King's character was by no means certain, for he was a very complex man, full of contradictions. For all his charm and bonhomie and for all the affection that he desired and gave, it is hard to think of any tangible acts of selfless action performed by him.[4] Like many a king, and despite all he already owned, he wanted more. What his eye saw and liked, he possessed, whether it was a woman or a palace. Yet he could be given over to self-pity, believing himself unjustly treated by the Almighty. His earlier naiveté gave way to increasing bombast and swagger. His former delight in close companions gathered a growing undertow of suspicion. He showed extraordinary physical bravery at the jousts but fled both his court and family for weeks on end if the sweating sickness threatened. He projected immense power and confidence but was at times beset by indecision. He saw himself as an amateur theologian and humanist prince in the modern fashion, defending the Church against Lutheranism and gaining the title *fidei defensor* from the Pope. His actions nevertheless opened the door to Lutheranism in the English Church, however much he fulminated against it. The last person he spoke to often swayed him: making him too easily susceptible to factions at court.

On a number of occasions, he threw his most loyal servants to their wolf-like enemies, coming later to regret it. Thomas Cromwell had earlier predicted that the King would exchange his head for a castle, and it was true. Henry was inordinately affected by the style of Francis I of France and sought to imitate and surpass him in opulence. Keeping up with the French was as important as defeating France in battle. He lived in an age when he had two contemporary rival kings, Francis I and Charles V, both of whom could outshine him. This was the character, swathed in velvet and cloth of gold, of the King who was to pilot both Church and state into one of their most formative periods, and who would prove an unforgettable life force in the English monarchy.

It is not surprising that in the early years of his reign Henry needed a Wolsey to conduct government for him. The rise of Wolsey in Henry's court may only be inexactly chronicled. Wolsey came from humble origins in Ipswich, had a stellar career as a student at Magdalen College Oxford, was a chaplain to the Archbishop of Canterbury before Warham's appointment, and then became a protégé of Bishop Foxe of Winchester, arriving at the court of Henry VII as almoner in November 1509. Promising, young, quick-witted churchmen were often used in diplomacy and this was also true of Wolsey, who soon became involved in an embassy to the Holy Roman Emperor Maximilian in 1508. It was an extraordinarily speedy trip: just three and a half days to Dordrecht and back. Wolsey's talents were recognized by the new king, who needed a loyal and able official to do his business while he immersed himself in revels, jousting and hunting. Wolsey's ability, diligence and vast capacity for work meant that he accrued more and more power and appointments during the next eighteen years, becoming Bishop of Winchester, Archbishop of York and, most coveted of all, Papal Legate (in 1518) and Lord Chancellor. He conducted the King's policy, or the policy he thought the King should have, with almost complete freedom. However, along with his remarkable administrative talent came a love of ostentation, personal power and pomp. He kept a concubine and had at least two children. He loved to walk down the streets around Westminster and York Place, his London palace, wearing his scarlet cardinal's robes, smelling an orange with a cross carried before him and his clerical assistants surrounding him. No cleric before or after him loved the trappings of power and patronage more, or endeavoured more to increase both. In sponsoring education, Wolsey suppressed thirty monasteries and used their wealth to found the college of Christ Church, Oxford.

In the early part of Henry's reign, the cornerstone of Wolsey's policies was to restrain, as far as possible, the King's desire to emulate Henry V in defeating France, and to support the papacy. Restraining Henry's desire for military conquest was not possible, however, for the King looked for fulfilment in foreign wars. The first campaign against France yielded only the seizure of Tournai—after the much-hyped Battle of the Spurs in which the French fled the field spurring on their charges—and a marriage between Mary, Henry's sister, and the much older Louis XII. From Mary's viewpoint, it was a mercy when Louis died within three months of their marriage, releasing her to secretly marry her lover, Brandon.

Louis was succeeded by Henry's great rival and adversary, Francis I—the very epitome of a late Renaissance prince.

In 1518, Wolsey, now the papal legate to England, supported the Pope's call for a Crusade against the Turks and personally united the warring nations in the short-lived peace of the Treaty of London in the same year. This reconciliation between England and France was celebrated with a sumptuous meeting of the two kings at the Field of the Cloth of Gold in 1520. The extravagance and display of this meeting went far beyond anything seen before or since. Yet war with France was irresistible, and after forging an alliance with Charles V, his wife Catherine's uncle, France was again attacked in 1522–3, following the Treaty of Bruges, made secretly with Charles V in 1521. The English campaign certainly drew off some of Francis's troops, better enabling Charles V to comprehensively defeat Francis in an historic victory at Pavia in northern Italy in 1525. Francis himself was captured and kept in Madrid, while Charles V was left supreme in Europe at the very time that Henry began to think of a divorce from Catherine.

As a churchman, Wolsey was far from typical. He had huge ambition and sought to extend his power into every crevice of court and nation, yet he also had some compassion for the poor. As papal legate, he was the senior cleric in England, even more senior than Warham, the Archbishop of Canterbury, with whom he had an uneasy working relationship. Wolsey was of the new humanist learning and sought a measure of church and monastic reform, most of all in bringing independent-minded orders like the Franciscan Observant community under his rule. He used the courts to control the nobility, especially those of Chancery and the Star Chamber, and extended his jurisdiction whenever possible, even, for instance, insisting on proving all wills himself. He was resented by the nobility for his control and influence over the King, especially by the conservative nobility of the court, whose power he had displaced. In 1526, Wolsey tried to reform the running of the court and council through his Eltham Ordinances. He sought to displace his opponents there and made enemies of the Howard and Boleyn faction in the process. Yet there was a softer side to his administration, for when faced with bad harvests, Wolsey forced the sale of surplus grain on the market, imposing strong penalties on merchants who failed to do this, thereby helping the poor.

Wolsey was conservative in religious outlook, doctrine and practice. When Lutheranism surfaced in the capital in 1521, he was the first to advocate book burnings in the courtyard of St Paul's Cathedral, whilst inside the cathedral Lutheranism was strongly condemned from the pulpit. These book burnings began in 1520 following the first circulation of Luther's works in England in 1519. Like others in his network, Wolsey was a reforming Roman Catholic with a clear humanist or classical education, but also strong ties to the papacy (even wanting to be pope himself). He in no way approved of Luther, far from it. Like Archbishop Warham, Thomas More and the King, he sought to stamp out Lutheran tendencies from early on.

After Charles V's defeat of Francis at Pavia, Henry had hoped to carve up France while Francis was a prisoner in Madrid. He expected that this would be his reward for his support of Charles V in his campaign in Italy. No such reward was forthcoming. But Charles did not wish to increase Henry's power on the continent and was himself preoccupied with checking the Turks after their massive victory at Mohacs on the Danube in Hungary in August 1526. Lutheranism and the Turks were more than enough to contend with, without also changing the political map of Europe. Furthermore, a new compelling factor had entered into foreign policy from 1527, and indeed into every aspect of royal policy thereafter: Henry's marriage to Catherine of Aragon.

The King's Great Matter and the winds of change

Henry married Catherine after the death of his older brother Arthur, Prince of Wales, to please his father Henry VII. The daughter of Ferdinand II of Aragon—of the ancient Trastámara dynasty—was a catch for the new upstart Tudor dynasty. After Arthur's untimely death in 1501, Catherine remained in England, holding the titles of Ambassador of the Aragonese court to England and Dowager Princess of Wales. She was in fact a pawn in future marriage negotiations between her father-in-law, Henry VII, and her own father, Ferdinand II of Aragon and Ferdinand V of Castile. Her lady-in-waiting, Dona Elvira, assured Ferdinand that Catherine, despite six months' marriage to Arthur, had remained a virgin. This was to be an important point in the future, at the time of her divorce from Henry VIII. Seven years after Arthur's death, Catherine married Henry VIII on 11 June 1509, just after he acceded to the throne. They were married quietly at the chapel of the Observant Friars at Greenwich. Catherine was by then accustomed to life in England, was a devout Catholic, and a pretty, cultured, loyal, playful and willing wife to Henry.

For the next few years, Henry and Catherine enjoyed their marriage. Catherine accompanied Henry to every feast and entered into his charades and revels. She watched the jousting at which Henry emblazoned her initials on his sleeve and called himself "Sir Loyal Heart". He confided in her, showed her off and, returning from France after his first campaign, laid the keys of the cities he had captured—such as they were—at her feet. Yet the passing of the years and the absence of a male heir—many were born, but all died tragically soon after birth—increased the restlessness and anxiety of the King. If a male heir had survived—as in the case of the child born to Catherine on New Year's Day 1511—then quite probably England would have remained a Roman Catholic country. However, despite great celebrations, that child, christened Henry, died on 23 February that same year. Princess Mary was born to Catherine and Henry in 1516. Over time, Henry VIII's own passionate nature and the easy opportunities to find sexual partners at court gave way to adultery. First there was Elizabeth Blount, a lady-in-waiting of the Queen, who bore him a son in 1519, later to be the Duke of Richmond. Other mistresses would follow, including Anne Boleyn's sister Mary: "the other Boleyn girl".

By 1527, Henry's marriage to Catherine had grown cold, although it would probably have survived had there been a male heir. Bearing in mind the dynastic struggle of the Wars of the Roses, from which the Tudor dynasty had only recently emerged, and given the only prior example of a female ruler of England was Matilda, whose reign had ended in civil war, Henry believed that *at all costs* he must provide a legitimate male heir. The only way forward was therefore a divorce, and the only ground for a divorce was the fact that he had married his brother's wife, and in doing so had disobeyed, he supposed, the scriptural injunction not to do so. In this issue lay "The King's Great Matter", which became the dominant driver of government policy both domestically and internationally from 1527, and which led in the end to the break with Rome, although not automatically to the setting up of a Protestant national church.

The King's religious frame of mind was a curious one. He was essentially a medieval Catholic steeped in the ceremony and theology of the medieval Roman Catholic Church. He was very religious: he "heard three masses daily when he hunted, and sometimes five on other days", and he usually joined the Queen for Compline and Vespers.[5] He loved to debate the New Learning with Erasmus, the great humanist scholar from Rotterdam, who dedicated to Henry and Catherine his fresh translation of the Greek New Testament into Latin, which supplanted the Vulgate (the old Latin translation of the scriptures initiated by Jerome). Henry was also an amateur theologian who enjoyed thoughtfully discussing issues with his bishops, courtiers and academics. Yet all this religious interest lived side by side with his frequent sexual liaisons and his constant use of the executioner to strike down those who had served him unsparingly, but who crossed his will in matters of "morality". The King's Great Matter or his search for a divorce was the one issue on which he would brook no opposition.

The issue of the divorce turned on a number of points: whether in marrying Catherine he had contravened scripture (not normally a great problem for Henry); whether Catherine was a virgin at the time of their marriage; and whether the Pope had acted correctly in annulling Catherine's marriage to Arthur and allowing her to marry again. All of these points were controversial, and the universities, courts and councils of the whole of Europe were drawn into the debate. All this was given heightened piquancy and urgency by the King's complete infatuation with Anne Boleyn from 1525 onwards.

The scriptural debate about the legitimacy of Henry's marriage to Catherine turned on three Old Testament texts. The first two, taken from Leviticus, prohibited the marrying of one's brother's wife: "You shall not uncover the nakedness of your brother's wife: it is your brother's nakedness" (Leviticus 18:16) and "if a man shall take his brother's wife, it is an impurity: he has uncovered his brother's nakedness; they shall be childless" (Leviticus 20:21). The force of the penalty for marrying one's brother's wife was not lost on Henry, who, discounting his daughter Mary, believed the frequent deaths of his male children by Catherine were punishment for transgressing this commandment. The other text, which was from Deuteronomy, appeared to contradict the Leviticus passages: "When brethren dwell together, and one of them dies without children, the wife of the deceased shall not marry another; but his brother shall marry her, and raise up children for his brother" (Deuteronomy 25:5). The simplest way of reconciling these passages was to say that the Leviticus passages applied when both brothers were alive, while the other (the so-called Levirate marriage, a deeply-rooted Hebrew tradition) reflected the duty of a brother to marry his deceased brother's wife in order to raise issue (as it were) to him after his death. This was common practice in the community of Israel (e.g. the Book of Ruth). This apparent contradiction was far from simple to resolve, and all of Europe was consulted. Cranmer, not yet the archbishop, but an up-and-coming Cambridge Fellow of Jesus College, advocated consulting universities throughout Europe, and himself shared the King's scruples about marrying Catherine in the first place. Luther, who was strongly opposed to divorce, supported Catherine, and suggested, surprisingly, that Henry commit bigamy.[6] Melanchthon bizarrely added that Henry should get a papal dispensation for committing bigamy. Juan Luis Vives, a Spanish Roman Catholic Renaissance scholar, and later tutor to Princess Mary, wrote in favour of Catherine, as did

John Fisher, Bishop of Rochester, who held the palm for his trenchant support of Catherine by writing a seven-volume work in her defence. Motives for exegesis are not hard to discern: the King saw Leviticus as a reason for divorce; Luther saw no justification; Cranmer, who perhaps saw the opportunity for reform, supported the King; while the Pope, a virtual prisoner of Charles V, was opposed. Europe was divided.

Meanwhile, the second and even more humiliating issue for Catherine was the question over whether she was a virgin at the time of marrying Henry. If she was a virgin, it meant her previous marriage had not been consummated. It then followed that the text of Leviticus could not serve as a ground for divorce, since in Roman Catholic thinking there had been no marriage and hence no problem of affinity. Catherine maintained strongly she was "intact" and Henry, who probably prided himself in these matters, having had not a few women, the opposite (and given his infatuation with Anne Boleyn, the temptation is to say "he would believe that, wouldn't he?"). It was an impasse. People believed whomever they chose.

The last piece of the divorce jigsaw was the issue of the validity of the dispensation Pope Julius II had granted Henry to marry Catherine in the first place, given the teaching of scripture (or at least one interpretation thereof). Some maintained that Julius's decision to grant such a dispensation was *ultra vires* (i.e. beyond his jurisdiction), but this could not be so. The precedents were long established by Innocent III in the thirteenth century, who granted dispensations for most royal houses in Europe, who were then often inter-related and marrying each other for dynastic reasons. They frequently had recourse to the papacy to provide licences for their marriages. The papacy was a royal marriage clearing house. Marrying a dead brother's wife was unusual but not exceptional. In terms of the degrees of affinity it was no worse than many other dispensations granted. Canon law dispensations were "exact and exacting", and few would have seen the original dispensation as invalid. Perhaps too little was made by Henry of another argument, based not on affinity being produced by sexual union, but simply a marriage being truly created by living together. This was the earlier argument of Thomas Aquinas, and therefore marrying your dead brother's wife was more a transgression of *public honesty* (i.e. what it looks like to the public). Although Henry argued that sexual union had taken place between Arthur and Catherine and hence the rules of affinity had been breached, it was not a problem in his eyes to marry Anne Boleyn after having had sex with her sister Mary, although this would come back to haunt him and Thomas Cranmer as well. In other words, the casuistry of his case was holed beneath the moral water line by a clear case of hypocrisy, but it was fed by a superstitious conscience, a passionate infatuation with Anne, and a deep desire to procure a legitimate male heir and be rid of Catherine, the innocent party. Henry sought freedom to remarry in order to provide a male heir, although the reason for the break with Rome was dressed up in many other clothes.

Procuring the divorce was the priority of Henry's government. In 1527, Charles V's troops mutinied in Rome whilst fighting the League of Cognac, which included France, Venice, Clement VII (the Pope) and England. They sacked the city and sent the Pope in flight to Castel Sant' Angelo, where he became the virtual prisoner of Charles, the nephew of Catherine. This did not augur well for the divorce. Wolsey's policy of siding with the Pope against Charles had not worked. An embassy to the Pope was planned to prepare for the divorce, and William Knight was sent to Rome to secure permission, but failed. A further embassy made up of Provost Foxe of King's, Cambridge and Bishop Gardiner, both powerful men, was sent to Pope Clement, now at Orvieto. Despite being alternately cajoled and bullied, Pope Clement stood his ground and only granted that a commission be sent to England to hear the case. He would not yet authorize a decretal commission with power to dissolve the marriage without leave of appeal by an injured party (e.g. Catherine). The papal legate Campeggio was despatched to England and, after many twists and turns, the legatine court opened in June 1529 at Blackfriars, London, with Catherine present and Henry represented.

In many ways this event was the crux of Henry's reign, full of drama and great consequence for England and its future. The court at Blackfriars opened on 18 June 1529. Many political manoeuvrings had preceded its opening, with great pressure to comply with Henry exerted on both Catherine and the papal legates, Wolsey and Campeggio. Wolsey in particular, for his job depended on it, heaped great pressure on Catherine to renounce her marriage and go into a nunnery. Yet Catherine remained hugely popular among the public and quietly and serenely determined. Henry dishonestly told a group of notables at Bridewell that should his marriage to Catherine be upheld by the court, there could be nothing "more pleasant nor more acceptable to me in my life".[7] Catherine refused to be intimidated by the King and the officials who were desperate to please him. Her plea was well prepared. She had procured a vital document that Henry did not have: the so-called "brief" of the original dispensation from Julius II allowing the marriage. She had assembled a powerful legal team to represent her. Fisher unleashed a thundering speech affirming the validity of the marriage. Catherine appealed to Rome that the case be heard there, and on 13 July Clement agreed to halt the legatine court in London. Copies of the revocation of the court were sent throughout Europe, as well as to Catherine and Henry. The very thing Henry had most wanted to prevent had occurred. The process would now be lost in the long grass of papal bureaucracy and Henry must obtain his divorce by other means. It would be four long years until, in 1533, the divorce was granted by Cranmer, in the unlikely place of Dunstable Abbey, and these were years in which Henry was besotted with Anne.

The immediate consequence of the failure of the legatine court at Blackfriars was the fall of Wolsey and the impeachment on a charge of *praemunire* of all English clergy. Wolsey, opposed by Anne Boleyn and the Duke of Norfolk and his faction, was commanded to hand over the Great Seal, although the King proffered him a ring through the Groom of the Stool, Sir William Norris, which was a sign of continuing affection. A legal charge of *praemunire* was brought against Wolsey in October 1529. Negotiations about the future status of Wolsey, his offices, palaces and income, were left between Thomas Cromwell, representing Wolsey, and the crown. Wolsey must give up Hampton Court, York House in London (soon to become Whitehall) and several of his appointments save the Archbishopric of York. He fought hard to retain his college at Oxford, later to become Christ Church, but lost the right to found a college in his home town of Ipswich. He travelled north to his diocese of York, which he had until then rarely visited. At Peterborough, on Maundy Thursday, he washed the feet of fifty-nine poor men. By July, the charge of *praemunire* was extended against fourteen other leading churchmen, including eight bishops and three abbots. Henry's assault on the Church continued to put pressure on the Pope to acquiesce over the divorce. Wolsey was then "attainted" for treason and commanded to stand trial. It was while he progressed to London that he fell ill at Shrewsbury. The governor of the Tower, Sir William Kingston, had come to escort him. One of the most perceptive observers of the English political scene, the French ambassador du Bellay, had realized the key to understanding Thomas Wolsey was that he loved his master more than himself, and maybe even more than his God. With Wolsey, the late medieval age of Henry's reign ended. A period marked by chivalry, jousts and war with France passed. The next part of his reign was to be dominated by the divorce, the break with Rome, emerging Protestantism and the effort to retain some of conservative Catholicism, while simultaneously dismantling the larger part of medieval religion, from the monasteries to the doctrine of purgatory.

Elsewhere on the continent, the winds of theological change were blowing a storm. In 1517, Martin Luther had pinned his *95 Theses* on indulgences to the door of the Castle Church in Wittenberg, and events thereafter moved fast. Disputations followed at Heidelberg and Leipzig in 1518 and 1519 in which Luther attacked scholastic theology, the role of indulgences, and the doctrine of purgatory. He debated with Van Eyck, a professor of theology at Ingolstadt. Luther's theology was the result of the internal pilgrimage he himself had followed since becoming a monk. (After a terrifying storm enveloped him in July 1505, Luther had famously presented himself at the door of the Augustinian monastery in Erfurt.) Out of a sense of there being more to faith than rounds of monastic prayer, a theology of fear arising from church discipline, and the regular observance of the mass, Luther searched the scriptures for an understanding of the Christian faith beyond the accretions of the Church. For a time, God became the hangman and jailer of his soul. Luther then found enlightenment and understanding through his lectures on the Psalms, Romans and Galatians, and from the new translation of the Vulgate New Testament by Erasmus.[8] These were to be seminal texts in which Luther, a brilliant linguist, rediscovered the doctrine of justification by faith. He experienced an explosion of certainty, a deep conversion to the all-sufficiency of Christ and scripture alone. From then on, the tenets of Lutheranism, and indeed of Evangelicalism, were to be *solus Christus, sola fide, sola scriptura and sola gratia.* This was the heart of Luther's confession and, from 1517 onwards, just twelve years after his first entry into a monastery, it was expressed in blistering publications from the printing presses of Wittenberg.

In fact, Wittenberg provided all that Luther needed: the protection of Friedrich III, the Elector who hid Luther from the danger of arrest in Wartburg Castle, the illustrative skills of Cranach the Elder and the Younger, and the linguistic genius of Philipp Melanchthon. In Wittenberg, there was also the new university where Luther now taught, and his wife Katharina von Bora lived there too, initially as a nun. From 1520, publications of peculiar power poured forth from his pen: *To the Christian Nobility of the German Nation, On the Babylonian Captivity of the Church* and *The Freedom of a Christian Man.* In the same year, Luther burnt the papal bull, *Exsurge Dominus,* in which the Pope warned that unless Luther recanted, he would be excommunicated. Luther burnt the bull publicly on 10 December 1520. Summoned to the Diet of Worms, where thousands awaited him, he defied the Emperor and the Pope, declaring: "I am bound by the Scriptures I have quoted and my conscience is captive to the word of God. I cannot and will not recant anything since it is neither safe nor right to go against conscience. May God help me." On his return from Worms he was hidden in Wartburg Castle, where in just a few weeks he translated the New Testament into German. Many more translations and editions of the Bible were to follow.

Europe was set ablaze by Luther's defiance, and the repercussions were irreversible. Cuthbert Tunstall, an English cleric, later to be Bishop of London and then of Durham, attended the Diet of Worms and reported back to Archbishop

Warham. In England, Luther's ideas, which quickly came to London and the universities, especially Cambridge, were extirpated wherever found. Wolsey, and later Thomas More, saw to that.

Over the coming years, the English would divide into four different groups holding very general religious allegiances. These were the die-hard conservative Roman Catholics, such as John Fisher of Rochester, Wolsey, Stokesley, Bishop of London, and Thomas More, who were loyal to the Pope; the more acquiescent Catholics, such as Cuthbert Tunstall of Durham, who would accept the supremacy of Henry over the English Church; the Evangelicals, who accepted Henry as head of the English Church and wished for moderate reform; and lastly, the more extreme Evangelicals—to be called Puritans—who wanted an end to all ceremony, symbols and the episcopal government of the Church. The divisions were not hard and fast: some of the conservatives, like More and Wolsey, wanted reform of the Church and had strong humanist leanings, but their sticking point was loyalty to Rome. As events progressed, the allegiances of each group would become clear and the hard choices starker, and life-threatening.

Thomas Cromwell and Anne Boleyn

Following the hearing at Blackfriars which Henry regarded as a disaster and where the divorce or annulment was referred to the labyrinthine papal courts in Rome, the King re-doubled his efforts to procure an annulment, only by different means. He began an all-out assault on the Church, in part to bully Pope Clement into issuing the annulment, and he also led the anticlericalism that was rife in parts of England. Ever since John of Gaunt and Wyclif, a strong strain of anticlericalism had existed in the country: i.e. resentment of foreign control of the Church, dislike of its judicial privileges, and resistance to the drain of money abroad. There was also jealousy of the large landholdings of the Church, especially the monasteries. All of these were about to be attacked.

Henry strengthened his grip over the Church and became more imperious by the month. Wolsey was sacked and threatened with charges of treason, but he escaped before he was tried—by dying. Thomas More was appointed Chancellor in his place in October 1529 and what became the Reformation Parliament was called in the autumn of the same year. Henry took an active role therein, and gradually succumbed to the notion that England was an empire and therefore not susceptible to any jurisdiction from Rome. Indeed one of Henry's ships was called *Henry Imperial*. He gave credence to the Arthurian legends and to the writings of Geoffrey of Monmouth, who claimed that the early English kings were the descendants of Aeneas of Troy. From quite another source, and one despised by Thomas More, he appreciated Tyndale's *Obedience of the Christian Man*, which argued that Christians should be obedient to their monarch—music to Henry's ears. Anne Boleyn gave *Obedience* to him, and having read it, with its call for obedience to magistrates and the crown as a hallmark of true faith and salvation, Henry said: "This is a book for me and for all kings to read."[9] Although he may have approved of his views, which on this matter coincided with his own, Henry never fully took to Tyndale, and continued to regard him as a heretic. With this brew of ideas swirling in Henry's head and his heart firmly attached to Anne Boleyn, he promoted in practice what he now embraced intellectually and emotionally—he was an emperor who could be bound by no one, not even the Church. Indeed, in emending the Act in Restraint of Appeals, Cromwell added the notion that "the bill derived and dependeth frome and of the same Imperiall Crowne".[10] This was just what Henry wanted to see.

Henry's mission was to make England an empire again and legislation to this end followed. The famous Supplication against the Ordinaries, which sounds prosaic enough, was a pure piece of anticlericalism. Drawn up by the King in Parliament, it listed many complaints of the crown against the Church. The King demanded that in future no church law made in Convocation should proceed without his consent, that all obnoxious constitutions from the past be annulled, and that all resolutions approved by Convocation required his assent. After initial resistance, Convocation caved in during May of 1532. Likewise, the Southern Convocation was put on a *praemunire* charge for its support of the disgraced Wolsey, and only pardoned after the payment of £100,000. Although the King drove this early charge against the Church, by 1532 Thomas Cromwell had clearly become the successor to Wolsey, although with a very different agenda of curtailing the power, privilege and papal control of the Church in England.

Like his master Wolsey, Thomas Cromwell came from humble origins. His father was at various times a blacksmith, brewer and a fuller (cloth dresser) in Putney. Like many a young man, Cromwell had travelled abroad in the Low Countries and Italy, which, unlike many of his more insular fellow Englishmen, he loved. Of such insular English, Andreas Franciscus wrote that they "not only despise the way in which Italians live, but actually curse them with uncontrolled hatred".[11] Not so Thomas, who revelled in the colour and life in Italy. On his return, Thomas married Elizabeth Williams, the widow of a Yeoman of the Guard, and soon became involved in the cloth trade, gaining well-honed skills as a commercial fixer and lawyer. In 1517, he was travelling again, this time on behalf of the Guild of Our Lady from St Botolph of Boston, in order to obtain from the Pope in Rome the right to sell indulgences. Like Luther, he was visiting Rome at the height of its Renaissance greatness, shortly after the completion of the Sistine Chapel ceiling by Michelangelo in 1512. With typical ingenuity, Thomas gained an audience with the Pope and secured the licence for the Guild of St Botolph's. Demonstrating what a polymath he was, Thomas eased the tedium of the journey back by learning by heart Erasmus's new translation of the Vulgate New Testament. He was a man of the New Learning, a lawyer in Gray's Inn, and by no means a conservative Catholic. By 1516, he had entered Wolsey's service, at first as an informal acquaintance, acting as a lawyer, diplomat and resourceful negotiator. He made a few close friends, such as Stephen Vaughan, a prosperous merchant and diplomat, and Thomas Elyot, who was clerk to the Privy Council. Cromwell's circle consisted of intelligent men of the New Learning; some, but not all, with Evangelical sympathies, and like him ambitious. In 1522, Cromwell moved to the old Augustinian friary of Austin Friars, where later some meetings of the Privy Council were held. In 1523, he was elected a Burgess to the Commons, possibly for a part of London, and later on was re-elected for Taunton. He became the principal official in Wolsey's house, and the person with whom the King dealt over Wolsey's fall. After he came to the King's notice, he was appointed to the Privy Council in the closing months of 1530 and would take centre stage soon after. His rise was crab-like; he filled holes as they appeared, moving from Master of the Jewels to Clerk of the Hanaper (1532), to Master of the Rolls (1534), to Lord Privy Seal, and supremely to Vicegerent in Spirituals and Vicar General (1534)—second only to Henry in the governing of the Church. Before his final nemesis, Cromwell was given extensive lands and titles, including the Earldom of Essex, and was made a Knight of the Garter. Also, his son's marriage into the Seymour family made Cromwell an uncle by marriage to the King. He was building a dynasty, but it was not to last.

The figure who was shaping events alongside Cromwell, and sometimes in competition with him, because she held the King's heart, was Anne Boleyn. She was the tragic figure at the centre of Henry's reign who had ignited the King's passionate desire for a divorce. She was the woman who fascinated and tormented him and with whom he wanted to have a male heir. At the court joust on Shrove Tuesday in 1526, the King had the motto *"Declare je nos"* embroidered on his jousting costume of gold and silver cloth, with a man's heart engulfed in flames depicted above it. Although such things were common in the practice of courtly love, in this instance it meant that the King had fallen passionately in love with someone other than Queen Catherine. Anne Boleyn was a lady-in-waiting to

Catherine and arrived at court from France, where she had been a lady-in-waiting to the French queen. She was a member of the powerful Howard/Boleyn family: her grandfather on her mother's side was the Duke of Norfolk, from one of the most influential, religiously conservative families at court. Anne was intelligent, quick-witted and full of repartee, and while not strikingly beautiful, she dazzled and fascinated with her jet-black eyes and vivacious manner: a Cleopatra of the court. Yet her haughty ways and her intense jealousy and dislike of the Queen made her many enemies, both at home and abroad. She was not popular. Unlike her sister Mary, who had been the King's mistress, she was no easy picking, and resisted the insistent advances of the King for at least six years. On a visit to Calais and having been very regularly in the King's company for nearly two years, she became pregnant. By January 1533, the time for waiting on the Pope's ruling was over, and Henry married Anne secretly on 25 January. By March, Henry was fulminating to the Imperial ambassador Chapuys against the Holy See and its usurping of power. With the prospect of Anne giving birth in a few months, the divorce or annulment had to be procured, the severance with Rome and the papacy executed, and the supremacy of Henry over the Church enshrined in law. It was time for Cromwell to enact this process in law.

The Reformation Parliament was the means of achieving these ends, and Cromwell piloted the legislation through in the fiery presence of the King. Firstly, in March, the Act in Restraint of Appeals, which proclaimed England's jurisdictional self-sufficiency, was enacted. There were to be no legal appeals from England to Rome, including any to do with the King's marriage. This ended the Pope's jurisdiction in English church affairs and severed all legal ties. On 5 April, the Southern Convocation, the church assembly in the province of Canterbury, gave its assent to the King's divorce. There were twenty-five dissentients led by John Fisher, Bishop of Rochester. Fortuitously for Henry, the old conservative Archbishop Warham died in 1532, and in his place the King appointed Thomas Cranmer, because of his support for the King's quest for a divorce or annulment. On 23 May 1533, in the unlikely and conveniently out-of-the-way priory at Dunstable, Cranmer heard the case for Henry's divorce and quietly and "legally" ended the marriage, declaring it null and void. Catherine, following royal precedence, reverted to being the dowager widow of Prince Arthur. Mary was declared for a time illegitimate, and Anne became the Queen. In May, the Conditional Restraint of Annates was passed by royal letters patent, reducing the flow of funds to Rome to a trickle. In Rome, Pope Clement solemnly condemned the divorce, and thereafter the threat of excommunication hung over Henry. Further epoch-making legislation was enacted during the next sessions of Parliament. The Act of

Dispensation provided for all licences and faculties to be made in England. An Act in Absolute Restraint of Annates stopped all payments to Rome. The Submission of the Clergy required all clergy to fulfil the terms of their surrender to Henry, as described in the Convocation of 1533. The Heresy Act declared that it was no longer heretical to deny papal primacy, and then in 1534 all this was topped off with the Act of Supremacy, in which the King was made head on earth of the English Church, to which all office-holders had to swear an oath of acceptance applied by the King's officials. The umbilical cord between Rome and England, present since the mission of Augustine in 597, had been cut.

On 7 September 1533, the longed-for child of Henry and Anne was born: a girl, Elizabeth. Even during her confinement, Henry had been unfaithful to Anne, although the name of his *inamorata* is unknown. Unlike Catherine, Anne created a scene. She was not an acquiescent wife as her predecessor had been, or as her successor, Jane Seymour, would be. Nor would she take Henry's counsel to "shut her eyes and endure as her betters had done".[12] Understandably, this had the makings of an unhappy marriage, which was to deteriorate over the next two years, affected by the lack of a male heir, the unfaithfulness of Henry and Anne's unwillingness to be cowed by him. Indeed, because of her undaunted spirit—the very thing that Henry had previously admired in their long courtship and which had teased and entranced him—Henry came to despise her and withdraw from her company, so much so that he wanted to be rid of her. With the connivance and orchestration of Cromwell, who disliked Anne's influence on the King, particularly in foreign policy because she favoured France rather than Spain, Anne was accused of adultery. It was a charge made on the flimsiest of evidence, based on words spoken in jest or out of courtly love to a number of her courtiers. Mark Smeaton, her brother Lord Rochford (with whom she was accused of incest), Sir Francis Weston, Sir Thomas Wyatt, Sir Richard Page and William Brereton were all arrested and several were executed on false charges. Within ten days of being accused, Anne herself was executed by sword at Tower Green at 9 a.m. on Friday, 19 May 1536. Her final words, following the etiquette of executions, did not protest her innocence, but extraordinarily spoke of the King's gentleness:

> For according to the law and by the law I am judged to die, and therefore I will speak nothing against it. I am come hither to accuse no man, nor to speak that whereof I am accused and condemned to die, but I pray God save the king and send him long to reign over you, for a gentler nor a more merciful prince was there never, and to me he was ever a good, a gentle, and a sovereign lord. And if any persons will meddle of my cause, I require

them to judge the best. And thus I take my leave of the world and of you
all, I heartily desire you all pray for me.[13]

Anne of a thousand days was a history-maker; quite apart from being the mother
of Elizabeth, one of England's most successful monarchs, she was *the* figure, along
with Catherine of Aragon, at the centre of the King's divorce and the break with
Rome. Despised by Catholic Europe, Anne was a rallying point for the English
reformers, and yet in terms of personality there is an enigma or paradox at her
heart: she was "religious yet aggressive, calculating yet emotional, having the
light touch of the courtier [e.g. poetry and courtly love] yet the strong grip of
the politician".[14] She was of the New Learning, but more than that she preferred
the young English reformers, those who were innovators and modern rather
than conservative churchmen. It was she who put Tyndale's works into the King's
hands. She promoted or recruited chaplains and clergy, such as William Butts,
Hugh Latimer, William Latimer (her personal chaplain), John Skip and Matthew
Parker (later to be her daughter's archbishop). She read the Bible mostly in French,
but by 1534 she had a copy of Tyndale's New Testament. Her affinity was not
so much with the doyen of the new humanist learning, Erasmus, but with the
French Christian humanists such as Lefèvre, d'Etaples, who translated the Bible
into French at Antwerp and Strasbourg, and Louis de Berquin. The verses copied
into the front of her own French Bible betray her Evangelical leanings and include
John 1:17: "For the Law was given through Moses: grace and truth came through
Jesus Christ" (NIV). Anne read her Bible, encouraged her chaplains, distributed
charity in large amounts to the poor and was involved in church appointments,
not least because of her close ties to Archbishop Cranmer. She was undoubtedly
a force for Reformation at the centre of court, but with her execution, Cromwell,
who had connived at it, held the field.

On 20 May 1536, the day after Anne's execution, Henry was betrothed in a
ceremony at Hampton Court to the demure and compliant Jane Seymour. She was
everything that Anne was not: submissive, unquestioning and calm. Ten days later,
Bishop Gardiner of Winchester married Henry and Jane in the Queen's closet in
Whitehall. Cranmer was deeply shocked by Anne's sudden arrest and execution,
for she had been his patron, and on hearing of the arrest wrote to the King that "I
never had better opinion in woman, than I had in her".[15] Just over a year later, on
12 October 1537, Edward, Prince of Wales, was born and the King at last had a
legitimate son, but twelve days after that his mother Jane died from an infection.

For the next four years, until Cromwell's own fall from power following
the disastrous recommendation of Anne of Cleves as a new wife for the King,

Cromwell and Cranmer were able to push forward the Reformation. Theologically, this meant the promulgation of the Ten Articles by Convocation in 1536, which was a mixture of the reaffirmation of conservative Catholic doctrine and the introduction of more Evangelical doctrines. In the former case were baptism of infants, the real presence of the body and blood of Christ in the mass, the requirement for penance and auricular confession. The latter included justification by faith, the repudiation of images and saints, and the overturning of prayers for the dead, especially private masses. It was Reformation by steady progress and the slow process of moving forward Evangelical ideas in a deeply divided Bench of Bishops. If the King did not find Protestant theology appealing in several aspects, the notion of the dissolution of the monasteries and the destruction of some shrines, like Thomas Becket's at Canterbury, was much more to his taste, especially as the monasteries had great monetary value for the crown. It was Cromwell's policy to move ahead incrementally. In advocating the dissolution of the monasteries, he adopted a cautious policy, advising the King, "mine advice is that it should be done by little and little, nor suddenly by Parliament". In fact, it was to be a combination of the two.

Cromwell and Henry had in mind the greatest land grab since the Norman Conquest. A number of monasteries had already been dissolved by Wolsey in order to finance his new colleges at Oxford and Ipswich, although in the case of Christ Church, the project had been temporarily abandoned at his fall, while Ipswich College was never to come about. As ever, Cromwell set about the task systematically, and with all the great administrative power at his disposal. A valuation of all the monasteries was made by the *Valor Ecclesiasticus* in 1535, a piece of work valuing church assets much like the Domesday Book had done for the whole country. This audit was likewise completed in just a few months. It was prepared by commissioners who toured the country, recording the assets and noting the shortcomings of the monasteries. Twenty-two volumes in Latin noted their wealth and these can still be found in the National Archive in Kew. This work formed the basis of the Act of Parliament for the Suppression of Religious Houses, which was enacted later that year. Houses with income below £200 (£65,000 in present money) were first suppressed, before Cromwell turned to larger houses like St Albans, Bury St Edmunds, Glastonbury, Fountains, Rievaulx and Tintern. A Court of Augmentations was set up to receive the vast revenues accruing to the crown, and from this land transfers were made to some of the crown's new men, such as the Herberts (of Wilton Abbey) and the Russells (of Woburn Abbey). The effects of the dissolution were great: the crown received a vast augmentation in wealth (largely squandered); new families had a vested interest in the Reformation;

thousands of monks found themselves with no livelihood, so some became secular priests. Parts of the country, especially in the north where for centuries the monastery had been part of the fabric of life, were suddenly robbed of these communities. For local people it must have been a disorientating change.

In 1536, possibly the most tempestuous and dangerous year in Henry's reign, in which Anne was executed and Catherine of Aragon died, the North rebelled in what was called the Pilgrimage of Grace. It was a revolt against all the changes, religious and social—especially the dissolution of the monasteries—that had come about in Henry's reign. Led by Robert Aske, it was a formidable threat to an ill-defended realm. Henry employed the same tactic that Richard II had used against the Peasants' Revolt in 1381. He promised to consider their grievances and played for time until he had gathered sufficient forces to suppress them. When he did so, some three hundred were hung, executed or burnt: about the same number as would be executed in Mary's reign some twenty years later. The Tudors always suppressed rebellions harshly and in each of their reigns Tudor monarchs faced rebellions.

During this period, three men, born within sixteen years of each other, came to typify both the struggle and the far-reaching effects of these years on England, and indeed on the English language. They were Sir Thomas More, Thomas Cranmer and William Tyndale, and they exemplify the struggles and the achievements of the period.

More, Tyndale and Cranmer

Each of these men came to a violent end because of their beliefs and work, although they were by no means on the same side of the argument. Two were Evangelical Reformers; the third, Thomas More, was a conservative humanist Catholic. All three were executed or burnt during this turbulent period, Cranmer in Mary's reign.

Thomas More was a Londoner born in 1478 in Milk Street, just yards from his namesake Thomas Becket's home, on the corner of Ironmonger Lane and Cheapside. More's world was defined by status and structure, which called pre-eminently for qualities of loyalty and duty. He was born into a prosperous family of lawyers, and his father, Sir John More, became a judge in King's Bench. Thomas was educated at St Anthony's School, one of London's finest. Here he would have conversed in Latin, received grammatical instruction, been taught to write, and given what was virtually an unchanged classical education in music, geometry, grammar, rhetoric, astronomy and Latin literature. So taught, and precocious in his studies, More was soon placed by his ambitious father in the household of Archbishop Morton, a leading figure in Henry VII's reign. From there he entered Oxford University, where he studied civil and ecclesiastical law. It was here too that medieval logic that "came close to the enclosed and self-referential qualities of modern mathematics" became his milieu.[16] He imbibed the law and relished the ceremonies of university and church. He was steeped in the scholastic tradition in which he felt at home and in which he circulated with his own seemingly detached demeanour. It was only a short step from the schools at the university to the Inns of Court in London. It was, and is, a well-travelled route. He went to New Inn and on 12 February 1496 was admitted to Lincoln's Inn, where his father was a senior member. His legal training would have taken six years.

Thomas was more than a lawyer: he was a serious oblate (or would-be monk) and a humanist. In other words, he considered following the life of a monk, although in the end he chose family life, as he was not able to commit to celibacy or sexual abstinence. He immersed himself in the New Learning from Renaissance Italy and the continent. For nearly four years he lived in monastic conditions and gave himself to devotion and prayer alongside his legal work in the Charterhouse of London. He followed Catholic devotions. He attended mass every day. He read the spiritual classics. He critiqued Italian humanists like Pico de Mirandola and Marsilio Ficino. He lectured on Augustine's *City of God*. He also came to know well the leading English humanists of the day: William Grocyn, John Colet, Thomas Linacre and especially Erasmus: all brilliant linguists and scholars who knew and taught the classical languages. None of them wanted a root and branch reform of medieval piety and the Roman Catholic Church. What they wanted was a purified faith, a greater understanding, a simpler but informed eloquence, yet all within the edifice of the Catholic faith and its structures.

More wrote continuously from this perspective. He wrote works on the use of power, such as his life of Richard III. His most famous work, *Utopia*, was of an imaginary political paradise. Added to these and later on he wrote lengthy religious works against the new movement of Protestantism. In *Utopia* (meaning literally *no place*) a traveller from the Low Countries called Hythlodaius recalls the orderly and harmonious life of a place of good government, social harmony and optimism: an island called Utopia. It was written while More was acting as a diplomat in Leuven and Antwerp in 1515. It was a piece of creative writing by a rising intellectual star, similar to his friend Erasmus's *In Praise of Folly*, a satirical attack on the Church and on traditions of European society which was published in 1511. Indeed, More and Erasmus had together rendered translations in Latin of the Greek playwright Lucian of Samosata. By 1521, More had become part of

Wolsey's household and further engaged in diplomacy with Charles V. In 1523 he was an MP and, at the fall of Wolsey in 1529, became Lord Chancellor, the chief legal officer of the realm. His rise was therefore meteoric.

When Luther published his 95 Theses and his blistering attacks on the papacy and medieval piety in 1520, More responded in kind. He used the law, the King's religious conservatism and his own pen to strike down Lutheranism and its heretical notions wherever he found them. Indeed, More has been characterized as "driven by a murderous panic about heresy rooted less in objective reality than in his own psychosexual pathology".[17] The truth may be simpler: he wanted to uphold medieval religion and its structures and theology at all costs, despite his humanist abilities and occasional intellectual playfulness. Against the Evangelicals, Tyndale and others, he wrote *A Dialogue Concerning Heresies*. Running to four books, it presented More as "an eager and determined hunter and interrogator of heretics".[18] When Simon Fish, an English Evangelical, wrote a tract, *The Supplication of Beggars*, against the English Church in Antwerp, accusing it of rapacity and debauchery, More replied with a response ten times in length. In response to Tyndale's work, More wrote *The Confutation of Tyndale's Answer*, the longest religious polemic in the English language. Wherever he could, More traced and tracked down, denounced and brought to trial these Lutheran heretics, some of whom recanted, having been made to carry faggots to a place of execution. He led raids on the Steelyard of London, a German ghetto rife with Lutheran influence, and made arrests there. With Cuthbert Tunstall, the Bishop of London, John Fisher and Cardinal Wolsey, More presided over the burning of Lutheran books in the churchyard of St Paul's, while one Robert Barnes, an Evangelical preacher from Ely, and four Germans were made to kneel and confess their guilt with faggots on their backs. Some, like Thomas Bilney and James Bainham, were executed during this period. Bilney, who preached an Evangelical faith, was burnt at the Lollard pit in Norwich in 1531 after More's own investigation of his earlier recantation. More himself imprisoned suspects, had them flogged at his house in Cheyney Walk, restrained them in the stocks and possibly tortured those complicit in the trafficking of Lutheran books. He was determined to break the ring of Lutheran book traders in London. More felt that if left to its course, Lutheranism would bring social chaos and religious anarchy; the order of the Church must prevail, even if it needed reforming.

When the King sought to annul his marriage to Catherine at Blackfriars in 1529, More realized that his office as chancellor would soon be untenable. He disapproved of the annulment and the manner in which Henry went about obtaining it. He refused to put his name to a letter to the Pope, Clement VII, requesting an annulment. As Lord Chancellor and Speaker of the House of Lords, it was an invidious position to be in. He would not countenance a break with Rome, but he was prepared vehemently to persecute the Lutherans. Together with Archbishop Warham and Bishop Stokesley of London, he prosecuted the Cambridge Evangelical, John Frith, a friend of William Tyndale. Frith was burnt for heresy, for not believing in either purgatory or transubstantiation.

The net was closing in on More himself, however: he refused to go to Anne's coronation. He sided with Elizabeth Barton, the nun of Kent who prophesied dire consequences for Henry's actions, and who had gained a wide following. An Act of Succession was brought to Parliament in 1534, disinheriting Catherine's daughter Mary and validating Anne's children as true heirs. More was taken by boat to Lambeth Palace, where he was expected to swear the oath to this Act. Cromwell, Cranmer, Audley and the Abbot of Westminster, William Benson, awaited him there; it must have been a highly dramatic meeting. He refused, saying "unto the oath that here is offered to me I cannot swear without the jeoparding of my soul to perpetual damnation".[19] He was given a second chance and shown a print roll with the names of all who had signed. Despite last-minute attempts between Cromwell and Cranmer to lessen the extent of the oath, Henry was having none of it. Only the full oath would do. On 18 April, More was taken to the Tower from Westminster by the river and entered by the Traitors' Gate. Two days later, Elizabeth Barton was dragged through the streets of London, lashed to a hurdle, and hung at Tyburn. More sought solace and distraction in writing. He wrote a book called *A Dialogue of Comfort against Tribulation*, based on the experience of the Hungarians after their defeat by the Turks at Mohacs in 1526. More's last work in the Tower was entitled *The Sadness of Christ*.

The initial kindness with which More was treated by Cromwell, in the hope he would swear the Oath of Succession, did not last, and More's distance from Henry's regime only deepened. An Act of Supremacy was passed to which a further oath was needed declaring Henry Supreme Head of the *Anglicana Ecclesia*. Furthermore, a Treason Act was passed, making it treasonable to write or speak against the King, thereby depriving the King "of his dignity, title, or name of their royal estates".[20] The state had moved into a form of parliamentary monarchical tyranny. A bill of attainder was then passed against Fisher and More, both of whom were imprisoned in the Tower. More was tried before his peers for treason, with Richard Rich claiming that More had said Parliament did not have the authority to make Henry head of the English Church, thus contravening the Treason Act. More denied saying this and accused Rich, once apprenticed to him, of perjury. More was condemned to death, to be hung, drawn and quartered, although this was later commuted to execution by decapitation. It was one of the most celebrated trials in English history and secured More's reputation for courageous resistance to the state. More was executed by one stroke of the axe on 6 July 1535. His head was boiled and put on London Bridge. A year later, one of his main opponents, William Tyndale, would be strangled and burnt at Vilvorde near Antwerp. More was essentially a conservative but reforming Catholic, implacably opposed to the doctrines of Lutheranism and the reforms of the King leading to the break with Rome. For this resistance he was prepared to give his life.

William Tyndale had a very different upbringing from that of Thomas More. He was born in Gloucestershire, quite probably near Dursley and not far from Berkeley Castle, the ill-fated place where Edward II perished in a grotesque murder. Tyndale's family were landowners in the vicinity of Slimbridge and played their part in the county.[21] Tyndale therefore grew up with an ear for the common dialect, and the ordinary man or woman's ability to encapsulate wisdom in brief proverbial sayings. This was to stand him in good stead in crafting memorable phrases or sayings. After a local schooling he went to Oxford in about 1506, taking a BA in 1512 and in 1515 an MA from Magdalen Hall. Those were heady days in Oxford: Erasmus, Colet, Grocyn and Thomas Wolsey were all teaching there. John Anwykyll, Master of Magdalen, had brought out a revolutionary Latin grammar entitled *Compendium Totius Grammatice*, while the twenty-nine-year-old Colet lectured on Paul's Epistles. Disliking the aridity of scholasticism and the arcane form of university disputations, Tyndale longed to immerse himself in the scriptures by themselves, and to write in English rather than the customary Latin. To further his studies, he decided to go to Cambridge.

He may have gone to Cambridge for a little more freedom to study and to pursue his interests, given Oxford tended to be more in the public eye. A group of like-minded Protestant dons or students meeting at the White Horse pub in Cambridge is perhaps more a romantic image than the reality, but there were certainly several men of Lutheran leanings in the university. Tyndale would thus have met some like-minded Evangelicals there. He translated Basil of Caesarea's commentary on Isaiah into Latin and likewise the Greek writer, Lucian, who had wide influence at the time. Then, to make a living, Tyndale left Cambridge to tutor two boys of the Walsh family in Chipping Sodbury, not far from his home. Here, in peaceful surroundings, he read and translated into English Erasmus's *Enchiridion*, a time-honoured title used by Augustine of Hippo as a manual on the Christian faith.

Recognizing the need to translate the scriptures into his mother tongue, Tyndale sought a patron who would protect him. In 1522, he approached

Cuthbert Tunstall, the Bishop of London. Tunstall was a humanist scholar who knew the New Learning well and had also attended the Diet of Worms as an observer the year before, when Luther had been condemned. Tyndale may have provided his translation of Isocrates for Tunstall as an example of his work, but no such patronage from Tunstall was forthcoming. Attitudes against Luther were hardening in the capital, and soon a more aggressively anti-Evangelical Bishop of London, John Stokesley, would succeed Tunstall in 1530 after Wolsey's fall. Stokesley was to become Tyndale's implacable opponent and possibly his nemesis. In 1525, already sensing the way the wind was blowing, Tyndale left for Cologne. He would never live in England again, and it is worth remembering that the English scriptures were constructed in Germany and Antwerp, printed in France and sent into England for use.

The work of translating the New Testament proceeded swiftly in Cologne. Tyndale began with Matthew, giving English readers his familiar cadences and avoiding some of the more jarring literalness of Luther's translation. An example follows:

> When he saw the people he went up into a mountain, and when he was set,
> his disciples came unto him, and he opened his mouth, and taught them
> saying: Blessed are the poor in spirit: for theirs is the kingdom of heaven.
> Blessed are they that mourn: for they shall be comforted.

So began Tyndale's translation of the Beatitudes: rhythmic, poetic, memorable and conveying admirably the sense of the original Greek. In translation, Tyndale was his own man. He consulted Luther but did not slavishly follow him. He knew the Vulgate and the Greek text thoroughly, but he also knew his audience, and with a genius for a memorable phrase and pleasing cadence he sought above all to convey the meaning of the text with absolute clarity.

The printing of Tyndale's New Testament, with the rather erratic assistance of William Roye, began in Cologne, but had only progressed as far as Matthew 22 before news of an impending arrest by the Cologne authorities caused them to flee to Worms. Thus, in January 1526, in the printing works of Peter Schoeffer, a simple, small, octavo (hymn book size) New Testament was produced. It had 700 pages, and there was a print-run of three to six thousand copies, a huge first run. By February 1526, they were being sold in London by Master Garrett, Curate of All Hallows in Honey Lane. Only two copies of this edition survive. The printing of the New Testament in English was like an explosion detonated in the capital. Never before had the *entire* New Testament been available in English. Other works, such as an introduction to the Epistle to the Romans, would follow from the same press in Worms before Tyndale moved to Antwerp. Romans, Galatians and the Psalms followed; these books were, after all, the main sources for Lutheran and Evangelical theology, being centred on the doctrine of justification by faith alone.

The reception of Tyndale's New Testament in London and England was shrill. Tunstall preached against it, saying it contained at least 2,000 errors. Booksellers were summoned and forbidden to import Lutheran books. As Tyndale said of Tunstall, "He burnt the New Testament calling it 'strange learning.'"[22] This was a great shock to Tyndale, since Tunstall, a scholar, had after all worked with Erasmus on his ground-breaking new Latin translation of the Greek New Testament. The Pope had already commanded the faithful to burn Luther's books in his 1520 bull, *Exsurge Domine*, and the hierarchy implemented his will. It was at this point that Thomas More was arresting Germans in the Steelyard in London, questioning them and punishing them with public penance. More objected to Tyndale's translation of the New Testament and to the replacement of the term "priest" with "elder", "church" with "congregation" and "charity" with "love". In 1531, Tyndale's friend and colleague John Frith, who wrote persuasively against purgatory, was burnt. In 1528, Miles Coverdale fled to the continent, and was later to take part in the production of the Great Bible of 1536.

Titles from Tyndale were mounting up: *Wicked Mammon, The Obedience of a Christian Man* and *The Practice of Prelates*. Not all of them met with an indignant reception from the hierarchy; indeed, as we have noted, the King was given *Obedience of a Christian Man* by Anne Boleyn and liked it, since it argued that the Church should be subservient to the state. From 1530, Tyndale began his next great work of translation, the Pentateuch. How Tyndale learnt Hebrew we do not know. Only a very few scholars in England had any acquaintance with it. Corpus Christi, Oxford, one of the most advanced colleges in biblical studies, had only one book on Hebrew in its library in 1537, *De Rudimentis hebriaichis* by Johann Reuchlin, Melanchthon's great uncle and one of the great humanist scholars of the Renaissance. Surely it must have been from the German scholars in his network that Tyndale learnt Hebrew, whether in Cologne, Worms, Wittenberg, Hamburg or Antwerp. Once again Tyndale's translation of the Pentateuch gave the English a book that was memorable, vivid and at times haunting. His translation of the creation narratives was strikingly new, clear, colloquial and long-lasting. Thus, in the Garden of Eden, when Eve tells the serpent of God's penalty of death if she eats the forbidden fruit, the serpent replies: "Tush, you will not die." In his prologue to Deuteronomy, Tyndale writes:

This is a book [Deuteronomy] worthy to be read in day and night and never to be out of hands. For it is the most excellent of all the Books of Moses. It is easy also and light and a very pure gospel that is to know, a preaching of faith and love: deducing the love to God out of faith, and the love of man's neighbour out of the love of God.[23]

Tyndale found a synergy between English and Hebrew: "The properties of the Hebrew tongue agreed a thousand times more with English than with the Latin."[24] Once again copies of his Pentateuch were printed in Antwerp and sent to London, but by 1534 the atmosphere was changing. With the ascendancy of Cromwell, the idea of an English Bible, of which the King was the patron, was gaining ground. In 1534, Tyndale revised his original New Testament amidst pirate copies produced by printers in Antwerp and by his erstwhile colleague Joye.

In May 1535, Tyndale was arrested, betrayed to the Catholic authorities by Henry Phillips, who was quite possibly working on the instructions of Stokesley, Bishop of London. He was held for eighteen months in Vilvorde Castle, six miles from Brussels. The officers of the Emperor Charles V accused him of being a Lutheran and seventeen commissioners tried him on heresy charges. His main opponent was Jacobus Latomus from the University of Leuven. The proceedings took up three volumes of minutes, and Tyndale made his own defence. In a famous letter sent by Tyndale to his captors, he asked for warm clothes for the winter, but most of all for his Hebrew Bible, his Hebrew dictionary and his Hebrew grammar. His imprisonment was not to interrupt his work. He concluded: "I will be patient, abiding the will of God, to the glory of my Lord Jesus Christ: whose Spirit I pray may ever direct your heart."[25] Despite Thomas Cromwell's pleas for his life, Tyndale was found guilty of heresy and sentenced to die by burning. On 6 October 1536, he was strangled at the stake and burnt at Vilvorde. Would he have been surprised at the subsequent turn of events?

In 1537, the second complete English Bible, called *Matthew's Bible*, was printed in Antwerp, Matthew being a pseudonym for Tyndale. It comprised Tyndale's New Testament, his Pentateuch, and those historical books of the Old Testament he had translated. It was to be the primary source or version of the English Bible. The Great Bible of 1539 was then commissioned by Henry VIII at the invitation of Convocation and was edited and assembled on the continent by Miles Coverdale, who was also based at Antwerp and Paris before taking a pastorate in Saxony. It was first printed in Paris, overseen by Coverdale, and then printed by Grafton and Whitchurch in Antwerp and London. Within four years of Tyndale's death, every parish church of England had the Great Bible chained to its lectern. Since Tyndale's translation formed the major part of the Great Bible and in turn the Authorised Version of 1611, it was he who shaped both the spirituality and the language of the English nation over the years. His language transcended his life and it served to convey the message and narrative of scripture into the very soul of the nation. Archbishop Cranmer wrote a preface, commending the Bible to all its readers.

Thomas Cranmer was a pivotal figure in the closing years of Henry's reign. In some ways he was an unlikely person to emerge as the leading cleric. He did not have startling qualities of scholarship or leadership, but Henry knew Cranmer had supported him in his divorce from Catherine of Aragon and that he was utterly loyal. Born in Aslockton in Nottinghamshire in 1489, he was a member of the minor gentry of the county. His early life was spent entirely in Cambridge. He took eight years to receive his Bachelor of Arts degree and by 1515 he received his MA and was elected to a fellowship in Jesus College. Not yet a priest, Cranmer married a girl named Joan, a consequence of which was losing the fellowship at Jesus. Tragically, she died in her first childbirth and Cranmer was then reinstated as a fellow, ordained in 1520, and took a doctorate in divinity in 1526. He spent nigh on three decades in Cambridge and was undoubtedly familiar with the new humanist learning sweeping the universities, although there is little evidence of close association with the Evangelical fraternity. There is evidence in some of his annotated books that Cranmer was anti-Luther in 1523. He was prepared to support the Pope, although he advocated church councils. His main influence in Cambridge was the uncle of Nicholas Ridley, one Dr Robert Ridley. Later, Cranmer would be burnt alongside Nicholas Ridley. (Robert Ridley was a conservative humanist and secretary to the arch-conservative Cuthbert Tunstall.)

Soon, Cranmer was to enter the King's service. There was a well-worn route for academics from the universities to become involved with royal diplomacy and, by 1527, this was the case with Cranmer. By 1529, Cranmer was being actively consulted by Gardiner and Foxe over the King's Great Matter. He had come into contact with the Boleyn family and in particular Anne Boleyn, with whom he was in favour. He was drafted into the great cause of the annulment of the marriage and moved to Durham Place in London, one of Wolsey's palaces, where he formed part of a team sent to Bologna to argue the case for the annulment with the Emperor and the Pope. He was also given new posts, like the Rectory of Bredon in Worcestershire. Papers called Determinations were produced in support of an annulment of the King's marriage, in conjunction with the Italian universities and his own research into Aquinas's position on marriage. This investigation led Cranmer to the conclusion that marriage could be fun and was not just an institution created for the suppression of lust. Perhaps it was this idea that led him most incautiously to marry again in 1533, quite against Catholic teaching and the expressed wishes of the King. Or it may have been that he was having increasing contact with Evangelical Reformers on the continent, particularly Martin Bucer of Strasbourg, for whom marriage was the natural right of all Christians, ordained or lay. The brilliant Greek scholar Simon Grynaeus, from Hungary and Heidelberg but staying in London, initiated these relationships between Cranmer and the continental Reformers.

In 1533, while he was still in Italy, Cranmer was informed that he had been appointed Archbishop of Canterbury on the death of Warham. He would remain archbishop until his imprisonment by Mary in 1553. It would be a tempestuous twenty years, during which he would annul four of Henry's marriages (Catherine for affinity, Anne Boleyn for adultery, Anne of Cleves for affinity and Catherine Howard for adultery) and serve three monarchs. To some historians he "cravenly" followed his master Henry VIII's wishes; to others he was loyal to a fault. Perhaps in Cranmer's mind, he, like Esther in the Bible, had unexpectedly risen to such eminence through the providence of God in order to usher in and cautiously pilot the English Reformation. He was by character cautious. He was a laborious scholar and gifted as an editor rather than an original thinker: well-positioned to deal with the art of the possible and operate within the polarities of a king who fancied himself as theologian, a court dominated by one faction or another, a Parliament that must enact change, and a Convocation of clergy filled with a mixture of conservatives and Evangelicals. It is no surprise that during these latter years of Henry's reign (1533–47), progress in reform was often stuttering and uncertain. A new dawning of reform would follow under Edward's rule, before it was extinguished by Mary.

Progress in reform during Cranmer's years as Henry's archbishop was like a waltz: one step forward, two steps back but then a step forward, but the overall direction was forward. Having dealt with the annulment of Catherine's marriage at Dunstable, there was space to pursue reform. Until the fall of Anne Boleyn in 1536, with Cranmer as archbishop and Cromwell as vicegerent, there was momentum for change. Cromwell recruited Hugh Latimer, a plain-speaking Englishman, as a Reformation publicist. The King sought a middle course in preaching, not "seduced with the filthy and corrupt abominations of the bishop of Rome, nor yet by the setting forth of novelties".[26] A new primer was issued by Marshall with radical departures from the old prayer books, for it left out the "Dirige" and contained no prayers for the dead. A later edition returned them, following an outcry. In June 1536, Convocation opened with a blistering attack by Latimer on the old religion. Clearly in his sights were saints, shrines, images, lights, relics, holy days, pilgrimages, pardons and purgatory. Two weeks later Convocation produced the high-water mark of Evangelical Reformation in Henry's reign, the Ten Articles, which formed part of the *Bishops' Book*. In them, only three sacraments were approved: Baptism, the Eucharist and Penance. A form of justification by faith was affirmed, and qualified approval was given to the veneration of images and prayers for the dead. When holy days such as St Wilfrid's Day at Beverley were abrogated, as very many were, there was a riot and a refusal to abolish it. The day had been a local holiday for centuries, after all. In response, Cromwell produced injunctions insisting on the changes. With a bench of bishops sharply divided between conservative or traditionalist and Evangelical, there was no uniform implementation. A further primer (i.e. prayer book) was produced in 1537, which had English versions of the Epistles and Gospels based on Tyndale's New Testament. Some changes were slow, others readily agreed. The practice of eating white meat in Lent was readily adopted for instance, although traditionalists found such changes shocking. One baker in Windsor said: "by the grace of God, no eggs shall come into my belly before Easter."[27] Cromwell issued further injunctions in 1538, calling for quarterly sermons and the instruction of the laity in the Creed, Ten Commandments and Paternoster in English. These injunctions were far stronger against images, shrines, pilgrimages and the whole cult of the saints.

Then, just when everything seemed to be all going one way, in November 1538, Henry issued a Royal Proclamation that put the brakes on, indeed reversed, the process. This was a devastating setback, although the King finally sounded the death knell to the shrine of Becket at Canterbury, instructing that his name should be erased from all liturgies. Once again, bishops of differing persuasions implemented these injunctions unevenly. Miles Coverdale reported that in Newbury the Pope's name and titles still stood in the Matins book in 1538. By 1539, Henry, writing in his own hand, believed that unfettered Bible reading had led to "murmur, malice and malignity".[28] This was a clear indication that Henry had determined to throw his not inconsiderable weight on the side of traditional religion.

Despite poor health in the final years of his reign, and an open, weeping ulcer on his leg, Henry did not slacken in pace, and in many ways reverted to traditional policies of English kingship: invading Scotland to tie down "England's back door", invading France to get glory, and further incorporating Wales and Ireland into the realm. Scotland was defeated at the Battle of Solway Moss in 1542, but the campaign in France yielded only Boulogne as a gain and it was soon traded by his son Edward's advisers. The two campaigns bankrupted the King. On a personal front, another of Henry's marriages, this time to Catherine Howard, ended disastrously. A teenage beauty, and a member of the arch-conservative Howard family of the Duke of Norfolk, Catherine was already used to the ways of love. Finding herself married to the bulk of an old King, she preferred the charms of the courtier Thomas Culpeper. It was Cranmer who broke the news of Catherine's adultery to an anguished King. However, by 1543 he had found a much more suitable match in Catherine Parr: religious, serious and thoughtful, she was able with some skill to gather his estranged children together.

By 1539, Henry was troubled by the numerous religious opinions abroad in the realm and irritated by the sermonizing of German emissaries of the Schmalkalden League. In typically draconian fashion, he introduced the Six Articles, which upheld the doctrine of the mass, communion in one kind, the celibacy of the priesthood, private masses for the dead and auricular confession. Indeed, so strongly was the King opposed to marriage of the clergy that Cranmer most probably had his wife sent away to Ford, one of his most remote palaces. The Articles sought to shore up medieval piety, draw a line under reform and prevent any further changes. They represented the decline of Thomas Cromwell's authority. Cromwell would be executed the following year, mostly because of the Anne of Cleves marriage debacle, which provided an opportunity for the scheming of his enemies, notably the Duke of Norfolk. The fact that Henry had to plead non-consummation as the basis for an annulment of his marriage to Anne was humiliating for the King and the reason given was because he could not even approach Anne because of her looks, rather than any lack of prowess on his part. Humiliating the King on this score was enough to seal Cromwell's death. On the day that Cromwell was executed, Henry married the seventeen-year-old and sexually experienced Catherine Howard. News of her later sexual betrayal of Henry for her cousin, the courtier Thomas Culpeper, was communicated by Cranmer, and she too was executed in 1542. In many ways Henry's final wedding to Catherine Parr in 1543 was to prove his best match.

The final years of Henry's reign saw a retrenchment of conservatism from the high-water mark of reform in 1540, the time of Cromwell's execution. At the passing of the conservative Six Articles, Bishop Shaxton of Salisbury and Latimer of Worcester both resigned and Latimer was imprisoned in the Tower for a while. For Henry, pursuing the "middle way" between Evangelicals and Catholics meant executing equal numbers of both, so as not to be seen to be favouring either. As in 1540, when along with others the courageous and outspoken Evangelical Robert Barnes was burnt, Catholics tended to be executed by being hung, drawn and quartered. Evangelicals were burnt as heretics. Evangelical preachers were often chastened and some burnt. Private reading of scripture was prohibited, even though there were English Bibles available in every parish from 1540. In 1539, Cromwell's greatest legacy was a full-scale revision of the *Matthew Bible* and its presentation to all 9,000 parish churches in the kingdom. Then, in 1543, a plot was hatched in Kent to remove Cranmer for heresy. The prebendaries (or canons) of Canterbury Cathedral led this scheme. Cranmer survived because the King remained unswervingly loyal to him. Religious conservatism was then further entrenched by the *King's Book*, a successor to the *Bishops' Book*, only more conservative in theology. Images were once again permitted, provided they were not worshipped. At the same time, Cranmer brought out his litany: a form of prayer used on Wednesdays and Fridays and a precursor to his own prayer book of 1549. On 29 May 1545, the official English primer, or *King's Primer*, came out. It represented a notable blow to traditional religion, with its reduction of saints' days, its simplicity of language and use of scripture. The calendar in the primer radically stripped out many saints' days, although Cranmer tried to intrude some unlikely new ones, such as Hezekiah and Epiphanius of Salamis, Cyprus, the heresy hunter of the fifth century, but they did not catch on. Prayers to the Virgin were replaced; scriptures such as the Beatitudes were introduced. In subtle and incremental ways, the cause of reform went on even in the twilight of Henry's reign and the half-light of his own mercurial theology.

In January 1547, ill health got the better of Henry and he now faced his end. He had asked those around him whether "the mercy of Christ was able to pardon me all my sins, though they were greater than they be".[29] On 27 January, he called for Cranmer, who was at Croydon. By the time Cranmer reached the King's bedside, Henry had lost his speech. If he had been conscious and able to speak, doubtless Cranmer would have heard his confession. Instead he told the King to give him a sign that he trusted God; whereupon, "holding him with his hand, he did wring his hand in his as hard as he could".[30] Time would tell whether the great events of his reign would bring irreversible change to England: the break with Rome, the destruction of the monasteries, the assault upon medieval religion—especially on shrines, pilgrimages, processions, saints' days, purgatory and some images—the advent of an English Bible and the first steps towards an English Prayer Book. For now, Henry left a male heir, albeit a young boy, in the hands of a Council. In the short term it looked like Henry's reforms were to be the start of a greater reformation of conservative Catholic religion by Edward's government. However, Mary would demonstrate that the depth of the Reformation was superficial and still regarded as novel by the population at large. It was the long reign of Elizabeth that would consolidate the changes her father and brother had begun.

CHAPTER 12

Forth and Back: Edward VI and Mary

When Henry VIII died, his son and heir, Edward VI, was confident of his father's eternal destiny: "It consoles us," he wrote to his stepmother Catherine Parr, "that he is now in heaven, and that he hath gone out of this miserable world into a happy and everlasting blessedness. For whoever here leads a virtuous life, and governs the state aright, as my noble father has done, whoever promoted piety and banished all ignorance hath a most certain journey into heaven."[1] Henry's body did not enjoy the same easy progress as his soul! "The leaden coffin" built around Henry's vast frame "being cleft by the shaking of the carriage, the pavement of the church was wetted with his blood."[2] Plumbers repaired the coffin while it lay in transit in the chapel of Syon Abbey, which had been closed by Cromwell. Henry was then buried next to Jane Seymour, Edward's mother, on 15 February 1547 in St George's, Windsor. They lie in the choir of the Garter Chapel to this day.

Three fundamental factors established the politics of Edward's reign: his youth (he was only nine when he succeeded), his relatives (the Seymour family of Wolf Hall, who were determined to advance both the Protestant cause and their own family interests), and the completion of what his father Henry unintentionally had begun in establishing an Evangelical or reformed Church. These factors, together with the economic and social changes resulting from inflation and a debased coinage, defined the character of Edward's reign, not to mention the growing Evangelicalism and confidence of the young monarch himself. His reign was short, just a few months over six years, and yet it left an indelible mark on the realm.

Henry had taken care to establish a Council of Ministers around his young son before his death. At the time of Henry's death, the conservative Catholic faction led by the Duke of Norfolk was on the back foot: Thomas, Duke of Norfolk, was in the Tower, and his son, Henry, Earl of Surrey, had been executed for conspiring against King Henry. The principal councillors were William Paget, the King's ever-secretive secretary; Edward Seymour, the King's uncle who was soon to style himself the Protector; John Dudley, Earl of Warwick; and Edward Seymour's brother Thomas, the Lord Admiral, who sought advancement by seduction and marriage, marrying Catherine Parr, Henry VIII's widow, and making advances on a susceptible teenage Princess Elizabeth. Henry's will provided for sixteen executors, and decisions were to be taken by a majority vote. The will, which was drawn up in December 1546, made provision for the succession of Mary and then Elizabeth if each died without issue. It excluded Mary Queen of Scots, who had been Henry's choice of a bride for Edward, which had led to the "rough wooing" of Scotland, even though a more unlikely combination of man and wife could hardly be imagined.

Henry's will was contested by Mary Queen of Scots as it had not been signed, only dry stamped. Despite the checks and balances created by Henry, Edward Seymour, with the support of Paget, moved swiftly to take control of government as soon as he could, grandly taking the title Protector. The rest of the councillors quickly ennobled themselves, scattering peerages like confetti over their own heads. The coronation of the nine-year-old king took place with restrained grandeur in Westminster Abbey on 20 February 1547.

Cranmer preached a remarkable sermon explaining the revised liturgy of the coronation that he himself had devised. He told Edward he was "to reward virtue, to revenge sin, to justify the innocent, to relieve the poor, to procure peace, to repress violence, and to execute justice throughout your realms".[3] Edward was proclaimed by Cranmer the new Josiah, after the King of Judah who had cleansed that nation of idolatry. The mood music was unmistakable; Edward was the supreme governor of the Church and he would complete what his father had begun, under advice from his sagacious councillors and the Archbishop of Canterbury.

By 1547, the continental Reformation had reached a turning point. It was thirty years since Luther had pinned his *95 Theses* to the door of the Castle Church in Wittenberg. Luther died in February 1546. After the initial sensational protest against the corruption and venality of the Church and papacy, the Reformed churches now found their own structures and discipline entering a more difficult and fractious period. The wineskin in which this new heady wine was to be kept must be renewed, but how to do so? Divergence of opinion soon emerged over church structure, articles of faith or confession, the retention of symbols and images, and, most importantly, the doctrine of the Eucharist. The extreme action of the Anabaptists, led by Jan Beukels (or John of Leiden), in taking control of Münster in 1534 and waiting for the end times, had shocked both Protestant and Catholic Europe. It was clear that a common declaration was required to define Lutheran faith, and this was achieved by Philipp Melanchthon in the Augsburg

Confession of 1530, which was subscribed to by several German states led by the Elector of Saxony.

Not all Reformation leaders fell in behind the Augsburg Confession, however. The Swiss, led by Zwingli and then Bullinger of Zurich, Bucer of Strasbourg, and later Calvin of Geneva, created a Reformed Protestantism which broke with Luther, particularly over the doctrine of the Eucharist, thus creating a real breach in Protestant Europe. The Swiss, who later came together at the Consensus of Tigurinus, created an important united front, but it was clear that Lutheranism and the Swiss Reformers, in conjunction with Strasbourg, marched to different drums. In general terms, Cranmer, who had extensive continental contacts with the Reformers, as did many of the Evangelical English, was closer to Bucer and Melanchthon, so he invited Bucer to England to become Regius Professor of Divinity at Cambridge in April 1549, early on in Edward's reign.

Divisions over the Eucharist quickly surfaced among the Reformers in England, not least between émigrés teaching in England, notably between Bucer in Cambridge and an Italian, Peter Martyr Vermigli, who was Regius Professor at Oxford and a strong Calvinist. Bucer was irenic in spirit, seeking unity wherever possible, and was a great support to Cranmer in his work of reforming the English Church, and in particular its liturgy.

Now that the handbrake of Henry's caution had been fully lifted, the reformation of the English Church proceeded apace. Knowing he had the support of Protector Somerset, the Council and the young King himself, Cranmer set about establishing a new church that had just a few of the visible characteristics of the old. The method of reforming the Church was thorough, and the results were shockingly extensive. On 15 July 1547, in a homily entitled "Good Works", delivered only months into the new reign, Cranmer gave notice of his intentions. Ungodly and "counterfeit religion" was to be swept away by the reforms of the new Josiah.[4] This ungodliness included all papistical superstitions, beads, lady psalters, rosaries, masses satisfactory (i.e. according to wills for the souls of individuals), stations, teachings on purgatory, feigned relics, bells, breads, holy waters, fastings, observations of Lent pardons through indulgences, burnings of lights in shrines, images of saints, particularly Mary, kissing of relics and pilgrimages. The lot were to go in an orgy of iconoclasm.

In other words, almost all facets of medieval religion, which had accompanied the people since time immemorial, were to be abolished. Most of these practices and objects were outlawed by injunctions passed in 1547. Some of these injunctions were first issued in 1538 against such things as "wandering to pilgrimages or kissing of relics", but now they were greatly extended. In 1547, all processions were abolished and images, pictures and paintings of "feigned miracles" were to be destroyed. In the church in Eisenach which Luther had attended as a boy, the rood screen remains to this day. In 1548, thirty commissioners were appointed to enforce these injunctions. They divided into six teams covering the whole country and set to work on their purifying and iconoclastic work. The process began in St Paul's Cathedral in September 1548, where all images except the rood (the cross) and the figures of Mary and John were removed. By mid-September the image-breaking was out of hand and the Council tried to redress the enactment of the policy, but local enthusiasm tied to legal injunctions had gone beyond that which was originally intended.

Another assault on medieval religion was the dissolution of the chantries. Chantries were part of the paraphernalia of purgatory, the doctrine of which had underpinned medieval religion. Wealthy people provided for a chantry priest to say masses for their souls or those of their loved ones for decades to follow. To pay for these priests and masses, land and resources such as plate were often entailed. Over the country this comprised a huge acreage, third only to monastic and church lands. There was thus now a handy conjunction of interests for the government: by objecting to chantries on religious grounds, the government was able to requisition a great many resources, including land. Although much was promised from this abolition of chantries in the form of funding for local education and amenities, little was in fact passed on. The chantries themselves were closed, such as the one to Prince Arthur (Henry VIII's older brother) in Worcester Cathedral, and the images therein were defaced on the instructions of the commissioners. No one was too great to escape. The links between guilds, chantries and parish were broken, severely disrupting a commercial and personal nexus of interests in local communities.

The imposition of these injunctions by the commissioners was a further demonstration of the power of the English government, a power that had been seen as long ago as Saxon times when the bureaucracy was able to raise vast sums of Danegeld to pay off the Vikings. It was seen also in the extraordinary production of the Domesday Book, assessing in short order the wealth of England and ascertaining the landholdings of tenants of the crown. It was seen again in Thomas Cromwell's assessment of ecclesiastical wealth before the dissolution of the monasteries in the hastily assembled but comprehensive in scope *Valor Ecclesiasticus* of 1534. Now it appeared once more in this centralized abolition of medieval religion. In Stanford, in the Vale of Oxfordshire, the Marian church wardens recorded that the schism in the realm was caused not so much by the breach with Rome (not mourned by many Englishmen), but during the "second year of King Edward the syxt",[5] when local customs and piety were affected. The cause of the schism was not some far-off change of administration, but the abolition of what had been seen, expected, cherished and relied upon for centuries—that was painful. But from the Reformers point of view, excision was necessary.

Now there were no Candlemas ceremonies, no ashes, no paschal candle, no palms, no creeping to the cross on Good Friday, no blessing of the font, no processions about the field or in the churchyard. From 1549, Christianity may have become a more word-centred faith, but the ending of visual symbols and community events drove a wedge between church and ordinary working people. It is arguable that the close identification between church and community was never again so close as at the beginning of the fifteenth century.

If the early years of Edward's reign saw the stripping away of medieval religion in the forms described, through a combination of Cranmer's homilies, injunctions issued by the Council or Convocation, and a strong political will emanating from King and Council, they also saw the beginnings of a new church order. Cranmer's intention, spurred on by his continental friends, and especially Bucer and Zwingli, was to establish a new uniform liturgy reflecting Evangelical or Reformed understanding of the Eucharist. In his first full-length publication of 1550, which he had been working on for two years, Cranmer fleshed out his *Defence of the True and Catholic Doctrine of the Sacrament of the Body and Blood of Christ*. This work reflected his thinking that the doctrine of transubstantiation was incorrect. The notion that the *substance* of the bread and wine actually become the body and blood of Christ—and likewise consubstantiation, which was the Lutheran view that the real presence of Christ is alongside (*con*) the bread and wine—were deemed wrong by Cranmer. What Cranmer maintained was that there was a *true presence* of Christ, made real by the Holy Spirit at the point of reception of the bread and wine. This was distinct also from the more literal Zwinglian view that the Eucharist was simply a memorial with no further elaboration of the spiritual presence of Christ in the service. In all there were thus four views of the efficacy and spiritual mechanics of the sacrament. As so often is the case, and as the Church Fathers discovered, human language was stretched to the limit in describing divine activity, whether the Trinity, the Incarnation, the Person of Christ—human and divine—or the Atonement by Christ. How to nail down theologically exactly what happened in the Eucharist was another case in point.

As with so many theological disputes, the more definition is attempted, the more a theologian is open to the charge of inadequately reflecting the profound reality that lies at the heart of the matter discussed. What is clear is that the Reformers wanted a clear move from the doctrine of transubstantiation in which it was claimed that, in an Aristotelian sense, the bread and wine *became* the actual body and blood of Christ, were venerated as such, and were therefore consumed only rarely because of their intense holiness.

On the back of this new freedom to jettison the traditional Roman Catholic position on the Eucharist that Henry VIII had retained, despite his other reforms, Cranmer and the Council quickly moved to reform both the doctrine and liturgy. At the end of Henry VIII's reign, Cranmer had already begun the process of liturgical revision. On 27 May 1544, the processional service of intercession known as the litany was the first vernacular service to be officially authorized in England. It was an extended service of prayer with penitence at its heart.

Cranmer's gifts of editing, combining and simplifying were evident in this revision and translation into English: "Its wonderfully sonorous language conceals the fact that, like all Cranmer's compositions, it is an ingenious effort of scissors and paste out of previous texts."[6] Cranmer's sources were many: from Chrysostom to Luther, from the Sarum Rite to William Marshall's *Godly Primer* of 1535, and from Cardinal Quinones, who himself had produced a new Roman Catholic breviary (prayer book), to Cardinal Cajetan.[7] Just because a source was Roman Catholic did not mean Cranmer considered it off limits, so long as the teaching was orthodox. This revised litany in English would survive, with only a few modifications, in the Book of Common Prayer. For Cranmer this work, the litany, was thus a "sighter" for the much larger challenge of producing the services and offices of the Prayer Book.

By December 1548, Parliament was debating the doctrine of the Eucharist. Four days were given to this debate. On 19 December, there was a debate in the Lords to tether the Book of Common Prayer to an Act of Uniformity, thus making it obligatory to use only *this form of service or worship* in the Church. The influence of Bullinger and Bucer may be seen in the Prayer Book, but not, in Bucer's case, without reservations. It seems that Cranmer had moved to a doctrine of true or spiritual presence at communion mediated by the Holy Spirit, and communicants were to receive communion in both kinds (bread and wine) *kneeling*. By March 1549, when Parliament rose, the new Prayer Book had been adopted. At the same time, Hugh Latimer preached one of his most politically pointed sermons in front of the young King, calling for the execution of the Protector's brother, Thomas Seymour, for his philandering and conspiracies. He also denigrated Catherine Parr, the widow of Henry VIII and then wife of Thomas Seymour, as a whore and called for the suspension of conservative bishops such as Gardiner of Winchester, Bonner of London and Heath of Worcester.

At Whitsun of 1549, the Book of Common Prayer became the authorized liturgy of the Church of England and this would be extended to Wales and Ireland by 1567. In some London parishes, including St Paul's, it had been piloted from Lent of that year. The Prayer Book contained morning and evening prayer, reduced in content to include more reading of scripture, the litany (see above), holy communion, and the occasional services of baptism, marriage, funerals and visiting the sick. There was a full lectionary, including collects, epistles and gospels for the communion services throughout the year, and in Coverdale's translation, the psalter. It was a radical departure from what had gone before, bulldozing away most of the features of the liturgical year. No longer included were the twelve offices of canonical hours which had been used in monastic worship. Now there were just two: morning (Matins) and evening prayer (Vespers). On the one hand it was a revolutionary change for the whole of medieval England, provoking a rebellion in Cornwall—the Prayer Book Rebellion of 1549—while on the other hand, the rubrics (instructions to the priest or minister printed in red) retained too many elements of the mass for the more Protestant members of the Council, Parliament and Convocation. The 1549 Prayer Book had enemies on both sides, showing the ever-present dangers of liturgical revision. It was probably never Cranmer's intention to leave the 1549 Prayer Book as it was, however. It was the beginning of liturgical reform.

All along, Cranmer's policy of introducing the Reformation to the English Church was one of gradual, even incremental, change, although it is true that previously Henry had regularly applied a theological handbrake after times of rapid ecclesiastical reform. Indeed, on the wider front Cranmer was always ready to put up with reverses, or even collude with political power in order to secure the Reformation of the Church (e.g. his acceptance of Anne Boleyn's fictional adultery and his annulment of Henry's marriage to Anne on grounds of affinity in light of Henry's sexual intercourse with Anne's sister Mary). The case of the Prayer Book was a further demonstration of both radical change and continuity in Cranmer's approach. Bucer considered the 1549 Prayer Book true to Evangelical principles "particularly considering the time at which it was done".[8] In a homily at the back of the Prayer Book, Cranmer argues why "some ceremonies be abolished and some retained".[9] There were two constituencies to address: those who wanted as much novelty and as few ceremonies as possible, and those who looked for reassuring continuity with the past. Cranmer gave indication of further revision to come in his statement that ceremonies objected to may "under just causes be altered and changed".[10] Bucer said that he was satisfied with the Prayer Book as it upheld justification by faith, it was read in the vernacular tongue, and the

Eucharist was administered as Christ taught with no private masses in the future or even separate masses in side chapels. The 1549 Eucharist was based on the Old Sarum rite, on German rites compiled by the Archbishop of Cologne, von Weid, in his *Pia Deliberatio*, and on Eastern Orthodox liturgies available to Cranmer in Greek. The liturgy makes it clear the congregation offers nothing to God; instead God offers himself to his people through bread and wine, thereby recalling the single sacrifice of Christ for human sin, all made real by calling on the Holy Spirit (*epiklesis*) to consecrate the elements of bread and wine. Gone were the old ceremonies of the parish procession, the elevation at the sacring, the pax and the sharing of holy bread.

Alongside Cranmer's revised Eucharistic liturgy, morning and evening prayer, and the occasional offices of baptism, marriage and funerals, were the collects— surely one of the glories of the Prayer Book. They are distinguished by concise expression, quite unlike the more fulsome continental liturgical prayers going back to Carolingian Christianity of the early medieval period. These ancient English prayers, originally in Latin, are made up of sixty-seven collects from the Sarum Rite and twenty-four original collects, including Advent I and II. Composed in the mid-sixteenth century, they have proved one of the most enduring characteristics of Anglican worship, especially alongside the collects of morning and evening prayer. How liturgically impoverished we would be if we did not have the third collect of Evensong that begins:

> Lyghten our darkenes, we beseche thee, O Lord, and by thy great mercy defende us from all perilles and daungers of thys nyght, for the loue of thy onely sonne, our sauiour Jes Christ.

So too the collect for Advent Sunday:

> Almightye God, geue us grace, that we may cast awaye the works of darkness, and put upon us the armour of light, now in the tyme of this mortall lyfe, (in whiche thy sonne Jesus Christe came to visite us in great humilitie;) that in the last daye when he shal come again in his glorious maiestye to judge bothe quicke and the dead, we maye ryse to the lyfe immortal, through him who liveth and reigneth with thee and the holy ghoste now and for euer. Amen.

Both collects were composed by Cranmer and reflect his great gift for compressing spiritual truth into resonating cadences. The immediate result of the imposition of the new Prayer Book via an Act of Uniformity was a rebellion in Cornwall, however. It was to be one of a number of rebellions, or "commotions" as they were called, during Edward's brief reign. In April 1547 there had already been signs of revolt in Cornwall. A local chantry commissioner, William Body, had been stabbed to death. Cornishmen wanted no further change to the religious order until Edward reached the age of twenty-one. The imposition of the Prayer Book was a trigger for rebellion in a region of Britain tired of change and of economic hardship. The flashpoint came in Stamford Courtney in Devon, when the new service was used on Whit Sunday of 1549. Two thousand rebels marched on Exeter, which was closed against them. Some of their leaders were robed; they were chanting and carrying the pyx beneath a canopy. It was truly a religious demonstration. At the centre of this litany was a banner of the five wounds of Christ. The rebels wanted the burning of the Prayer Books, a return to the Six Articles, restoration of the Latin mass and relief from the economic pressures caused by inflation, landlord rent increases, and taxation on woollen cloth and sheep. A number of violent confrontations ensued at Fenny Bridges, Woodbury Common and Clyst St Mary. Many hundreds were killed by the forces led by John Russell, first Earl of Bedford, who had been sent by Protector Somerset. Finally, at Stamford Courtney where the rebellion had begun, the Cornish were swept away by the combined forces of Russell, William Herbert and Lord Grey. The conflict was to leave a bitter feeling in the hearts of Cornishmen for generations to come.

Rebellion and "commotion" were not restricted to the West Country, however. Risings sprang up in Essex, Suffolk, Sussex, Hertfordshire, Oxfordshire and Buckinghamshire. The causes were mainly economic pressure, enclosures of land by landlords and taxation. Among the rebels were Evangelical preachers who preached a notion of commonwealth in which the people shared the wealth of the nation. They set up camps, becoming "camp men", and issued petitions to Protector Somerset that included verses of scripture. This was a foreshadowing of the role of the Levellers in the Civil War of the seventeenth century. Somerset responded with surprising leniency, even admitting that their grievances were valid, but in so doing lost the confidence of the ruling Council. By trying to ride the dragon of popular opinion he forfeited the confidence of his co-rulers, who were fearful that the popular uprising would get out of hand. When the most dangerous rebellion occurred in Norwich under Kett, the Council was severely rattled. Paget, the King's secretary, and William Paulet, the ever-surviving treasurer, withdrew their support. John Dudley, Earl of Warwick, who had harshly put down Kett's rebellion, including executing the two brothers who gave the movement its name, emerged as leader in the Council in opposition to Somerset.

Somerset was a mixture of people's hero and ambitious politician furthering his family's interests. He built the beautifully proportioned Renaissance palace of Somerset House in London at the cost of considerable house and church clearances in the area. He was a further example of a ruler with strong Protestant convictions linked to great personal ambition. This combination originated from the values of the Seymours of Wolf Hall, but also contained the seeds for his demise. After his rival Dudley attempted to get rid of him, Somerset was executed for felony in the Tower of London in 1552. Once more Cranmer typically urged mercy, but power politics won out and Somerset was executed. Dudley, Somerset's equally Protestant and no less ambitious rival and successor, promptly made himself Duke of Northumberland. He continued the Reformation of the English Church to the point of challenging Cranmer's reforming credentials.

With the rise of Dudley, the Reformation of the English Church would be taken to a new level. Already the movement towards further reform of the Church was underway. In 1550, the Act of Uniformity was further applied to the banning of all service books other than the 1549 Prayer Book. Legislative provision was made for the revision of canon law, although in the end it came to nothing. A new ordinal was passed for the three orders of the Church: bishops, priests and deacons replaced the eight medieval orders of ministers. Outside Parliament the order had gone out to destroy the altars. Princess Mary was asked to desist in using the mass in her own household, though she truculently refused. Many conservative bishops were replaced, e.g. Bonner of London, Gardiner of Winchester and Heath of Worcester. Nicholas Ridley was appointed to London and immediately began a clear out of popish ways. John Hooper, an out-and-out Evangelical, was appointed to Gloucester and typically insisted on not wearing episcopal robes at his consecration. The King settled the matter by telling Hooper he would need his robes at court but could do what he liked in his diocese. The issue of clergy robes was to run and run and would become a bone of contention between Puritans, Church and crown, especially in Elizabeth's reign and beyond. The issue revealed a deeper question about reform. How far should it go? Was the Church in England to be a mirror of the Reformed churches in Geneva, Zurich and Strasbourg?

The pressure that Cranmer was under to abandon more of the ceremonies and symbols of the Catholic Church was intense. In general terms, Cranmer sought to retain some of the outward appearance of Catholic worship whilst reforming the teaching and liturgy (in word) in line with Evangelical convictions. This teaching was expressed in the Articles of Religion (to be called the Thirty-nine Articles), which formed part of the Prayer Book, and in the words of the communion service and the homilies. One example of the pressure on Cranmer comes from an incident with John Knox, the Scottish Calvinist Reformer, who had become a protégé of Robert Dudley, Duke of Northumberland. The publication of the new 1552 edition of the Book of Common Prayer was delayed because of a passionate disagreement between Knox and Cranmer over whether communicants should kneel at communion. Cranmer kept the familiarity of Catholic ritual during a time of change and believed communicants should kneel. Knox, by contrast, found no scriptural warrant for the practice and believed kneeling could be interpreted as worship of the sacrament rather than of the Saviour. "In this contest Cranmer only defeated Knox by some passionately confrontational politicking with the Privy Council, and by the addition to the Prayer Book text of the so-called 'black rubric', making it clear that kneeling at communion did not imply adoration of the Eucharistic elements."[11] (The rubric was black simply because in the rush to print the 1552 Prayer Book there was no time to use the red ink with which rubrics were normally printed.)

The revision of the 1549 Prayer Book was complete in 1552 and passed into law in April of that year along with a new Act of Uniformity to enforce its use. The process of revision had involved consulting the chief refugee theologians, Martyn Bucer in Cambridge and Peter Martyr in Oxford, Regius Professors of Theology from Strasbourg and Lucca respectively. Their comments were not slavishly followed by Cranmer but were nonetheless influential. One change, reminiscent of the liturgical practice in Valerand Poullain's French refugee congregation that had been set up by Protector Somerset in Glastonbury, was the recitation of the Ten Commandments, together with responses at the start of the communion service. Other changes were the removal of the intercessions from the central section or canon of the service, less emphasis on the departed, and alterations to the words of administration. These last were provoked by Stephen Gardiner's strong critique of the eucharistic theology of the 1549 Prayer Book: the communicant was now directed to think with gratitude and faith on the sacrifice of Christ.

Further changes were made to the sequence or printing of the service. The removal of printed crosses in the text (formerly used to denote a holy moment) lessened theology of consecration at a precise moment in time. There were also modifications to the funeral service: i.e. less praying for the dead (although Hugh Latimer would continue this practice), virtually no focus on the body, much more attention to the mourners, and no provision for communion, thus undergirding the concept of the Church militant on earth and triumphant in heaven.

So, with just a little revision in 1662, and fully endorsed by Elizabeth in her long reign, the 1552 service passed into the heart of the English nation *via the ear rather than the eye*. If the mass had once been a piece of visual theatre with questionable theology, the Book of Common Prayer was an appeal to understanding by hearing. It would not find acceptance from the Roman Catholic community, who were looking for the certainty and familiarity of the Roman mass, nor would it be accepted by the Puritans, who were looking for a more radical simplicity. It did become the engine of Anglicanism in England and world-wide, however. Together with the singing or saying of the Psalms, which were translated by Coverdale, and the reading of the scriptures, largely translated by Tyndale, the Book of Common Prayer became the bulwark of the expression of national English faith.

The fact that, along with the Authorised Version of the Bible, the Prayer Book remained largely unaltered for about four hundred years is testimony to the resonance that both works found with the English, although not all was sweetness and light. As Eamon Duffy has shown, parish records in Morebath in Devon tell a tale of dislocation and decline of church life over these years: "The destruction of treasured objects, the disruption of immemorial custom and the festal calendar, the pressing problems of debt and the narrowing range of options to meet them, all this was replicated in parishes up and down the land."[12] Demoralization accompanying sudden and violent change was commonplace. The trauma of these years broke up the many-layered devotional and communal lives of church and people that had built up over centuries, and which would not be quickly, if ever, replaced. If a word-centred faith now came to replace a visually oriented faith, could it ever be as effective in drawing church and community together? Would the cost of a greater purity of faith be a weakening of relationship with the community that faith sought to change, especially if that community could not or did not read?

After the publication of the second Prayer Book, the final two years of Edward's rule were notable for the monarch's growing confidence in faith and government, but also for his growing sickness. In one celebrated story Edward sent for Nicholas Ridley after hearing his sermon exhorting charity and asked what he might do. The result was the royal palace of Bridewell being re-founded as Christ's Hospital for the urban poor. Grammar schools were founded in cities in increasing numbers from the monies gained from chantry sales, although not nearly as many as promised or expected. The founding of London hospitals, discussed from 1544, was given further encouragement. Edward himself, now fifteen years old, showed great progress in Latin and Greek, made notes on sermons, kept a daily diary, and brought tears to the eyes of Cranmer over his progress in the faith and his intellectual attainment. His library held books in six languages, including thirty-three volumes on modern Reformed theology. He was also stalked by illness, and in April 1553 suffered an attack of smallpox from which he recovered, although other illnesses were soon to follow. Because his half-sister Mary, a staunch and inveterate Roman Catholic, would succeed him, thereby imperilling all the changes Edward had overseen, Edward and his government sought ways of preventing that from happening.

Edward himself devised what he called his "device for succession", written in his own hand. There was no time for a variation of succession to be approved by Parliament. So, in order to overturn his father's provision for succession of 1543 (Henry's Third Act of Succession)—that Princess Mary should succeed in the event of Edward having no issue—some other means must be found. The device hit upon was for Lady Jane Grey, a granddaughter of the other Mary Tudor—i.e. the youngest sister of Henry VIII who was briefly married to Louis of France and then to the Duke of Suffolk—to succeed. Jane was a thoughtful, devout Evangelical, sixteen years of age, who considered her role of heir as a religious vocation. She was married to the Duke of Northumberland's younger son, Lord Guildford Dudley, in May 1553. On 6 July, still aged only fifteen, Edward died from tuberculosis and the device, issued by Royal Letters Patent, was put into action, supported by Northumberland, Cranmer, and initially also by the Council, with its young secretary, William Cecil.

The device was not deemed legal even in the eyes of the judges summoned to Edward's bedside to endorse it and support quickly fell away. Jane Grey was queen for only nine days. Crowned in the Tower in a pitiful ceremony, she awaited events. Mary was given popular support. The device concocted by her half-brother to deny her the crown crumbled, and Mary soon became Queen, bringing with her a powerful drive to restore the old Catholic faith and reverse the humiliation suffered by her mother, Catherine of Aragon, at the hands of the Tudors. It would prove a tragic cocktail.

Queen Mary

Like her half-sister Elizabeth, Mary was the product of an uneasy and sometimes traumatic childhood. Born in 1516, she was already thirty-seven when she became Queen. She remembered her father as doting on her in her early childhood, but all that was to change as she grew up. Her most distressing childhood event was her father's divorce from her mother on the grounds of consanguinity, which had been conducted by Cranmer in May 1531 in an ecclesiastical court in the unlikely place of the abbey at Dunstable. Catherine of Aragon was humiliated by Henry and sent to live in isolation in Kimbolton Castle in Huntingdonshire, where she existed, more or less, in a single room, wearing a hair shirt as she prepared for what she supposed would be an early death, which duly came in 1536.

It was in effect five years of imprisonment for failing to bear a son. She was buried without honours in Peterborough Cathedral, but mourned by the nation. Catherine's rival and supplanter, Anne Boleyn, despised her and was jealous of any attention paid her by Henry before the annulment. Yet to Henry she had been a loyal and forgiving wife. At the time of the divorce Princess Mary was necessarily declared illegitimate by her father and banished from her mother's presence for the last five years of Catherine's life. Mary did not recognize Henry's supremacy over the Church and saw it as a ruse to divorce her mother. The effect of her loyalty to her mother and her refusal to accept Henry's supremacy meant that she was banished from her father's presence until, under pressure from Thomas Cromwell, she surrendered on 22 June 1536. With these words she made herself subservient to her father's will: "I do most humbly beseech the King's Highness, my father whom I have obstinately and inobediently offended in the denial of the same heretofore, to forgive mine offence therein, and take me to his most gracious majesty."[13] The drafting of this famous submission was probably the work of Thomas Cromwell, who may even have had designs on her as a future wife, so great was his ambition.

These events had a deep effect on Mary. She had a long-standing tendency to see things in black and white, and such a personal history only increased this tendency. Her estrangement from the English court only reinforced her Spanish allegiances and her dependence on her cousin Charles V, the Emperor. The memory of her mother's religious devotion reinforced her desire to re-establish Roman Catholicism in England. Her tutor in the 1520s was the notable Spanish humanist Jan Luis Vives. Coming from Valencia, Vives studied in Paris at the College de Montaigu and then at Louvain University. Under his tutelage Mary studied the text of the Bible in Latin and the Church Fathers, although with limited understanding. Vives wrote *On the Formation of a Christian Woman* for Mary. It was a slightly ambivalent work, because in his heart Vives never really believed in female monarchy. The purpose, however, was to prepare her for the possibility of wearing the crown.[14] Stolid in her dedication to the task in hand, Mary had neither the intellectual power of her half-sister Elizabeth, nor flexibility of mind. Mary had straightforward loyalties and alongside those the strength of purpose to carry them through. She had poor health and suffered from frequent illnesses, some quite possibly psychologically generated by the way she had been treated, while her menstrual cycle was frequently irregular and difficult. She sought enduring and steadfast relationships, but was not to find this in her marriage, while her later phantom pregnancies heaped humiliation and anxiety upon her.

Mary came to the throne as the first female monarch in English history since Matilda, the daughter of Henry I, whose reign had led to civil war with Stephen of Blois. She quickly overcame the "devise" of her half-brother Edward with the evident and spontaneous support of the commons and most of the peerage. The reason for this was that the Reformation was still mostly the preserve of the elite merchant classes and not of the rest of the population. Even before she heard of Edward's death, and before any army could assemble against her, Mary moved to shore up her base in East Anglia. When a small force commanded by Robert Dudley came to her home at Hunsdon House in Hertfordshire, Mary had already fled, first to Kenninghall and then to Framlingham in Suffolk. People rallied to her; first local gentry, and then towns like Bury St Edmunds in Suffolk, which had seen the dismantling of its great abbey. Six ships carrying men and an ordinance commissioned by Northumberland agreed to serve Mary rather than the Council headed by Northumberland. This was the biggest blow of all.

Northumberland, hesitant in Cambridge, did not press the attack and the momentum shifted to Mary, who, buoyed by her popular reception, began the march on London. Peers began to declare for Mary: Arundel, Oxford, Shrewsbury and Pembroke. *Te Deums* were sung in her support in London. Meanwhile in Cambridge, Northumberland resigned to the inevitable and proclaimed Mary Queen, while Jane Grey was marooned and isolated in the Tower, the victim of a plot designed by her father, the Duke of Suffolk, her cousin Edward VI, and Northumberland. A pious and dutiful girl of fifteen, caught up in a scheme well beyond her years, she awaited her fate with prayerful equanimity.

On 24 July, with her welcome secure, Mary set out with her army from Framlingham in what became a victory procession to London. She entered the capital on 3 August 1553, riding on a palfrey with gold embroidered trappings that reached the ground. Five days later Edward was buried in Westminster Abbey. The irony was that although it was Mary's sweet hour of victory, she was never again to be as popular or as commanding.

Mary was not bent on vengeance against Lady Jane and, but for a rebellion led by Thomas Wyatt the Younger, a poet and soldier, into which Jane was drawn, she might have survived with her head. Instead both were executed along with Jane's husband, Guildford Dudley. After a long exclusion, the realm was then Mary's. She had two aims: to restore the Roman Catholic religion, including restoring the Pope as head of the Church, and to produce an heir. She was to fail in both.

The Catholic marriage to Philip of Spain

As a woman and queen, Mary faced the same choice her half-sister Elizabeth would meet just a few years later, although she resolved it very differently. She could marry a subject or a foreign prince. Unable to see the potential danger to her own rule and driven into the arms of her Spanish cousins on her mother's side by her treatment over the years, Mary chose to marry Philip of Spain. He was the son of her cousin, Emperor Charles V, who in turn was the nephew of her mother, Catherine of Aragon. Spain was a traditional ally of England going back to John of Gaunt, but the idea of a queen ruling in England who also gave wifely allegiance to a foreign monarch was fraught with difficulty, compounded only by the problem of the novelty of a female monarch. How would England avoid becoming an adjunct of Spanish policy if Mary married a foreign monarch, and how might his influence over England be restrained or restricted?

However, in order to provide an heir, Mary must marry, and on 25 July 1554, less than a year after her accession, she married Philip at Winchester Cathedral in a service led by Bishop Stephen Gardiner (an old war-horse of conservative Catholic theology who had been in the Tower at the time of Mary's accession). At her wedding, Mary pointedly took the right side of the cathedral and Philip the left, to remind her spouse that in England he was the Queen's husband and not king in his own right. The marriage was preceded by a treaty in which a clear separation was made between Philip's rights in England, which were only to assist the Queen in her rule, and Mary's rights in Spain or Hapsburg territories, which were none. Despite this treaty or matrimonial agreement of limitations, the Spanish marriage was unpopular in England. The English were deeply distrustful of the foreign king, his entourage, and his Spanish customs and ways. Although Philip did little to alienate the English, his very presence was a spur to hostility. Furthermore, England got caught up with Philip's continental wars, in particular in France and the Low Countries. This led to English troops being deployed at English expense, while the failure of the campaign in France led in the end to the loss of Calais, England's only possession in France. The marriage also provoked Wyatt's rebellion and the cry of "no foreign king". (A sentiment that would resound down the ages!) On a more personal level, and despite Mary's longing for a fulfilling marriage, it was always a dynastic alliance rather than an intimate relationship, although Philip did show gratifying concern for Mary's health, using Cardinal Pole as the conduit for his care.

Mary's phantom pregnancies in 1554 and 1557 led to humiliation and depression when it transpired she had never been pregnant at all. Philip's continued absences abroad, fighting in the Low Countries and in France, led to further deep unhappiness for Mary. While Philip provided sensible advice on what was achievable, in particular concerning the re-establishment of Roman Catholicism, he viewed England as simply another territory to govern rather than a country to be cherished. The fact that Philip was eleven years younger than Mary and had vast territories to administer elsewhere rendered the marriage vulnerable from the start.

The re-establishment of Catholicism

If Mary failed to provide an heir and lost favour through an unpopular marriage, her other great objective was the re-establishment of Roman Catholicism in England. Despite her initial popularity, this goal was also to become deeply problematic and forever tarnished by the 300 Protestant martyrs she created. Mary had firmly-held convictions, nurtured by her treatment as a teenager, and by the very black-and-white views she held. She wanted to restore the Church to its former worship and to the position it had held in the earlier part of her father's reign. She also wanted to restore the Pope's supremacy and the Church's assets, which had been stripped away by Henry himself, through his minister Thomas Cromwell, and by her half-brother Edward and his Council. Restoring Roman Catholicism was no easy matter, however, especially since Mary wished to proceed through Parliament as her father had done. At least two of these objectives were unpopular, and one nigh impossible. Imposition of papal control over the Church in England was resented by many since the papacy was seen as a foreign power interfering with the commonwealth of England. The restitution of lands sold by the crown that had been taken from monasteries, dioceses and chantries was nigh on impossible. However sympathetic conservatives might be to the restoration of the papacy, returning land to the Church, which they had only recently gained and bought, was too high a price for religious change. The land transfers of Henry and Edward's reigns had given many a stake in the "new order", which they refused to yield. There was no going back to the *status quo ante*. Mary may have wished for this, but Philip and the Council saw that it was not practical. To give them their due, both Charles V and Philip saw that such a policy would only make the task of restoring Catholicism more difficult.

As for restoring the jurisdiction of the papacy, this too called for caution. Gardiner, the long-term opponent of Cranmer and Thomas Cromwell, and now Lord Chancellor and Bishop of Winchester, saw the dangers of too hasty a restitution of papal authority at the same time as introducing a new Spanish consort in Philip. Indeed, Mary remained head of the Church in England until 1554, however much she disliked the title, and she used this executive power to clear out the bishops of whom she disapproved.

In April 1554, Gardiner brought forward a legislative programme in Parliament which would set the tone for Mary's reign. The heresy laws that had been abandoned by Edward VI were revived. A bill for the restitution of papal authority was brought forward, but the papal legate, Cardinal Pole, a long-term opponent of Henry's reforms, was not yet in England to speak for the Pope. The House of Lords, made up of about seventy peers and those bishops who remained, rejected the Roman Obedience Bill on its third reading. It was not until November 1554, when Pole eventually arrived in England, that forgiveness for schism was formally and officially pronounced by the cardinal in Parliament, itself as an act of reconciliation, and the Pope's jurisdiction was re-established. Earlier in the year, the Book of Common Prayer had been proscribed, the Act of Uniformity repealed, and the Church in England returned to Catholic worship and the mass.

Following this legislative programme, heresy and treason trials began, and these were to spark a period of religious violence that defined Mary's reign thereafter. Cranmer and others were arrested and imprisoned at the start of Mary's reign for their attempt to overturn Henry's Succession Act—a treasonable offence. The heresy laws, first passed in the reign of Henry IV to elicit the support of the Church against Lollardism, and which had been repealed by Edward VI, were now restored.

A succession of Evangelicals were now tried by these laws, over whether they recognized the authority of the Pope as well as various teachings of the Church, especially the doctrine of transubstantiation. By January 1555, the trials were underway, prosecuted by Cardinal Pole and the Chancellor, Bishop Gardiner. Sitting judicially at his house in St Mary's Overy, by virtue of Pole's legatine commission, Gardiner convicted John Hooper, Bishop of Gloucester, and several others for heresy. Hooper was burnt on a slow fire (an extended death) in Gloucester and John Rogers was burnt at Smithfield. Rogers, a clergyman from St Sepulchre's in the City of London, had helped Tyndale translate the Bible for the Matthew Edition. He was a close friend of Philipp Melanchthon and a graduate of the University of Wittenberg. His final words at the stake were, "that which I have preached, I seal with my blood".[15] Many others were to follow. Some, like John Cardmaker, recanted and submitted, but Gardiner was surprised how many went to their deaths, which served only to increase popular unrest.

The policy of burning continued. Although Gardiner saw that it was likely to backfire, his colleague Bishop Bonner of London was far more committed to the process. Bonner was being advised by Bartolomé de Carranza, who had worked with the Spanish Inquisition. Carranza and Pole worked hard to reintroduce Catholicism to the English Church through a synod in 1556, which became a model for the later Council of Trent. Burning was part of medieval life, from which England was only gradually being weaned. It was the traditional punishment in Europe for heresy from the early Middle Ages onwards, although there is no record of its use in the early centuries of the Church.

Heresy was seen as an attack, not only on the immortal soul of the individual from which he or she might be saved by burning, but also on the very fabric of society. Astonishing to our minds, burning was a religious punishment exercised by the civil authorities on the say so of the Church: it was almost part of a liturgy of cleansing by fire. A sermon would quite often be preached before the fire was lit. Sometimes the victims would have a pouch of gunpowder tied around their necks to hasten death. This was the case for Nicholas Ridley and Hugh Latimer in October 1555 when they were burnt at Oxford. Latimer, stripped to his shroud, according to Foxe, and within sight of Cranmer who was being held in the Bocardo gatehouse or prison near Balliol College, stood erect and famously said to his compatriot Ridley: "Be of good comfort, Master Ridley, and play the man; we shall this day light such a candle by God's grace in England, as (I trust) shall never be put out."[16] Latimer was sixty-eight years old when he was burnt, a former Bishop of Worcester and Fellow of Clare College, Cambridge. He too had preached at burnings: as on the occasion of the gruesome burning of John Forest, who had wooden "idols" taken from Wales set alight beneath him. Ridley, the academic, former Master of Pembroke Cambridge and co-author of the Prayer Book, was only fifty.

The re-imposition of Catholicism in England did not only involve burnings, it also represented a change in the treatment of the Reformers by the Catholic hierarchy. In Mary's reign the Reformers were burnt, while in Edward's reign conservative Catholic leaders were simply removed from office. For instance, the month after Latimer and Ridley were burnt at the stake, the great survivor of the episcopal bench, Stephen Gardiner, died in his bed. Henry VIII had kept a kind of theological equivalence in his burning of Evangelicals and Catholics, despising, as he saw it, both extremes. The *via media* for Henry was burning equal numbers of both. We would be wrong to see Catholicism in 1550 as a monolithic structure with homogenous views in response to the onslaught of the Reformation, however. It too was undergoing reform, beginning tacitly to acknowledge its weakness and corruption, as well as redefining its future by its willingness to consider reform. There were nevertheless many eddies and currents in its course.

Catholicism and the need for change

The so-called Counter Reformation (the movement to reform the Roman Catholic Church in the light of the Reformation) was getting underway, albeit accompanied by a good deal of suspicion. The new Pope Paul IV (Giovanni Pietro Carafa), elected in 1555, was an arch-conservative Italian who sought complete obedience to the traditional discipline of the Church. He also hated the Spaniards, and in particular Philip II of Spain, Mary's husband, a hatred based on the Spanish government of his native home of Naples when he had been archbishop there. Cardinal Pole, who had nearly been elected Pope in 1548, also came under suspicion because of his emphasis on understanding the Bible as well as the necessity for church discipline, which made him, in the eyes of Rome, a kind of crypto-Protestant, although in England his pursuit of Evangelicals was unrelenting. The Spanish Ambassador in London at the court of Queen Mary thought Pole lukewarm in his Roman Catholic convictions. Yet Pole was a friend of the new star of Catholicism Ignatius Loyola (1491–1556) and his newly-founded Jesuit movement. Nevertheless, the cross currents of Roman Catholicism needed better charting and navigating.

On 13 December 1545, the long-awaited Council of Trent began and continued on and off to 1563. Like a snowball rolling downhill, it would gather in size and momentum as time passed. Although initially beset by problems, Trent succeeded in its mission of stabilizing and renewing the Roman Catholic Church: indeed "the medieval western church had been a house of many mansions: now they were all to be tidied up and given uniform Tridentine colour-scheme in a Roman Catholic Church".[17] Ironically, a major contributor to the council was Archbishop Carranza, who was a powerful voice in England in 1556. He wrote a breviary (a book of daily prayers and offices for priests and religious) in 1568 based on his work in England for the Council of Trent, but he completed it in a gaol in Toledo, where he was imprisoned for seventeen years by the Spanish Inquisition on the charge that he had read too much heretical Protestant literature in the cause of combatting it! At this stage of the Counter Reformation, old scores, ethnic jealousies, power politics and mishandling of spiritual truth led to much suspicion and uncertainty about the verities of Roman Catholicism. The Church persecuted those who departed from its medieval traditions but had yet to define what these verities were for the age the world had entered. Trent was to take this next step into the future.

Roman Catholicism in England

In England, Mary's reign saw the re-imposition of Roman Catholic teaching or, at the very least, the Catholicism of her father. Some historians see this as a uniformly backward step, the imprisonment of the country in cultural and religious sterility. Others see the Marian church settlement as a creative reconstruction of Catholicism in the face of the recent onslaught by the Reformers. Although ceremonies were reintroduced, along with the signs of the mass, the Roman Catholic English hierarchy realized that they could not go on as before. Bonner, the Bishop of London, introduced a requirement to catechize the flock in "the true meaning of the ceremonies of the Church".[18] The Marian clergy now produced homilies not dissimilar in purpose to those provided in Cranmer's Prayer Book. Some dealt with fundamental issues, such as the Creation and the Fall, the nature of Christ's redeeming work, the sinfulness of humankind and the need for charity; others dealt with the papacy, the authority of the Church and the presence of Christ in the sacraments.

Bishop Bonner's chaplains, John Harpsfield and Henry Pendleton, wrote these homilies. They were part of a larger project of instruction called *A Profitable and Necessary Doctrine,* which set out to explain the fundamentals of the faith: the Apostles' Creed, the Ten Commandments, the seven deadly sins, the seven sacraments, the Lord's Prayer and the Hail Mary. Although Roman Catholic in tenor, these homilies highlight the view, common to the age, that to explain is to understand and that ceremonies are not enough in themselves. Alongside these reforms was Pole's emphasis on scriptural preaching, for which he would be arraigned by the Inquisition, accused of Lutheran teaching. Pole also put in hand the printing of primers (prayer books) based on the Old Sarum Rite, containing at least sixty devotional prayers printed in English. There is no doubt that the Catholic hierarchy in England made a real attempt to turn medieval religion into a restored Catholicism, but it was blighted by the restoration of heresy trials and the deaths of hundreds: 300 were burnt, 100 died in prison and over 800 fled in exile to the continent. The most celebrated of the martyrs was Archbishop Thomas Cranmer.

The burning of Thomas Cranmer

Cranmer had earlier been arrested for treason for his complicity in placing Lady Jane Grey on the throne, and was attainted (deprived of his titles, estates and chattels) on Mary's accession. Like his colleagues, Latimer and Ridley, he was tried for heresy in Oxford. The trial appears, at least initially, to have been a protracted theological debate or disputation in which the teachings of the three were judged for heresy. Cranmer came off worst of the three in his cross-examination by Thomas Martin. Pressure was then exerted on Cranmer, who seemed to want to come to some accommodation with the Queen. Ridley and Latimer were burnt just outside the Bocardo gaol where Cranmer was being held on Broad Street, Oxford. He was forced to watch and found the burning of Ridley traumatizing, not least because Ridley's brother-in-law, George Shipside, inadvertently slowed the progress of the flames by adding more wood.

Cranmer was further examined by the Spanish Dominican theologian Pedro de Soto and Juan de Villagarcia, another Dominican who came to England with Carranza. They set to work to see if Cranmer would retract his views on the papacy, the mass and transubstantiation. On 31 December 1555, their meetings began, now in the more congenial surroundings of Christ Church, Oxford. After some stormy meetings, Cranmer showed his fragility and indeed his isolation by attending mass in the cathedral without protest. Soon afterwards Cranmer signed his first recantation: "I am content to take the Pope for chief head of the Church of England, so far as God's laws and the laws and customs of this realm will permit."[19] Another strand of his humiliation was complete.

Far away in Rome, Cranmer was stripped of the office of archbishop by the papal consistory court on 4 December, and Cardinal Pole was appointed in his place. Back in Oxford, formal and theatrical evidence was given of Cranmer's fall. His degradation as archbishop was given in the rood-loft of Christ Church Cathedral, where he stood for all to see. John Harpsfield preached the sermon and Bonner produced a diatribe. Cranmer shouted out in Latin and English, "I appeal to the next General Council." It was a piece of ecclesiastical pantomime, laughable if the consequences had not been so dire, but also painful and full of foreboding for the future. Cranmer was an old man, sixty-six years old and broken in spirit. On 26 February 1556, he signed a document, most probably drawn up by Villagarcia, in which he anathematized Luther and Zwingli, acknowledged the doctrine of transubstantiation, the seven sacraments and the truth of purgatory. It appeared that his inquisitors' relentless pressure, combined with his own isolation, had succeeded. He was given More's *Dialogue of Comfort*, which More had written in the Tower when he was awaiting execution. Cranmer's own burning was delayed from the first weekend of March, but Mary could not be persuaded to rescind his punishment on the basis of his recantation. His heresy was too great. Cranmer began to set his affairs in order, thinking of his son and making provision for him. He even signed another recantation, his sixth and fullest, on 18 March, publicly confessing his guilt.

Likening himself to the penitent thief, he confessed the crimes of masterminding the divorce from Catherine, denying the real presence of Christ in the Eucharist, and rejecting the Pope's authority. He implored the forgiveness of the Queen and the Pope, but it availed him nothing. Three days later he was burnt, but not before one final dramatic twist arising from something as mundane as the English weather.

As the day determined for his burning was wet, the "pre-burning service" (yes) was held inside in the University Church. Cranmer, who had submitted his text to the authorities in advance, was to preach a sermon of penitence and contrition. But departing from the text, he overthrew all his previous recantations and, as commotion took hold in the church, he cried out, "As for the Pope I refuse him, as Christ's enemy, and Antichrist with all his false doctrine."[20] He was dragged from the pulpit and burnt, but not before extending the hand which had signed the recantations into the flames, saying: "Forasmuch as my hand offended, writing contrary to my heart, my hand shall first be punished there-for."[21] Like Stephen, the first martyr, he then spoke the words: "Lord Jesus receive my Spirit." (The gaolers accounts for the cost of burning Cranmer, itemizing the wood, the post and the labour, may be seen still in the Parker Library at Corpus Christi College in Cambridge.)

In the end, Cranmer had cheated Mary's regime of its greatest religious victory, its greatest trophy. Like Samson, in his dying moments Cranmer had brought down the temple (Judges 16). Maybe prayer and the message of his sister, a staunch Protestant, brought about Cranmer's change of heart in the final days before his burning. In many ways Cranmer's final recantation of his recantations was a talisman of Mary's reign: cheated of an heir through phantom pregnancies, cheated of a happy marriage through a preoccupied husband, and in the end cheated of the affections of her people that she had too easily squandered—she remains one of the pitiable losers in life. The people had welcomed her warmly at the outset, but she had spent all their affection. Two years after Cranmer's burning Mary died, with the loss of Calais graven on her heart, it is said. On the same day, her archbishop, Cardinal Pole, died of a flu epidemic. A new regime had arrived with Elizabeth. The herald would have cried, uniquely in English history: "The Queen is dead! Long live the Queen!"

CHAPTER 13

The Elizabethan Church Settlement: The *Via Media*

When Elizabeth succeeded to the throne following the death of her half-sister Mary, she was twenty-five years old, already experienced in the dangers of being on the edges of power, and increasingly wary of being used by others in their unscrupulous plots. It was still the age when a monarch's religious convictions determined the faith of the nation: her father had broken with Rome, yet sought to retain the cardinal doctrines of the Roman Catholic Church; Edward had led a Protestant revolution stirring up opposition; and Mary had tried to re-impose Catholicism, although at the cost of alienating many of her people and creating hosts of Protestant martyrs. Each Tudor monarch had shaped the faith of the nation, and it now remained to be seen what Elizabeth would do. Elizabeth's style was to love her people rather than tyrannize them as her father had done; to keep her options open until she really had to decide; and to rule through wise and good counsel. Where she could, she would procrastinate rather than decide. Whenever she could economize and be parsimonious, she would tighten the purse strings. Where possible, she hid her intentions behind elusive speeches filled with allusions, prepared and written by herself. She became the mistress of political camouflage.

When she appointed William Cecil as her chief adviser—a man of great capacity, integrity, intellectual ability and clear determination—she charged him with these loaded words on 18 November 1558:

> I give you this charge, that you shall be of my Privy Council, and content yourself to take pains for me and my realm. This judgement I have of you, that you will not be corrupted with any manner of gift, and that you will be favourable to the state, and that without respect of my private will, you will

give me that counsel that you think best. And if you shall know anything necessary to be declared to me of secrecy, you shall show it to myself only, and assure yourself I will not fail to keep taciturnity therein.[1]

Her charge was remarkably mature and prescient for a twenty-five-year-old. This then would be the tenor of her government and what she required of her most trusted adviser. There were two great issues before Elizabeth: the question of the religious settlement she would make and her succession. One concerned the whole body politic, the other her own body and her heirs. In both she would be cautious, circumspect and often infuriatingly opaque. Much of this circumspection came from the lessons of her early years.

The young Elizabeth

The first twenty-five years of Elizabeth's life had been turbulent, and she came close to losing her life on at least two occasions. Her mother, Anne Boleyn, whom Henry had moved heaven and earth to marry, had been executed on Henry's orders barely three years into their marriage. Thomas Cromwell had orchestrated trumped-up allegations of adultery against Anne. Despite the loss of her mother, Elizabeth continued to reveal many of her mother's lively characteristics: vivacity; a love of colour, show and theatre; sharpness of wit and mind; a love of learning and more than a hint of imperiousness. Combined with inherited characteristics from her father, she was a potent force, but set on a sea of deep insecurity. It was this insecurity, so present in her childhood and early adulthood, that arranged the talents of her personality and marked her for life. It was "an insecurity of both external political reality and, so far as it is possible to tell, her internal psychological landscape was the defining feature of Elizabeth's life".[2] This point needs to be grasped, not only for understanding the way she ruled, but for understanding the religious settlement she made.

From the time of her mother's execution, Elizabeth was raised in her own household. She wrote or uttered not a single word about her mother's death—which must have been an extraordinary act of self-discipline. She was in the charge of Lady Bryan, an experienced "governess" of royal children. Jane Seymour was not an unkindly stepmother, and Elizabeth was given the best of educations, encouraged by her own precociousness. Her tutors, Roger Ascham and William Grindal, were Cambridge scholars. She learnt Latin, Greek, French and Italian and expressed herself fluently in all. Her mind was probably the most wide-ranging and perceptive of all Henry's children. She was at home in the classics and Christian teaching, was familiar with Reformed teaching through Melanchthon's works, but may not have given it the same undivided loyalty as her half-brother Edward. She certainly did not have the outlook, perspective and insensitivity of her half-sister Mary. Henry's final wife, Catherine Parr, made it her business to bring the half-siblings together, albeit with limited success.

Elizabeth was thirteen when her father died on 28 January 1547. The final two years of Henry's life had been Elizabeth's happiest. It would be twelve years before she acceded to the throne, and for that to happen both Edward and Mary must die childless. It was one of the ironies of Henry's life that despite six marriages he had no grandchildren; perhaps that was an act of providence. It was during these years that Elizabeth learnt extreme caution and harsh lessons about whom she could and could not trust, amidst the politics of conspiracy that swirled around her. Despite her youthfulness, she was an important piece on the chessboard of Tudor politics, but there were few moves she could make with impunity, and many wanted to position her on the board of politics in pursuit of their own interests.

During her half-sister Mary's reign, Elizabeth's position became more dangerous. There were occasions when she came close to losing her life. In January 1554, when it was known that Queen Mary and Philip of Spain were to marry, Wyatt raised a rebellion with the object of replacing Mary with Elizabeth. These were dangerous times for Mary, but in a rallying speech at the Guildhall, delivered in her best Tudor style, she inspired loyalty from the burghers of London. By February, the rebellion had been put down. Executions began of Lady Jane Grey and her husband Guildford Dudley. Others followed, and even Elizabeth wondered what kind of execution she might request: whether by axe or by the sword as her mother had been (in the French way). By February, Elizabeth was a virtual prisoner in Whitehall. On Saturday, 18 March, she was escorted to the Tower, whereupon she pleaded to Mary for her life.

For Protestants, and for John Foxe in particular, the author of *Acts and Monuments*, or *Foxe's Book of Martyrs*, Elizabeth's survival in the Tower was nothing short of miraculous. She stayed in the accommodation used by her mother prior to being crowned as Queen and also, a few years later, before her execution. The Council interrogated Elizabeth about her intentions during the uprising, and why she was going to her castle at Donnington near Newbury. Wyatt, who was himself executed on 11 April, had never implicated her, so Elizabeth escaped with her life. She was then taken by stages to Woodstock near Oxford, where she was placed under house arrest, guarded by Sir Henry Bedingfield, a Norfolk supporter of Queen Mary. There Elizabeth held a mini court in exile, gave the performance of a devoted Catholic, but kept an English Bible and a copy of Cranmer's *Litany*, and continued to avow her innocence.

In October 1555, she was released from this house arrest and allowed to go to her own estates at Hatfield. In danger of being drawn into hot-headed plots to put her on the throne, she had a precarious existence: but as Mary grew older Elizabeth's position strengthened.

In the meantime, Elizabeth was once again put under gentle house arrest with new guardians, Sir Thomas Pope and Robert Gage. She was not left in peace, however, for now it was the turn of Philip to propose a husband for her: Emmanuel Philibert, Duke of Savoy—Catholic and a Spaniard. If she declined, she was to look forward to imprisonment, disinheritance and even death. Elizabeth would not be bullied, however. She knew her rank. She knew her destiny and would only marry the person *she chose* to marry. So she declined, much to the exasperation of Philip and Mary. But by 1558 Mary was running out of life and time.

At twenty-five, Elizabeth had thus been uncommonly tested. She was wary about giving her name to her supporters' conspiracies in case she was ill-used. She refused to marry any but one of her own choice. She knew how to act a part until it suited her to do otherwise. She could rarely relax. She was able to obfuscate with the best, yet she could also write convincing letters or addresses with emotional effect. She grew accustomed to the loneliness of leadership, but she was a young woman of great intelligence, social skill and wit, and, when she wanted to be, of magnetic attraction. How could she satisfy these two sides of her nature: her longing for intelligent association—intimacy even—and her duty to England? We know how, through circumstances and the passage of time, she decided. Two issues primarily confronted her: who to marry and how to settle the issue of the nation's Church and faith. Everything would depend on the church settlement: her heir, her alliances, her enemies and her ongoing vulnerability.

Elizabeth and her Church: Puritans and Catholics

High on Cecil's "to do list", or more formally, his first memorandum of "things to be done", written on the first day of his sovereign's reign, was the selection of a preacher for St Paul's Cross, the great open-air preaching space north of the cathedral. The sermon was to set the tone for the coming religious settlement. On 20 November 1558, the diarist and great sermon sampler, Henry Machyn, wrote that William Bill, Elizabeth's chaplain, "made a goodly sermon": no doubt supporting Elizabeth and preparing the way for change. Elizabeth, Protestant in conviction if Roman Catholic in some matters of ceremonial style, educated as she was by Philipp Melanchthon's *Loci Communes*—a summary of Evangelical theology—needed to act. In William Cecil she had the man to bring forward the necessary parliamentary legislation. If there was any doubt about the immediate need for this, Cecil arranged for several eminent people to urge Elizabeth to get on with it. Parliament was called and met in January 1559. The Upper House, which numbered only sixty, had many conservative peers, who, together with the Catholic Marian bench of bishops, were hostile to change. The House of Commons, by contrast, had about four hundred members newly elected and was ready to get on with change. The composition of the Commons in this historic parliament is important. About one third would have served under Mary in previous parliaments, and a number, perhaps twenty, were exiles who had returned from the continent—in particular Calvin's Geneva—after Mary's reign: making a hundred who would have been sympathetic to a reformed Church. Basically, legislation to reform the Church would carry the Commons easily, but in the Lords it was likely to fail.

Records of that first parliament are scanty and a comprehensive understanding of the business of Parliament cannot be found. Nevertheless, the *Commons Journal* records that the Supremacy Bill was brought forward by the government on 9 February 1559. It was at least the fourth bill concerning Supremacy to come before Parliament since 1534. In committee, it was drastically amended. It appears to have been amended to include both an Act of Uniformity and of Supremacy. No doubt the returning exiles in the Commons lobbied hard for greater simplicity of worship and an end to Roman ceremonies and vestments. The 1552 Prayer Book was to be reinstated as *the* common worship of the Church of England. Edward VI's second Act of Uniformity was to be re-enacted, but this required more time, was opposed by the Lords, and was thus detached from the Supremacy Bill.

By 22 March, just before Easter, the Act of Supremacy alone was passed by both houses and particular provision was made for Easter communicants to receive communion of both kinds: the bread and the wine. The Lords had massacred the bill, however, in reducing it to a minimum. Catholic opposition had proven too strong. Elizabeth refused to give her consent to the emasculated legislation and prorogued Parliament, taking all by surprise. So often cautious, she now imperiously expected her royal will to be observed. What is more, in her own Chapel Royal she used the Prayer Book for her Easter liturgy, signalling the direction of her mind. Parliament knew what was coming.

Elizabeth and the Council realized that greater force must be used to bring the Lords Spiritual in particular to heel. As a preliminary to any further parliamentary debate, a conference of eight Catholics and eight Protestants (four lay doctors of divinity and four bishops on each side) was held at Westminster with the purpose of persuading Elizabeth that one tradition, either Catholic or Protestant, was truly of the Word of God. The debate descended into farce and acrimony, and two Catholic bishops, White of Winchester and Watson of Lincoln, were sent to the Tower. It was pure coercion, but this was mild after the reigns of Henry VIII and Mary.

When Parliament opened on 3 April, both sides of the debate had had time to assess their position. Elizabeth began with a concession. In view of her sex, she was content to be known in the Supremacy Bill as "Supreme Governor" and not "Supreme Head", a title that had stuck in the throats of Puritans and Roman Catholics alike. In the Prayer Book, the words of administration from the Prayer Books of 1549 and 1552 were combined to give the now deeply-loved words: "The Body of our Lord Jesus Christ, which was given for thee, preserve thy body and soul unto everlasting life (1549) . . . Take and eat this in remembrance that Christ died for thee, and feed on him in thy heart by faith with thanksgiving (1552)." The first sentence emphasizes the real presence of Christ, the latter the commemorative aspect of communion. The combination was intended to satisfy both sides, but probably didn't. The Bills of Uniformity and Supremacy were presented separately, while debate about the Prayer Book led to claims it was unscriptural or heretical. The black rubric (about kneeling at communion) was omitted but kneeling for communion was kept and a rubric permitting the use of ornaments was included. The Act of Uniformity finally passed by three votes, with two Lords Spiritual handily kept in the Tower. Elizabeth and Cecil had scraped home, but it had been an honourable defeat for the Catholic bishops.

Now Cecil and Parker, the new Archbishop of Canterbury, would clear the bench of bishops of the old Catholics, although in a humane way for the most part. Most were deprived of their sees. Bonner was sent to Marshalsea Prison, but none were executed. Many saw out their days in quiet comfort under the eye of another bishop, much like the aged Tunstall and Archbishop Heath of York, who retired to Heath's house in Cobham. In 1559 large quantities of Marian church items were burnt on 23 August at Smithfield during the Bartholomew Fair, but the following year Elizabeth insisted that Lent be observed properly, and cartloads of meat were thus confiscated.

A commission was set up to apply the new settlement, and royal injunctions were drawn up by Cecil to be applied around the country. Instructions were laid down on matters such as clerical dress and attitudes in worship, e.g. kneeling at communion and bowing the head when uttering the name of Jesus in the Creed.

The government required that no parish priest could marry before the bishop and two justices of the peace had interviewed his intended! Like her father, Elizabeth preferred her clergy not to marry at all. The task now was to make this *via media* stick under challenges from both Puritans and Catholics.

The Puritans

The arrival of Puritanism can first be discerned in some of the more Protestant members of the Church who found even Edward's religious settlement deficient. One such person had been Bishop Hooper of Gloucester, who contested the use of clerical robes with Cranmer and was later burnt by Mary. During Mary's reign some five hundred clergy and laity fled her persecution to the continent, and as soon as she died, they returned. Some, like Bishop White of Winchester, who preached at Mary's funeral, said: "The wolves be coming out of Geneva and other places of Germany and have sent their books before, full of pestilent doctrines, blasphemy, and heresy to infect the people."[3] These émigrés had attended the best Reformed churches in the cities of Germany or Switzerland they lived in. Not only that, but using the 1552 Prayer Book, they had worshipped freely in Aarau (between Basel and Zurich), Basel, Strasbourg, Worms, Frankfurt and other places. A bishop had not overseen these churches; they had assembled freely; they could choose how to worship; and they were familiar with the works of the great continental reformers near where they lived. The first editions of Calvin's *Institutes* were published in 1536, 1539, 1543, and the final version in 1559. It would become the most influential work of Evangelical theology and would be known by many of these émigrés. John Knox, who had been in England during Edward's reign when he had sparred with Cranmer about further reform of the liturgy, was back in Geneva in 1558, writing a stirring address to the commonalty of Scotland. *Persona non grata* in England since writing his *Blasts* against the "Monstrous Regiment of Women" (i.e. the three Queens: Mary Tudor, Elizabeth and Mary Queen of Scots), he was nonetheless used by Cecil to go to Scotland as an antidote to the French-Catholic influences there, and to hasten Reformation. Just as Lenin was sent by the Germans to Russia to hasten the revolution in 1917, so too Knox was spirited into Scotland to stir up the Scots to overthrow Catholicism. He did not disappoint.

The stereotypical meaning of Puritanism is well-embedded in public consciousness and is generally taken as "the fear that someone somewhere might be having fun!" If this is how Puritanism is popularly (or unpopularly) remembered, it does not tell the whole story. In fact, the defining features of Puritanism are well-expressed in the Thirty-Nine Articles, which form the core of the doctrine of the Prayer Book and the Elizabethan religious settlement. The articles begin by affirming the reality of the Trinity and the truth of the Resurrection (i–v); the all-sufficiency and authority of the Word of God, the Bible and the Creeds (vi–viii); the way of salvation predicated on the reality of original sin and human depravity, including the powerlessness of free will, and hence the requirement for justification by faith (ix–xi). These are followed by the necessity for good works to evidence faith (xii–xiii); and the nature of sin (xiv–xvi) and predestination, the longest of all the articles (xvii). The remaining articles focus on the Church: its authority, sacraments, orders and civil responsibilities (xvii–xxxix).

For the Puritan, these statements were good as far as they went, but they wanted more clarity about the godly life and about family life; about simplicity in worship, i.e. no symbols, ceremonies or vestments; about the power of the bishop and its limitations; and about the rights of the congregation. In a word, they wanted purity of life and purity of worship. These Puritan émigrés had experienced much of this in exile and they wanted to see it established likewise in the English Church. Over the next hundred years, Puritans would engage in a struggle to obtain these things, until they were enforced by law in the Commonwealth. Paradoxically, at the very moment these aims were realized in England, the political power that undergirded the Puritans drained away. At that point (and indeed before), new churches reflecting their values began in England and were called non-conformist. Others, despairing of finding religious freedom in England, set sail across the Atlantic to new territories to begin again.

The returning Puritan émigrés found the House of Commons to their taste and a natural place to launch repeated assaults against what they saw as Elizabeth's halfway-house settlement over the next forty years. Some of them were formidable operators, like Sir Anthony Cooke, Sir Nicholas Bacon and Sir Francis Knollys: all parliamentarians either steeped in law or the humanities and Protestant, if not Puritan, to the core (and it's a fine line between the two). The areas of controversy with either the government (i.e. the Queen's Council) or the church hierarchy they would repeatedly come up against had to do with ceremonies, vestments, the power of the bishop, preaching and the independence of the clergy. Throughout Elizabeth's reign these matters would be raised frequently, both in and out of Parliament. In the reigns of her successors they would become even more acute, until only violence was left.

There were thirteen parliaments in Elizabeth's reign (most called for less than a year), and in many the matter of religion took up a good deal of time, second only to the question of succession. Religion was a hot topic in 1566 and 1571, focussing on the Articles of Religion, the quality of ministers, non-residency and ceremonies. In 1566, Bishop Horne of Winchester wrote to the Swiss reformer Rudolph of Zurich, saying that he hoped to appeal the injunction to wear the hated caps and surplices. Others, like Bullinger, also of Zurich, and Theodore Beza of Geneva, lamented the doleful effects of papist practices in the English Church. On the other side of the Puritan balance, the Thirty-Nine Articles were caught up in a Bill and passed only after considerable parliamentary horse trading with Elizabeth. By that year, 1571, the temperature of religious debate had been raised by the excommunication of the Queen by the Pope and the flight of Mary Queen of Scots to England in 1568, both significant events which we will return to later. The bishops were hoping for further reform of the Church, but the Queen refused. Instead, a new advocate of Presbyterianism and of Geneva arose in one Thomas Cartwright, the Lady Margaret Professor of Divinity at Cambridge. He famously lectured on the pattern of church government found in the Acts of the Apostles, and he did not find in favour of bishops. He was well-supported by the Earl of Leicester. A few Puritan firebrands had entered the Commons, such as Peter Wentworth of Lillingstone-Lovell, a man of "whet and vehement spirit", who ended up in the Tower, and Strickland "the Stinger" from Scarborough, and there were calls for further reform of the Church, especially because of the Catholic threat of the time.

Archbishop Matthew Parker, who was appointed soon after Elizabeth's accession, found it hard to restrain the Puritan movement. Stolidly Anglican, and not an inspiring leader, he laboured to demonstrate that the English Church had always been independent of Rome; in this he sought to confirm that *Ecclesia Anglicana* had always been an entity somewhat independent, a kind of uniate church. He was nevertheless against further reform, especially any which was the result of radical pressure. On the vestment controversy, he issued his *Advertisements*, an attempt to hold the line on clergy dress and practices. For his fussy inquisitiveness about clerical conduct, he earned the sobriquet "nosey Parker". A careful academic at heart, who had a large part in fashioning the Thirty-Nine Articles, he gathered together a priceless collection of early English manuscripts at Corpus Christi, Cambridge. He lamented the radical zeal of Wentworth, who called the bishops "mini popes", and with whom he had a complete disconnection of temperament.

Parker was succeeded by Edmund Grindal in 1575, another Marian exile. Grindal had spent those years in Strasbourg and Frankfurt before being made Bishop of London at Elizabeth's accession. By 1571, the Puritan presence, both on the Council and in Parliament, had grown in strength and its exponents were ready to experiment further with reform. The movement was widely supported by powerful aristocrats, such as the Duchess of Suffolk and Lady Ann Bacon, and Councillors such as Sir Francis Walsingham and Sir Walter Mildmay. During this period a new feature of Puritanism was on the increase, namely "prophesyings". These were periodic meetings of ministers for the purpose of biblical exposition and were held under a moderator or chairman. Lay people were also able to attend. To outside observers such as Elizabeth, these gatherings looked suspiciously like churches, and when Peter Wentworth offered the sacrament in the Geneva fashion at his house at Lillingstone-Lovell, there appeared good reason for the suspicion. Elizabeth wanted these prophesyings suspended, because of their resemblance to churches, but Grindal was reluctant to alienate their members. He was then himself suspended. Archbishop Whitgift succeeded him in 1583, being a man closer in outlook and spirituality to Elizabeth, although not rated by the Puritans in his own day or later.

In the later parliaments of Elizabeth's reign, from 1581 onwards, anti-Catholic legislation became the centrepiece of religious business. Following powerful speeches in the house by Robert Norton and Sir Walter Mildmay, heavier fines were imposed on recusant Catholics for non-attendance at the parish church. Failure to attend church incurred a fine of £20 and failure to receive communion twice a year resulted in a fine of £20 for the first offence, and up to £100 for the fourth. These fines were ruinous. The saying or hearing of mass also became a felony, with a sliding scale of penalties ranging from a fine to imprisonment, or even death. Although the Queen famously did not want to make windows into the hearts of men, nevertheless if their secret thoughts led to disobedience there was a price to pay. Furthermore, Robert Norton called for a Sedition Bill which made it a "seditious rumour" to question the doctrine of the Church of England or say that it was in any way heretical.[4] This too was passed.

Although the Queen would countenance enforcing uniformity, she was not willing to extend religion into new areas; in 1584, she vetoed a "Right Use of the Sabbath" Bill. Nor did she take kindly to ministerial classes lobbying Parliament for further reform after their own investigations into the fitness of the clergy. The Commons seized on this, however, proposing the need for qualifications for ministers. The Puritans also presented a Bill that protected clergy from being removed from their benefices by a zealous Archbishop Whitgift, who wanted complete agreement (from Puritans in fact who thought the Articles deficient) with all Thirty-Nine Articles. Appealed to by Whitgift, the Queen vetoed all three Bills, supporting the archbishop even against her old favourite, the Earl of Leicester, who spoke in favour of the Bills in the House of Lords.

In the Parliament of 1586, which followed the failure of a plot against Elizabeth called the Babington Plot, and the arrest of Mary Queen of Scots, who was implicated therein, the Puritans in Parliament once again used the momentum of those dangerous days to look for further reform. Sir Anthony Cope and his colleagues brought forward a Bill to reform the Prayer Book with a new Puritan Book that would highlight the sermon and extempore prayer, and which would bring into being a Presbyterian church without bishops. On this occasion the Queen literally confiscated the Bill and sent Cope and his ringleaders to the Tower. This of course brought into question the rights and privileges of MPs in relation to the crown, an issue raised by the firebrand Wentworth. The MPs were released from imprisonment and no more was heard about the Bill. The desire for a new Presbyterian Reformation did not go away, and the Queen was petitioned for a debate on the subject. Not only that, but satirical tracts, rather in the manner of the later Dean Swift, were anonymously and illegally circulated on the streets of London. Called the Martin Marprelate Tracts, they essentially attacked the bishops, going so far as to call them embodiments of the antichrist. Although there was no possibility of such a debate about a Presbyterian church being granted, the request did prompt Whitgift to audit the effectiveness and preaching capacity of his clergy. A Bill was then attempted to prevent clergy from holding a plurality of livings (i.e. several parishes). Even Lord Burghley spoke in favour of restricting a clergyman to two, but he must have known the Queen would veto this. She did. She was the Governor of the Church.

There were two subjects that were anathema or taboo for Elizabeth: her succession and meddling with the Church. Whenever anyone tried to discuss such matters, as occurred in 1593, she closed down the debate. In the Parliament of 1593, Puritans contested the efficacy of including Presbyterian separatists in the recusancy Bill of 1581. Recusants were also forbidden from moving more than five miles from their homes on pain of losing all their goods or even death and this was to last for generations. Catholic priests who would not identify themselves were likewise liable to execution. By now the Tudor state had become one of extreme surveillance and, for many, of terror. In the final Parliament of Elizabeth's reign in 1601, a Bill was proposed to fine those above the age of twelve who were absent from church at the charge of one shilling a service. Justices of the peace or church wardens were empowered to collect the fines and distribute the money to the poor, so they became the eyes and ears of the crown.

Internationally, the Elizabethan church settlement put England firmly in the Protestant camp, and as such it became a heretical state in the eyes of the Catholic powers of Europe. Foreign policy was increasingly affected by the Protestant church settlement in England, especially after the Pope's excommunication of Elizabeth in the bull, or papal declaration, *Regnans in Excelsis*, which was issued in the spring of 1570. This excommunication made it a religious duty for Catholics to get rid of Elizabeth. On the one hand this encouraged Spain to launch a Crusade against England, as it eventually did under Philip II with the Armada, while on the other it provoked Catholics in England to plot for a Catholic successor to Elizabeth in the person of Mary Queen of Scots. Once Mary Queen of Scots arrived in England as a refugee from her Scottish opponents, she became the focus of continuous plotting by Catholics in England seeking to replace Elizabeth.

The Protestant settlement of the English Church also made England a likely ally with Protestant causes in Europe. This had the dual effect of prompting England to intervene to support Holland in its Protestant struggle for independence from its imperial Catholic masters, Spain, and also to support the French Protestants, called Huguenots, in their bitter and violent struggle with French Catholic powers. After a period of confusion in the Netherlands, the Union of Utrecht was signed in January 1579 by rival groups, who thereby created an entity that was clearly Protestant as well as anti-Spanish. However, in 1584, the Prince of Orange, the Dutch Protestant leader, was assassinated. Spain, under the Duke of Parma, retook Antwerp and England could no longer procrastinate about involvement. Robert Dudley, Earl of Leicester, the Queen's favourite, raised an army and so began a protracted and unsuccessful campaign, underfinanced and with ambivalent support from the Queen, until eventually the campaign was side-lined by the more urgent necessity of defeating the Armada.

Relations with France were equally confused while France went through a period of bitter and bloody religious wars. The great houses of Guise, Montmorency and Valois/Bourbon were divided on religious lines: Guise and Montmorency were Catholic, the Bourbons were Huguenot. And from 1560, with the sudden death of the teenage King Francis II, Mary Queen of Scots' first husband, France descended into a period of religious and dynastic struggle. Not until 1598 and Henry IV's Edict of Nantes, which provided protection for French Huguenots, would there be an end to the bloodletting, which reached its peak in the Massacre of St Bartholomew's Day on 24 August 1572. Having murdered the Protestant leader, Admiral Coligny, the Guise faction incited the murder of around 10,000 Protestants in Paris and beyond. It was a foretaste of the revolutionary bloodletting that would come two centuries later.

At the news of this massacre the English court went into mourning, and the Queen and her courtiers wore black. After a further labyrinthine set of dynastic struggles, Henry of Navarre emerged as the Protestant heir to the French throne.

Henry IV was from the House of Bourbon and had a wife, Margaret, from the House of Valois. Henry won his inheritance by force of arms in defeating the Guise faction, but to heal his nation's divisions he announced his own conversion to Roman Catholicism in 1593, four years after his accession in 1589, famously saying *"Paris vaut bien une messe"* ("Paris is well worth a mass"). Despite Henry's success, the years had taken their toll on the French Protestant population. Many fled to England and formed French Protestant communities in London, one of which settled in Glastonbury during the Protectorate of Edward VI. Likewise, many other refugees came from the Low Countries to settle in Norwich. They were called "strangers", were mostly weavers, and boosted the city's industry. They brought with them canaries that sang while they worked, giving the city a new and enduring symbol (passed on to its present football club, Norwich City, with its canary symbol).

If the Elizabethan church settlement provided the basis for English foreign policy, producing both alliances and enemies, it was even more determinative of the succession. Only a Protestant might succeed. (Indeed, only in 2013 did discrimination against a Catholic inheriting the British crown end with the Succession to the Crown Act of that year.) The issue of Protestant succession was to dominate English politics for the next three centuries. Two hundred years on, the mere thought of a Catholic succession was enough to bring a mob out onto the streets of London in the Gordon Riots in 1780, opposed as they were to any slackening of the anti-Catholic stance in public life.

The great question in English public life from the time of Elizabeth's accession until her final years was whom she would marry and/or who would be her heir. It was a question that concerned the population at large as they gathered to gossip in the taverns of London and beyond. The issue concerned Elizabeth's ministers and Parliament even more. For Elizabeth it was a topic not to be discussed by Council or by Parliament. Time and again she addressed the Houses of Parliament with her own opaque prose, obfuscating her intentions, and closing down the subject.

Suitors, she had many. She turned down the Duke of Savoy and later, in 1579, the Duke of Anjou, whom she called "the little frog". Pamphlets such as "The Moste Strange Wedding of the Frogge and the Mouse" circulated against that prospective union. But the most serious relationship was with Robert Dudley, the Earl of Leicester, to whom she lost her heart. But in the end, she denied her affections, not wanting to sow seeds of discord or jealousy among the English nobility. And towards the end of her reign there was Essex: but he was more an immature "toy boy" than a serious potential partner. Anyhow he fell badly out of favour having invaded the Queen's bedroom and was executed in 1601. In the end, the succession was settled by an unspoken policy that Mary Queen of Scots' son, James VI of Scotland, would succeed, which Cecil made sure of through the Treaty of Berwick in 1586.

The Catholics

For the last twenty years, from 1536 and the break with Rome, the parishes of England had faced a bewildering, and probably stomach-turning, roller coaster of religious change. From the high-water mark of the Henrician reform in the late 1530s to the Protestant revolution of Edward VI, with the imposition of the Prayer Book in 1549 and its revision in 1552, to the reversal of everything under Queen Mary and the restoration of the mass, parish life in England was anything but calm. And now, with the accession of Elizabeth I, further change from the Catholicism of Mary and her bishops could be expected. As noted previously, the conservative Marian bishops were for the most part quietly retired. The Act of Supremacy and Uniformity, as in Edward's day, was passed in Parliament in April 1559. The bishops and the crown handed down injunctions about the conduct of liturgy and church life. Most parishioners with a modicum of English phlegm might well have quietly muttered to themselves "here we go again" and probably hedged their bets. Until Henry's Act of Supremacy, every worshipper in every parish church knew themselves to be part of the one Catholic Church. The Sarum Rite (an early medieval liturgy of the eleventh century), with some regional variations, had been the staple of parish eucharistic worship for centuries. After the sudden changes under Edward and Mary, a wary public wondered what the future would hold under Elizabeth I. For instance, when William Woodman of Eye in Suffolk made a will two days after Mary's death, leaving twenty ounces of silver to his parish church to make a silver processional cross, he did so with the proviso "yf the laws of the realme will permit and suffer the same".[5] If souls were no longer in limbo because of the official ending of purgatory, there was a sense in which the average parishioner felt herself in limbo with the accession of a new monarch until it became clear which way the religious wind was blowing.

The composition of a distinctly Roman Catholic grouping in the body spiritual of the realm took time to form. It was less distinct the further down the social scale you went. And it was formed by events beyond the control of most people. It is estimated that out of a population of three to four million, approximately 40,000 called themselves Roman Catholic. Elizabeth's settlement was not as stark as Edward's. She authorized the same Prayer Book, but kept more outward ceremony, such as use of the cope in the Eucharist, singing of polyphonic music rather than just plain chant, the use of the sign of the cross and even prayers for the repose of the dead. However, the commissioners who were to enforce the injunctions were empowered to dismantle rood screens and get rid of patronal statues, holy water stoups and any missals or manuals produced in Mary's reign. The resulting ferreting across 9,000 parishes took time, and the enforcement proceeded for at least twenty years and then not uniformly. There would be more left for the Cromwellian soldiers to do during and after the Civil War.

There seems to have been a slow and often reluctant conformity to the rules imposed from above. Age-long practices in funeral services or rogation services (praying for the land) were hard to eliminate. Some parish priests used some of the symbolic actions of the mass with the new liturgy, but they received no more than admonishment. On the other hand, the cycles of mystery plays were effectively banned. As the years went by, the majority of parishioners acceded to the new way of doing things: the Prayer Book established itself, the simple liturgy with some ceremony became familiar, and, as new generations arrived who knew nothing about what went before, the new became the norm. This was not the case for everyone, however.

While many took the line of least resistance and complied with Elizabeth's new religious settlement, it was not acceptable to all. Some Catholics were occasional attenders at the parish church, others were recusants. Later in the sixteenth century, the Catholic religious leader William Allen thought as many as two thirds of the population were still at heart Catholic, but in truth, as I have suggested, the number was much smaller. Only the old aristocratic families and the gentry could afford to pay the punishing fines after 1581 for recusancy (i.e. for non-attendance at the parish church). Catholics were a small minority of the overall population, found mostly in the North and the East of the country, but nonetheless they formed an influential proportion of the Elizabethan elite.

As Elizabeth's reign wore on, the dilemma of the Catholic population only increased, and pressure on them became intense. Many may have chosen to be loyal subjects of the crown were it not for international pressure: the papal bull, the parliamentary legislative response, the conspiracies surrounding the claim of Mary Queen of Scots to the English crown. Then there was the sending of Catholic missionaries to England and aggressive Spanish intentions resulting in the Armada. Lastly, support for James as the heir to the English throne only increased pressure on Catholics. Then, in 1581, the Act "to retain the queen's majesty's subjects in their due obedience" defined anyone converting to Rome or seeking to convert others as a traitor, whilst at the same time increasing the penalties for saying or hearing mass or failing to attend church. What we can see in Elizabeth's reign is a ratcheting up of the risk to Elizabeth from Catholics and the corresponding increase of penalties against them. It was a spiral that did no favours to the Catholic community over the years, and it sowed deep discord for the future.

At the outset of her reign it had not been Elizabeth's policy to turn the whole Catholic community against her. Her policy of not making "windows into the souls of men" made her initially unwilling to judge the religious affiliations of others, but this was not the policy of her Councillors, such as William Cecil, for whom such a determination was crucial. Even less was it the policy of her spymaster, Francis Walsingham, for whom such disinterest in human souls was criminal. As Elizabeth's reign continued, as plots thickened and grew more numerous, the screw was turned ever more tightly on her Catholic subjects. At first, she resisted the imposition of recusancy fines proposed by Parliament, but by 1581 this had changed. In the intervening years, the threat to Elizabeth had increased with the arrival of Mary Queen of Scots on English soil, the uprising of the Northern Earls in 1571, the papal bull *Regnans in Excelsis* of the same year, the growing threat of missionary Catholic priests in England, and the intentions of Spain. Together, the confluence of these factors posed a lethal threat to an insecure queen.

The arrival of Mary Queen of Scots on English soil in 1568, as a refugee from Scottish internal divisions, was not welcomed by Cecil or those supporting the Protestant cause in England. As the granddaughter of Margaret Tudor, Henry VIII's sister, Mary was the closest heir to the English throne, only she was Catholic and half French. Her life before her arrival in England was marked by a series of tragic misfortunes. Her husband, the French Dauphin, died soon after becoming King Francis II. Returning to Scotland, a tall and flamboyant beauty, she married the elegant but dissolute Darnley, with whom she had a son, James, in 1566. The following year an explosion in his castle killed Darnley, whereupon Mary married Bothwell, a man who had been implicated in her husband's death. At this point, having been defeated at Carberry Hill, Mary was forced to abdicate by the Confederate Lords (a group of Protestant lowland lords) in favour of her son James, who would then be raised by this Protestant association. Mary escaped her imprisonment in Loch Leven Castle and fled to England in 1568, where she became the focus of Catholic plots against Elizabeth. From early on William Cecil made Mary's destruction a cardinal element of his policy for preserving Elizabeth as Queen, but this was never Elizabeth's desire.

The situation for Elizabeth was becoming graver by the year. In 1571, the Ridolfi Plot was hatched against her by an international Italian banker of that name. The intention was to replace Elizabeth with Mary with the support of the Duke of Norfolk and Spanish troops. Through Walsingham's unsleeping diligence, the plot was uncovered. Norfolk was executed and Mary put under ever more watchful guard. Elizabeth's security was weakened far more by the Pope's bull, *Regnans in Excelsis*.

The papal bull came out of a clear blue sky. Neither King Philip of Spain nor the Emperor Maximilian had been told of Pope Pius V's intention to excommunicate Elizabeth. And indeed, when they were told, they did not publish it in their countries. Not only did the bull excommunicate Elizabeth, it also made treason against her a religious duty: her removal from the throne was now the obligation of all faithful Catholics. It was this that led to at least thirty years of what would be called today "religious terrorist plots" against the realm—because the realm was deemed to be led by a deviant power. The Pope freed all peers, office-holders and people from having to obey her laws, directions and commands. Furthermore, engineering her death had become a moral duty. The effect on the Catholic community was as devastating, perhaps even more so, than on Elizabeth herself. If Catholics remained obedient and loyal to the Pope, they immediately became probable traitors. If they were obedient citizens, they were in peril, as they saw it, of losing salvation. The conditions of English Catholics worsened: they were exposed to the charge of treason if they obeyed the Pope and, if they didn't, they were exposed to the corresponding risk of excommunication. It was precisely into these conditions of plotting around Mary Queen of Scots and responding to this bull that a new phenomenon emerged: the sending of Catholic missionaries into England to strengthen Catholic resistance and advance the re-conversion of England to Catholicism.

William Allen, Douai College and the Jesuits

The period from the papal bull to the end of Elizabeth's reign was tragic for relations between her government and the Catholic community, both in England and abroad. Neither would it improve in the early years of her successor James I's reign, beginning as it did with the Gunpowder Plot of 1605. This breakdown between crown and subject reaped a bitter whirlwind. On Elizabeth's side, her minister William Cecil, working with her "chief of police", Francis Walsingham, sought to thwart any plot against her, traumatized as they were by the massacre in Paris on St Bartholomew's Day. They now saw Catholic priests not simply as spiritual leaders, but as political agents seeking to bring down the monarchy and return England to the Roman Catholic fold. It was a bitter divide with violence used or planned on both sides, and into its vortex both the noble and the ignoble were drawn, with repercussions to relations between both communities that would last for hundreds of years.

One of the chief proponents of the conversion of England to Catholicism was Cardinal William Allen. Born in Fleetwood in Lancashire in 1532, he was only eighteen when he was elected to a Fellowship of Oriel College, Oxford, which, as a university, had remained more Catholic during the Tudor period than Cambridge. Between 1559 and 1561, all but one of the Catholic heads of colleges were ejected by Elizabeth. Allen also left his post as Principal of St Mary's Hall. With the advent of Elizabeth's church settlement, Allen refused to take the Oath of Supremacy, left England for a while, before returning under cover to persuade Catholics not to attend Anglican worship and to continue faithful to their Church and worship. He was of the opinion that only force kept the Elizabethan church settlement in place, and if that force or the monarch were removed, then England would return to Catholicism.

It was with this in mind that he founded a training college for English Catholic priests at Douai in northern France on the borders with the Low Countries. For this he had the support of Pope Paul IV—an unpopular pope who established a Jewish ghetto in Rome—Philip II of Spain, and the Guise family, relatives of Mary Queen of Scots.

It was this mixture of the spiritual and the political that made Allen's mission so problematic. Yet it was a world in which political power and religious convictions were hopelessly intertwined. From 1574, Allen sent a stream of idealistic young priests from his college to prison, execution and torture in England, first from Douai, then Rheims. Their mission was literally to go and die. They were regarded as a group of "missionary stormtroopers". By May 1576, there were eighty students in the college; by September 1576 there were 120. By then, harbouring a priest in England was treason and so too was being one. By implication, not recognizing the Queen as the Governor of the Church was also treasonable. From 1572, Allen was actively involved in a series of plots for the overthrowal of Elizabeth and the forcible re-conversion of England. "By any standard recognized in Elizabethan England Allen was a traitor."[6] He proved as much by his very active involvement in what was called on the continent "Enterprise England", which ended with the Spanish Armada.

Over the course of Elizabeth's reign, some four hundred young priests were sent to England on missions initiated by Douai, often in conjunction with the Jesuits, by now the premier missionary order in the Catholic Church. (Fearless and uncompromising, the order had been founded by Ignatius Loyola in 1540.) Of these four hundred, about three hundred were executed, often after torture and imprisonment. The walls of the English College in Rome, or the *Venerabile*, were covered with scenes of priests being arrested, tortured and executed whilst on mission in England—a sobering prospect for any would-be ordinand. Some of these priests, like Robert Persons (1546–1610), failed to capture the support of the English Catholic community, being too extreme. Persons was born in Nether Stowey in the Quantocks and educated at St Mary's Hall and Balliol in Oxford, which he left after 1574 to become a Jesuit priest in Rome. He was castigated in 1610 by the poet and Dean of St Paul's, John Donne, who in his work *Pseudo-Martyr* criticized the Catholic practice of martyrdom.

While Persons died in peace in the English College in Rome, his fellow Jesuit and missionary, Edmund Campion, inspired a devoted Roman Catholic following. Campion was an outstanding academic and rhetorician at Oxford during Mary's reign. He was formally chosen to welcome Elizabeth to Oxford in 1556 before her accession. Despite initially joining Anglican orders, he left England and joined the Jesuits in Rome. Arriving on a mission to England in 1581, he was discovered at Lyford Grange in Berkshire in June 1581. Arrested and tried by three Privy Councillors and tortured on the rack, he was condemned to death as a traitor: hung, drawn and quartered. He became a paragon of sacrificial Catholic mission, inspiring many others in his wake. He regarded his own execution as a denial of the Catholic Church in England, which had been founded by St Augustine's mission in 597, and of which he saw himself a faithful representative. He captured the imagination of the English Catholics in a way Persons had not.

By the late sixteenth century, not only was there a stream of young Catholic priests willing to go on mission to England—and risk their lives in doing so—but there was also a new literature that they were to disseminate. English Roman Catholic scholars had not been idle, and chief among them was Gregory Martin, one of a number of Catholic intellectual luminaries exiled to the continent. Others included Nicholas Sanders, Thomas Stapleton, Thomas Harding and Persons, who were either Catholic theologians based at Louvain or, in the case of Sanders, partakers in a holy war to repossess England for Rome via an invasion through Ireland.

Martin was another product of Marian Oxford, a scholar of St John's, who joined Allen at Douai. He founded the curriculum of study for the students there and his great work was the translation of the Bible into English for a Catholic audience. Unlike Tyndale's, it was a translation based on the Latin Vulgate, rather than the Greek and Hebrew. Many clumsy renderings resulted. Thus 1 Corinthians

5:7 is translated as "Purge the old leaven, that you may be a new paste, as you are azymes. For our Pasche, Christ, is immolated."[7] The Rheims Bible, as Martin's translation was called, precipitated a veritable industry of Puritan rebuttals by Thomas Cartwright of Cambridge, William Whittaker and William Fulke, the Master of Pembroke, Cambridge. The battle against the English translation of the Bible had been well and truly lost, but for Martin it was now a question of rendering the scriptures in line with Catholic tradition.

Martin also sought to stiffen Roman Catholic resolve against Elizabeth by publishing his *Treatise of Schisme*. Along with others, he sought sterner restrictions on those Catholic lay people who were occasional conformists (i.e. merely occasional attenders of Prayer Book services in their parishes). Inspired by his time in Rome, Martin sought to reclaim that city's ancient traditions, its Christian history, architecture and the writings of the Church Fathers, as a further basis for establishing Roman Catholic integrity. The resulting book, *Roma Sancta*, was a kind of answer to Foxe's *Acts and Monuments*, commonly called *Foxe's Book of Martyrs*, which was the publishing event of the 1560s, listing martyrs from earliest times, but concentrating on the Protestant martyrs of the sixteenth century. Both sides of the Reformation divide claimed the early martyrs of the Church as their own. In his *Roma Sancta*, Martin sought to show that there was an unbroken tradition of faith, architecture, history and suffering from the early Church to the Council of Trent, whereas the Protestant Church sought to demonstrate that the Catholic Church had departed from its origins and that the Reformed Church was the true successor to the martyrs of the first four centuries.

It was in the end a fruitless argument. Indeed, the father of Western theology, Augustine of Hippo, could be found on both sides: on the one hand he was an advocate of the requirement for grace alone to grant salvation because of the power of original sin, and damnation (here the heart of Reformed theology was played out by Augustine in the Pelagian controversy). On the other, Augustine's teaching against the Donatists argues that the efficacy of the sacraments is not dependent on the purity of the minister, which supports the Roman Catholic position, i.e. although popes and clergy err, this failing does not impair the efficacy of the Church's ministry.

Martin sought to validate the present from his research into the past. In the same way, Thomas Stapleton reissued the works of Bede, emphasizing Bede's English or Anglo-Saxon pedigree, but also his commitment to Rome. Armed with this literature, and with a renewed commitment to prayer in the form of the new Ignatian spiritual disciplines, Roman Catholic devotion increased with its uncompromising attitude to the Elizabethan Church and towards Elizabeth herself. The Catholic threat to the Elizabethan Church was intense, and never more so than in the final years of her reign.

Elizabeth's final years

The Catholic threat to Elizabeth came to a head in her final years. In 1584, a Catholic fanatic fatally shot William of Orange, the leader of the Dutch Protestants, at his home in Delft, causing consternation in England. In the Parliament of 1584–5, the Bond of Association to protect the Queen's majesty was given legal force in the Act for the Queen's Surety. A year later, the final move, the Babington Plot, which implicated Mary Queen of Scots, was discovered by Walsingham, who deciphered encrypted messages made up of a curious assortment of Greek and Arabic letters. Proof was provided of Mary's involvement with a foreign power, Spain, to remove and supplant Elizabeth. Mary was tried by twenty-four nobles and Privy Councillors, an event orchestrated by her long-term opponent, William Cecil, at Fotheringhay Castle in Northamptonshire. On 4 December 1586, she was found guilty. On 5 February 1587, in spite of Elizabeth's extreme reluctance to sign the death warrant at the behest of Cecil, Mary was executed in the castle hall in scenes of utmost drama. On hearing the news of Mary's death, Elizabeth flew into a tantrum of rage, guilt and grief. She exiled Cecil from the court and locked herself away for days. Yet the reality of the challenge was unquestionable, for the following year England faced its greatest threat in the form of the Spanish Armada.

The purpose of the Armada was to convey an army of 17,000 to England, where it would then invade the south coast under the Duke of Parma, who was waiting to cross the Channel from the Low Countries. On 19 July 1588, the Armada was sighted off the Isles of Scilly. Meanwhile, Elizabeth rallied her troops at Tilbury for a defence of the realm. In an age of poetry, prose and military daring, the age of Shakespeare, Edmund Spenser and Sir Philip Sidney, her words captured the spirit of the moment and the genius of her rule.

In a reign studded with England's greatest playwrights, Shakespeare himself could not have composed better. At Tilbury Elizabeth exhorted her troops with the words, "I know I have the body of a weak and feeble woman; but I have the heart and stomach of a king, and of a king of England too". Elizabeth's words inspired, while a gale and her sea captains—Drake in the *Revenge*, Hawkins in the *Victory* and Frobisher in the *Triumph* under the Lord Admiral Howard of Effingham in the *Ark Royal*—did the rest. Every Protestant believed that God had breathed and the enemy was scattered. The commemorative medallion for the defeat of the Armada read *Deus flavit et dissipati sunt* (God blew and they were scattered). They were scattered all round the coast of the British Isles.

The final years of Elizabeth's reign were marked by strong repression and control. There was continuing severe treatment of Catholics and ongoing attempts by Puritans to create a Calvinist church within the Church of England, particularly by the great organizer of the *classis* system, John Field, who sought a "presbytery with an episcopacy".[8] Both attempts were resisted by the state. Questions of succession to Elizabeth were never far from Parliament's mind, but although Elizabeth would never discuss it, there was quiet acceptance that James VI of Scotland would succeed her and he had already been given a retaining pension of £3,000 a year by the Council.

As well as greater peace, there was also widespread poverty in the country. Inflation, a growing population and the reduction in common land due to enclosures all took their toll. Beggars were a frequent sight in the cities, with as many as 12,000 in the City of London alone, while vagrants on the roads were a common sight between towns. A combination of repressive legislation and the administration of the Poor Rate were introduced to address the problem, but two thirds of the population existed on or below the poverty line. The poor were divided into the labouring poor, the impotent poor (disabled and disadvantaged) and the idle poor, with the severest penalties of branding or even mutilation reserved for the idle poor. There is no doubt it was a harsh regime, although leavened for some by the growing opportunity for entertainment at the Globe and Rose theatres in London, where playwrights Johnson, Marlowe and Shakespeare entranced their audiences. No one elucidated more vividly in drama both political and personal dilemmas than Shakespeare. Ambition, rivalry, slander, love, truth and falsehood, depression, jealousy, revenge and sheer humour at human foibles grace the pages of his plays, which arise from both realistic scepticism about, and deep engagement with, the human story. It was an age of vivid reflection on life in all its ribaldry, chance and unfairness—giving a voice to monarch and pauper alike.

Forty years after its re-establishment by Elizabeth in 1559, the Church of England now found two apologists to answer both its Puritan and Catholic critics. Both extremes judged Anglicanism either heretical (Catholic) or wanting (Puritan), but two men, John Jewel (1522–71), Bishop of Salisbury, and Richard Hooker (1554–1600), a priest, sought to set out the Church of England's orthodoxy.

Jewel, the older of the two, was educated at Corpus Christi Oxford and was a close follower of the Italian Reformer Pietro Vermigli. During Mary's reign, having seen the burnings of the Oxford martyrs, he fled to Germany, although he later rued his timidity. On his return he took part in the disputation with the conservative Catholics during Elizabeth's first Parliament in 1559, before the Acts of Supremacy and Uniformity were carried. His argument, as expressed in his *Apology of the Church of England*, was that the Church of England was built solidly on the teaching of scripture, the Apostles, the Church Fathers and councils. He upheld the teaching of the Reformers on the doctrine of justification by faith— indeed he hoped the Anglican settlement might go further in expressing it. He taught that the sacraments are a seal of God's grace in the heart of the believer when received with faith. He maintained that the sacraments are "visible words, seals of righteousness, tokens of grace".[9] The Roman Catholic Church had become a "den of robbers", and it was thus necessary to leave it to ensure continuing orthodoxy.

Richard Hooker, another Devonian from Heavitree outside Exeter, was a protégé of Jewel, who had gained him admittance to Corpus Christi Oxford, where Hooker became a Fellow in 1577. From there he went to the Temple Church in London before settling in two parishes in Wiltshire and finally near Canterbury. His teaching was criticized by the Puritans, who suspected him of Rome-ish tendencies, in part because he argued that Roman Catholics could be saved whilst remaining in the Catholic Church. Hooker's great work was *The Laws of Ecclesiastical Polity*, published in several sections over seven years. The first four books appeared in 1593, the fifth in 1597 and the remaining work posthumously. A survey of these five books reveals a systematic, erudite and exhaustive defence of the establishment and ministry of the Church of England, especially in light of the Puritan challenge. He suggests there are laws which should govern our lives: the Eternal Law, Celestial Laws which regulate angelic and spirit life, the Law of Reason, the Law of Scripture and Civic Law. Where necessary, we are to live in accordance with these laws. In broad terms, he uses in his defence of Anglican orders that threefold cord which was to mark the distinctiveness of Anglicanism thereafter: scripture, tradition and reason. Concerning the Puritan challenge, "that what is not explicitly stated in scripture should not be done", Hooker answers that if something is not inimical to the tenets of scripture, and is in line with tradition and reason, then it may be permitted or welcomed. The issue is that God "blessed the creative process of human reasoning and the peaceful ordering of human society" with clear lines of authority, providing the outcomes do not contradict scripture. With this principle established on the foundation of reason, including use of classical philosophers such as Aristotle, Hooker commends that which is harmonious with scripture, tradition and reason. He was no slouch when it came to knowledge of the biblical languages, the classics and the early

Fathers. Copious references may be found in his writing to Athanasius, Gregory Nazianzen, Augustine of Hippo and many others.

The fifth book, which came out somewhat later than the first four, is a detailed defence of the practice of Anglicanism against the Puritan criticism of such matters as the use of fine church buildings, the use of singing and music in worship, the appropriate length of a service as neither too short nor too long, for "words be they never so few are too many when they benefit not the hearer", etc. And then controversially, and at length, Hooker supports women performing baptism, upholding the practice that midwives might baptize children who are sickly (since many infants died close to birth or before), thus giving comfort to their parents. Presumably this practice was rejected by the Puritans, not so much on grounds of objection to infant baptism, since after all both Luther and Calvin commended infant baptism, but on the grounds that since women cannot teach in church, they certainly cannot baptize. In a lengthy argument from the Church Fathers, Hooker says that the standing and hence sex of the person (i.e. the one baptizing) does not vitiate the efficacy of the sacrament if it is received with understanding and faith.[10] This is in many ways a clear example of Hooker's method of combining reason, scripture and tradition with compassionate pastoral action. The subject would come up again at the Hampton Court Conference in 1604, where even King James I crassly rejected the practice, saying "that he rather his child be baptized by an ape than by a woman".[11]

Finally, Hooker defended the use of festival days, fasting, spiritual power bestowed upon ministers through the laying on of hands, and the Anglican marriage service. The Puritans objected to the use of a ring in marriage and the words, "With this ring I thee wed, with my body I thee worship", maintaining that neither a ring nor worship were fitting. Hooker cites in response Tertullian's argument that engagement rings were used in the Early Church and that worship simply meant reverence and duty towards a wife.[12]

Hooker's great work is impressive for its erudition, reasonableness and orthodoxy, but it was not popular. It could not match the sheer breadth and scale of either Aquinas or Calvin in their dogmatic works of *Summa* and *Institutes* respectively. It was also peculiarly English, being clearly orthodox in faith, Protestant in outlook, but deeply founded on the Church Fathers (tradition) and on the classics, in particular Aristotle (reason). It would serve as a defence of the Elizabethan church settlement or Anglicanism in the seventeenth and subsequent centuries, but it could never compete with the racy, iconoclastic, populist Puritan pamphlets that demanded change and the overthrow of the *status quo*. It had been quietly produced in Anglican rectories in Wiltshire and Kent by Hooker, after a period of preparation at the Temple Church and at Oxford University, and in that sense too it was a quintessentially Anglican and English production, fusing controversy in scriptural reasonableness.

As Elizabeth's reign drew to a close at the start of the seventeenth century, there was some respite from her foes. Famously, on 30 November 1601, she addressed Parliament for the last time in what became known as her "Golden Speech". It was printed and circulated by Robert Barker. Demurring greatness, she said:

> You must not beguile yourselves, nor wrong us, to think that the glossy lustre of a glittering glory of a king's title may so extol us that we think all is lawful what we list, nor caring what we do. Lord, how far should you be off from our conceits![13]

Ever circumspect, ever playing the part of a dutiful and loving queen, she ruled by acknowledging her weakness, but nevertheless expected complete loyalty and devotion in return. She had a fist of iron in a well-adorned velvet glove.

There was by then already a sense of a passing age: the Earl of Essex, her last favourite, had been executed for treason; Drake and Hawkins had died in an expedition to the New World; and William Cecil, Lord Burleigh, had been succeeded by his son Robert. The contours of English Christianity had been set in a state of continual dynamic struggle. It was a three-way split: the Church of England by law established; the Catholics fostered by continental hopes, but shackled in England; and the Puritans ever seeking to overturn Elizabeth's religious settlement. The Church of England had, at its centre, a paradox. It was reformed in doctrine, but modestly Catholic in outward appearance, and its liturgy, in the words of Lord Burleigh, was "a mingle-mangle"—even if this jibe is a little unfair on Cranmer's efforts. Just as Elizabeth loved colour, texture and a sense of theatre and glory about her person, so too in her Church she wanted something similar: song inspired by Tallis, Byrd and Taverner, the great Elizabethan composers, for example, and wit in her preachers. She loved words herself, she expected no less from others. For Elizabeth, the Church should appeal to the intellect as well as to the emotions, the spirit as well as to the soul, the ear as well as to the eye. She was able to ride these competing horses in an artful and beguiling way; her successors did not have the same skill, nor could call on the same loyalty as the bulwark between a Protestant church and Spain.

On 24 March 1603, the seventy-year-old queen breathed her last. Only then did she intimate her successor with the words: "Who should succeed me but a king?"[14] It was her roundabout way of nominating James VI of Scotland. That night Robert Carey began a three-day journey to Edinburgh, carrying with him a blue sapphire, a pre-arranged sign of Elizabeth's death, and greeted James as the new King of England. The Stuarts had succeeded the Tudors; a future as equally tempestuous as the past awaited.

CHAPTER 14

Puritanism and Revolution

When James heard that he was to succeed Elizabeth in 1603, he must have thought that Christmas had come early. Indeed, in the early years of his reign he must have thought that Christmas had come every day! Others in his entourage would have felt the same way, for his procession south from Edinburgh to London was a surreal pageant of celebration. His generosity delighted his contemporaries: the landlord at the Beer in Doncaster received a valuable royal lease; he knighted no fewer than 906 men; and he showered peerages on the leaders of Elizabeth's administration. In Lincolnshire, a hundred men on stilts greeted him, and knowing his passion for hunting he was invited to view game and take part in the chase wherever he could. There was joy in having a king to succeed Elizabeth, not least a Protestant one who would continue her policies. As for James, he was entering into almost unimagined wealth, although on closer inspection there were plenty of snags as well: not least a large financial deficit bequeathed by Elizabeth.

When James succeeded to the English throne, he was thirty-six years old and had been King James VI of Scotland since 1567. Like Elizabeth's, his childhood and upbringing had been tempestuous. He was separated from his mother, Mary Queen of Scots, when he was only thirteen months old and she was forced to abdicate and much later flee to England. He became King of Scotland in a ceremony at which John Knox preached, and he was brought up in Stirling Castle under the supervision of the Earl and Countess of Mar. His main tutor was the redoubtable George Buchanan, one of the greatest Latin scholars of his age. Starved of consistent female nurture, it is not surprising that his sexuality was ambiguous, as we shall see. Nevertheless, he married Anne of Denmark when she was fifteen, and they had three surviving children: Henry, who died as Prince of Wales, Elizabeth, who married the Elector of the Palatine—whose daughter Sophia married the Elector of Hannover and was the mother of George I—and Charles, who became Charles I, King of Great Britain and Ireland.

James himself was an unusual character. He had a passion for hunting and spending days on end in seclusion with a few male friends in pursuit of game. He also regarded himself as a theologian and philosopher. In 1598, he had written *The True Law of Free Monarchies* to correct the endless miseries of "our long disordered, and distracted Commonwealth". In it he argued against extremes: the radical Calvinists he knew from Scotland and the belligerent Catholic League known to him from the Guise family on his mother's side. He was a man of peace, who sought the middle ground. He also firmly believed in his divine right to rule, and that was to become a fatal flaw in the thinking of the Stuart monarchy. It was not that the Tudors did not have the same implicit view, but it had been more readily believed even fifty years before and was assumed rather than explicitly stated. James gave his eldest son Henry (who predeceased James) a handbook to monarchy which he had written, called *Basilikon Doron*, meaning "a Royal Gift". It reiterates the concept of a king's divine right to rule, but hedges it about with much practical everyday advice on good government. Alongside James's more theological views, expressed in the stylish Latin of which he was a master, were less circumspect traits. He was generous to a fault, rewarding his Scottish cronies with hefty pensions drawn from the English exchequer and thus causing resentment. He also put off doing business whenever possible, preferring to drink and hunt.

James's religious policy

James confronted the same issues as Elizabeth: a Puritan party strong in Parliament, who wanted further reform of the Church of England and would not rest until this was accomplished, *and* a Roman Catholic missionary movement that sought to bring down the Protestant monarchy or, at the least, simply to bolster Catholics in England. Like Elizabeth, James wanted to pursue a middle way, but he faced the extremes of both wings.

On his accession, the Puritans had high hopes of further reform. After all, James had been surrounded from the cradle by the Scottish Calvinism of John Knox, who sought a church along the lines of Calvin's Geneva. Even before James was crowned, the Puritans presented their Millenary Petition. It contained the usual Puritan demands: no signing of the cross at baptism; no confirmation; no bowing at the name of Jesus; no use of midwives to baptize infants; no wearing of vestments; no defiling the Lord's Day; no ring to be used in weddings; and no immoderation in the use of church music and singing. This is not an exhaustive list, but it more than catches the flavour of their demands. In response, James called the Hampton Court Conference in 1604. The Puritans had high hopes of change.

James took centre stage at the conference. Happy to be in the limelight and to debate with all comers, he displayed his knowledge of the scriptures, the Church Fathers and Reformed theology, but he rejected extremes and held fast to the middle way. He was like a theological Catherine wheel, firing in all directions. In response to a movement towards Presbyterianism—meaning the local government of the Church and the abolition of bishops—he cried "no bishop no king". The King would not move one step away from episcopacy to Presbyterianism. The one great gain from the conference was the King's commission of a new and authoritative translation of the Bible into English. It was to be called the King James Bible and its translation was to be overseen by Richard Bancroft, who succeeded John Whitgift as archbishop when the latter died shortly after the end of the conference. Like his predecessor, Bancroft was no friend of the Puritan lobby.

The King James Bible

By any standards this new authorized translation of the Bible was a milestone in English Church and national life. It would build on all those translations that had preceded it in the last eighty years: Tyndale and Coverdale's translation found in the Matthew Bible, which was then re-published as the Great Bible in 1539 under Thomas Cromwell; the Genevan Bible; and lastly the Bishops' Bible. This last Bible had been produced by the bishops of the Church of England during Elizabeth's reign under the leadership of Matthew Parker, having its final revision in 1602. It was intended to counter-balance the more Presbyterian Geneva Bible of 1575, which the returning exiles had grown accustomed to during their years of exile in Mary's reign. The Geneva Bible, translated by English scholars residing in Geneva and Switzerland, was the translation of choice for Puritans for many years to come. Some of its language was loaded, as in the case of the word "tyrant", which occurred 400 times in the text, and it had extensive Puritan marginal notes which James loathed. James and the bishops wanted a translation that grew out of its predecessors, in particular the work of Tyndale, a Bible for the whole Church: both its Puritan and more sacramental wings. In other words, it was to be the authorized version for the whole Church of England, prepared at the governor's command, so having his authority.

Under the presidency of Archbishop Bancroft and the linguistic leadership of the brilliant and complex Lancelot Andrewes, Master of Pembroke College and

Bishop of Chichester from 1605, the project was carried forward. In many ways, Andrewes was the driving force. He was a multi-layered individual: a great lover of English, probing, investigative, politically sensitive, outwardly showy, but inwardly plagued by guilt. In Andrewes, the company had a scholar who was sensitive to the symbolic and mystical aspects of prayer and theology: at home with the mystical Cappadocian Gregory of Nyssa, and comfortable also with the more doctrinal and intellectual side of the faith. In effect, Andrewes was the convener of the forty-seven translators, who were divided into six companies, each responsible for different parts of the Bible. It says much for the scholarship that resided in the universities and in the Church that such a gifted group of linguists could now come together in England.

Clear instructions were given to the translators by the King and archbishop: the Bishops' Bible was to be the translators' guiding text; there were to be no marginal notes except in relation to translation of words; the old word "church" must be kept and not replaced with "congregation"; all divisions of chapters were to be retained; and difficulties in translation were to be answered at regular meetings of the six companies where translations of chapters were submitted.

The translators met for the most part in their companies: two in Oxford, two in Cambridge and two in Westminster. They were not short of talent. There was the brilliant but bruising George Abbott, with one brother serving as Master of Balliol, the other as Lord Mayor of London. Abbott was archbishop between 1611 and 1633, at once Puritan and strongly episcopal. He was known to have had 140 undergraduates arrested for not removing their hats when entering St Mary's Church. Another translator was Sir Henry Savile: handsome, charismatic, scholarly, and an intellectual buccaneer. He was a Fellow of Merton and later Provost of Eton. At Merton, he lectured on Ptolemy's *Almagest*, and also increased the library by 700 books. He collected Patristic manuscripts and was a dedicated student of Chrysostom. If Savile was at one end of the flamboyance scale, his opposite was John Bois, of the second Cambridge company. Bois was a lecturer in Greek at Cambridge and familiar with Hebrew. He was the vicar of Boxworth and walked twenty miles to Cambridge each day, cogitating over the Greek text. Small in stature, meticulous in habit, quiet and earnest in demeanour, he was secretary to the Revising Committee. Where Savile brought linguistic panache to the task, Bois brought myopic attention to detail, and took infinite pains.

These men and many other talented linguists in ancient languages had completed the task by 1611. For three and a half centuries, the Authorised Version remained the gold standard of biblical translation in the English language. The cadence, wit and faithfulness of Tyndale's translation were preserved and enhanced. Phrases like "fighting the good fight", "ill-gotten gains", "fullness of time", "a law unto themselves", "cast the first stone", "measure for measure", "fall on one's sword", "put your house in order", and "the land of nod" passed into common parlance. More importantly, common people had the word of God on their tongue, as Tyndale had dreamt. Yet in the midst of this great work, the nation was plunged into its greatest crisis of the reign.

Citizens or terrorists? The ambiguity of Catholics

Just as the Puritans looked to James for further change in the national Church, the Catholic community looked to the King for some let-up from the fierce Elizabethan recusancy laws. James was minded to ease penalties against practising Catholics in the interests of a peaceful realm, although the Puritans were set against it. Any thought of relaxing penalties against Catholics for practising their faith was stopped in its tracks by the Gunpowder Plot of 4 November 1605. Thirty-six barrels of gunpowder were assembled in an undercroft adjoining the Palace of Westminster, where the Houses of Parliament met. Had they exploded they would have caused untold damage and killed many MPs, peers and bishops, as the explosion was timed for the opening of Parliament by the King. The leader of the plotters was Robert Catesby, a member of the gentry with land at Chastleton House in the Oxfordshire Cotswolds. Other plotters included Guy Fawkes, who had served in the Spanish army and been baptized at St Michael-le-Belfry, York, next to the minster. The conspirators were pursued: some were killed; others, like Fawkes, tortured in the Tower and then executed as traitors. The discovery of the plot through an anonymous letter sent to Lord Mounteagle, a member of the House of Peers, caused a sensation. Members of Parliament wept, and a national day of deliverance was declared on 5 November, when bonfires were lit and sermons preached. For centuries after, the London mob could be brought out at the mention of a popish plot. Lord Chancellor Ellesmere declared of Catholics: "I am ashamed they are English; I am ashamed they be Christians, but at least they be Roman Christians."[1]

The possibility of Catholics being accepted as genuine citizens had been set back years, if not generations. A "Guy" became synonymous with an image to be burnt annually. Catholics were driven underground. For James, the event at least had the effect of uniting the Puritan faction in Parliament behind him. The Commons voted £400,000 towards the King's expenses and his extravagant court with its many pensions for Scots—this was a huge sum. James's shock and anger soon abated. He philosophized and theologized too much and let off steam hunting. He was no Henry VIII, brooding endlessly on slights to his majesty. He continued to seek to winnow off Catholics from an extreme position through an oath by which they could forswear the Pope's right to call for his deposition and instead swear allegiance to James as the rightful king. Later in his reign, in 1622, James suspended the penalties on Catholics, much to the chagrin of the Commons, but his reign was cut short by his death in 1625. What had become clear was that if England was to make any continental alliances with Catholic powers, her treatment of Catholics would come up in any treaty arrangements.

Marriages and continental alliances

Knowing the expense of war and, not unlike his predecessor Elizabeth, baulking at its cost, wherever possible James sought peaceful alliances with his continental neighbours. After years of warfare with Spain, both in the set piece Armada and in the sporadic attacks by English buccaneer sailors on the Spanish treasure fleet bringing silver and gold from South America, James gained peace with Spain in 1604. More than that, he sought a dynastic marriage for his son Charles from either Spain or France.

The map of Europe was divided along Protestant and Catholic lines. Scandinavia and northern Germany were broadly Lutheran, while the south and west of Europe, except Switzerland and eastern France at Strasbourg, were Catholic. James and Anne of Demark had three surviving children, Henry, Elizabeth and Charles, having lost several others. James's oldest son Henry tragically died aged sixteen in 1612. Left with daughter Elizabeth and his son Charles, who would succeed as Charles I, he sought dynastic marriages for both. Elizabeth, later known as the Winter Queen, married a Protestant—Frederick the Elector Palatine and later King of Bohemia—and Charles, after considerable shenanigans, married a Catholic, Henrietta Maria—the daughter of Henry IV of France. Both marriages were to have considerable repercussions for England.

Elizabeth's husband was Frederick V, the Elector Palatine, whose seat was in the gracious city of Heidelberg. Born in Scotland in 1596, she married Frederick in 1613, a year after the loss of her brother Henry, of whom she was especially fond. It was a popular match, since Frederick was Protestant, but it was a marriage that would entangle England in the tempestuous events of Europe. This was especially the case after Frederick was offered and accepted the Kingdom of Bohemia, with its capital in Prague, a flashpoint in the origins of the Thirty Years' War.

The Thirty Years' War, which burst upon Europe from 1618, was the most devastating conflict that the continent had known. A third to a half of the male population in Germany would be killed by war and famine—an even higher mortality rate than in the First World War. Its principal cause was the attempt by Emperor Ferdinand II, a fervent Catholic, to eradicate Protestantism in his territories by the sword. In 1618, Bohemia joined the revolt against the Catholic Hapsburgs with Protestant rebels throwing Czech imperial officials out of the windows of Prague Castle in an incident that came to be known as the Defenestration of Prague. In the course of the reprisals, Frederick, Elizabeth's husband, was defeated at the Battle of White Mountain in 1620, forcing Elizabeth to flee to Holland. After her brief rule, she would be called the Winter Queen.

This chain of events overthrew James's carefully nurtured policy of being the moderator between Protestants and Catholics. Trade was disrupted and James, now allied to the anti-Catholic cause, was drawn into expensive support for his son-in-law, Frederick. Parliament was pleased to vote funds for this in 1621, since it was a Protestant cause, but to little avail. It was only when the Protestant Gustavus Adolphus, King of Sweden, urged Richelieu, the first minister of France, to bring France into the war as a counterweight to the Hapsburgs, that there was any hope of peace. Elizabeth had gone into exile in Holland in 1620, where she continued to have children—thirteen in all—of whom Prince Rupert of the Rhine was one and Sophia, who married the Elector of Hannover, another. Rupert would be the main cavalry commander of Charles I in the English Civil War, while Sophia's son, George of Hannover, would later become George I of England. If nothing else, Elizabeth, a strong and engaging character, provided the bloodline for the Protestant succession in England.

Her brother Charles would set about his marriage in a quite different style. The nation was shocked to hear that the Duke of Buckingham, the King's favourite and chief minister, had crossed the Channel in February 1623 to travel *incognito* to the Spanish court and win the hand of the *infanta*. James "wept, fasted and prayed" for the safe return of the Prince without a Spanish wife. Charles and Buckingham arrived in Madrid during Lent and it was only the formality and coldness of the Spanish court that prevented a love-struck Charles from pursuing his suit. To great rejoicing, especially in Parliament, Charles returned single to England, but he was married by proxy to the fifteen-year-old Henrietta Maria of France just two months after his father's death in March 1625. Henrietta was the daughter of the great Henry IV of France, who had ended the religious wars in France before being assassinated in 1610. Her life was to be even more tempestuous than that of her sister-in-law, Elizabeth. She was to be the daughter of an assassinated father, wife of an executed husband, mother of two kings, the constant focus of Puritan opprobrium, and an exile from her adopted country before eventual restoration. It was a life of extraordinary contrasts and controversies.

Playwrights, poets, philosophers and pilgrims in Jacobean England

By the start of the seventeenth century, the canopy of medieval religion had been well and truly pierced in England. The Renaissance, with its emphasis on the humanities and the liberal arts, and the Reformation had seen to that. With the accession of James I, who thought of himself as a philosopher-theologian, published extensively and preferred the religious *via media*, there was more space for a considered Christianity commingling with the liberal arts.

James despised extreme Calvinism on the one hand and extreme Catholicism on the other. Indeed, he banned Jesuit missionaries from England in 1604 and kept in check Puritan demands, as we have seen. It is not surprising, then, that in this atmosphere of relative calm, plays, poetry and philosophy flourished. We might wonder at the sheer galaxy of literary stars in England in the early seventeenth century in the persons of Shakespeare (1564–1616), Ben Johnson (1572–1637), George Herbert (1593–1633), John Donne (1571–1631), John Milton (1608–72) and, a little later, Henry Vaughan (1621–95). Of a similar period was the political philosopher, Thomas Hobbes (1588–1679).

Shakespeare was at the height of his powers at the accession of James, having written many of his great history plays and tragedies by 1603. Indeed, the golden years of his writing were from 1594 to 1603, during which time he wrote *Romeo and Juliet, Richard II, Henry IV, Parts II and I, Henry V, The Merchant of Venice* and *Hamlet*. In true Renaissance style, he explored the humanity of men and women: their faults and triumphs and their loves and losses, seen through the prism of their ever-real human motivations of desire for power, yearning for glory, consuming love and the reality of death. The fundamental question Shakespeare posed had to do with the nature and destiny of humanity, as illustrated in a line of Benedict's in *Much Ado About Nothing*, "Man is a giddy thing, and this is my conclusion" (Act 5), or in the deduction of a dejected Macbeth, who says at the end: "Life's but a walking shadow, a poor player that struts and frets his hour upon the stage, and then is heard no more. It is a tale told by an idiot full of sound and fury, signifying nothing" (Act 5: Scene 5).

If Shakespeare posed the ultimate questions of life through a host of plays, unsurpassed in their dramatic power and perception, then the poets from the Jacobean period, steeped in classical learning and Christian insight, gave their own telling answers. It is not far-fetched to think that Donne, Milton and Shakespeare may have met in the streets, taverns or churches of crowded, teeming London, as they were all Londoners and more or less contemporaries. Shakespeare, the renowned player-manager, Donne, now theatrical Dean of St Paul's, and Milton, the precocious Cambridge student.

John Donne (1572–1631) could have been a Shakespearean character himself. He was pursued by an irate father-in-law, Sir George More, for secretly marrying More's socially higher-ranking daughter Anne, for which act Donne was sent to the Fleet prison. He was under suspicion from the authorities because his brother Henry harboured a Catholic priest—a treasonable offence—for which Henry was arrested and tortured before dying in prison from his wounds and starvation. Donne penned steamy love poems, which would have sat well with those of Ovid, which in Ovid's case led to exile to Tomis on the Black Sea on the orders of Emperor Augustus.

Although Donne ranked as a metaphysical poet, in his earlier life he could have been considered a purely physical one. His youthful portrait in the National Portrait Gallery shows a sensitive and sensuous figure more than capable of breaking hearts. The poem "Elegy XIX: To His Mistress Going to Bed" is as suggestive as any erotic poem. His marriage to Anne and their ten surviving children created a need for more remunerative work and an endless round of childcare, however. After scraping a living as an impecunious lawyer, he gained new patronage and became a Member of Parliament. Now known to King James I, he was urged to train for ordination. He became a royal chaplain and by 1621 was Dean of St Paul's. His was another journey from untamed youth to influential office. St Paul's gave context to Donne's theatrical gifts, allowing him to display his rhetorical verve and metaphysical verse on a prestigious platform.

If Donne had any preoccupation in his later years, it was with the overshadowing of death and the transforming power of God's love. In preparation for the reality of death, he even lay in a coffin. Most famously, in his *Devotions Upon Emergent Occasions*, published in 1623, he wrote a further meditation on death (No. XVII):

> No man is an island, entire of itself; every man is a piece of the continent,
> a part of the main. If a clod be washed away by the sea, Europe is the less,
> as well as if a promontory were, as well as if a manor of thy friend's or of
> thine own were: any man's death diminishes me, because I am involved

in mankind, and therefore never send to know for whom the bell tolls; it
tolls for thee.[2]

Yet in face of one's mortality, a person might still feel the ravishing presence of
God's love. In his *Holy Sonnet XIV*, entitled "Batter my Heart", Donne transposes
feelings of love normally considered erotic to his relationship with God. In
this sense he stands in the tradition of Christian mystics exemplified by the
Cappadocian Church Father Gregory of Nyssa, and in the tradition of the Bible
exemplified in the Song of Songs.

  Elsewhere in England, and an exact contemporary, was another poet-minister,
George Herbert (1593–1633). Whereas Donne came from a Catholic family with
an ironmonger father, Herbert came from one of the grandest in the land, the
family of the Earl of Pembroke, the Herberts of Wilton. His mother, Magdalen
Herbert, was described by Donne as having "holy cheerfulness and religious
alacrity" and was renowned for her wit. Brought up in Montgomeryshire, George's
father was high sheriff of the county for several years. After a university education
at Cambridge, he became the university public orator. An accomplished Latinist,
lutenist and musician, and a Fellow of Trinity College, Cambridge, his poetry was
intricate and lucid, and also deeply devotional. This was no more so than in his
poem "Love III", with its tender personal tone:

> Love bade me welcome: yet my heart drew back
> Guilty of dust and sin,
> But quick-ey'd Love, observing me grow slack
> From my first entrance in,
> Drew nearer to me, sweetly questioning
> If I lacked anything.

In his later years Herbert moved from the heady university life of Cambridge,
where he composed pieces for visiting dignitaries, to the more rural rhythms
of an English parish life in Wiltshire, with its pastoral and liturgical rounds. As
university orator he had been given the difficult task of composing an address in
praise of the King's favourite, the Duke of Buckingham, when made Chancellor
of the University in 1623, and had welcomed home the Prince of Wales from his
abortive courtship of the *infanta* in Madrid. Then, in 1626, Herbert left Cambridge
for the parish of Leighton Bromswold, where he held a prebendary (a cathedral
appointment connected to a parish) close to his friend Nicholas Ferrar, who had

set up a religious community in Little Gidding, which was to prove a great support to Herbert.

For the last three years of his life, from 1630, Herbert was the rector of two parishes on the edge of the Wilton estate in Wiltshire. It was here that he gave expression to his love of music, flowers, the church building, locality and ecclesiastical year, and where he wrote poetry and hymns with scarcely a wafer of difference between them. He appreciated the customs of the parish: processions, hospitality, the church's year and liturgy. To summarize, he said: "Love is [my] business"—no doubt reflecting his experience of and expressions for God's love. His luminous poetry won many admirers and imitators, including Henry Vaughan, who found in the hills of Wales his own cathedral inspiring praise.

Such was the variety of Christian artistic expression at the time that it embraced not only the theatricality of Donne's preaching with an hourglass by his side at St Paul's Cathedral (to mark the shortness of time before death), but also the lambent luminosity of Herbert's verse as he gave sensitive praise to God in all things, great and small. Now a third joined this gathering of Christian literary expression in the early part of the seventeenth century, and this time with a fierce uncompromising brilliance.

He was John Milton, born not far from St Paul's in Bread Street in the City of London in 1608. After his studies at Christ's College, Cambridge, he embarked on a period of private study financed by his father, who was a successful scrivener (writer of legal documents) and musician. By this time Milton had become proficient in seven languages and was deeply familiar with the Bible in its original Hebrew and Greek, as well as with the classics, and in particular Plato. Milton's early poems include a reflection on Christ's birth called *On the Morning of Christ's Nativity*, *Comus* and *Lycidas*. *Comus*, after the Greek god of revelry, was written as a masque in praise of chastity for the Earl of Bridgewater at Ludlow Castle in 1634, and already the rendering of Comus had about it something of the disturbing brilliance of Satan in *Paradise Lost*. Another of his early poems, *Lycidas*, one of the greatest English poems, was written as an elegy to a lost friend, Edward King, who drowned in the Irish Sea in 1637, and carries within it the hope of resurrection.

In 1638, Milton went on tour in Europe, following these and other acclaimed poems he had written or published, for what would be a highly influential experience just before the breakdown of relations between King and Parliament in England. In Paris he met, among others, Hugo Grotius, an outstanding Dutch law professor and playwright, who gave himself to seeking unity among the numerous Protestant confessions or churches on the continent. But it was a meeting in Rome with the great astronomer Galileo—just after a meeting with Cardinal

Francesco Barberini, a spiritual guide to Queen Henrietta Maria—that would be the most influential meeting for Milton. Galileo was under virtual house arrest by the Inquisition for maintaining, quite rightly, the Copernican revolution in astronomy that held the earth travelled around the sun and not the other way around. Galileo, now blind, as Milton would become many years later, had been intellectually and scientifically muzzled by the Church. He was forced to recant his belief in the Copernican theory of the universe and uphold instead the erroneous proposition that the earth was the centre of everything. More than anything else, this was an affront to freedom.

For Milton, it was a further example of the suffocating intellectual presence of the Church, just at a time when Charles I, along with Archbishop Laud, sought to impose the English Prayer Book on the Scots, provoking war in 1639. Freedom would forever after be Milton's tune, and for freedom he would compose, rebut, pour scorn, ridicule, proclaim and suffer in an unparalleled corpus of work. He would link himself to the Commonwealth and the cause of Oliver Cromwell, as we shall see; however disappointing that would turn out to be.

But there were some for whom freedom meant a complete physical change, a voyage, or exile from home. These were the pilgrims. While the Puritans had denigrated pilgrimage as a practice in the Middle Ages, here was a different sort of pilgrimage of which they approved. This was not about travelling to a shrine in Europe; it was about starting afresh in an atmosphere of religious freedom, across the Atlantic in a Christian community at Plymouth, Massachusetts.

During the Elizabethan era, English seamen had explored the world: Drake had circumnavigated the earth from 1577–80 on the *Golden Hind*; the Virginia Colony Company had begun in 1607 (later becoming a Crown Colony in 1624), of which John Donne was a member of the ruling council, with Walter Raleigh instrumental in its beginnings. In 1620, the *Mayflower* landed in Massachusetts Bay with the Pilgrim Fathers aboard. Some of these pilgrims had come from a congregation in Leyden in the Netherlands; others were "strangers", and for the most part from East Anglia. They survived the first winter and gave thanks in a Puritan feast called Thanksgiving, which would be celebrated every year in November thereafter. Others were to follow, such as John Winthrop in 1630 aboard the *Arabella*. He preached in mid-Atlantic that they had come "to be a city set upon a hill that cannot be hid".[3] It is estimated that as many as 20,000 emigrated to the New World during the early years of the seventeenth century. By 1636, the colonists had founded Harvard College, devoting half the colony's taxes to the project, so great was the Puritan regard for education. In scarcely 150 years the colonies of Virginia and Massachusetts would fight for independence from the British crown. There was Maryland, a colony founded in memory of Queen Henrietta Maria; Carolina in memory of King Charles; and much later Pennsylvania, founded by William Penn, would follow, together with colonies seized from the Dutch, such as New Amsterdam (New York). From these small, intrepid beginnings the English-speaking Episcopal, Presbyterian, Quaker and Baptist churches of the United States would become some of the most influential Christian movements in the world.

While Milton was meeting Galileo, and making a lifetime commitment to freedom, while Herbert was quietly composing lucid verses that linger long in the human spirit, and while the Pilgrim Fathers courageously sought freedom of life and worship across the Atlantic, the coming conflagration in England provoked a controversial philosopher to describe the contract between governor (monarch) and governed with new urgency. His name was Thomas Hobbes. Born in 1588, educated at Oxford, where he grew proficient in the classics by translating Euripides's *Medea*, his great work was *Leviathan*. Begun at the outset of the Civil War, and no doubt provoked by it, Hobbes analyses the human condition: all men are naturally equal, easily given to fear, and desire to preserve their liberty and avoid violent death. All also seek dominion over others.[4] To prevent anarchy, there must be a clear contract between the people and the government, else human life will always be "solitary, poor, nasty, brutish and short". For there to be peaceable government there must be a *single undivided power*, whether an individual or an assembly. Because in England power had been divided between the crown, the Commons and the Lords, civil unrest and war followed. The Church, Hobbes argues, must be submissive to the sovereign, although scripture rightly understood is the only true test of truth, for all else is ignorance and darkness. Hobbes would be succeeded by Locke some forty years later, yet Hobbes's pessimistic analysis of the human condition, which he considered requires strong government to obviate its worst consequences, was a milestone in political philosophy. He was regarded as *enfant terrible* by the Church because of his mechanistic view of humankind without expressing a clear faith himself. The events of 1629, to the execution of the King and after, were to provide a political laboratory for Hobbes, in which his ideas could be tested. Kingship was an authority given by the people, and in return the King or Leviathan gave protection from anarchy and abject misery. Yet what happens when the King makes war on the people? In England in 1640 such a conflagration was about to begin.

The Descent into Civil War

By the seventeenth century, there was a systemic tension at the heart of government. The crown could no longer afford to govern. The medieval system of crown lands, which included regular subsidies such as tonnage and poundage, as voted by Parliament, which had been sufficient to maintain government, defence and an occasional continental or British war (i.e. in Scotland, or Ireland), no longer worked. For all her husbanding of resources, Elizabeth faced increasing debts and likewise James I. By 1617, the crown's debt was £700,000 and rising inexorably. The cost of fielding an army on the continent for the support of the Protestants in the Netherlands or Germany, say, was approaching a million pounds annually. In addition, James ran an expensive court. Inflation was rising with the import of precious metals into Europe by Spain. As much as 40 per cent of the population, which was now about four million and growing, was poor. In Norwich, over ten per cent of the adult population qualified for poor relief, and there were 12,000 beggars in the City of London alone. With these constraints the crown had to look for any possible method of raising money.

The crown needed funds. The Puritans controlled the House of Commons. Every time Parliament met, it looked to assert its privileges, to uphold the right of the citizen to resist unwarranted taxation and illegal arrest, and to impugn the King's ministers. The story of these years is a combination of these demands rubbing up against the King's theory of the divine right to rule unquestioned by his subjects. It was a combination that made for conflict.

James's first Parliament was called in 1605. The House of Commons, which had been gaining in authority throughout the Tudor period, now mustered 450 members, many of whom were new. The gentry dominated the Commons, and a majority were Puritan. Thanks to the fact both Parliament and King had escaped the Gunpowder Plot, the former was in a mood to be generous to the latter. James was granted £450,000 in taxation. Stiffer penalties were applied to recusant Catholics, rising from £20 to £60 a year, although there were still limits. Parliament refused James's cherished request to unite the countries of England and Scotland in a union: this would have to wait a hundred years. In a xenophobic age there were still deep suspicions of James's Scottish roots and Scottish advisers, who now populated his court and were on generous pensions paid for by the English.

James's government was erratic to say the least. While Robert Cecil, Earl of Salisbury, was alive he continued to manage Parliament as effectively as his father, William Cecil, had before him—although not even Robert was always successful. But James's compulsive choice of favourites landed him in a series of scandals:

first through Robert Carr, Earl of Somerset, and then even more through George Villiers, created Duke of Buckingham. In pursuing the scheme seeking a marriage for Charles, Prince of Wales, with the Spanish *infanta* and failing to support the French Protestants, Buckingham lost the support of Parliament.

If relations between Parliament and James were frustrating and bad for both sides, they would only decline further under Charles, who had succeeded his father in 1625. Early on in his reign Charles came to the decision not to summon Parliament at all unless facing extreme financial difficulty. The relationship did not get off to a good start when Parliament refused to grant Charles the traditional right of taxation on imports (called tonnage and poundage, it equated to 12 pence in the pound on specified goods). Charles nevertheless continued to levy the tax by Royal Prerogative. The powers of Parliament and the Royal Prerogative were on a collision course. Charles's second Parliament was called in 1626, but by then suspicions against Buckingham, the King's favourite, were accumulating. The Puritan Pym was gaining ascendancy in the House and becoming ever more demanding of change.

A whiff of Pelagianism was now invading the Church of England through the teachings of Arminius, a Dutch Reformed theologian, who surprisingly, given his origins, denied the total depravity of humanity and argued instead for people's ability to contribute to their own salvation. It was a re-run of the Pelagian controversy of the fifth century, in which Augustine of Hippo denounced the British monk Pelagius for the same doctrines.

Now Pym moved against Buckingham, seeking his impeachment, not only for military failures in Spain, such as the raid on Cadiz, but for favouring this new, deeply suspect trend in the Church. Formal charges were laid against Buckingham in Parliament on 8 May 1626. At this point Charles dissolved Parliament on 15 June. A third Parliament was called in March 1628 in an atmosphere of crisis: Buckingham was being openly attacked by the mob in London; another costly naval military expedition against France at La Rochelle to relieve the Huguenots had failed disastrously, seen off by Cardinal Richelieu; and the King was out of money. What Pym had intended to do constitutionally against Buckingham, a disgruntled sailor called John Felton did instead: he took Buckingham's life in a Portsmouth pub called the Greyhound, stabbing him to death.

At the opening of Parliament in March 1628, the King was on the back foot, despite being dressed in chocolate black silk trimmed with gold. The normal pattern followed. Parliament presented its grievances. If the King agreed to redress them, money would be voted. On this occasion a Petition of Rights was drawn up for the King to accept: to uphold *habeas corpus* (the right of a citizen not to be imprisoned without trial), not to levy forced loans or billet soldiers compulsorily, and not to use martial law against citizens. The charge of "popery" was laid against the government because of its military failure (as in Joshua 7 and the failure to take Ai). Charles's response was to prorogue Parliament in June 1628. The fall of La Rochelle in October to Louis XIII and the killing or starving of near on 20,000 Protestant inhabitants by the French government forces of Louis gave an air of incompetence to Charles's government. The second session of this Parliament ended in uproar. With the Commons pressing its case on the crown, the Speaker, Sir John Finch, still at this point representing the crown, wanted to end the debate, but was forcibly held in his chair by MPs, and wept while the session continued against his will. The crown arrested Sir John Eliot, the leader of the Commons. He died in the Tower and, vindictively, his body was not released to his family for burial. Charles dissolved Parliament and would not call another until 1640; during this period tension in the country only increased.

There were three things in particular that increased pressure in the nation to explosion point: taxation by Royal Prerogative, the increase of "popery" in the national Church, and the actions of two royal servants, Archbishop Laud and Thomas Strafford, Earl of Wentworth, who became hated public figures.

By 1629, the government's deficit was £2 million and rising. Although peace with Spain and France had been concluded by 1630, Charles still needed substantial sums of money. He sold crown estates to the value of £600,000; he levied a forced loan, which was contested in the courts; and in 1634 he extended ship money to pay for the navy across the country (i.e. far away from the ports where it should be raised), although this was contested by Sir John Hampden, a leading parliamentarian. If this taxation provoked a sense of growing grievance among the landed gentry, an even more visceral hatred was sparked by changes in the Church.

Suspicion of growing popery or Catholicism was the trigger for growing discontent in Parliament and the country. It was caused by the marriage of Charles to Henrietta Maria, the sister of Louis XIII of France, whose forces England had so recently fought. In 1625, Charles was married by proxy to this plucky, fifteen-year-old princess. She arrived on English soil in 1626 with a large retinue of French courtiers. Many of these were summarily dismissed by Charles, but after initial difficulties, theirs was to be a loyal and devoted marriage with seven surviving children. Their union, so intimate compared to the more stylized projection of power caught by Holbein in his rendering of the Tudors, was frequently caught on canvas by Van Dyck.

Even before the marriage, Henrietta Maria had given assurances to Pope Urban VIII that she would do all in her power to restore Catholicism in England. There was even a papal legate attached to her household called George Con. She had her own chaplains, heard the mass and was permitted in the marriage treaty to bring up her children in the Catholic faith. By 1638 she was vilified by the London mob, slandered by the Puritan lawyer William Prynne (for which crime his ears were cut off), and generally made a byword for all that was wrong in the government. Still only twenty-seven at the outbreak of the Civil War, she sold her jewels to raise forces for the crown, personally brought troops from the continent to Bridlington in Yorkshire and marched them across England in support of her husband. She was generally considered to be like Margaret of Anjou, the wife of Henry VI in the Wars of the Roses, although Charles proved more resolute than Henry.

If Henrietta Maria became the butt of much Puritan suspicion, Archbishop Laud was still more disliked, indeed hated. He was appointed Archbishop of Canterbury in 1633, in succession to George Abbot (1611–33), who by contrast had Puritan instincts and had been one of the translators of the King James Bible. Aged sixty by the time he became archbishop, Laud had an agenda to establish the ceremonies of the Church of England, suppress Puritanism and, whilst by no means Roman Catholic, introduce "the beauty of holiness" into Anglican worship. Laud was a stickler for enforcing the canons of the Church introduced by Archbishop Bancroft (1604–10), such as kneeling for communion, railing off the communion table or altar, buying or making silver chalices and patens for communion, doffing one's hat (men) on entering the church, making lowly reverence at the name of Jesus, and wearing a "comely surplice". For the Puritan, these ceremonies were the dregs of popery. Lastly, Laud suppressed the Puritan preaching system by ending Puritan lectureships (a way of avoiding the accusation of licensing illegal preachers) wherever they appeared. These lectureships were essentially preachers being paid by subscription to assist in the parishes. For Laud they were dangerous, outside the control of the bishops, and likely to teach ecclesiastical doctrine prejudicial to the Church of England. For all these actions and for using the church courts to fine offenders one shilling for non-attendance at church, Laud became the most hated man in England. He had a lawyer's eye for detail, an indefatigable energy to prosecute any person who crossed a ceremonial or canonical line in the church courts or Star Chamber. What Laud pursued so zealously was anathema to the Puritans. He was the supreme enforcer and the silencer of disputatious matters, then deemed closed by him.[5] He was as much against Catholicism as he was against Puritanism; he upheld ceremonial Anglicanism to its last detail. He sought to bring in line bishops such as John

Williams of Lincoln who followed their own lights too independently. Having stirred up such animosity, it was not surprising that he was accused of treason by the Long Parliament in the Grand Remonstrance of 1641. William Prynne, once punished for his vocal opposition to the Queen, was, in a piece of intentional irony, appointed by Parliament to try Laud. Condemned to death, Laud was executed in his seventies in 1645, having been kept in the Tower during the Civil War. He was the last of five Archbishops of Canterbury to be violently killed: the others were Alphege, Becket, Sudbury and Cranmer.

The "personal rule" of Charles came to an end with the summoning of Parliament in 1640. Once again Charles needed money. This time the trigger for the summoning of Parliament came from war with Scotland, the result of an ill-advised attempt to impose the English Prayer Book on that nation. When the Bishop of Edinburgh announced its use in Scotland and read its prayers in his sonorous tones, he was greeted with cries of "Woe, Woe", while a three-legged stool flew through the air, narrowly missing the dean of the chapel. The bishop barely escaped with his life. The Covenanter Scots, representing the Calvinist kirk under Alexander Leslie, who had fought alongside the Swedish King Gustavus Adolphus in the Thirty Years' War—as had many Scots—now threatened England with 16,000 troops. After a stand-off in 1639, the Scots invaded England, taking Durham and Northumberland and interrupting the supply of coal from Newcastle to London. Charles had no alternative but to summon Parliament. He needed money for a crisis of his own making.

Looking to Parliament for support, Charles found only the opposite. All the old grievances were raised exhaustively, and his Chief Minister Strafford and Archbishop Laud were attainted (accused of treason). There were powerful voices raised against the crown in both Lords and Commons: Essex, Warwick, Saye and Sele in the Lords and Pym and Hampden in the Commons. They argued that "popery eroded the fabric of the English church and financial mismanagement the fabric of the English state".[6] There were increasing numbers of disturbances on the streets of London, caused by apprentices whipped up by Puritan preaching by the likes of John Lilburn in Coleman Street. Initially, Parliament sat for three weeks from April to May 1640 (called the Short Parliament) but had to be recalled in what became known as the Long Parliament, which would last until 1660 after the death of Oliver Cromwell. It ranks as one of the most significant Parliaments in English history (along with the Reformation Parliament, the Parliament of the Great Reform Act of 1832 and the Parliament of 1940 which replaced Neville Chamberlain with Winston Churchill).

The Long Parliament began with the trial of Thomas Wentworth, Earl of Strafford, for treason. Strafford had threatened to bring Irish troops to England to quell opposition to the crown and repel the Scots. He then encouraged the King to rule without Parliament by using his Royal Prerogative. Strafford was tried by Bill of Attainder, which required a majority in both houses and the King's assent for his indictment. Both Houses of Parliament condemned Strafford. The mob in the capital was now near hysterical. In the end Charles gave way to pressure, signed the Bill of Attainder, and a vast crowd of 300,000 watched his chief minister's execution. It was an action for which Charles believed he was punished later by his own execution, for he felt he had betrayed Strafford. Not content with Strafford's head, Parliament now pressed a raft of measures upon Charles. "Most of the lasting achievements of the English Revolution came during the first two hundred days of the Long Parliament":[7] the abolition of the prerogative courts—Star Chamber, the Court of Wards, the High Commission, the Council of the North—the abolition of taxation without the consent of Parliament, the removal of the bishops from the House of Lords, the Triennial Acts requiring the calling of Parliaments every three years, and a Grand Remonstrance detailing all Charles's abuses of power. This last act was printed and circulated in London in an atmosphere of febrile excitement. In short order, the power of the royal executive was drastically reduced, the legislature greatly strengthened, and the crown humiliated. Charles attempted to arrest Pym, Hampden, Holles, Haselrig and Strode, the leaders in the Commons, on 22 November 1641; but, as he famously said, it was not possible because "the birds had flown". Nine months later, by August 1642, there was civil war. The irony was that at the end of the Civil War and on the orders of Cromwell, on 7 December 1648, Colonel Pride arrested forty-one Members of Parliament who were Presbyterian in outlook (in favour of a national and not an independent church) and who would not support the execution of the King. What Charles had attempted, namely the exclusion of Members of Parliament, Cromwell and the army did.

The Civil War

The Civil War can be divided into three parts or phases spread over three kingdoms, eventually including Scotland and Ireland and lasting overall until 1651. The first phase involved the defeat of the King and his forces by 1646. The second was the invasion of England by the Scots in support of Charles I, defeated at Preston in 1648. The third phase took place in 1650 with a rebellion in Scotland

and a continuing revolt in Ireland. From the outset Parliament was in the stronger position: controlling London, the Home Counties and the south-eastern part of England. The Royalist cause was strongest in the west, the south-west and the north; the eastern side of the country, including London and north to the Humber, was Parliamentarian. But whatever the geographical division of Royalist and Parliamentarian, the Civil War bitterly divided families, communities and regions.

The Parliamentary side was Puritan-led, but it would divide into a plethora of Protestant sects: Presbyterians, Independents, Quakers, Anabaptists and Fifth Monarchists, as well as other socio-religious, revolutionary groups, such as the Levellers and Diggers that would be spawned by the army. The Royalists, on the other hand, were a mixture of Anglican, Roman Catholic and continental Lutherans—like Prince Rupert of the Rhine, the cavalry commander whose father was the Elector of the Rhineland Palatinate and Charles's nephew, a son of his sister Elizabeth. They all upheld bishop and king. The Royalists' watchword was loyalty, while Parliament's was liberty. The Royalists upheld the Church by law established, but with increasing ceremony; Parliament wanted a purified Church. The Civil War forced people to choose one set of values over another.

The war itself was fought along conventional lines: winter quarters followed by spring to autumn campaigns, but it was to be a devastating conflict for the three nations of England, Scotland and Ireland. Oxford was the headquarters for the King; London for Parliament. There were a number of set-piece battles, principally Edgehill in Warwickshire on 23 October 1642, Marston Moor in Yorkshire on 2 July 1644, and finally Naseby on 14 June 1645. Sometimes the Royalists won handsomely, as at Lostwithiel in September 1644, where they took 4,000 prisoners, but the pressure on Parliamentary forces could not be sustained. Between the pitched battles were frequent engagements, sieges and skirmishes: little of the Midlands, North and West was left untouched. Exhaustion of the armies, of the nation and of the land inevitably followed. As time wore on, the resources and discipline of the Parliamentary forces grew. Cromwell emerged as a brilliant and effective cavalry commander. The New Model Army, formed in 1645, became the first truly disciplined standing army of professional soldiers in England, with a strongly Puritan ethos, where prayer meetings were more frequent than parade ground drills. Initially, Parliamentary commanders were drawn from any with experience, such as Lord Essex, Lord Manchester and Sir William Waller, but that was all to change as a more tightly-drawn group of Puritan commanders, such as Cromwell, Fairfax and Ireton, took over and there was division between those who held a seat in Parliament and those who held a commission in the army (to be addressed in the Self-denying Ordinance of 1644 which aimed to separate a commission in the army from membership of Parliament).

In May 1646, with no hope of continuing the war, Charles gave himself up to the Scots, with whom Parliament had earlier agreed a Solemn League and Covenant, pioneered by Pym before his untimely death from cancer and by Sir Henry Vane. In January 1647, Charles was handed over to Parliament by the Scots for £400,000, and would remain a prisoner until his execution, apart from a short spell of freedom when he slipped out of Hampton Court only to be recaptured and made a prisoner at Carisbrooke Castle on the Isle of Wight. With the first phase of this costly and brutal civil war finished, new and inevitable questions opened up: what kind of a peace was envisaged and what role was envisaged for the King, the Church, the Houses of Parliament and the army? These questions would take time to answer.

A revolution in the making

What is clear is that there were many voices, many differing visions for the future, and many emphases in both religious conviction and views on constitutional structure of the realm. Beyond that there were two centres of authority in England: one was in Parliament, the House of Lords (for a while) and House of Commons, soon to be without a king; the other was in the New Model Army, created by Oliver Cromwell as an efficient and religiously-motivated fighting machine, which had remained victorious in the field after the Battle of Naseby. The Self-denying Ordinance of April 1644 had separated the army from Parliament, with no Parliamentarian able to hold a commission in the army. Here Cromwell was the exception, because he could not be spared by either side. He alone formed a bridge between Parliament and army. As the first phase of the Civil War came to an end with the capture of the King, the army resisted disbandment. There was still a rebellion in Ireland and the army was owed money. Indeed, Parliament would soon need the army to resist the Scots again, for they had forged a new alliance with Charles and his son, the Prince of Wales (Charles II), called "The Engagement", in the wake of failure to persuade Parliament to commit to Presbyterianism. These forces invaded England led by the Duke of Hamilton and Earl Holland but were defeated at Preston in August 1648 by Cromwell and the New Model Army. Tired of the prevarications of Parliament, the Scots army had marched on London in 1647.

The events that followed would lead to the execution of the King in January 1649. The army, deeply penetrated by Independent and Presbyterian religious convictions, wanted the immediate dissolution of the Church of England and the outlawing of its bishops. Parliament was split three ways when it came to a religious settlement: there were reforming Episcopalians, Presbyterians and Independents. Some expected a New Jerusalem to be created immediately. Millenarian thinking that the Second Coming of Christ was imminent abounded. Others, like the Fifth Monarchists, expected the immediate monarchy of Jesus Christ on earth through the preaching of the gospel, and wanted to hasten that reality by using Parliament.

With the air thick with intrigue, Cromwell, reluctantly, and the army less so, marched on London in 1647, brandishing a new constitution called the Heads of Proposals. Like Caesar crossing the Rubicon, the army had decided to exert its power over Parliament. The Putney Debates about the nature of a future constitution chaired by Cromwell followed and they considered ideas as radical as universal suffrage and the trial of the King. By then agitators had been appointed by radicals in every regiment to provoke political, social and religious change. The war had created a new social and religious radicalism, and chief among the radicals were the Levellers. A new law or motto was promulgated called *Salus populi est Suprema lex*, the "Safety of the People is the Highest Law".[8] More practically, soldiers were owed substantial arrears by Parliament and negotiation with the King over terms appeared to be going nowhere. This had been declared as such in the Vote of No Addresses in January 1648. Cromwell had been called away to fight the Scots at Preston in August. While he was away, on 6 December 1648, Colonel Pride stood on the steps of Westminster and arrested forty-five MPs, kept 145 out of the chamber and allowed seventy-five in to do the army's bidding, which was to bring the King to trial. The army had taken control, far more effectively than Charles had ever done. Parliament was purged, and those left were to try the King. The irony was that Cromwell had done what Parliament had rejected, when Charles had sought tyrannically to arrest the five in 1642.

The trial and execution of Charles I was both a political and religious act. It was political in that it ended (for the time being) a form of monarchical government, which in the eyes of Parliament had prevented freedom. It was religious in that the regicides did it in the name of God. The issue of liberty was central: "England", said Charles at his trial, "was never an elected kingdom, but an heredity kingdom for near these thousand years, therefore let me know by what authority I am called thither. I do stand more for the liberty of my people than any that come be my pretended judges."[9] It was a powerful statement.

A purged group of sixty-eight Parliamentarians, who would deliver the verdict the army expected, tried Charles I. Charles himself would not plead or recognize the court. Witnesses were called over three days, with Charles absent. Cromwell regarded Charles's death as a "cruel necessity". Like Old Testament kings deserted by God, Charles, it was argued, had forfeited the right to govern by waging war on Parliament. Fifty-nine commissioners, later called regicides, signed his death warrant. On the day of his execution Charles was calm. He wore two shirts so that he would not shiver in the January cold, and this be mistaken for fear. It was snowing. The execution took place on a scaffold outside the Banqueting House that had been designed by Inigo Jones for James I. The day before Charles had spent time with his two children still in England, Elizabeth and Henry, and in prayer with Archbishop Juxon. When he was executed a deep moan arose from the crowd and his head was *not* held up by the executioner with the customary shout, "the head of a traitor".[10] Among his last words Charles said: "I declare before you all I die a Christian according to the profession of the Church of England as I found it left me by my father."[11] That church regarded him a martyr, and the Commonwealth as a murderer. It was a division of opinion that would take centuries to surmount, and in some quarters has not been.

If at one level the execution of the King fulfilled the expectations of the radicals in the revolution, it also marked a point of no return. It alienated the Royalists and the conservative Parliamentarians who had worked for a settlement with the Presbyterian Church, but who had been steadfastly rejected by Charles. The Levellers, a new political movement that permeated the army, had also resisted the execution of the King, seeing the emergence of a new dictatorship that would threaten freedom, and social and religious change. They eyed the new regime with the greatest of suspicion and would soon rise in revolt against it.

The Levellers were the leading movement for radical political reform in the nation and their influence mostly rested in the army. Cromwell had largely recruited his New Model Army for its Puritan credentials, including unusual levels of commitment. He realized that a Puritan army would be much more motivated to destroy the Royalist forces, but now they had won, the Levellers turned to considering the kind of state they had fought for. Furthermore, the moderating influence of Lord Manchester, Lord Holland and others had been removed by the Self-denying Ordinance of 1644, which separated parliamentary office from military rank. Having executed the King, Cromwell faced an equally serious threat from the Levellers, for they had a formidable leader and powerful political ideas.

John Lilburne, called "Freeborn John" and originally a landowner in County Durham, was the leader of the Levellers. Puritan in background, he was radical in politics, forging an alliance between biblical ideas and political change that would powerfully re-surface in the nineteenth century and in Christian socialism thereafter. He had already fallen foul of Charles I's government for publishing unlicensed tracts and would no longer be silent under Cromwell. He opposed Pride's Purge, the drift to compliance with Cromwell, and the Council of State appointed by the seriously reduced Rump Parliament. When others in the movement drifted away, Lilburne held fast to the values of the Levellers. Their interests were present in their name—Levellers—for they wanted to remove social and political barriers between people. Their programme revolved around poor relief, redistribution of wealth (although they recognized the right of property ownership), legal and political reform, and greatly extended suffrage. In 1649, Lilburne published *England's New Chains Discovered*, an attack on the newly formed Commonwealth and its illegitimate power. He encouraged the soldiers to mutiny against "the lords of army", stoking their grievances about pay arrears, about being sent to Ireland to fight, and about their views being ignored in the army councils. One Leveller pamphlet issued on 21 March 1649 stated: "You will scarce speak to Cromwell but he will lay his hand on his heart, elevate his eyes and call God to record; he will weep, howl and repent even while he doth smite you under the fifth rib. O, Cromwell! Wither are you aspiring?"[12] In the end, the army commanders at Burford put down a mutiny of 900 soldiers in 1649.

A turning point had been reached in which Cromwell had turned his back on the Levellers and any further radical reform. Lilburne was arrested and, until his death in 1657, most of the rest of his life was spent either in exile in Holland or in prison, inveighing against the regime he had fought to put in place.

A fellow radical from Lancashire with similar ideas, but a more unorthodox spirituality, was Gerard Winstanley, the leader of a group that became known as the Diggers. They did not pose the same political threat to the Commonwealth; they were instead more of a spiritual and moral danger. Winstanley, whose business failed in London when he was unable to collect his debts, abandoned London and settled at St George's Hill in Surrey and then at Cobham. In both places he formed an agricultural commune with shared property ownership. Like the Levellers he wanted poor relief and redistribution of wealth but founded on the basis of the rights of people to share property rather than on private ownership. His religious views were unorthodox; he was given to visions and he did not believe in the Trinity, predestination or the Second Coming. The government opposed the Diggers and the vision of shared ownership did not succeed. Later in life, much like Lilburne, Winstanley moved towards Quakerism, and at the time of the Restoration took up positions in local government.

Both the Levellers and Diggers (or True Levellers as they were sometimes called) were representative of more radical ideas present in the country and also reflected the ideas manifest in the Peasants' Revolt of 1381, the commotions against enclosures in the reign of Edward VI, and in particular, Kett's rebellion of 1549 in Norfolk. All of them drew powerfully on ideas of community, of sharing and of the rights and liberties of the individual found in the Bible. But for Oliver Cromwell, essentially a pragmatist and not a theoretician or intellectual, although a practical Puritan, these were *not* ideas to be entertained at a time of acute political threat. In 1650 there were rebellions in Scotland and Ireland to put down, and the politics of the post-royalist nation of England to settle.

Commonwealth and Protectorate (1649–60)

Following the execution of the King, the Commonwealth had to be secured, not only from internal rifts of policy in the army and Parliament, but in the two kingdoms of Scotland and Ireland. There were armed rebellions in both places. Ireland had been in sporadic revolt against England since the late Elizabethan period, and the late queen's favourite, the Earl of Essex, lost his reputation as a soldier there in 1599 when with an army of 16,000 he failed to confront and defeat Hugh O'Neill, the Earl of Tyrone, the leader of the Irish who was eventually driven from his lands. Since then a policy of settling Protestant lowland Scots in Ulster was put in place at the instigation of the Attorney General of Ireland, Sir John Davies. The policy, from which England reaped a mixed and bitter harvest in the following centuries, was to clear Irish inhabitants from six counties in the north and replace them entirely with English and Scots. (The plan was to build a new English community on Protestant lines. Freehold land was offered to settlers on preferential terms under James I and, by 1613, eighty-four parliamentary boroughs were created throughout the country with representation in an Irish Parliament, giving them effective control.) By 1641, Ireland was once more descending into conflict, between the Irish, the Old English (Catholic) and Ulster's Protestant forces. The motto of the Irish and Old English was "a United Ireland". There were wars and atrocities on both sides, a warning sign of centuries of division to come.

By 1647, the Rump Parliament decided to subjugate Ireland, fearing it might function as a back door for the Royalist cause in England. Cromwell was sent with the New Model Army to "pacify Ireland". He faced a complicated situation in which Owen Roe O'Neill and the royalist Duke of Ormonde opposed him. Cromwell attacked the city of Drogheda on the east coast, north of Dublin, with 10,000 troops and artillery. All the inhabitants were executed, but still worse, all the inhabitants of Wexford were massacred in a subsequent siege. Cromwell, in writing to Speaker Lenthal at Westminster, saw it as exemplary punishment, and considered his success the blessing of the Lord. It would take a further three years to subjugate Ireland, before the loss of Henry Ireton, the revolution's theoretician, from plague. The result of this "pacification" was centuries of bitter resentment towards the English. Cromwellian commanders like Colonel Warden were rewarded with thousands of acres, in his case around Burnchurch in Kilkenny, later marrying into the Flood family and becoming part of the Protestant Ascendancy for nearly three hundred years.

In 1650, Cromwell was urgently withdrawn from Ireland to go to Scotland. Charles II had accepted the invitation of the Scots to become their king if he accepted Presbyterianism in Scotland. Showing more flexibility than his father, Charles obliged by offering a Presbyterian church in England should they succeed in helping him regain the crown. Cromwell had other ideas, however, and on 3 September 1650 inflicted a crushing defeat on Scottish forces at Dunbar, where 4,000 Scots were killed. A further defeat was inflicted at Stirling. Charles II marched south with his troops as far as Worcester, where they too were defeated. Charles II escaped capture by hiding in the ubiquitous Royal Oak, and Cromwell returned to London having set all his enemies to flight. What now to do with the peace?

Following Pride's Purge and the execution of the King, the Rump Parliament of some one hundred and twenty Members of Parliament retained a distinctly Puritan flavour. The celebration of Christmas (and Easter and Whitsun) had been abolished in 1647, with no plum pudding or minced pies or feasting allowed. Shopkeepers who closed on Christmas Day were punished; some were put in the stocks. Christmas riots in Kent followed. Legislation punishing adultery and incest with death was passed in May 1650, a new blasphemy law established, and fornication made subject to three months in prison. The bishops and the House of Lords were abolished. The Prayer Book had been replaced in 1645 with a rather lightweight *Directory of Public Worship*, which authorized services with a minimum of liturgy. Licences to preach were issued by a committee of Parliament. Despite this raft of Puritan legislation, there was uncertainty about the overall direction of government.

Cromwell, it was said, was "not wedded or glued" to any form of government. He allowed the Rump Parliament to linger on. This encouraged trade and colonial projects effectively, but in 1653 Cromwell famously said, "You are no Parliament, I say you are no Parliament" and "You have sat too long for any good you have been doing lately, I say depart; and let us have done with you."[13] Instead, a new Parliament was devised, known as the Barebones Parliament (named after one of its members, Praise-God Barebones, from the City of London). Cromwell had high hopes for this assembly, which was essentially a hand-picked Parliament of godly men, 140 in all, from around the country. It was said to be modelled on the Jewish Sanhedrin, and it busied itself debating the reorganization of church life, the abolition of tithes, the control of sects and the treatment of radicals like the Leveller, Lilburne. The debates became increasingly arcane and it lasted for barely eight months. At Cromwell's request it voted itself out of existence. It is said that this failure was a great blow to Cromwell's idealism and what he had hoped for from the Revolution. With the failure of the Barebones Parliament, Cromwell no longer hoped to realize the rule of God's people in England: he now saw himself as "a constable whose task was to prevent Englishmen from flying at one another's throats".[14] A more conservative constitution was drawn up, based on the Instrument of Government, which required a constitutional leader or Protector, Parliament, liberty of conscience and a standing army controlled and financed by Parliament and the Protector.

To the chagrin of the radicals, Cromwell was king in all but name, but he now had an army with which to control the country, a force more costly than anything Charles I ever had. It was financed by a decimation tax on the Royalists, but their resources would run out. The Revolution was over. For a time in 1655, and between Parliaments, the country was divided into districts governed by eleven Major Generals. Alehouses were closed, horse racing and cock fighting prohibited, and a Puritan lifestyle was imposed wherever possible. Two more Protectorate Parliaments sat, resulting in a new attempt at a constitution in February 1657, called a Humble Petition and Advice, but Cromwell steadfastly refused to be called king. He died, worn out, in 1658, and the Commonwealth staggered on for two more years, but the experiment was running out of steam.

The Church in the Commonwealth

The state of affairs of the Church during the Commonwealth years was as confused as the political situation, but it was to change the landscape of the Church in England forever. There were nevertheless years of struggle ahead to achieve religious toleration and the liberty to worship as a congregation chose.

What was clear from the outset was that the Roman Catholic Church would continue to be suppressed as papist and heretical for the time being, and it was so, in fact, for two centuries. The leaders of the Commonwealth had only revulsion for Catholicism. But now the Anglican Church, or Church of England, was to be almost similarly treated. The office of bishop was abolished, the Prayer Book was denounced, and there was no longer uniformity of worship. Not only that, but the Puritan army was able to destroy any vestiges of Catholicism in the parish churches and cathedrals of England, completing for the most part the iconoclasm begun in Edward VI's reign. The ring was at last banned in the marriage service, the signing of the cross on a baby was forbidden at baptism, the churching of women ended, the body at a funeral was virtually ignored, with no prayers near the corpse, all altars or rails in churches were dismantled and all effigies destroyed, whether in stone, glass or wood.

It is always comparatively easy to destroy what exists, but quite another thing to replace it; and the issue of what kind of church settlement should be provided was repeatedly to tear open the Commonwealth, especially since it became clear that a uniform solution was not desired. What was undisputed was that Roman Catholicism must still be actively opposed, its traces in the Church of England removed, and the episcopal government and uniformity of worship abolished. Yet the debate about what should replace the Elizabethan Established Church raged throughout the period.

Initially the Presbyterians in Parliament wanted a national church on the Calvinist Scottish model, based on the exhaustive Westminster Confession of Faith of 1647. This church would be controlled by Parliament with its own assembly and with ministers licensed by it, but with no bishops. Bishops had been the sticking point for both James I and Charles I: their view of monarchy was bound to them. "No bishop no king" was their cry. Yet the Presbyterian model was resisted by the Independents, of whom Cromwell was one. They wanted more autonomy for the local congregation and a more federated solution, although this too had its difficulties of control and quality.

The initial idea of the Puritans for the national church was that the parish system should be kept but grouped into "classes" resembling the brilliant organization of John Field, the Presbyterian leader of the late Elizabethan period. It was one thing to envisage, quite another to deliver; very few of these classes grouped as a network got off the ground, except in parts of Wiltshire and Lancashire. Only eight of forty counties even bothered to organize the Church in this way, and even fewer responded to Parliament's inquiries into what was happening on the ground. Organized religion of the Roman Catholic and Anglican kind had required bishops, archdeacons, rural deans, diocesan officials, church courts and church wardens. A replacement system would not be found quickly. The truth of the matter was that most parishes carried on as before, muddling their way through till clearer days emerged. Indeed, for the hundred years since Henry VIII, this had been the tactic, for local people still needed to be baptized, married and buried, whatever the bigwigs on high thought, however they theologized and whether or not a mitre or a black hat was proscribed. Control of ministers and their licensing was erratic. Committees of Triers overseen by Parliament were set up to examine and appoint ministers, but this too was implemented haphazardly.

What Cromwell did not abolish was the system of tithes and patronage, which had undergirded church administration since Saxon times and had proved remarkably enduring. Patronage was the right of a landlord to present a minister to a vacant parish, which in one form or another survives even to this day in the Church of England. "Degrees of ministers" (i.e. deacon, presbyter and bishop) had been defended by Hooker in his *Ecclesiastical Polity* Book V, as indeed had the system of tithes (the giving of money or produce for the upkeep of ministry). Having built his case for tithes on Old Testament and New Testament teaching on giving, Hooker quotes Charles the Great (Charlemagne), who said: "The goods of the Church are sacred endowments of God, [and] to the Lord our God we offer and dedicate whatsoever we deliver unto his church." But for too many among the Levellers and others, the tithe system was a gross affront to spiritual liberty. Nevertheless, Cromwell would not abolish the tithe system and plunge the Church into financial chaos; he was too practical for that and also not sufficiently ideologically driven. If tithes had practical merit if not ideological support, he would not abolish them, much to the disappointment and anger of the radical reformers during the Commonwealth.

Into this semi-vacuum of church governance, a whole range of new forms of church, worship and organization sprang into being (or sometimes there was nothing at all). Some did not last, like the Diggers and the Muggletonians, the latter a sect led by two London tailors. One of these, Lodowicke Muggleton, believed that the pair were the last prophets named in Revelation 11. They were pacifist, anti-authoritarian and apolitical. Another group, called the Ranters, regarded themselves as free from the law and from any authority, be it scriptural or moral, and in particular they considered themselves free from sexual standards.

These more extreme groups came and went, but three in particular would have lasting impact on the nation and would flourish. They were the Independents, who morphed into the Congregationalist Church, the Baptists, who started as Anabaptists, and the Quakers. Each was defined by particular beliefs or practices. The Congregationalists had their origins among the Independent Puritans. They based their beliefs on the Savoy Confession, which came out of the Savoy Conference of October 1658 in London (close to the present-day Savoy Hotel). Their leaders were the notable Puritan writers Thomas Goodwin and John Owen, to whom we shall return. The Baptists sprang from the single defining doctrine that believers should be baptized as adults, and thus broke from the practice of infant baptism, and indeed from Lutheran and Calvinist teaching on infant baptism. In time, they were to have a powerful social impact on the nation's life.

Finally, the Quakers, or the Society of Friends, emerged out of the Leveller movement, which was both Puritan and political in character. Believing in the power of the Holy Spirit to move any member of the community to speak and convey God's word (evidenced by quaking or shaking), they quickly became a refuge for disappointed Levellers and agitators, and even for Lilburne himself. In line with Leveller philosophy, Quakers sought a non-hierarchical community in which any could thus speak when moved. Their aims of education, pacifism, opposition to slavery, relief of poverty and economic progress were to have a remarkable and enduring impact on English national life, not least in the nineteenth century in banking and manufacturing, especially of chocolate and shoes, to which we shall also return.

At the outset, the Quakers could seem extreme and unorthodox. One James Nayler, for example, a friend of George Fox, the founder of Quakerism, rode into Bristol in a re-enactment of Palm Sunday in October 1656. He was tried for blasphemy in a sensational trial, for setting himself up as a Christ figure, and was convicted and then branded with a B for blasphemer. He also had his tongue bored through with a red-hot poker. Although Fox deeply disapproved of Nayler's actions, the two were reconciled on Nayler's plea for forgiveness; itself a testimony to the peace-loving nature of the Friends. All of these movements, which would be grouped together as Dissenters or Non-Conformists in the coming Restoration period, had their origins in the Commonwealth or before.

Not only was there a plethora of new churches in England pursuing a variety of callings in the seventeenth century, but the first half of that century saw an unprecedented quantity of Christian publishing by the leading Puritan divines. These works were mostly biblical exposition, doctrinal elucidation and pastoral encouragement. Among the chief writers were Richard Sibbe, a Puritan Anglican expositor from Suffolk, William Gurnall, another Anglican from Kings Lynn, whose book on Ephesians 6, *Christian Armour*, became a classic in devotional literature, and William Perkins. Perkins taught theology at Christ's, Cambridge at the end of the sixteenth century and influenced a whole cohort of great Puritan writers and ministers. But perhaps the princes among these writers and ministers were John Owen (1616–83) and Thomas Goodwin (1600–80). Goodwin, a chaplain to Cromwell who had been influenced by John Preston, another Cambridge Divine, contributed to the Westminster Assembly and left behind five volumes of sermons, which have been reprinted forty-seven times.

Interestingly, his devotional writings on the heart of Jesus have been an inspiration to Catholics and Puritans alike.

John Owen, another chaplain to Cromwell, was the most prolific of the Puritan authors. Made Vice-Chancellor of Oxford University and Dean of Christ Church in 1651, he was nonetheless at heart an Independent. Almost uniquely among the Puritans, he wrote on the work of the Holy Spirit, his person and gifts, and emphasized the power of the Spirit to bring the student of the Bible into a proper understanding of spiritual truth. Reading Owen's rather laboured writings requires perseverance, however. If we were to add to these authors the works of later Puritans, such as John Bunyan and Richard Baxter, there is little doubt about the scope and profound influence of these men.

By 1660, the Commonwealth had run its course. High taxation to maintain a standing army burdened the population, especially the merchant and landowning classes. On seeing the incapacity to govern of Oliver Cromwell's son, Richard, one of the generals of the army, General Monck, made contact with Charles II in the Hague. He negotiated an amnesty for Parliamentarians who had opposed his father and religious toleration was also proposed, but these provisions would be worked out in the coming months less advantageously both for the regicides, who were pursued and executed when apprehended, and for those outside the Church of England, henceforth called Dissenters, who would be penalized. The agreement was called the Declaration of Breda, and on its basis Charles II was restored. To tumultuous acclaim Charles arrived in London, just twenty months after the death of Oliver Cromwell, and a new age had begun.

CHAPTER 15

Restoration, Repression and Revolution

The hardest thing to achieve was a prevailing wind to bring Charles and his advisers back to England. He eventually arrived at Dover on the *Royal Charles* (previously called the *Naseby*!) on 25 May 1660. He delayed his arrival in London until the 29th, his thirtieth birthday, reviewed the army—which now numbered 40,000—*en route* on Blackheath, and then rode to Westminster to huge popular acclaim. He dated his accession from the execution of his father eleven years earlier. Standing six feet, two inches tall, dark and swarthy, he cut an easily recognizable figure. He inherited the crowns of three countries, England, Ireland and Scotland, all vastly changed by the experience of civil war and Cromwell's government.

The English Revolution never had a revolutionary ideology such as that supplied to the French by Rousseau or to the Russians by Marx and Lenin. It had all been about the restraint of power, the rule of law and of Parliament, and the general pursuit of liberty. In the event, liberty was hardest to achieve. Cromwell had sought toleration but found he must control radical and extreme ideas and hold the middle ground. This exertion of control, which at times depended entirely upon the army, as in the period of rule by the Major Generals, was seen as a betrayal by some of the causes for which they had fought. Cromwell clung tenaciously to the idea of toleration as long as the person or group had the "heart of the matter" (meaning true Christian conviction) in them. He opposed subversion of the social order on religious grounds, as proposed by the Levellers, and also the immorality of the Ranters. At the same time, he wanted an independent church free of central control.

Puritan thought had inspired and directed the revolution. Whatever social class Puritans had come from—and they came from all—they had undergone the same process of conversion, which could be explained in the purely biblical terms of grace, faith in Christ, scripture and purity. They had failed, not as a religious movement, but in the task for which they were unprepared, that of handling power and ruling a nation that did not all hold to the same ideals. If they were unable to establish the revolution in the institutions of government—with a fatal rift between the army and Parliament—some barriers had been incontrovertibly crossed and these would mark the new fabric of the nation which Charles came to rule.

Power had shifted from the central administration to the country squire: the landowning gentry, who prized liberty, were the patrons of local churches, and the JPs on the local bench. They resented overweening control from the centre and were empowered by their property, which became the bulwark and basis of local authority. Other barriers had been crossed also. Judges were now more accountable to Parliament, although the tension between legislature and executive and judiciary would always be uneasy. Intellectually, people had moved and were moving from the realm of magic to science. The last execution of a witch took place in 1685, the last trial in 1717. With new confidence in the providence of God and his rule of the universe, the motivation to study mathematics, physics, astronomy and chemistry was given fresh impetus. This was the social fabric that Charles came to govern.

For these undergirding reasons, the next twenty-five years of government were some of the most influential in our history. The Royal Society was founded in 1662. Sir Isaac Newton wrote his seminal work *Philosophiae Naturalis Principia Mathematica* in 1687. Great spiritual writers, such as Milton, Bunyan and Baxter, flourished in difficult circumstances. Against the backdrop of an expensive continental war with the French, public finances were set on a new footing with the establishment of the Bank of England in 1694, somewhat later under William and Mary. This was established through a royal charter and with Parliamentary support organized by Charles Montague. In this way, the financing of the nation's debt was revolutionized. Over a thousand people contributed to the bank's capital, with a generous eight per cent annual rate of interest on their deposit. Although the standing army was stood down, disciplines that had been acquired for military campaigns were effectively passed on. The navy was rebuilt to take on Holland first and then France, in a global struggle for trade and to maintain a balance of power on the continent of Europe. Finally, the political fabric of the nation was laid down with the establishment of two parties: Whigs and Tories. Both were terms of abuse, one drawn from Scotland (Whigs) and the other (Tories) from Ireland (perhaps indicating the public's cynical view of politicians). The City of London was decimated by plague in 1665 and then gutted by fire in 1666, before a spectacular rebuild of its greatest landmarks, most notably St Paul's Cathedral, orchestrated by Christopher Wren. Given his head, Wren would have redesigned the whole city. The greatest challenge to the incoming government of Charles was, however, the religious settlement.

The religious settlement

The Parliament that enacted the transition from the Protectorate to the restoration of Charles II was called the Convention Parliament. Charles and his chief minister Hyde, or the Earl of Clarendon as he was shortly to become, were in control of government business. The Parliament was royalist, with full representations from the boroughs. The House of Lords was restored and likewise the Church of England, with bishops reappointed. A conference was held at Worcester House to plan the nature of the future church. This was followed by the Savoy Conference, which made only superficial changes to the 1652 Prayer Book. Richard Baxter, one of the leading Puritans, attended, and the hope was for a comprehensive church in which the Protestant majority might feel comfortable. An Act of Indemnity and Oblivion was passed through which restoration of property was to be pursued where possible and amnesty granted to most Parliamentarians, although not the regicides. Of the fifty-nine regicides who had signed the King's death warrant some had fled, some had died, and nine were hung, drawn and quartered for treason. Major General Thomas Harrison, the Fifth Monarchist, was the first to be executed. He resolutely went to his death, sure that judgement would come on the King and his court—curiously, from providence's point of view, a notoriously immoral king was allowed to flourish in his lifetime, but not his heirs. The body of Cromwell was exhumed from Westminster Abbey where he had been laid to rest in a sumptuous funeral worthy of a monarch and instead was hung in chains at Tyburn, along with Ireton and John Bradshaw, who had presided at Charles I's trial.

After this first Parliament, which to the Royalists was the Convention Parliament, the King called a new one, the Cavalier Parliament, that met in May 1661, and which was to last eighteen years: the longest of all English parliaments. It would enact the religious settlement, which would prove so divisive.

In the Declaration of Breda, the King had promised liberty of conscience and religious toleration, at least to the non-Roman Catholic Church. The Worcester House Conference sought a church that would accommodate the Presbyterians, but the Cavalier Parliament, with its overwhelmingly royalist and reactionary flavour, decided to impose a severe religious settlement on the dissenting or non-conformist community as well as on the Catholics. In the case of the Protestant churches outside the Church of England, this settlement was contrary to the hopes of the King and Clarendon. The King was for toleration and Clarendon for comprehension (i.e. inclusion). But the settlement consisted of four Parliamentary Acts, which effectively abandoned the attempt to provide a single church for all the non-Catholic parts of the nation. These four Acts were called the Clarendon Code, as they were passed on Lord Clarendon's watch, although not always with his support, and they effectively excluded all but Church of England members from government and from freely meeting for worship. The Corporation Act denied membership to any who had not for the previous twelve months taken the sacrament of the Lord's Supper in the Established Church. This legislation effectively prevented Presbyterians and others from holding office. The Act of Uniformity of 1662 required all clergy to use only the forms of service prescribed by the Prayer Book and to forswear any involvement in the Solemn League and Covenant, the instrument of the Presbyterian Church. The result was that over nine hundred clergy in the Church of England refused to comply and were ejected from their parishes, including a third of the clergy in London. It was at this point that Richard Baxter, probably one of the most effective and reasonable parish priests in England, resigned his living (parish), becoming thereafter a writer supported by his wife's income.

More harsh legislation was to follow. The Conventicle Act of 1664 prevented the gathering for worship of more than five people other than immediate family outside the Church of England. This Act was designed to prevent the growth of non-conformism, but it was hard to enforce and the King himself was known to be unsupportive. When Jews came to him complaining that the law restricted their meetings, he assured them he would turn a blind eye and the Privy Council agreed. Furthermore, the penal laws against transgressing this law were mitigated by the Declaration of Indulgence of 1672, which made the concession of licensing dissenting chapels. The final piece of legislation in this code was the Five Mile Act of 1665, which forbade a clergyman from living within five miles of a congregation or parish from which he had been expelled, or in the town in which that church or congregation was situated. By breaking the physical bond between congregation and minister, it was hoped to hold in check the growth of dissenting congregations.

Further legislation, although not ostensibly part of the Clarendon Code, followed. An Act against Quakers was passed in 1662 suppressing their meetings, although the absence of ministers (any Quaker could receive the "inner light" and teach from the Bible) made such meetings difficult to identify and prohibit. Although persecuted in the 1660s, with many leading lights imprisoned, over time Quakers gained the respect of the wider community. George Fox was a tireless and fearless leader. He organized monthly meetings; schools were set up for Quaker (and other) children; and Quakers were generous in the face of need. Despite persecution, and criticism of their outmoded dress, and of elders who pried into people's lives, they exhibited an infectious and attractive spirituality. One Robert Barclay, a Calvinist Scot, found the motto "In stillness there is fullness; in fullness there is nothingness and in nothingness there are all things" especially beguiling.

The most famous of the Quakers, apart from George Fox their founder, was William Penn, the son of Admiral Penn. Well-educated at Christ Church, Oxford and known to the court as a sincere Quaker, he was leased a grant of land by the crown south of New Jersey and Pennsylvania, where he set up a colony based on liberty of conscience, respect for the Native Americans and an early form of democracy. The early promise of the venture faced the inevitable human greed, ambition and deception, and soon civil laws with harsh penalties were needed to restrain crime. Penn found his own vision tested to breaking point. Finally, in this tranche of religious and related legislation, the Cavalier Parliament passed a Licensing Act preventing the printing of any seditious libel that had religious implications.

What was the effect of this legislation or the so-called Clarendon Code? The King and Clarendon had hoped for a more comprehensive and inclusive church settlement. The legislation passed resulted in many dissenting ministers going to gaol and their goods seized, which sometimes reduced them to poverty and hunger. They were separated from their communities and congregations. Most famously, John Bunyan was tried for preaching without a licence at a conventicle in Bedford, an unlicensed meeting of more than five persons, thus transgressing the Conventicle Act. He was arraigned "for devilishly and perniciously abstaining from coming to church to hear divine service".[1] Bunyan was to remain imprisoned in Bedford gaol for twelve years. It was in gaol that he wrote *Grace Abounding* and began *The Pilgrim's Progress*. He was released in 1672. By then the King had issued his Declaration of Indulgence, which allowed for greater toleration and the licensing of dissenting chapels. Bunyan became the minister of the Bedford meeting, but also travelled extensively. *The Pilgrim's Progress* has undergone over a thousand editions and in Bunyan's lifetime sold at least 100,000 copies, perhaps, after the prison letters of St Paul, one of the finest examples of Christian prison literature.

The persecution of the dissenters did not substantially diminish their numbers, whether Baptist, Quaker, Independent or Presbyterian. Indeed, congregations began meeting in barns, fields and caves. Ministers were quickly spirited away when the constables arrived. There was no disguising the hardship of many.

Some, like Mr Chadwick in Somerset, as Richard Baxter recalled, lived with their family on rye bread, water and the gifts of the faithful. As so often with persecution, the fervency of their faith was enhanced by the severity of their persecution and, if anything, dissenter numbers increased whilst the Church of England's popularity declined. It is a fair summary to say that the Church of England was not established in the hearts of the people, as the laws of Parliament in the Clarendon Code had hoped. The Established Church would have longed for the warmth and commitment of the non-conformist fellowship over against the perfunctory formality of so much Anglican worship. In 1676, an official census reported 108,678 adult dissenters in the country. This was probably a severe case of under-reporting by the government, aimed at belittling the issue of dissent. By contrast, a Quaker census in the early eighteenth century reported 638 Presbyterian congregations, 203 Independent, 211 Particular or Seventh Day Baptist, 122 General Baptist and 672 Quaker. In addition, there were at least 50,000 Huguenots in their own French or Walloon congregations in several of the major cities. The Roman Catholics, to whom we will come, also numbered roughly 50,000 in the country. If the dissenting church survived, indeed flourished in places, it did so at a cost: its leadership was hampered; it was rendered narrower in its social appeal; and in the case of the Presbyterian Church, its nationwide network of synods was almost obliterated.

If the first years of Charles II's reign were taken up with the Restoration Settlement, especially of the Church, and the paying back of old scores and the shoring up of government finances, the years 1665–7 saw a number of defining disasters: the Great Plague of 1665; the Great Fire of London of 1666; and the second Anglo-Dutch War, which in the end humiliated the government. The Great Plague of London killed nearly a quarter of the population of the city, i.e. about 100,000 people. There had been other plagues in recent years: 1603, 1625, 1636, but this was the worst. Samuel Pepys, along with the even more prolific diarist John Evelyn, recorded that walking down a city street, there was scarcely anyone to be seen. A year later, the Great Fire of London struck, starting in Pudding Lane. The flames spread along the Thames from the Tower of London to the Temple. The fire destroyed nearly 14,000 houses, eighty-seven parish churches and St Paul's Cathedral.

The third setback to the nation was the humiliation of the English in the Second Dutch War. The first had been concluded in 1654 during the Commonwealth. The purpose was to protect English trade and it was enforced by the Navigation Act of 1651, which was renewed in 1663. The principal to be followed was "English trade in English ships" and this was the foundation to imperial trade for 200 years.

The war also demonstrated that, although the Dutch were co-religionists and soon to be part of the English monarchy with the accession of William of Orange to the throne in 1688, trade outweighed religious affiliations! In defence of these Navigation Acts, England went to war with uneven results. James, Duke of York, the King's brother who would become James II, by then an avowed Catholic, was the Lord High Admiral. Although he would win a naval engagement off Lowestoft in 1665, further inconclusive engagements were fought until, humiliatingly for England, the Dutch sailed up the Medway in June 1666, breaking through the chain barrier across the river and destroying fifteen ships of the line, including the *Royal Charles*, the ship once called *Naseby*, that had brought Charles to England in 1660. Such was the humiliation of this event that Clarendon went into exile, while Arlington, and a group known as The Cabal, succeeded him. One silver lining to the defeat by the Dutch was that, at the concluding Treaty of Breda, Charles was able to retain the colony of New Amsterdam in North America, which had been seized from the Dutch. The King renamed it New York, after the Duke of York, his brother.

The reign which had begun so propitiously in 1660 now faced a crisis. Puritan gentry wondered what might have provoked such judgement on the country as to produce the Great Plague, the Great Fire of London and a degrading military defeat. To the Puritan mind, a King whose court was a veritable "school for scandal",[2] the reappearance of Roman Catholicism, and a compromised government were all probable causes. Also, Charles II had taken several mistresses, most famously Barbara Palmer (nee Villiers) and the actress Nell Gwyn. He was to sire at least nine illegitimate children, but had no heirs from his infertile and cruelly-treated Portuguese wife, Catherine of Braganza. Barbara Villiers, a twenty-year-old beauty, who was married to Sir Roger Palmer, the cuckolded squire of Dorney Court, had five children by Charles in five years, and one other by John Churchill, later Duke of Marlborough. The merry court of the so-called "merry king" was a continuous offence to the censorious high churchman Clarendon, and to the Whig Puritan, Shaftesbury.

A change in principal minister followed the sinking of the English fleet at Medway. Clarendon fled into exile in France, although his family was never far from the centre of power. Clarendon's daughter, Anne Hyde, had married the heir to the throne, James, Duke of York and was mother of Princess Mary, wife of William of Orange, and Princess Anne, who as queen would be the last Stuart monarch. The so-called Cabal ministry succeeded Clarendon and included Clifford, Arlington, Buckingham, Ashley Cooper (Shaftesbury) and Lauderdale (hence "Cabal" as an acronym). The most important member of the Cabal would be the one-time Roundhead, Lord Shaftesbury (1621–83)—Anthony Ashley Cooper—who was determined to resist the growing influence of the Catholics in court and government and whose secretary was the philosopher John Locke. The worst fear of the Puritan gentry was a Catholic absolute monarch with a standing army, as had emerged in France in the person of Louis XIV (ruled 1643–1715). As Spain had been England's chief enemy in the sixteenth century, now a resurgent, absolutist, Catholic France was the new terror of Protestant Europe.

The Roman Catholic threat

In the years after Clarendon's fall, the fairly ineffective government of the Cabal alienated opinion by its frequent quarrels. From 1667, Charles II was showing signs of moving away from simply being a "merry monarch" to wanting to pursue his own policies and more actively manage Parliament. At the same time there was a growing groundswell of suspicion that Roman Catholicism was intruding into the policies of government and the office-holders of the administration were being corrupted, just as it had with Charles's father during his personal rule. James, Duke of York, was known to be a Roman Catholic, Sir Thomas Clifford, a member of the Cabal, was a crypto-Catholic and was given the Treasury, while Charles II was in the process of making the 1670 Treaty of Dover with Louis XIV, in which he agreed to renew fighting the Dutch (France's enemy), took a pension from the French king of £225,000, and removed penalties against English Catholics from the Clarendon Code. It was viewed as a slippery slope to Catholicism and Absolutism.

When Charles used his royal prerogative in 1672 and issued the Declaration of Indulgence, waiving the restrictions of worship on both dissenters and Roman Catholics, all the worst fears of Shaftesbury and others like him were confirmed. After the very costly rebuilding of the navy and a very expensive third Dutch war, fears of a Catholic conspiracy to take over the state took hold. In response, the House of Commons called for the rescinding of the Declaration of Indulgence and Thomas Osborne, Lord Danby, by now the main leader in the House of Commons, made voting any funds for the King dependent on full and untrammelled support for the Church of England. A blunt Yorkshireman and country Tory, not beyond feathering his own nest, but at the same time suspicious of corruption in government, Danby was determined to see restrictions imposed on dissenters and Catholics. In 1672, and then again in 1678, the Test Act was passed. This required all office-holders in government, the forces, corporations and Parliament to swear they were communicant members of the Church of England and to reject the doctrine of transubstantiation. When this Act was extended in 1678 to cover the peerage, James, Duke of York resigned his post of Lord High Admiral. Worse was to follow; general hysteria took hold against Catholics, enflamed by the "Popish Plot".

The Popish Plot was designed to whip up deep-seated fears that a plot to put a Roman Catholic on the throne of England and a move to a foreign-aided absolute government was imminent. Everything that had been fought for since 1640 would be irretrievably lost. The plot itself was convoluted, based on mendacious allegations, and designed to feed the latent fear of a Catholic takeover of the realm orchestrated by Louis XIV. One Titus Oates, a charlatan and con-artist, compulsive liar and attention-seeker, was at the heart of the plot. On 28 September 1678—some years after he had been sent down from Cambridge without a degree, accused of buggery on a naval vessel in Morocco, and received into the Catholic Church— Oates laid charges before the Privy Council of a popish plot to assassinate Charles II. Eighty-one people were accused, including James Coleman, secretary to the Duke of York's new Catholic wife, Mary of Modena. Quite by chance, Coleman was found to have in his possession letters that referred to a French triumph over England—the very thing the populace most feared. Oates continued to accuse people caught up in this conspiracy, under oath and in court. When the judge before whom he gave this evidence, Edmund Berry Godfrey, was found dead in a ditch at the bottom of Primrose Hill, anti-popish fever became hysterical. Twenty-four people were executed, and an astonishing 1,200 Catholics were prosecuted in London. One of the final victims of this plot was the Archbishop of Armagh, Oliver Plunkett, who was hung, drawn and quartered.

In response, Parliament passed a second Test Act, which extended the oath to all Catholics in the peerage, except James, Duke of York, barring them from office or from membership of the House of Lords. The poet Andrew Marvell, author of "To His Coy Mistress" and successor to Milton as Secretary of Foreign Tongues under Cromwell, wrote at this time, "for divers years a design has been carried on to change the lawful government of England into an absolute tyranny and convert the established Protestant religion into downright Popery".[3] In the end Oates was arrested and tried in James II's reign. He was imprisoned, heavily fined, and sentenced to public whipping through the streets of London on five days a year for the remainder of his life.

Suspicions generated by the Popish Plot produced a lasting political consequence. Lord Danby was arraigned for disbelieving the plot, rightly as it turned out, but such was public fear that he was forced to resign in 1679 and was later even accused of the murder of Judge Godfrey. In this frenzied atmosphere, the Earl of Shaftesbury came to the fore and urged Charles to exclude his brother, the Duke of York, from succeeding him on the grounds he was a confessed Catholic. In this way the Popish Plot morphed into the Exclusion Crisis, and the outlines of two political parties emerged: the Whigs and Tories. The leader of the Whigs was an intellectual Protestant who detested the thought of the return of Catholicism, Anthony Ashley Cooper, Earl of Shaftesbury. He had been a Parliamentarian during the Civil War. He now urged Charles II to divorce Catherine of Braganza, as no heir was forthcoming, and to exclude James, Duke of York, from the succession.

In the parliamentary elections of 1679, the Whigs coalesced as a party. They stood for a Protestant succession, the safety of the people (*salus populi*), and a contract theory of government between people and ruler, supported by the philosopher John Locke, who was also Shaftesbury's secretary. Whigs were widely supported by the merchant classes, Protestant landowners and dissenters. By contrast, the Tories were the party of the crown, the divine right of kings, and the Established Church. The two parties, born out of the Popish Plot and the Exclusion Crisis, would shape English politics for the next two centuries. For now, they met in London coffee houses, and planned their next moves in the country and Parliament.

Shaftesbury's attempt to exclude James, Duke of York, from the succession fell on the tin ear of Charles II. In the face of this campaign to exclude his brother, Charles discovered that he cared for legitimate succession to the crown more than anything else. He refused to countenance an exclusion bill introduced into the new Parliament of 1679, which itself lasted only months before being prorogued. Charles now starved the Whigs of any parliamentary air, reducing the temperature of their opposition. When a plot was discovered in 1683, this time led by some prominent Whigs, the boot was on the other foot. The plan had been to assassinate the King and the Duke of York on their return from Newmarket races at Rye House in Hertfordshire. The plot, now called the Rye House Plot, failed, but leading Whigs were implicated: Lord Russell and Algernon Sidney were executed, and Shaftesbury, though not directly implicated, was arrested for treason. A sympathetic jury would not return an indictment, however.

During these years Catholics faced increased hostility and abuse. When a moderate Tory pamphleteer, Roger L'Estrange, sought to get at the truth of the Popish Plot, he was swiftly condemned as a papist by fevered popular opinion. Pope burnings were revived, and recusancy fines against Catholics increased, as in Wiltshire in 1683. Likewise, fines for non-attendance at Anglican worship against dissenters rose after the Rye House Plot. In the whole of Lancashire, the value of recusancy fines for Catholics was £3,000 on estates with an annual national total figure of approximately £30,000. It was still expensive to be a Catholic. With the accession of James II, new dangers were to reach a critical point. Popular opinion, not least in the scientific and philosophical community, was deeply suspicious of what lay ahead and any tendency to either Catholicism or Absolutism.

Faith, science and reason

The Restoration period witnessed an explosion of literature, science and philosophy. Some of the greatest poets, scientists and thinkers in English history lived during this time; much of their work was part of the legacy of Puritanism, and the principles it laid down in thought and observation. The novelty of Puritanism, which in many respects underlay this movement in science and literature, lay in its deep sense of God as lawgiver, of the universe being therefore rational, such that through observation and empirical experiment it would yield its workings and laws. The desire to grasp God's purposes drove the Puritans to science and to history, and to reveal thereby the wisdom of God. Isaac Newton could not be described as a Puritan, although his science was underscored by a deeply theist outlook, while the spiritual writer Richard Baxter and the poet John Milton were examples of the best of Puritan literature.

John Milton had served the Commonwealth as Secretary of Foreign Tongues, using his ability in Latin to communicate the policies and propaganda of the government to the rulers of Europe. By 1657, and blind, he handed on this work to Andrew Marvell and others. His blindness precipitated one of his greatest sonnets, *When I Consider How My Light Is Spent,* with its famous and poignant last line, "They also serve who only stand and wait."[4] At the time of the Restoration, Milton was in danger of being tried for treason and hung, drawn and quartered for his support of the Commonwealth. He was briefly imprisoned, fined, and then moved to a cottage in Chalfont St Giles, Buckinghamshire, where he lived with his three daughters and third wife, Elizabeth. It was here, in great simplicity of life, that he dictated *Paradise Lost,* his lifetime's work that had been gestating in him since his youth. An epic in the style of Homer's *Iliad* and *Odyssey,* it chronicled the Fall of man through Satan's temptation of Adam and Eve. Satan is depicted as protean and fatally brilliant.

Divided into twelve books, *Paradise Lost* grapples with the rebellion of Satan, his fall to earth and the tempting of Adam and Eve. Each night Milton would compose the next section in his head, and then dictate it to one of his daughters the following day. John Aubrey, a contemporary who wrote *Brief Lives*, said of him: "He had a very good memory; but I believe that his excellent method of thinking and disposing did much to helpe his memorie."[5] *Paradise Regained* (which he was encouraged to write as an afterthought to *Paradise Lost*) was to follow, with *Samson Agonistes*, a tragedy focussed on Samson's life and blindness—with which Milton identified—and his final act of destruction of the Philistines. Extraordinary knowledge of the classics and proficiency in Hebrew, which he read every day in the Old Testament on waking at 4 a.m., as well as Latin and Greek, equipped him to be, after Shakespeare, the greatest of English poets.

A very different writer from the same Puritan stable was Richard Baxter (1615–91). In 1641, the Vicar of Kidderminster appointed Baxter preacher for £60 a year at St Mary's and All Saints, Kidderminster, where he remained for nearly twenty years. During the Civil War, he took opportunities to preach to the army and had some contact with Oliver Cromwell. He was a man of sensitive humanity, independent thought, great diligence and courage. Of a Puritan background, although not a strict Calvinist, he was able to see faults on both sides in the Civil War. He was not a party man. He refused to call the Pope the Anti-Christ, and guilelessly asked Cromwell what had been wrong with the monarchy.

Following the Civil War and during the Restoration Settlement, as defined by the repressive Clarendon Code, Baxter was willing to be classified a non-conformist. As such he could not be licensed to a parish and joined the large number of former clergy ejected from their parishes. He took part in the Savoy Conference as a leading figure of the non-conformist churches. He was not especially averse to the Church of England. He was willing to attend Prayer Book services and recognized the reformed nature of the Church's liturgy and articles. He simply wanted greater freedom to devise services and worship according to local desires. In fact, soon after the Restoration, he was offered the bishopric of Hereford, but was unable to accept. He believed strongly that churches should be grouped together in associations to provide stimulation and accountability. Yet for all his moderation, he was attacked for his independence, and was often hauled before magistrates for breaking the Conventicle Act by speaking to meetings of more than five adults. In 1685, when he was approaching seventy, Judge Jeffreys fined him and threw him into prison, in an extraordinary act of unwarranted judicial ineptitude.

Baxter is mostly remembered as author of over eighty books that he wrote in the long period after the Restoration. They are based largely upon his period as minister of Kidderminster, where he was supported by his wealthy wife, who had brought £1,650 to the marriage in her dowry. *The Reformed Pastor* remains a classic of ministry and is drawn from his practice of devoting seven hours a week to interviewing families about their spiritual lives. The nineteenth-century edition of his *Christian Directory* of teaching and pastoral practice runs into over twenty volumes. His book *The Saints' Everlasting Rest* is a luminous work on the contemplation of heaven. Perhaps the saying he loved to use most, which he borrowed from Peter Meiderlin, serves as a fitting epithet to his labours over the years: "Unity in all things necessary, liberty in all things unnecessary, and charity in all." He neither condemned the Pope, nor considered the Puritan Church the kingdom of God on earth. He simply sought by preaching, prayer and pastoral practice to establish salvation in ordinary people's hearts.

If Bunyan, Baxter and Milton were stars in the firmament of spiritual writing in England from 1660, there was also an explosion of research and discovery in mathematics, the natural and physical sciences, astronomy and philosophy.

For all his libertine lifestyle, the King had more than a passing interest in the developments of science. The Royal Society was founded on 28 November 1660, the brainchild of Robert Boyle and other natural philosophers who had already formed what was called the Invisible College, which met initially in Gresham's College in the City. By 1662, the society had royal patronage and a royal charter. John Evelyn, the diarist and polymath, was an early member, and diarist Samuel Pepys was proposed a member in 1665 by his Admiralty friend, Thomas Povey. The great scientist Robert Boyle (1627–91), son of the Earl of Cork, who discovered Boyle's Law, in which pressure multiplied by volume is a constant in an ideal gas, was also a member. He went on to found annual lectures confuting atheism with science to be delivered in a London church. His assistant at Oxford, Robert Hooke (1635–1703), became Curator of Experiments to the Royal Society. He demonstrated an air pump capable of creating a vacuum and showed the effects of air (or lack of it) on life, to fascinated royal visitors to the society. Flamstead, the royal astronomer, would be elected later, as would John Ray (1627–1705), the father of modern botany, who was elected to the society in 1667. Ray provided the first definition of species and, among many other works, wrote *The Wisdom of God Manifested in Works of Creation*. The three members on whom we shall especially focus, however, are Sir Christopher Wren, Sir Isaac Newton and John Locke. The scale of their work forever changed the way we perceive the world; and each of them worked within the framework of their faith, which varied considerably in understanding.

It is one of those mysteries of history that a man or woman of particular genius is often ready at the moment their gifts are most needed. It was just such a time when Christopher Wren (1632–1723), mathematician and geometrician turned architect, was at hand after the Great Fire of London in 1666. Within ten days of the fire Wren was ready with a scheme to redesign London, although his radical proposals were not taken up. Instead he had to content himself with redesigning St Paul's Cathedral in its present form, along with fifty-two other churches in the capital!

Wren's family was royalist in background. His father, also Christopher Wren, was a protégé of Lancelot Andrewes, the great brain behind the King James version of the Bible. Wren senior became Dean of Windsor and Chaplain to the Knights of the Garter. Wren junior's uncle Matthew Wren was Bishop of Ely, a Laudian churchman who was imprisoned during the Commonwealth. He later commissioned his nephew, Christopher, to design the chapel at Pembroke College, Cambridge. Wren junior was a mathematician by training and was elected to a Fellowship at All Souls, Oxford in 1653. It was his mathematics and astronomical work that gained him entrance to the Royal Society as a founder member. In 1661, he was elected Professor of Astronomy at Oxford. Until 1668, Wren was based in Oxford, but in 1669 he was appointed Surveyor General of the King's Works. From this period the plethora of buildings designed by his office began: Pembroke College, the Sheldonian at Oxford, Tom Tower at Christ Church, Oxford, the City churches, St Paul's Cathedral, repairs to Salisbury Cathedral, Trinity College Library, Cambridge, Emmanuel College, Cambridge, the Royal Hospital at Greenwich, the Royal Military Hospital Chelsea, new state rooms at Windsor Castle, the south front of Hampton Court, the east front of Kensington Palace, and Windsor Guildhall. Virtually no part of London, royal, military or civic, and neither university, was untouched by his designs.

Wren's achievement was awesome by any standard, but it was all the more extraordinary since it coincided with a time of great political turbulence. Nevertheless, it was this turbulence that gave him the opportunity to re-craft in built form the aspirations of the nation at the time of the Restoration. The Great Fire of London extended this project further. Just as Vermeer in Holland used light and perspective to give new definition to the values of Dutch life, so Wren through his buildings gave light and vistas to the hopes of the new era. His work was continued well beyond his own efforts by his talented colleague Sir John Vanbrugh, an architect and dramatist.

Another member of the Royal Society who was to alter, not the constructed landscape of England, but the view that people would take of the universe and its laws, was Isaac Newton. Born on Christmas Day in 1642, in his early years he witnessed the horror of the Civil War. His father was a yeoman farmer who inherited a fine property at Woolsthorpe in Lincolnshire.[6] His father died three months before Newton's birth and his stepfather was an ageing rector of a Lincolnshire parish. Newton disliked his stepfather and resented his mother's remarriage. Mostly looked after by his maternal grandmother, he was schooled at Grantham Grammar School and then at Trinity, Cambridge, where his maternal uncle had studied. Absorbed with making mechanical devices, he was nevertheless a deeply unhappy child. Throughout his life he would be given to fits of anger and defensiveness, no doubt born of his childhood experience of loss and parental absence. But contrariwise, his mistrust of others created room for long periods of study and thought, the breeding ground for his mathematical and inventive genius. He was brought up in a religious setting, as was customary in the period for one of his background, which gave him an acute sense of right and wrong, of guilt, and a sense that God was a distant deity with whom it was difficult to form a loving friendship. His peculiar faith would be a powerful force throughout his life, as we shall see.

Newton's time at Trinity College, Cambridge began in 1661. John Pearson, the author of the influential *Exposition of the Creed*, was Master at the time. Although Newton followed the standard course of study prescribed for an undergraduate, with the usual helpings of theological and Aristotelian literature, his interest in mathematics may have been sparked by the lectures of the Lucasian Professor of Mathematics, Isaac Barrow. It was an exhilarating time for astronomy and mathematics, stimulated by the discoveries of Kepler, Galileo and Copernicus. These scientists had demonstrated the heliocentric nature (sun-centredness) of our solar system, and the trajectory of the planets, which are controlled by mathematical laws expressed in geometric equations (e.g. Kepler's Third Law). At the same time Newton was reading Descartes' *Géometrie*. It was also a stimulating time to be a student. Perhaps it was at this time, around 1665, that the fall of an apple provoked Newton to reflect on whether laws of motion on earth corresponded to laws of motion in the heavens, and that a similar force controlled motion in both. In his notebooks of this period, he recorded over a hundred axioms of motion.

Newton's work on calculus, optics, light, refraction and the existence of ether as a basis for life continued, and in 1669 he was offered the Lucasian Chair of Mathematics at Cambridge. This presented a challenge to Newton's faith. Normally, he would be called on to be ordained at this point in his teaching career and swear his agreement to the doctrine of the Church of England. He demurred, however, partly on grounds of needing more time for research, but more especially because of his reluctance to agree to the doctrine of the Trinity. Newton's understanding of Christianity was not orthodox. He was a deist: he believed God was the Creator but did not hold to belief in the Trinity. At some point he became a radical anti-Trinitarian. His studies of the Church Fathers, which were extensive, led him to think the doctrine of the Trinity was a human invention. From then on, he would hide his religious opinions from others. This did not mean he sidestepped the Bible; he simply interpreted it in his own way. He saw the Book of Revelation as the story of the judgement of God on a corrupt Roman Catholic Church. This judgement was heralded by the trumpets of Revelation, which began as far back as the Vandals' assault on the Roman Empire in the fourth century, continued until the Reformation, and included the Turkish Empire and the Saracens purifying the Church. Indeed, even as Newton was putting his finishing touches to his great *Principia*, he was writing about how Revelation foretold the judgement on the Catholic Church.

In doctrinal terms, Newton was a latter-day Arian (i.e. he did not believe in the full divinity of Christ as consubstantial with the Father and the Spirit). Rather, Newton believed that Christ was himself a created being, not pre-existent to his incarnation or divine, but adopted as a model of humanity to carry divine power and purpose in God's plan for his creation. Newton was not incredulous, however; he believed other things we would find hard to countenance. He sought the chemical or the process that would turn other substances to gold (alchemy). He believed in the reality of souls, both in people as well as in things (like Plato and Origen). He drew a connection between memory and the existence of the soul.[7] Equally, he saw imagination as a faculty of the soul capable of being spoilt by gluttony, drunkenness or "dizzinesse" brought on by too much meditation.

For all his forays into philosophical and theological speculation, Newton's great work and the fruit of years of study was the *Principia Mathematica*, published in 1687 and presented to the Royal Society. Although it became a byword for impenetrability, it offered the stunning conclusion "that each and every massive body in the universe attracted every other body".[8] This was Newton's inverse square law of universal gravitation. It marked the beginning of modern science, to be superseded only by Einstein's Law of Relativity, more than two hundred years later.

The third great contributor to human thought during this period was the philosopher John Locke (1632–1704). Like Newton he was to combine public office with natural philosophy. Locke became Warden of the Mint in 1696 and, to alleviate the corruption of the coinage, he recommended paper money supported by the newly created Bank of England (1694). Locke was secretary to the mercurial and important politician Lord Shaftesbury, the founder of the Whig party, a Parliamentarian in the Civil War, the political opponent of Danby, and the one, more than any other, who sought to exclude James II from succeeding to the crown.

Locke was born in Wrington, Somerset in 1632 into a Puritan family.[9] Although his Puritan background provided an anchor and perspective for the whole of his life, it was more a platform from which to spring than a room to explore. His father was clerk to the justices of the peace in Somerset, but through his good connections, Locke was able to go to Westminster School and then Christ Church, Oxford. Whilst at Oxford he met and fraternized with Boyle, Hooke and a medical researcher named Sydenham. Locke adopted Sydenham's dictum that "knowledge grew first in the world by experience and rational observation" and from that laid down maxims that operate in nature. This was the very basis of scientific method: observation, experience, deductive reasoning and the formulation of laws. At the same time Locke was deeply influenced by René Descartes (1596–1650) and Pierre Gassendi (1592–1655). From Descartes he learnt to reduce things to their most basic principles, to strip away the accretions of custom and mere tradition, and in particular to search for fundamental truths and describe the knowledge of which humanity was capable.

Broadly speaking, there are three main areas of work for which Locke is well known: his work on government, most thoroughly expressed in his *Two Treatises of Government*, his *Letter on Toleration* and his *Essay concerning Human Understanding*. The most fundamental of the three is perhaps the last, for this *Essay* is concerned with our understanding of knowledge and of ourselves. In a letter to his friend, William Molyneux, justifying his research and labours, Locke writes, "I am convinced on the contrary: I know there is a truth opposite to falsehood, that it may be found if people will, and it is worth the seeking, and is not only the most valuable, but the pleasantest thing in the world."[10] Locke held there are three types of knowledge: intuitive, demonstrative and sensitive. Knowledge of our existence is intuitive, or as Descartes said, "I think therefore I am." Mathematical truth is demonstrative and, for Locke, the most important truth to know is the knowledge of God. This can come through revelation arising from the life of Christ and teaching about him, as he explains in a later work, *The Reasonableness of Christianity*. In fact, Jesus himself proclaimed the law of faith, demanding obedience and promising salvation in return. This revelation comes through trust: faith is a form of trust; it is beyond reason but is not against reason. In turn, this trust will be demonstrated in morality. If this thinking would later be questioned during the Enlightenment, so would his theory of knowledge coming through the senses, and whether what is observed and described with our words in fact corresponds to what is there. Locke did not doubt the validity of sense experience on which our experience of pleasure or pain is grounded. Philosophers since have nevertheless questioned whether our ideas of reality match the true reality of those things; for "to deal effectively with nature does not demand knowledge, it merely demands skilful guessing".[11] For Locke, however, it was a matter of reason and trust.

If what was novel about Locke was his willingness to argue for truth on the basis of our capacity to know, rather than accept tradition or some internal inscription of truth—"thus using the candle of reason"—his writing on both government and toleration was ground-breaking. His work on the philosophy of government was all of a piece with the times. He had grown up in the Civil War. He had been a young man, aged thirty, at the time of the Restoration and then worked for Shaftesbury, the leading politician of the age, to exclude the Catholic Duke of York (the future James II). Together with Shaftesbury, between the years 1667 and 1683 Locke faced the realities of political life. After the Rye House Plot affected the careers of some Whigs, Shaftesbury went into exile and soon died. Locke fled in the summer of 1683, having written the *Two Treatises on Government*. As far as the government was concerned, it was a seditious work.

At the nub of the *Two Treatises* is the notion that governments rule by a contract with the people. It is not a question of the divine right to government of a particular monarchy, but government, whoever it is, having been contracted by the people to govern. Not only that, but the government, as his *Letter on Toleration* argues, must respect the rights of people to worship as they choose. To do otherwise is "blasphemously presumptuous". Of course, he was opposed by the crown and by inveterate Anglicans like Edward Stillingfleet, the Bishop of Worcester, a powerful advocate of religious intolerance (or rather of Anglicans having the field to themselves on the grounds of security). Although Locke did not quite extend his concept of toleration to Catholics because of their misapprehensions, his principle was that religious freedom meant freedom to be religious in one's own way. After all, each individual is responsible for his own salvation. The movement that Locke began was connected to the view that religious worship was a matter of an individual's choice and conscience, not government diktat. Locke also realized, on the other side of the argument, that government must rule in such a way as to prevent anarchy. The reconciliation of these at times conflicting principles of freedom and control was not fully answered by Locke, and for that matter they are a moving target for all governments and societies. Yet Locke nevertheless argued that toleration by inclusivity was more likely to create peace.

The *Two Treatises* is rendered as answer to a royalist philosopher, Sir Robert Filmer, who was the devout equivalent of Thomas Hobbes, and who argued for the divine right of authority, which could in no circumstances be overthrown. It was not a human contract between two parties, but a divine appointment. For his part, Locke proposed that there were rights and duties: the right of the ruler to exact obedience is circumscribed by the worthiness of his rule, and the duty of the subject to obey is circumscribed by the justness of the ruler. Indeed, by being or becoming a citizen of a state, tacit consent is given to the contract of government already existing in that society, and that relationship is undergirded by trust. Furthermore, the subjects' rights to property are the reward of ownership for labour, and that right is inalienable as it is granted by God, except it be abused by crime. Locke stressed the individual's right to life or a fair trial if accused, to holding property as a reward for labour, to a pension accrued from labour when younger, and also to resisting unjust political authorities or slavery. In so saying, Locke was opening the door to Western political theory from then on. His views would be taken further by Thomas Paine and by Jean-Jacques Rousseau and the Enlightenment thinkers, but in their cases without Locke's undergirding of Christianity. In a matter of years, with the threat of James II's tendency to absolutism and his lack of toleration, Locke's theory of rights and duties, toleration and contract would be put to a very real and practical test.

The last Catholic monarch and the Glorious Revolution

The final years of Charles II's reign, until the accession of James II in 1685, were marked by increasing signs of James's influence as his brother's health failed. The Whig-inspired Rye House Plot of 1683 had marked the high tide of Whig influence. Charles II had by then secured the succession of his brother James, seeing off the Exclusion Crisis orchestrated by Shaftesbury, who had gone into exile. James sought to strengthen the court party or Tories in Parliament by a reissuing of warrants to corporations, giving them the right to nominate Members of Parliament.[12] Likewise, the American colonies, New York and New Jersey, were taken from the Dutch and the power of the crown rolled out.

Charles II died of apoplexy, after converting to Catholicism on his deathbed. His reign had been marked by the restoration of the Church of England, the emergence of parliamentary parties, Whig and Tory, the repression of the dissenters, a court renowned for licentiousness, and an unshakeable resolve to maintain the Stuart succession at all costs. When James came to the throne, he was warmly greeted with high hopes, but in little more than three years he was forced to flee and was succeeded by his eldest daughter, Mary, and her Protestant, campaigning husband,

William of Orange. James's nemesis was his stubborn desire to return England to the Catholic faith and rule, not through Parliament, but with the royal prerogative. This choice took England to the brink of another civil war.

From the outset, James was able to garner popular support because of the attempt by the Protestant Duke of Monmouth to invade England to depose him. Monmouth, who was Charles II's eldest illegitimate child, landed with a motley crew of officers and men at Lyme Regis, where he gathered thousands more from the West Country. After marching around Somerset, his force was soon defeated at Sedgemoor and the rebels were subsequently brutally punished by Judge Jeffreys, James's cynical and cruel enforcer. Jeffreys had 300 rebels executed and around 700 deported to the West Indies as slaves or indentured labour. The military commander who had defeated Monmouth was John Churchill, later to be the Duke of Marlborough, the victor of Blenheim and husband of Sarah Churchill, the favourite of Queen Anne.

James's plan to rehabilitate the Catholic Church and accrue greater power to himself was not slow in coming. He had been a Catholic secretly since 1668, and openly since 1678, at which point he no longer attended Anglican worship. At his first Parliament, James made moves to establish a standing army, waive the Test Act so that Catholics might hold military commissions, and repeal the Acts designed to repress both dissenting congregations and Roman Catholicism. Parliament firmly expressed its unwillingness to cooperate and the beginnings of a crisis took shape. James prorogued Parliament, which would never meet again in his reign, and sought to further his aims by royal prerogative.

James's policy of religious toleration had a single purpose: the return of England to Catholicism. He used a royal power called "a dispensing power", whereby, in certain circumstances, he could abrogate laws in pursuance of royal policy. James now used this prerogative to issue a Declaration of Indulgence. The Declaration had the effect of enabling Roman Catholics to be appointed by royal patronage and absolved of penalties for recusancy (not attending Anglican worship).

James insisted that his Declaration of Indulgence be read from every pulpit in the land. However, neither the clergy nor the Bench of Bishops were minded to comply and they decided not to obey the royal order. They based their decision on the legal entitlement of the King to so act, rather than any objection to the content of the Declaration. The principal bishops, including the pious and gentle Archbishop Sancroft, instigator of the new St Paul's Cathedral, were brought before the Council, and called to appear before the Court of the King's Bench on the charge of seditious libel (for publishing their refusal to read the Declaration). In the meantime, they were sent to the Tower. As the bishops were taken in a boat downstream to the Tower, people thronged the banks in support.

On 29 June 1688, the bishops were acquitted after the jury considered their verdict for ten hours. Five months later, James was, in practice, no longer King. On 11 December, he fled London by boat at the news of the success of Prince William of Orange's approach, pathetically throwing his Great Seal of Office into the Thames. Even in the seventeenth century, six months was a long time in politics. No amount of rowing back from his policies in the intervening months could save James. A revolution had been set in motion that could not be halted.

The truth was that both Whig and Tory had been alienated by James: the Tories by James's betrayal of the Church of England and his circumvention of the Test Acts, and the Whigs, although welcoming toleration towards dissenters, through their fear of an absolute Catholic monarchy in the style of Louis XIV. The crisis was made more pressing by the birth on 10 June 1688 to James and his second wife, Mary of Modena, of a son, James, who became the Catholic heir to the throne. In the heated political atmosphere of the day, some people thought that the baby had been smuggled into his mother's bed in a bedpan, but he was a genuine son and heir and became the Jacobite Old Pretender. As a result, an invitation to take the throne was made on 30 June by seven senior politicians to William of Orange and to Mary Stuart, the oldest daughter of James's first marriage. Among them was the Bishop of London, Henry Compton. William saw his opportunity not simply to take the English throne with Mary, but to procure considerable resources to pursue the defence of Holland against Louis XIV's incursions.

Within months William had assembled an invasion force of some size: 20,000 soldiers, 5,000 horses and 500 vessels. It was the largest invasion of England since Julius Caesar's second invasion of Britain in 54 BC.[13] When William finally set sail, he was blessed with a "Protestant Wind" like the one that dispersed the Spanish Armada, and which drove him westwards down the Channel to Devon. He disembarked at Brixham, an arrival point totally unexpected by James, and on the propitious Protestant date of 5 November! Faced by the forces William had assembled, but more especially by the sense of welcome for William's arrival, James, despite leading forces of at least 25,000, completely lost his nerve. Two of James's commanders, John Churchill, later Duke of Marlborough, and the Duke of Grafton (another illegitimate son of Charles II) went over to William, and James fled to France, where he was welcomed by Louis XIV, thereby sparing England another civil war.

After some preliminary negotiations with William, a Convention Parliament was called. It dealt swiftly with the constitutional issues that confronted the nation. Archbishop Sancroft and several of the bishops, amazingly despite their recent experiences, followed a doctrine of non-resistance, indefeasible hereditary succession and the rule of law and sought the restoration of James II. Others sought a regency while James lived, while still others argued that by fleeing James had abdicated and that Mary, the blood relative of James, should be crowned Queen. William insisted that he should be jointly crowned with Mary, however. The formulation of James's flight as abdication and therefore creating a vacancy into which William and Mary stepped won the day and Mary, ever the faithful wife, agreed to William's joint coronation.

William and Mary were crowned on the basis of the Whigian notion of contract, given expression by John Locke, although it took time to establish their rule. Some of the bishops led by Sancroft refused on principle to swear an oath of allegiance to William and Mary, having done so previously to James. They became known as the "non-juror" bishops. They were relieved of their offices and served out their days quietly. Bishop Ken of Bath and Wells, a most saintly man, who at Winchester had refused accommodation to Nell Gwyn, one of Charles II's most famous mistresses, now lived out his days at Longleat, writing and encouraging Lord Bath in philanthropic projects.

When the deposed James sought to retake his throne the following year by bringing an army to Ireland that was resourced by Louis XIV and the French, William went over to Ireland to fight him and, having lifted the siege of Londonderry (which gave Northern Ireland the iconic slogan of "No Surrender"), defeated James close to Dublin at the Boyne. The poorly trained, ill-equipped, diffuse Jacobite army was no match for William's well-schooled regulars, jointly commanded by William and the Duke of Schomberg. The convincing victory won by William has forever after been a rallying point for the Orange Orders and Protestants of Northern Ireland.

William III and Mary II were to reign uniquely as joint monarchs of England, Ireland and Scotland (with the usual claim to the French throne kept as a "formality"). William was single-minded in his pursuit of Dutch interests, and England was drawn remorselessly into the campaign against the French that became known as the Nine Years' War. He firmly supported the Act of Toleration of May 1689, which followed the Bill of Rights, and which granted freedom of worship to dissenters, permitting their congregations to worship wherever a local Anglican bishop licensed them to do so. In fact, William's toleration was further demonstrated by his attempt to obtain generous surrender terms for the combatant Catholics in Ireland, although he was frustrated in this by the Protestant Parliament in Dublin. The only downsides to William's rule were his rather prosaic court; his plain and reserved style; his favouring of Dutch comrades, such as Willem Bentinck (later made the Duke of Portland) and the handsome Joost Van Keppel; his earlier affair with the squinting Elizabeth Villiers and his neglect of Mary. But ironically, when Mary died of smallpox in 1694, no one was more distraught and broken than William himself.

Mary, the eldest daughter of James II and Anne Hyde, had been married to William at the age of fifteen. She never had an heir. She was a High Anglican devoted to the Church of England in its more ceremonial style. She loved music, especially the composer Purcell, glittering occasions and fun. She was plainly spoken and enjoyed collecting porcelain and knitting. She was involved in extending Hampton Court and building Greenwich Naval Hospital with the help of Wren. This unpretentious queen with simple tastes was greatly loved by the people and when she died, after only five years' reign, the mourning was great and heartfelt. John Evelyn wrote, "never was there so universal mourning." Together with William, Mary's philanthropy and compassion were especially noticeable in the £39,000 given from the Civil List to the Huguenots between 1689 and 1693. After the repeal of the Edict of Nantes by Louis XIV, the Huguenots had arrived in England in great numbers, many as destitute refugees.

The Huguenots

On 22 October 1685, Louis XIV repealed the Edict of Nantes. The edict granted by Henry IV in 1598 had given security to the French Protestants, called Huguenots, at the end of the religious wars in France, which had been so violent and had culminated in the Massacre of St Bartholomew's Day in 1572. The repeal of the edict, and the new persecution of Huguenots in France by Louis XIV's regime, precipitated a mass exodus of Huguenots to Germany, the Low Countries and England. The new nationalist Gallican church, led by Bossuet, Bishop of Meaux, saw Louis XIV as a new Theodosius eradicating heresy. French military called *dragonnades* were often used to clear Huguenots from the towns and villages of France. It is estimated that 200,000 Huguenots left France after the Revocation.

French Protestants had been coming in numbers to England since the reign of Edward VI, and congregations of French could be found in London, Canterbury, Norwich, Bristol and even Glastonbury for a time. Others came in Elizabeth's reign. Support for Huguenots during Charles I's reign often misfired, as in the Duke of Buckingham's disastrous campaign to relieve the Huguenot citizens of La Rochelle in 1628. Following the Revocation in 1685, some 50,000 Huguenots, many destitute, arrived in England. Out of a population of nearly six million, they represented nearly one per cent, and were mostly concentrated in the south-east and south-west of England. They came to practise their faith freely, to use their varied skills and to make permanent homes. They were first and foremost refugees. Many were prevented from leaving France and severely punished if caught. There were stories of great suffering and courage. They represented the largest wave of immigration into England since the Conquest and would remain so until the Irish and the Jewish immigrations from Russia in the nineteenth century.

The Huguenots were given a mixed reception by the English. As co-religionists in an established Protestant state, they were welcomed, but they hardly wanted to fit into the structures of the Church of England. For the most part they established their own congregations in London. Huguenot congregations, like the wider church in England, divided into conformists, who used a French translation of the Prayer Book and similar ceremonies as the Anglican Church, and non-conformists, who were like the dissenting English churches. During Charles I's reign, many of the London congregations, as in the case of the nine Spitalfields churches, had been non-conformist. Others, like the earlier Savoy Church, followed Anglican lines. Huguenot non-conforming churches would often have long sermons of at least an hour, which Pepys reported as being tedious—how readily he understood we are not told—and they did not observe the ceremonies of the Church of England when it came to dress and liturgy. But in Bishop Henry Compton of London (bishop from 1675 to 1713), the Huguenots found a supporter and advocate.

Compton had strong Protestant credentials, being one of the "immortals" who had invited William and Mary to replace James II. He was more than willing to license and permit Huguenot congregations in his diocese. He sought to persuade fellow bishops and towns to do the same. In 1682, he raised £6,684 17s 8d for their welfare through voluntary giving, with King Charles II's encouragement. There were prejudices and fears to overcome: religiously because some Huguenots did strange things like speaking in tongues (not just in French!) or claiming to be prophets; and, more generally, because many Huguenots were talented craftsmen whose skills threatened, or seemed to threaten, the livelihoods of the indigenous English.

One of the unique characteristics of the Huguenots, besides their faith and perseverance in great difficulties, was their skilfulness. These skills were allied to qualities of hard work, thrift and business acumen. Add these things together and the Huguenots presented a powerful economic force in England just at a time when the nation's economic fortunes were about to burgeon. They brought with them great expertise in almost all the higher-value crafts: silk weaving; clothing and textile manufacturing (e.g. the Courtauld family); fashionable draperies and "worsted" made in Norwich; stocking making (which would employ 100,000 people part-time); calico printing; banking (contributing to the newly founded Bank of England); gold and silversmithing; glass making; paper making (e.g the Portals); furniture and cabinet making; and printing. They contributed also to the arts: on the stage, David Garrick; on canvas, Adrien Carpentiers; and in sculpture, Louis Francois Roubillac. There was hardly a trade or profession untouched by their presence, and great fortunes would be made. Not only did the Huguenots flourish in these and other trades and professions, they also flourished in the military like Ligonier, fighting their old enemy, Louis XIV, only now serving under Queen Anne's great military commander, John Churchill, the Duke of Marlborough. Indeed, one Huguenot, Field Marshal Lord Ligonier, would come to command British forces in the Seven Years' War.

The last Stuart monarch: Queen Anne

After the death of Queen Mary II from smallpox in 1694, William ruled until 8 March 1702, whereupon Anne succeeded. Anne was Mary's younger sister, likewise the daughter of James II's first marriage to Anne Hyde. In 1683, at the age of eighteen, Anne married George of Denmark, a Protestant prince and cousin. Almost yearly pregnancies until 1702 produced no surviving heir.[14] It is thought that Anne had seventeen pregnancies, which resulted either in miscarriages, stillbirths or early deaths. By the time of her accession, her childbearing days were over, although she was only thirty-seven.

In some ways, the pattern of her reign was laid down early on. A number of issues faced her, including the continual fear of a Jacobite conspiracy on behalf of her half-brother, the Old Pretender, James Edward Stuart, who was fourteen years old at her coronation (her father, James II, having died in 1701). The war with France and Louis XIV flared up once again on the occasion of the Spanish succession, and there was need to prevent France claiming the Spanish crown and all its dependencies for itself, thereby making itself an almost unassailable power in Europe. English foreign policy as usual sought to prevent a dominant power on the continent, so, at great cost to England, the army, led by John Churchill, now Earl of Marlborough, sought to prevent French control of northern Europe. The war, called the War of the Spanish Succession, yielded great victories to the English armies with their Dutch and Prussian allies under Marlborough's command, especially at Blenheim on the Danube in 1704.

Anne was a staunch defender of the Anglican Church and its interests and had little regard for the toleration granted by William III. She was not afraid to intervene in ecclesiastical appointments, as she did in 1707 in the Bishopric Crisis, where she made appointments of which the Whigs did not approve. She also established a fund in 1704 called Queen Anne's Bounty, taken from her royal revenues, to support poorer clergy and Anglican ministry in general, which was administered by the Church Commissioners. Moreover, Anne gave support to the High Church Tories led by Harley and Henry St John, Viscount Bolingbroke, who refused to allow "Occasional Conformity", a means whereby Roman Catholics and dissenters could, by "Occasional Conformity" or attendance at a Church of England eucharist, obtain the right to hold public office, despite the Test and Corporation Acts. The Whigs had supported the scheme of "Occasional Conformity" in Parliament, but by 1711 the Tories succeeded in their design to prevent the concession of "Occasional Conformity" by passing the Occasional Conformity and Schism Acts, which closed down all dissenting schools and forced all future dissenting teachers to obtain a licence from the local diocesan bishop. This, as it turned out temporary, victory for High Church Tories had been in part fuelled by a church campaign with the slogan "Church in danger".

Two eccentric but influential figures were responsible for this campaign and the sense of crisis that it engendered. They were Henry Sacheverell and Francis Atterbury. Sacheverell, a Fellow of Magdalen College, Oxford, preached an incendiary sermon at St Paul's in 1709, full of half concealed insults aimed at the bishops and Whig ministers who had placed the Church in danger. He went on to preach that no subject had the right to resist a monarch and by so doing he brought into question the whole principle of the Glorious Revolution and the removal of James II. The response of the government under the Whig-leaning Godolphin was to call for Sacheverell's impeachment. This gave Sacheverell the best publicity he could have wished for. He was put on trial in Westminster Hall with capacity seating and a royal box: it was the biggest show in town. A young man in his thirties, Sacheverell was popular with the ladies, and they brought their cold chicken along to picnic on and watch the proceedings. Before the Lord Chancellor and twelve judges, Sacheverell arrived "like an ambassador making his entry, rather than like a criminal conducted to his trial".[15] The London mob supported Sacheverell. Robert Walpole was counsel for the prosecution, and after ten days' consideration the Peers gave their decision against Sacheverell, but with a majority of only seventeen. It was a Pyrrhic victory for the Whigs. Another soon-to-be-Jacobite clergyman, Francis Atterbury, a high Tory friend of Lord Bolingbroke, whipped up hysteria over the Church with his pamphlet campaign in the city. He supported the clergy and Lower House of Convocation against the bishops. For it was the bishops who had shielded the low church and dissenters and betrayed the principles of the Church of England.[16] For a time the High Church Tories had their day.

As Anne's reign drew to a close, the Treaty of Utrecht with the French concluded the War of Spanish Succession. This treaty consolidated English overseas gains, and gave England virtual governance of the seas, including the strategic port of Gibraltar. On hearing that James III, the Old Pretender, would remain a Catholic, Harley stuck to the Act of Succession of 1701, making the Electress Sophia of Hanover and her children heirs to the triple throne of England, Scotland and Ireland. Sophia died in May 1714 just before Queen Anne's death, and her son Prince George of Hanover became the first Hanoverian King of England. He could speak no English.

PART V

The Church in the Hanoverian Age 1714–1901

CHAPTER 16

Expansion, Enthusiasm and Loss

The Hanoverian Age began in 1714 with the accession of George I, aged fifty-four. The following year the attempt by the Old Pretender, James Stuart, to retake the crown failed, petering out in Scotland.[1] A Whig government was returned to power following the elections of 1715. The Whigs would remain the governing party for nearly half a century; they successfully branded the Tories closet Jacobites and therefore not to be trusted. Since the Whigs were supremely the party of the Protestant Succession, it is no surprise that George I would find them the more congenial. Sir Robert Walpole and Lords Townshend, Stanhope and Sunderland led the government. Walpole had emerged as the effective Prime Minister by 1721 and remained as such until 1742, when he was succeeded by what was called the "Broad Bottom Ministry" of Henry Pelham. The years of Walpole's ministry were dubbed by the satirists as the years of "Robinocracy" (Robin being the pet name for Robert Walpole). The final years of Tory government led by Robert Harley, the Earl of Oxford, and Henry St John, Lord Bolingbroke at the end of Queen Anne's reign were now well and truly eclipsed. Some Tories, dispossessed of influence by a once-again triumphant Whig party, continued to look across the water to the Jacobite James III, ensconced at St Germain by Louis XIV, who would himself die soon in 1715. The general landscape of Christian England was settled in broad outline in 1715 and was to last until the middle of the century and the birth of Methodism.

The period of the Tudors and Stuarts had seen a revolution in English Christianity. Medieval religion had been replaced, a process hastened by the theology of the Reformation; the advent of the printing press; knowledge of biblical languages; and a political desire for an autonomous or self-governing church in England, without interference from the papacy. The Roman Catholic Church in England had become a rump, restricted to a few landed families and their retainers, to continental embassies in London, and to particular regions like

Lancashire, north Norfolk and Somerset. The Commonwealth under Cromwell had seen the proliferation of Protestant churches of various hues: Independents, Baptists, Quakers, Presbyterians and Congregationalists, and these had become known collectively as the Dissenters. They were persecuted along with the Catholics after the Restoration of Monarchy in 1660 and the strengthening of the Church of England by the so-called Clarendon Code. The need to prevent James II from returning England to Catholicism had led to William and Mary's invitation to take the throne, a decision underpinned by John Locke's new political theory of a contract between governors and governed. This contract was expressed in the Bill of Rights.

At the centre of the religious settlement of the times was the Church of England, established by law and furnished with its credentials by the Tudor state in the form of the Book of Common Prayer, the Authorized Version of the Bible (largely based on the translation by Tyndale, but authorized by King James I) and the Thirty-Nine Articles. The Church of England was a hybrid church, having the inner convictions of Protestantism, but some of the outer ceremonies of Catholicism, although its ritual was much reduced. It refused, for example, any semblance of the mass. It was a church reinvented at the Restoration to support the authority of the monarchy and was equally fearful of popery and Puritanism.

By the end of Queen Anne's reign, the churches were gaining a more settled existence, even if Dissenters and Catholics still had the status of second-class religious citizens or worse. Under the Toleration Act of 1689, Dissenters could be licensed to worship in their own chapels, however. In general, the elite classes tended to support the Established Church, while some of the middle classes and labourers supported the Dissenting Church, especially in the market towns and in London. There would be occasional extreme reactions to Catholicism, as in the Gordon Riots of 1780 and during the Jacobite rebellions. Dissenters continued to be prevented from taking public office until the Occasional Conformity Act (which prevented Dissenters from holding public office by *occasionally attending* Anglican worship) was reversed, as it quickly would be by the Whigs under George I.

The Church of England was not, and would not be, however, a uniform community. The events of the Restoration and the Glorious Revolution, together with the internal contradictions of Protestant theology and Catholic ceremony, would result in a fragmented institution. Furthermore, the advent of Deism, or anti-Trinitarian doctrine, under the scientific advances of the period, as personified in Isaac Newton, meant that a third strain of "rationalism unbounded" or latitudinarianism sheltered in a church founded on scripture, tradition and reason. As the eighteenth century went on this latitudinarianism would find many supporters. Unitarianism would be the eventual product of this intellectual movement, but within the Church of England there would be many who put reason first, above tradition and scripture. And as academics needed to be part of the Church of England to hold office, they were in no hurry to leave unless especially conscientious.

Each of these streams reflected a foundational value of the Church of England, as defined by Hooker: the Low Church held to scripture and the Articles of Religion, the High Church held to tradition and the latitudinarians held to reason, yet they all sought to be part of one church community as they jostled each other for supremacy. Thus Sacheverell, the High Church preacher of passive obedience to the divine right of kings, defined the characteristics of the high churchman as follows:

> He is high for the divine right of Episcopacy, High for the uninterrupted Succession, High for Liturgies against extempore prayers, High for the primitive Doctrine and Discipline of the Ancient Church. He believes separation from the Church of England to be a damning Schism, and Dissenters to be in a very dangerous state, notwithstanding the toleration. He always bows very low before the Altar and at the name of Jesus.[2]

Leadership of these different emphases in the Church came from its different parts. Whereas in the reigns of William and Mary and Anne, the High Church leaders were found among the clergy, many Low Church leaders were to be found among the bishops, such as Bishop Compton of London, Archbishop Tenison and Bishop Burnet. They had strong Whig connections, and had firmly supported the Act of Succession. They recognized that no Catholic could be a monarch of England, and that freedom from tyranny and quiet possession of property depended on a Protestant succession contracted by Parliament.

For all its internal contradictions and external pressures, at the start of the eighteenth century the Church of England exhibited two important features: a new kind of social confidence and, in places, an outward-looking sense of mission. For good or ill, the Established Church took its place in the fabric of rural life in the nation, in its villages and market towns, supported by the Tory squirearchy. It would be a different story in the emerging towns of the Industrial Revolution towards the end of the century. It was Dean Swift, one of the great satirists of the age, along with John Gay, Alexander Pope and Daniel Defoe, who, with characteristic humour, put his finger on an emerging pattern of pastoral presence in the villages of England, both beneficial and bucolic. Swift, an Anglican clergyman and Dean of St Patrick's Cathedral in Dublin, was from a royalist background and criticized the exploitation of man in his satire *Gulliver's Travels* of 1727, and most notably the exploitation of the Irish. From a dissenting background, Defoe saw his famous character Robinson Crusoe as the epitome of an imperial voyager bringing civilization to an unexplored island and its inhabitant, Friday. Swift's piece quoted here reflects a social pecking order of squire and rector in the village. This rural relationship was to last 200 years, until the First World War. In his *Country Parson*, Swift writes:

> Parson, these things are in thy possessing
> Are better than the bishop's blessing.
> A wife that makes conserves; a steed
> That carries double when there's need;
> October store and best Virginia,
> Tythe pig and mortuary guinea;
> Gazettes sent 'gratis' down and franked,
> For which the patron's weekly thanked;
> A large concordance bound long since;
> Sermons to Charles the First, when Prince;
> A chronicle of ancient standing;
> A Chrysostom to smooth thy band in.[3]
> He that has these, may pass his life,
> Drink with the squire, and kiss his wife;
> On Sundays preach, and eat his fill;
> And fast on Fridays—if he will;
> Toast Church and Queen, explain the news;
> Talk with churchwardens about the pews;
> Pray heartily for some new gift,
> And shake his head at Doctor Swift.[4]

If this mild satire of Anglican rural ministry conveys a sense of the settled hierarchy of the eighteenth-century village after all the turbulence of the previous hundred years or more, it was accompanied elsewhere in the wider church with a sense of mission. Bucolic Church of England ministry providing a type of settled and conservative cohesion in the countryside was not the whole story.

In 1699, four laymen met in London to found the Society for Promoting Christian Knowledge and, two years later, the Society for Propagating the Gospel in Foreign Parts was founded. Thomas Bray (1656–1730), an early abolitionist (of slavery) and Anglican clergyman, was active in both societies together with an American, Henry Newman. They gave unstinting effort to the furtherance of ministry in the American colonies and in India, and to the opening of charity schools in England and Wales. Henry Compton, Bishop of London, supported Bray initially. Bray began parish libraries in Maryland and elsewhere, encouraged a scheme to settle ex-offenders in the new state of Georgia, and, on his return from the American colonies, became Rector of St Botolph's, Aldgate, from 1708–22. With the expansion of English colonies and trading posts abroad, this work only increased, and in future days many more missionary societies would be founded for overseas work. The incidence of philanthropy, pastoral guidance and preaching also increased in England itself.

Nation, society and politics in Georgian England

George I, the first Hanoverian English king, was generally thought to be a lucky monarch. He was chosen, through the workings of the Act of Settlement in 1701, for what he wasn't, rather than for what he was. He was not a Catholic. He was not French, nor was he controlled by the French. He was not a Stuart and so not of suspect heredity. He had little charisma; was divorced from his wife, Sophia; had a steady mistress, Melusine von der Schulenburg (created Duchess of Kendal and known as "the Maypole" as she was once so tall and thin); had a feud with his son, the Prince of Wales (which would be typical of Hanoverian kings); and sought the advancement of Hanover using the resources of England. Hanover gained the territories of Breden and Verden from Sweden and sought to retain, with England's help and money, a balance of power on the continent. George was served by a trio of young and able politicians: Sunderland, aged thirty-nine, James Stanhope at forty-two, and Robert Walpole, aged thirty-eight. All Whig to the core, they tarnished all Tories as potential Jacobites. Between them they would manage the greater part of George's reign, although not in harmony. Stanhope, with his military background and knowledge of French—a common language with the King—was George's favourite. Walpole was the more effective manager of the Commons, however, and had greater ability in harnessing the finances of the City and trade.

In 1688, the national debt was nil, but with the founding of the Bank of England and the ability to raise loans with interest, it ballooned to £36 million by 1715. Speculation was in the air and the wealthy, and not so wealthy, looked for quick profits. The South Sea Company was a speculative venture designed in part to reduce this national debt, but it collapsed spectacularly, ruining many investors. Walpole steadied the nation after the collapse of the South Sea Company, which had been licensed to trade with Spain in the West Indies and South America in 1720. This was a Tory venture that had sought to reduce the national debt by £9 million by encouraging investment in its activities and was seen as a financial antidote to the Whig-inspired Bank of England. At first it seemed like an alchemist's dream, turning all to gold, but it quickly turned to farce and then to tragedy as thousands of investors lost everything. Walpole had to screen the government and crown from meltdown, which he did. The later years of George's reign were taken up with continental concerns, such as creating alliances to prevent greater Austrian-Spanish power. Then, in 1727, George died, his reputation higher on the continent than in England. He was barely mourned in England, as he had been perceived as remote, and because he was a Hanoverian German.

By the early part of the eighteenth century, the population of England was about six million. At last it had begun to grow, having kept to two to three million until the seventeenth century. By comparison with France, now registering sixteen million, it was small. By the middle of the century research work had been done on relative incomes in the nation. Joseph Massie, an eighteenth-century economist, reckoned that 2,070 landowners and squires had incomes of £800 or more; 4,800 gentlemen had £400–799 per annum; 2,000 senior clergy, lawyers and army officers, of which there were 22,000 in all, earned about £80–199 p.a., as did 45,000 farmers and freeholders; 9,000 junior clergy were on £50–79 p.a. and 218,000 labourers and soldiers were on £14 or less p.a. Fees for Eton College were £50 a year. An average labourer's wage was 7d a day without food or drink. Despite the evidence of real poverty, there was clearly a growing middle class.

A distinctive middle-class culture was also forming in the country. China plates and mahogany furniture were familiar items. The Staffordshire pottery industry was becoming established, including Worcester and Derby porcelain. Textiles were being produced in Lancashire, and "cotton-gentry" were emerging in the region. Periodicals and literature were becoming common. Some of the first novels, such as Henry Fielding's *Tom Jones*, were among a number of books to be published. Fielding, also a judge, would go on with his brother John to provide security for London with the establishment of the Bow Street Runners and a more effective urban magistracy. *The Gentleman's Magazine* (1731) and *The London Magazine* (1732) began, and political pamphlets proliferated. Spa towns were becoming common throughout the country for leisure and socializing, as in Harrogate, Malvern, Bath and Cheltenham. Birmingham was becoming a manufacturing base for nails, which were exported to the colonies. With the increase of towns there came a rise in dissenting congregations. Of the twenty-one places of worship built in Birmingham between 1730 and 1795, only five belonged to the Established Church. By far the greater number of churches or chapels in urban Britain during this period were those of dissenting congregations.

Besides the conspicuous wealth of the upper middle class, the great landowners and the comfortable, burgeoning middle class, there was a great swathe of poor people in the land. The early part of the century saw relatively good harvests and plentiful availability of food, but after 1740 there was a higher incidence of food riots and the end of cheap food. A combination of state intervention and an upsurge in charitable work by church societies and philanthropists began to make a difference in care for the poor. In 1723, a new Poor Law Act was passed, which permitted parishes to cooperate in the establishment of workhouses, which were to become a staple of state provision for the poor. The poor were divided into "sturdy beggars" able to work outside, who were given outdoor relief, or a wage for labour, and the old, infirm and the young, for whom the workhouses provided.

By 1776, there were around 2,000 of these institutions with a capacity of 90,000. Contractors, who were brought in by parishes, used (and often exploited) the labour in the workhouses for their own enterprises. By 1748, annual provision from the Poor Rate raised from the better off in the parishes amounted to £700,000 a year. Vagrancy was a continual problem, with vagrants returned to their parishes of origin (if known), or otherwise subjected to hard labour or transportation.

In addition, philanthropists provided for education and medical care where possible. By 1723, there were 1,329 charity schools in the country, many begun in the early part of the eighteenth century, with a fall-off in the reign of George II (1727–60). Sponsorship for schools was invited by a national campaign run by the Society for Promoting Christian Knowledge. Hospitals with very rudimentary ideas about medicine were started. Some of the great London hospitals date their existence from this period: the London, Westminster, St George's and Middlesex began in the 1730s and 40s. By 1785, the London was admitting 7,000 patients a year. Outside in the provinces, hospitals were begun in significant cities such as Liverpool, Chester, Newcastle, York, Birmingham, Worcester, Bristol and Winchester, among others. The Lock Hospital for venereal disease was sponsored by Lady Huntingdon, but its Methodist chaplain, Martin Madan, had to resign in a scandal over promoting polygamy! Hospitals for the insane were started at the Bethlehem (Bedlam) and later at St Luke's in 1751. Two new foundations attracted the philanthropy of the great and the good: the Foundling Hospital (1742) for abandoned children was begun by the remarkable Thomas Coram, sea captain and philanthropist, and the Magdalen for reformed prostitutes. Handel composed pieces for the Foundling Hospital and contributed a number of performances of *Messiah* as well as leaving his score of *Messiah* in his will. Hogarth exhibited pictures there, making it into a kind of public gallery. The hospital combined care of abandoned infants with promotion of the arts, notably music and painting, in a unique synergy.

Finally, with regard to the poor and the wider general population, there was a concerted drive to change their manners and drinking habits. The London Society for the Reformation of Manners, founded in 1691, mobilized ordinary citizens in the enforcement of laws against immorality. In the early part of the eighteenth century, as a result of the momentum built up in the previous century, there were a large number of prosecutions for drunkenness, prostitution, gaming and profanation of the Sabbath. There were as many as 7,251 in 1722, although by the time of George II's reign these had markedly fallen off. Gin consumption had become widespread, even rampant in places, especially in London. In times of plentiful harvests, farmers or brewers used the residue of barley or "long malt" to produce gin, which was cheaper than beer. In 1745, total domestic consumption of spirits was 7,886,000 gallons, but in years of leaner harvests it fell to almost half that. It was still a considerable intake. "Mother Gin" succoured the poor but was also the cause of great misery. Hogarth captured its effect in vivid colours, especially in his picture *Gin Lane* (1751), which followed his satirical series of pictures on aristocratic marriage, titled *Marriage a-la-Mode* (1741–3). The government tried to restrict use of gin by licensing retailers and placing excises on its sale, but so despised were these charges by the population at large that they nearly brought the government down. The 1733 Excise Crisis occurred when Walpole sought to relieve the gentry of the Land Tax by switching it to excises on imports and goods, including alcohol. He only managed to survive by rescinding the increases and climbing down.[5]

The reign of George II and his talented and quick-witted, if manipulative, wife, Caroline of Ansbach, was ushered in by Handel's new work, "Zadok the Priest", composed for George's coronation in 1727.[6] Although the anthem became part of all coronations thereafter, the choir at the coronation seems to have performed less well. The reign was to last until 1760. In the first fourteen years, Walpole managed to avoid an extensive war, but by 1741 England was drawn with Hanover into the War of Austrian Succession.

At home, the Jacobite threat had returned with the arrival of Bonnie Prince Charlie at Arisaig in Scotland in 1745, and the calling together of the Highland clans at Glenfinnan to retake the crown. By 16 April 1746, Cumberland had caught up with the Jacobite army at Culloden in the Highlands. Some 7,000 Jacobites faced a far superior force of 9,000 well-trained and seasoned troops. The battle lasted half an hour, in which time the Jacobites lost some 2,000 and Cumberland 350. It was a devastating defeat, followed up by ruthless harrying of those who would not lay down their arms, and the disarming of the Highlanders both then and in the years to come was remorseless. It ended the Stuart cause in Britain and the twenty-five-year-old Cumberland, youngest son of the King, was forever tarnished with the epithet "Butcher" for his destruction of the Stuart army.

Henry Pelham, the Prime Minister, led the so-called "Broad Bottom Ministry" from the Peace of Aix-la-Chapelle at the end of the War of Austrian Succession until his death in 1754. Released from the exigencies of war, the government had time to focus on domestic policy. During his administration, the Marriage Act of 1753 was passed, requiring, for the first time, that a marriage be solemnized in a formal, public ceremony, rather than simply after the calling of banns and a virtually private event involving an Anglican clergyman. Thus, the state, rather than simply canon law, controlled the validation of marriages and births (or baptisms). Marriages and deaths had become a point of taxation in William and Mary's reign, with parish registration of both marriages and deaths, and returns of both to the government, becoming a legal responsibility.

A further important piece of legislation was the Jew Act of 1753, which provided for the naturalization of Jews in England. Jews had been settling in England since the time of the Commonwealth. They had supported the government during the 1745 Jacobite rebellion and were rewarded now with citizenship or naturalization on application to Parliament. Although the Act passed the Lords easily, the Tories opposed it in the Commons as anti-Christian, while the Whigs supported it on the basis of their principle of toleration. Earlier Bills in 1747, 1748 and 1751 had been defeated, but despite popular protest over the numbers of immigrants in recent years—not least the Huguenots, with the attendant threat to English jobs and professions—the 1753 Jew Bill was passed. But a torrent of anti-Semitism resulted and in the following parliamentary session the Act was repealed. Naturalization and emancipation would have to wait a further century until 1846, and the Religious Opinions Relief Act. The natural suspicions of the English about immigration were not quickly allayed.

One Act that was passed more easily entailed the adoption of the continental Gregorian calendar, used in Europe since 1582. Unlike the Julian calendar, the Gregorian calendar worked with a leap year, which included an extra day every four years to accommodate a year's length being 365.2422 days for the earth's annual revolution around the sun. After 200 years England decided to ally its calendar with that of the continent. A justifiable reflection might be that it took time for the English to integrate their ways with those of the continent, but in the end they did. It did mean that eleven days went missing when England underwent its realignment of calendars in 1752.

The court of George II reflected many of the attitudes of the time. George II had a bluff exterior which belied his ability to oversee political negotiations, in particular the difficult task of melding the interests of England and Hanover, something not always accomplished to the satisfaction of English politicians or Parliament. He was conscientious and dutiful in his administration of business. His reign was thirty-three years long, despite his coming to the throne at the relatively advanced age of forty-four.

While George took the role of a military-minded administrator, his wife Caroline of Ansbach provided the court with a certain *frisson*. Caroline had been brought up in the Enlightenment court of Frederick I and Queen Charlotte of Prussia. Charlotte was a friend of the philosopher Leibniz, a relationship that Caroline continued. Caroline displayed a combination of liberal ideas and natural charm. She associated with men of ideas and science, was praised by the poet and classicist Alexander Pope, and made the acquaintance of Isaac Newton, among others. A close associate of Walpole and with strong Whig sympathies, she was regarded by the gossip and court diarist Lord John Hervey as very influential in government and a focus for liberal ideas. Caroline's health deteriorated in 1735; she was afflicted by gout and had to be wheeled around the court. She lived only two more years.

Her infirmity, however, did not prevent George from taking a new mistress, following his relationship with Henrietta Howard. This time it was one Madame Walmolden, who lived in Hanover. Surprisingly, Hervey records that "the King acquainted the Queen of this new engagement by letter, and of every step he took in it, of the growth of his passion, the progress of his applications, and their success".[7] The King's weekly letters from Hanover to the Queen were forty to sixty pages long.

This then was the court and nation when, in May 1738, a year after the Queen's death, one John Wesley had a spiritual experience that was to have a profound impact on the outlook and aspirations of the nation, and one that would set in motion one of the greatest Christian revivals the country has experienced.

The Evangelical Revival and Catholic consolidation

The religious atmosphere in the early eighteenth century was marked by a number of factors: a benevolent negligence of spiritual matters by the Hanoverian government; a pragmatic and sceptical outlook on the part of Walpole and his ministers; a desire by the government for dependability rather than innovation from the Bench of Bishops who sat in the Lords; and a religious toleration which was marked compared with the continent, as fines were not uniformly imposed on Catholics for recusancy. With the repeal of the Occasional Conformity Act in 1719, it was once again possible for dissenters who occasionally attended Anglican communion services to hold office. And many of the laws designed to penalize dissenters were not implemented, so although the law had the appearance of rigour, in fact it was a neglected armoury.

In culture generally, and in education particularly, there was a marked interest in the classics and the virtues of the ancient world—as evidenced by Gibbon's *Decline and Fall of the Roman Empire* (1776)—alongside the steady march of reason, which favoured Deism and the anti-Trinitarian stance that had crept into the Church. The Archbishop of Canterbury, William Wake (1715–37), was more interested in defending Anglican orders against any charge of unorthodoxy by the Catholic Church than in promoting lay participation or growth by conversion. By contrast, Bishop Benjamin Hoadly, eventually Bishop of Winchester, a strong Whig supporter and lover of politics and the court, impugned the orthodox credentials of the Church of England and proclaimed the rights of the state over it. Given the High Church was often associated with the Jacobites, George I accepted Hoadly's view and his criticism of the non-jurors. Added to this mix was the popularity of the Deist writer and philosopher Matthew Tindal, who openly questioned the concept of revelation and advocated knowledge based on reason, rather than faith. Against this background, it is not surprising the Church was crying out for fresh divine inspiration. It was getting bogged down in a mixture of dry rationality, political Protestantism, social conservatism and state control. Inspiration was not long in coming.

The sources of this inspiration, humanly speaking, were an Oxford academic and an innkeeper's son from Gloucester. They were John Wesley and George Whitfield, who together with their associates and the rise of Methodism had a profound effect on English Christianity in the eighteenth century and beyond, even though the two by no means agreed on the workings of grace or its effects on the believer. Like Luther, they subscribed to the same doctrines of Christ alone (*solus Christus*), only through scripture (*sola scriptura*), only through grace (*sola gratia*) and only by faith (*sola fide*), which they believed had become lost in the religious controversies of recent times, and through the march of pure reason.

Wesley came from good clerical stock, with clerical families on both sides of the family who had been ejected following Charles II's Restoration, but who had found their way back into Church of England ministry. John's father, Samuel, was the Vicar of Epworth in Lincolnshire. He came to Epworth in 1697 aged thirty-four, having been a chaplain to Lord Normanby for a short time. He had hoped for higher things, but was consigned to this corner of Lincolnshire for forty years. Here he immersed himself in parish duties, raising a large family and writing, appropriately as it happens, *Dissertations on the Book of Job*. The subject matter was appropriate because the family often faced debt, were treated with hostility by several of the local inhabitants and suffered the occasional tragedy. When the completed work was presented at court, the Queen much admired the binding!

The Reverend Samuel Wesley was not only a prolific author but also a prodigious breeder. He had nineteen children, of whom nine survived. Many of his books and projects were destroyed in a fire in February 1709, from which his son Jackey (or John) was wonderfully saved, together with the rest of the children. John Wesley often reminisced later in life that he was saved as "a brand plucked out of the fire". Samuel's wife Susanna was the daughter of a dissenting minister based in Bishopsgate, London, called Samuel Annesley, and was herself the youngest of twenty-five children, or was it twenty-four? Her father admitted in conversation with a son-in-law that he was unsure whether the count was "two dozen or a quarter of a hundred!"[8] Susanna's upbringing of her children became proverbial. Asked in later life to recall her method, she wrote the following about the period the family returned to their rebuilt house after the fire:

> We entered on a strict reform; and then was begun the custom of singing psalms at the beginning and leaving school, morning and evening. Then also of a general retirement at five o'clock was entered upon, when the oldest took the youngest that could speak, and the second the next, to whom they read psalms for the day, and a chapter of the New Testament—as in the morning they were directed to read the psalms and a chapter in the Old Testament, after which they went to their private prayers, before they got their breakfast.[9]

Allowing for the fact that when this was written Susanna was sixty-three and there could have been some tidying up of the past, it is nevertheless a powerful tradition and one that would become legendary in Methodist child-rearing in the future.

Susanna's influence was not only present in the discipline of a daily devotional life, but also in her spiritual teaching and the reading she recommended to her children. She much admired Pascal's *Pensées*, for example, and implanted a love of the mystics in her son, John. When her husband was away in London, and because she disapproved of the curate, she led meetings in her kitchen, where she taught the assembled company. There is no doubt that her character formed and shaped the young John, as well as giving him a similar love of learning and discipline of conduct.

What is clear is that when John Wesley left home, inculcated with this devotional discipline by his mother, along with his father's teaching of Latin and Greek, he was ready for the study of theology at Charterhouse and then Oxford. He entered Christ Church, Oxford in June 1720, aged seventeen. Five years later he would be ordained. Although part of the university, which was "Royalist" in predilection and Jacobite in sympathy, Christ Church nevertheless boasted the greatest of the Puritan divines from the previous century, John Owen as Dean and the greatest of the Whig philosophers, John Locke. For John Wesley, Christ Church would be the unlikely cauldron for forging his own spiritual search.

John Wesley's fellow evangelist, sometime theological sparring partner and near contemporary was George Whitfield. Born in 1714, he came from a very different background. He was the fifth son and seventh child of Thomas Whitfield, the keeper of the Bell Inn in Gloucester. George had a talent for acting and storytelling, and a mother who sought for her son the advantages of Oxford. With the support of a family friend, she procured a place for George at Pembroke College as a servitor undergraduate. (Servitors were the poorest type of student and earned their keep by serving wealthier students.) George went to Oxford in 1732, where, already sensing the call of God on his life to preach, he joined the Holy Club founded by John and Charles Wesley.

The common spiritual paths of John and Charles Wesley and George Whitfield not only included membership of the Holy Club at Oxford, but also appointments as clergymen in the American colonies. For them, the Holy Club was a powerful *negative* experience, in that it confirmed—in retrospect—the necessity for grace and the spiritual freedom that comes *only* through forgiveness and new birth in the Spirit.

By 1730, the Holy Club was underway. John Wesley had by then been elected a Fellow of Lincoln in March 1726. He was College Lecturer and Moderator of Greek. He had also fallen in love with Sally Kirkham, nicknamed Varanese, whom he had met in 1725, and noted in his diary. She was one of a Cotswold set, all given classical nicknames by Wesley and his friends. For his part Wesley had been given the name Cyrus. Their friendship would continue even after Sally's marriage to the local schoolmaster, and it was a relationship that unsurprisingly did not lack intensity. For two years or more after his appointment at Lincoln College, and with the permission of the college, Wesley helped out in various parishes, but returned in 1729 with a renewed desire to join the Holy Club set up by his now "reformed" brother Charles. The club was a group of like-minded young men who ardently pursued "holiness" in the hope of reaching a higher plane of spiritual life. Along with his brother Charles, members included George Whitfield from Pembroke College, William Morgan, the son of a prominent Dublin lawyer, and several others. The club became well known, and they were often mocked in Oxford as "Methodists"—already a term of abuse generally applied to serious and non-conformist religion.

The club held a weekly sacrament read the mystics—particularly Thomas à Kempis, Jeremy Taylor's *Rule and Exercises in Holy Living* and William Law's *Serious Call to Devout and Holy Living*. They studied for at least six hours a day, observed rigorous fasting twice a week and subjected themselves to critical self-examination and confession. With early rising leaving little time for socializing in the evenings, they became a rather isolated group. They engaged in prison and sick visiting; and then in August 1732 disaster struck the club. Following a period of mental instability and hallucinations, William Morgan, one of the principal members of the club, died at home in Dublin. Despite this tragedy, William's father committed his second son Richard to Oxford and into Wesley's care, but asked that he be spared the rigours of the Holy Club. When Richard Morgan complained of Wesley's heavy-handedness, and when Wesley's father was dying in Epworth without his son being willing to help him out financially, it seemed that the Holy Club had strained at gnats and swallowed camels. Uncompromising in his pursuit of holiness and prepared to impose the same standards on others, however unwilling, in the interest of their salvation, Wesley saw the fruits of the club turn to ashes. So, when offered a chance to go with SPCK to an appointment in the newly-formed colony of Georgia, Wesley jumped at the opportunity—although he took with him the same principles of severe religious expectation that had guided him at Oxford.

Ministry in Georgia was to be his wilderness time. In October 1735, both John and Charles sailed on the *Simmonds* from Gravesend in Kent to Savannah, Georgia. Georgia had only recently been founded by General Oglethorpe as a proprietary colony governed by trustees under licence from the crown and was a haven for those convicted of debt. Oglethorpe and the trustees permitted indentured labour, but not slavery, and banned liquor. It was for such an idealistic colony that Wesley was bound with his brother and two other members of the Holy Club, Delamotte and Ingham. On the voyage, Wesley and his colleagues continued to fast fiercely. Then, when facing severe storms, Wesley attended the worship on board of twenty-six German Pietists called Moravians. He was impressed by their quiet calm in the face of danger, their singing of the psalms, their extempore preaching, and the prayers of their leaders.

This was also the time when Wesley began his journal: beginning on 14 October 1735, he kept it up until 24 October 1790, writing daily until just four months before he died. His journal was more about his "doings" than his feelings: there is no mention of his marriage or his later love affair with Grace Murray, nor of the love he had for Sophy Hopkey, a bright, devout eighteen-year-old who lived with her aunt and uncle Tom Causton, the former chief magistrate of Savannah. In fact, Wesley proposed marriage to her, but she only appears in the journals as a litigant against him.

Wesley's ministry in Georgia was marked by several disputes, which arose from his desire to enforce a strict observance of the rubrics or rules of church life and worship. Another running sore was his jilted love for Sophy Hopkey, who married another and then was banned from holy communion by him for failing to have her banns read. Subsequently this escalated into a court case with Sophy's uncle. In the meantime, church attendance declined. Wesley resolved to leave, despite the protests of Causton, who wanted his day in court and Wesley's full conviction. Wesley slipped away, writing in his diary:

> I saw clearly the hour was come for leaving this place: and as soon as evening prayers were over, about eight o'clock, the tide then serving, I shook off the dust of my feet and left Georgia after having preached the gospel there (not as I aught but as I was able) one year and nearly nine months.[10]

There is no doubt that the German Pietists or Moravians who came from the estates of Count Zinzendorf in eastern Germany had already had a profound effect on Wesley. As he sailed back to England through further storms and trials, the thought came to him: "I went to America to convert Indians; but oh! Who shall convert me?"[11] The answer was not slow in coming. He had a number of conversations with Peter Böhler in Georgia. Then, back in England at the beginning of 1738, Wesley joined a society of brethren led by Böhler, which met in Fetter Lane in the City of London. Having agreed to its demanding rules of conduct, he settled into its fellowship. On 24 May 1738, at a meeting of the group, and when he was listening to a reading from Martin Luther's preface to his *Commentary on Romans*, Wesley famously records:

> About a quarter before nine, while he [Martin Luther] was describing the change which God works in the heart through faith in Jesus Christ, I felt my heart strangely warmed. I felt I did trust Christ, Christ alone, for salvation: and an assurance was given me he had taken away my sins, **even mine** [Wesley's emphasis in his diary] and saved me from the law of sin and death.[12]

At the same time, Wesley gave a long account of his religious life hitherto and its deficiencies. Rather like Augustine, who after his conversion went on a retreat with friends to Cassiacum in north Italy, Wesley now went with his friends, including his old friend from Oxford, Benjamin Ingham, to visit the Moravian community in Germany. Although ill, Wesley met Count Zinzendorf, their leader and founder, and heard him teach on the meaning and working of justification by faith. He would not always support Zinzendorf, but on this point Wesley was all ears and eyes. He stayed some months at Herrnhut, the centre of the Moravian community, absorbing everything he experienced, but not uncritical of some practices, such as silent prayer, which he found too mystical (and mysticism, despite his mother, was something he now disavowed). He returned to England at the end of 1738 and began preaching justification by faith in Christ alone and new birth in the Spirit.

Although Wesley's conversion was one of the most significant starting points in the Evangelical Revival of the eighteenth century, it was not the only one. Wesley said that there were only ten Anglican clergy who truly understood the gospel and one or two Presbyterians. Many were Deists; many did not believe in the Trinity and were on their way to beginning Unitarianism, founded by Joseph Priestley (1733–1804) towards the end of the century. There were others, however, who understood both justification by faith and the need for new birth in Christ. The most influential of these were George Whitfield, Howell Harris (1714–73) from Wales, and the Countess of Huntingdon (1707–91). Whitfield, as noted above, had been a member of the Holy Club, but in April 1735, aged twenty-one, experienced joy, confidence in God and relief from the guilt of sin while reading a book by a godly former Bishop of Norwich, Joseph Hall (1574–1656), titled *Contemplations on the Old and New Testament*.[13] So, at just twenty-one, Martin Benson, Bishop of Gloucester, ordained him. With considerable gifts of oratory, a clear voice that carried far—Benjamin Franklin reckoned Whitfield could be heard by 10,000 people—and with a heart that was more than warmed by the love of God, Whitfield began to preach in Gloucester and then London. Like Wesley before him, Whitfield went for a time to Savannah, and then to some of the northern American states. By 1740, a revival had begun on both sides of the Atlantic. What then were its main characteristics?

One of the unique, and for some disturbing, characteristics of this revival was the deeply emotional response to the preaching of Wesley and Whitfield. In 1738, when denied a pulpit in Islington, Whitfield took to the open spaces of Moorfields, Kennington Common, Hackney Marsh and Marylebone Fields, where he gathered vast crowds. It was clear from this huge popular reaction that his preaching and message were deeply affecting. Wesley would more cautiously follow suit and similar responses would attend his gatherings. So, for instance, on 30 April 1739, in the Weavers Hall in Bristol, Wesley records how "seven or eight persons were constrained to roar aloud while the sword of the Spirit was dividing asunder their souls and spirits. But they were all relieved upon prayer, and sang praises unto our God."[14] Nor was this in any way unusual. Although often unmoved himself, the effect of Wesley's preaching was marked. A few weeks later he wrote in Bristol that "a young woman sunk down at Rose-Green, in a violent agony of body and mind; so did five or six persons in the evening, at the New-Room, at whose cries many were greatly offended".[15] Nor was such a response confined to women. The miners of Kingswood, Bristol heard him in numbers, and their tears made channels down their coal-blackened faces. At Bath, to a more aristocratic audience, Wesley spelt out his message that sinners require grace with uncompromising clarity. He was given rapt attention. At other times he preached in the street, as in Pontypool, where he told five or six hundred attentive hearers to "believe in the Lord Jesus, that they might be saved".[16] The response of falling, groaning, crying out or exuberant joy was to be an issue for many.

The reaction to this outpouring of grace through the preaching of Whitfield, Wesley and others was broadly fourfold. In the first instance, there was the growing establishment of Methodist meeting chapels throughout the country for those touched or converted by the preaching. By the time of Wesley's death there would be some 470. It is hard to estimate numbers precisely, but by the end of the century there were 72,476 Methodists in England. (These were to split along Calvinist or Arminian lines, to which we shall return.) As a result of Wesley's extensive preaching tours between 1740 and 1780, in which he is said to have covered 250,000 miles on horseback, throughout the British Isles, including Cornwall, the Midlands, the North-East and North-West, Methodist societies would start throughout the country. The distinctiveness of Methodism, beyond Protestant Christianity as defined by Luther, was the creation of a "class" system.

This system was characterized by mutual submission and spiritual accountability within small groups; the appointment of lay preachers, including women; a strong emphasis on an ethical response to the Gospel, which helped the poor; an eschewing of alcohol, gambling and the exploitation of others, especially slavery; praying extemporaneously; and the formation of societies as part of the Methodist Connexion. Wesley himself was clear about generosity to the poor and the ending of slavery. His motto of "gain all you can; save all you can; give all you can" was long-lasting. His emphasis on honesty, when writing against smuggling in *A Word to a Smuggler* and to electors in his *Word to a Freeholder*, was clear. These were among more than 200 publications that Wesley wrote. It was this defining in writing of the implications of the Gospel for lifestyle that divided Wesley from Whitfield, along with their differences over Calvinism's doctrine of predestination, which, unlike Whitfield, Wesley could not accept.

The reaction of the Established Church and population to Methodism was mixed. As both Wesley brothers and Whitfield were ordained priests in the Church of England, their preaching and conduct was firstly a matter for the church hierarchy and for the congregations and ministers at large. The hierarchy itself, as ever in the Church of England, was hardly uniform in its opinions. Bishop Warburton of Gloucester, a great admirer of the poet and classicist Alexander Pope, and a considerable literary figure himself, was cautious about the "enthusiasm". The famous philosopher Bishop Butler (1692–1752), author of *Analogy of Religion*, friend of Queen Caroline, Dean of St Paul's and then Bishop of Durham, was sceptical and shocked at Wesley's claims of inspiration. He famously said in his interview with Wesley on 16 August 1739, "the pretending of extraordinary gifts and revelations of the Holy Ghost is a horrid thing, a very horrid thing."[17] But Wesley was complimentary about Butler's principal work, *Analogy of Religion*, saying it was "well wrote" although "too deep for the understanding of his [Butler's] readers".[18] The main problem for the hierarchy, aside from the emotion and enthusiasm wrought by Wesley's preaching (which in fact subsided over the years, as the *Journals* clearly show), was how to treat the societies and the lay preachers. Wesley wanted the societies and their buildings accepted as outposts of Anglicanism. He would not say they were dissenting chapels, which would have given them standing under the Act of Toleration, but nor were they accepted as Anglican churches, since they existed outside the parish system and were only accountable to Wesley, and later to the Preachers' Conference and not the bishops. Nor would Robert Lowth, the sympathetic Bishop of London from 1777–87, ordain Methodist lay preachers as Anglican clergy. In his lifetime Wesley acted as the overall bishop, although not in name, of the whole movement, while considering himself still an Anglican. It was almost inevitable that after his death, the societies, the Conference of Methodist Preachers, and the spiritual disciplines of Methodism should result in the formation of a new denomination. For his part, by 1770, George III regarded Methodists as virtuous and loyal citizens.

If for these reasons the societies founded by Wesley, in response to his and his colleagues' preaching and ministries, were never at the time absorbed into the Church of England, there was nevertheless a revival of Evangelicalism in the Church of England also, which has lasted until today. Just as Richard Baxter did his utmost to remain true to his beliefs *and* stay in the Church of England—although he was in fact ejected—there were a number of Anglican clergy in the eighteenth century who remained true to their Evangelicalism and carved out effective ministries within the Church, and as such provided a template for such ministry in generations to come. This was to prove one of the most enduring results of the eighteenth-century Evangelical Revival. Underlying the resolution of such Anglican clergymen to stay in the Church of England and *not* join the Countess of Huntingdon's Connexion or Wesley's Methodist Societies, was an unwillingness to put themselves under the sway of either of those powerful and somewhat dictatorial figures. Instead, they would work out their Evangelical beliefs and mission in the relative independence of Anglican freehold incumbency. This gave them legal entitlement to pursue worship and mission in a parish and to have legal possession of vicarage or rectory and the parish church, with the support of church wardens and of the church or vestry council. Given this structure, many clergy who had been touched by the Evangelical movement decided to stay within this system, whatever the other drawbacks of the Church of England might be. Exemplifying this pattern were men such as John Fletcher of Madeley in Shropshire, Augustus Toplady of Broadhembury in Devon, and William Grimshaw of Rochdale and then Haworth (still remembered at Haworth when the Brontë sisters and their vicar father were there). These were the precursors of the late eighteenth-century Evangelicals, such as the Clapham Sect and Charles Simeon of Cambridge. They would become a considerable influence at the end of the century, and we shall return to them. In many ways subsequent Evangelical Anglicans owe their inspiration to *these* models of parish ministry, albeit fashioned as they were in a much more deferential, authoritarian and masculine age.

As we have seen, Wesley and Whitfield were not immune from theological controversy and physical conflict, some of the former being of their own making. Quite often both men faced attacks by threatening mobs. Wesley records such an attack at Wrangle in Cheshire on 7 August 1752:

> The Constables led me out to a large mob, who carried me, and threw me into standing water, and as often as I tried to come out, they pitched me in again. At last some of them said I should come out, and kept the others off, till I got up the bank. I found myself very happy all the time; for I knew I was in the Lord's hand. I got back to the house where I lodged and went to bed. But in less than an hour the mob came again, broke open the doors of the house and the chamber and dragged me away with them. They carried me to a great pond, which was railed round, being ten or twelve feet deep. Then four men took me by my legs and arms. I felt the flesh shrink a little at first; but it was soon over, and I did not care whether I lived or died; just as I pleased the Lord. They swung me backward and forward two or three times, and then threw me as far as they could into the water. The fall took away my senses, so that I felt nothing more.[19]

Wesley was fished out by others using a long pole, but he was still driven out of the town half-naked. For a man who was nearly fifty, it must have been a great physical shock, but Wesley shook off the effects. Alongside these physical bouts were more extended theological conflicts on doctrine. Wesley was a convinced Arminian, which meant that he believed people had a genuine choice as to whether they were saved or redeemed. In other words, "it was up to them". Calvinists, by contrast, proposed that only those elected or predestined could be saved and therefore among the elect. On the side of the Calvinists was Augustus Montague Toplady and George Whitfield, who regarded Wesley's Arminianism as deeply suspect, on the other side was Wesley and his close associates. Both sides of the argument raged in pamphlets and publications. Wesley summarized Toplady's ominous-sounding and lengthy publication *Absolute Predestination* in blistering fashion:

> The sum of all is this: one in twenty (suppose) of mankind are elected; nineteen in twenty are reprobated (damned). The elect shall be saved, do what they will; the reprobate will be damned, do what they can. Reader believe this or be damned. Witness my hand Augustus.[20]

Wesley was taken to task by the extreme Calvinists and the more moderate Prayer Book Anglicans, who regarded him as a Jesuit with the dictatorial manner of a pope. Worse was to come, however, when, in 1770, Wesley overemphasized the need for works to be added to faith for salvation and held to the doctrine that an individual could be perfected by love. Both teachings seemed to impugn the central Evangelical doctrine of justification by faith alone, "not by works lest any man should boast" (Ephesians 2:9), and he was further reviled. None other than the redoubtable Countess of Huntingdon sought a retraction, confronted Wesley, and asked for a rewriting of the offending conference minutes, which was finally offered.

Wesley was without doubt one of the most influential figures in the eighteenth century. Whereas Whitfield may have been the greater preacher, he split his time between England and America, where he eventually died in Newport, Massachusetts, on 30 September 1770. In the end Whitfield had less lasting influence in England than Wesley. After the heady and emotional responses to their preaching in the early 1740s, the Evangelical movement became one that was based upon the Moravian spiritual disciplines of prayer, Bible study and mutual accountability, which was then worked into a system of small groups. These in turn made up the Methodist Societies that were overseen by Wesley, lay preachers and the Methodist Conference. Wesley was a man of formidable energy and organizational grip: he oversaw and checked up on the numbers in each society he went to. He was a prolific author, a compulsive reader, and a man of wide-ranging interests. In between preaching, which usually began at 5 a.m., he would read the classics, betraying the academic's love of learning. He records reading the Greek historian Xenophon in his seventy-fifth year, at a time when he says he felt no weaker than in his twenty-fifth year.[21] Later he records reading a French author, Le Vrayer, and his *Animadversions on the Ancient Historians*.[22] He lambasted Henry VIII when preaching near Walsingham for the wanton destruction of the abbey there. He used or recommended electricity as a cure for illness. He was interested in human health, illness and scientific cures. In effect, he was ceaselessly thinking.

Wesley's relationships with women were not so fulfilling, however. Although attractive to women, often counselling them and appointing them preachers, as in the case of Bathsheba Hall in Bristol, he was unable to form a long-lasting and happy partnership with a woman. As we have seen, he enjoyed the society of young women of the Cotswolds set whilst at Oxford. His relationship with Sophy Hopkey in Georgia badly misfired and then, perhaps most devastatingly of all, a deep love of Grace Murray, when Wesley was forty-five, never developed. She was a young widow in her twenties from Newcastle and a member of the Methodist fellowship. Wesley's brother Charles thought she was beneath him socially and intervened personally and clumsily to prevent the match. Grace had another suitor, John Bennet, also a Methodist preacher, whom she had nursed in the Orphan House in Newcastle over six months. They would marry. Wesley's uncertainty over whether marriage to Grace was the Lord's will, Charles's interference and Bennet's suit together prevented the marriage. This combination of circumstances persuaded Grace herself against the idea of marrying Wesley, leaving him bewildered, emotionally battered and bruised. Six months later, in what seems like a classic rebound, he married Molly Vazeille, a widow of forty-one from London. She could not cope with Wesley's incessant itinerant ministry and, since she was not a meek or compliant woman, she resented his authoritarian ways, preferring a more comfortable life in Threadneedle Street. Neither could compromise, so neither could give the other what each looked for. In the end they parted in January 1758, married but separated until the end of their lives. On 12 October 1781, Molly died and Wesley wrote, "I came to London, and was informed that my wife died on Monday. This evening she was buried, though I was not informed of it till a day or two after."[23] At the end of his life, confiding to Henry Moore, an early biographer, Wesley reckoned that if he had had a happy marriage, "he might have been unfaithful to the great work to which God had called him",[24] surely a rationalization decked out in providential clothing. It is no surprise that in front of Wesley's house on City Road there is a statue, not of a wife, but his mother, Susannah, the paragon he followed and publicised.

Meanwhile, the Roman Catholic Church was quietly consolidating its position in England, having been proscribed nationally for over two hundred years, and its members prevented from holding any public office since 1673 with the passing of the Test Act. Catholics were now divided into four districts, with each overseen by a Vicar Apostolic. These districts were London, the Midlands, the North and the West. Dioceses would not be formed until 1850. Influences on English Catholics came from the Gallican Church in France, which was sober in style but intransigently Catholic in doctrine and which was led at the beginning of the eighteenth century by Jacques-Bénigne Bossuet, who had preached at the funeral of Henrietta Maria and was thus a firm supporter of the Jacobites.

The most influential figure in the English Roman Catholic Church during the eighteenth century was Richard Challoner (1691–1781). Trained at the English College at Douai, he determined to return to England as a missionary priest, which he did in 1730. Working among the poor of London, he led services secretly in alehouses such as the Sign of the Ship in Gate Street and the Cockpit in Drury Lane. He read voraciously and wrote prolifically; some eighty works in total. Most famous was his new translation of the Douai Bible. As a whole, Roman Catholics had greater room to breathe, but from time to time bigotry and open hostility flared up, not least in the Gordon Riots: a Protestant-led response to the Papist Acts of 1778, the first attempt to bring relief to Catholics such as they enjoyed elsewhere in the colonies and, in particular, in Canada. The reaction to Catholic relief was violent: some 40,000 Londoners marched on Parliament, led by Lord Gordon, the head of the Protestant Association. The mob was fired on by troops, there being no police force, and over 200 were shot dead and as many wounded. It would be nearly fifty years before Catholic emancipation could be thought of and acted on again.

Hymns and music

No study of eighteenth-century Christianity would be complete without acknowledging the extraordinary upsurge of church music, oratorios and hymn singing during the period. Probably the greatest English hymn composers were writing at that time: whether Charles Wesley, John Newton, William Cowper or Isaac Watts. Between them they wrote the greatest English hymns.[25] It is worth observing that almost none of John Wesley's pamphlets are now known, but Charles Wesley's hymns are probably sung by hundreds of thousands world-wide every Sunday, and in many ways their verse, condensed theological expression and spiritual insight have not been surpassed. What is true of Charles Wesley is also true of the other hymn writers of the period. *Amazing Grace* by John Newton is quite possibly the best-known hymn of all time, even sung solo by former American President Barack Obama in June 2015 to a group of grieving Southern Baptists in Pinckney, South Carolina, and known as much outside the Church as in it.

Two of these great hymn writers were friends and close neighbours in the village of Olney in Buckinghamshire. They were William Cowper and John Newton. Newton was the converted slave trader who became curate at Olney before a long incumbency at St Mary Woolnoth. He was famously to describe himself as "an infidel and libertine and servant of slaves in Africa [who] was by the rich mercy of Jesus Christ preserved, restored and pardoned and appointed to preach the faith he had long laboured to destroy" (Taken from the memorial in St Mary Woolnoth in the City of London). He was a regular correspondent with and pastor to William Cowper, a gentle, erudite, sensitive and sometimes whimsical poet and Christian. Periodically overcome with depression, Cowper was nonetheless a charming companion: "He was so gregarious and so affectionate that he made a friend of an animal if he could not find a human being."[26] Indeed he kept hares at home that he tenderly nursed, and a cat about whom he wrote. He gave us the humorous tale of *John Gilpin*, poems about the death of a Robin Redbreast, a eulogy to William Wilberforce and letters galore to John Newton, a rather demanding spiritual mentor, and to his much-loved cousin Lady Hesketh, whose "letters were the joy of [his] heart".[27] From this quiet Buckinghamshire village came hymns, poems, letters and aspirations that have quite literally lit up and comforted the world.

Alongside this extraordinary outpouring of hymns inspired by the Revival in the eighteenth century is the music that was created in the early part of the century, and by Handel in particular. Since the days of King Henry VIII, the Chapel Royal was the womb that developed some of the greatest English and continental composers. Thomas Tallis (1505–85) was a composer to Henry VIII and was joined by William Byrd (1540–1625) in Elizabeth's reign. They were to be succeeded by Henry Purcell (1659–95), another Chapel Royal composer who played and sang at the coronation of Charles II. Purcell's early death deprived England of one of her greatest composers until the arrival of the twentieth-century clutch of composers such as Edward Elgar, Ralph Vaughan Williams and Benjamin Britten.

A German who became a naturalized British citizen, George Frederick Handel dominated the first half of the eighteenth century in England musically. He was born in the same year as Johann Sebastian Bach, whom he never met. A musical prodigy from an early age, he developed "an acute sensitivity to the echo and the association of words and images".[28] Coming from Halle in Saxony, he was born into a professional and Protestant family, his father Georg being court physician to the Elector of Brandenburg. He joined the Hanoverian court in 1710 as Kapellmeister before settling in England during Queen Anne's reign.

For the next forty years, he would light up English music. For the coronation of George II, he wrote "Zadok the Priest", which was subsequently sung at every coronation, and then the *Water Music* for a royal water procession and *Music for Royal Fireworks*. By the 1730s, Handel forsook opera for oratorios, working with the librettist Charles Jennens. A series of oratorios based on the story of the Jews were produced, in which England came to see itself as the new Israel. In fact, Handel saw Hanoverian, Protestant England as a second and better Israel. The pinnacle of these oratorios was to be the *Messiah*, performed first in Dublin on 13 April 1742 at the invitation of the Duke of Devonshire, the Lord Lieutenant, and then subsequently in London at the Foundling Hospital and elsewhere. Its opening performance was an unqualified success (although Jennens was disappointed with the score!). As one reviewer wrote, "The Sublime, the Grand, and the Tender, adapted to the most elevated, majestick and moving Words, conspired to transport and charm the ravished Heart and Ear."[29] It has done so ever since.

Patriotism, expansion and loss

The period from the end of the Pelham ministry in 1754 until the accession of George III and beyond saw a change of tempo in British political life. Parts of the population and the elite had become tired of the political principles of first Walpole and then the Pelhams (Henry Pelham and his brother, who succeeded him as the Duke of Newcastle). Walpole had been the Stanley Baldwin of his age, following a similar policy of "safety first" and to that end avoiding involvement with conflicts abroad, while shoring up financial policy at home through the arts of political fixing in the House of Commons, and of keeping the financiers of the City sweet. This was the Whig combination of prospering trade and keeping the Whig grandees of the Hanoverian succession on side. It could lead to insipid results when there were cries for greater expansion, aggression and dominance, fired by patriotism. The Treaty of Aix-la-Chapelle had concluded the War of Austrian Succession, which had enabled Empress Maria Theresa to succeed to the throne of Austria. This had been a European land war, in which the interests of Hanover were uppermost in preventing the dominance of France, but in which Prussia had, under Frederick the Great, seized Silesia from Austria.

By 1746, a new political voice was being heard, capturing the mood of the moment, and this was the voice of William Pitt the Elder. He was opposed to the pursuit of Hanoverian interests on the continent, so no friend of George II, nor later of George III. There is truth in the commentator and *literati* Samuel Johnson's saying that, "Walpole was a minister given by the King to the people, but Pitt was a minister given by the people to the King."[30] With his heady rhetoric and powerful personality, Pitt provided leadership in the Commons to the "old Whigs" and the leaderless Tories. He led a new charge for the expansion of English interests abroad, especially in Canada and India, principally against the French, through a world-wide war in theatres of conflict mostly in North America and India. For British interests, 1759 was described as an *annus mirabilis* and the beginnings of a formidable empire in the East and West.

Pitt tapped into a growing patriotism in Britain. In 1745, patriotic songs, which were to become part of the nation's repertoire, made their first appearance in theatres and concert halls of London. It was in a London theatre, against the fear of the looming Jacobite invasion, that these words were first sung:

> God save our noble King
> God save great George our King
> God save the King

Send him victorious
Happy and Glorious
Long to reign over us
God save the King

O Lord our God arise,
Scatter his enemies
And make them fall:
Confound their politicks,
Frustrate their knavish tricks,
On him our hopes are fixed
O save us all.

Nor was the future national anthem the only patriotic hymn. There was an equal sense of being "God's favourite" in what came to be known as *Rule Britannia*:

When Britain first at heaven's command
Arose from out the azure main
This was the charter of the land.
And guardian angels sing this strain;

Rule Britannia, rule the waves.
Britons never will be slaves.

"Britannia" was a Roman word for Britain, portrayed as a female martial figure with helmet and trident ruling the waves on coins from the early eighteenth century.

Content to enslave others in 1745, the British were not prepared to countenance such a future for themselves. Patriotism was further stoked and elaborated by the frequent formation of patriotic societies. One such group that formed in 1745 was the Laudable Association of Anti-Gallicans, founded by tradesmen in London. Its aim was to "discourage by precept and example, the importation and consumption of French produce and manufactures, and to encourage the produce and manufactures of Great Britain". There were more than shades of a trade war with France. The Society of Arts was formed to develop national culture and by 1764 it had 2,100 supporters. The Marine Society founded at the outset of the Seven Years' War on 25 June 1756 provided a supply of recruits for the navy, but was funded by private subscription. George II gave £1,000 and the Prince of Wales, the future George III, £300.

Patriotism was furtherer widened in meaning, and in a controversial manner, by the radical journalist John Wilkes. If the patriotic songs and societies wrapped themselves in the flag of the Protestant Hanoverian succession, and resistance to the French and Jacobite claim to the English throne, Wilkes stood for a very English idea of freedom in the tradition of Pym, Hampden, John Lilburne of the Levellers and the extreme Whig Algernon Sydney. In his publication of *The North Briton*, he attacked first George III's favourite new minister, Lord Bute, generally lampooned for his close relationship with George III's mother, the Dowager Princess of Wales. Even worse, in issue number 45 of *The North Briton*, he criticized King George III himself, for his pusillanimous conduct at the Peace of Paris which concluded the Seven Years' War. Wilkes was arrested under a general warrant, but then elected to the House of Commons by the voters of Middlesex in 1768. The House of Commons refused him entry, as he was an outlaw at the time of his election. Furthermore, in a riot in his support, seven men were killed and fifteen wounded in what became known as the St George's Field Massacre. It came as no surprise that Wilkes and Edmund Burke, the political philosopher and secretary to the Whig politician Lord Rockingham, were both supporters of Locke's theory of a contract between the government and the governed.

After the success of the Seven Years' War and the acquisition of territory in Canada, in India, on the continent of Europe at Gibraltar and Menorca, in the Caribbean, in Florida and in the Pacific, this fledgling empire was about to be dealt its severest blow: the loss of the thirteen American colonies. That a nation which had so conclusively defeated its major rival, France, in most of these areas should be defeated by an inexperienced militia of farmers and tradesmen seems inexplicable. But these were not inconsiderable colonies. Between 1601 and 1701, emigration to the American colonies totalled 700,000 people, nearly half as indentured European labour. The population of the colonies was 2.5 million by 1775, a third of that of Britain. In fact, Britain slid into war with its American colonies because of a half-thought-through policy of colonial taxation. Reeling from the costs of the Seven Years' War, the motley group of ministers advising the new King George III sought to raise money from the colonies through taxation and to bring them to heel under British Parliamentary control. Since trade with the colonies accounted for 20 per cent of exports and 30 per cent of imports, war was a risky business. The country, both in and out of Parliament, was divided. The reaction of independent-minded, eighteenth-century Americans, not unlike Pym or Hampden, resented taxation without representation. The refusal to pay the stamp tax levied on documents and newspapers and the tea tax sparked a rejection of the British Parliament and a refusal to take British or colonial goods. On 19 April 1775, at Lexington Green, Massachusetts, British Redcoats exchanged fire with colonial Minutemen or militia. By October 1781, after a protracted campaign during which Britain increasingly had other conflicts to worry about, the British Army commanded by Lord Cornwallis surrendered at Yorktown. The American Declaration of Independence, a document much inspired by John Locke, which had been approved on 4 July 1776 by all thirteen states, summed up the new nation's noble aspirations. Its second sentence, crafted mostly by Thomas Jefferson, has since become a beacon for freedom and human rights:

> We hold these truths to be self-evident, that all men are created equal, that they are endowed by their Creator with certain inalienable Rights, that among these are Life, Liberty and the pursuit of Happiness.

It is ironic that the Parliament that fought so hard for similar rights in seventeenth-century England should find itself, with the crown, preventing its former citizens from enjoying the same rights. After all the successes of recent years, the loss of the colonies was a profound shock. In March 1782, Lord North resigned, following a motion of "no confidence" in Parliament. James Gillray, the great cartoonist of his age, portrayed North and his cronies as a bunch of incompetent tinkers trying to fix the national kettle, with the King praising their work. The United States, which would pass through its own vicissitudes a century later in the Civil War, would be a foil and inspiration to the Church in England over the next two centuries, and would militarily come to the support of the Allies twice in their continental struggles in the twentieth century.

CHAPTER 17

War and Peace

By 1783, there had been a remarkable change of attitude towards King George III. In 1775, after criss-crossing the country with his preaching, John Wesley recorded that "the bulk of the people in every city, town, and village . . . heartily despise his Majesty, and hate him with a perfect hatred".[1] Yet surprisingly, although he was unpopular in the 1760s and 1770s, after the loss of the American colonies at the Peace of Versailles in 1783 he grew gradually in the affections and estimation of his subjects.

Unlike his grandfather, George II, this third George considered himself a true Englishman, not a Hanoverian as his forbears had done. In fact, George III never visited Hanover. He was hardworking and devout; he spent hours in prayer each week and was faithful to his wife, Charlotte, a German princess with whom he had fifteen children. With his simple tastes, he was sometimes mistaken for a farmer. He gave to the nation the first real model of a royal family, although several of his seven surviving sons failed to live up to his standards (particularly the Prince Regent, later George IV, and the Duke of York). Although he suffered from bouts of madness—especially in 1788, 1801 and 1810—for which he received awful treatments, such as blistering, the then normal application of leeches, and a straitjacket administered by a clergyman and his son, George III nevertheless found a special place in the affections of his people. By the time of his jubilee in 1810, he was blind and had reached the apotheosis of his long reign. The reasons for George's growing popularity were complex: they included his steady, hardworking family life, his vulnerability to mental illness, and his consistent espousal of the Protestant faith. England was at war with France for over twenty years during his reign, and he was liked for being a counterpoint to everything French. His two sons, George IV and William IV, would succeed him, while his granddaughter Victoria carried forward many of his values.

While the ideal of a royal family can be traced back to George, his family relations were far from perfect. Several of his sons were markedly wayward and, as with all Hanoverian monarchs, his relations with his heir were decidedly rocky. George III's father, Frederick, Prince of Wales, who died before he acceded to the throne, had been at odds with his father, George II. (He held an alternative court at Leicester House, was an enthusiastic patron of the arts, and gathered opposition politicians around him to the great suspicion of his father.) Now the same thing would happen with George III: his eldest son, the Prince Regent, complained bitterly of his treatment by the King, who often refused to speak to him. He said he was suffocated by court life and that he had nothing to do. Instead, the Prince Regent spent lavishly, gambled extensively, womanized continually, and in the end married Maria Fitzherbert, a well-to-do widow and a Roman Catholic, in a drawing room with only an Anglican clergyman present. It was a marriage never recognized in law. The Prince Regent espoused the Whig cause, led by Charles James Fox in opposition to Pitt, and was surrounded by Whig *glitterati* and their aristocratic connections: the Grenvilles, Rockinghams, Devonshires, Spensers, Churchills, Pelhams, Bedfords, Herveys and Lansdownes.

George was also more than choosy about the ministers who would serve him and would be one of the last monarchs to choose his own, rather than have Parliament thrust them upon him. When the coalition of Lord North and Charles James Fox (whom George initially detested) ended in 1783, a new and essentially Tory prime minister came to the fore. He was William Pitt, son of the Earl of Chatham, the former prime minister who had seen England victorious in the Seven Years' War. Pitt was Chancellor at twenty-three, and at twenty-four was the youngest prime minster Britain ever had. He would be prime minister for almost twenty years. Few kings were better served by a prime minister who would face the gravest threat from post-Revolutionary France in Napoleon's attempt to invade and subjugate England.

Over the next forty years, from 1784 onwards, England would face two revolutions of great significance for the nation, in the body politic and the Church.

The Industrial Revolution

While the Industrial Revolution began slowly, the exigencies of war, the result of inventions, growing capital investment, availability of labour, and the Act of Unions with Scotland and Ireland would thrust the United Kingdom into pole position as an industrialized nation by the middle of the nineteenth century.

The process began with improved travel. A series of inland Navigation Acts passed in the 1760s and 1770s heralded the canal age. At the same time, hundreds of Turnpike Acts licensed individuals or corporations to collect fees in return for building and maintaining roads. There were 170 Turnpike Acts in the 1750s and 1760s, and the mid-eighteenth century became an age of turnpike mania. Fifty-two per cent of the total mileage constructed between 1696 and 1836 was authorized between 1750 and 1770. Journey times were greatly reduced as a great network of inns and carrier coach services operated across the land. A timetable evolved with clear journey times between towns. Likewise, the canal system conveyed goods across the country, including imported goods like cotton and locally mined coal, as on the Bridgewater Canal, which was owned and constructed by the third Duke of Bridgewater. By the mid-nineteenth century, there would be 19,000 barges operating in Britain.

At the same time, Richard Arkwright's invention of the loom or spinning frame increased growth in the new population centres. The looms would later be driven by steam engines designed by James Watt in 1778. What happened in the North-West was then replicated in other new industries: in the Potteries, where china and pottery were manufactured by Sir Josiah Wedgwood (1730–95), and in Birmingham, through the production of iron in new smelting processes. A whole new industrialized Britain was emerging. This development would be enhanced by more than twenty years of war, and the need to equip the army that was fighting Napoleon on the continent, and an ever-growing navy at sea. During a protracted war, the demand for clothes and iron was insatiable: war drove the industrialization of Britain.

The result of all this was rapid population growth. By the end of the eighteenth century, the population of London was near on a million, and it became the largest city in Europe and probably the Western world. Other cities would also increase greatly, e.g. Bristol, Bath, Newcastle, Sunderland, Liverpool, Manchester and Birmingham. Old centres of manufacture that were less well located, such as Tiverton, Salisbury, Canterbury, Norwich and Worcester, declined. Lincoln was another to decline and was described by one customs officer as "the meanest city this day in all England". The population of the United Kingdom, which since the Act of Union in 1800 included Ireland, was 16 million in 1801, but by 1821 it was 21 million. In the same period, the population of Manchester increased from 75,000 to 126,000; Birmingham from 71,000 to 102,000; Liverpool from 82,000 to 138,000; and Glasgow from 77,000 to 147,000. These were large increases that were set to rise even further. Because England was at the centre of an ever-developing trade based around an expanding empire, shipping also increased throughout the great sea ports of the kingdom, and most of all in London, where, in this period, the West India Docks (1802), the East India Docks (1803), the London Docks (1805) and the Surrey Commercial Docks (1807) were all constructed.

Such sudden population surges created accompanying social, sanitary, spiritual and political problems, which would only increase as the new century wore on. It would be some time before housing would keep pace with population, with the resulting appearance of slums in many cities and most of all in London. Slum parishes arose in Shoreditch, Hackney, Bethnal Green, Stepney, Ratcliffe, Shadwell and Limehouse. Further slums appeared in other industrialized cities, or wherever the labouring population grew rapidly. It would not be until the mid or late nineteenth century that water, sewage and lighting would come to these areas and we will trace the progress of that inventive march of the great Victorian engineers. Before such improvement, conditions had become so grave that by the 1830s emigration had turned to a flood. In 1832, i.e. at the end of the period dealt with in this chapter, 100,000 had departed to destinations outside Europe. The reason for this was that there were few signs of improvement in the quality of life for ordinary people in England, either in the towns or in the countryside. The latter was itself subject to new limitations of mechanization and the enclosure of common ground, which in turn provoked rural movements of protest that were often brutally suppressed. The Swing Riots of 1830 and the Tolpuddle Martyrs of 1834 were the product of great rural unrest, the increased mechanization of farming, and the harsh imprint of the Poor Law. Not only was there an acute need for improved living conditions, but these new urban populations also needed to be properly represented in Parliament through the redistribution of parliamentary seats.

Industrialization also presented one of the greatest challenges to the Church, which had become a pillar of patriotism in a society threatened by Napoleon and the French Revolution. With its privileged position in the fabric of the nation, the Church of England was failing to keep pace with the growth and shifting distribution patterns in the population. For instance, in 1800, there were a thousand parishes in rural and agricultural Norfolk, but only seventy in industrialized and urbanizing Lancashire. The former reflected the rural medieval economy based on sheep, the latter the industrialized economy of cotton and coal. Later we shall see the attempts of Lord Liverpool's government to plug this hole with the building of urban churches and parishes, but it is arguable that the Church of England never really made up the lost ground in pastoring and evangelizing the new urban populations.

Non-Conformist churches had a better record, although, as with Anglicanism, parts of Methodism failed to identify or campaign adequately for the needs of the working man. Jabez Bunting (1779–1858), a Methodist leader in Manchester, for example, exchanged revivalism for authoritarianism because he disapproved of movements for social change. In 1810, the Primitive Methodists, a revivalist branch emanating from a new spiritual movement in America, separated from the main body of Methodists. Drawn mainly from the working class, they saw themselves returning to the pure beginnings of Methodism, with open-air meetings and a deep concern for personal holiness. In general, the churches were slow to come to terms with the needs and opportunities of industrialization, and the question must be asked whether they ever managed to minister effectively to these new industrialized communities in England.

The French Revolution

Alongside the Industrial Revolution, which would change the face of England, another revolution not only presented a deep challenge to political and religious thinking in England, but also caught the country up in one of its lengthiest wars.

The liberal and artistic communities of England initially greeted the storming of the Bastille on 14 July 1789 with excitement and hope, for the Bastille was a symbol of autocratic France. From his school at Christ's Hospital, the sixteen-year-old Samuel Taylor Coleridge wrote *The Destruction of the Bastille*, his first substantial and original poem, in which he records the universal cry for liberty. Hundreds of such odes to liberty were penned in England, and William Wordsworth famously wrote in his autobiographical *Prelude*, "Bliss was it in that dawn to be alive. But to be young was very heaven."[2] Later and in partnership with Robert Southey, Coleridge wrote a play, *The Fall of Robespierre* (1794), which reflected a greater ambivalence about the Revolution, for it praised Robespierre as a destroyer of despotism while accusing him of becoming a tyrant himself. In later years, all three of these Romantic Lake Poets would become critical of the Revolution and its effects. Robert Southey was appointed Poet Laureate by the Tory government of Lord Liverpool and became virtually reactionary by 1817.

On the political front, Edmund Burke (1729–97), the Irish-born statesman, churchman and politician, had early misgivings about the actions of the French. Although Whig in his principles and a supporter of the concept of liberty, he espoused *evolution* rather than *revolution* as a truer means of achieving freedom. He criticized the French Enlightenment philosophers, Rousseau, Voltaire and

Turgot, for rejecting concepts of original sin and of a supreme and divine moral order. His views were powerfully expressed in his *Reflections on the French Revolution*, a pamphlet written in November 1790, early on in the Revolution. Other liberal-minded philosophers, church leaders or writers did *not* universally applaud Burke. In an electrifying 1789 sermon, entitled *Discourse on the Love of Our Country*, the leading Non-Conformist preacher, Richard Price (1723–91), proposed that the principles of the Glorious Revolution of 1688 were now finally being fulfilled in France. Others, like Tom Paine (1723–1809), author of *Rights of Man*, and Mary Wollstonecraft (1759–97), author of *A Vindication of the Rights of Woman*, leapt to Price's defence. As the Revolution wore on, however, devouring its children as well as King Louis XVI and Marie Antoinette in 1793, their praise was shown to be premature. By October 1793, a campaign to replace Christianity with a pagan calendar and classical virtues revealed the Revolution in its true colours.[3] In turn the Revolution was consumed by the Terror. By 1793, England was at war with France, an almost continuous conflict that would last for more than twenty years until 1815. At times England was a whisker away from being invaded by the forces of the Revolution's greatest heir, Napoleon Bonaparte. What began for some as a Romantic fulfilment of all their aspirations for liberty turned into an existential threat to the whole English way of life.

The danger of invasion was also real, with attempts made in Pembrokeshire, Wales, in 1797 and, more seriously, through Ireland in 1796 and 1798. A more direct attack on England was threatened from Boulogne in 1805.

Ireland was a disaffected nation that Pitt sought to cajole with carrot and stick. In 1798, some 30,000 Irish rebels who supported a French invasion had died. In response, Pitt passed the Act of Union between Britain and Ireland in 1800, implementing direct rule from Westminster and abolishing the Irish Parliament in Dublin, which had been open only to Protestant or Church of Ireland members. This Act was to have fateful implications for the British government in the nineteenth and twentieth centuries. To placate the Irish, Pitt sought to emancipate Catholics so that they might vote and themselves be elected, but he met implacable opposition from George III, which forced his resignation in 1801. George III felt his coronation oath meant he had to uphold the Church of England, and continue suppressing Roman Catholics in national life, in Ireland as in England.

The final and most dangerous threat of invasion came in 1805. War had resumed after the brief Peace of Amiens of 1803 and after a row with the British Ambassador, Lord Charles Whitworth. The British navy continued to blockade French ports, while Napoleon tried to strangle British trade with his "Continental System", hitting England where it hurt most as a "nation of shopkeepers". He assembled a force of 100,000 at Boulogne, but he did not command the seas, so in the end he secretly abandoned this plan, to challenge others instead. When Nelson defeated the combined French and Spanish navies at Trafalgar on 21 October 1805, all possibility of invasion had gone. At the same time, having withdrawn his *grande armée* from the Channel ports, Napoleon defeated the Russian and Austrian armies at Austerlitz on 2 December 1805. Pitt heard the news from Lord Castlereagh while he was in Bath taking a cure as a sick man. William Wilberforce, Pitt's close friend, maintained that it broke the Prime Minister's spirit: "Roll up that map. It will not be wanted these ten years," was Pitt's insightful and prophetic response. It would indeed be almost ten years before Napoleon was finally defeated at Waterloo by the Duke of Wellington and the Prussian army, and even then it was "a damn close-run thing".

The effect of the long years of war was to turn Britain into an armed camp, leaving no aspect of society untouched, including the Church. The first effect of this long period of increased danger from revolutionary France was to increase patriotism, almost out of a sense of relief after the humiliation of the American War of Independence. Here was something to define Britain; here was something to fight for. The allegory of Britannia was reborn, as depicted in paint by Benjamin West, a British North American and second President of the Royal Academy. A more populist portrayal of British identity came from cartoonists Hogarth, Gillray, Rowlandson and Cruikshank, who offered John Bull, the quintessential Briton: stubborn, bucolic, steady and opinionated. In one cartoon, this rustic figure carries the severed head of Napoleon on his pitchfork. Bull was undoubtedly Protestant and knew all the patriotic dates from Magna Carta to the Glorious Revolution of 1688. He studied his Almanac carefully, which sold like hot cakes in those days, and knew all the historic turning points of English or British history and their significance. He would also fight to defend them. As Handel had done earlier in the eighteenth century, Israel was readily replaced by Great Britain in the biblical narrative. Indeed, Isaac Watts, the great hymn writer, dissenting minister and creator of "When I Survey the Wondrous Cross", translated the Psalms replacing references to Israel with Great Britain: to him they were one and the same. So too the visionary William Blake, who sought to "build Jerusalem in England's green and pleasant land", a task for which bow and chariot were needed.

Blake was a supporter of revolution and social change, but his poem was quickly requisitioned for more patriotic aims. Thus, by 1810, we have "Jerusalem", "God Save the King" and "Rule Britannia" all struggling for a share of John Bull's lungs. "Jerusalem" would wait a further hundred years until Hubert Parry, himself inspired by Edward Elgar, would add music to complete the emotional pull of its words, but there was no doubting the general patriotism as nation and faith fused in the furnace of national danger. "Jerusalem" was resurrected during the First World War to inspire the nation. While the Protestant Church, in its established and non-conformist manifestation—although tinged with the pacifism of Quakerism—formed a bulwark of the state, the clergy were seemingly the quiet backbone of England in the parishes.

In her novels of English upper- and middle-class life, Jane Austen focussed with delicious humour on the formation of relationships and marriages, rather than on the dangers of war. Soldiers were depicted more for their dashing uniforms than their military capability. Her novels were set in Hampshire and Bath, yet were written during the Napoleonic Wars. Like most parish clergy, her father, the Vicar of Steventon, was responsible for keeping a register of possible volunteers for the militia. He noted that thirty-five men would volunteer from his parish, also revealing that, of its 150 inhabitants, all but six worked on the land. By and large, local villagers responded to this national mobilization that was overseen by clergy and recruiting officers, as villagers do everywhere, with "stolid unconcern, marked suspicion, dumb resentment and sometimes with downright resistance".[4] In the end, about a sixth of the adult population was under arms and recruited into the militia, an early version of the Home Guard that would be formed in the Second World War. The cost in lives from the Napoleonic Wars was great: about 210,000 men would die. The clergy provided sermons and information to promote the cause against Napoleon and led the nation in mourning.

While these great events of war and peace unfurled in the late eighteenth century and at the beginning of the nineteenth century, three great movements of change were underway: the Abolition of the Slave Trade, the Emancipation of Roman Catholics and the Reform of Parliament. In an age of revolution, these all had to do with freedom, none more so than the ending of the slave trade, the greatest stain on British life.

The abolition of the slave trade

The abolition of the slave trade was the noblest of all the movements in this period. It was a national and parliamentary response to a great evil that had grown up over preceding generations, and the campaign to end the trade in human beings was spearheaded in the House of Commons by William Wilberforce.

The Portuguese began the Atlantic slave trade in the sixteenth century, although slavery had been part of human life from time immemorial. The Portuguese traders took African people from the West African seaboard, who were then sold by African slave traders, and took them to Brazil. The British, the Dutch, the Spanish and the French soon followed. The British enslaved people from the West Africa coast and its interior and took them to the colonies of the British West Indies, notably Jamaica, to work the sugar plantations. Some also went to the American colonies to grow cotton and clear the ground, while others went as servants to England. It is estimated that some 300,000 slave traders were involved from the start of the slave trade in the seventeenth century to its abolition. A highly profitable triangular system emerged: goods from Europe, including guns, were traded with African kings and slave traders; slaves were then sold or exchanged and taken to the West Indies or American colonies; and on the return journey, cotton, sugar, molasses, tobacco and rum were exported to Britain and Europe. It is estimated that by 1772 some 52,000 people were being taken to the Caribbean as slaves each year. By the mid-eighteenth century, Britain and France had become the largest slave-trading nations.

A bald description of the extent of the trade by the mid-eighteenth century cannot convey the indescribable misery of the trade and the conditions that pertained, both in the ships and on the plantations. In 1840, Joseph Mallord William Turner sought to depict the horror of the trade in a picture called *The Slave Ship*, which was based on the true account of a slave-trading vessel called the *Zong*. Back in 1783, the *Zong*, a British slave ship bound for Jamaica, was hit by an epidemic (not uncommon in the terrible conditions of slave ships, where slaves lay for weeks on end below decks). The captain, Luke Collingwood, knowing that his insurance policy only covered slaves lost at sea, and that his stocks of water were running low, decided to solve both his problems by casting 133 sick slaves into the sea. At root, he failed to recognize his cargo were human beings and committed mass murder. It was this scene, caught in the act, which Turner shows in his picture of the limbs of desperate slaves threshing in the water, before sinking to a watery grave. Turner's intention was "to represent the doom of slavery". Indeed, slavery itself, not simply the trade, had just been rendered illegal. John Ruskin, the art critic, bought Turner's picture, but quickly sold it on, because he found it unbearable to look at.

The trade underwrote the commercial and colonial development of Britain. The British went on throughout the eighteenth century supplying approximately 23,000 slaves a year to their colonies. While trumpeting freedom at home, the nation enslaved a people abroad: it was blind or wilful, or both. Thomas Jefferson, the chief composer of the American Declaration of Independence, accused George III of conducting "a cruel war against human nature itself, violating its most sacred rights of life and liberty in the persons of a distant people who never offended him, captivating and carrying them into slavery in another hemisphere".[5] By the 1780s there was the stirring, not only of profound revulsion at the trade, but also a desire to end it, as a number of factors came together to make this possible. Nevertheless, there would still be a titanic struggle against the forces of vested interest and commerce.

The movement to end the slave trade had many parts, personalities and contributors, but it had one spearhead uniquely placed to bring the campaign to a successful conclusion: William Wilberforce. Others had prepared the ground— Samuel Johnson and Adam Smith, the social and political commentator and economist respectively—by speaking against it. John Wesley wrote a powerful pamphlet entitled *Thoughts on Slavery* in which he also declared against it.[6] On 11 October 1787, Wesley wrote to a leading actor in the abolition movement, Granville Sharpe, saying, "Ever since I heard of it first, I felt a perfect detestation of the horrid trade."[7] Granville Sharpe (1735–1813) was a civil servant and political reformer who formed the Society for Effecting the Abolition of the Slave Trade in 1787. He brought together a powerful group of reformers including, among others, John Wesley, John Newton, William Wilberforce, Josiah Wedgwood, Hannah More, Baron Grenville, Zachary Macaulay (a former plantation owner and father of the famous Whig historian, Thomas Babington Macaulay, the great educationalist of the Raj in India) and the former slave and writer, Olaudah Equiano. Each would bring insight, wisdom, biblical teaching, voluminous evidence, knowledge and experience to bear on the case for abolition, which had to be moved in the nation, the media and, supremely, in Parliament.

By the 1780s, a national movement for the abolition of the slave trade was coalescing in England. In 1783, the Quakers presented the first anti-slavery petition to Parliament. Four years later, the Society for Effecting the Abolition of the Slave Trade was founded. Then, in 1788, Manchester pointedly began a mass campaign petitioning against the trade. In the same year, Josiah Wedgwood produced his famous cameo medallion with a picture of a chained slave pleading for liberty. The words inscribed below the kneeling figure were: "Am I not a Man and a Brother?" It was to become a truly iconic symbol of the campaign, produced by one of the great industrialists of the age. Elsewhere in London, a group of dedicated Evangelical Christians emerged, who came to be called the Clapham Sect. The group was founded by Henry Venn and was continued by his son John Venn, the Rector of Holy Trinity Clapham. Among the members were Henry Thornton, MP for Southwark, and Thomas Fowell Buxton, the brewer and later MP who was related to the Norfolk Quaker families of Gurneys and

Frys. Buxton was to carry forward the legislation for the abolition of slavery in all the British dominions. Collectively, the Clapham Sect was a resourceful and determined group who gave comfort and support, both spiritual and personal, to their parliamentary leader, William Wilberforce.

Few men could have been better equipped for the task of abolition than Wilberforce. His blend of spiritual, personal and mental qualities combined in a man of great attractiveness, personal integrity, persuasive oratory and Christian vision would sustain the campaign over the next twenty years. He was born and raised in Hull, the son of a wealthy merchant family, and was partly educated in London before going to St John's, Cambridge. It was there that he met his lifelong friend and the future prime minister, William Pitt. Liked for his witty conversation, his playful disposition and his carefree lifestyle at Cambridge, along with Pitt he soon aspired to a life in national politics and was elected MP for Hull in 1781, while still a student. Extraordinarily, his Cambridge friend Pitt was prime minister just three years later, having already been Chancellor in the government of Lord Shelburne following the failure of the North-Fox coalition and Lord Rockingham's brief government, in the aftermath of the loss of the American colonies. By 1784, Pitt was prime minister, and Wilberforce was about to undergo a more fundamental change.

Wilberforce had been pondering the deeper questions of life, seeking more than his privileged background, natural talents and unusual opportunities had already given him. Although he was an MP at the age of twenty-two, he was not satisfied. Together with his mother, two sisters, and two female cousins who were in need of a tonic, Wilberforce set out on the continental tour so beloved of the eighteenth-century elite. For male company he invited along Isaac Milner, a man of physically large presence, gentle wit and great intellect. Milner was the Jacksonian Professor of Natural Philosophy at Cambridge, and also an ordained and avowed Evangelical Christian of clear convictions. Having read Philip Doddridge's *Rise and Progress of Religion in the Soul* and the Greek New Testament, Wilberforce found that, in the Swiss Alps during that autumn of 1785, he too came to believe and hope in Christ. His conversion followed the classic pattern of self-examination leading to a sense of inadequacy and sinfulness, followed by the assurance of forgiveness and acceptance through the redemption of Christ—a process that took time but was solidly born. Wilberforce's conversion took place over those months when he was travelling on the continent. (The journey was interrupted from April to August, however, when Wilberforce returned to London to support the new prime minister, William Pitt, in his unsuccessful bid for parliamentary reform and a more successful quest for a new trading relationship with Ireland.) What began during those months of sabbatical would motivate and shape Wilberforce's response to the cause of abolition over the next twenty years. He would remain spiritually self-critical, combining deep devotion with personal humility, and he never tired of the grace of Christ. In 1787, Wilberforce was asked by Thomas Clarkson and others to head the parliamentary campaign to abolish the slave trade. He gladly agreed, because he was convinced of the need. He was further encouraged to do so by Pitt himself, who feared Wilberforce might otherwise retreat from national politics, and who thus encouraged him to convert his new-found faith into action for the public good.

The campaign would continue for twenty years as part of some of the most tempestuous years of British national life, i.e. the period of the Napoleonic Wars. Indeed, William Pitt, who would serve as prime minister for nearly twenty-two years, would die exhausted from his service in 1806, a year before Abolition was passed. At times, Wilberforce could not support Pitt in his path to war—hoping and voting for peace—and progress towards Abolition was slow and tortuous.

By 1783, the movement was well underway. That year, Granville Sharpe had brought the action of Captain Collingwood in the infamous case of the *Zong* slave ship to court. The case was heard by Lord Mansfield, the Lord Chief Justice, who had ruled in the case of Somerset in June 1772. In that case, it had been decided that the ownership of a slave by Charles Stewart, an American customs officer, was illegal, and that owning a slave in England or transporting a slave *out* of England was against the law. It was a landmark ruling, but did not in itself make the slave trade illegal outside of England. In 1784, the Reverend James Ramsey, a Quaker, published two powerful pamphlets based on twenty-one years' research into the slave trade in the West Indies. They were entitled *An Essay on the Treatment and Conversion of African Slaves in the British Sugar Colonies* and *An Inquiry into the Effects of the Abolition of the Slave Trade* respectively. Many of the arguments which would be developed in the years ahead were in these two pamphlets by Ramsey. In 1786, following persuasion by Ramsey, Clarkson, Sir Charles and Lady Middleton of Teston, Kent, John Newton and many others, Wilberforce took up the cause. When visiting Pitt at his house at Holwood, Kent, and sitting under an oak tree with William Grenville, later also prime minister, Pitt encouraged Wilberforce with these words:

> Wilberforce, why don't you give notice of a motion on the subject of the slave trade? You have already taken great pains to collect evidence, and are therefore fully entitled to the credit which doing so will ensure you. Do not lose time, or the ground may be occupied by another.[8]

At the end of the year Wilberforce wrote, "God Almighty has sent before me two great objects, the suppression of the slave trade and the reformation of manners."[9] These two objectives would become the central purposes of his life.

The campaign for Abolition was lengthy: Parliamentary hearings and a commission collected evidence. In April 1791, Wilberforce brought forward the first Bill for Abolition, speaking for four hours. On his side were many heavyweights, including Pitt, Charles James Fox and Edmund Burke. On 20 April 1791, the House divided. Slightly less than half the members were there, and the "Nos" were 163 and the "Ayes" eighty-eight. The vote was lost by seventy-five. A further Bill was brought back in 1792, which proposed that the trade be gradually abolished. Although passed by a large majority, it was in essence a ruse to delay Abolition. By now war with France was dominating Commons business, including the passing of the Gagging Acts, the suspension of *habeas corpus*, and measures to finance the war. There was less urgency for, or interest in, Abolition, although Wilberforce continued to introduce new Bills. Then, in 1804, Thomas Clarkson renewed the campaign. More confident of resisting the revolutionary ideas coming from France, Parliament was likewise more willing to countenance a change in the slave trade. Opposition was lessening discernibly, and a Bill introduced in May 1804 was denied by a majority of just forty-nine. The new Irish MPs were solidly for Abolition. Soon there was a majority of seventy-five in the Commons, and it seemed like the tide was turning.

The campaign was more than injurious to Wilberforce's health, however. Often weak, ill and dependent on opiates, he would find consolation in his family, whom he adored, and in times of respite in the English countryside. In September 1804, he revelled in a visit to Lyme Regis: "For Wilberforce reading, travelling, and gazing on the countryside joined together as a splendid opportunity to learn and contemplate his actions."[10] It would be another two years before the Parliamentary victory he yearned for was achieved. In that time there would be the victory of Trafalgar and the loss of Pitt, who, worn down by the war years, died too soon and in office. Reflecting on this great loss, Wilberforce wrote to William Hey on 12 February 1806: "For personal purity, disinterestedness, integrity and love of country, I have never known his equal."[11]

The Bill for Abolition was reintroduced in 1806 with the support of the new government led by Grenville. The Bill passed the Commons and was introduced by Grenville himself in the Lords, where it also passed. It was returned to the Commons for the final reading and vote on 23 February 1807. With tears streaming down his face, Wilberforce heard that the Bill had been carried by 283 to sixteen. With royal assent, it became law. The slave trade was abolished in all British territories and the Royal Navy would seek to end it wherever it could. "It was the culmination of one of the greatest campaigns of British history."[12] Freetown in Sierra Leone, founded as a colony in 1792 with John Clarkson, the younger brother of abolitionist Thomas Clarkson, as governor, became the place where many of those caught up in the trade were set free.

Following the great victory in Parliament, Wilberforce would remain active in public life and in the many causes with which he was connected. His commitment to the Reformation of Manners remained unchanged and was reflected in his 1796 publication *A Practical View of the Prevailing Religious System of Professed Christians, in the Higher and Middle Classes in this Country, Contrasted with Real Christianity*. This laboured title was indicative of a rather discursive work of over five hundred pages, but it was quickly taken up, selling 7,500 copies. The general view was that Wilberforce was better in speech than in print. He supported Hannah More and her Sunday School project in Somerset and joined Jeremy Bentham in prison reform. He also supported Pitt in the Botany Bay project in Australia with its transportation of convicts, which proved better in theory than in practice. He got behind the foundation of the Baptist Missionary Society, begun by William Carey, and sought Anglican support for this also. He was a founding member of the British and Foreign Bible Society in 1804, and he discussed the beginnings of an Anglican Missionary Society with Charles Simeon, Charles Grant and Henry Thornton at the Castle and Falcon in Battersea Rise. From this conversation in 1799, the Church Mission Society was born. He lobbied the government that missionaries should be given leave to work in India when the East India Company charter came up for renewal in 1806, and he wrote to the Duke of Wellington in support of this cause. Few could have been involved in more societies with Christian mission or human betterment in view; indeed, a "Bettering Society" was founded—a scientific investigation into the causes of poverty—led by Thomas Bernard and Bishop Barrington, Bishop of Durham, among others. As for slavery, total abolition of the practice itself, rather than the trade in slaves, would not happen until 1833 when new legislation was brought forward by Fowell Buxton. Wilberforce was nevertheless still alive to hear the news that Parliament, setting aside a fund of £20 million for the redemption of slaves, and to purchase and procure their freedom, abolished slavery in all Britain's colonies. Four days later he died.

A costly peace

The early years of the nineteenth century were taken up almost entirely with the defeat of France. The victory over the French and Spanish navies at Trafalgar by Lord Nelson ensured England was safe from invasion. The Peninsular War, which began in 1807, saw British land forces fully committed to waging war against Napoleon's forces under Marshals Junot and Massena in Portugal and Spain. Despite setbacks—politically at the Convention of Sintra in 1808 and militarily in General Moore's famous retreat to Corunna—the campaigns in both Portugal and Spain would eventually prove successful. After a long campaign involving extensive guerrilla warfare, Wellington crossed the Pyrenees into France near Orthez in 1814. Meanwhile, Napoleon had taken the *Grande Armée*, numbering 680,000 troops, on a catastrophic invasion of Russia—testimony to Napoleon's extraordinary ability to inspire even in a reckless campaign.

On the retreat from Moscow, which had been burnt to the ground, and facing a scorched-earth policy from the Russians and relentless attacks by marauding Cossacks, men froze overnight by their horses or bivouacs. The *Grande Armée* struggled home: only 27,000 remained, and soon Napoleon abdicated. Tsar Alexander I entered Paris and was received in London almost like a messiah. Napoleon was sent to Elba, from where he escaped, and in the following hundred days raised an army to face Wellington's British and Prussian forces at Waterloo on Sunday, 18 June 1815. It was a defining battle with great consequences for Britain, for Europe, and indeed the world, with the unassailable establishment of the British Empire. As Wellington said at the end of the battle, "Well, thank God, I don't know what it is to lose a battle, but certainly nothing can be more painful than to gain one with the loss of so many of one's friends."[13] On both sides there were more than 40,000 casualties.

In France, the Bourbon monarchy was restored. Allied forces occupied the country for three years while reparations were paid following the Treaty of Paris. Wellington was the British Ambassador to France and virtually reigned supreme. Lord Castlereagh represented Britain at the Congress of Vienna, a diplomatic junket that redrew the map of Europe. The English, and especially their ladies, were criticized for their lack of style. Lord and Lady Castlereagh, the British Foreign Secretary and his wife, were to be seen "everywhere in the streets and their shops walking arm-in-arm, [going] in every single shop, have everything the establishment contains shown them, and then leave without purchasing a single item!"[14]

These were the final years of the Napoleonic Wars, years of the Regency of Prince George—later George IV—whose father was slipping into madness, senility and blindness. Doctors attending the declining King managed to sequester £271,691 in total fees from the Queen from 1812.[15] When George III died on 29 January 1820, there was national mourning however, with 30,000 attending his funeral at Windsor. Sir George Wraxall summed up the national feeling, saying that although he had not been seen for many years by the public, "his presence suspended or averted national calamities", such was the religious and sentimental affection for him.

The end of the Napoleonic Wars left Britain victorious but exhausted. As a result of the victory, Britain became pre-eminent in Europe and its huge navy, which would only increase, dominated the seas and secured the ever-growing empire with its trade. The wars also left the country vulnerable. As with the end of any great war, social forces were at work that required attention. Yet the governments that followed the victory of Waterloo were by and large conservative, sometimes repressive, and sought to maintain the *status quo*. Fear of civil disorder leading to revolution, as had occurred in France, was very real. To those seeking social change—e.g. William Cobbett and John Wade, author of *The Black Book*, a two-volume work on corruption in the state in the form of an exposé of sinecures and placement—reform was desperately needed.

It seemed that government was mired in profligacy and sunk in corruption. The country faced a severe post-war recession, yet many had their hands in the till and their snouts in the trough. At the same time, tens of thousands of demobilized soldiers were cast on the labour market with little hope of work, and an economy overburdened with debt tipped into recession. There were as many as 20,000 unemployed weavers in Spitalfields, London, alone. When, on 16 August 1819, the cavalry charged a demonstration of 60–80,000 people listening to the radical orator, Hunt, arguing for parliamentary reform in St Peter's Square, Manchester, killing fifteen and injuring between four and seven hundred, the fears of the government were realized. The event was ironically called Peterloo and took place only four years after Waterloo.

Government reacted by passing the Six Acts or Gagging Acts aimed at preventing revolution and unrest among other things, and by suspending *habeas corpus* and banning meetings of over fifty people unless they were registered with the magistrate. In such circumstances, the challenge to the Church was clear: where was it on the great issues of the day, namely industrial and parliamentary reform and the Emancipation of Roman Catholics?

An age of reform

The remaining years of this period—until the accession of Queen Victoria in 1837—were marked by a period of prosperity in the mid-1820s, when policies of reduced taxation and growing free trade pioneered by William Huskisson paid off, and a spell of renewed economic and political tension in the 1830s. Lord Liverpool (Prime Minister, 1812–27), the political manager of a very able, if fractious, Cabinet, steered the ship of state into calmer waters after the radical protests of the years following Waterloo. At different times the Cabinet included men of great ability, such as Vansittart the Chancellor, the Duke of Wellington, Lord Castlereagh, Canning, Peel and Lord Bathurst, the Colonial Secretary. The greatest storm that faced the government in 1820 was George IV's desire for a divorce from his promiscuous wife, Caroline of Brunswick, whom he detested. This plan provoked the unlikely sympathy of the London mob, who saw Caroline as an abused wife, and of radical Whigs who saw their chance to rattle the government of Lord Liverpool and to punish the new king. Legislation in Parliament was required for the divorce, which was eventually dropped when it became clear such a proceeding was likely to expose the King's own uniquely extravagant and equally promiscuous lifestyle. Later the press tired of Caroline's antics, and the following rhyme appeared after Thomas Denman, her solicitor general, effectively admitted her fault by alluding to the woman caught in adultery in John's Gospel (John 7:53–8:11):

> Most Gracious queen we thee implore
> To go away and sin no more;
> Or if that effort be too great,
> To go away at any rate.[16]

Excluded from the coronation, Caroline died a few months later in August 1821.

In 1827, Lord Liverpool died after a stroke while still prime minister. A succession of short governments took office under Canning, Goderich and Wellington, during which time the issue of Catholic Emancipation once more came to the fore. The trend towards religious toleration had been growing.

As early as 1812, Liverpool's government had brought forward a Toleration Bill, which specifically sought to protect Methodists from religious discrimination and from being registered as dissenters. Relief from the various ancient legal restrictions placed upon them was thus provided both to Methodists and other dissenters. However, it was not long before the issue of Roman Catholic Emancipation returned.

Roman Catholics were not permitted freedom to worship, and they could not build parish churches or have a hierarchy in England. They were confined to worshipping in family chapels or foreign embassies, or to requisitioning public spaces in public houses or halls. More drastically, they could not attend or teach at universities, hold public office, have a commission in the army (although several did) or be MPs. All these activities were forbidden unless they became communicant members of the Church of England and foreswore the Catholic theology of the mass. George III had been implacably and crucially opposed to the notion of emancipation, and likewise—although with less conviction than prejudice—George IV. The Hanoverians were brought to the British throne because they were Protestants, and Catholic France was Hanover's and England's arch-enemy, even though France's aspirations had been checked. As far as George III and the Tories were concerned, Roman Catholics were not to be trusted.

If the establishment in the court and the House of Lords was against Roman Catholic Emancipation, it was not so in the Commons. In fact, following the Act of Union with Ireland and the direct rule of Ireland by the British Parliament in 1800, it had been William Pitt's plan to give greater Irish representation by waiving the rule against Catholic electors in Ireland. Yet merely suggesting this to George III, who was so implacably opposed to Roman Catholics, was enough to bring Pitt's government down in 1801. For if Irish Catholic electors were permitted in Ireland, and Catholic MPs were returned to Westminster, how could similar concessions reasonably be withheld in England? Equally, how could Irish Catholics who had fought in the British army against France, giving their blood and lives, now be refused the right to take part in, or elect, a government. As William Plunkett, MP for Dublin University and a Tory barrister, said with heavy irony in a Commons debate:

> While you were binding the wreath around the brow of the conqueror (the Duke of Wellington), you assured him that his victorious followers must never expect to participate in the fruits of his valour, but that they who had shed their blood in achieving conquests were to be the only persons who were not to share in the profits of success in the rights of citizens.[17]

By the 1820s, the House of Commons was moving towards relief from repressive legislation for Roman Catholics: only 250 MPs were by then against such relief. There were however 170 MPs of the Ultra-Tories who were implacably opposed.

In the Lords, the Duke of Wellington, with his knowledge of Ireland—his brother, Richard Marquess Wellesley, was Lord Lieutenant of Ireland from 1821—refused to join the Orange Order and was likewise edging towards Emancipation. The appearance of the Catholic Association in 1823, led by the robust and eloquent Kerryman, Daniel O'Connell, who powerfully advocated Catholic representation in Westminster, brought matters to a head, saying: either risk more violence in Ireland or bring Catholic Emancipation to pass in the United Kingdom. Once again, the nation was at the interface of religious scruples and political realities, a frequent situation in government. When O'Connell was elected to Westminster as MP for County Clare in 1828, the issue of discrimination preventing progress in the democratic process was well and truly in the fire.

Wellington, who had become Prime Minister in January 1828, and who was supported by Robert Peel in the Commons, now had to choose between violence in Ireland or Emancipation. Opinion in England had also been shifting. By 1831, there were 580,000 Irish labourers in England, a figure set to grow greatly in the 1840s as a result of the famine. The nation was no longer so zealously Protestant, although that did not prevent petitions expressing anti-Catholic sentiment being sent to Parliament by the thousands. Over 3,000 were sent in 1828–9. Along with parliamentary reform, the Corn Laws and slavery, Emancipation was the cause that touched the identity of the nation most deeply. The response to each of these issues would define the outlook and perspective of the realm. The Establishment and the more Protestant section of the Church, as well as the Anglican hierarchy, were against Emancipation. The King, a vociferous minority of peers, the bishops, the Ultra-Tories, and less educated folk, especially women, were also equally fiercely opposed; but the educated, commercial and professional classes were more relaxed.

Wellington was now determined to bring forward a Catholic Relief and an Emancipation Bill, despite fierce opposition in some quarters, not least from George IV, who, like his father, cherished Protestant principles in this matter (although they did not much influence his lifestyle!). By May 1828, the old Test and Corporation Acts preventing Catholic involvement in public corporations were repealed. For his part in this, Wellington was denounced as a die-hard traitor—the Iron Duke of all people—by Lord Winchilsea and accused of re-establishing popery, abandoning the King, and forcing the latter to violate his coronation oath to uphold the Anglican Church. Over such a slur, Wellington and Winchilsea fought a duel on Battersea Common, with Wellington coming through unscathed. Both Peel and Wellington resigned briefly on 4 March 1829 during a five-hour argument in which they sought the King's support. The Relief

Bill was finally passed in the Commons on 30 March by 320 to 142, a majority of 178. Peel introduced it with a formidable four-hour speech, and while in the past he had opposed the measure, he now saw the political necessity. The Relief Bill passed in the Lords on 10 April by 217 to 112. In many ways it was Wellington's finest political (as opposed to military) hour. For the first time since 1558, Roman Catholics could worship freely and hold office without penalty in England and the United Kingdom. It would be some time, however, before Roman Catholicism was fully re-established in England with its own hierarchy, and a longer time still before prejudices and suspicions that Catholics were a fifth column of foreign powers in the realm were allayed. From a Protestant point of view, the Roman Catholic allegiance to the Pope and their understanding of the mass and priesthood were still deeply suspect.

As Shakespeare wrote, when sorrows come "they come not singly but in battalions" (*Hamlet* Act IV, Scene V, Claudius), for just a few years later, Parliament, the government and nation faced a greater test: this time over parliamentary reform. The last of the great issues to come, namely the price of corn and free trade, would be more than ten years later in 1845, when it would be Wellington's turn to support Peel.

If the Acts repealing the slave trade and slavery were ones of civil rights and liberty, and the freedom of Roman Catholics to worship and serve the state unmolested had to do with religious toleration, the Reform of Parliament was all about democracy and the right to representation. Compared to universal suffrage for all adult men and women, the Reform Bill was modest, although at the time it seemed like radical politics. It was not a religious or Christian issue *per se*, but the response of the Church was indicative of the attitude of the Church in England to greater parliamentary representation. During the period of the Civil War, the Levellers, led by John Lilburne and others, and drawing on biblical tenets, had clearly upheld in their political philosophy the right of citizens to vote and participate in government. Nearly two hundred years later, this was far from an accepted principle in the Church. It would be almost a hundred years before universal suffrage for adult men and women, regardless of property, came into effect. And at the outset large swathes of opinion in the Church of England especially was against any reform at all. They liked things as they were.

What came to be known as the Great Reform Bill was passed into law by Parliament in 1832, just three years after Catholic Emancipation and amidst a welter of controversy. The movement for parliamentary reform was nationwide. It had been brewing for at least two or three generations, being first tentatively proposed by the Earl of Chatham in the 1760s, and then considered by his son,

William Pitt, in the 1780s, before the outbreak of the French Revolution. The pressure for reform built steadily with population change, the establishing of Corresponding Societies to act as pressure groups, and the Radical movement led by William Cobbett (1763–1835)—campaigner for civil liberties and parliamentary reform. The Irish Parliamentarian Henry Flood (son of the Lord Chief Justice of Ireland, Warden Flood) headed up the Society for Constitutional Information in Westminster in the 1790s, a group that advocated reform and an increase in the electorate.

Those seeking reform wanted a restructuring of the British electoral system and legislature. In a word, the distribution of parliamentary seats was anachronistic. It did not reflect the vast shifts of population to the great manufacturing areas in the late eighteenth and early nineteenth centuries. Many parliamentary seats were in the gift of landlords and had few electors: hence they were called pocket or rotten boroughs, although they did have the advantage of being available to give a leg up to an aspiring young politician like William Gladstone, who took the Duke of Newcastle's pocket-borough seat in Newark in 1832. The Church of England—slow to make its presence felt in these manufacturing areas—was seen as the landowning and rural class at prayer. It was instinctively conservative rather than reforming. Indeed, the record of the bishops in the House of Lords was decidedly reactionary. John Wade wrote in his *Black Book* on the old corruption that "the Clergy, from superior education, from their wealth and sacred profession, possess greater influence than any other order of men, and all the influence they possess is as subservient to government as the army or navy, or any other branch of public service". He continued: "Whenever a loyal address is to be obtained, a popular petition opposed, or a hard measure against the poor, it is almost certain that some reverend rector, very reverend dean, or venerable archdeacon, will make himself conspicuous."[18] The clergy of the Church of England basically wanted to support the hand that fed and promoted them.

In 1829, after the more prosperous middle years of the 1820s, the movement for reform gathered pace once more. Voluminous petitions for reform were sent to Parliament. Yet Wellington, so flexible in supporting Catholic Emancipation, was implacably opposed to reform. Writing to the Duke of Buckingham following the Reform Act, he was gloom personified: "The Government of England is destroyed. A Parliament will be returned, by the means of which no set of men will be able to conduct the administration of affairs, and to protect the lives and properties of the King's subjects."[19] A general election took place in August 1830 after the death of George IV, which did not improve Wellington's position. The new king, William IV, more used to the sea than politics and as eccentric and supercilious as his brother George IV was extravagant, was also against reform. The Tories were divided between the Ultras, led by Wellington now, and, until his untimely death after being run over by a train, Huskisson. In November 1830, Wellington had refused parliamentary reform, was defeated and resigned. Lord Grey became Prime Minister and the Whigs returned to power. Although more blue-blooded and landed than the Tory squirearchy, the Whigs had always espoused a relationship with commerce, supported progress, been a friend of dissenters and would advocate reform to save themselves from anything more radical. Earl Grey in the Lords and Lord Russell (having a purely honorary title, hence in the Commons) brought forward the Reform Bill, but it was thwarted in the Lords three times until Britain came extremely close to revolution in May 1832. Grey promised to flood the Lords with peers unless the House supported the Bill. Wellington's London abode, Apsley House, was stoned repeatedly. On 7 June 1832, the Great Reform Bill became law. Archbishop Howley had a dead cat thrown at him in August 1832, while the Bishop of Bristol's palace was burned down, an act which led to the hanging of four men. In October 1831, the bishops had helped kill off the Reform Bill and, like other peers, had to be persuaded by the threat of mass appointments of reform-minded clergy to their ranks.

The upshot of the passing of the Reform Bill in 1832 was a modest change to the electoral system, but a great change in the political atmosphere of the nation. The electorate increased from 12.7 per cent of the male property-owning population to 18 per cent. In England, fifty-six borough constituencies lost their representation and forty-one new boroughs with one or two seats were created. County representation increased. As John Bright, the future Radical MP, said: "It was not a good bill but it was a great bill when it passed." It enabled Britain, alone among the great powers of Europe, to avoid revolution, extend the franchise and maintain government stability. In 1834, there would be three changes of prime minister and the Houses of Parliament would burn down in October when an overzealous clerk incinerated tally sticks in a wood-burning stove in the basement. In 1835, the unprincipled but charming Melbourne took office again, and was prime minister at Queen Victoria's accession in 1837.

The final years of William IV's reign were marked by a number of important pieces of social legislation. The Poor Law Act of 1834 was to have a profound effect on later Victorian society, giving us the phenomenon of the institutional workhouse. The Act resulted from a royal commission set up in 1832 and was passed by Lord Grey's government to effect economies in the relief of the poor. It replaced the Elizabethan Poor Law Act of 1601, which had led to rising costs in outdoor poor relief especially, and which was the responsibility of the parishes and the Poor Rate. Now, those incapable of work, orphans, and sometimes the insane, were all grouped together in workhouses where cruel and abusive conditions often prevailed. It is estimated that up to six per cent of the population were "cared for" in workhouses. Punishment was meted out to the disorderly in the form of severely reduced rations; inspections were intermittent; and all too often the master or matron, although responsible to a board, which included a chaplain, became caught up in petty corruption. The most celebrated exposé of the workhouse was Dickens's second novel *Oliver Twist* (1839): the boy who dared to ask for "more" food. The guiding light among the Commissioners for the Poor was Edwin Chadwick, a disciple of Jeremy Bentham. He remains a controversial social reformer, for he is sometimes accused of creating an inadequately supervised system that trapped people in institutions from which it was hard to break free. Workhouses would remain a feature of British society until the emergence of the Welfare State post-1945. Their buildings, which were substantial, were then taken over by universities in some cases, while others became expensive urban accommodation! Workhouses failed in their objective of enabling the poor, creating instead conditions of dependency and exploitation, all too prone to abuse.

In the 1830s, the first stirrings of reform in factories, mines and private households were felt. Primary education was only just beginning—and in a piecemeal way—and would not be established nationally and compulsorily until 1870, when education was provided for children between five and ten years of age. In the 1830s, education was pioneered by religious societies, the government, private groups or philanthropists, as in the case of the Ragged Schools. The resulting gap was quickly filled by child employment or exploitation. Small girls and boys of only five or six were forced up chimneys for sweeping, endured long hours working in factories, and were sent down the mines. It was Lord Shaftesbury (1801–85), the Christian Parliamentarian, who supported schools for the poor, and was instrumental in bringing in a Factory Act in 1833, restricting children aged nine from thirteen to eight hours work a day, and no more than forty-eight hours a week! Likewise, the Mines Act of 1842, prepared by Shaftesbury and others, prevented the employment of girls, or indeed any child under the age of ten, down the mines. Reforms begun in this period were to continue throughout the Victorian period, and Shaftesbury was to be instrumental in many of them.

The ministry of the Church

There can be little doubt that in the period from 1780 to 1837, the Church was becoming ever more varied in its expressions, and deeply in need of reform itself—not least the Church of England. Just as parliamentary representation had failed to keep step with a shifting population and the process of industrialization, so too the Church, and in particular the Anglican Church, was finding it hard to adjust to a new set of circumstances. Like trees that appear suddenly bare after winter in bright spring sunlight, the Anglican Church at this time seemed quite unprepared for a way of life that now affected increasing numbers of citizens. The structures were medieval and the challenges unprecedented—after all, no one had ever lived in an industrialized society before. The diocese of Norwich had over a thousand parishes, whereas Rochester diocese had only eighty-three. Yet it was government, more than the church hierarchy, that was aware of the challenge. Political leaders saw the Church as a bulwark against the revolutionary ideas that had been coming in from France. They wanted to increase provision of churches, and indeed this is what happened, and with government financial support.

In 1815, the Reverend Richard Yates calculated that, given that the population in England was 17 million and rising rapidly (by 1830 it would be 24 million), the capacity of church buildings needed to be increased by 60 per cent if the population was to be able to attend church on any given Sunday during the year. This was church growth through central planning: in a believing age, more space meant more congregations. In the aftermath of Waterloo, the country thus enjoyed a boom in church building. Indeed, in direct thanksgiving for that great victory, four Waterloo churches were built in South London: St Luke's Norwood, St Matthew's Brixton, St Mark's Kennington and St John's Waterloo. And it is amazing to the modern mind that the government of Lord Liverpool provided £1 million for this building programme, including up to £20,000 for a single church building (at least £3 million in present-day money). The Church Commissioners, who had been brought into being for this purpose, handled the distribution of these grants.

This was the just the start; more money was granted in 1820. For thirty years from 1830 onwards, some two thousand Anglican churches were built, this being the greatest period of church building since the fifteenth century. Most were built in the preferred Victorian style of gothic: generous edifices of brick or stone, with soaring roofs visible from a distance. This style would entail great heating costs for less hardy future congregations, but with space enough to combine worship with cafes today, something not envisaged by the Victorian architects.

If church buildings were the initial answer to the issue of keeping the Church abreast of a changing population, the staffing and resourcing questions could not be neglected, nor were they. Once again, it was the government that re-ordered the Church, rather than the Church re-ordering itself. In fact, Sir Robert Peel, as with so much else, turned his formidable mind to the need for church reform. In February 1835, during his first short premiership of 120 days, the Ecclesiastical Commissioners met in Peel's home to address discrepancies in pay and lifestyle among the clergy. They had much work to do in those early years sharing the revenues of the Church more equitably and providing for mission in the urban centres of the nation.

At the end of the eighteenth century, there still were some clerical eccentrics, none more so than the Earl Bishop Augustus Hervey, Bishop of Derry. A scion of the Whig Hervey dynasty from Ickworth, Suffolk, he had a passion for building of all kinds, which earned him the epithet "the Edifying Bishop". Commended by Wesley for his generosity and conduct of worship early in his episcopacy, his ministry was in the end overwhelmed by his desire to acquire art for a mansion he was building at Ickworth. His daughter Bess lived in a *ménage a trois* with the Duke of Devonshire and his first wife Georgiana, before herself becoming the Duchess of Devonshire, while his youngest daughter, Louisa, became the virtuous and beloved wife of the Prime Minister, Lord Liverpool.

The Archbishop of Canterbury was paid £19,000 a year (about over £2 million per annum in today's money), while some bishops held multiple posts, such as canonries in other cathedrals. It was time for reform, since some clergy with large families barely subsisted, while the wider population wrestled with paying tithes and were aghast at such wealth. In 1836, tithes, in terms of payment in kind, were commuted to payments in rents through the Tithe Commutation Act. Episcopal salaries were pegged at £4,000—still a tidy £400,000 in today's terms. Legislation preventing the plurality of livings (holding two posts concurrently more than ten miles apart) was brought forward, while many non-residential cathedral appointments were abolished. All of this reduced what was termed the "Old Corruption" in the Church and the political world of sinecures and pensions.

In the parishes, there was a mixture of a conventional middle-of-the-road Anglicanism, concerned with little more than discharging pastoral obligations, and a more thoroughgoing evangelical working of the parish.

Spiritual aspiration had been effectively swallowed by social convention. But the quiet devotion of a Jane Austen could be overlooked, since it had no strong doctrinal clothing. In a prayer now framed in her bedroom at Chawton, Hampshire, she wrote reflectively:

> Have we thought irreverently of thee, have we neglected any known duty, or willingly given pain to any human being? Incline our hearts to ask these questions, oh God, to save us from deceiving ourselves by pride or vanity.

Hers was a spirituality of careful self-examination: not surprising in one who was so quick to recognize human foibles and inconsistencies in her ironic and highly perceptive writing.

An example of an Evangelical parish ministry with wide influence was that of Charles Simeon (1759–1836). Educated at Eton College and King's College Cambridge, he was made a Fellow of King's in 1782 and Vicar of Holy Trinity, Cambridge in 1783, and would remain vicar there for the rest of his life. A staunch Anglican, Simeon steered a middle course between Calvin's strong teaching on predestination and irresistible grace and the need for the individual to work out his own salvation in faith and godly fear. His especial skill was taking all the elements of parish ministry—preaching, prayer, liturgy, pastoral care and the sacraments—and using them purposefully in the forming of Christ in the life of each individual. By bringing Evangelical purpose within the parameters of Anglicanism, he forged a pattern of ministry that was to be widely followed. His preaching classes were well-attended, and he made possible the extension of this ministry beyond his life in the wider church through the purchase of patronage. (Patronage was the right to present a candidate to the bishop as an incumbent for a parish during a vacancy. The right to do this through advowsons—patronage—was commonplace. The right could then be vested in a trust, which still operates effectively today nearly two hundred years later. Indeed, advowsons could be bought on the open market. Other patronage trusts, representing different interests in the Church of England, also exist today.)

Simeon was not only influential at home; his influence overseas was just as great. At the end of the Napoleonic Wars, Britain had established the foundations of empire, emerging from its haphazard beginnings into more cohesive entity. The abolition of the slave trade had put in place new priorities and values, not least the conversion of peoples to Christianity. From the end of the eighteenth century, this was to be a powerful motivation in colonizing new territories, as it had been in the seventeenth century. In 1776, the *Evangelical Magazine* announced the need to send the gospel of Christ to the "benighted" continent of Africa. Missionary societies were quickly founded: the Baptist Society for Propagating of the Gospel among the Heathen, the London Missionary Society in 1795, and the Anglican Church Mission Society in 1799. Many others would follow. From Cambridge, Simeon supported not a few missionaries: Henry Martyn in Persia, David Brown in Calcutta, and Daniel Corrie, the first bishop in Madras. There were many others besides, and throughout the nineteenth century Cambridge would supply its missionary graduates to the "field", perhaps culminating in the "Cambridge Seven", who went to China in 1885. What became a missionary flood in the nineteenth century had its origins in these early years in Cambridge, Clapham and elsewhere.

By 1837, and the death of William IV, it is fair to say that the nation had been set on a course which the later nineteenth century would develop. For some, "the 1830s were the pivotal years of the nineteenth century".[20] Slavery had been abolished; the Catholics emancipated; reform of the Church of England begun; parliamentary reform and the modest increase of the electorate undertaken; local government in the Municipal Corporation Acts established; the Metropolitan Police Force begun by Robert Peel; some prison reform initiated by Elizabeth Fry; and the Combination Acts had been rescinded in 1824, providing for the foundation of trade unions. The role of women was enhanced by notable campaigners, thinkers and artists: Elizabeth Fry, Jane Austen, Mrs Delaney, Fanny Burney and the Brontë sisters, for example. Most of them were practising Christians. And in the nation's consciousness the early death of Princess Charlotte, the heir to George IV, created unprecedented mourning: "It really was as if every household throughout Great Britain had lost a favourite child."[21] By the 1830s a start had been made in social, economic and religious reform. It would take nearly a century for the benefits to be felt by the population as a whole. For the greater part of that century a woman aged just eighteen when she came to the throne gave her name to an age that was tempestuous, controversial and deeply religious. She was Queen Victoria.

CHAPTER 1 8

The Early Victorian Church

On 20 June 1837, Victoria became queen, and on that day the age to which she gave her name began. Both her upbringing and her route to the throne were unusual. She was, after all, the only child of the fourth son of George III, the Duke of Kent, and his German wife, Victoria of Saxe-Coburg-Saalfeld, Duchess of Kent. Victoria's father died when she was a few months old, and she was brought up in what became known as the "Kensington system" by her mother and her mother's adviser and unscrupulous friend, Sir John Conroy. Knowing that Victoria would be queen, both sought to micro-manage her life and control her destiny to their advantage. It was a childhood that would mar her relationships with her own family in years to come.

Despite, or maybe because of, her upbringing, Victoria decidedly wanted to be her own person and govern alone, until that is Lord Melbourne, the Prime Minister, and then Prince Albert sought to help. In the meantime, her closest companion was her diary, which ran, in the end, to 141 volumes and in which she wrote every day, including on her wedding day.

By 1837, the country had undergone considerable change and reform. The Reform Bill of 1832, with all its surrounding furore, was now well in place. Roman Catholics had been emancipated, although this reform was hedged about with anxious restrictions. Anti-papist feeling still existed and could be quickly roused. Slavery was in the process of being fully abolished, with Melbourne taking forward some final legislation, albeit it without much conviction. Social conditions in factory and farm, which had been a source of conflict for several years, called for urgent attention. In 1833, Melbourne was particularly opposed to the Swing Riots in the countryside, which led to the destruction of threshing machines and hayricks, and protests against tithes, the working of the Poor Laws, rents and low wages. One "Swing Rioter", William Winterbourne, was condemned to death at Reading Assizes in 1830. As Winterbourne was a former resident of Kintbury, the vicar, Fulwar Craven Rowle, collected his body from Reading Gaol and buried him in Kintbury churchyard.

These riots, frequent in the southern counties of England, were also mirrored in the actions of the Tolpuddle Martyrs of 1833–4, led by a Methodist preacher, George Loveless, who demanded higher wages of ten shillings a week. For combining in a union called the Friendly Society of Agricultural Labourers, the Tolpuddle Martyrs were prosecuted during Melbourne's government under a piece of wartime legislation called the Unlawful Oaths Act of 1797 and they were sent to Australia for seven years' penal servitude. They were harsh times.

At the same time, the industrialization of England moved inexorably ahead. Despite the tragic accidental death of William Huskisson, President of the Board of Trade, at the opening of the Manchester and Liverpool Railway in 1830, nothing could stop the advance of the locomotive. In 1835, there were only 338 miles of railway open in Britain, but by 1841 the figure had risen to 17,775 miles, with most of the main lines completed. It was an astonishing expansion of track and train. Wellington was as ill-disposed towards railways as he had been to reform. He felt they encouraged the lower classes "to travel about"! Meanwhile, the population of England, Wales and Scotland increased from 16.2 million in 1831 to 18.5 million in 1841. In fact, in 1841, the population of the British Isles, including Ireland, was twice what it had been in 1783. This too was unprecedented growth and formed the prequel to what would be called the "Hungry Forties", when famine stalked Ireland with tragic consequences and also appeared in England, although less vehemently.

Industrialization proceeded on two levels: in many areas, such as Birmingham, it meant the proliferation of small workshops, often operating in extreme squalor, while elsewhere, the cotton industry of Lancashire developed large factories. By 1841, there were a thousand spinning and weaving firms in Lancashire, but only twenty-five employed more than a thousand workers. Along with the concentration of population in urban areas without decent housing, running water and sanitation came inevitable squalor and with it disease, especially cholera. Days of prayer were called for by King William IV, for places suffering from outbreaks of cholera, and it would be some time before practical intervention prevented the disease. The King called for a national day of fasting and humiliation to be held on 21 March 1832, and this would be repeated, albeit reluctantly, under Melbourne's government, beginning in 1834. General Sir Charles Napier, an enlightened General and Commander of the Northern District, wrote: "Would that I had gone to Australia and thus been saved this work, produced by Tory injustice and Whig imbecility; this doctrine of slowly reforming when men are starving is of all things the most silly; famishing men cannot wait."[1]

By the start of Victoria's reign, some of the great reforming legislation had been completed. A fierce battle over freedom of trade against the landed Tories remained to be fought by Peel's government in 1846, against the backdrop of the repeal of the Corn Laws. Reform had also come to the Church of England under Peel's brief government of 1834, but there was still much more to do, and the slowness of this reform boded ill for the Church's popularity among the working classes.

The Church at the beginning of Victoria's reign

At the start of Victoria's reign, there were three conspicuous parts to the Church: the Church of England (with Anglican churches now spreading in the empire), the Dissenters or Non-Conformists, and the Roman Catholic Church, which had been brought in from the cold by the Catholic Relief Bill of 1829. The Tory die-hards were against the Reform Bill and Catholic relief and saw the destruction by fire of the old Houses of Parliament in 1834 as God's wrathful judgement on Catholic Emancipation.

The Church of England was a reluctant reformer: it sat too prettily in the established position given it by law to want to reform easily. It was intrinsically conservative; only two bishops, hardly radical, had voted for the Reform Bill initially: Bishop Maltby, a Whig, later Bishop of Durham, and the eighty-seven-year-old Bishop Bathurst of Norwich. Maltby would later engage in controversial ecumenical relations with Unitarians, who could hardly be called Christians, since they did not believe in the Trinity. He was also sufficiently absent-minded to present the orb at the wrong moment during Victoria's coronation. He had also amassed huge wealth, based on an income of up to £21,000 per annum from Durham Diocese, until it was reduced. The Archbishop of Canterbury at the time was William Howley (1828–48), a scholarly high churchman with a hesitant manner: "He acted so firmly that others almost felt him to be a leader and looked so feeble that they wanted to rally round and surround him with their shields."[2] Like most bishops, he had actively opposed the Reform Bill, and had his carriage pelted in the street.

If reform did not come naturally to the Church of England, the need for it was obvious to all but the church leaders themselves. When Thomas Arnold, the lateral-thinking headmaster of Rugby, wrote a pamphlet called *The Principles of*

Church Reform, he destroyed any prospects of his advancement in the Church. His plan was to open the doors of the Church to dissenters and so establish a broad-based Church, one that was less dogmatic, more diverse and inclusive. He argued new dioceses should be created so that every significant town would have one. Received with a mixture of bafflement and contempt, the pamphlet was no less radical than Lord Henley's 1832 plans for reform, which included turning cathedrals into parish churches, redistributing their assets, reducing crown patronage and abolishing bishops in the House of Lords! Neither report chimed with William Gladstone's almost opaque work of 1838, titled *The State in its Relations to the Church*, in which he argued that church and state should act together in unison. He felt that the state possessed a conscience that could discern between truth and error, and the state could make provision for true worship of God by the Established Church, which was uniquely equipped to do so. Unlike Henley, his aim was to strengthen rather than dismember the Church of England. Many church leaders, such as Archbishop Howley and Charles Blomfield, the very capable Bishop of London from 1826–56, approved of Gladstone's ideas, as did Newman and Keble, the leaders of the Oxford or Tractarian movement. Nevertheless, reform could not be put off, and amidst these high-flown ideas about the Church's place in society, there were pressing problems to be addressed.

The practical problems that confronted the Church of England were of a more everyday nature. Foremost among them was the payment of church rate, a tax on parish property-holders to maintain the upkeep of church buildings. The church rate had been part of the warp and woof of medieval England when everything revolved around the parish church. Some property-holders in parishes were responsible for the upkeep of at least part of the church building. From the Commonwealth onwards, however, and the spawning of new "dissenting churches" in parishes, the church rate was seen as an unjust tax on people of middle England who had no time for the Established Church and did not wish to pay for its upkeep, especially if they were at odds with the practices of the Church of England and already supported a dissenting church instead. Case after case of parishes being unable to raise the church rate now arose. The government wrestled with the idea of scrapping the rate and instead paying for the upkeep of churches from the national budget. That was the intention of Melbourne's government in May 1835, but, come 1836, Whig leaders were no longer content with this plan. Another plan from the Chancellor of the Exchequer, Thomas Spring Rice, was to take surplus money from the Church (i.e. its dioceses and cathedrals) and commute this into a maintenance fund of £250,000. Yet if this happened it would stymy the Ecclesiastical Commissioners so recently founded by Peel, who wanted to take the same money and use it for founding new dioceses in poorer or less well-endowed industrial areas. In the face of Church opposition and narrow votes in the Commons, the government abandoned the proposed scheme. In the meantime, cases against church rate were piling up in the ecclesiastical courts, with few people knowing how to deal with them, and martyrs being made of the protesters.

One notorious case was that of Thorogood, a Chelmsford cobbler. In September 1838, he was summoned before the magistrates for failing to pay church rate of 5s 6d. He maintained that to pay this sum was inconsistent with his religious beliefs. His case was taken to the consistory court in London, where he was summoned in November 1838. He failed to appear and Judge Lushington, himself an opponent of church rate, was forced to imprison Thorogood for contempt of court. It required a special Act of Parliament to release him. The defiant Thorogood languished in gaol, unwilling to admit to contempt of court, while Prime Minister Lord John Russell brought forward an antiquated law about the royal prerogative in order to release him. So, in July 1840, Parliament ruled that after six months' imprisonment for contempt, the prisoner might be released. This had all the ingredients of a Victorian saga fit for a novel by Trollope: an antiquated financial system, a robust man of conscience, and a labyrinthine legal tangle from which only the Prime Minister and Parliament could extract the undeserving prisoner. It was not the last time that such a thing would happen, but it was certainly grist to the mill of the great Victorian novelist of church and state Anthony Trollope, whose novels about both would soon start rolling. Less literary, but more campaigning, was William Baines's journal *The Nonconformist*, which sought to highlight the grievances of dissenters against the Established Church. Baines was determined to liberate the Church from state control. His aim was to "ring a peal in the ears of drowsy dissenters".[3] Meanwhile, in East Anglia, the powerful Courtauld family took on their local parishes and refused to pay the rate. They could well afford it, but principles prevented such acquiescence.

Another grievance of dissenters against the Established Church was the conduct and registrations of marriages and baptisms. Dissenters wanted to be married in their own chapels without recourse to Anglican parishes and clergy, but since "their ministers were of insecure tenure, their chapels impermanent and their registers chaotic", they could not do so.[4] Only the local vicar could register births (baptisms), marriages and deaths. Already Lord Russell and Sir Robert Peel had attempted reform. Eventually the necessary legislation passed, and by 1 March 1837 marriages were permitted in chapels using the parish registers. Incidentally, in a moment of gallantry, the House of Lords struck out the clause that the bride must state her age. The preponderance of weddings nevertheless still took place in parish churches. In 1845, there were 14,228 marriages in Roman Catholic or Protestant chapels. In the same year, Anglican marriages were recorded at 129,515.

If dissenters were on a campaign to gain full independence from the Established Church, Roman Catholics were on a slow and still more fragile march to acceptance. In 1828, the repeal of the Test Acts, which prevented dissenters from holding office, also prepared them to be more open to Catholic Emancipation the following year. Although freed from penalties by the Relief Act of 1829, Catholicism was going through a kind of twilight zone: from emancipation to the re-establishment of a Roman Catholic hierarchy, which would take place in 1850. There was still a deeply held common suspicion that Roman Catholics were a fifth column within English society and could not be trusted. Although English Catholics were not fully integrated into the Roman Catholic Church world-wide, they were still viewed with suspicion as having allegiance to foreign Catholic powers in a generally Protestant country. No Roman Catholic could be sovereign, Lord Chancellor, Lord Lieutenant of Ireland, or High Commissioner to the General Assembly of the Church of Scotland, although Roman Catholic MPs, especially from Ireland, could take their place in the Commons. They had to swear an oath, problematic for some, that they must not subvert the establishment of the Church of England. The four Vicars Apostolic of the Catholic Church granted permission for the oath to be taken, but the Pope was more reticent. All male members of communities such as the Jesuits were obliged by law to register with a justice of the peace. No one could become a Jesuit without a penalty. No Catholic could wear a religious habit at a civil ceremony. In a word, it was a slow route to acceptance, revealing the insecurities and fears of the Protestant state, which had all but proscribed Roman Catholicism for nearly 300 years. Nor was the path to acceptance smooth. It was to get worse before it got better when the hierarchy of the Roman Catholic Church was re-established mid-century.

At the outset of Victoria's reign, the Church of England was undergoing gentle reform and remained the church of the Tory party. Were it not for politicians like Peel, the reform might have been far too little too late. The rest of the century would see an ongoing tussle between dissenters and the Established Church, especially over education. The Roman Catholic Church was on a slow path to re-incorporation into the social and political fabric of the nation. Yet unforeseen movements were about to overtake the religious settlement of the times, creating new divisions in the Church of England, revealing the limitations of the courts and legislation in relation to the Church, and producing new tensions between Roman Catholicism and Anglicanism. The trigger for all this was a group of

Oxford academics seeking to reactivate the past. They came to be called the Oxford or Tractarian Movement.

The Oxford Movement

It is one of the extraordinary features of the Victorian world that in the midst of a dynamic movement of progress and industrialization, which would be celebrated remarkably in the Great Exhibition of 1851, there was an equally passionate movement to gain inspiration from the past: the gothic, the medieval, the romantic and the chivalrous.

This was a Europe-wide movement idealizing the medieval past. In Aix-la-Chapelle (Aachen), the home of Charlemagne's court, the Rathaus (or town hall) was decorated by Alfred Rethel between 1847 and 1851 with a new set of murals depicting Charlemagne's life, in a classic example of idolizing a heroic past to inspire the present. When Sir Charles Barry redesigned the Palace of Westminster, the gothic palace we know so well was the result. Then, when it was decorated inside, the work was done by Augustus Pugin (1812–52), who had himself converted to Roman Catholicism in 1834 and worked with Barry on the design. Pugin was nothing if not an evangelist of gothic architecture and decoration. Alongside the nostalgic trend in architecture were the novels of Walter Scott (1771–1832), which idealized and romanticized Scottish history; the poetry of Wordsworth; and the painting of the Pre-Raphaelite Brotherhood founded in 1848 by Holman Hunt, John Everett Millais and Dante Gabriel Rossetti. All of these looked either to the natural world or to a medieval past for inspiration. "Religious men wanted poetry of the heart in their hymns, sacramental sensibility in their worship, recovery of symbolism in art and architecture" and a theology to go with it.[5] Whether it was the visual elements that gave rise to theology, or whether theology produced the visual, is debatable, but there was nevertheless a desire to put the visual elements that had been lost in the Reformation back into worship. The forcing ground for these things was Oxford.

Alongside the romantic movement was the utilitarian movement, which was primarily concerned with social change and individual liberty. This movement was pioneered by Jeremy Bentham (1748–1832), the utilitarian philosopher and founder of University College London, and John Stuart Mill. Bentham deplored the Church of England for sharing in a discredited legal and political system, and saw its attempts at reaching the new industrial class as merely "another way of perpetuating its abuses".[6] Bentham's pupil and follower was John Stuart Mill

(1806–73), a strong advocate of liberty and the right of the individual to choose, so long as doing so did not cause harm to others. He espoused universal suffrage for women and their liberation from male domination and believed that bringing forward a debate on women's suffrage in Parliament in 1866 was one of his greatest contributions to public life.

For its part, the Oxford Movement was more of a revisionist movement than a utilitarian one, a renewed quarrying of the teaching of the Church Fathers. It looked back in order to look forward. Compared with the fenland scholarship of Cambridge, well known for its Puritan priorities and scientific brilliance, Oxford in the nineteenth century does seem to have had an infectious miasma of religious reworking, even revanchism. Oxford has an ambivalent place in English religious history: it was the place where Cranmer, Latimer and Ridley were tried and burnt, where Wolsey and Laud were formed, and where the Oxford Movement would now find traction. It was where Wesley embarked on the Holy Club until finding greater enlightenment through the Moravians. Now an indication of rough weather ahead in Oxford was given by the furore over the appointment by Lord Melbourne of a new Regius Professor of Divinity, Dr Hampden, in 1836, a year before Victoria's accession. Not noted for his Christian convictions, Hampden had given a series of lectures in 1834 entitled *Observations of Religious Dissent*. Sober and dull, these lectures nonetheless gave *reason* an important place in religious doctrine, with Hampden questioning the need to subscribe to the Thirty-Nine Articles in order to teach at Oxford. Because of these lectures, his appointment was opposed by a growing group of Oxford church leaders, including Newman, Pusey and Keble. The ultra-high churchman Bishop Phillpotts of Exeter joined the fray, giving students of Exeter College, over which he had jurisdiction, the right to abscond from Hampden's lectures. Despite the furore, Hampden would remain professor until made Bishop of Hereford in 1847 by Lord Russell's government. What the upset did show was that there was a group in Oxford who saw the need to revive Anglicanism as they understood it, and especially its more Catholic elements. They were to form the kernel of the Oxford Movement.

The principal members of the Oxford Movement were the pastor and poet John Keble (1792–1866), the professor of Hebrew and sacramentalist Edward Pusey (1800–82), and the writer and theologian John Newman (1801–90). All of them were for a time Fellows of Oriel College, where another Fellow, Richard Whatley, an eccentric logician known as the White Bear—who wore a white hat and a white coat while exercising a white dog—proved a great influence, especially on Newman. "Whatley dissected the truths of religion like an anatomist."[7] He gave Newman confidence in the power of logic but was removed from Oxford to become Archbishop of Dublin in 1831, soon after Newman's election to Oriel. Another influence in Oriel College on this group was Hurrell Froude, who was also to have a profound effect on Newman.

Froude's friendship was to have a sifting effect on Newman: both loved the romantic novels of Walter Scott with their rose-tinted picture of medieval times; both sought a renaissance of Catholicism; and they travelled together. Newman sensed a different call, however.[8] Their friendship was both established and limited by a voyage they took to the Mediterranean in 1833, visiting Malta, Patras, Sicily, Naples and Rome. During the voyage Newman experienced a profound sense of calling and an awareness of his ambivalence towards Catholicism.[9] He penned what would become his most famous hymn, "Lead, Kindly Light", sensing God's calling "in the encircling gloom", but recognizing that his progress would be deliberate: "one step enough for me." Froude died of ill health aged thirty-three on 28 February 1836, and Newman helped publish his *Remains*, "a candid and intimate journal about Froude's opinions and ascetic mortifications to quell temptations".[10] In time, these leaders of the Oxford or Tractarian Movement would hold important posts in the university: Keble as Professor of Poetry, Pusey as Professor of Hebrew and Newman as Vicar of the University Church. From this academic and pastoral platform, they would launch a call to church and state that would change the Church of England.

The trigger for the Oxford Movement was the reform of the Church of England by Parliament in the 1830s. By then, church leaders had become more than a little unnerved by the succession of pieces of legislation that had changed the *status quo* in the religious settlement of England that had been concluded at the restoration of the monarchy. Discrimination against dissenters and Roman Catholics had ended in 1828 and 1829 respectively. The Reform Bill changed the political *status quo*, and was much opposed by most Anglican clergy, and nearly all the bishops. The Church Temporalities Act of Ireland of 1833 suppressed ten bishoprics in Ireland, including those at Cashel and Tuam, redeploying revenues possibly for Catholic education. Whilst in Naples, Newman sarcastically wrote of Lord Grey, the Whig Prime Minister, "Well done! My blind Premier confiscate and rob till, like Samson, you pull down the political structure on your head."[11] More importantly, the Bill was the trigger for the Assize Sermon on 14 July 1833 of John Keble, Professor of Poetry at Oxford and author of the popular *Christian Year*. The Assize Sermon was in retrospect the starting gun for the Oxford Movement, for it advocated the renaissance of Catholicism in its widest sense in the Anglican Church. Keble deplored the fact that the Church should be submissive to the state and that it could be shaped and formed by a political power. This was nothing less than "national apostasy", in his view. Keble was to become the model pastor, in this envisaged Anglican Church, content to live the life of a rural parson at Hursley in Gloucestershire, with Pusey its ascetic guide and Newman its publicist. Newman now took up the campaign by issuing *Tracts for the Times*.

John Henry Newman's life spanned almost the whole of the nineteenth century, and as such he was one of the eminent Victorians. Half his life he was an Anglican and the other half, from 1845, a Roman Catholic. He started his spiritual journey as an Evangelical, and never lost aspects of that outlook. His father was a banker who was ruined in 1816, and thereafter failed in his attempts to manage a brewery. Whilst at school in Ealing, Newman was deeply influenced by an Evangelical teacher and never lost the sense of God's providential care. He was impressed by Joseph Milner's *History of the Church of Christ*, and while he grasped the Evangelical doctrine of justification by faith alone, he later came to express its working in the individual differently. It was in going up to Trinity College, Oxford, that he was exposed to wider influences and reading which moved him to a more sacramental and catholic theology.

In 1824, Newman was ordained deacon at Christ Church; in 1826, he became a Fellow of Oriel—the centre of intellectual life in Oxford at the time—and in 1828 was made Vicar of St Mary's University Church, with its attached parish of Littlemore on the edge of Oxford. Already deeply immersed in theology, he published his first full-length book, *The Arians of the Fourth Century*. His study and appreciation of this fourth-century church controversy would profoundly affect his approach to theology. No libertarian, he decided to turn his back on the latitudinarian or liberal stance of the Church, as it had been expressed by men like Benjamin Hoadley, Bishop of Bangor, in the previous century, with the Church reduced to an arm of government, "an instrument for social control and amelioration".[12] Instead, Newman appealed to revealed truth as discerned, formulated and made known by the scriptures and the Church Fathers. Indeed, his appeal to the Church Fathers, and in particular Athanasius and Ambrose, who had confronted the Arians in the fourth and fifth centuries, was characteristic of his approach.

The means whereby Newman sought to awake the Church in his day was through preaching and publishing. For all his shy, almost feminine and undemonstrative style, he was a born campaigner and publicist. As a preacher, Newman was to have a powerful hold on the university, even though he read his intense and well-crafted sermons haltingly. "Undergraduates paid him the compliment of crowding his sermons."[13] His appeal was frequently to holiness of living, and his sermons were filled with references to scripture. By 1837, Pusey and Newman were said to govern the university. It was the fulfilment of that sense of calling he had when touring the Mediterranean and writing, "Lead kindly light in this encircling gloom." He had thrown off his physical weakness and religious blues and was enjoying what, looking back, he considered the time of his life. He described it as "a time of plenty".

Tracts for the Times were published between 1833 and 1841 and comprised ninety publications on themes connected to the Oxford Movement. There were about a dozen contributing authors, including Newman, Pusey and Keble. In the first two years, 1833 and 1834, there were fifty tracts on subjects as wide-ranging as suggested alterations to the liturgy for the Burial of the Dead (no. 3) and Apostolic Succession (nos. 4, 15 and 19). Indeed, the *Tracts* poured forth on the orders of the Church (i.e. bishops, priests and deacons), the Athanasian Creed, frequency of communion and the reform of the Church. The Church of England had not known such detailed pastoral, liturgical, sacramental and doctrinal output, directed at the clergy and laity alike. But the production came to a screeching crescendo and halt in the final *Tract XC*, on the Thirty-Nine Articles.

A tract on the Thirty-Nine Articles was deemed an assault on the very citadel of the Church of England. The Articles defined the Protestantism of the English Church and were its foundational document. Newman, whose great focus was to make the Church of England consciously catholic, appealed particularly to the Church Fathers, to Richard Hooker and to the Caroline sacramental divines, such as Archbishop Laud, as representatives of true catholicity. For Newman, something was catholic if it could be proven to be in accord with the teaching of the Church Fathers. *Tract XC* took fourteen articles and treated them legally, although in doing so Newman was not trying to reconcile them with the Church of Rome. In some respects, he believed Roman Catholicism to be in error, but he did seek to demonstrate that the articles were catholic, and as such could be celebrated as part of the one true catholic Church. What Newman underestimated, to his great cost, was that when most people heard the word "catholic", they understood it to mean Roman Catholic, rather than simply the catholic or universal faith as taught by scripture and the Church Fathers. As Chadwick writes, "Not even the university was accustomed to the word Catholic as not meaning Roman Catholic."[14] Indeed, Newman was expecting a high level of knowledge of the Church Fathers when he said that the truly catholic was protestant and the protestant truly catholic. What many heard instead was that the Articles were truly Roman Catholic. The balloon went up. It was a case of the academic Newman being unaware, and of a statement turning into a misconception and the misconception then gaining a life and course of its own.

The effect of *Tract XC* was immediate theological and ecclesiastical combustion. The thought that the House of Commons might embark on redefining the Thirty-Nine Articles, bolstered by Irish Catholics led by O'Connell since Catholic emancipation, produced waves of anxiety in the Church. The Evangelical Bishop Golightly (splendid name) was horrified. He went around Oxford condemning the tract and waving it about. Oxford became a cauldron of controversy. Senior members of the university wanted a formal rejection of Newman. On 16 March 1841, the vice-chancellor published a declaration of the hebdomadal board in the press saying that the *Tracts* in no way represented the thinking of the university. Newman wrote to his sister, "I fear I am clean dished."[15] Later he would write to her, "We are ducks on a pond, knocked over but not knocked out."[16] The Bishop of Oxford, Bishop Bagot—no serious divine but a "courteous aristocratic Tory pluralist"—was besieged with demands that Newman be tried in an ecclesiastical court. The compromise solution was that production of the *Tracts* should cease. The controversy spread. Whigs and liberals saw the need to loosen the grip of the Articles, while the Tories and the establishment invoked their necessity.

In all, the controversy had more than enough material for several Trollope novels, with its heady mixture of characters, theologies, party politics and the architecture and arcane ways of Oxford. The controversy ended Newman's "usefulness" to the Church of England. Four years later, in 1845, he would join the Roman Catholic Church, where he was received as an errant sheep who had found his way back to the true flock. He now retreated more and more to his almost monastic community at Littlemore, along with like-minded companions. Bad blood continued in Oxford, with Pusey suspended from preaching for two years in 1843 for using sacramental language suggestive of the Real Presence and, in 1845, W. G. Ward, an unstable, liberal Fellow of Balliol, publishing his *Ideal of a Christian Church*, which gave the impression that "the Church of Rome preserved devotional treasures that the Church of England had lost".[17] For this he was condemned by the MAs of the university and stripped of his degrees. It seemed the Oxford Movement had run its course.

What did the Oxford Movement bring to the Church of England? It was a search for the ways and beliefs of the Church from its earliest centuries and their reinstatement in Anglicanism. The movement set itself the task of showing that either Anglicanism still retained some of those features, or that they needed to be reaffirmed or reinstated. At its heart, the Oxford Movement meant greater emphasis on the Eucharist. Previously relegated to a service held four times a year in most parishes, the Eucharist became a central feature of Tractarian worship. The doctrine of Real Presence—meaning that the body and blood of Christ were present in more than simply a spiritual form—if not explicitly held at the outset of the movement, soon became the implicit understanding of Tractarian Anglicanism. Decoration, theatre, colour, gothic architecture (as exemplified by Butterfield), vestments, surplices and candles accompanied the rite. Confession was reintroduced, although it existed only embryonically in the Prayer Book service as part of the Visitation of the Sick. More profoundly, in his understanding of justification by faith alone, Newman linked this doctrine, not as Evangelicals did to belief in the promise of Christ through faith in his Word alone, but rather in the appropriation of the presence of Christ in the sacrament of the Eucharist. If Protestants made trust in the *Word* the defining essence of justification, Newman opted for trust in the *sign* of bread and wine (given meaning by the Word and received by faith). If it seems a rather precise difference, it in fact led to a significant development in ritual. If the celebration of the sacrament bore such significance, then dramatizing it became its corollary.

Furthermore, Newman stressed that the result of such faith would be costly discipleship. He himself embraced a world-renouncing practice, which for him involved sexual abstinence and celibacy. As such, he was following the monk bishops of the Early Church: Ambrose, Athanasius and Chrysostom. Thus, even if the atmosphere in Oxford was filled with controversy in the mid-1840s, in later years these principles caught on up and down the land. For instance, in the Berkshire village of Inkpen, a rood screen was reintroduced in the late nineteenth century, an altar rail fixed, the east end raised, colour and decoration abounded, and "the altar" (a word that was studiously avoided by the Prayer Book as reeking of theology of the mass) was made of decorated stone. In other words, the work of Edward VI's commissioners in removing images and vestiges of the mass was reversed and the "beauty of holiness" re-established. From the standpoint of Evangelicals, however, images had crept back.

The effect of the Oxford Movement was undoubtedly to increase party and dissension in the Established Church. If saying the movement Balkanized the Church of England into warring parties is an overstatement, there were times when this seemed only too true. One famous incident that reveals the intensity of the stand-off between High Church or Tractarian Anglicanism and the more Evangelical clergy was the Gorham case that sprang to public notice in 1848. All that was needed to create a rift was an immovable high church bishop and an intransigent Evangelical or low church vicar, or vice versa.

Such a state of affairs came to the fore when George Cornelius Gorham, former Fellow of Queen's College Cambridge—where he had become a committed Evangelical—moved to the diocese of Exeter, and the bailiwick of the most high church of all bishops, Phillpotts of Exeter. Gorham was previously the Rector of St Just in west Cornwall but wanted to be closer to a town where he could educate his children. He moved to the Exeter diocese, where the staunchest defender and most outspoken advocate of the sacramental theology of the Church of England, Henry Phillpotts, resided as bishop. Phillpotts caught the whiff of Gorham's hostility to sacramentalism in the Church of England when he advertised for a curate "free from Tractarian error". Phillpotts went into battle. At all costs he would defend the liturgy and doctrine of the Church of England. He refused to licence Gorham to the parish of Bramford Speke near Exeter until Gorham had been fully examined on his understanding of baptismal regeneration, which is indicated in the Anglican liturgy of infant baptism. The idea that a baptized child was *ipso facto* born again or regenerate by virtue of the rite of baptism was expressed in the Book of Common Prayer, although not held by many Evangelicals, except in certain circumstances.

Gorham was examined on this point for fourteen hours between 8 and 10 March 1848. The bishop required answers to 149 questions. By 3 April, news of the examination had reached Parliament, where there was at first amusement and then growing consternation. Gorham now wrote a public piece citing "a cruel exercise of episcopal power" and, in June 1848, asked the Court of Arches to compel the bishop to license him. The case was delayed for six months. A search was made of the writings of Augustine, Luther, the Augsburg Confession and English Divines over the centuries concerning the efficacy of baptismal regeneration. On 2 August 1848, the old Dean of Arches was carried into court by two footmen in a chair to deliver his verdict: there could be no doubt that an infant was regenerated through baptism.

The Evangelical party was appalled: it seemed as if the necessity for repentance and faith was overturned by the rite of baptism. Both archbishops rallied to support Gorham. The case was referred to the Judicial Committee of the Privy Council. On 11 December 1849, the committee met for five days of hearings, and judgement was eventually delivered in March 1850. The committee, by a majority verdict, was satisfied that Gorham had not contradicted the formularies of the Church of England. He was vindicated. Public meetings followed, attended by thousands on both sides of the argument; the high church party threatened to leave for Rome, and many did so. Keble, Manning, Pusey and Henry Wilberforce declared the Privy Council heretical. Above all, this case, as others would do, showed that the Church needed its own body to resolve its own disputes, whether doctrinal or legal, as Convocation (an assembly of clergy) had done, but which had, for the most part, been suspended by Parliament since the time of Oliver Cromwell.

Such a body would be a long time coming. Although there was a campaign to re-establish Convocations, initial meetings in the 1850s were intermittent and desultory. Indeed, it was not fully established until 1919 and was later superseded by General Synod in 1970. It was typical of the Victorian period that, as one part of the nation was in ferment about the doctrine of baptism, across the water in Ireland another part of the British Isles was threatened with starvation.

The "Hungry Forties"

If Victoria's early years were marked by theological controversy, they were also marked by hardship, hunger and a degree of helplessness in the burgeoning industrial cities of the country. Melbourne's influence on the young Queen waned with the advent of her "beautiful" first cousin Albert, whom she married on 10 February 1840 in the Chapel Royal, St James'—a small affair by today's royal wedding standards. Melbourne grew increasingly tired in office, even falling asleep in the Queen's presence, and was defeated in the election of 1841, when Sir Robert Peel became prime minister.

This was Peel's second government: the first was formed in 1834 as a minority. It had lasted only a few months, but one of its main achievements had been the establishment of the forerunner to the Church Commissioners, which began the process of reform of the Church of England. Peel was offered a second chance to form a government in 1839, but this foundered on the so-called "Bedchamber Crisis" when Victoria refused to exchange her Whig ladies-in-waiting for Tory ones. Matters were made worse when Victoria accused Lady Flora Hastings, one of her ladies-in-waiting, of being pregnant by Victoria's *bête noire*, Sir John Conroy, the man who had imposed the Kensington system on her in her youth. To clear her name Lady Flora underwent a medical test and was found to be a virgin. Both episodes indicated that Victoria's court was not going to be like those of her Hanoverian forbears, with the nearest in moral rectitude the court of George III.

In 1841, Peel formed the first majority Tory government. After a slow start he would grow in the affections of Victoria, because of Prince Albert's admiration for him as an enlightened and effective reformer. His government was to be tempestuous. Having a brilliant mind, with a double first in classics and maths, he was also a man of action, but possessed little in the way of personal charm. Disraeli, his later great political opponent, said his smile was like "a silver plate on a coffin". Disraeli knew how to wound. Peel was an unadventurous Anglican who hardly ever spoke of his faith.[18] He had an instinctive Protestant opposition to Roman

Catholicism, but in order to rule a more united kingdom—and in particular to make Ireland more fully part of the union—he supported Catholic Emancipation in 1829 and later put forward a Bill to grant funds to the Roman Catholic seminary at Maynooth in Ireland. The Bill was carried in 1845 in the teeth of great Tory opposition: "The Bill will pass", wrote Peel, "but our party is destroyed."[19] All these actions marked him out as a reformer, and as one who overcame his original Tory principles, which were either illiberal or discriminatory, and which he also judged to be not in the national interest. His greatest test would be in relation to the Corn Laws and Free Trade.

In 1840, and still for some years to come, the largest part of the economy was agriculture. More people were employed in the fields than in the factories, with the second largest form of employment being domestic service. Factories, coal mining and the railways still came collectively third. The squirearchy, as opposed to the great landed Whig estates, was mostly Tory and Anglican, as it had been since the Restoration in 1666, nearly two hundred years previously. The squirearchy would add to its interests service in the army, especially in the empire. Given the size of the agricultural interest, the extent of domestic service, and the need for cheap bread in the burgeoning cities, the price of corn was critical. The landlord depended on the price of corn for his crops, and likewise his tenants to pay their rent. And through a skewed electoral system, they were able to return MPs who reflected this vested interest.

The price of corn had been protected by the Corn Laws since the Napoleonic era. A section of the Tory party, i.e. early liberals, such as Huskisson and Palmerston, sought some reform of the Corn Laws. In 1813, imported grain was prohibited until a quarter of wheat reached eighty shillings. Later, in Wellington's government, Huskisson passed a sliding scale of duties: the higher the price of corn at home, the lower the duty. In 1838, the Anti-Corn Law League, led by Richard Cobden, was formed and became, like the anti-slavery movement, one of the most popular movements in the country and, not surprisingly, in the towns. In Manchester, over 5,000 working people came together to lobby for repeal. Repeal was seen by the leaders of the league as a panacea for many ills and the message was increasingly sounded. Although Peel had voted for the Corn Laws on several previous occasions, the momentum for repeal was growing and the Irish potato famine, which took hold in 1845, presented him with a deepening tragedy on his doorstep, and a moral reason for changing his mind.

After the Black Death, the Irish potato famine was the single worst human calamity in the British Isles until the losses of the Great War. It is worth remembering that all of Ireland had been ruled directly by Westminster since the Act of Union of 1801, brought in by William Pitt during the Napoleonic Wars. This strategy had necessitated the end of discrimination against Catholics and meant that legislation in Westminster applied to all four countries of the union. Given this legislative arrangement, the British prime minister would be legislating for the price of corn in all of Britain. Eighty per cent of the population of Ireland lived close to poverty and were Roman Catholic. In describing the Irish problem in 1844, a year before the first signs of the failure of the potato crop, Benjamin Disraeli said: "You have a starving population, an absentee aristocracy, an alien Church [the Anglican Church of Ireland], and in addition the weakest executive in the world. That is the Irish Question."[20]

In 1845, the potato blight (*phytophthora infestans*) destroyed most of the potato crop. With much of the population subsisting on small tenanted farms of a few acres, and dependent on the potato as almost their sole source of food, large sections of the population faced starvation and disease. With successive failures of the crop in the following years, the situation was devastating. Peel was far from immune to the impending tragedy. He imported Indian corn from the United States to Ireland—known as "flint corn", it was too hard to mill easily. In 1845, he attempted to repeal the Corn Laws, but was defeated. In 1846, he tried again and, with Whig support, succeeded with a comfortable majority, but split his own party. In the same year, he was defeated in Parliament when bringing an Irish Coercion Bill removing *habeas corpus* in an attempt to ensure order in a country on the edge of breakdown. Now out of office, the Tories would not have a majority again until Disraeli's government of 1866, twenty years later, apart from some brief tenures as a minority government when the Whigs collapsed.

Relief in Ireland failed to halt death by disease and starvation. Absentee landlords who owned large swathes of the country resorted to evicting tenants who could not pay rent. Relief in terms of civil works was patchy and ill-managed. The Poor Law was inflexible as a tool for relief. Churches, particularly the Quakers, provided soup kitchens in Ireland and Liverpool, encouraged diversification of crops, and started model farms. Of all the churches, the Quakers were the most imaginative and effective. As with the Black Death, the Roman Catholic Church in Ireland was as disabled by illness as the community it served. Although there are no fixed figures, nearly a million died from disease and starvation, and the same number emigrated both to the United States and to England. The famine was yet another chapter in the long history of pain between England and Ireland. Nor was it the last, for others were to follow. One effect was large-scale migration of Irish people to Liverpool, Glasgow and London, for the British economy was expanding rapidly, especially with the building of the railways. This also meant that a large number of Catholics swelled the Roman Catholic Church in England, with historic consequences.

The 1850s: Confidence, Catholics and Non-Conformists

Under their long-lasting leader, Lord Russell, the Whigs would be in the driving seat for twenty years after the 1846 collapse of Peel's government. The Peelites were led first by Lord Aberdeen and then Gladstone, who eventually formed the Liberal Party. Peel died in a fall from his horse in 1850, and Gladstone, an uneasy and intermittent colleague of Lord Palmerston, finally took over the reins of government from Lord Russell, who lasted until 1865, with one short break of opposition. Palmerston would be the first prime minister to be in office at the age of eighty. The period from 1850–65 would be characterized by the discarding for the present of any further electoral reform, and the gradual demise of the Chartist movement from 1848,[21] the re-establishment of the Roman Catholic hierarchy in England, the Great Exhibition, the census of 1851, limited social reform, war against Russia in the Crimea, and the effect of the Indian Mutiny. It was a heady series of events.

These were the middle years of Victoria's reign. It was a time of flux when the Peelites and the Irish held the balance of power in the Commons and either decried the cliquishness of the Whigs and their grand ways, or the Tories for their love of the establishment, and in particular the Church of England. The old guard of the Duke of Wellington and Peel had passed; the new guard of Gladstone and Disraeli was emerging; and Palmerston was the man of the moment.

The Great Exhibition of 1851 was the climax of Prince Albert's influence. Along with Henry Cole, he was the great visionary behind the exhibition. It is indicative of the Victorian age that, only two years after the end of the great famine in Ireland, such a splendid and optimistic exhibition could be staged in the capital city of London. Famine and feast jostled side by side; instability and invention both demanded attention. When Queen Victoria entered the great Crystal Palace, designed by Paxton, the Duke of Devonshire's chief designer and gardener, she recorded her feelings: "It was the happiest, proudest day of my life, and I can think of nothing else. Albert's dearest name is immortalized with this great conception, his own, and my own dear country showed she was worthy of it."[22] Among the myriad of exhibits showing off new inventions, manufactured goods, implements and foods was one displaying Bibles translated into 130 languages. At the outset, Albert had been less than enthusiastic about including a display of Bibles: he stood for moral and scientific progress rather than religious publications. The Bible, it was said, had nothing to do with the spirit of progress, industry and science showcased by the exhibition. Only after a lengthy correspondence between Lord Shaftesbury and Albert himself were the Bibles allowed, demonstrating thereby, according to Albert, human intellectual prowess in translation. They were given space but "in an obscure back room off a side passage upstairs",[23] whereas the art of Pugin was shown to best advantage.

Worse was to come: it was proposed that the exhibition be opened on Sundays. A delegation of church leaders, including Sumner, the Archbishop of Canterbury, and Bishop Blomfield of London, petitioned the government. As a result, the exhibition remained closed on Sundays. Then, when the Crystal Palace moved from Kensington to Sydenham, a petition was made that fig leaves be used to cover nude statuary. The directors yielded to modesty and fig leaves were duly affixed. Millions visited the Great Exhibition and with the takings permanent museums were built: the Victoria and Albert, the Natural History and the Science Museum, now the glory of South Kensington, were built on the site of the original Crystal Palace. Albert's ideals were of human harmony, scientific progress and liberal enquiry, linked to moral rectitude, self-discipline and duty. These ideals, as much as the objects in the exhibition, were to have a lasting impact.

If the Great Exhibition demonstrated creativity, scientific progress and the extent of human ability, the census of 1851, enacted by Lord Russell's government, revealed the size and disposition of the population, and in particular its religious leanings. It was decided to ask the population about their religious affiliations and habits of worship. On 30 March 1851, every minister was asked to fill in a form detailing frequency of worship services, capacity of buildings used, and numbers present at each service. It was a prodigious undertaking, overseen by Horace Mann and opposed by suspicious clergymen like Bishop Sam Wilberforce in Oxford, who was of the "damned lies and statistics" frame of mind. Mann had an "indefinable air of the historical amateur" and was a "well-meaning warm-hearted latitudinarian".[24]

The result was revealing, with Mann making allowances for the return of blank forms by suspicious clergy. With Victorian confidence, he estimated the following attendance at churches in England and Wales for 30 March 1851: 5,292,551 Anglicans; 383,630 Roman Catholics; and 4,536,264 Dissenters (e.g. Presbyterian, Methodist, Congregationalist and Baptist). The population of England and Wales was 17,927,609 in total. Having made deductions for under-ten-year-olds (three million), the sick or infirm with carers (one million) and other deductions for those with occupations on Sundays, Mann estimated that 58 per cent of the population were in a church on Sunday. It was a high figure.

After the Roman Catholic Relief Act of 1829, Roman Catholics were like owls blinking in the daylight, having existed in England in a type of social darkness for centuries. From 1838 until 1851, there were eight vicars apostolic with regional pastoral responsibilities. The ending of discrimination in 1829 meant penalties were now removed and new possibilities unfolded. The Catholic Church proved attractive to an intellectual milieu that lauded the country's medieval past and sought to invoke the teaching of the Church Fathers from the earliest centuries. Add to that the arrival of hundreds of thousands of Irish Catholics in Liverpool, Manchester and then Birmingham and London, and the numbers of Catholics were suddenly burgeoning. The Church struggled to know how best to proceed.

The English Catholic Church faced a dilemma. It could continue its accustomed retiring style of going unnoticed, or it could embrace a more conspicuous and demanding role, advocating a resurgent papacy. For centuries, the Roman Catholic Church in England had been virtually a banned organization, in a kind of exile. English Catholics had grown accustomed to a constitutional and social darkness and lived within that. They practised their faith unobtrusively around landed Catholic families and foreign embassies, or even in pubs and disused factories in London. Now they could "come out" into the open and take their place in national life. The mood, in some quarters, was for a more conspicuously Catholic presence; churches were sought with gilded decorations, gothic exteriors and a medieval atmosphere. The Catholic Earl of Shrewsbury built such edifices with the help of Pugin, a newly converted Catholic. For Pugin, colour and style were everything and the only true Christian architecture was gothic! He is reported to have said: "How will you convert England if you wear a chasuble (a cope) like that?" If you like, ecclesiastical bling was part of the "wow" factor of unleashed Catholicism.

Further afield, Rome was embracing a policy of papal assertion. With origins in the eighteenth century, this movement sought to develop the prerogative power of the Pope and would find its fulfilment in the First Vatican Council of 1870. It was then that the infallibility of the Pope and his encyclicals was first fully pronounced. Catholics in England were split: some preferred the once-Anglican archdeacon, Henry Manning, who was ultramontane, while others were closer to the intellectual Cardinal Newman. Manning converted to Catholicism, from being an Anglican archdeacon, in 1851 and espoused a telling mixture of papal power, Catholic discipline and social justice, focussed on the poor of London. Shocked by the outcome of the Gorham case, in which an Evangelical view of baptism had been upheld by the Privy Council, he had converted to Catholicism.

For his part, Newman had also converted in 1845, not so much out of positive feelings for Catholicism (although he was moving in that direction), but because of his treatment by the University of Oxford and his sense that the Catholic Church best approximated to the ancient Church of the Fathers. Some embraced a resurgent, disciplined and conspicuous Catholicism; others, like Newman, were more cautious, embracing a more variegated, but still convinced, Catholic stance. Mistrust grew between some English Catholics and Rome over Rome's desire to foist its Italian religious culture on the English.

Two events made the government and nation wary of a retrenched Catholicism in England. The first was the re-establishment of a Roman Catholic hierarchy, and the other was an inflammatory pastoral letter from Cardinal Wiseman. There was an internal logic to this: in order to have greater autonomy in the future, the Church needed to be fully constituted with its own bishops. Until 1851, it had been administered by eight vicars apostolic, but to get over its provisional and missionary status, and the consequent over-dependence on Rome, the Church needed its own hierarchy. The way this was done made it look as though an assault was being made on the Queen, the archbishop, and the English Church, whether Catholic or Protestant. Cardinal Wiseman was at the centre of this policy.

Born in Seville of Irish parents and educated in Waterford, Ireland, before attending Ushaw College in County Durham, Wiseman became Rector of the English College in Rome in 1828 and was an undoubted scholar of the Early Church. He was also ambitious for position. Although about to lose its papal lands to Victor Emmanuel II in 1860, because of the unification of Italy, the Catholic Church was nevertheless centralizing its authority under ultramontane policies to increase the spiritual power of the papacy. This would be achieved by Pope Pius IX, the longest-serving pope in history (1846–78), who had moved from a liberal to a more conservative position. It was during his papacy that the bull *Universalis Ecclesiae*, promulgating the infallibility of the Pope, was issued, and an exultant Wiseman was appointed Cardinal Archbishop of Westminster, with seven other sees created.

When, on 7 October 1850, Cardinal Wiseman produced a pastoral letter to all English Catholics entitled "From out of the Flaminian Gate", he fomented opinion in England against himself and the actions of his Church. In this letter, Wiseman wrote, "Your beloved country has received a place among the fair churches, which, normally constituted, form the splendid aggregate of Catholic communion: Catholic England has been restored to its orbit in the ecclesiastical firmament, from which its light had long vanished."[25] In many quarters the letter was seen as meddlesome, provocative and insensitive. There were renewed calls for "No Popery", disturbances in Liverpool and elsewhere, and petitions handed to the Queen complaining of "Papal Aggression". Lord Russell's government reacted by passing the Ecclesiastical Titles Bill of 1851, preventing the Roman Catholic Church from using any title currently used by the Church of England with its medieval provenance. It was never used, however, and repealed in 1871.

Wiseman thought that following the formal re-establishment of the Roman Catholic Church in England, streams of converts would come to Catholicism. Some did, like Newman, Manning and Faber, but many, like Keble and Pusey, did not, preferring to bring a more sacramental theology to the Church of England than take on the full panoply and discipline of Roman Catholicism. It would take time for Roman Catholicism to find appropriate standing in England, once out of the shadows. Traditional English Catholics were wary of the ways and ambitions of Rome. Recent converts like Pugin, Faber and, to a lesser extent, Newman were ready to press for the antiquity, doctrines, traditions, claims and colour of full-blown Roman Catholicism. In Pugin's case, such aspirations were well vested in medieval romance and intricate decoration. But in truth Catholics were still a minority faith in an overwhelmingly Protestant nation, with the census of church attendance taken in 1851 revealing ten times as many Non-Conformists, let alone Anglicans, as Catholics.

Methodists were the most numerous Non-Conformist Christians in England, numbering well over a million by 1851. The seeds of difficulties were present in their formation, however, for two forms of Methodism soon emerged: conservative and radical. These two outlooks were held in tension at Wesley's inception of Methodism. On the one hand he never broke with the Anglican Church but set up a separate organization within it—the Methodist Connexion with its conference, preachers and doctrinal values. On the other hand, he was critical of Anglicanism and more drawn to poorer urban communities and to a less educated leadership. The conservative Methodists remained close to the Anglicans, while the radicals sought a more independent style of ministry. There was an intractable conflict between those who valued order and organization and those who wanted freedom and independence. It is an old tension in church life. The Tractarian Movement, with its censorious view of those who worshipped in Methodist and Evangelical Anglican churches, only increased unease between the Methodist Conference and their part of the Church of England.

There were also plenty of opportunities for powerful leaders to emerge from the structure of Methodism. Jabez Bunting, as we have seen, rose as the much-needed manager of the Conference. By 1820, he was president and remained a dominant force for years. One irritated Mancunian complained that "the whole Methodist

Conference is buttoned up in a single pair of breeches".[26] There was deep tension between the desire for free-spirited ministry, evangelism and deployment, and a more organized structure. Some wanted full-blooded training of ministers; others the raising up of leaders by the Spirit. Some wanted organization, others inspiration; some wanted fervour and charismata, others order and agendas. Inevitably this led to a power struggle in the Conference and outside: showers of pamphlets were produced against the autocracy of Bunting by Dr Samuel Warren, for example, and more lay involvement was demanded. In some districts, especially Cornwall, teetotalism emerged, with its adherents organizing themselves into a separate group in the Conference in 1842. Primitive Methodists wanted to return to original field preaching and expected signs of the Spirit, as at the beginning, such as crying out, ranting and falling. The Conference was uneasy. American Methodists, such as James Caughey, came to England with new methods of ministry and, while they were extolled by many English congregations, they were considered suspect and contrived by others. Then, from 1834, a disgruntled preacher called James Everett started producing an anonymous series of pamphlets, later called *Fly Sheets*, that vilified the Conference in general and Bunting in particular. These attacks continued until it was agreed by Conference to reply to the *Fly Sheets* with other anonymous pamphlets. A full-scale pamphlet war ensued, until brought to an end by the Conference in 1849, when it expelled Everett and others whom Conference believed responsible. The Conference was criticized for these expulsions by the national press and compared to the court of the Star Chamber.

By 1850, Methodists were not a happy collective, with many groups seceding. By far the largest group were the Primitive Methodists, founded by Hugh Bourne and William Clowes in 1811. By the time of the census in 1851, 229,646 were attending Primitive Methodist chapels. These were strongest in the Potteries, among Durham and Northumberland miners, in the West Riding, Hull and Lincolnshire and Norfolk. Among their characteristics were open-air preaching, communal hymn singing, uncompromising denunciation of sin, demands for instant conversion and full sanctification and visible signs of the Spirit's presence. For all their "primitiveness in spirit" and structure (or lack of structure), they were a church nearest to the working man. Other secessionists besides the Primitives included the Temperance Methodists, the New Connexion or Kilhamites, the Wesleyan Association and the Bible Christians, to name a few. It seems that a church born out of secession had the possibility for further secession deep in its genes.

While Methodists were the largest single grouping of Non-Conformists, other churches included the Baptists, Independents, Quakers, Presbyterians and

Unitarians. Many had their origins in the England of the seventeenth century, so had weathered many storms. Others, like the Unitarians, had evolved as a rationalist offshoot from the Presbyterians. Between 1830 and 1860, chapels of Congregationalists or Independents became a modern denomination. In 1851, members may have numbered as many as 515,071. Well-educated and better paid than many Anglican clergy on £500–700 a year, their leaders were more deeply rooted than Methodist preachers. They had, in the London Missionary Society, an organization of great repute. The Union of Congregations began in 1831 under the warm-hearted leadership of Algernon Wells, but fell into more troubled waters after 1845.

Baptists were independents who disapproved of infant baptism. Similar to Congregationalists in most other ways, they valued extempore prayer and long sermons based on scripture, often delivered without notes. They were suspicious or hostile towards the Anglican Church. Yet divisions plagued them also, especially over who should be admitted to communion: only the baptized or believers not yet baptized. Strict and Particular Baptists formed and proliferated in East Anglia as a result, and likewise in the North-West. In Manchester, one William Gadsby, an extreme Calvinist and ribbon weaver by profession, had his own following called the Gadsbyites. Their chapels were called "Zoar", and they expected special providence from God to uphold their cause. So, when a minister's wife was struck dumb for four days after condemning a Strict and Particular pastor, they gave praise to God.

The greatest of the Victorian Baptists was Charles Haddon Spurgeon, and someone more different from the leaders of the Oxford Movement could not be found. Born in 1834, in Kelvedon, Essex, he was converted from nominal Anglicanism when attending a Primitive Methodist meeting in Colchester. The sermon could not have been plainer; indeed, the preacher for the day was detained by a snowstorm and an unstudied shoemaker took his place. His text was "Look unto me and be saved". Addressing Spurgeon directly from his preacher's box, he said: "'Young Man, you look very miserable. And you will always be miserable in life and in death if you don't obey my text.' Then lifting up his hands he shouted as only a Primitive Methodist can: 'Young Man, Look to Jesus Christ. Look! Look! Look! You are having nothing to do but to look and live!'"[27] Little did the unknown shoemaker know the effect he would have that day. Spurgeon preached his first sermon at Teversham aged sixteen and became a pastor of a small Baptist church at Waterbeach in Cambridgeshire aged nineteen, before moving to London and New Park Street Chapel in Southwark in 1854. The congregation outgrew the premises in Park Street, so he moved to Exeter Hall—one of the largest meeting rooms in

London—and then to Surrey Gardens Music Hall, both of which accommodated thousands. On 19 October 1856, a fire broke out during one of his services and several people died, affecting Spurgeon deeply. Once it was repaired, he remained at Surrey Gardens for several more years until, in 1861, he moved to the newly opened Metropolitan Tabernacle at Elephant and Castle. The building could take 5,000 and a further thousand standing. He would remain there preaching several times a week to full auditoriums until his death in 1892. His influence was incalculable: David Livingstone and James Hudson Taylor were affected, and hundreds of students, bound for Non-Conformist ministry, trained at his South Norwood College.

If Spurgeon was the prince of Victorian preachers, arousing tens of thousands through his preaching, by 1851 the Quakers were quietly declining in numbers, although still an influential social force. The effect of their policy of denouncing any who married outside the Friends was a serious handicap and was condemned by the Parliamentarian and Quaker John Bright. What Spurgeon was to preaching, Joseph Rowntree (1836–1925) would become to social care and justice. Joseph never forgot his visit to Ireland during the great famine, along with his father, a Quaker grocer from York. After working in his father's business, in 1869 Rowntree would join his brother Henry in the chocolate business, which would grow to be one of the largest manufacturers in England. Elsewhere, in Warwickshire, John Cadbury, another Quaker, would set up Cadbury's chocolate in Bridge Street, Birmingham. The business models these Quakers provided would become deeply influential. Chocolate and banking became the preserve of the Quakers in York, Birmingham and Norfolk (banking—the Barclays and Gurneys). Elizabeth Fry, married to another chocolate-maker, Joseph Fry, and having had eleven children, devoted herself to improving conditions in prisons like Newgate and on transportation ships.

By the 1850s, there was a relaxation of the Quaker rules on marriage, on wearing the garb (the simple Quaker smock), and on the pre-eminence of silence over teaching in meetings. There was also greater willingness to debate issues of concern, and to train ministers instead of relying on spontaneous inspiration. In the second half of the century, numbers were increasing again.

By the early part of the nineteenth century, many of the previously Presbyterian congregations in England had become Unitarian. In England, Unitarianism can be traced back to the writings of Joseph Priestley (1733–1804), a natural philosopher and a remarkable chemist, who isolated "an air" and demonstrated this in front of Lavoisier in Paris. Lavoisier would go on to identify it as oxygen. Priestley represented an Enlightenment rationalism in a religious form: he overturned the doctrine of the Trinity, the notion of original sin, predestination and the authority of the Bible. Instead, reason and empirical testing replaced mere "believing". His was a rationalist religion that could hardly be said to be Christian and which corresponded to the Arianism (the belief that Jesus was not fully God) that had plagued the Church in the fourth century. Unitarianism became popular in late eighteenth-century society, because of its high view of scientific advancement and the premium it placed on education. Priestley had a patron in Lord Shelburne and a laboratory at Bowood House near Chippenham. Together with a colleague, Theophilus Lindsey, he started the first Unitarian meeting in London. These meetings spread quickly, even developing connections with Unitarian churches in Transylvania and Romania. When a trust fund producing nearly £3,000 a year from a Presbyterian philanthropist, Lady Hewley (1627–1710), fell into the hands of Unitarian trustees, legislation in Parliament had to be brought in by Peel. Called the Dissenters' Chapels Bill (1844), it enabled Unitarians to legitimately access the trust. This Bill caused a controversy, as Evangelicals, Wesleyans and others believed that the trust was being misapplied to "heretics". Despite the furore, the Bill was passed, and many saw it as a further extension of the religious toleration that had already been given to Roman Catholics and dissenters.

By the middle of the nineteenth century, the variety of churches in England was greater than it had ever been, and most were now permitted to function legally. In addition, Latter-day Saints or Mormons arrived in England in the 1840s. The Brethren movement, which began in Ireland, was to spread to England by the 1830s, splitting in 1848 into the Open and Exclusive Brethren. The latter was led by John Nelson Darby, who espoused Dispensationalism, which divided God's revelation through history into different watertight compartments.[28] Anomalies to do with toleration still remained, for instance with tithes, and with restrictions in the universities where only Anglican lecturers were permitted. A watershed had been reached by the 1850s; now it remained to be seen how this large-scale, diverse Christian presence would affect education and social and medical care. The answer was "slowly", as scientific knowledge progressed and ideas about raising living standards gradually took hold in the country.

Education, social reform and medical care

In England, education had always been connected to the Christian faith. Indeed, the original purpose of education was to teach Christianity. By the early nineteenth century, there was a movement to extend education more widely, not only in scope, but also to provide a national education system. In 1811, the National Society for Promoting the Education of the Poor in the Principles of the Established Church was founded, and in 1814, the British and Foreign Schools Society was formed. The National Society was in effect controlled by Anglicans and the British and Foreign by dissenters. The state granted money to both, but only in proportion to the amount raised by each. Since, not surprisingly, the National Society raised more money, it received a larger government grant, and this was of course deemed unfair. Lord John Russell proposed a modest increase in the government's educational grant from £20,000 to £30,000, but attached it to a new Board of Education with its own secretary, the redoubtable Dr Kay Shuttleworth, thought to be a liberal and formerly a dissenter, who had now come over to the Church of England. This Board of Education was a sub-committee of the Privy Council, with government appointees, which deliberately excluded bishops, who greatly resented this. Neither Phillpotts of Exeter nor Blomfield of London approved. Worse was to come: receiving money from the board depended on agreeing to allow government inspectors into schools. The thought that money was dependent on inspection, and that inspectors were evaluating religious education provided by Anglican clergy, was too much for some. One vicar of East Brent in Somerset truculently declared that the Church should "reject their thirty pieces of silver" and threatened that if the inspector came again, he would be thrown into the pond! The provision of education across the country for all primary-aged boys and girls was to be an ongoing challenge to government, and in particular to appease a sense of injustice among the dissenting community. From its inception, primary school education had been started by religious organizations and the issue was how two ideas of education, Anglican and dissenting, could be reconciled and fairly supported by government provision. First steps had been taken, but there was a long way to go, and the issue would dog the education system for the remainder of the century, and indeed to the Butler Education Act of 1944.

Social reform was mildly on the agenda of the Whig governments up to 1865. For a brief spell Palmerston had been home secretary in the 1850s. Known better for his gun-toting foreign policy, he generally had a *laissez faire* attitude to social reform. In 1853, cholera once again swept Britain. Fasting and prayer were called for, but Palmerston preferred civic action to beseeching prayers. He attempted to improve drainage through a Board of Health and a Commissioner of Sewers was appointed, but the development became "bogged down" in bureaucratic infighting. With the stimulus of his relative by marriage, the great Christian social reformer Lord Ashley (later Earl Shaftesbury), he sought to restrict children working down the mines. Only a modest change resulted, however, which was the exclusion of children under twelve from night shifts after 6 p.m. In the daytime, children were still used down the mines. Ashley was to tire of Palmerston's ineffectiveness in piloting legislation through Parliament, such as the Public Health Bill, the Juvenile Mendicancy Bill and the Chimney Sweep Bill. It was as though, having welcomed the idea of reform, legislation rarely resulted.[29] Palmerston had too great a reliance on the market to regulate industry by legislation. It was also probably because his heart was mostly in foreign affairs and, in March 1854, the nation was busy embarking on war against the Russians in Crimea.

An unexpected by-product of the nightmare of the Crimean War was the invention of modern nursing by Florence Nightingale. The war was intended to prevent further encroachment by Russia into the Ottoman Empire: already Russia had moved into Bessarabia and Wallachia in present-day Romania and Moldova. An alliance of England, France, the Ottomans and Sardinia took on Russia. The war lasted for two and a half years from October 1853 to March 1855 and initially involved stalemate battles at Sevastopol and Inkerman, until Sevastopol fell after a lengthy siege. The war became known for three things: the unprofessionalism of Britain's military leaders (leading for instance to "The Charge of the Light Brigade", immortalized by Tennyson); the institution of the Victoria Cross, the highest medal thereafter for gallantry; and the nursing regime of Florence Nightingale with its future impact on hospital care.

Florence Nightingale (1820–1910) was a singular character. She came from an upper middle-class family based at Embley Park in Hampshire, family friends of the Palmerstons, who lived at nearby Broadlands.[30] She was intellectually curious and enjoyed family tours on the continent, making a close friend of the English salon hostess in Paris, Mary Clarke (later Mary Mohl), known as "Clarkey", whose friends included the authors George Eliot and Elizabeth Gaskell.

In 1853, now thirty-three, Florence realized her hope of useful service and took up the post of Superintendent of the Institute for the Care of Sick Gentlewomen in Upper Harley Street. Her father supported her financially with £500 a year, as he would throughout her life. Her nursing career had begun. Given her adventurous spirit and her indomitable will, it was perhaps not surprising that the following year she responded to reports of terrible conditions in the Crimean campaign, and with the support of the Secretary of War, her friend Sidney Herbert,[31] embarked for the Crimea with thirty-eight nurses and a group of Roman Catholic nuns. During the embarkation her pet owl, Athena, found at the Parthenon in Athens, died. It was as if one part of her life had ended and her defining work was about to begin.

Florence's nursing system in the Crimea became legendary. Death rates from cholera and typhus were far greater than from fighting in the campaign. Florence had already studied nursing methods elsewhere and in particular at the Kaiserswerth Institution in Germany in 1851. She later criticized its hygiene but praised its devotion and discipline. What she brought to the nursing challenge in Scutari was immense discipline: she redesigned the lay-out of the hospital beds (indeed, she even had a new hospital prefabricated in England by Brunel and shipped out to Scutari), she created spacious airy wards, gave out clean clothing, attended to the wives and widows of the soldiers and cleaned, cleaned, cleaned. Little was understood about the science of infection until the French chemist Louis Pasteur (1822–95) discovered the microbiology of disease, but Florence accounted for the transference of disease by a "miasma" based on lack of hygiene and she supported this conjecture with copious statistics. Her work was reported on and painted for the people back in Britain. She was a ray of professionalism in an otherwise debilitating and unprofessional campaign. To the nation she was "the Lady with the Lamp", as depicted by *The Times*: an icon of attentive care of sick and wounded soldiers. She caught the heart of a sentimental nation ready to believe in the power of feminine care and devotion to duty.

Only thirty-five at the end of the Crimean War, Florence had a long life ahead of her. She had become a household name. She met Queen Victoria and Prince Albert in Balmoral for over two hours and lobbied the government relentlessly to set up a royal commission on sanitation in the army. Too often she met with procrastination, male resentment and obfuscation. Yet her charm and persistence were always intransigently deployed, and in 1857 the commission began sitting. She wrote *Notes on Matters Affecting the Health, Efficiency and Hospital Administration of the British Army*, and founded through public subscription the first nursing school in the world at St Thomas's Hospital. Her health then began to deteriorate. Living as she did in an annexe of three rooms off a London hotel, there was little time for relaxation, but she soldiered on until her ninetieth year. Not a feminist in the sense of wanting to press women's rights, as her friend Harriet Martineau did, she nonetheless opened a whole new sphere of work to women in nursing, and in time this would spread to all positions in medicine. She remained a member of the Church of England, holding robust and typically unorthodox views. She especially believed in the reconciling mercy of God.

There is no doubt that this period from 1837 to 1860 established the basis of the Victorian world. As far as the Church was concerned, the national Christian community existed now in three broad ways: the Anglican Church, the Non-Conformist churches and the newly emancipated and reconstituted Roman Catholic Church. Each would face the growing challenge of reason and science. The Church of England had re-examined its roots through the Oxford Movement and its relationship with the Church Fathers of the first five centuries; the Roman Catholics were an uneasy alliance of Old Catholics, new converts and the Irish. Each of the churches now faced the challenge of increasing industrialization and urbanization at home and new missionary opportunities abroad. They also faced tests as to their response to social change, injustice and empire: how much would they bless the *status quo* or how much would they be harbingers of the kingdom of God, how much would they imbibe new scientific learning and how much resist it? These challenges lay ahead.

CHAPTER 19

The Church in the Modern World

The Victorian world changed in the early 1860s. On 14 December 1861, at around 11 p.m., Prince Albert died after a short illness, quite probably of pneumonia brought on by typhoid and from premature ageing through overwork.[1] Sir Charles Phipps, an equerry to the Queen, reported to Prime Minister Palmerston that "The Queen, though in an agony of grief, is perfectly collected, and shows a self-control that is quite extraordinary. Alas! She has not realized her loss—and when the full consciousness comes upon her—I tremble—but only for the depth of her grief."[2]

How right he was. The Queen was plunged into protracted mourning which caught up her family, and then the nation, in a prolonged psychodrama of grief. Her family was trapped by it. Her eldest daughter, Vicky, married to the Prussian Crown Prince Frederick, wrote to her husband Fritz, "Where shall I look to for advice (now)? I am only 21 and things here [Berlin] wear a threatening aspect! God will help; He will not desert us—'Seek and ye shall find, knock and it shall be opened to you.'"[3] Vicky's young son, later to be Kaiser Wilhelm II and Britain's adversary in the Great War, was barely two. Bertie, the Prince of Wales, was blamed by Queen Victoria for his father's death, since he had caused great consternation through his "fall" only weeks before whilst on military exercises at the Curragh, Dublin, where he had lost his virginity to Nellie Clifden, a courtesan in Ireland. Albert had then caught a cold while walking near Cambridge with his eldest son and talking over the affair, and being assured of Bertie's contrition.

The cold would develop into a more severe illness from which Albert would die. The Queen, beside herself with grief, sank into an isolation from which it would take years to emerge. Apart from opening Parliament occasionally, and a thanksgiving service at St Paul's for the deliverance of the Prince of Wales from typhoid on 27 February 1872—twelve years later—she did not appear in public, and only then at Gladstone's insistence.[4]

The influence of Albert was gone and within four years Palmerston would die in office: that hardworking, raffish, gunboat-threatening, liberal statesman who had dominated the previous ten years and was more like an eighteenth-century Whig politician than the serious-minded Liberal and Conservative reformers who were to follow. By 1865, a new age of Victorian Britain had begun: an age of empire, expansion, industrialization, sanitation and electoral reform, but also of science, religious doubt and a changing map in Europe. As Dickens said in the opening lines of his *Tale of Two Cities*, "It was the best of times, it was worst of times . . . it was the season of Light, it was the season of Darkness."[5] In many ways, these words summed up the Victorian experience.

The Church in Mid-Victorian England

By the 1860s, the Church of England had settled into its three constituent parts of Evangelical or Low Church, Sacramental or High Church and Liberal or Broad Church. The jibe that the Church of England was like Turl Street in Oxford— going from the High Street to Broad Street and passing Jesus (College) on the way—was typical of the Evangelical complaint about Anglicanism. These three factions reflected the way each party gave pre-eminence to a constituent part of Anglicanism's formulation. Evangelicals put scripture first; the Sacramentalists put tradition first; and the Broad Church put reason first. All of them jostled for pre-eminence.

By the mid-Victorian period, the Evangelicals had mobilized their forces. The Evangelical Alliance, which combined Evangelicals of all denominational persuasions in England and abroad, was founded in 1846 by the missionary-minded Edward Bickersteth, later Bishop of Exeter, the Jewish Christian Ridley Herschell, and Sir Culling Eardley, Bt. It still flourishes today and coordinates Evangelical responses to issues affecting Church and nation. At the same time, the Church Pastoral Aid Society was begun in 1836 by Lord Shaftesbury and others to support curates and lay workers in Evangelical parishes. Some bishops, like Phillpotts of Exeter and Samuel Wilberforce, resigned their initial membership because the society was too narrowly focussed on Evangelical clergy and lay workers, but it had the support, among others, of Archbishop Sumner (1848–62), his brother Bishop Sumner of Winchester (1827–69, and incidentally the father-in-law of Mary Sumner, the founder of the Mothers' Union) and old Bishop Bathurst of Norwich. By 1858, the significant sum of £48,000 was being granted to curates and lay workers in Evangelical parishes. Evangelicals were well supported by members of the aristocracy: ladies like the Duchesses of Gordon, Manchester, Beaufort and Sutherland attended the fashionable proprietary chapel of St Mary's, Brighton, where the thoughtful and popular ministry of Henry Venn Elliott continued for thirty-eight years. Not only this, but Lord Palmerston, with his family connection to the Evangelical Lord Shaftesbury, continued to promote Evangelical bishops. Both sought the appointments, not of scholars, but of godly pastors.

Likewise, the Tractarian or High Church party sought to establish themselves in both the hierarchy and the parishes of the Church of England. After the conversion to Rome of Newman and Manning and others, such as Robert and Henry Wilberforce, both sons of William Wilberforce, a time of Tractarian retrenchment was needed within Anglicanism. Leaders like Edward Pusey (1800–82) wanted Anglo-Catholicism to live and thrive within Anglicanism. With the conversion of Newman to Roman Catholicism there came a sense of betrayal among many High Church Anglicans, who now sought a more secure niche in the Church of England.

There were some clergy who campaigned for the sacramentalism of the Tractarian Movement to be better established in the Church of England. One such was the Archdeacon of Wells, George Denison, who, in line with ancient Catholic teaching, sought to impose on ordinands (those going forward to ordination) the belief that the inward reality of the sacrament could be received by the wicked as well as the faithful, although many found this view antithetical to Article 29 of the Church of England and its teaching on the sacraments. At this point a legal case was called for and the prosecution of Denison proceeded through the labyrinthine maze of the ecclesiastical courts until it failed on a technicality.

In fact, Denison became a hero in the Diocese of Bath and Wells: parishioners met him on his return to his parish and personally drew his coach to his church and vicarage. Evangelicals were defeated in the courts "partly because the prosecution seemed so persistent, partly because dissenting money helped to finance the attack upon an Anglican archdeacon, and partly because Archbishop Sumner appeared before the world as an archbishop in a muddle".[6] Furthermore, the word "altar" (instead of "holy table"), along with candles and ornaments, was allowed by decision of the Privy Council in 1857 on the grounds that nothing in the Prayer Book prohibited the use of organs, pews, pulpit cloth and cassocks, nor the word "altar" or lights. Such a judgement opened the door to pretty much anything, unless it was inimical to the Articles. By such means, decorations and the vocabulary of sacramentalism and ceremonies were readmitted to the Church and could be pursued in worship. Nor did Parliament want to interfere by defining what was permissible or by setting a scale of punishments for miscreants. The redecoration of churches was further fuelled by the Ecclesiological Society in 1839, with its own publication on architecture, liturgy and decoration. The Tractarian Movement was to be embedded in the stonework and decoration of parish churches up and down England over the remaining sixty years of the century. The High Church movement would be proclaimed in the Eucharist, nurtured by confession, and applied in pastoral care through anointing and the use of the rosary.

Finally, the liberal stream of the Church of England, also called the Broad Church—a term disliked by many liberals because of their passionate espousal of equality and social change—developed during this period. This stream in Anglicanism received a boost from the writing and preaching of F. D. Maurice (1805–72), a man of humble background with Unitarian and dissenting parents, and to that extent an outsider in relation to the establishment. He attended both Cambridge and Oxford universities, had a notable intellect, and was ordained in 1834. Maurice disliked Evangelical doctrine, but looked for the building of the kingdom of God on earth *now*. He was influenced by the movements for political freedom so evident in Europe in 1848 and was a founder and spokesperson for Christian Socialism. In 1853, he published *Theological Essays*, which was considered unorthodox, particularly with regard to future judgement and eternal punishment. Before returning to Cambridge as a professor of moral theology in 1866, he founded a Working Men's College in London in 1854 and sought to educate working men in theology and the liberal arts. Other colleges were linked together in the Society for Promoting Working Men's Associations. Into this circle came liberal luminaries, such as author and Regius Professor of History at Cambridge, Charles Kingsley, along with Matthew Arnold, John Ruskin, Dante Gabriel Rossetti and Thomas Carlyle. However difficult it was to pin Maurice down, he did represent a school of thought that held Christianity should lead to socialism and political engagement so that there might be equal opportunities for all. In a word, he preached a social gospel in which Christianity properly understood was to bring liberation from the effects of poverty. This trajectory was to be an important ingredient in the future Labour Party, which came into existence towards the end of the century (1893) and of which one of its founders, Keir Hardie (1856–1915), said: "I claim for socialism that it is the embodiment of Christianity in our industrial system."[7]

A less intellectual response to the needs of the urban poor in mid-Victorian society came from two other sources. The first was the preaching and ministry of William Booth and his wife Catherine (née Mumford) Booth. William was originally a Methodist, to which denomination he was converted in 1844. Two years later, he became a street preacher and quickly expanded his ministry. By 1868, Booth controlled thirteen preaching stations in East London. He found an audience by singing hymns and not by preaching alone. By 1875, there was a constitution, and, at a subsequent annual meeting or conference, the banner of the Salvation Army was painted across the platform. With that, a new movement was formed, not of education and political empowerment as envisaged by Christian Socialism, but of spiritual reform and community action among the poor communities of the nation. Soon, the Salvation Army would spread around the world with its distinctive brass bands—originally used to drown out the opposition—military uniforms and hierarchy, and a value system based on simple preaching and compassionate care. It was also to inspire Wilson Carlile to birth the Church Army in the Anglican Church as a body of lay evangelists.

Another ministry among the poor came from the opposite wing of the Church: traditional Roman Catholicism. If Newman was the intellectual Catholic, his sparring partner Henry Manning, also a convert to Catholicism at the time of the Gorham case, was no less committed to Catholicism, although of a more authoritarian kind. Manning, previously an Anglican archdeacon, looked on the surface as different from the Salvation Army as possible, yet he approved of its work among the poor. He was austere and rigorous when it came to canon law, as unbending in his devotion to the Holy See as he was critical of insular Old English Catholics, and self-assured to the point of arrogance. Manning could never agree with the principles of pure socialism: the poor needed help, but not at the expense of property ownership—that would be killing the patient to cure his ills. Instead, injustice must be alleviated by governments or employers and aid provided to help the poor, both spiritually and materially. He personally gave whatever he could to the poor. His reputation lent him authority, and it was through his intervention that the London Dock Strike was ended in 1890. On his death, thousands attended his lying-in-state and as many his funeral.

However diverse Christianity had become, its basic foundations in revelation were now to be challenged by scientific progress and critical, rationalist thought.

Evolution, biblical criticism and the issue of doubt

It is hard for us, who have grown accustomed to trusting in the veracity of scientific knowledge, to appreciate the effect of Darwin's publication in 1859 of *On the Origin of Species by Means of Natural Selection*. At that time, it was still widely held that the world was little more than 6,000 years old and that famously, according to Archbishop Ussher's work on the genealogies of Genesis in 1654, earth and human life came into existence on 23 October 4004 BC! Indeed, such a date was supported near enough as to make little difference by the Venerable Bede, Johannes Kepler and even Sir Isaac Newton. As a result of his observations whilst voyaging around South America and the Pacific on the *Beagle* from 1831–6, Darwin concluded that a process of evolution spaced over millions of years was the means whereby species both originated and developed. He sat on his ideas for twenty years before publishing them in 1859, delaying their publication because he knew the quarrel that publication would cause with the Church, and the stress it would cause his devout wife Emma (née Wedgwood). In the end, any further failure to publish meant that he would be overtaken by others, so he published.

The reaction of the Church to Darwin's findings was varied. The more liberal, like Charles Kingsley, welcomed the findings, but others saw them as deeply problematic, especially when such theories were applied to the creation of humankind. The debate of the British Association that took place in Oxford between Bishop Sam Wilberforce (son of William Wilberforce and known as "Soapy Sam") and the biologist Thomas Huxley was, in many ways, characteristic of the entire Victorian conflict over evolution.

On the one side was the rhetorical and obscurantist bishop with little knowledge of science and, on the other, the empirically minded and instructed professor. Wilberforce hoped to use ridicule to belittle the scientist's case, famously asking whether Huxley was descended from an ape on his father or mother's side. One professor in the audience responded that he "would rather be descended from an ape than a bishop!"[8] In 1871, Darwin published *The Descent of Man, and Selection in Relation to Sex*, in which he drew a continuity between animals and humans, and showed that visual display, culture and social standing affected sexual selection in the interests of breeding fitter descendants. It was in this work that the line between the animal world and human creation was blurred.

What Darwin's work did was heighten tension between theology and science, and especially between what the Bible was thought to tell us and what science was beginning to show through natural evidence. On the scientific side, people like the Ulsterman John Tyndall (1820–93) underscored the limits of religion in relation to the laws of nature. For Tyndall, prayer could not alter the physical universe, improve harvests, avert bad weather or heal the sick. Others, such as Clerk Maxwell (1831–79), the Cavendish Professor of Physics at Cambridge University and one of the pioneers of electrical engineering and quantum mechanics, had a different view. He saw no conflict between the Bible and the outcomes of research, between divine and physical laws. The scientist was thinking God's thoughts after him. Likewise, among the clergy and theologians there were various responses to Darwinian theories of evolution: some opposed it with all they had; others doubted the Bible because of it; still others took the view "we will hear you more on this" and sought to interpret Genesis in light of scientific research. Bishop Ryle, the Evangelical Bishop of Liverpool, believed in all the information of the Old Testament. Ellicott of Gloucester, the biblical commentator, condemned the theory that man was part of an evolutionary process. By contrast, Frederick Temple, another brilliant academic from Balliol, Oxford, controversially made Bishop of Exeter, Bishop of London and later Archbishop of Canterbury from 1897, assumed evolution in his Bampton Lectures of 1884. Still, there was some hostility towards Christianity, spearheaded by Thomas Huxley, John Tyndall and the polymath Francis Galton. Men like Temple were able to meld science to faith, doing justice to each. It was a dialectic which would be repeated more or less felicitously in the years to come. Meanwhile, there were other battles to fight closer to home; and also over the Bible.

The mid-nineteenth century saw the birth of biblical criticism and the beginnings of the search for the historical Jesus in the New Testament. This so-called academic "search" would last for at least a hundred years and resulted from burgeoning scholarship, especially in the German universities. In Germany, there was much greater knowledge and availability of the manuscript texts of the Bible, combined with an underlying philosophy of rational, scientific materialism which *a priori* disbelieved the miraculous. The Germans were much more willing to question previously held presuppositions. While the roots of this movement may be found in the mid-Victorian period, it went on to reach well into the second half of the twentieth century.

Firstly, there was renewed interest in the text of the Bible. In the 1840s and 50s, the Vatican had practically refused entry to scholars wanting to study *Codex Vaticanus*. Then, in February 1859, the scholar Constantin von Tischendorf, working for the Tsar of Russia, located a late fourth-century New Testament manuscript of exceptional quality and provenance at St Catherine's Monastery in Sinai. He persuaded the abbot to part with it in exchange for a large payment by the Tsar. The discovery of *Codex Sinaiticus* was to New Testament studies what the discovery of Tutankhamun was to Egyptology. In 1933, the Stalinist government sold the *Codex* to the British Museum for £100,000, where it now resides with a third great codex, *Codex Alexandrinus*, which also includes much of the Septuagint.

Soon, a critical text of the New Testament was published by S. P. Tregalles, and then in 1881, Westcott and Hort published a revised text of the New Testament. A re-established text gave rise to the possibility of a new translation of the Bible to replace the Authorized King James Version. One MP, Charles Buxton, suggested that Queen Victoria and the President of the United States should sponsor such a venture, but others, more conservative, did not want to destabilize people's faith and familiarity with the King James version. A new translation was undertaken with Hort, Westcott and Bishops Lightfoot of Durham and Ellicott of Gloucester (and earlier of Bristol) taking part. The task was completed in 1881, but was given a cool reception. Interestingly, Lightfoot had called for a change in the Lord's Prayer from "deliver us from evil" to "deliver us from the evil one". And in 1 Corinthians 13 the translators changed "charity" to "love". Of course, such changes provoked controversy.

J. W. Burgon, the Dean of Chichester, and chief conservative, wanted not a jot or a tittle changed. Bishop Wordsworth of Lincoln went for the compromise, suggesting that possible changes be annotated in the margins of the Authorized Version. The conservatives won, and when Burgon lay dying he rejoiced that "he had crushed the revised version of the New Testament, so that I believe it will never lift up its head again".[9] In truth, the Revised Version never flew. It exemplified the dilemma of biblical translation, in fact, for, as Gladstone said, "You will sacrifice truth if you don't read it, and you will sacrifice people if you do."[10] Only in 1899 was it authorized by Convocation to be read in church, although many chose not to!

If establishing a new text of the New Testament was hard enough, dealing with criticism of the text was still more disruptive. From the German universities innovative theories abounded: Julius Wellhausen (1844–1918) published his *Prolegomena to the History of Israel* in 1885, in which the historicity of Old Testament narratives was questioned, and which led to some thinking the great part of early Hebrew history was simply legend. Somewhat earlier, David Strauss (1808–74) wrote a *Life of Jesus* that was published in 1835. Much liked by Princess Alice of Hesse (1843–78), the second daughter of Queen Victoria and the maternal great-grandmother of Prince Philip, this is a devotional work in which Jesus is detached from the miraculous to give us a sympathetic and perfect man, rather than an authoritative, all-powerful Son of God.

Other *Lives* of Jesus followed, including that of the Frenchman Ernest Renan, whose Jesus is depicted as "an original genius, a great soul and an incomparable artist".[11] In England, a similar book called *Ecce Homo* was published anonymously in 1865. It transpired that it was written by J. R. Seeley, a professor of Latin at University College. It did not cause much of a stir until Lord Shaftesbury said at the 1866 annual meeting of the Church Pastoral Aid Society that it "was the most pestilential book ever vomited, I think, from the jaws of hell". A further 1,000 copies were quickly sold—always the result of controversy. Two other *Lives* of Christ followed, both of which proved popular and were less critical: F. W. Farrar's *Life of Christ* of 1874 and Alfred Eddersheim's *Life and Times of Jesus the Messiah* in 1883. In 1874, a book that was more critical of the New Testament called *Supernatural Religion* was published anonymously. It was a free-thinking piece, but shallow, and Lightfoot soon exposed its tendentious scholarship. The greatest challenge to conservative theological thinking came from two other books: *Essays and Reviews* and *Lux Mundi*.

The purpose of *Essays and Reviews* of March 1860 was to open up a debate on the new criticism of the Bible. The main movers of this project were the soon-to-be Master of Balliol, Benjamin Jowett, and Frederick Temple. Seven academic contributions were sought: six clerical and one lay. The authors held that since all truth belongs to God, there should be no fear of investigation. Miracles may not have been historical, but they nevertheless teach spiritual truths. The truth of revelation lies in its moral impact and not in questionable "legendary episodes". In many ways this was the classic liberal position of separating faith from fact, of showing facts that are incapable of substantiation, and so holding on to the Christ of faith while detaching him from the moorings of history. Jowett, who as Regius Professor of Greek was both a Platonic philosopher and textual scholar, employed a dialectic which oscillated between these two approaches: Platonism and particularity.

The reaction to *Essays and Reviews* was furious. In 1861, Archbishop Sumner denounced the work. Many asked how such people could retain their status as clergy and how such views could be reconciled with the Articles of the Church of England. The bishops were almost united in their condemnation. Prosecutions were brought, and one of the essayists, Henry Wilson of St John's College, Oxford, was suspended from his post for one year for denying the inspiration of scripture and the doctrine of eternal punishment. The case then went higher, to the Privy Council, and in 1864 two contributors to *Essays and Reviews*, Rowland Williams and H. B. Wilson, were cleared with the support of the Bishop of London, Archibald Tait, another scholar from Balliol and later Archbishop of Canterbury.

Now the hierarchy resorted to declarations of condemnation, but a gulf was opening between the intelligent layman and the pronouncements of the Church. Frederick Temple was nominated by Gladstone to the see of Exeter in 1869, but at the same time Temple allowed his essay to be withdrawn from future publications of *Essays and Reviews*, thus gaining support for his appointment as bishop there.

In 1889, there was to be a re-run of the same issues with the publication of *Lux Mundi*. Edited by Charles Gore, the Principal of Pusey House, it sought to suggest that adherence to the divine inspiration of scripture is compatible with suggestions that Jonah and David were narrators of *myth* rather than historical events. Such a debunking of the history of the Old Testament was vigorously resisted by Henry Liddon of St Paul's, the Tractarian preacher and Professor of Exegesis at Oxford, the Tractarian Archdeacon Denison of Taunton, Bishop Hervey of Bath and Wells, Ryle of Liverpool and Ellicott of Gloucester. One colonel, speaking at his diocesan conference in 1890, proposed that criticism of the Old Testament was not even compatible with Christianity. But for all the protest, interest in new ideas, and the progress of science and biblical criticism emanating from Germany in particular, meant that by 1894 "nearly all the intelligent young men stood behind Gore".[12] Gore had helped his cause by apologizing for any perceived criticism of Christ for holding literal views of the Old Testament, and by giving a series of thoroughly orthodox Bampton Lectures on the incarnation.

Nonetheless, the late Victorian age had many who wrestled with doubt. George Eliot, the brilliant novelist, was an agnostic. Tennyson found faith difficult whilst reflecting on the vastness of the universe but resolved his doubts in his poem "Crossing the Bar", in which he hoped to see "his pilot face to face". The MP Charles Bradlaugh was an avowed atheist who could not take his seat in the House of Commons for six years because he would not take an oath on the Bible, thereby creating a political furore. His friend Annie Besant (1847–1933), who lived in Gipsy Hill, London, joined him in the National Secular Society and criticized Christianity for its suppression of women's rights. She advocated home rule for Ireland like Gladstone, independence for India and contraception for women. Matthew Arnold, the son of the Headmaster of Rugby—a latitudinarian whom Queen Victoria and Prince Albert had admired—was an Anglican who became first a doubter, then a Roman Catholic, then an Anglican again, and finally a Roman Catholic! Thus, for some it was a restless age where new discoveries meant shifting trajectories of belief. It was also an age of huge social change and the battle of the great titans of Victorian politics.

Politics and social change (1868–92)

The population of Britain continued to grow between 1851 and 1861, despite decline in Ireland from the ravages of the Great Famine. In England, the population in this period went from 21 to 23 million. By 1871, it would reach 26 million. Despite the repeal of the Corn Laws, farming was more prosperous than ever, and would remain so until the advent of the steam ship in the 1890s facilitated imports from the United States. Railway tracks doubled. Exports grew at 11 per cent a year in mid-Victorian England. Cheap cloth, steel and iron abounded. Prosperity increased for the middle classes. At the same time, working hours gradually began to decrease for factory workers. However, the quality of life in the towns remained dreadful: malnutrition was rife; housing was grossly overcrowded; and outbreaks of disease common. By 1885, the Royal Commission on the Housing of the Working Classes reported alarming overcrowding. The census of 1891 showed one tenth of the population was living more than two per room, and in London this rose to 20 per cent. Sanitation was so bad in the cities and London that a sitting of Parliament had to be suspended in July 1858 due to the "Great Stink". Workhouses continued to institutionalize the poor, and in particular the aged poor. Congregational minister Andrew Mearns published a work entitled *The Bitter Cry of Outcast London*, drawing attention to the deplorable squalor of Bermondsey.

The campaigning journalist and publisher W. T. Stead drew attention to the extent of prostitution in the cities through his sensational and indignant style of journalism. The forerunners of the tabloids of the twentieth century, Stead's newspapers raised issues in unmistakeable ways: sensational, arresting and vivid. Nor did they need to search hard for shocking material when, in November 1888, Jack the Ripper went on a brutal killing spree of prostitutes in the East End of London. England was a nation of deep contrasts: rising prosperity and stubborn poverty; a growing middle class and an untouched underclass, with about 30 per cent of the population struggling to escape the bonds of destitution. It was to such a population that the Church tried to minister, with what results we shall see.

It was in these national circumstances that two of the great political titans of the Victorian age were to vie for power: Gladstone and Disraeli. Not only did Gladstone and Disraeli have sharply differing political outlooks, but their characters were just as contrasting. Disraeli was brilliant, waspish, sickly, an opportunist and imperialist, while Gladstone was comprehensive, emotional, rugged, religious and remorseless in his quest for change. Gladstone liked chopping down trees and espousing unjust causes; Disraeli liked writing novels of uneven quality and conversing in London clubs. Disraeli flattered the Queen; Gladstone lectured her, for which she hated him, calling him "half mad". Gladstone was a High Church Anglican who immersed himself in theology and even flagellated himself for misdemeanours when out seeking prostitutes to save. Disraeli was a Jew who had become a nominal Anglican. They would spar with each other from the end of Peel's government until Disraeli's death in 1881: the central years of Victoria's reign.

Following the demise of Palmerston and his reluctance to continue with parliamentary reform, the Liberals led by Russell in the Lords and Gladstone in the Commons brought a second Reform Bill to increase the electorate, but the Liberals split over the extent of the reform, thus allowing the government to be defeated in June 1866. The Tories now formed a minority administration with Disraeli as Chancellor of the Exchequer in the Commons, and Lord Derby in the Lords as Prime Minister: the famous combination of the jockey (in fact racehorse owner) and the Jew. A new Reform Bill was brought forward by Disraeli in the Commons in March 1867. He was determined to succeed and end the Conservative period in the political wilderness. It also enabled the Conservatives to steal a march on the Liberals when it came to electoral reform. In a virtuoso performance of parliamentary leadership, Disraeli succeeded in "this leap in the dark" and the second Reform Act reached the statute book. As a result, the electorate increased by 90 per cent to two million, about ten per cent of the population.[13] The bishops were nevertheless slow to support reform and, despite the second Reform Act, the Conservatives were defeated in 1868 by an increased electorate now looking for greater social reform and Gladstone was voted into office for his first premiership from 1868–74. It was to be one of the great reforming administrations in modern political history.

When, whilst chopping down trees at Hawarden, his home in Flintshire, Gladstone received the news that he had handsomely won the election of 1868, he turned to Evelyn Ashley, who was with him, and famously said: "My mission is to pacify Ireland", that is, to bring peace to Ireland's fractious life. Ireland was front and centre in Gladstone's first two administrations (1868–74 and 1880–85), and it would end his last. As a first step in this campaign to "pacify Ireland", Gladstone brought forward the Irish Church Act of 1869 to disestablish the Protestant Church there (from which we get the word "disestablishment"). It was now to be separated from the Church of England. Irish bishops could no longer sit in the House of Lords. Tithes were to be abolished in return for an annual stipend, and endowments greatly reduced. The Queen disliked the Act when she understood what was intended. The Commons approved, while the bishops in the House of Lords abstained. Yet piloted by Gladstone, who between fits of nervous illness drafted the legislation and so commanded the detail, the Act passed both Houses. Further reforms followed in a cascade: the Irish Land Bill (a less successful measure to tip the balance of land ownership towards Irish rather than English by turning tenants into owners); a Ballot Act enabling a secret ballot in all general elections; the Universities Tests Act of 1871, removing the bar against non-Anglicans teaching at the universities; and an Education Act. The Education Act introduced by William Forster provided a framework for primary school education. Those not yet in either state-aided or voluntary schools, some two million children, were now to be placed in Board Schools. A sensible settlement on religious education was made through the Cowper-Temple amendment, in which some Bible teaching and hymns were required in the Board Schools, rather than a strictly Anglican approach to religious education. This was more acceptable to Non-Conformists and the system lasted until the Balfour Education Act of 1902 and the creation of local education authorities.

Despite this welter of reforms, which even included the establishment of a professional civil service with its own entrance examination and the end of sales of commissions in the army, Gladstone was defeated by Disraeli in 1874. He had split his party by seeking to establish a Catholic University in Dublin led by the Jesuits—it was one Roman Catholic project too far, as Maynooth had been under Peel. He had attempted to pacify Ireland at the cost of his own party, something that would be repeated with the Irish Home Rule Bill with still greater political repercussions for the future.

In the election of 1874, the Tories gained their first overall majority since 1841. Disraeli succeeded in governing with a heady mixture of ameliorating conditions for the working man and woman and by furthering the advance of an increasingly popular empire. A comprehensive Factory Act was passed, in which factories and workshops were to be more rigorously regulated and children of school years excluded from employment. (Part-time employment was permitted for children over ten, if their schoolwork was satisfactory.) At the same time, in November 1875, the government purchased a majority holding of shares in the Suez Canal from a bankrupt Khedive of Egypt, Isma'il Pasha, funded by the Rothschilds. It was presented as a *fait accompli* to the admiring Queen.

Queen Victoria was even more admiring of Disraeli when his government gave her the title Empress of India in the Royal Titles Act of 1876. Victoria, who was easily predisposed to ceremonial slights, could now level with the Tsar of Russia and the Prussian Emperor (her son-in-law) as an empress also.[14] This was especially important when both these emperors in later years were her own grandsons. Disraeli also had success at the Congress of Berlin in 1878, where he helped broker a deal between Russia and the Ottoman Turks over Bulgaria and came away with the island of Cyprus as a British protectorate. Disraeli, now Lord Beaconsfield since 1876, was in failing health: plagued by asthma, general fragility and the effects of the burden of office. The mood of the nation in the 1880 election was less gung-ho, sobered by several poor harvests, and in the event Disraeli was defeated. He died the following year.

Gladstone, aged sixty-nine, returned to the fray having left the Commons following his defeat in 1874, and now, in November 1879, fought his famous Midlothian campaign for a seat in the bailiwick of Lord Roseberry. He denounced the showy imperialism of Disraeli and the recent imperial wars among the Zulus and the Afghans. He spoke to thousands at the Edinburgh Corn Exchange and in the Waverley Market. He was anti-plutocrat in invective, if not anti-wealth in principle. He was provoked by injustice, having in 1876 famously espoused the cause of the Bulgars, who had been downtrodden by the Ottoman Turks in their bid for freedom, with vehement passion. He would do the same for the Armenians at the end of the century when they faced ethnic cleansing in Constantinople. Both were struggling Christian nations seeking self-determination. Gladstone was re-elected, much to the horror of Queen Victoria, and his second premiership (1880–6) was mired down in colonial problems which reached their and his nemesis in the failure to relieve General Gordon in Khartoum in 1885. In the eyes of the press, the Grand Old Man (GOM) had become the Murderer of Gordon (MOG). But he had managed to pass a further Reform Act in 1885 in which seats more precisely reflected population.

Lord Salisbury now became the Tory Prime Minister in a minority government. With the Irish vote in the Commons holding the balance of power, his grasp on power was precarious. Gladstone was returned to government in 1886 and brought forward an Irish Home Rule Bill which split his party into Liberals and Liberal Unionists: the Unionists would later join with the Conservatives. The Liberals would remain weak until 1900, apart from a fourth and final Gladstonian administration from 1892–4.

By now Gladstone was eighty-two years old. A second Home Rule Bill was brought forward in 1893, passed in the Commons, but overwhelmingly defeated in the Lords. In 1894, Gladstone finally left office. He set up a residential library in Hawarden for the clergy, donating 32,000 volumes. Complex and deeply Christian, with a conscience nurtured by the Church Fathers and scripture, he could not, in the end, persuade the vested interests of the landowning elite to give Ireland its head, or abandon it to a Catholic majority. This was his downfall, and the issue was to return with a vengeance in the early twentieth century. One lesson from nineteenth-century politics is germane for today: great causes split political parties. Parties were split by Catholic Emancipation (the Tories), by the repeal of the Corn Laws (the Tories), by Home Rule (the Liberals) and by Free Trade (the Tories). Parties divide around great issues, just as they have done over relations with Europe today.

The Church and the Empire

Whether people liked it or not, the British Empire did provide an unparalleled opportunity for mission and the carrying of the gospel to the ends of the earth (Matthew 28:19). It was certainly an opportunity that energized the churches and mission societies in Britain. It is said that England woke up and found it had an empire. The settlements in the Americas in the sixteenth and seventeenth centuries were largely religiously motivated, although with added commercial interests, as in the case of Virginia. Land holdings expanded, and by 1763 were secured in North America by General Amherst, and by Clive and the East India Company in India, although the American colonies were lost shortly before Britain secured dominance on the seas following Trafalgar and the defeat of Napoleon. The abolition of the slave trade was then pursued with the same zest as its inception had been embraced. England was one of the principal slave-trading nations, with trade emanating from Bristol and Liverpool. It was one thing to abolish the slave trade; it was another to implement that abolition. Winston Churchill, no less, pointed out the pitfalls of empire-building, noting that the practice of empire often betrayed any noble vision that underpinned it: "The inevitable gap between conquest and dominion becomes filled with the figures of the greedy trader, the inopportune missionary, the ambitious soldier, and the lying speculator."[15] In other words, the failures of empire-building could not be overlooked. They were many, from opium sold by thousands of tons to China, through one-sided imperial wars—in which machine guns took on spears—and the removal of peoples from their lands, to the exploitation of labour, whether it be freed Africans from Freetown, Sierra Leone, or unskilled Chinese workers in South Africa.

By the mid-Victorian age, the haphazard acquisition of lands brought about by trade, religion, exploration and sheer imperialism had coalesced into a sense of an empire administered as part of the foreign policy of Britain. The Colonial Office in 1816 was responsible for forty-three colonies and had a staff smaller than that of the Foreign Office with just twenty-eight men. By 1860, it had increased considerably, though still modest in size. The Indian Mutiny of 1857 had shocked the nation into taking direct control of the government of India from the East India Company. Henceforward India would have an Empress, a Viceroy with a semi-regal court, an Indian army under the control of the crown, and a civil service with a rigorous entrance exam, as well as being staffed by some notable minds and administrators. The Empire now spread around Canada, the West Indies, Australia, New Zealand, India (including Pakistan, Burma and Ceylon), Hong Kong, Singapore and a host of other ports and islands. Then began the scramble for Africa—until, all told, a quarter of the land surface of the world was part of the British Empire.

With all its faults or misconceived ideas, the Empire was nevertheless a place for Christian mission and social transformation. The abolition of the slave trade became part of the mission of the Church and the British government throughout the Empire. Abolition began with Wilberforce and the Clapham Sect from their spiritual home at Holy Trinity Church, Clapham. Zachary Macaulay had helped stamp out the trade in Sierra Leone, and Freetown was the place of release for slaves seized by the Royal Navy. Palm oil for the manufacture of soap replaced the trade in slaves, and from this Lever Bros and Port Sunlight were born on the Wirral. Missionary societies proliferated from the turn of the nineteenth century. The London Missionary Society had been formed in 1795. Its mission in Kuruman, 600 miles north-east of Cape Town, was typical of its work: a Scottish-like village with a thatched kirk, white-washed cottages and a red post box. There Africans were brought to faith, education was given, a new mode of dress prescribed. Monogamy was encouraged, and hygiene and better housing were offered. This work was reported to supporters back home, in an account that made clear cleanliness was next to godliness: "The people are now dressed in British manufacture and make a very respectable appearance in the house of God. The children who formerly went naked and presented a disgusting appearance are decently clothed . . . Instead of huts resembling a pigsty we now have a regular village."[16] This report exemplified the values at the heart of much of the missionary work in Africa, as personified in the towering figure of the Scottish missionary David Livingstone. Reflecting on the causes of the Indian Mutiny in an address in the Cambridge University Senate House in December 1857, Livingstone coined the phrase "those two pioneers of civilization, Christianity and commerce, should ever be inseparable".[17]

Livingstone was born in the Scottish textile town of Blantyre in Lanarkshire. He was a prodigious autodidact, who taught himself Latin and the rudiments of

Greek. The two great Scottish intellectual currents, an Enlightenment reverence for science and a Calvinist sense of providence and mission, met in him. These two streams dictated his own destiny, and when answering a question in the London Missionary Society questionnaire, he spoke of his desire "to make known the Gospel by preaching, exhortation, conversion and instruction" thereby introducing the arts and sciences of civilization to those among whom he laboured. He was aware too of the hardships and dangers of the missionary life, but depended on the "assistance of the Holy Spirit".[18] He gained a medical licence from the Glasgow College of Physicians and Surgeons and married Mary Moffat, the daughter of a missionary with whom he later served.

Livingstone went to Kuruman in South Africa, but found it hard going. The response was slow; there was little missionary success. He moved north to present-day Botswana and by 1848 virtually ceased being a missionary, becoming instead an explorer in the region of the Zambezi, and discovering the Victoria Falls and the Batoka Plateau. By 1858, he had resigned from the missionary society. In that year he led a government-sponsored exploration of the resources of the Zambezi Basin and then, from 1866, a further exploration to seek the source of the Nile. After being totally isolated for years, Henry Morton Stanley was sent to find him and did so in 1871, uttering the legendary or mythical words, "Dr Livingstone, I presume". As a symbol of indestructible Victorian endeavour, Livingstone found it almost impossible to cooperate with fellow countrymen, did not find the source of the Nile, or convert more than a handful of Africans. Yet he fired the imagination of Victorian England and the lives of countless missionaries, explorers and colonialists seeking to combine Christianity and commerce on the African continent. His was a curious mixture of herculean endeavour, heroic failure and heart-warming inspiration. In fact, his example was straight from the playbook of eminent Victorians.

Countless missionaries did go to Africa and very many died from disease, persecution or malnutrition, whether in West, East or Central Africa or the Sudan. Their courage was unquestionable. In the later part of the nineteenth century, there was a constant stream of missionaries departing Britain for southern, eastern and western Africa. They either preceded or followed British arms. The principal Anglican missionary societies were the Church Mission Society (CMS) and the Society for the Propagation of the Gospel in Foreign Parts (SPG, renamed United Society for the Propagation of the Gospel (USPG) in 1965), which then reproduced their values and styles, their foibles and cultural spirituality in the churches they planted. Anglican churches and dioceses were established and then given coherence by the Lambeth Conference, a meeting of Anglican bishops first organized in 1876, with seventy-six bishops present.

The interior of East Africa was opened up for mission. Zanzibar, which had been cleared of slave trade in 1822, became a British Protectorate in 1890 and then, with Mombasa, became a staging post to the East African territories. After an initial encouraging invitation from the King of Buganda, Mutesa I, the CMS sent missionaries to Uganda: firstly Alexander Mackay and then James Hannington. Subsequently, King (Kabaka) Mwanga turned on the missionaries and Hannington was killed and many Ugandan Christians burnt, some for refusing homosexual relations with the King. For a short while Hannington was the first Anglican Bishop of East Africa. The Sudan Interior Mission started linking the area north of Uganda with Khartoum and then Egypt, while the Roman Catholic African mission led by the White Fathers suffered similar hardships in Uganda. In 1888, the British East African Company administered the colony and Frederick Lugard reached an accommodation with the Kabaka.

Meanwhile, in the Calabar region of Nigeria, a Scottish Presbyterian missionary, Mary Slessor, saved children from exposure in the bush and preached Christ. Having faced almost interminable disease, she died in the Old Calabar or Arochukwu region in 1915 among the Efik people, at a time when Frederick Lugard had become the Governor of Southern Nigeria. In Nigeria, Samuel Ajayi Crowther (1809–91), who had been freed by the British from a captured Portuguese slave ship, became a Christian while being cared for by the CMS in Sierra Leone. He studied English and trained for the priesthood in England, worked with the CMS among the Yoruba and Hausa Africans, and translated the scriptures. He was consecrated in 1864 by Archbishop Charles Longley and was the first indigenous Nigerian—and indeed the first black African—bishop to be thus appointed.

Asia, and in particular India and China, would also yield rich opportunities for mission, and no one was more motivated to seize the opportunity than James Hudson Taylor (1832–1905). Born in Barnsley, Yorkshire, the son of a Methodist lay preacher, he learnt his earliest spiritual lessons in Hull as a medical assistant and while ministering among the poor. Following a call to go to China, he began learning Mandarin and went there with the Chinese Evangelization Society founded by the Prussian Karl Gützlaff in 1865. He soon founded his own missionary society, the China Inland Mission (CIM), which proved the most successful of all the faith missions in which individual missionaries raised their own support.

For Hudson Taylor, God's work done in God's ways would never lack support. Soon, over six hundred missionaries would go to China, among them the Cambridge Seven, which included C. T. Studd (1860–1931), the English cricketer who gave away his inheritance to pursue this calling. In 1882, Studd had scored 118 runs in one innings against Australia and taken five wickets. Like Hudson Taylor himself, many missionaries adopted Chinese dress, agreed a simple doctrinal creed, did not necessarily have advanced education, and came from any or no denomination. Hudson Taylor undertook eleven tours of ministry in China, interspersed with preaching tours in England and the United States to raise support and awareness. By 1882, all the provinces had been visited, and missionaries were resident in all but three of them. Most converts were from humble backgrounds and one, Pastor Hsi, himself a converted opium addict, set up refuges where, through faith, prayer and the appropriate use of medicine, many were delivered from addiction. In that respect it was a forerunner to Jackie Pullinger's work in Hong Kong since 1966, and the foundation of St Stephen's House. Other missions sprang from CIM, like the Heart of Africa mission started by C. T. Studd, which developed into the World Evangelization Crusade (WEC International), also begun by Studd in 1913 in Upper Norwood, and subsequently taken forward by Gilbert Barclay and Norman Grubb.

The situation for mission in India was more complex still. Until the Indian Mutiny of 1857, the East India Company had run a commercial and expansionist company on pragmatic lines with no commitment to Christian mission: and that was Livingstone's criticism. By 1813, the East India Act made possible the sending of missionaries to India, while a bishop was appointed in Calcutta and three archdeacons in Bengal and beyond. By the 1830s, there were fifty-eight CMS preachers active in India. They saw themselves struggling with deep forces of darkness: the caste system, child labour, female circumcision and sati (or sutee), the self-immolation of a Hindu widow on her husband's funeral pyre. By 1839, magistrates and indigenous rulers sought to stamp out the practice, but with mixed results. Thousands of women died in Bengal and beyond between 1813 and 1825. The Mutiny produced heroic and lurid tales: Henry Lawrence, the Resident of Lucknow, who perished there, had inscribed on his tomb the words, "Here lies Henry Lawrence who tried to do his duty." Others, including British women and children, were massacred. Spurgeon, in London, responded to the Mutiny with the words, "If my religion consisted of bestiality, infanticide and murder, I should have no right to it unless I was prepared to be hanged." Revenge was taken for the Mutiny: some rebel Indians being made to lick the blood of their white victims before being executed. If some in government rued the policy of evangelizing Indians, others saw the Mutiny as a reason for increasing mission. The London Mission Society resolved to send out twenty missionaries and was met with a fervent and generous response: within a year, all the costs of their sending had been met.

On the other side of the world, a mission begun by Allen Gardiner, called the Patagonian Missionary Society, had a tumultuous beginning. A first exploratory mission was sent to Patagonia in 1850, setting sail from Liverpool in September that year. By the following year, Gardiner and his companions had all died from hunger, cast ashore with dwindling supplies on Picton Island at the tip of South America. Discovered by HMS *Dido* the following year, in January 1852, Gardiner's diary of his last days was made known: a story of utter sacrifice and courage. Once again, the Church at home responded, and the South American Missionary Society, a twin of the CMS, was born. Once more, the home church in Britain was invigorated by great vicissitudes abroad.

The Church in England: Town and country

In the mid-nineteenth century, the greatest part of the English population still lived in the countryside, and hence in villages and market towns. By the end of the century, this would no longer be the case. Two and a half million people laboured in the fields in unmechanized agriculture. As an entity, they comprised the largest workforce in the country. In many ways the system of pastoral care in the parish had remained unchanged for 300 years or more. The Book of Common Prayer provided uniformity of worship, as it was intended to. The Authorized Version of the Bible, with its familiar cadences and set lectionary readings, gave familiarity. The squire or landlord built the church, or extended it, for which he had rights of patronage, presenting a new incumbent to the bishop in a vacancy. Indeed, the rights of patronage (advowsons) were still mostly in the hands of private landlords in the middle of the nineteenth century, although, now as a saleable item, they were being bought by patronage bodies to influence appointments in the Church. There was much nepotism in appointments. In 1878, a ninth (753) of the total number of private patronage livings (6,228) were occupied by the patron himself.

Who were these Victorian rural clergy? By 1887, there were some 13,000 beneficed Church of England clergy and many thousands of assistant clergy. In all, in 1891, there were 24,232 Anglican clergy, with 814 ordinations as deacons in 1886. There were 52,000 clergy across all denominations by 1890. Anglican clergy were paid on average less than £300 a year, and after 1840 these salaries were falling, as tithes had been commuted to salaries with a loss of 25 per cent of income. Curates' salaries were on average £145 a year. By and large, incumbents resided in large houses which they were not always able to keep up.

The role of the parish priest in the countryside is best described by J. J. Blunt in his much-published book, which ran to four editions, *The Duties of a Parish Priest*. It was first published in 1856. Blunt outlines the nature of parochial ministry, which still meant "rural ministry". The parson should be well-informed, the Authorized Version his basic tool of ministry, and much time should be spent in preparing sermons. He should enable as many as possible to participate; he should be a man of prayer; he should conduct the civil affairs of the parish; encourage education at the state or church school; not be diverted by hunting, dining or balls, nor be engaged in money-making activities such as bazaars. Other writers, like W. C. E. Newbolt, warned against seeking preferment, saying that clergy should seek a "withdrawn life" of study, prayer and spiritual counsel.

There were examples of both the active and the more reflective among the thousands of rural parish clergy: there was plenty of scope for entrepreneurial mission in the Victorian parish. John Bond in Bath Weston (Vicar, 1826–82) rebuilt the parish church with more spacious seating, started a new voluntary school in 1846, and began a Working Man's Association. Like many others, he "faithfully and unobtrusively fulfilled from day to day his sacred round of duties in the parish".[19] Another, Robert Elrington (1855–89), rebuilt the parish church of Lower Brixham in Devon, made a new vicarage and school, was chairman of the local school board, dealt single-handed with a cholera epidemic in Brixham and almost died from an outbreak of scarlet fever. Francis Kilvert (1840–79) provides vivid insight into rural ministry in Bredwardine in Herefordshire in his voluminous and entertaining diaries. More typical of the rural minister who may have been criticized by J. J. Blunt was Bartholomew Edwards, Rector of Ashill in Norfolk, who rode to hounds regularly, was an excellent judge of a horse, and was only absent for three Sundays between 1859 and 1889, dying in post just nine days before his hundredth birthday!

In some villages, Victorian clergy had so few parishioners they had time for other things: George Bayldon, the Vicar of Cowling (1850–94), spoke nine languages and published a dictionary of the Icelandic language. Others were botanists, geologists, beekeepers, collectors of fossils and writers. Nevertheless, there was disenchantment in the country parishes: between country labourers and the village parson; between growing numbers of agnostics and traditional village piety; and between more educated labourers with increased learning and the parson who had previously been the fount of all knowledge. J. C. Ryle, the

Evangelical Bishop of Liverpool, put this state of affairs down to livings held in plurality, inadequate sermons, locked churches and parsons who were invariably on the side of the squire. No wonder he said the Non-Conformist ministers in the village were better guides to heaven.

The fabric of parish life in the countryside was now well-developed. The school (primary) together with church, chapel, village hall and churchyard, overseen by the Church and later parish council from 1886, were the main institutions of the rural parish. While no Voluntary School was set up by the Established Church under Forster's Education Act of 1870, in Gladstone's first administration, Board Schools began. With a focus on teaching the Bible and hymns rather than Anglican practice, the schools were more appealing to dissenters' families, although children in a denominational school could still be withdrawn from religious education under a conscience clause.

By 1887, there were more than two million children being taught in Anglican schools, and only 7,890 were withdrawn from religious instruction. Alongside schools, the Mothers' Union became active in supporting family life and was prevalent in dioceses. Founded in 1876 in Alresford in Hampshire by Mary Sumner (née Heywood, 1828–1921)—a lady of aristocratic principles and driving energy, who took cold baths daily, refused either a telephone or car when invented, and thought that herrings were food for cats and should not be served in the vicarage—the Mothers' Union brought unerring focus to the need for sound family life. The Union was against any further weakening of the Divorce Act of 1857 (previous to which divorce could only be obtained through an Act of Parliament). Mary managed to join mothers, whether from the hall or the cottage, in meetings focussed on the rearing of children and family life. The Mothers' Union was to spread throughout England, and become firmly connected to Anglican dioceses overseas, especially in Africa.

If provision for education was sometimes controversial, so was provision for the dead. In rural areas the churchyard was invariably provided by the Church of England. There were instances where burials of dissenting parishioners created conflict thanks to the far from generous attitude of some Anglican clergy. In general, dissenting clergy could not use their liturgies in Anglican village churchyards. Either silence or an Anglican service was therefore prescribed. One vicar in Oxford insisted that his curate read the Anglican service over a Baptist mother who already had six children buried there; no Baptist minister or liturgy was allowed. On another occasion, a grieving Wesleyan minister was not allowed wording on his daughter's tombstone saying she was the daughter of the Reverend H. Keet. The incumbent vicar and Bishop Wordsworth of Lincoln (1869–85) objected to a dissenting minister being termed "Reverend". The prohibition was only rescinded when the family appealed to a higher court in 1876. Such conflicts were not uncommon.

In 1880, 15,500 Anglican clergy petitioned Parliament against allowing Non-Conformist ministers to conduct burials in Anglican churchyards, but that year Lord Chancellor Selborne passed an Act that enabled relatives of the deceased to inform the incumbent that a burial would take place in the churchyard without the Prayer Book service. Such a service must be orderly, Christian and contain no address bringing contempt on any denomination. The first such service passed off peaceably in Beckenham, led by the Baptist minister of Penge. Thus, the churchyard eventually became a place of peace and not of denominational conflict.

Relations between church and chapel in the villages varied according to the personalities or respective ministers involved. From the 1830s, many villages had Methodist or Primitive Methodist, Baptist or Congregational chapels. In Cornwall, chapels predominated. From 1850, Roman Catholic churches were restricted to the towns. In villages, chapel and church were often divided on social grounds, the one not speaking to the other because of social convention and snobbery. A rector of Oswestry said: "I make it a principle never to speak to dissenters about religious matters. But I have a good garden with a southern slope, and I send them baskets of early vegetables, and by this means I have brought several over to the church."[20] Chapels, by contrast, had hearty hymn singing, extempore prayer about sickness, the weather, the crops, and informative prayers to the Almighty, such as one for Mr Barker, in which God was told "it had not rained for two weeks on Mr Barker's plot and that his carrot bed was getting mortal dry".[21] Gradually, the old issues between church and chapel eased: as in religious education in the school, the levy of church rate, the use of the churchyard, joint Sunday school outings. By the end of the century, there were more grounds for unity than division, but it was a different story in the towns.

The population in England grew from 19 million in 1861 to 30 million in 1901: three million in each decade. Most of this growth was in the towns and cities. By the end of the century, population growth was slowing as contraceptive practices spread from the middle classes to the aspiring working class. There is no doubt that in the earlier part of this period there had been rapid growth and, with it, stubborn levels of poverty in the cities and especially in London. After the "Great Stink" from the River Thames closed a sitting of Parliament in 1858, work on the London sewage system began under Joseph Bazalgette. Hundreds of miles of sewers were constructed in the 1860s which serve the capital today. Sebohm Rowntree, the scion of the Quaker chocolate business, found that one third of York's population was living in poverty. This was not atypical for great manufacturing cities, such as Liverpool, Manchester, Birmingham, Leeds, Sheffield and Newcastle. Businesses led by Non-Conformist families, like the Cadburys of Birmingham, the Colmans of Norwich, the Courtaulds of Chelmsford, the Reckitts of Hull, and the Wedgwoods of Stoke on Trent, among many others, provided better social conditions for their employees. The question for the Church was whether models of ministry worked out in the social fabric of the countryside could be transferred to the towns.

All denominations increased their membership in the cities, especially in the suburbs. (It was estimated that about seventy new parishes and ninety-seven new clergymen were needed every year in the Church of England alone, when the population increased by 14 per cent between 1871 and 1881.) Between 1840 and 1876, 1,727 new Anglican churches were built in England and Wales. The Roman Catholic Church benefitted from the influx of Irish to Lancashire and Cheshire, where they numbered 240,653. Many chapels were likewise built for Non-Conformist congregations. The number of Anglican confirmations increased from 117,852 in 1872 to 244,030 in 1911. This increase may be partly accounted for by bishops travelling increasingly by train during the period. Also, the formation of new dioceses in the Church of England made for greater proximity of bishops to their flocks: Truro, Liverpool, Leeds, Manchester, Newcastle and Wakefield were all Victorian creations.

Baptisms in the Church of England remained more or less constant in the period. In 1885, there were 623 baptisms for every thousand live births, and in 1912, 678 per thousand. Marriages mostly took place in Anglican churches: for every thousand marriages in 1864, 782 were in parish churches, forty-seven in Roman Catholic churches and eighty-seven in other churches. By 1904, this figure had dropped to 642 in Anglican churches, forty-one in Roman Catholic and 131 in others. Civil ceremonies more than doubled in the same period, from 81 to 179. In 1891, Archbishop Benson said that "throughout the country the number of those who attend church has largely increased and is still increasing".[22] This was undoubtedly true, but as a percentage of the overall population churchgoing numbers were falling, especially between 1886 and 1902, although the Non-Conformist churches reported a steady increase along with the size of the population. By 1881, the proportion of the population attending church was 37.93 per cent. On the basis of his census in 1854, Horace Mann had calculated that 58 per cent of the population attended church. It must be admitted, however, that this calculation was an inexact science, although there was an observable trend.

The ministry of the Church proceeded along both familiar and novel lines. Clergy became more recognizable in the community, wearing clerical attire (e.g.

collars), except for Baptists and Congregationalists. Sunday schools increased in number for both children and teenagers. In 1887, the Church of England had 2.2 million children on its books and Non-Conformist churches approximately 3.1 million. In some places, there were adult Bible classes, as in Rochdale, with people remaining part of them even until death. A Sunday school in Stockport had 5,000 members and was led by non-denominational leaders. In Cambridge, the Jesus Lane Sunday School had a staff of 160, including four Fellows of Trinity Cambridge. In the same city, Handley Moule, the great biblical scholar and later Bishop of Durham, held Bible classes for railway employees in the second-class waiting room of Cambridge station. There were more radical forms of ministry also: Keir Hardie, the Christian Socialist and founder member of the Labour Party, preached a Christmas Day message in 1897 in which he said: "[Do we] not see Christ's image being crucified in every hungry child . . . We have no right to a merry Christmas which so many of our fellows cannot share."[23]

By the 1890s, almost every denomination had within it a socialist movement. The Anglican Church had F. D. Maurice and Charles Kingsley advocating a somewhat institutional form of ecclesiastical socialism, lacking teeth. Likewise, Scott Holland, the Regius Professor of Divinity at Oxford from 1910, saw unrestrained capitalism as the cause of urban poverty. Other ministers, such as the Congregationalist Ben Tillett from Stockport, believed that it was the Church's task, and not that of government, to liberate the urban poor.

Alongside theorists on social intervention were the practical activists who sought to relieve physical suffering, working particularly among children and women, often the most disadvantaged in society. In 1884, two church leaders, the Reverend Edward Rudolf, a vicar from Kennington, and Benjamin Waugh, a Congregationalist minister, began the London Society for the Prevention of Cruelty to Children, the forerunner of the NSPCC. It started by providing a home for "waifs and strays" in Dulwich and, by the 1890s, the society was involved with 10,000 cases a year. In the East End, Thomas Barnardo, a Dubliner by birth, whose mother was a member of the Plymouth Brethren and whose father was a Sephardic Jew, began to help orphans of the 1860s cholera epidemic. Archbishop Tait (1868–82) had also intervened to help. Barnardo prematurely ended his medical training at the London Hospital to begin a mission to children, and, in 1870, opened his first home for orphans in Stepney. He lost three of his seven children in infancy, but his daughter Syrie married Henry Solomon Wellcome— the pharmaceutical entrepreneur and a founder of the Wellcome Trust and of GlaxoSmithKline. On Thomas's death, the Barnardo charity was well-endowed, with the work set on a permanent footing.

Despite these efforts, child mortality rates remained stubbornly high throughout the century. In 1899, the figure stood at 163 deaths per thousand births, no lower than it had been sixty years before. Paradoxically, the celebration of childhood was never higher than then with the publication of J. M. Barrie's *Peter Pan* (1904), Beatrix Potter's *Tale of Peter Rabbit* (1902) and Kenneth Grahame's *Wind in the Willows* (1908). A. A Milne's *Winnie the Pooh* was soon to follow in 1926.

Work to improve the lot of women was taken forward by the campaigner Josephine Butler (1828–1906), who felt the injustices done to her gender acutely. Married to an Anglican clergyman and academic, she and her husband often prayed for the establishment of the kingdom of God on earth. From the early 1860s, she campaigned on several fronts for women's rights and well-being. She combined at different times with other campaigners, such as Florence Nightingale, Harriet Martineau, Florence Soper Booth, the novelist Elizabeth Gaskell, Elizabeth Wolstenholme and the journalist W. T. Stead. Josephine personally supported prostitutes suffering from venereal disease, and objected to the forced inspection of women, which she called "steel rape". To this end she sought to repeal the Contagious Diseases Act which had made women responsible for transmitting sexual diseases and had subjected them to forced inspections and a kind of internment. She also exposed and campaigned against child prostitution and human trafficking from England to the continent.

In 1885, as a result of this campaigning, the age of consent for girls was raised from thirteen to sixteen, where it remains. In 1886, after a long struggle, the Contagious Diseases Act was repealed, and women were spared forcible examination and virtual imprisonment in "lock hospitals". Taking her inspiration from Catherine of Siena, about whom she wrote, Josephine Butler also participated in the movement for women's education and suffrage from the 1870s onwards.

The Roman Catholic Church in the late nineteenth century

Victorian society moved forward with extraordinary energy from the 1860s onwards, and the re-establishment of the Roman Catholic Church was part of this. Catholic emancipation in 1829 and the re-establishment of the hierarchy in 1850, which followed Cardinal Wiseman's letter "From out of the Flaminian Gate" or "Porta del Popolo", were the basis for Catholic expansion. The main ingredients in Catholic renewal were large-scale immigration of the Irish, conversion to Catholicism of several leading Anglican thinkers and administrators, and a new phase of papal assertion in light of the unification of Italy, which had threatened the temporal power of the Holy See. In fact, these strands made for an uneasy period both for English Catholicism and the Church's ministry in England.

The main centres of Catholicism now lay in the cities, where the greater number of Catholic immigrants had arrived, mainly from Ireland. London, Liverpool and Birmingham had large communities of Irish Catholics, and new Catholic dioceses were created in Yorkshire, namely in Leeds and Middlesbrough. In 1882, Portsmouth was created out of Southwark. Estimates of the Catholic population were 700,000 in 1840 and 1.5 million by the end of the century. Of these, Cardinal Manning estimated that approximately 200,000 were English. Catholics constituted the minority of worshippers in major towns at 7.7 per cent, compared with Anglicans at 37 per cent and Non-Conformists at 55. Catholic churches increased from 798 in 1862 to 1,536 in 1901. As for priests, in 1860 there were 1,077, but by 1900 there were 2,856. The increase was rapid: in fact, in most respects the church was almost unrecognizable from its state seventy years before.

Below the surface there were several streams of Catholicism, some in contention with others. Firstly, there were the Old Catholics, whose families had survived recusancy or worse, followed by discrimination. These Old Catholics included the Duke of Norfolk, Lords Mowbray, Vaux of Harrowden, Arundell of Wardour, Howard of Glossop and Lord Shrewsbury. Some, like Lord Shrewsbury, whose residence was at Alton Towers, had a love of a flamboyant Catholicism of the Pugin and Wiseman kind, while a senior Catholic layman like the Duke of Norfolk was more sober, circumspect and restrained in his religious expression, the effect of generations of accommodation to an English Protestant state. These examples point to the spectrum of Catholic expression in England.

A clearer fault line in Catholic expression and priorities would emerge towards the end of the century, exemplified by the gulf between Cardinal Manning and John Henry Newman. Both had been converted to Catholicism from Anglicanism at the time of the Oxford Movement, but each would follow a different trajectory. Manning, who in 1865 succeeded Wiseman as the Cardinal Archbishop of Westminster, was very much a papal appointee. He was devoted to Pius IX and approved the move towards the doctrine of infallibility. Contrastingly, Newman opposed infallibility, had no wish to be part of the hierarchy, and did not want to be made a bishop. However, in death Newman has overtaken Manning in the sanctity stakes, being made a saint in 2019.

At first, Manning was received cautiously by the Old Catholics, but soon built support both among the Catholic poor of London and the traditional Catholics of the English establishment. Where possible, he was generous about Protestant opinion and ministry, especially the Salvation Army, which he admired. He played the part of a prince of the church, dressing accordingly, yet paradoxically eschewing expectations of formality. He remained an active theologian, and regularly published pamphlets on pastoral theology and catholic doctrine. He was a Tory in his political sympathies, opposed Gladstone's Home Rule Bill, wanted the Irish represented in Westminster, and was friendly with both the Prince of Wales (Edward VII) and Queen Victoria. Because of his support for the establishment, ambassadors were exchanged for the first time between the Court of St James and the Vatican.

Compared with the well-positioned convictions of Manning, which linked him with crown, Tory party and papacy (although without in any way disregarding the poor and social justice), Newman seemed more of a tortured soul. If Manning was the activist and politician, Newman was the thinker and educationalist who made his spiritual journey and struggles the subject of intense introspection and engaging literature. After the furore in Anglican quarters provoked by his turning to Rome, he found a spiritual home with the Oratorians. Yet even among the Oratorians there was tension for Newman, who saw the religious life as one of growth and development, while others, like his fellow Oratorian and convert from Anglicanism, Frederick Faber, saw it as submission to authority. Newman had a problem with authoritarianism, whether it be the doctrine of papal infallibility or ultramontanism. Other troubles dogged him in these middle years of the nineteenth century: he endured a libel trial for criticizing a Dominican monk, Giacinto Achilli, for sexual misdemeanours, which he unjustly lost—but "crowd funding" enabled Newman to pay the fine—and he failed in his plan to set up a Catholic university in Dublin. He had the *Idea of a University* in conceptual form, but could not turn it into reality. The purpose of such a university was to train gentlemen: that is, people who would cause no pain in life and would have the capacity to think "uselessly", as he put it. A university should not be a tool of church or state. This was a romantic rather than utilitarian ideal, so initially the project failed and Newman returned to Birmingham in 1858. By 1882, however, the Jesuits had taken up the project and created University College.

Severe trial seemed to bring the best out of Newman. When, in 1863, he was criticized by Charles Kingsley of *Water Babies* fame, he replied magisterially with his *Apologia*. Kingsley, a complex man who had fallen under Newman's spell in Oxford in the 1830s and who resented while at Oxford Newman's seemingly ambivalent sexuality, was offloading long-held angst dating back to their Oxford days.[24] The *Apologia Pro Vita Sua*, to give the work its full title, was part defence of Newman's spiritual journey and part proclamation of his convictions. It was a defence against Kingsley's accusation in 1863 that Catholics play fast and loose with truth, and too often use cunning in their arguments.

At the *Apologia*'s heart was the idea of continuity and discontinuity. Newman narrated both the history of Christianity from antiquity (always his starting point) and the story of the Church of England, to show that Anglicanism was in error. The Church of England, like the Donatists of Augustine of Hippo's era, was, in his view, separated from the true Church, and despite all its protestations of orthodoxy, was also therefore separate from the true stream of spiritual life. Despite these conclusions, Newman's *Apologia* was well-received, with the Bishop of Winchester writing that Kingsley would go down in history "as the embedded fly in the clear amber of his antagonist's *Apology*".[25]

In the 1870s, now in his seventies, Newman was readmitted to Oxford as an Honorary Fellow of Trinity College. He was made cardinal in the same year of 1878 by Leo XIII, and given warm support by the Duke of Norfolk, despite being critical of the First Vatican Council of 1869–70, with its push for infallibility. His poem, "The Dream of Gerontius" (1865), was set to music by Edward Elgar in 1900. By the end of the century, Roman Catholics were more at peace among themselves, and part of the religious settlement in England constructed seventy years before. Newman had shown that Catholics cared for truth, and had entered into a contented old age, becoming even lovable.

One of Newman's later pupils was the poet Gerard Manley Hopkins (1844–89), who was received into the Roman Catholic Church by Newman in 1866. He studied at Balliol, where he obtained a First in Greats, before training for the priesthood at St Bueno's, North Wales. As a Jesuit, he was kept on the move as a schoolteacher, pastor and priest. As a poet, his brilliance placed him among the greatest exponents of the English language. Along with Milton, Herbert and Cowper, he elucidated Christian themes in language of intense appreciation of the created order and of Christ's redemptive power.[26] His poems "God's Grandeur", "Wreck of the Deutschland" and "The Windhover" exalted these themes. Like the philosopher Duns Scotus, he saw the *essence of things* in particulars, as in his poem "Binsey Poplars", in which he mourns the loss of God's creation in the destruction of some beloved trees. Stalked by feelings of depression, his last years of teaching at University College Dublin (founded by Newman) led to moments of great desolation, before he rose above them in one of his last poems, "That Nature is a Heraclitean Fire and of the comfort of the Resurrection", in which he saw himself in Christ as an "immortal diamond". Hopkins died from typhus aged just forty-four. Published posthumously in 1918 by his Oxford friend, and then Poet Laureate, Robert Bridges, his poems were deeply influential on those who followed, including T. S. Eliot, W. H. Auden and Dylan Thomas. He was a bright star in the firmament of Christian spirituality, loving creation and seeking God in its grandeur.

Fin de Siècle

By the time of Gerard Manley Hopkins's death in 1889, the Victorian era was drawing to a close. Queen Victoria had entered into a mellow old age, putting behind her the twenty or so years of oppressive mourning that kept her from her people and dominated her family, most of all Bertie, her heir. For years, Bertie (the future Edward VII) had gone on a rampage of females, feasts and pheasant shooting, satiating those appetites that had been so repressed in childhood. The Empire reached its apogee in the late Victorian period, but carried with it the seeds of its own demise. Politics swung from the passions and obsessions of Gladstone to the more temperate conservatism of Salisbury, and then toward the more philosophical detachment of Arthur Balfour, his nephew, before returning to the Liberals in the 1906 election. Inventions, leisure and feminism were beginning to shape the modern era and modern England, and with that the Church.

By the time of her Golden Jubilee in 1887, Victoria had been restored to her nation's affections. On the day of those celebrations she held a reception for fifty heads of state and held a service of thanksgiving in Westminster Abbey. By then, her favourite had become a Hindustani attendant called "the Munshi", replacing John Brown, her Scottish companion who had died in 1883 and whose picture was placed in her coffin at her own command, along with a plaster cast of Albert's hand.

In 1897, Victoria celebrated her Diamond Jubilee and became the longest-ever reigning English monarch until her great-great-granddaughter, Elizabeth II, overtook her in 2015. By then Victoria had forty-two grandchildren, including the heads of state of Russia and Prussia—Nicholas II (in fact a great-grandson) and Kaiser Wilhelm II respectively—and several queens of European states, including Romania, Greece, Norway, Spain and Sweden.

Victoria died on 22 January 1901 at Osborne House on the Isle of Wight, which had been built for her by her beloved Albert. There were emotional scenes at the last. Archbishop Randall Davidson read her favourite hymn by Cardinal Newman, "Lead, Kindly Light in the Encircling Gloom", which well suited Victoria's approach to faith and life. She was reconciled to Bertie, whom she had blamed all along for her precious Albert's death, and all the while her despised grandson, Kaiser

Wilhelm II, knelt by her bedside and prayed. In just fourteen years, he would lead his armies against most of her relatives. She left behind a diary to which she had committed thousands of words each day and which would be redacted at her command by her faithful daughter, Beatrice. Bertie succeeded. Excluded by Victoria from official business, although prime ministers, especially Gladstone, drew him in where they could, Bertie had pursued his pleasures in house parties, at spas, in Paris and in travel; but now he became a punctilious and perceptive king.

When Victoria died, the Empire was at its zenith, having become the pride of *most* of the British public. In 1876, Victoria had been made Empress of India. Try as Gladstone and, to a lesser extent, his Conservative successor Salisbury might to restrain imperial ambitions, the proconsuls, such as Cecil Rhodes in southern Africa, and later Curzon in India, Milner in South Africa and Lugard in West Africa, had their own plans and drew the government remorselessly into them. Milner had said: "I am an imperialist and not a little Englander, because I am a British Race Patriot."[27] He was convinced of the superiority of the British race. And frequently the 1880s Tory squires found their greatest moment of fulfilment serving the crown in imperial wars. Under General Wolsey, a numerically inferior British Army (although equipped with superior weapons) took on 20,000 Egyptians at Tel-el-Kebir in September 1882. It was there that cavalry officers like Major Hanford Flood and subalterns like William Edwards found their military ambitions fulfilled: the former being General Wolsey's galloper (message-taker), the latter winning a VC for charging down an Egyptian battery.[28] The casualties speak for themselves, however: nine British and 2,000 Egyptians perished. No wonder the Mahdi raised a religious, Islamic rebellion against the British presence in Egypt and the Sudan, pinning down the semi-messianic General Gordon in Khartoum, where he was killed. Failure to relieve Gordon in Khartoum brought Gladstone's government down in 1885. The imperial tail certainly wagged the Liberal dog. A force was sent to retake Khartoum, and it was there that the young Winston Churchill, serving under General Kitchener, first saw action in Africa in the Battle of Omdurman. The Mahdi lost 12,000 dead, with 13,000 wounded and 5,000 captured. The British lost forty-seven. The Maxim machine gun had done its work. "Omdurman was the acme of Imperial overkill."[29]

The nemesis of the Empire turned out to be the Boer War, or the second Boer War to be precise (1899–1902). Indeed, Rudyard Kipling sensed the passing of glory in his poem/hymn entitled "Recessional", written for the Diamond Jubilee of 1897. The Colonial Secretary in Salisbury's government, Joseph Chamberlain, together with Milner and Rhodes in South Africa, determined to take over the Boer republics in the Transvaal and form a unitary state under British control.

To this end a war was provoked that was to prove costly to the British in terms of reputation, treasure and military competence. It cost 45,000 British lives, mostly from disease, and £250 million. What Vietnam was to the United States, the Boer War nearly was to the British. The Boers were likewise an implacable enemy: disciplined and well-armed—essentially another European army on African soil.

After initial successes, the Boers were overwhelmed and resorted to guerrilla warfare. The relief of a besieged Mafeking by Colonel Baden Powell was the stuff of Victorian imperial legend. Eventually, increased resources, new generals in the form of Lord Roberts and Kitchener, an army of 400,000, a scorched earth policy, and use of concentration camps (in which Boer families were interned and in which there were some 20,000 casualties, mostly from disease) were the price of victory. By 1929, the Boers were to take control of the enlarged republic and enforce segregation of the races in South Africa: the black or coloured peoples were excluded from the franchise; apartheid had begun. Fifty thousand Chinese labourers were imported to South Africa by Lord Milner to work down the mines: gold and diamonds were too tempting a prize to resist. They were paid virtually nothing and forced to live in compounds where disease, drugs and promiscuity abounded.

At home, the Boer War divided the main political parties. An election called the "Khaki Election", capitalizing on public concern about the war, was called by the Conservatives in 1900 under Salisbury. The Liberals under Campbell-Bannerman fiercely opposed the war, calling it "barbaric". Chamberlain, the Colonial Secretary, denounced all Liberals as unpatriotic, with the slogan, "A vote for the liberals is a vote for the Boers". The Established Church in the person of Archbishop Davidson, close friend of Queen Victoria, remained quiet, enjoying the pleasures of the Athenaeum. The song "Land of Hope and Glory" by A. C. Benson (1902), with music by Elgar, was added to the patriotic repertoire. Likewise, Blake's "Jerusalem", set to music first by Hubert Parry, would follow in 1916 as a way of encouraging the nation in the midst of the First World War. Blake's words were given new significance by the context, but originally they were intended as a romantic and metaphorical yearning for a spiritual Jerusalem to be created in the English countryside, in the face of increasing industrialization.

In 1900, the Conservatives and the Liberal Unionists (i.e. those Liberals who had not supported Home Rule and gone over to the Conservatives in a pact) won a comfortable majority of 130 seats. Nevertheless, the Liberals were slowly climbing back from the low point of their defeat after Gladstone's last administration in 1894. Churchill, although not uncritical of the conduct of the Boer War—of which he had first-hand experience from various vantage points as reporter, internee, escaped prisoner of war and soldier—was returned as a Conservative MP. The Conservative years of political dominance were coming to an end, however; split by issues of free trade or protection and under the more languorous leadership of Balfour, time was running out and the world was also changing.

The final years of the nineteenth century saw the beginnings of unprecedented changes, which would be as much a challenge to the churches as to the politicians. The changes were not yet full-blown, but their influence was starting to be felt. Women were much more influential outside the home, for they now made up a third of the total workforce. Apart from domestic service, between them the textile mills and clothing manufacturers employed three million women. Women were needed in large numbers as teachers and nurses. In the latter occupation they were encouraged by the example of the new Queen Alexandra. With the invention of the typewriter and the telephone in the 1890s, a new sphere of work opened up for women as typists and telephonists. They did not yet have the vote and in 1897 the National Union of Women's Suffrage Societies was formed. The suffragette movement was underway. Girls' secondary education was increasing greatly. Women in their thousands were present in the arts as actresses, musicians and artists. Universities were slow to change, with degrees only being conferred on women at Oxford in 1920 and at Cambridge as late as 1947. New universities were being founded, though, with more liberal approaches taken in Bristol, Birmingham, Sheffield, Liverpool, Manchester and Leeds. Durham University, University College London (secular) and King's College London (Christian) had been founded earlier in the century.

Great advances were also made in leisure, communications and health. Bank holiday legislation of 1871 and 1875 established days off through the year. Factories closed on Saturday afternoons. Professional football developed, as did Rugby Union and Rugby League. The Olympic Games were revived in 1896 in Athens, while Wimbledon began in 1877 and the Ashes Test match series (England versus Australia at cricket) in 1882. Light opera, by Gilbert and Sullivan, for example, and plays by Oscar Wilde and Bernard Shaw were brought to the stage. Alongside sport and entertainment, new inventions improved the quality of life. Newspapers doubled in circulation. With Edison's invention of the light bulb, electric lighting replaced gas lamps in the 1880s. Mains water was provided in Birmingham, Liverpool, London and elsewhere. The Elan Valley reservoirs carried water by gravity to Birmingham in 1906, and still do. Marconi invented the wireless in 1896, successfully transmitting a message from Cornwall to Newfoundland in 1901. London and Birmingham were linked by the telephone by 1890. The first petrol motor car was invented by Karl Benz in 1885 and the Channel was flown by Louis Blériot in 1909. The modern age had begun.

In 1906, the Liberal Party led by Campbell-Bannerman, succeeded by Herbert Asquith and then Lloyd George—both Liberals—won a landslide in the general election, one of the great landslide results of the twentieth century. The Labour Party won twenty-nine seats. The country would now face constitutional change, civil unrest, the gathering clouds of war on the continent of Europe, a demand for the vote for women, and a nationalist rebellion in Ireland. The Church would face a public whose hopes were shattered by war, and who were no longer willing to follow convention, as they were now offered pastimes their forbears could only have dreamed of. In the next sixty years, the old world was deconstructed and a new one was precariously built. Unprecedented progress was followed by unprecedented change.

PART VI

A Nation Slips its Moorings

CHAPTER 20

Faith and Conflict

During the sixty years from 1906 to 1966, the world and Britain would undergo unprecedented change. Some of these years will be covered in the next chapter, but most of them in this one. During this period, Britain and its empire would endure the costliest of wars in blood and treasure in its history. The nation would shed most of its empire in quick order, creating a Commonwealth of Nations in its place. Britain would be surpassed by the United States as the world's greatest superpower. Indeed, as early as 1899, Rudyard Kipling, the Empire's greatest poet, wrote as follows about the United States: "Take up the White Man's Burden, and reap his old reward: the blame of those ye better, the hate of those ye guard."[1] Exploration would continue at great cost, with Scott's expedition succumbing to the cold of the Antarctic and the loss of all his party in March 1912. Then, just weeks later, on April 14, the "unsinkable" *Titanic* struck an iceberg on her maiden voyage and sank, with the loss of more than 1,500 lives. These were tragic openings to the new century.

Both world wars gave a kick-start to further social change. Financial crises produced deep unemployment and the emergence of a new political party, the Labour Party, which became central to British politics, surpassing the Liberals in 1923 with numbers of MPs. It was based around organized labour and the trade union movement. In 1918, women over thirty were enfranchised after a long and at times violent campaign. It is worth remembering, however, that Christabel Pankhurst, the leading suffragette, suspended this campaign throughout the First World War. The electorate increased to 28 million when women over twenty-one gained the vote in 1928 (they were then 53 per cent of the electorate), all but completing a process of electoral change begun in 1832. In 1969, the voting age was reduced to eighteen for women and men, where it remains today.

By 1905, the long years of Conservative rule were coming to an end for the time being. The institutions that Lord Salisbury, the Prime Minister, especially cherished, such as the Established Church, the British Empire, the House of Lords, High Tory and High Church, Oxford, crown prerogatives, the aristocracy and the Act of Union (with Ireland), were all coming under fire. Salisbury had died in 1902, to be succeeded by his nephew Arthur Balfour during Salisbury's final illness. (Balfour succeeded, people said, because "Bob's—Lord Robert Salisbury—your uncle!") Balfour, a part-time philosopher and a member of the Cambridge Souls group, with interests in the paranormal and modern inventions like the motor car, cut a languid and aristocratic figure on the front bench of the Commons. His government lasted until 1904, riven by issues relating to education, free trade and Irish land reform. In the end Balfour had to hand over the government to the Liberal leader, Campbell-Bannerman, who called an election in January 1906. The Liberals were returned with a large majority. Two years later, Henry Asquith, a one-time lawyer and member of Gladstone's last government in 1892, took over, and would remain prime minister until 1918, when he was overturned by his fellow Liberal, David Lloyd George, in a coalition war-time government with the Tories.

After the long years of Tory conservatism, Asquith's government was necessarily a reforming one and sought better social provision for the working class. On the one hand it had to maintain naval defence spending, and build costly Dreadnought ships to match German spending, but on the other it needed to improve the lot of the working poor.[2] The People's Budget of 1909 increased direct taxation, attacked the conservative "Beerage" (the beer magnates) by reducing licensing hours, and paved the way for a National Insurance Act to provide financial support for the unemployed and the sick. A struggle had ensued over the reform of the Poor Law in a royal commission set up in 1905, with Helen Bosanquet advocating that new agencies run the old system. Beatrice Webb wanted to cover the unemployed and provide sickness benefit through the provision of labour exchanges and National Insurance on a voluntary basis. Churchill, who was shortly to be home secretary, supported a scheme of compulsory insurance with government contributions.

In November 1909, the House of Lords threw out the People's Budget, precipitating a constitutional crisis. Asquith, Lloyd George and Churchill campaigned for its acceptance. Social reform depended on the People's Budget. Asquith called two general elections on the issue in 1910 and brought forward a Parliament Act curtailing the power of the Lords to reject a money bill, or indeed any bill, from the Commons for more than two years, and threatened, with Edward VII's permission, to create enough Liberal peers to swamp the Conservatives in the Lords. Asquith won both elections, brought forward the Parliament Act having secured the reluctant support of the new King George V, and the House of Lords climbed down. The bishops in the House of Lords led by Randall Davidson—although instinctively conservative and influenced by the leading laymen of the Church, such as Lord Selburne and Hugh Cecil (both Cecils!)—nevertheless spoke up for the Bill, which passed by 131 to 114.

One major issue the Asquith government faced was the suffragette movement. Asquith, like most of the press, was reluctant to give women the vote and was unmoved when Emily Davison, an Oxford graduate and passionate Christian, threw herself in front of the King's horse in the Derby on 4 June 1913, dying a few days later. Her funeral procession, which numbered 50,000 and carried the motto "Fight on, God will give the Victory", was led by twelve clergymen surrounding her coffin on an open carriage.

The other major issue was Ireland. Once the resistance from the House of Lords had been removed, there was hope of passing a Home Rule for Ireland Bill, which had been Gladstone's ambition. But resistance was to come from another quarter. Sir Edward Carson, the leader of the Irish Unionists in Parliament, supported by Bonar Law, the new Conservative leader, resisted any notion of Home Rule and also organized resistance in Ireland. In 1911, Carson, who had a background as a successful barrister and who had prosecuted Oscar Wilde, leading to his imprisonment, raised the prospect of a separate Northern Ireland or Ulster made up of the Six Counties, buttressed by the Orange Orders and an Ulster Defence Force of Volunteers. Although Home Rule passed both Houses of Parliament in Westminster, it could not be implemented without the possibility of civil war and a mutiny among British officers at the Curragh. This rendered the ability of British forces to suppress civil unrest unlikely. Then the First World War intervened, and any further settlement had to wait for its end. The Easter Rising of April 1916 showed the passion of Republicanism and the strength of Sinn Fein led by Michael Collins (1890–1922). Finally, in 1921, Ireland was partitioned.

The Church leading up to the Great War

The early years of the twentieth century had already proved defining for the constitution and future shape of the United Kingdom. With the advent of war in 1914, this movement of social and constitutional change would only increase. The Church would not be unaffected. It is well to remember that leadership in both the political and religious spheres was by men who were Victorian in upbringing, and this would remain so until the late 1950s.

The churches enjoyed a momentum given to them by the last quarter of the nineteenth century, which thrust them forward into the first years of the twentieth. At the end of the nineteenth century, the clergy in the Church of England, whether Evangelical or Tractarian, undertook their pastoral ministry with "deep seriousness and mounting efficiency".[3] There were more Anglican baptisms per thousand live births in 1917 than in 1885, even if numbers of Anglican-conducted marriages were declining slightly. In 1919, there were 519 Anglican marriages per thousand, and in 1917, 705 baptisms per thousand live births. It was still an astonishing percentage. In 1911, there were 2,293,000 Easter communicants in the Church of England, up by a million on the 1881 figure, and there were still around 23,000 Anglican clergy, the high-water mark of ministry.

New dioceses were being formed in the period: Birmingham in 1905, Chelmsford in 1914, St Edmundsbury and Ipswich in 1914, Coventry in 1918, Bradford in 1920, Blackburn in 1926, and Portsmouth in 1927. They were to be the last. Despite this increase, the percentage of the population attending the Anglican church was starting to decline. In the cities, total attendance at *all churches* was around 40 per cent of the adult population in 1881, and it was higher in the villages. The attendance was far higher in the suburbs than in the inner cities, where by 1920 the attendance rate had fallen to around 20 per cent. In Tyneside in 1928, 20 per cent of the adult population attended church: 15 per cent went to Anglican churches, 42 per cent to Roman Catholic, and 43 per cent to Non-Conformist. In London, 29 per cent of Sydenham and Dulwich went to church, half being Anglican and the rest Non-Conformist, whereas in inner-city Walworth six per cent of the population attended, of which 90 per cent were Non-Conformist.[4] Perhaps unsurprisingly, in South Kensington 34.5 per cent of the population worshipped in Anglican churches.

Clearly immigration (e.g. Catholic Irish) and social status had much to do with choice of church. What is nevertheless clear is that by 1920, between 60 and 80 per cent of the *population in the cities* attended *no church* regularly. The Church of England acted as the chaplain to the nation for hatch, match and despatch, but those occasional services did not often convert into regular worship.

The Church of England had by now clearly divided into three streams: the Tractarian or High Church, which prized the sacraments, and especially the Eucharist, first; the Evangelical, which placed scripture first; and the Liberal, which placed reason foremost. Resistance to Tractarianism was gradually overcome by the end of the nineteenth century. The Victorian habit of going to law over unorthodox worship was now on the wane. In 1888, the Church Association had taken the godly Edward King, Bishop of Lincoln, to court for breaching ecclesiastical law on seven points: mixing the chalice with wine and water, adopting an eastward position at the altar, performing manual acts, allowing the singing of the *Agnus Dei*, taking ablutions in the sanctuary (i.e. washing his hands), placing lighted candles on the altar (or holy table as the Prayer Book described it), and making the sign of the cross in the blessing. He was tried, reluctantly, by Archbishop Benson over a nine-month period from July 1889, with five other bishops, and found guilty on three counts: the mixed chalice, making manual acts, and making the sign of the cross in the blessing. Bishop King immediately altered his practice out of obedience to his archbishop, but this did not prevent the onward march of ritual in the Church of England. A succession of bishops under Archbishop Davidson, who had been a close confidant of Queen Victoria, Dean of Windsor and Archbishop from 1903–28, moved Anglo-Catholic practice forward. "He was a man of remarkable balance of judgement, intellectual humility, sense of responsibility and capacity for work."[5] On his watch, the catholicizing of the Church of England proceeded not by advocacy, but by allowing others their head. Gore, Cosmo Lang (Davidson's successor at Canterbury), Winnington Ingram in London, and Cyril Garbett were all more committed to the ceremony and theology of Anglo-Catholicism. When Garbett was appointed Archbishop of York in 1908, he advocated the legalization of the six points: eucharistic vestments, the lighting of candles on the altar, the use of wafers, the eastward position of the celebrant, the mixing of water and wine in the chalice, and the use of incense, and all were adopted. If Davidson favoured the Anglo-Catholic way, "it was not because he was at heart a catholic but because there was no alternative in sight".[6]

The Evangelical party in the Church of England had few advocates at this time, apart from the well-named Bishop Edmund Knox of Manchester (1903–21), a Protestant Tory of the old school who would countenance neither Non-Conformism nor Catholicism and who petitioned against both, whether in education or ceremony. To his consternation, two of his sons had Anglo-Catholic tendencies, one of whom—Ronnie—became a celebrated Roman Catholic priest, to which he responded by saying, "Between ourselves Winnie (his wife) and I cannot understand what it is that the dear boys see in the Blessed Virgin Mary."[7] For his part, Ronnie would be a brilliant academic, a classicist at Oxford, and an author. The fact was that, in the war years, the old consensus that the religion of England was lay, Protestant, middle-class and scriptural would no longer hold. It had been changing and was about to change still more.

Evangelicals among the clergy and laity instead found fellowship in missionary societies, the Keswick Movement and the Christian Unions at universities, especially Cambridge. Evangelicals were still volunteering in numbers for the mission field and were being strategically led by J. H. Oldham and J. R. Mott, the former Scottish and the latter an American layman who sought to direct world mission on an ecumenical basis, and to fulfil the motto "evangelization of the world in this generation". To this end they organized the important Edinburgh Missionary Conference in 1910, with its first steps towards ecumenical cooperation among Protestant churches. They realized that evangelization needed to be achieved with strategies relating to education, colonial policy, the effects of war, and political engagement. Examples of this policy-making included, for instance, Oldham alerting Archbishop Davidson in 1919 to the need to lobby the government about German missionary property being exempted from reparations in the Versailles Treaty, and that freedom of conscience and the practice of religion should be mentioned in the League of Nations charter. These were important interventions that came from political engagement pioneered by Oldham in particular.

Not all Evangelicals were easy about too deep an involvement with politics or social concerns, and this division would affect the Evangelical movement until the 1970s. This was in part due to the success of the Student Christian Movement (SCM). The student population in England had grown to 50,000 by 1900 and the SCM, begun in the 1890s, grew with it. At its start, the SCM had a missionary outlook, a concern for holiness of life and a commitment to Jesus as God the Son and Saviour of the World. The movement provided a bridge between most Protestant denominations, but as it grew to 10,000 members, it moved away from its roots: Anglo-Catholics joined; there were more political and social concerns; it was less Keswick-based (with its annual Bible teaching conference); and generally more diverse. The Cambridge Christian Union or CICCU, once a constituent part of the SCM, was now a self-appointed guardian of Evangelical credentials. In 1910, the very year of the Edinburgh Conference, the CICCU's executive group decided to disaffiliate from the SCM by a margin of seventeen to five. It was a significant rift between Evangelicals, with many moving from a wider socio-political and social engagement to an Evangelical gospel, focussed on the authority of scripture, the atonement and personal conversion. It would not be until the 1970s, and the teaching of John Stott, the internationalist rector of All Souls, Langham Place, that the rift would be overcome. For Stott, social engagement and biblical teaching were not to be separated.

At the start of the twentieth century, the relationship between the Established and the Non-Conformist or Free Churches continued in much the same way as it had in the past: there was a certain arrogance on one side matched by a slight bitterness on the other. The "superiority" of the Established Church resulted from privileges going back to 1660, the Restoration of the Monarchy and the establishment of the Church of England; the sense of bitterness in Non-Conformity because they had been persecuted by the establishment, had to fight for their rights, whether in education or in the state, every inch of the way. There was a continual interplay between the state, Church and dissent, between Erastian (i.e. a church governed by the state) and Free Church, between Episcopalian and Non-Conformist, and between church and chapel.

Non-Conformity remained strong at the turn of the century and in some areas was increasing in reach. Later in the twentieth century, the Non-Conformist churches were to be joined by the Elim Pentecostal or Four-Square Church, which started life in Sunderland in the parish of Monkwearmouth where Alexander Boddy was vicar. George Jeffreys, who had been deeply influenced by the Welsh Revival of 1904, brought Pentecostalism there. The Methodists remained strong in the North of England, Cornwall, and on the Isle of Wight. In 1907, there were over a million children in Methodist Sunday schools, almost half a million in the Primitive Methodist schools, and half a million with the Baptists. In fact, there were 3,180,820 pupils in Free Church Sunday schools, over against 2,334,000 in Church of England Sunday schools. In today's terms, over five million children attending Sunday schools is an astonishing figure.

The characteristics of the Free Churches were generally these: they were strongly Protestant in flavour, if split between Calvinist (Baptist, Presbyterian and Congregationalist) and non-Calvinist (Methodist and Primitive Methodist); and strict in terms of morality, especially in relation to gambling, alcohol and free association of young men and women. And by 1907, there was evidence of the fissiparous Methodism of the early nineteenth century coming together again. As for worship, scripture and preaching were paramount, and this was expressed in communal hymn singing—there were now a great many hymns—and extempore prayer.

The Non-Conformist churches were often the womb of political activism. In fact, it is hard to overestimate the influence of Christian Socialism in the inception of the Cooperative movement, the Trade Union movement and the foundation of the Labour Party. By 1891, the Cooperatives Wholesale Societies had 1.5 million members. In 1920, the local secretary of the Darlington National Union of Railwaymen was Simeon Hardwick, a Primitive Methodist, a Sunday school and Young Men's Bible School teacher, and a circuit steward for the church. From 1918, he was the first chairman of the Darlington Labour Party. It was a typical progression. Indeed, it was a Non-Conformist background that was the genesis of such liberal papers as *The Manchester Guardian*. Founded in 1821, with C. P.

Scott as editor for forty-eight years, *The Manchester Guardian* represented dissent in its most secular, principled and pioneering form.

In the early part of the twentieth century, the Non-Conformist churches developed in their social engagement, political involvement and theological reflection. A great example of such social engagement was John Scott Lidgett, sometimes called the greatest Methodist since Wesley. For fifty years, he presided over a Methodist colony in Bermondsey, London. It was ecumenical, Evangelical and with the broadest possible educational and social aims. He was on the Senate of London University, becoming its vice-chancellor, and was deeply involved in the social health of Bermondsey. His was a profound social engagement, born out of gospel-held principles, working ecumenically where possible, and with considerable self-sacrifice.

More formal political engagement was sometimes less principled. In 1906, 185 Liberal politicians came from Free Church backgrounds, including individuals such as Asquith, Lloyd George, Haldane, Sir John Simon and Birrell. Although wanting Free Church votes, as politicians they hardly subscribed to strict Free Church morals. Brought up in stringent Victorian households, they were more at home with Edwardian moral latitude. When leaders of the Free Church General Assembly sought assurances from Lloyd George that he did not play golf on Sundays, they were unaware when they arrived at Downing Street that he may have just come down from his mistress's bed to greet them.

The early twentieth century saw the emergence of the greatest Free Church theologian of the period, P. T. Forsyth (1848–1921). In an age in which there was a danger of Christianity becoming an ethical soup, Forsyth gave depth and substance to theology. Like Karl Barth a little later on, Forsyth stood for the counterblast of gospel fundamentals against relativism or simply human amelioration: sin, the incarnation and redemption were profoundly stressed. In a pithy but telling phrase, he said: "Unless there is within us that which is above us, we shall soon yield to that which is around us." In a world that looked for a new theodicy in face of the carnage of the First World War, he found the justification of God and humanity in the atonement, in the Cross of Christ. Rather than becoming detached from the nostrums of the faith, he reburnished them for contemporary use. He did this while Principal of Hackney College, London from 1901 to 1921. And not far away in South London was F. B. Meyer, the great pastor and devotional writer, humble and ecumenical in spirit, who was secretary of the National Free Church Council in 1910. The two were shining examples of Free Church thought and ministry.

For the Roman Catholic Church, the early twentieth century was a period of consolidation, growth and definition. In 1910, there were 3,835 priests in England and Wales; by 1940, there would be 5,652, and the number would rise further still. There were two million Catholics in England and Wales. It was a community with by far the greatest number of members from the working class (unlike the Church of England), mostly from Liverpool, Lancashire and the London area, with just a few very aristocratic laymen at its head, such as the Duke of Norfolk and Lord Acton. There were 400,000 children in Catholic schools. The institutional church was also greatly strengthened in its organizational capacity in this period, and its worship was mostly centred on the mass, Friday abstinence, the confessional, candle-lighting in front of a replica of the Virgin Mary, pilgrimages to Lourdes, garish pictures of the Sacred Heart in the home, and the rosary. The sermon had become an afterthought in Catholic worship. Catholic morality was much freer than that of the Free Churches, especially when it came to alcohol, gambling and dancing: all pillars of Irish community life. If these practices were an unchanging staple of working-class Catholicism, there was still some dispute about what other content there should be to Catholic faith. In London and Oxford, there existed a form of Catholic continental internationalism centred on individuals like Francis de Zulueta, Regius Professor of Civil Law in Oxford from 1919. More ultramontane was Merry de Val, a Spanish Catholic, who had a strong influence on Monsignor Talbot and over upper-class English Catholics. The English College at Rome, or Venerabile, was to become the breeding ground for the English Catholic episcopacy, although Romanizing English Catholics was always fraught, and often resisted. Manning had despised the effete intellectualism of Newman with its Oxford influence. What Manning wanted was "downright, masculine and decided Catholics—more Roman than Rome, and more ultramontane than the Pope himself".[8]

There was also a creative side to Catholic theology of the modernist kind, which was at odds with traditional Catholicism and willing to engage with the Bible in the contemporary context. Such modernists, who were implacably opposed by the ultramontane traditionalists, included Baron von Hügel, an aristocratic Austrian Catholic married to an English aristocrat, Lady Mary Herbert, and George Tyrell, an Irish Jesuit influenced by the French biblical scholar Alfred Loisy. Tyrell rejected traditional Catholic teaching and liberal Protestantism, adopted modern biblical scholarship, and questioned the authority of Pope Pius X, who was a quiet traditionalist. For his temerity, Tyrell was expelled from the Jesuits, was unable to celebrate the mass, and was finally refused a Catholic burial. Buried by Abbé Brémond at Storrington Cemetery on 21 July 1909, "no other English Christian of the twentieth century has been so harshly treated, none other privileged to share so utterly in the condemnation and lonely death of the Saviour".[9]

Two others to escape such condemnation were Catholic laymen with no superior to please save their own conscience: G. K. Chesterton (1874–1936) and Hilaire Belloc. They made a formidable literary duo. Chesterton, who converted to Catholicism from High Anglicanism, was a large, ebullient man weighing twenty stone. When challenged by a lady as to why he was not out on the Front, he replied that if she would step round to the side of him, she would see that he was! An apologist for the faith, he debated with H. G. Wells, Bernard Shaw and others in an age of increasing scepticism, especially after the Great War. He held to orthodox beliefs with witty and memorable phraseology and was essentially an early C. S. Lewis. (The latter found Chesterton's book *Orthodoxy* powerfully illuminating and compellingly attractive.) Chesterton was also a lover of paradox. Typically, he said of rebellious sceptics, "by rebelling against everything, [the rebel] has lost his right to rebel against anything".[10] Again, he famously said that the Christian ideal has not been tried and found wanting; it has been found too difficult and left untried. Belloc (1870–1953), a naturalized Englishman of French origin, who suffered many losses in his family, was a bright star in the Catholic firmament. His brilliant mind was in the end overwhelmed by his own prejudices. He exulted in authoritarian symbols, whether Napoleon or the Catholic hierarchy, and by the 1930s he harboured anti-Semitic views. His foil would be R. H. Tawney (1880–1962), whose insights were forged in the black slime and mud of the First World War. Both were brilliant scholars from Balliol, but only one gave a true vision of a progressive society. All this was soon to be overtaken by war.

The First World War and its aftermath

The assassination of Archduke Ferdinand of Austria and his wife in Sarajevo by the nineteen-year-old Bosnian Serb, Gavrilo Princip, on 28 June 1914, sparked the beginning of the First World War, or the "Great War", as it was then called. The alliances that had been built up over preceding years took over. In this Balkan confrontation between Austria-Hungary and Serbia, others would soon take sides. Russia supported Serbia, its Orthodox-believing ally. Germany would not restrain its ally, Austria-Hungary, and seeing its chance to attack Belgium and humiliate France, invaded Belgium en route to Paris. Britain was willing to intervene in support of her ally, France, and to redress the violation of Belgium.[11] Thus the Great Powers, who had slowly accumulated grievances between themselves in preceding years, virtually sleepwalked into war. Apart from some regional conflicts in the Crimea and the Balkans, Europe had been free of a continental war for a hundred years. Now the worst war in European and English history was about to begin.

As far back as 1890, Helmuth von Moltke, who planned German victories in the age of German unification, warned: "All we have now is people's war, and any prudent government will hesitate to bring about a war of this nature, with all its incalculable consequences."[12] There was little restraining prudence, and not much understanding of the complexities and aspirations of different nations. "The majority of Europeans, as far as it is possible to tell, were simply stupefied at the speed and finality with which Europe's peace had ended."[13] The British government prepared for conflict. Lord Kitchener went to the War Office, becoming more famous for his recruitment poster, "Your Country Needs You", than for anything else, and General Sir John French, the commander of the British forces, thought the war, as many did, would be over by Christmas. By the end of 1914, the war having begun in August, the French had lost 255,000 and the British 90,000. The years of hope and progress came to a shuddering halt and the Church, in all its parts, had become the chaplain to the nation at war.

The course and characteristics of the war are well-known, but its awfulness is hard to grasp. By the end of 1914, the opposing forces had dug in from Switzerland to the Channel, in a continuous line of trenches. They were to remain there for almost four years of hell. The Eastern Front stretched from the Gulf of Riga in the Baltic to the Black Sea. The characteristics of the war in Europe soon became apparent: the continuous shelling and bombardment of positions, "softening up" for an attack, the use of gas and flame-throwers on both sides, the mining of positions and huge explosions, continual sniping, the preparations for an assault, the dreadful slaughter by machine guns and mortars, the use of bayonets and entrenching tools in hand-to-hand combat. On a more personal level, soldiers in the trenches faced desolate sights of a pitted landscape, lice on their bodies, trench foot, rats that ate food and bodies, screaming horses in the throes of death, excruciating death from chlorine or mustard gas, a sense of isolation on home leave, mental breakdown, shell shock, death all around—in shell holes or with bodies hanging in the trees, blown there by explosives. And then mud, mud and more mud—enough to drown in if you missed your footing. And this terror was for all those soldiers pitted by their governments to fight each other. Fraternizing, as in the Christmas truce of 1914 when football was played and German and English carols were sung, was frowned upon: the purpose of war was to kill each other, not to socialize. The war was a catastrophic failure of government and diplomacy.

The strategic course of the war on the Western Front involved a slaughter beyond imagining. The scale of the war memorials tells the story. It was decided early on *not* to repatriate dead combatants. Instead, if found, soldiers were buried near to where they fell. Yet the Menin Gate at Ypres bears the names of 54,000 officers and men whose bodies were *not found*, and every night there the "Last Post" is played by the local fire brigade for those lost, and those lost and never found. On the first day of the Battle of the Somme in 1916, 21,000 soldiers were killed within the first hour: the casualties that day, including the wounded, were 60,000—half the size of the original Expeditionary Force sent at the outset of the war. The Battle of the Somme lasted from 1 July to 18 November 1916 and would cost over 600,000 casualties: both British and Commonwealth soldiers. The Memorial at Thiepval designed by Lutyens remembers in poignant solitude the 72,000 names of soldiers *not found*. The following year, in 1917, the Third Battle of Ypres or Passchendaele consumed some 300,000 British and Commonwealth casualties. It rained for a month in midsummer, the mud was liquid treacle: deep enough to drown in, stronger than an enveloping python. Controversial from the first, and advocated by the new commander Douglas Haig, Passchendaele was regarded as a disaster by the new Prime Minister, Lloyd George, who had taken over from Asquith with Tory support in 1916. The cemetery and memorial for Passchendaele at Tyne Cot, the largest of British and Commonwealth cemeteries, bears the names of 35,000 soldiers *not found*. In 1917, Russia withdrew from the war, consumed by the Revolution and the overthrow and execution of the Tsar and his family. In the same year, the United States, provoked by German submarine attacks on transatlantic shipping, entered the war and an exhausted, starving and on-the-brink-of-revolution Germany soon sued for peace. German casualties on both fronts had been 1.8 million dead; Britain's were 774,000. Every town and village in Britain bears on memorials the record of their dead.

There were other theatres of war. In the North Sea, the Battle of Jutland in April 1916 had the effect—if not of outright victory—of keeping the German navy in port thereafter. The Gallipoli Campaign of 1915 resulted in tragic loss of life among Australians and New Zealanders, especially from Turkish fire on exposed positions, and the temporary political fall of Churchill from the government.

In Palestine, General Allenby's troops succeeded in taking Jerusalem from the Ottoman-appointed ruler on 9 December 1917. When Allenby took the surrender of the city, he walked in, so as not to appear a vindictive aggressor. In the same campaign, Lawrence of Arabia, working with Faisal and the Arab tribes, delivered Damascus to the Allies, but the outcome of French control of Damascus, the Arab pearl, through the Sykes-Picot pact seemed to Lawrence a betrayal of the

Arab cause. He bitterly reflected on this in his great account, *The Seven Pillars of Wisdom*. Elsewhere in Africa, the British took over German colonies.

The war gave rise to profound questions about the way it was conducted: the abominable waste, why supposedly Christian powers contrived such slaughter against each other, why clergy and school chaplains at home encouraged young men to die, why political leaders failed to prevent it and where God was in it all. Besides war machines and armies, the war drew in artists, poets, writers, nurses and thinkers. The archaeologist, mountaineer, explorer and later diplomat, Gertrude Bell, settled herself in at the Wounded and Mission Enquiry Department at Boulogne and sought to match details of casualties with the anxious enquiries of relatives.[14] The nurse Edith Cavell went to Belgium out of Christian conviction to nurse the wounded, and was captured by the Germans and vindictively executed. Her sacrifice is remembered in Norwich and Peterborough and is especially recalled in the cathedrals there. The artist Stanley Spencer—friend of the great war artist Paul Nash, who painted the grotesque landscapes of war-torn countryside—painted a memorial chapel in Burghclere, Berkshire, recalling his own experiences as an orderly in Thessalonica on the Eastern Front. His east-end wall painting depicts a resurrection scene of the war dead, with animals too, in a fresco of hope and redemption. (When first revealed, some objected to the resurrection of the animals as being ill-founded theologically!) Spencer's faith was sparked by a chaplain, Desmond Chute, who gave him a copy of Augustine's *Confessions* when he was working as a hospital orderly in Bristol. The poet John Masefield, who was to succeed Robert Bridges as Poet Laureate in 1930 and remain so for thirty-seven years, went as a Red Cross orderly to Arc-en-Barrois, sixty miles from the Front. He was soon helping with an amputation, administering chloroform, and writing to his wife, "My dearest Con, this is not a question of being 'noble' or 'being spared', it is a question of going through a little hardship to save the lives of beautiful human beings. I do more hard work . . . but I can do it and was never better in my life."[15] Later he would confide his experience as a war recorder at the Somme to his godmother, Annie Hanford-Flood, but he struggled to find comfort through faith.[16]

The most poignant legacy of the war and the most abiding literary monument—besides the endless white headstones in faultless ranks in the cemeteries of Flanders—was the verse of the war poets themselves: Siegfried Sassoon, Wilfred Owen, Robert Graves, Edmund Blunden and others. They observed as participants and recorded what they saw for posterity in immortal lines. What they witnessed was terrible waste, expressed in patriotism and honour.

How could the Church minister in such carnage? Some clergy did: humanely, quietly and sacrificially. Many did not, according to Graves and Sassoon. The Reverend Geoffrey Studdert Kennedy, known as Woodbine Willie, was close to the men. He offered cigarettes, he swore like them and wrote simple verse that resonated with the Tommies. His theme was often the suffering of God for the world and its inhumanity. One of his poems, "The Sorrows of God", includes these lines:

> I wonder if that's what it really means,
> The figure what 'angs on the Cross.
> I remember I seed one the other day
> As I stood with the Captain's 'oss . . .
> Well, what if 'e came to earth today,
> Came walking about this trench,
> 'Ow 'is 'eart would bleed for the sights 'e seed
> I' the mud and the blood and the stench.[17]

And in Poperinge, the Reverend Tubby Clayton opened Talbot House as a sanctuary for all ranks: a homely place with time for tea, games, humorous shows and, on the top floor, a chapel where many received communion, some were baptized and where, in simple familiarity, prayers and hope were offered. In army parlance it became known as Toc H, the signallers' call sign for Talbot House. Toc H founded a charity of the same name with houses throughout Britain that give support to returning soldiers. Robert Graves, no Christian, recalled half-forgotten lines of Psalm 91 that gave him comfort: "Though thousands languish and fall beside thee, And Ten thousand around thee perish, Yet still it shall not come nigh thee."[18] Yet by 1916, any comfort from chaplains or from the small Gospels given to the soldiers with a message from Lord Roberts to find solace therein was mingled with bitterness at the way the establishment conducted the war. Siegfried Sassoon recalled a "March Past" on Christmas Day 1916 with biting satire:

> In red and gold, the Corps-Commander stood
> With ribboned breast puffed out for all to see:
> He'd sworn to beat the Germans, if he could;
> For God had taught him strength and strategy.

He was our leader, and a judge of port –
Rode well to hounds, and was a damned good sort.

'Eyes right!' We passed him with a jaunty stare.
'Eyes front!' He'd watched his trusted legions go.
I wonder if he guessed how many there
Would get knocked out of time in next week's show.
'Eyes right!' The corpse-commander was a Mute;
And Death leered round him, taking our salute.[19]

For Sassoon, "And all this war's a sham, a stinking lie." Although the war had a just cause at the outset, the scale of loss and horror transformed its moral rectitude. Nothing could justify this. And the gap was between the men, the young officers and the establishment—old men who were politicians, generals, bishops and church leaders. By the time the literature of the war appeared in 1929, as in the case of *All Quiet on the Western Front* by Erich Maria Remarque, a German author who escaped Nazi Germany, or Robert Graves's *Goodbye to All That*, also in 1929, and the war poems and diaries of Wilfred Owen and Sassoon, the gap was rapidly becoming a chasm. Graves wrote, "Hardly one soldier in a hundred (in the trenches) was inspired by religious feeling of even the crudest kind."[20] Much later, in 1962, Benjamin Britten would compose *War Requiem*, putting into powerful music the war poems of Wilfred Owen; first performed in a restored Coventry Cathedral on 30 May 1962.

The lasting effect of the Great War was that it created for many emotional distance, and psychological buffers and spiritual numbness between front-line soldiers and their old leaders, creating the perception of lions led by donkeys. As Orwell wrote, "By 1918 everyone under forty was in bad temper with his elders, and the mood of anti-militarism which followed naturally upon the fighting was extended into a general revolt against orthodoxy and authority."[21] For the survivors, these men were truly the "Old Contemptibles". Succeeding generations wondered how they could have let it happen.

Peace came suddenly at 11 a.m. on 11 November 1918, but the wounds did not heal with the cessation of hostilities. Generals and their junior officers signed the Armistice agreement in French Commander Marshal Foch's railway carriage in a siding near Compiègne, and the peace was enforced a year later in Versailles.

The Treaty of Versailles, which changed the world, placed guilt on the German people and asked for astronomical war reparations, which were never paid. Internal convulsions precipitated by the war had claimed the royal families of Russia, Germany and Austria-Hungary, and others would follow: Greece, Romania and Bulgaria. Fostering the principles of self-determination embraced by the American President, Woodrow Wilson, new countries were formed out of old empires in Eastern Europe, and in particular the Ottoman Empire was divided into new Middle Eastern countries of Syria, Jordan, Iraq, Palestine and Lebanon, with a Jewish homeland thinly endorsed.[22] In a letter to Lord Rothschild on 2 November 1917, Balfour, as foreign secretary in Lloyd George's coalition, had granted a homeland to the Jews, but on the grounds that "nothing shall be done which may prejudice the civil and religious rights of existing non-Jewish communities in Palestine".[23] The League of Nations was also founded to police the peace, but it was short-lived.

The Versailles treaty would divide Christians then and in the future. Some, like Bishop Bell of Chichester, would be prevented in their condemnation of a resurgent Germany in the 1930s because of the treatment Germany had received from the Allies in the treaty: especially the war guilt clause and the reparations. English Christians would find themselves henceforward divided on how to protect Palestinian communities *and* support the Jewish state. The peace treaty was signed in an almost nonchalant way. Frances Stevenson, Lloyd George's secretary and mistress, said: "Everyone seems delighted with the peace terms and there is no fault to find with them on the ground that they are not severe enough."[24] It was signed in the Hall of Mirrors in Versailles—what images it would transmit! The greatest tragedy of the peace was that, in twenty years, Europe and the world would be at war again.

The Church in the 1920s

By the end of the war, there were 3.4 million in uniform; some had jobs to return to, many did not. Unemployment would stalk the land in the 1920s and 30s with industrial unrest and strikes, culminating in the General Strike in 1926. Women aged thirty who had "manned" the munitions industry through the war were given the vote. They had become accustomed to greater independence and a wage packet. There had been rebellion in Ireland in 1916 with the Easter Rising, repressed by the Black and Tans. The Irish Republican Army (IRA) was formed under Michael Collins, and the road to an independent Ireland and the separation of Ulster would take a further six years, when Collins would be murdered by his own side. The coalition government of Lloyd George Liberals (as opposed to Asquith Liberals) and Conservatives held until 1922, when a group of back bench Conservative MPs voted to secede (hence the 1922 Committee—now a weekly meeting of Conservative backbenchers). Lloyd George, an opportunistic war leader, had come to be seen as untrustworthy and corrupt, selling honours for influence. Bonar Law's Conservative government of 1922, dependent on Liberals, did not last long.

A Labour government in alliance with Asquith Liberals ruled under Ramsey MacDonald from 1923, but suspicions of dealing with the Soviet Union Communist Party and withdrawal of Liberal support ended the coalition. In 1924, a further election took place, and Baldwin leading the Conservatives, now with Lloyd George Liberals including Churchill, took office. It had been an unstable time with three elections in three years and would remain so for years to come. Churchill became Chancellor of the Exchequer under Baldwin and unwisely returned the pound to the Gold Standard, overvaluing it at $4.80 and exacerbating economic woes. The Wall Street Crash of 1929 would precipitate a National Government, and all the while the Nazi Party was gaining ground in Germany and Stalin was increasing his control through terror in the Soviet Union. The United States had gone into a period of international isolation. Among these seismic national and international events, how did the Church fare?

The post-war Church showed both outer calm and inner uncertainty. It would face great social unrest at home and powerful untamed movements in Europe, for which it was unprepared and which it did not understand. The old men were still in charge. Faced by the grinding poverty of much of northern working-class England, mineworkers and others looked for change and economic support. It did not come. The miners' strike was precipitated by the mine owners wanting more work for less pay, despite the already gruelling conditions, which got the response "not a penny off the pay, not an hour on the day". In Parliament, Churchill was severe in his condemnation.

Outwardly, the Church of England looked steady. New dioceses were formed in Blackburn and Leicester in 1926 and in Derby, Guildford and Portsmouth in 1927. Under Dean Milner-White, King's College Cambridge began the immensely popular Nine Lessons and Carols Christmas Eve service in 1918, which was broadcast from 1928. It would become part of the English religious tradition, mixing solemnity, beauty and the numinous with the Cenotaph Service on Remembrance Sunday. The Cenotaph, from the Greek word *kenotaphion*, meaning an empty tomb, was designed by Sir Edward Lutyens. There the war dead were remembered by the nation annually. The Church did there what it does best for the country: mixing the symbols of nation, royalty and faith in an environment of dramatic theatre and solemn remembrance. On the day it was first used, on 11

November 1920, with George V leading the mourning, the Unknown Soldier—an unidentified soldier dug up in France—was buried in Westminster Abbey.

If the Church had found a new role in leading the mourning of the nation, all was not so well beneath this outer carapace. These obsequies brought comfort but did not necessarily renew faith in God. The disconnect between the image of gaitered Anglican church leaders and the profound theological questions arising from the Great War grew in the 1920s and became increasingly apparent. By 1920, Archbishop Davidson had been in post seventeen years, and would remain so for another eight: conscientious, but increasingly out of touch. For twenty years Cosmo Lang was Archbishop of York, before spending a further fourteen as Archbishop of Canterbury (1928–42). Lang was a liberal Catholic who veered from support of the social reform enshrined in Lloyd George's People's Budget to sympathy towards the Kaiser at the outset of the war, and then to unbending censure of Edward VIII for asking for the hand of a twice-divorced woman, Wallis Simpson. Prevented by Baldwin and Davidson from doing so, Edward abdicated to marry her to the great consternation of the nation and the royal family.

In the 1920s, Anglo-Catholicism had reached its high-water mark in the Church of England, with leaders like Gore, Lang and Garbett. At the same time, the number of clergy would start falling by a hundred a year during the 1920s. Compulsory chapel at Oxbridge colleges ended in the 1920s. There were few Evangelical bishops in the Church of England, apart from Francis Chavasse, who took over from Bishop Ryle in Liverpool. One of his sons, Noel, had won two VCs and an MC in the war for rescuing soldiers in no-man's land in France, where he later died. The other son, Christopher, would become Bishop of Rochester. Both were Olympians in the 1908 Games.

The Evangelical movement in the universities, as epitomized by the Christian Union at Cambridge (CICCU), was at a low ebb compared with the heady missionary days of the late 1880s onwards and had fallen prey to the inspiring moralism of Frank Buchman, an attractive American who founded the Oxford Group or Moral Re-Armament. This group appealed to masculine pride and moral challenge but was in the end neither Christocentric nor dependent on grace. It is an interesting phenomenon that English Evangelicalism has often looked to American Evangelicalism for its future inspiration, perhaps finding it hard sometimes to accept leadership from within its own ranks.

In the 1920s, there were three discernible ways in which the Church responded to the times: an attempt at deeper social engagement, closer ecumenical relations, and reaction to theological modernism. The ecumenism was between the Free Churches and the more Protestant part of the Church of England. It was led by

John R. Mott, an American Methodist who had presided at the World Missionary Conference at Edinburgh in 1910. Unlike German Protestantism, which before the Great War had been a close companion to the English Protestant nexus of churches, Mott's variety of spirituality was practical, optimistic, well-supported financially and a bit naïve. Together with English church leaders like William Temple (later Archbishop of York and then Canterbury from 1942–4), Joseph Oldham, William Paton, Arthur Headlam and George Bell (later Bishop of Chichester), he arranged a further International Missionary Conference to be held in Jerusalem in 1928. The ecumenical focus of joint action and prayer was on international mission, social order and unity. Other conferences would be arranged at Lausanne in 1927, Edinburgh in 1937, and Madras in 1938.[25] A big superstructure of committees, the predecessor of the World Council of Churches, was arranged, but there was a danger that it would turn into a bureaucratic junket. In fact, from Germany there came a theological blast that would shake the Protestant world, namely Karl Barth's *Commentary on Romans* (1919), translated into English by Sir Edward Hoskyns in 1933. Indeed, by the 1920s, the effect of Barth's neo-Protestantism was making encounter with the Word in scripture central to Christian faith. Nevertheless, when asked to summarize his *Church Dogmatics*, which ran to six million words, Barth is reported to have said, "Jesus loves me this I know, for the Bible tells me so."

Although ecumenism was a necessary focus for the churches, given Christ's command to be one, it remained a matter of long-running debate as to how this could best be achieved. Conferences, committees and papers were one way, but something more existential was required. Equally, the Church's engagement with a society riven by inequality, poverty and discrimination was imperative. Once again William Temple saw the need and was intellectually well-prepared to respond. As a result, a Conference on Christian Politics, Economics and Citizenship was set up (COPEC). It met in April 1924 in Birmingham and had 1,400 delegates presided over by Temple, then in his prime aged forty-three. The danger with Temple, however, was that his attempt at conciliation between classes in society was ill-informed and easily fell into platitudes and amateurism. But if COPEC did little to highlight issues which society and government must tackle—and the General Strike was only two years away—it did alert some clergy involved to the need for massive social reform and a welfare state.

The General Strike of May 1926 produced a mixed response from the Church and a more intransigent response from the political establishment. Churchill, then Chancellor of the Exchequer and in pugnacious mood, founded a broadsheet called the *British Gazette* with a circulation from the start of 250,000.[26] The line of this paper was no compromise with the unions, but a settlement, if possible, with the miners. The miners numbered over a million. The Church's response, if there was such a thing, was conflicted. The Archbishop of Canterbury, now a very elderly Randall Davidson, who was sympathetic to the miners' position, was initially refused broadcasting rights by Lord Reith of the BBC, until this stance was overturned in the Commons. Cardinal Bourne of Westminster was forthright in his condemnation. The strike was a "sin against the obedience we owe to God".[27] The Roman Catholic Bishop of Liverpool, who was probably closer to the working man, wrote: "The poor must live and if private enterprise cannot provide the worker with a living, it must clear out for another system which can."[28] Only a few church leaders and more radical clergy supported such a view. Bishop Hensley Henson of Durham, critical of social reform and the COPEC movement, despised the notion of a living wage and thought the strike might lead to civil war.[29] To the miners, Henson looked like the friend of Baldwin, the friend of the mine owners, the proponent of unrestrained capitalism. No wonder they rendered their feelings in verse thus:

> Have you heard the parson preaching?
> Have you listened to his teaching?
> How the slaves in Egypt suffered long ago?
> But you heeded not his patter
> As you felt it didn't matter,
> For of mining how could any parson know?[30]

The Trades Union Council settled with the government, but the miners' strike continued painfully until they had to return to work. The answer came in 1929 when a Labour government was returned for the first time with 287 seats, almost an absolute majority. Five months later came the Stock Market Crash, and then a National Government led by Ramsay MacDonald.

Events in the more rarefied atmosphere of Anglican liturgical reform were also to prove problematic. It is said that in the house next door to the Russian revolutionaries of 1917, the Orthodox Church leaders were discussing how many fingers should be raised in a blessing. Now, in the fraught atmosphere of industrial unrest, the Church of England sought to revise its prayer book. It hoped to leave behind the language that marriage was instituted to temper the "passions of brute beasts" and to give brides the option of not obeying their husbands in their vows. The new revised Prayer Book was overwhelmingly passed in Church Assembly (by 253 to thirty-seven in the House of Clergy), although the House of Commons, incited by Sir William Joynson Hicks, the home secretary, and Thomas Inskip, later

Lord Caldecote, led the debate against the Prayer Book revision as a Romanizing reform. Twice the revised Prayer Book was thrown out by Parliament, brought down in the Commons by an alliance of Evangelicals with the Welsh, Scots and Ulstermen. The Church Assembly nevertheless approved its unauthorized (by Parliament) use. The mistake of the Church was that it was not an *alternative service book*, but rather a replacement for the Prayer Book of 1662, one of the foundations of the expressed faith of England. Loss of the *Book of Common Prayer* was not something that Parliament or country could stomach. And the whole episode showed the extent of the Erastian settlement in which the Church of England operated.

By the end of the decade, there was both hope and a sense of foreboding. In 1928, Alexander Fleming, who had served in the Medical Corps on the Western Front, had discovered penicillin. In 1929, in his rooms in Magdalen College Oxford, C. S. Lewis recorded that, "In the Trinity Term of 1929 I gave in, and admitted God was God, and knelt and prayed: perhaps, that night, the most dejected and reluctant convert in all England."[31] Lewis was to move from reluctant Deist to full Christian in 1931, bringing, in time, hope to millions and being himself surprised by joy. Meanwhile, in Germany, the Nazi Party in 1930 increased its representation in the Reichstag from twelve to 107 seats.[32]

The hope and horror of the 1930s

The 1930s came in with hope and went out in horror. In 1930, Pluto was identified in the outer darkness of space and sliced bread made its first appearance in the English diet. Following the great stock market crash of 1929, England was suffering increasing economic hardship, and unemployment rose to 2.5 million. While for the United States, F. D. Roosevelt announced the New Deal in 1932, spending the nation out of the Depression, no such remedy was open to Britain. Churchill, Chancellor of the Exchequer until 1929, said the government had neither the resources to counteract recession, nor the capacity to borrow. These economic conditions were to present some stark choices in England, as on the continent.

Meanwhile, for the churches it was a time of hopefulness; growth in some parts and in other parts steady decline. After the growing liberalism of the 1920s, the result of earlier liberal Protestantism coming from Germany, a resurgent creative orthodoxy followed in the 1930s. This was due to the appearance of a number of remarkable thinkers and biblical scholars. Foremost among them were

Reinhold Niebuhr, C. H. Dodd, William Temple and Michael Ramsey. Each was to contribute profoundly to the confidence of the Church at the time.

Niebuhr (1892–1971) was an American, but the son of an Evangelical German pastor. The influences on him were diverse: the family spoke German at home in Illinois, and Reinhold married an Englishwoman, an Oxford graduate in theology and history: Ursula Keppel Compton. As with Barth and Ramsey, he had little time for the social gospel and, influenced by Karl Barth and the gathering storm clouds in Germany, he pivoted away from that gospel in the 1930s. He opposed the bigotry of racism in the States and would be a strong influence on Dietrich Bonhoeffer and Martin Luther King. Writing on racism, he said: "We are admonished in Scripture to judge people by their fruits, not by their roots: and their fruits are their character, their deeds and their accomplishments."[33] It is to him that the well-known Serenity Prayer is generally attributed: "God grant me the serenity to accept the things I cannot change, Courage to change things I can, and wisdom to know the difference." Furthermore, "Niebuhr provided a gospel fully sensitive to social reality which yet escaped from entombment within any one single socio-political option."[34]

If Niebuhr gave leadership in Britain to an orthodoxy that was socially engaged, C. H. Dodd (1884–1973), a Congregationalist Free Church biblical scholar, together with Sir Edwyn Hoskyns, gave renewed hope of establishing the historical Jesus, who had been progressively shredded by liberal Protestantism (e.g. by Adolf von Harnack, Strauss and others). This new combination of Dodd and Niebuhr gave hope and new confidence to the Church, and it also gave rise to the quip: "Thou shalt love the lord thy Dodd, and thy Niebuhr as thyself."[35]

Alongside these two significant scholars, who burst onto the scene in the 1930s, were two upcoming Archbishops of Canterbury, William Temple (1881–1944) and Michael Ramsey (1904–88). Temple was a prodigiously talented thinker with a double first in Greats from Balliol Oxford who had been President of the Oxford Union. After a spell as headmaster of Repton, he became Bishop of Manchester and then succeeded Cosmo Lang at York in 1929. Although quite capable of writing fresh and compellingly lucid exposition of scripture, as he did in his commentaries on St John's Gospel, he concentrated his theological firepower on Christianity and the social order, with ecumenism firmly attached. All-embracing and positive in outlook, Temple was at the helm of a number of conferences both in the 1920s, as in COPEC, but supremely at the Oxford Conference of Life and Work in 1937.

This gathering was held in the face of growing Nazi oppression of the Jews and was immediately preceded by the arrest of one would-be delegate, Pastor Martin

Niemoeller, who would spend until 1945 in a concentration camp. The conference focussed on the Church's obligations to society, but was also the precursor to the foundation of the World Council of Churches in 1938, and was welcomed by the Church Assembly in 1940. Others who took part in the conference included Lesslie Newbigin, who would in time write forcefully on the gospel and culture, Max Warren of Holy Trinity Cambridge, William Paton, the powerful and selfless administrator, and the éminence grise of such gatherings, J. H. Oldham. They were a formidable team, and willingly led by Temple. But there was also a new star on the horizon.

In 1935, Michael Ramsey, then a vice-principal of Lincoln Theological College, published perhaps his greatest work, *The Gospel and the Catholic Church*. It was a plea for the Church to turn away from a focus on social improvement to a deeper gospel. "For the church exists for something deeper than philanthropy and reform, namely to teach men to die to self and to trust in a resurrection to a new life that, because it spans both this world and another world, can never be wholly understood here, and must puzzle this world's idealists."[36] For Ramsey, the Church, the Body of Christ, must be located and found in the passion and resurrection of Christ. This work was a re-statement of the Evangelical gospel, linked to the tradition of the catholic (universal) church as expressed in a biblical and episcopal church order. Ramsey's theology complemented Temple's of social engagement. From *this* theological base other works would follow from Ramsey, notably on the priesthood, the Holy Spirit and prayer. With a Congregationalist background and a Liberal political stance, Ramsey's time would fully come during the period of his episcopacies from 1952–74, to which we will return.

The work of church and society was also taken up in T. S. Eliot's addresses at Cambridge in 1939, published that year as *The Idea of a Christian Society*. Eliot had emerged from the post-war disillusionment expressed in *The Waste Land* and "The Hollow Men". And, following his conversion to Anglo-Catholic Christianity, he denounced in *Ash-Wednesday* the twin evils of fascism and communism. Eliot came to the conclusion that "only in humility, charity and purity—and most of all perhaps humility—can we best prepare to receive the grace of God, without which human operations are in vain".[37]

Furthermore, a powerful combination of Christian thinkers, including R. H. Tawney, J. H. Oldham, the philosopher, and the Master of Balliol A. D. Lindsay, produced the "Pilgrim Report", probably the best study on unemployment of the 1930s.

The three great blights on English society in the 1930s were unemployment, poor housing and ill health. Education was not far behind. No one would make this more real than George Orwell. In his book *The Road to Wigan Pier*, first published in 1937 by Victor Gollanz as an exposé of English life, especially in the North of England, Orwell recounts the deprivation he found: the hell of coal mining, the pittance of earnings of £115 11s 6d per annum, squalid and cramped slum housing where it was necessary to walk the length of the terrace to get to a toilet shared with as many as thirty-six others, and the shame and destitution of the dole. Orwell recalls the moment in Greenwood's play, *Love on the Dole*, when an out-of-work miner cries out in desperation, "O God, send me some work." In fact, the unpleasantness of mining undertaken with companions was better than the impotence of falling on the human slagheap of being unwanted and out of work.

Orwell, who confronted the political movements of fascism and communism, which were so stark in the 1930s, chose democratic socialism as the way forward. He demonstrated his ideals by fighting in the Spanish Civil War of 1936 in the International Brigades. Orwell was an agnostic, though fond of the institution of the Church of England, like some beneficent uncle. His grandfather (Blair) had been a clergyman.[38] He was nevertheless to remain one of the most prophetic voices of those times; a voice against the totalitarianism of his age, and of any age, and he warned of its threat most powerfully in his later works of *Animal Farm* and *1984*.

Against such a social and political background as the 1930s, how did the churches fare? The Roman Catholic Church, though hardly led by inspiring leaders like Cardinal Bourne of Westminster, who died in 1935, was still growing. Bourne was succeeded by Arthur Hinsley, who was thought to be ultramontane, but turned out to have a fresh approach and became a national figure during the war. Archbishop Lang had him accepted into the Athenaeum, creating the possibility of ongoing Anglican-Roman Catholic dialogue!

In Liverpool, still the greatest of Catholic strongholds, Archbishop Downey sought to promote the Catholic presence with a vast new cathedral, but it was too grand ever to be built, and was in time replaced by a smaller building, locally known as "Paddy's Wigwam". Nevertheless, the Catholic Church grew in England and Wales by nearly 2,000 priests from 1925 to 1940. The mixed marriage doctrine, ensuring that children of mixed marriages were brought up Catholics, resulted in increased membership. Yet in areas of greatest deprivation, in Newcastle and Liverpool, there was not much national support for social reform from the hierarchy. The Jarrow Hunger Marchers of 1936 drew little or no support from the churches.

While there was little engagement with working class needs, cultured intellectual Catholicism flourished. Ronald Knox, Evelyn Waugh, Graham Greene, Eric Gill (later arraigned for sexual abuse) and Frank Pakenham all shone. Their admiration of Catholicism was unquestioning of any authoritarianism or doctrinal anachronism, indeed "its very authoritativeness was what appealed".[39] Yet authoritarianism in Europe was taking on a sinister presence and the papacy would wake up too late to its full import.

Pius XI (1922–39) joined other "guilty men" in completely misreading the rise of Mussolini and Nazi Germany and realized only in 1939 that "he had terribly misjudged the times and the movements".[40] Once again, because of fear of communism and of Stalin, a leader—in this case the Pope—saw fascism as a bulwark against the march of communism, only to wake up too late to the reality of the beast he had allowed to develop. It was a common problem among the leaders in Europe.

If the Catholic Church was growing in England, but conflicted like most in its response to the great movements and issues of the day, the Free Churches were now declining. In the 1930s, Christian socialism as present in a figure like Isaac Foot, the MP for Bodmin, was morphing into the agnostic socialism represented by his son, Michael Foot, who would become leader of the Labour Party in the 1980s. Although different sections of the Protestant family were reassembling in federations—as were differing parts of the Free Church movement, e.g. Congregationalists and Methodists—this did not halt decline. A high-water mark had been reached in 1906. Baptists declined from 434,741 in 1906 to 354,900 in 1946. Sunday school attendance also declined. Indignation against the Established Church and its privileges faded as the state took over education more and more, and with that some of the glue that had held the Free Churches together—mistrust of the Established Church—loosened. Others "went over" and became Anglicans. One D. R. Davies started out with Congregationalism, proceeded to Marxism, grew disillusioned with socialism after the Spanish Civil War, in which he took part, because of Stalin, returned to Congregationalism and in the end settled for Anglicanism! If numbers were declining, the contribution by individual Free Churchmen such as C. H. Dodd, Maurice Powicke, J. H. Oldham and William Paton increased, while some newer Pentecostal churches, like Elim and the Assemblies of God, thrived.

The Church of England had gifted emerging leaders in the 1930s. The more Victorian bishops were gradually beginning to fade: individuals like Winnington Ingram in London, who was Bishop of London for thirty-nine years till 1939, Henson in Durham, who retired in 1939 aged seventy-five, Headlam in Gloucester and, most of all, Lang, who retired as Archbishop of Canterbury in 1942 aged seventy-eight. The old guard was passing. Initially progressive, Lang became an arch-establishment figure of liberal Catholic instincts. Clever, and a Fellow of All Souls, he was regarded as one of the best speakers on the bench of bishops, yet he gave little lead to the Church in those critical years when he was at the helm. He had been Archbishop of York and then Canterbury from 1909 until 1942, a lengthy rule. It would be left to younger men, such as William Temple, George Bell and Cyril Garbett, to give a more contemporary and responsive lead.

Outside the hierarchy, laymen and women and junior clergy were coming to the fore, including Dorothy L. Sayers, C. S. Lewis, J. R. R. Tolkien and R. H. Tawney. The Inklings, an informal literary group that included Lewis and Tolkien, met at the Eagle and Child pub in St Giles, Oxford. Their work was deeply to affect the spiritual aspirations of millions, helping them access the meaning of the Christian faith. Contrastingly, a little-known curate, E. J. H. Nash (1898–1982), was taken on by the Scripture Union. He was to start summer camps in 1940 at Iwerne Minster in Dorset, aimed at the top thirty public schools of the country. From these camps would come many of the principal leaders of the Evangelical wing of the Church of England in the post-war period. A man of humility and determination, he ran the camps in a military and single-minded style, with a simple, attractive and profound explanation of the Gospel. Although effective in training many future church leaders, the camps and their school's work sadly saw some leaders use its all-male preserve as a context for abuse.

By the end of the 1930s, there was growing confidence in dealing with some of the social conditions of the age, and in explaining the faith in fresh and new terms. This fresh ability to explain the faith was born of the unusual mixture of experience of the First World War and the conventions of Anglo-Saxon English or medieval courtly love, as in the cases of Tolkien and Lewis respectively. Their writings were to prove ever fresh in explaining the nature of Christian faith. At the same time, the background of German re-armament and aggression had moved to the foreground, and from 1936 there appeared to be the growing probability of war.

The path to and the effects of war

From 1933, Britain had a National Government in which the weakening Labour leader, Ramsay MacDonald, gave way to Stanley Baldwin. From 1935 until 1937, Baldwin was prime minister. In 1937, Neville Chamberlain took over from Baldwin. Together with Cosmo Lang, Baldwin had negotiated the abdication crisis, in which, after remarkably short coverage by a more deferential press, Edward VIII broadcast that it was impossible to do his duties without the support of "the woman I love", the twice-divorced Wallis Simpson. All the while, events from the continent were pressing in.

In 1933, Hitler had become Chancellor of Germany. In 1935, in contravention of the Treaty of Versailles, he announced conscription and began building the Luftwaffe. Under the fascist Mussolini, Italy invaded Abyssinia, and was condemned by Hensley Henson and Archbishop Lang. In July 1936, the Spanish Civil War began, and the likes of Orwell and Hemingway joined the Republican International Brigades which fought against the Fascists. On 26 April 1937, German bombers pounded Guernica, while Picasso painted an iconic picture of the sustained terror bombing of a civilian population, an awful harbinger of things to come. Meanwhile, across the world, the Japanese advanced into China. On the nights of 9 and 10 November 1938, a rampage of destruction was launched against German Jews on what became known as *Kristallnacht* (because of the breaking of so much glass). Thirty thousand Jews were arrested and placed in concentration camps such as Dachau, set up in March 1933.

The response in England to this growing catalogue of atrocities was conflicted. Baldwin had seen a war coming, but by 1937 was too tired to do much about it; he saw Churchill as the coming war leader. Chamberlain, Lord Halifax and several in the Cabinet acted as "appeasers" and were later called the "guilty men" in a pamphlet written by Michael Foot in 1940 for their failure to prepare for war. When Chamberlain returned from Munich in September 1938, with what he thought was "peace in our time", there was great relief in most quarters, but some clergy, like Dean Duncan-Jones of Chichester, saw Munich "as the most shameful betrayal [of Czechoslovakia] in English History".[41] Archbishop Lang contrastingly saw Munich as the "hand of God".[42] And at Oxford, the Christian Lord Hailsham stood in October 1938 in a by-election against the Master of Balliol, the left-wing Christian A. D. Lindsay. Lord Hailsham, or Quintin Hogg, was for appeasement, Lindsay for resistance. Hailsham narrowly won. Oxford was conflicted, the Church was conflicted, and the nation was conflicted in their response to Hitler: longing for peace, many could not prepare mentally for war.

Two clergy who held very different worldviews in the late 1930s were George Bell, Bishop of Chichester, and the Dean of Canterbury, Hewlett Johnston. Both were to become national figures for completely different reasons. By 1937, Johnston was intent on supporting and publicizing socialism wherever he found it. He went on a tour of Spain during the Civil War, supporting the Republicans, and was rebuked by Lang for eulogizing the Republican cause. In reply, Johnston wrote to the archbishop, "We have condoned an economic and social order [capitalism] which is sub-Christian. And now there arises another order [communism], more fundamentally Christian in essence, however much it repudiates the name. This suggestion of another order, where the service motive radically replaces the profit motive, and where class, sex and racial barriers disappear, has gripped the imagination."[43] In September 1937, Johnston went to Moscow and was entertained by VOKS, a Stalinist organization that aimed to persuade visiting intellectuals that communism was enlightened. In 1939, Johnston published *The Socialist Sixth of the World*, in which he extolled the Russian Revolution and the state-controlled economy. He never appreciated the totalitarianism of Stalin's Russia: the gulags, the terror, the purges and the famines. What was especially surprising was that a cleric in England's premier cathedral should remain convinced of these things for the rest of his life.

By contrast, George Bell (1883–1958), Bishop of Chichester, supported the Confessing Lutheran Church in Germany and its foremost leader, Dietrich Bonhoeffer. The two men shared 4 February as their birthday, although Bell was twenty years Bonhoeffer's senior.[44] Bell had previously been a student (don) at Christ Church, Oxford, chaplain to Archbishop Davidson, and then Dean of Canterbury, where he commissioned T. S. Eliot's *Murder in the Cathedral*, itself a critique of the overweening power of the Reich. He was appointed bishop in 1929 and died in office in 1958. Bell and Bonhoeffer first met on 21 November 1933 at Chichester and became firm friends. In 1942, Bonhoeffer wrote to Bell after they had briefly met in Sweden: "I think these days will remain in my memory as some of the greatest of my life. This spirit of fellowship and of Christian brotherliness will carry me through the darkest hours, and even if things get worse than we hope and expect, the light of these days will never extinguish in my heart."[45] Bonhoeffer sent his last message to Bell before he was executed in 1945, having been arrested for involvement in a conspiracy to kill Hitler.

Bell had always been anxious about the effects of the Treaty of Versailles, and the conditions of economic instability and national resentment it fostered in Germany, a narrative the Nazis always played to their own political advantage. Bell chaired the Committee for International Refugees, especially those who were

Jewish and Christian. He sheltered some in his home. When war came, he had deep reservations about the bombing of civilians—especially its final months as symbolized by Dresden—which, by the end of the war, had claimed 600,000 German civilians, a fifth of whom were children. He wrote to *The Times* as early as 1941 deploring bombing of German towns and spoke powerfully against it in the House of Lords in 1944, for which he was not popular. (Thirty-seven years after his death, child abuse allegations were made against Bishop Bell, but after lengthy enquiries these were found to be unfounded.)

War came in September 1939, but the existing government led by Chamberlain was in no position to prosecute it. Soon the Commons, led in fact by the Labour Party, turned to Churchill. His hour had come. Although no friend of the Church, Churchill had a sense of destiny, providence and the hand of the Almighty. He certainly believed he had been spared for this moment.

The shape of the war is well known, especially those parts that affected England. The rescue of the Expeditionary Force from Dunkirk under Lord Gort, VC, a hero of the Great War, seemed like a miracle. For nine days, 338,226 troops were evacuated. It was "a miracle of deliverance", Churchill said in his speech in the House of Commons on 4 June 1940. This was followed by the Battle of Britain from July to October 1940, when "so much was owed by so many to so few". And then the Blitz began in London and spread to Coventry, Liverpool, Plymouth, Hull, Southampton, Portsmouth and many other cities from September 1940. If Hitler could not defeat Britain on the continent, he and Hermann Goering would break her at home. The Blitz culminated with an attack on London on 10 May 1941 when Lambeth Palace, Westminster, the House of Commons and countless homes were badly damaged.

Churchill led the resistance with mental resolution, saying, "Every night I try myself by court martial to see if I have done anything effective during the day. I don't mean pawing the ground; anyone can go through the motions: but something really effective."[46] Not until 15 November 1942 did the tide turn against Nazi Germany at El Alamein, when church bells were permitted to ring. In the east at Stalingrad, the most disastrous of battles led to the encircling and surrender of Field Marshal Paulus's army group to the Russians. When on 7 December 1942 the Japanese attacked the US Pacific Fleet in Pearl Harbour, Roosevelt joined the war. Eighteen months later, on 6 June 1944, the Allies launched the largest invasion force in history on the Normandy beaches. In less than a year, despite stiff resistance, Germany surrendered. In the east, the war with Japan went on until 9 August 1945, when a second atomic bomb was dropped on Nagasaki, after the one on Hiroshima, with massive loss of life of 200,000 in the two cities.

The legacy of the war was incalculable. Over fifty million died. Civilian populations had been terrorized on all sides. The Holocaust, with all its appalling evil, was laid bare as armies liberated Auschwitz, Bergen Belsen, Dachau, Ravensbrück and other concentration camps. The map of Europe was once again politically redrawn; as Churchill said in his 1946 speech an "Iron Curtain" had come down from Stettin in the Baltic to Trieste on the Adriatic. Eastern Europe and its churches suffered from prolonged and sometimes brutal repression. Bibles were banned and had to be smuggled to the East.

There were also innumerable stories of humanity, Christian love and human care that came out of the war. The churches provided chaplains to the forces and care of the population at home. One chaplain, Graham Smith, was captured at Boulogne, where he was serving in the military hospital. He spent nearly five years in the POW camp at Obermassfeld, ministering to the prisoners, taking weekly services and acting as an orderly in the camp hospital. He was freed by American forces and rewarded with an MBE.[47] Bishop Wilson of Singapore, when faced with torture in a Japanese POW camp, remembered the floggings he had received at St John's, Leatherhead, which he regarded as good preparation for his POW experiences under the Japanese: "Well, thank heaven I went to St John's Leatherhead!", he responded with indefatigable humour. With great grace he saw his captors as they had once been, playful children, only now corrupted by a brutal system, so he prayed for them.[48]

Leonard Cheshire, who witnessed the dropping of the atomic bomb on Nagasaki, was haunted by it for the rest of his life, although he believed it was justified. He devoted himself to establishing Cheshire Homes for the disabled. His wife, Sue Ryder, Baroness Ryder of Warsaw, brought relief to that stricken city, where 200,000 died in the Warsaw Uprising.

William Alchin, a young soldier captured by the Japanese, first heard the Gospel preached at the camp on the River Kwai. To communicate with his guards, he learnt Japanese.

At the start of the war in France, a quartermaster sergeant recorded on 16 June 1940 that he "took Holy Communion at an 8 am service outside farmhouse with small table for altar. Received a great deal of consolation from it. The guns were silent during the service and the birds sang sweetly."[49]

On the way over to Normandy, on board the ship *Princess Ingrid*, a service was held, one of many, but it was less than consoling. The service was held in the bows, but the altar cloth flew off, and the cross fell to the deck and broke in two. Elsewhere men quietly read their Bibles.

In England, the churches were not idle in the war years. Ecumenism moved forward under the duress of war. Cardinal Archbishop Hinsley of Westminster (1865–1943), a man of unusual warmth and compassion, forged a strong bond with William Temple. The Sword and the Spirit Conference in the Stoll Theatre, London, in May 1941, brought together delegates from most denominations following the worst night of the Blitz. Archbishop Lang came to the conference through a gravely damaged Lambeth Palace. Bishop Bell said to Archbishop Hinsley, "Eminence, may we say the Our Father together."[50] Almost for the first time—as Roman Catholics hitherto would not pray with heretics—the company led by Cardinal Hinsley prayed the Lord's Prayer. Later, other Catholics reproved Hinsley, but he had broken the dam.

In March 1943, Temple spoke powerfully in the House of Lords, demanding that every assistance should be given to Jews in finding asylum in Britain or Palestine and that the railheads at Auschwitz should be bombed, but his words fell on deaf ears. Earlier, in 1938, the *Kindertransport* programme had rescued 10,000 children from Nazi Germany, at the instigation of British Jews and Quakers. One child thus transported was Rolf Harding, a German Jew from Hamburg. He became a Christian in England, was ordained and served with distinction, ably supported by his wife Elizabeth, in parishes in Essex and Bath.

Through the war, C. S. Lewis had begun publishing his Christian works: *The Problem of Pain*, succeeded by *The Screwtape Letters*. He had also become a frequent broadcaster on the BBC. Likewise, Temple's *Christianity and the Social Order*, Sayers's *The Man Born to Be King* and T. S. Eliot's "Little Gidding", completing *Four Quartets*, were all published in 1942. Pacifism, which had grown to be a movement in the 1930s under Dick Sheppard, a canon of St Paul's and a man of intense emotion but little analytical thinking, now had tens of thousands of followers. The remarkable Vera Brittain, a nurse during the First World War, a graduate of Somerville, Oxford, and mother of Shirley Williams, like many others was a practical pacifist working as a fire-warden and raising money for food relief.

During the war years, people deeply influenced by Christian faith worked out the shape of new social policy. Sir William Beveridge, while working with his Anglo-Catholic and socialist brother-in-law, R. H. Tawney, brought forward his Report, which would prove to be a foundation stone of the welfare state. Likewise, R. A. Butler, in close consultation with Temple, shaped his great Education Act of 1944, to which we shall return. Together, Beveridge, Butler and later Bevan formed the social basis of post-war English society. Temple, who died in 1944 soon after taking office as archbishop in 1942, was closely associated with this great work of educational reform.

Who could have guessed that the end of the war would usher in such dramatic political changes, constructing a sort of "New Deal" in the United Kingdom, in which the Church must find a distinct role? In the United States, Roosevelt died in April 1945. Stalin dominated Eastern Europe until his death in 1953. Both were to develop nuclear weapons. In July 1945, Churchill was voted out of office: the British public saw him as a great war leader and deliverer, but not a social reformer. Attlee succeeded Churchill and began constructing the fabric of social Britain as we now know it and disposing of the Empire, beginning with India. Within seven years, King George VI, exhausted by the war, died and a new Elizabethan age began.

CHAPTER 21

The Second Elizabethan Age

The election of 26 July 1945 saw Labour record a landslide victory: they gained nearly four hundred seats; the Conservatives won 210. Clement Attlee, Churchill's deputy in the war-time coalition, became prime minister, and so began an administration which, more than any other, shaped modern Britain (probably more so than the Thatcher administrations following 1979). The pillars of this new Britain were the establishment of the National Health Service pioneered by Aneurin Bevan, the construction of the welfare state based on the Beveridge Report, and the entrenchment of Butler's Education Act of 1944.

In foreign affairs, Ernest Bevin, one-time orphan and dock worker, became one of Britain's greatest foreign secretaries. He began the process of dismantling the Empire, beginning with India and Pakistan in 1947. Under his stewardship, the United Nations, World Bank and IMF began. He also coordinated the West's response to the Soviet Union under Stalin at the beginning of the Cold War by persuading President Truman to commit to the NATO Alliance, which then became the cornerstone of British foreign policy. Already in 1948, the Soviet Union had sought to choke Berlin of its supplies, precipitating the Berlin Airlift.

Attlee was a terse prime minister, with as few words as Churchill had many, and as little flourish as Churchill had much. If Churchill won the war, Attlee won the peace. Coming from a Christian home with Bible reading and prayer at the start of every day, he was the product of Haileybury School and Oxford.[1] From early on, he was drawn into encouraging social change, and helped to reform the Poor Law with the Webbs in 1909. He fought courageously in the First World War and took part in the Gallipoli campaign as a company commander in the South Lancashires, whose men were drawn from Warrington, Wigan and Liverpool. He was elected an MP in 1922, after being a reforming mayor of Stepney. He would become a unifying member of the Labour Party, giving support to Churchill, especially in May 1940.

When he came to power in July 1945, Attlee had a brilliant cabinet. Aneurin Bevan was determined to establish the National Health Service. He won over consultant doctors by allowing them to continue in private practice. He allayed the fears of the British Medical Association, 80 per cent of whose members opposed the NHS, and he championed the cause of "health for all" with inspiring oratory and a clear grasp of administration. Herbert Morrison, Sir Stafford Cripps— another Christian socialist—and Hugh Dalton oversaw the establishment of the welfare state with its "cradle to grave" provision based on National Insurance. Great swathes of the economy were nationalized in the next four years: mining, the railways, gas, electricity, the airlines, iron and steel. Millions of workers were paid by the government and more were needed from abroad, especially for the Health Service. Thus porters, orderlies and council workers were brought over from the West Indies on the SS *Windrush* and given rights of citizenship. (In an administrative fiasco in 2018 the citizenship of many was questioned, and some were threatened with deportation, in an egregious failure by the Home Office.) Forty years later, Margaret Thatcher's government privatized much of what had been nationalized, re-tilting the economy from state to privately-owned industries, but the foundations of the welfare state were established for good. Welfare, health and education were now firmly the government's responsibility. The Church, which had been so instrumental in the beginnings of education and health, had been a midwife to their birth. Future governments would change methods of delivery of these services, but a Rubicon had been crossed which could never be reversed.

Butler's Education Act passed in 1944 and provided the way forward for the nation's learning. Butler's great achievement was to bring a settlement to the sparring religious parties over education. It was his good fortune that he was able to work with a cooperative Archbishop Temple of Canterbury and the Labour shadow education secretary, James Chuter Ede. A system was devised whereby denominational schools could be taken under state control. These church schools could either opt for *voluntary controlled*—in effect fully funded by the state—or *voluntary aided*, in which schools had state subsidies, but could remain autonomous over admissions. Local education authorities (LEAs) took responsibility for providing a mix of secondary education: grammar schools (with an Eleven Plus examination), secondary moderns with no entry test, and technical schools providing vocational training.

By the 1960s, grammar and secondary schools in many LEAs were merged into comprehensives. By 1980, 90 per cent of secondary schools were comprehensives. The effect of Butler's changes was that the Church of England primary schools fell to being one in three of all primaries, and Roman Catholics increased their secondary schools to one in ten. Broadly speaking, the Roman Catholic Church was more unwilling to lose its independence, while the Anglican and Free Church schools were grateful for the support. The school leaving age went up to fifteen. An act of worship was expected each day in all schools, which soon became a bone of contention. Public or independent schools were endorsed, and a greater number of assisted places provided. Butler's Education Act stood for more or less forty years through the surge in comprehensive school education from the 1960s to the 1980s, until these were overtaken by new academy schools initiated by Tony Blair's government, with the accompanying diminution of influence of the LEAs.

The 1940s had been years of recovery and hardship following the war, of radical implementation of new social provision, and of social change. The winter of 1946-7 had been the harshest, and rationing was still enforced for food and clothing. Hardship followed peace, in the same way the flu pandemic of 1918-19 had followed the First World War (the epidemic claimed 59 million lives world-wide.) There were strict rules on taking currency outside the country, but gradually things were easing and there were signs of a new dawn: Princess Elizabeth married Prince Philip of Greece and the following year Prince Charles was born; the Olympics came to London in 1948; and in 1951 Churchill was returned to power in the hope of providing more affordable housing, the one weak spot of Attlee's government.

The 1950s: An Indian summer for the churches

Churchill's second premiership, which lasted from October 1951 until April 1955, was like "a vast commemorative pageant for the great days of the war".[2] This term was marked by ambitions for summitry that included four transatlantic visits, entering the nuclear arms race, building hundreds of thousands of houses under Macmillan's Ministry of Housing, and finally Churchill himself facing the onset of illness and of time running out. His successor, Sir Anthony Eden, risked all on intervening in Egypt in 1956, provoking the Suez Crisis and pitifully displaying the denouement of British imperial power. Having waited for the crown so long, Eden found it turned to dust and ashes on his head. Macmillan, "Super Mac", succeeded and continued the ending of empire, while assuring the public at home that "some of you have never had it so good".

By the mid-1950s, there was a sense of stability in the country and growing prosperity. There was full employment. For very many there was a weekly trip to the pictures. Cinemas in Britain could accommodate four million and cost only 10 pence a go (the equivalent of 4p today). The BBC had resumed its television broadcasts in 1946, while the *Third Programme* and the *Light Programme* began on the radio. The *Goon Show* was the Monty Python of the 1950s. The *Archers* also began at this time: a story of country folk in Ambridge which also tracked social change in rural England. In 1951, the Festival of Britain raised the nation's spirits. Then, after the sadness of George VI's premature death, deeply mourned by the nation, the coronation of Queen Elizabeth became a broadcasting milestone— suggested by the Queen herself—and was led by the awed tones of Richard Dimbleby. Elsewhere in the world, Hillary and Sherpa Tenzing were conquering Everest, while in Cambridge Crick and Watson were discovering the double helix as the basis for DNA. These were signals for a new age to begin. It would be one of the ironies of the age that no monarch had a more personal or vital Christian faith, but the nation, by degrees, sought to slip, either by intent or carelessness (or both), from its time-honoured Christian mooring.

In the 1950s, the Church experienced something of an Indian summer of faith. Intellectually, there was a mixture of ground-breaking Christian apologetics, brilliantly crafted by remarkable, artistic and imaginative talent, but opposed by an emerging, but not yet too aggressive, agnosticism or atheism. The great apologist for Christianity was C. S. Lewis. During the war, he saw evacuated children crowding the churches around Oxford where he lived with little understanding of the Christian faith, and so began the Narnia series, perhaps Lewis's greatest legacy. *The Lion, The Witch and the Wardrobe* was published in October 1950. Like the characters in his timeless stories, Lewis crossed a threshold from apologetics based on reason to one based in imagination; from intellectual propositions to mythical symbols capable of communicating truth more powerfully, viscerally and memorably in what was even then a less biblically literate age. Six more Narnia tales followed, culminating in 1956 in the seventh and final one: *The Last Battle*.

Likewise, Lewis's Oxford colleague, J. R. R. Tolkien, a devout Roman Catholic, published *The Lord of the Rings* in 1954–5, having previously written *The Hobbit*, published in 1937, for his own children. Tolkien had been at the Somme in 1916, and no doubt that experience of warfare coloured his description of giant forces at war. For Tolkien, mythology symbolized truth, and the continual struggle between good and evil in the world. His work *The Silmarillion* came closest to depicting the Christian story of incarnation and the consequent deliverance of humankind, and of a creation through harmony best symbolized by music (as suggested by Augustine's *De Musica*). Lewis and Tolkien gave the world a literature that transcended reason, and yet at the same time Lewis's *Mere Christianity* (1952) and *Surprised by Joy* (1955) offered a reasoned explanation for the faith based on personal reflection and experience—honestly related—that would influence and persuade millions.

The 1950s were an extraordinarily productive time for Christian literature. T. S. Eliot had become an acknowledged master poet, having published his most overtly Christian work, *Four Quartets*, in the 1940s. Drawing on the insights of mystics like Julian of Norwich and St John of the Cross, Eliot saw Christ, rather than science or reason, as the way to harmony and redemption (see especially *Burnt Norton* and *East Coker*). Other Catholic writers—although hardly orthodox—were Graham Greene and Evelyn Waugh. The most popular of Waugh's novels was *Brideshead Revisited*, later to be turned into a classic television series with a haunting soundtrack by Granada Television. The work charts the decline of an aristocratic Catholic dynasty personified in the woes of Lady Marchmain, who takes upon herself the failures of her family: Lord Marchmain's dissolute life in Venice, her daughter Julia's engagement to a political spiv, Rex Mottram MP, and her drunken second son Sebastian were collectively her cross to bear. "[She] took all these sorrows with her daily to church: it seemed her heart was transfixed with swords of her dolours, a living heart to match plaster and paint: what comfort she took home, God knows."[3] *Brideshead Revisited* remains a caricature of decaying elite Catholicism, a million miles from the experience of most Catholics living in Liverpool or Glasgow. The record was put right in Waugh's later war trilogy, *Sword of Honour*, where the Catholic hero, Guy Crouchback, is an unassuming Englishman whose love of tradition and heroism is not enough to secure his future in the modern world.

Alongside these spiritually inspired writers were great artists and composers. The artist Stanley Spencer depicted Christianity in a kind of modern miracle play in his *Christ Preaching at Cookham Regatta*. Benjamin Britten, the greatest modern English composer, composed *Noye's Fludde*, first performed in Orford Church in June 1958 and based on a fifteenth-century Chester mystery play. Graham Sutherland, Jacob Epstein—the father of modern British sculpture—Basil Spence, the architect, John Piper and Patrick Reyntiens came together to build and decorate the new cathedral at Coventry. And there, on what must have been an unforgettable occasion, Britten's *War Requiem* was performed on 30 May 1962, using the war poems of Wilfred Owen.

Against such an outpouring of inspired art, contextualized by the suffering and loss of life in two world wars, the agnosticism of the 1950s did not make significant or strident headway. Yes, there was the logical positivism of Oxford's A. J. Ayer (1910–89), who was essentially the heir to David Hume. For Ayer, propositions that could not be proven were meaningless. At the same time, in Cambridge, Ludwig Wittgenstein (1889–1951), the pupil of Bertrand Russell (1872–1970), was not comfortable following Russell's view of religion as being merely superstition. Although an agnostic himself, Wittgenstein would not follow the positivism of Ayer and sought to puncture this new orthodoxy. He left the door open to religious faith which the empirical positivists had sought to close off emphatically.

If these were some of the artistic, philosophical and Christian streams flowing through this period of fertile reflection in the aftermath of war, the churches themselves were experiencing a period of confidence and support in the context of greater general optimism. A new young queen with evident faith was also a powerful symbol of this hope for the future. As if to endorse this, the Church of England found itself led by a conservative administrator, Geoffrey Fisher, following the premature death of William Temple (Archbishop 1942–4). The more inspiring and interesting, but probably less well suited, Bishop Bell was passed over. Fisher's tenure would span the 1950s (1945–61). If archbishops can be divided into scholars, statesmen, pioneers, pastors and administrators, Fisher was definitely the headmaster-administrator to his fingertips, having been headmaster of Repton and then Bishop of London. It was a question of the administrator sandwiched between the statesman (Temple) and the scholar-theologian (Ramsey), and probably this alternation of talent responded to the needs of the Church. Fisher, born in a rectory, where his father served for forty-three years in a family living (parish) in Leicestershire, was Anglican to his fingertips. He pursued church unity, visiting Pope John XXIII in 1960, ruled by edict, formed the Church Commissioners, pooled all parish endowments in diocesan trusts, standardized clergy salaries (£500 p.a.), built churches in new post-war housing estates, and chaired two successful Lambeth Conferences. Politically, he opposed Eden's policy in Suez, denounced Macmillan's phrase "you have never had it so good", and described Archbishop Makarios, the leader of the Greek Cypriots in a time of struggle, as a "low character". He also exercised the right, soon to be discontinued, of seeing the prime minister when he wished. For a modern state it was an almost medieval style, certainly a Victorian one.

During Fisher's archiepiscopate, the Evangelical wing of the Church of England thrived, not so much because of his personal support, but because of the fruition of strategies put in place in the 1940s. There was a general sense that the nation needed to be re-evangelized after the war and, in 1945, the Church of England published the report *Towards the Conversion of England*. The commission that wrote it was chaired by Christopher Chavasse, the Bishop of Rochester. Clergy numbers had drastically fallen during the war, with numbers of curates reduced from 4,554 in 1938 to 2,189 in 1946. It was also still a rural church, with 41.7 per cent of clergy serving 11.2 per cent of the population. Pastoral reorganization began, ten-bedroomed vicarages were being sold, and the Parish and People movement advocated weekly communion as the central service on Sundays. However, the answer as to why the Church flourished in the 1950s came from elsewhere.

There were two events that turned the tide in the 1950s, both to do with individual ministries. The first was the 1950 appointment of John Stott as the Rector of All Souls, Langham Place after he had been curate there for five years. He had been led to faith in Christ whilst at Rugby School by Eric Nash, of whom we heard earlier. Stott would remain at All Souls as rector and then rector emeritus until 2007. We shall chart his profound influence on the Church during the next fifty years: suffice it now to say that he formed a pattern of Evangelical Anglican parish ministry that would become an example for hundreds, if not thousands, of other parish clergy. This pattern centred on faithful biblical preaching; engaging worship; sensitive pastoral care and nurture in groups; a personal Evangelical challenge to faith in Christ; and clear parochial strategies supported by efficient administration and developed from true knowledge (based on surveys) of a parish. In the early days of his work at All Souls, Stott drew into his team two curates who would also profoundly affect the Anglican Church and its mission. They were Michael Harper and John Collins. The other individual to have great impact on the Church in England was Billy Graham.

Billy Graham (1918–2018), who was given the support of the Queen from 1955, conducted a "Greater London Crusade" for three full months in the spring of 1954. The total audience over that period was 1.3 million, with the concluding night at Wembley Stadium and the White City having an audience of 180,000, with the Archbishop present. Graham's preaching was straightforward, biblical, clear, with attractive illustrations and tethered to the issues confronting the modern world. He always ended with an appeal to make a decision to follow Christ. His matinée good looks and charm made him a striking presence. His rallies were attended by large choirs in their thousands and well-organized "counsellors" who spoke at the end of the evening to those who "had come out of their seats" and made "a decision" to follow Christ. Over the coming three decades, until 1989, Graham would frequently return to England. The effects of this first mission, as well as other university missions at Oxford and Cambridge in the 1950s conducted by Stott and Graham, were the strengthening of the churches and, in the universities, of the Christian Unions, resulting in greater numbers of ordinands going forward for ministerial training.

Alongside these signs of the reinvigoration of Christian faith there was also evidence that parts of the Church were in the early stages of decline. In Sheffield, up to a third of church membership was lost over thirty years. In London, the great preachers, Leslie Weatherhead at the City Temple, W. E. Sangster at Central Hall Westminster, Donald Soper at the Kingsway Hall, and Dr Martyn Lloyd Jones (1899–1981) at Westminster Chapel, held sway. The latter, Lloyd Jones, became the doyenne of expository preaching in London. Each of these leaders had different emphases: Soper was socially more radical, Lloyd Jones more expository and Evangelical, Weatherhead more psychological and therapeutic, and Sangster was a well-crafted communicator of the gospel. Increasingly, their appeal was to a middle-class audience. By 1957, Methodist Sunday schools, which had numbered 1.3 million members in 1921, were at only 699,000.

At the same time, ecumenism between Anglicans and Free Churches was growing, if never brought to visible unity. Archbishop Fisher said: "What I desire is that I should freely be able to enter their churches, and they mine, in the sacraments of the Lord and in full worship and fellowship."[4] Following a report in 1963, a Methodist Anglican Union was suggested, but it was a project that was ultimately stillborn.

Perhaps a premonition of such an outcome came when, in 1951, the elder statesman of Methodism, Scott Lidgett, preached at the World Methodist Conference in Oxford at the University Church. Aged ninety-seven, he preached for forty minutes, but at the end "collapsed into unconsciousness".[5] Methodism had arrived, but at the same time showed signs of passing away! Literally thousands of chapels representing different streams of Methodism were threatened with closure. What could not be obtained in the way of union between Anglicanism and Methodism in England was successfully brought to fruition between the Anglican Church and the Church of South India, however. In the CSI, Anglicans, Methodists, Presbyterians and Congregationalists joined together, committed to future episcopal leadership, and were brought into communion with Anglicanism world-wide. What was achieved there was far harder in relation to Roman Catholicism, however.

During this period, the Roman Catholic Church remained a law unto itself. Geoffrey Fisher said in an outburst that the greatest hindrance to the advance of the kingdom of God among human beings was the intransigence of the Roman Catholic Church. Rome simply forbade inter-communion. Part of the cause of that isolation was the growing strength of the Catholic Church. The numbers of priests were up, Catholic marriages were up (12.7 per cent of all marriages in England and Wales were Catholic) and congregations were up. Polish refugees swelled the ranks of the faithful with ninety-two Polish priests. The White Fathers increased their missionary presence. There were also growing numbers of Catholics in London: the dioceses of Westminster and Southwark had 52 per cent of all Catholics in England; Liverpool's proportion was down from 58.4 per cent in 1911 to 37.8 in 1951. The influence of Catholic writing was growing, but the leadership of the Church was uninspiring. William Godfrey succeeded Bernard Griffin as Archbishop of Westminster. Both came from the English College in Rome to Westminster. Godfrey was the dominant ecclesiastic of the late 1950s, however "no one was surer of his own mind or had less to offer that was unexpected".[6] As the 1950s gave way to the 1960s, the post-war conservative mould was about to be broken.

The 1960s: All change

The 1960s sowed the seeds, for good and ill, that the rest of the century would reap. Under a conventional English façade, germs of revolution were being sown. Anyone looking at the politicians could see that they were white, male and mostly public school-educated. It was an Old Etonian Cabinet with a populist culture (some might argue that in 2020, little has changed!). Macmillan, the Prime Minister, was *outwardly* more relaxed than his predecessor, Anthony Eden, who had resigned following the Suez Crisis in 1957. Macmillan would be in office for six years, during which time the sun set more fully on the Empire, except for a recalcitrant Rhodesia. The country grew more prosperous; and the government was latterly enveloped in the Profumo scandal and the attractions of Christine Keeler. The Cold War reached a new height during the Cuba crisis of 1962, handled wisely by a new young President of the United States, John Kennedy.

In 1963, Kennedy visited Berlin and was shown the East/West divide at the Berlin Wall and the Brandenburg Gate by an equally young Brigade Commander, Rex Whitworth (the author's father); here Kennedy gave his famous "Ich bin ein Berliner" speech. Within six months, Kennedy was assassinated on 22 November 1963. The civil rights movement reached a new peak with Martin Luther King's speech in Washington in August 1963, when he declared that "I have a dream that one day this nation will rise up and live out the true meaning of its creed: 'we hold these to be self-evident: that all men are created equal'". Yet in less than five years, in April 1968, King would also be assassinated. In Britain, Macmillan, followed by Alec Douglas-Home, would give way to a new Labour government led by Harold Wilson, which arrived with a slim majority in 1963.

At the beginning of the decade, the British establishment looked as conventional as ever: bowler-hatted stockbrokers, pinstriped politicians, gaitered clergy and deference towards the professional classes. Part of the *zeitgeist* of the decade was its juxtaposition of the irreverent and the shocking against the conventional and staid. Political satire came in with *Beyond the Fringe*, brilliantly acted by Peter Cook, Dudley Moore, Alan Bennett and Jonathan Miller, followed by the television satire *That Was the Week that Was*. Much later there would be *Monty Python* and *Spitting Image*, both equally irreverent. The Church, politicians and the army were all sent up, among others. By the end of the decade, satire had been supplanted by protest. The musical *Hair*, heralding the "Age of Aquarius" with its contentious nudity scene, was a protest against repression and the injustice of the Vietnam War.

The culture of the 1960s was a heady mix of rock and pop, of the Beatles, the Rolling Stones, Bob Dylan, and Simon and Garfunkel, among many others. A spiritual quest, however confected, was expressed in transcendental meditation, eastern mysticism of Indian extraction, drugs—from marijuana to LSD and cocaine—and a search for new experiences, whether sexual, spiritual or political. Sexual permissiveness was made possible in part by the pill. The mini skirt and the Mini car were emblems of the 1960s in Britain and, in a surge of youthful aspiration, a transatlantic culture took shape in Boston and San Francisco as much as in Liverpool and London. John Lennon, killed in 1980, was the prophet and the martyr of this culture. His song "Imagine", which begins with the thought, "Imagine there is no heaven", is regularly voted the most popular song of the post-war era.

It was a culture fuelled by greater prosperity and the end of the restraint, rationing and austerity imposed by the sacrifice of the war. Yet it also took shape under the possibility of mutual nuclear destruction. In 1968, students from this culture took to the streets in Paris, the United States, Berlin and London, taking on dyed-in-the-wool governments and in particular protesting against the Vietnam War, now mired in the Viet Cong Tet Offensive. The repression of the Prague Spring that year was a reminder to the more romantic Marxists among the students that the Soviet Union had not grown any more mellow with age. Real freedom for Eastern Europe would not come for another twenty years with the tearing down of the Berlin Wall in 1989.

If the culture of the 1960s can be dismissed as a period of self-indulgence after long years of struggle, as many certainly do, there was an important philosophical shift going on as well, with profound repercussions for the Church and society in the coming years. Compared with Germany, France, and indeed Scotland,

England tends to pride itself on pragmatism and practicality, rather than being consciously driven by the twists and turns of philosophical thought. Broadly speaking, the Romantic movement of the early nineteenth century, which had succeeded the ideas of Kant about the primacy of pure reason, was in turn replaced by the utilitarianism of the mid-nineteenth century, that is, the view that human activity must give the greatest happiness to the greatest number. Parts of the Church in England had linked themselves with the Gothic Romantic movement, as expressed by Tractarianism in the mid-nineteenth century. Now, after two world wars, a new popular movement was taking root, superseding the empirical and logical positivist movement expressed by Bertrand Russell and A. J. Ayer, and the exaltation of power and will of Nietzsche, who had pronounced the death of God.

The relatively new philosophy was existentialism, as expressed by the Danish philosopher Søren Kierkegaard (1813–55). Above all, it was a philosophy that placed the individual *centre stage* along with the search for fulfilment through individual value systems and choices. The French writers Sartre and Camus would take up the central theme of existentialism: each person must find their own truth, and be true to their own existence, values and history. In a society that was becoming ever more plural, it was a form of thinking that allowed relativism and dispensed with the possibility of objective truth and a religious metanarrative of the world. There was no longer right or wrong ways of thinking, just ways of thinking that were right for each person provided they did not harm others. The anarchy of this position taken to extremes can be seen in the play *Look Back in Anger* (1956) by John Osborne, in the search for meaning of Samuel Beckett's *Waiting for Godot* (1955), for Godot never comes, and in the search for significance in *Happy Days* (1962), also by Beckett.

Harold Pinter continued this anarchic surge of writing: impugning governments, politicians and institutions. This shift in philosophy eventually took the name "postmodern", with an overarching inclusivity as its creed. Postmodernism posed an existential question for the Church about communicating the objective truths at its core to a generation that was in the process of overturning such thinking. Beneath the more superficial change in culture in the 1960s, deeper and more penetrating questions needed to be addressed. While it is clear that society was on the move, was the Church likewise? How could it hold to the objective truths that underpinned the Gospel and the way of life that followed from them?

The 1960s would also see a stream of socially liberalizing legislation that was in keeping with the movement of culture in society. Like all the governments of this period, the Labour government (1964–70) led by Harold Wilson struggled with economic issues: a weakening pound, devalued from £2.80 to £2.40 in 1967, relations with trade unions, inflation and a balance of payment deficit. The government sought also to harness the "white heat" of science and technology in the implementation of progress. Alongside this was the implementation of social reform, so that people might pursue their inclinations.

Roy Jenkins, who was home secretary, saw it as "civilizing society". The death penalty was abolished in 1965, while in 1966 the Abortion Act, a private member's bill sponsored by David Steel, came into law supported in a poll by 70 per cent of the electorate. In 2014, the figures for abortion remained fairly constant at 185,824 a year in England and Wales. In 1967, following the recommendations of the Wolfenden Report ten years previously, homosexual acts between consenting adults (over twenty-one) were legalized and a new Divorce Law Reform Act of 1969 replaced the concept of matrimonial offence (usually adultery) with that of breakdown of marriage. Within two years, the number of divorces doubled, and by the 1980s it stood at 160,000 a year. Thus, within a five-year period, the moral compass of the nation had been largely reset by a secular society. How would a church that had traditionally taught the sanctity of marriage respond? (For example, in 1955 and under pressure from Archbishop Fisher, Princess Margaret abandoned ideas of marrying the divorcée, Group Captain Peter Townsend. The Church had also condemned homosexual acts, taught celibacy outside marriage and faithfulness in it, and had championed the protection of the unborn child.) Further, how would the Church respond to a society which rapidly and *rightly* saw discrimination against people on the grounds of sex, race, religion and age as offensive, and in some cases even a criminal offence?

On 28 October 1958, white smoke rose above the Sistine Chapel and Cardinal Angelo Guiseppe Roncalli was elected Pope. He was seventy-six. It had taken eleven ballots to elect a pope, and it was thought that he would merely be a caretaker pope. Instead, he called the Second Vatican Council. The council and the pope were like a breath of fresh air. Pope John was of peasant stock, had been a sergeant in the First World War, and was of a practical, humorous and positive turn of mind. The council opened on 11 October 1962 in St Peter's. There was great anticipation world-wide. Theologians previously banned, including Karl Rahner, Teilhard de Chardin, Henri de Lubac and Hans Urs von Balthasar, were brought in from the cold. A young Hans Küng wrote expectantly of the council's prospects. The council reached out through the new Secretariat of Unity to other churches, including the Orthodox and Anglican. It provided for the Latin mass to be replaced by vernacular liturgies in mother tongues; it opened up issues for discussion; it consolidated a new body of doctrine based on scripture and the

Church Fathers, and a less monarchical view of the Church, now seen primarily as "the People of God", united by faith and the Holy Spirit, and by baptism and Eucharist rather than by government. In these ways the council caught both the dynamic of the New Testament and the spirit of the age. John died in June 1963, well before the end of the council, which was closed by his successor, Paul VI, in December 1965. Paul VI was a far more anxious and conflicted man—conflicted between his modernizing aspirations and his ultramontane convictions. When Michael Ramsey, the Archbishop of Canterbury, went to Rome in March 1966, the Pope and the Archbishop led a joint act of worship, and recited the "Our Father" together—a new age had come, a new warmth had arrived, and the Second Vatican Council had pioneered the way for churches to respond to each other on a different footing.

Michael Ramsey was Archbishop of Canterbury through almost all of the 1960s, from 1961 to 1974. He was the hundredth Archbishop of Canterbury, a scholar theologian who followed Fisher's gifts of headmasterly administration. It was for Ramsey to lead the response to the evident social and cultural changes in England, and to respond to the changes overseas, especially in Africa. Ramsey was a theologian with a deeply reflective nature and catholic/sacramental instincts, although his father had been a Congregational minister. He took a first in theology from Cambridge as an ordinand; later, in 1950, he became the Regius Professor of Divinity, lecturing on redemption and the New Testament. He was a liberal politically and became a popular and captivating speaker as President of the Cambridge Union in 1926. His gifts of thoughtfulness and devotion to scripture, to the tradition of the Church Fathers, and to reasonable explanation were now to be put to the test in the furnace of parliamentary reform.

Although Ramsey adhered to the moral orthodoxy of the Church, he found it hard to be judgemental of others or to campaign vigorously for that moral orthodoxy. He was also instinctively suspicious of large gatherings and the emotions they engendered. He had thus been cautious about the Billy Graham Crusades. He upheld orthodoxy concerning marriage (celibacy outside, faithfulness within), but he did not want to condemn those who lived in long-term stable partnerships without marrying. He upheld the sanctity of the foetus but did not call abortion infanticide. He was opposed to euthanasia but did not want to prolong life where there was no quality of life left. He supported the Bill for decriminalization of homosexuality, arguing against two of the most formidable lawyers in the House of Lords who opposed this Bill, Lords Dilhorne and Kilmuir. Kilmuir had prosecuted Nazi war criminals at Nuremberg and was no slouch at cross-examination. Ramsey did not bless homosexuality, but he did not want it to be criminalized. He voted for the abolition of capital punishment, unlike Fisher, who would keep it for certain types of murder. He opposed pornography, but found it difficult to campaign with the Festival of Light led by Lord Longford (Roman Catholic), Colonel Dobbie, Malcolm Muggeridge—a popular and brilliant Christian journalist—and Bishop Trevor Huddleston, fearing that it gave credence to the idea that lust was the worst sin, rather than greed, oppression or prejudice.

He opposed all racial prejudice, accepted immigration (earlier opposing Macmillan's cap in 1962) and was the chair of Wilson's National Committee for Commonwealth Immigrants in 1964. Before any substantial Race Relations Act was formulated, the committee collected evidence of racism and informed the government. Immigration was increasing from the Commonwealth and, in 1968, Kenya's Asians were expelled and came to England. A further 27,000 were to follow from Uganda in 1972. A Race Relations Act was passed in 1965, but in the process of supporting its necessity, Ramsey experienced the racism of many. The Act was timely: three years later, Enoch Powell made his "Rivers of Blood" speech predicting violence if immigration continued.

Although Ramsey sought to respond to the liberalizing agenda of the 1960s, the Church, and in particular the Church of England, was unsure in its response. The three wings of the Church—the sacramental, the liberal and the Evangelical—were notable for their differing approaches, and indeed as we shall see, that response was itself emerging because the Anglican Church faced a set of circumstances never experienced before.

The liberal response was headed by John Robinson. By liberal, I mean someone who sets reason over scripture and tradition. Robinson had become Bishop of Woolwich while Mervyn Stockwood was Bishop of Southwark. Stockwood was a well-known liberal Catholic and publicist. Robinson had previously served as Stockwood's curate in Bristol. A conservative scholar in his views on the authorship and dating of the New Testament, Robinson was nonetheless radical in theology and ethics. He took the stand for the defence in his role as bishop in the 1960 prosecution of Penguin Books, charged with obscenity for publishing D. H. Lawrence's *Lady Chatterley's Lover*. But he was at his most radical in the publication of *Honest to God* in 1963. That book sought to synthesize the teaching of Bonhoeffer and Tillich, with the missionary intention of interpreting Christianity to modern scientific, secular and materialist people. In so doing, Robinson described God, using Tillich's words, as "the Ground of our being". He adopted a new language, sought to abandon the supernatural, and jettisoned the idea of judgement. In a word, like much of the German school of biblical criticism advocated by Bultmann and taken up by Denis Nineham in Cambridge, he wanted to de-mythologize Christianity, although in so doing he appeared to abandon its very essence. He was an able writer and communicator, but in the desire to reach out to a great population of unchurched in South London—it was said that in Battersea in the 1960s less than one per cent attended any Anglican church—he raised as many questions as he answered. During this time, "South Bank religion", a theologically radical and ethically liberal view, was advocated by Eric James, John Robinson and Mervyn Stockwood. Soon this type of theology would be found in Cambridge, led by Don Cupitt, and in time would lead to the publication of *The Myth of God Incarnate* in 1977, edited by John Hick. This was a new form of Arianism for the twentieth century, promulgated in the hope of making Christianity more palatable to the modern mind. Others sought to bridge the gap between church and society by leaving pastoral ministry and immersing themselves in the pressing needs of housing, social or welfare work. Nicholas Stacey was one such pioneer in St Mary's, Woolwich.

Another response to the 1960s culture change came from the Evangelical wing of the Church and in surprising ways. This response was centred at All Souls Langham Place in the person of the rector, John Stott, and his staff in the late 1950s and 60s. Stott was himself on a well-considered journey of faith, and the issue that concerned him was the nature of mission. Having been Rector of All Souls for ten years, by the 1960s his ministry was becoming increasingly international, and, along with Billy Graham, he was considered one of the main leaders of world-wide Evangelicalism. Yet such exposure to the world through travel brought both development and change to his outlook on mission and the response to social needs in the world. In 1966, he attended the World Congress on Evangelism in Berlin with 1,200 delegates, practically all from Protestant churches.[7] One of the major issues was "the place of social action within the purpose of world evangelization". While giving three Bible expositions on the Great Commission, Stott noted that in evangelism there must be "compassionate identification" with the needs of people, and in the divided city of Berlin what could be more necessary? Inevitably, "identification" must result in alleviation. Failure to identify, Stott noted in Berlin, led to megaphone proclamation, which was "the greatest weakness" of Evangelicals today.

Looking back on his expositions, Stott believed he should have gone further in stressing compassionate service as integral to evangelism. A year later, at the Conference of Evangelical Anglicans in Keele, the same substantial point was made. The concluding statement endorsing social action as part of Christian mission was a watershed in the life of the Evangelical Church. In 1968, Stott went to the World Council of Churches in Uppsala as an observer, ironically having to defend his attendance in the *Church of England Newspaper*. Although critical of the WCC's use of scripture and its inadequacy in defining the spiritual needs of humanity, he was impressed by the commitment to compassionate social action in mission. As he later said, "I have come to a much more holistic position. At the first National Evangelical Anglican Congress (NEAC) in England—in 1967, still seven years before Lausanne—we issued a very clear statement that evangelism and social action belonged together in the church's compassionate and sacrificial mission."[8] It was a restatement of something that had been lost since the work of Wilberforce and the Victorian reformers, but was now regained, and was in many ways a turning point in post-war Evangelicalism in England. It was not embraced by all, however. Thus, when David Sheppard (former England cricket captain and later Bishop of Liverpool) spoke at a gathering of Evangelicals (Church of England Evangelical Council) in May 1972 on "Gospel and Social Justice", some of the delegates walked out, to be rebuked by Stott later in the conference.

The other response to the spiritual challenges of the 1960s was the beginning of the Charismatic Movement in the Anglican Church, which also, surprisingly, began at All Souls Langham Place, not through Stott, who was critical of its theology, but through Michael Harper, one of his curates. The Charismatic Movement was an offshoot of the Pentecostal Movement that began in Azusa Street in 1906. It had been represented by the Elim Church in England that was defined by the empowering of Christians by the Spirit and the bestowal of spiritual gifts, particularly tongues. In the 1950s, this movement spread to England again through the writings of Dennis Bennett, who in turn influenced Michael Harper, a Cambridge graduate and curate at All Souls from 1956 to 1964.

At its heart, the Charismatic Movement taught baptism in or filling by the Spirit and the use of *charismata*, spiritual gifts or droplets of grace, as explained in 1 Corinthians 12–14, including speaking in tongues, prophecy and healing. Stott wrote against the idea of a two-stage initiation, with the second stage being baptism in the Spirit, following initial conversion, but this did not prevent the growth of the movement, which was further inspired by the Fountain Trust begun by Harper in 1964. The trust acted as a rallying point for and midwife to the infant Charismatic Movement in the 1960s and '70s. It published *Renewal* magazine from 1968 and was greatly encouraged by a similar movement in the Roman Catholic Church, thereby providing another unofficial stream of ecumenism which was to develop strongly. A further encouragement to the Charismatic Movement came from John Collins, another curate at All Souls, who later established new models of charismatic ministry in parish life as an incumbent at Gillingham in Kent. These models were ably carried on and developed by curates of Collins: David Watson,

David MacInnes and Graham Cray. All were to make a significant contribution to Anglican ministry in the coming decades.

A third and more negative movement directed at Anglican Evangelicalism was the siren voices calling for Evangelicals to leave the Church of England and unite with like-minded Evangelicals outside it. This appeal was made somewhat precipitately by Martyn Lloyd-Jones at the National Assembly of Evangelicals in 1966 and was resisted by Stott. Yet the idea of leaving the Church of England, or at least proceeding separately from Anglican structures, remained appealing to those who felt that in either doctrine or ethics, or both, the Church had departed from gospel standards. Evangelicals made themselves the main arbiters of those standards. Unlike Michael Ramsey, they tended to adhere to the gospel, but sit loose to the universal Church.[9] In the tradition of the Reformers, if the gospel was compromised by the Church, the Church must be abandoned. The seeds of these three parts of Evangelical Anglican life (alleviating social need, developing charismatic life and withdrawing from fellowship) would grow through the coming years, and are still clearly identifiable today.

During the 1960s, the Church in England showed itself more active in addressing issues of social justice and relieving poverty in the world. In 1957, the British Council of Churches started Christian Aid Week to raise money to relieve poverty in the developing world, and from 1964 the organization was named Christian Aid. Oxfam, not a specifically Christian organization, had already been founded in Oxford in 1942. Other organizations soon followed. Hospices for the dying were begun by Dr Cicely Saunders, with St Christopher's in Sydenham being the first one in 1967. Charities like Shelter, the Samaritans, Amnesty International and the Cyrenians started. Amnesty was founded by Peter Benenson, a Roman Catholic of Jewish Russian descent, in 1961. The Samaritans began in 1953 with a single telephone line to the crypt of St Stephen Walbrook, answered by Chad Varah, who incidentally remained rector there until the age of ninety-three! CAFOD, the Roman Catholic aid agency, began in 1960 when a group of Catholic women raised money for a mother and baby centre in the Caribbean. TEAR Fund, started by George Hoffman and supported by Sir Cliff Richard, began in a small way in 1959–60 in World Refugee Year.[10]

Matters of social justice were never far from the agenda of Michael Ramsey when travelling overseas. He was the first truly travelling Anglican archbishop. He travelled to the United States in nine of his years as Archbishop of Canterbury. He visited South America and met General Pinochet in Chile, of which meeting he said, "I bore my testimony firmly, as I always do, specifically about human rights."[11] Ramsey's longest visit to Africa was in 1960. He visited Nyasaland (Malawi),

Zambia and Rhodesia, five years before Ian Smith's declaration of independence from Britain, which Ramsey would resolutely oppose. Other visits would follow to Biafra in 1965. Two years later, Biafra, the mainly Christian part of Nigeria which sought to secede from that country, a British-made state containing Christians with a Muslim majority, was embroiled in civil war (1967–70) with awful and haunting consequences of famine for the most vulnerable. Ramsey sought to bring peace and to end arms shipments, but also to not take sides: it was an impossibly difficult path to follow.

Finally, in 1970, Ramsey visited South Africa. Mandela had already been in prison on Robben Island for eight years; nineteen more would follow. "Wherever Ramsey went he tried to be religious rather than political: and yet to speak of society. He would talk of Christ and humanity, of all men and women as children of God, of Christianity as brotherhood between peoples, of the way in which Christian doctrine does not recognize racial separations of individuals and groups. He stuck to the truths of the Bible, and left his hearers to apply them to their condition."[12] On 27 November, he had a meeting with John Vorster, the Prime Minister of South Africa. For Ramsey, "It was the worst day of his life."[13] Ramsey opposed selling arms to South Africa; he criticized migratory labour practices for putting stress on African marriages; he defended priests whom Vorster called subversive, such as Huddleston and Reeves; and he questioned whether "Providence" had provided such a thing as white-only areas, which was the religious justification for apartheid.

The meeting was as frosty as it was adversarial. And for good measure, on the return home, Ramsey called in on Dr Milton Obote, the Ugandan dictator; a year before Obote would be ousted by Idi Amin. Whilst there, Ramsey met a young aid-worker working among refugees from South Sudan. His name was Terry Waite.

The 1970s: Decline and fall

In the 1970s, many of the trends which began in the 60s would take their full effect. They certainly did so economically, as successive governments wrestled with the effects of inflation on prices and incomes, and on relations with trade unions whose wage demands spiralled. Unemployment returned as a by-product of inflation, running at 16–20 per cent. Ted Heath won the 1970 general election, but his tenure as prime minister proved distinctly rocky. Despite success in taking Britain into the Common Market, a Conservative goal since Macmillan, the economy was at the mercy of inflation and wage demands as high as 30 per cent by the miners. In the end, a three-day working week, petrol rationing and the opposition of the unions, particularly the miners, brought the demise of his government. Labour under Wilson and then Callaghan was back, but so were economic difficulties. A referendum in 1975 confirmed Britain's commitment to joining the Common Market (the EU) but enabling legislation in Parliament depended on Wilson getting Conservative votes in the Commons. Chancellors of the Exchequer were dependent on loans from the International Monetary Fund (IMF) to shore up the economy.

When Wilson resigned and Callaghan was elected leader in 1976, the Labour government had not long to run and, following the Winter of Discontent (1978–9) in which bodies were not buried, rubbish not cleared and a sense of crisis gripped the country, Callaghan's government seemed moribund. Following the loss of a no-confidence motion in the Commons, a general election was called. All the while the terrorist campaign of the IRA on mainland Britain, and the mounting Troubles in Northern Ireland, gave a further siege mentality to the nation. In May 1979, Margaret Thatcher was elected the first female prime minister of Britain. England was a patient ready for reform, but the medicine applied by this most unsparing and honest of doctors was a bitter pill to swallow.

Overseas troubles were no better. In 1974, President Nixon had resigned following the Watergate scandal. Terrorism emanating from the Middle East was growing rapidly. The Palestinian terrorist group Black September murdered eleven members of the Israeli Olympic team at the Olympic Games in Munich in 1972. In 1973, the Yom Kippur War took place when surrounding Arab nations attacked Israel. Israel then turned the tables on its aggressors, retaking the Golan Heights from Syria and the Sinai from Egypt. As in the Six-Day War of 1967, Israel saw off its neighbours with speed and tenacity. In 1979, a revolution in Iran had exiled the Shah, the West's ally, and replaced him with Ayatollah Khomeini. Meanwhile, the Warsaw Pact and NATO continued the Cold War, with Brezhnev maintaining a conservative but stagnant Soviet Union.

Meanwhile, the Church in England was facing decline. In 1962, the average number of converts to the Roman Catholic Church was 12,490; by 1969–72 it was 4,436, a near 60 per cent drop in ten years. The reputational damage to the Catholic Church from Pope Paul VI's encyclical on contraception, *Humanae vitae*, of 29 July 1968, forbidding any artificial means of contraception, was great. Since then, the encyclical has been seen as a call to exercise conscience, to administer its teaching with compassion, and to recognize its prophetic intent in maintaining the sanctity of the family. Nevertheless, the response to *Humanae vitae* froze Pope Paul VI's leadership. Likewise, the final years in office of Cardinal Heenan of Westminster (1963–75) were ones of "bitter depression". The Roman Catholic Church was facing considerable losses: loss of religious houses; loss of intellectual priests such as Nicholas Lash (although he remained a Catholic), who became the Norris-Hulse Professor of Divinity at Cambridge, Anthony Kenny, an Oxford philosopher, and Peter de Rosa, a writer; and a loss of coherence.

There were also forces of conservative retrenchment at work in the Catholic Church. *Pro Fide*, following the lead of the ultraconservative Archbishop Marcel Lefebvre, wanted to turn the clock back to the Latin mass, discontinue ecumenical talks like ARCIC (the Anglican Roman Catholic International Commission) and restore the authority of the papacy. Given that, under the new conservative Pope John Paul II (Pope: 1978–2005), the papacy was loyal to the reforms of the council and that John Paul II was every inch a powerful, conservative and Evangelical apostle, their stance began to look unnecessary. On the other side there were those who wanted not so much restoration as *renewal*, and they formed the Catholic Renewal Movement. Renewal of doctrine came from the more radical and out-of-favour Hans Küng, and renewal of pastoral practice came from Dr Jack Dominion, who taught on marriage and supported contraception.

Pro Fide saw members of the Renewal Movement as wolves in sheep's clothing, but the movement nevertheless gradually provided a reforming agenda for most English Catholics. Between these sparring groups, the Catholic Charismatic Movement grew and, led by Cardinal Suenens, 22,000 attended a conference at Notre Dame in 1973. Amidst some institutional withering on the vine there was hope for the future, not least with the arrival in 1976 of Basil Hume as the next leader of English Catholics. Hume would quietly and softly stay with the Catholic Renewal Movement in the face of the new monarchical conservatism of John Paul II. Although the meeting of Archbishop Runcie and John Paul II in Canterbury Cathedral in 1982 was a moving moment (especially when the Pope enveloped Runcie in a bear hug), it did not signal an institutional rapprochement between the two communions.[14]

If relations between Roman Catholics and Anglicans were thawing in the face of secular pressure on the Christian faith at large, other churches were finding the period tough going. Methodist membership continued to fall: by 1977, it was 516,798, and by 1984 it was 458,206. By 2016, it would be just 188,000. Likewise, the United Reformed Church shrank by 30 per cent from 1973 to 1984, to 132,000. Much of the shrinkage was in the great northern cities of Manchester, Newcastle, Liverpool and Sheffield, leaving Roman Catholic congregations as the largest Christian presence in these places. In 1979, Open Christian Brethren numbered 64,000 and Fellowship of Independent Evangelical Churches members, 63,100.

What is clear is that traditional Non-Conformists were experiencing substantial losses, but Baptists and smaller Non-Conformist churches declined at a lesser rate, or had their own individual stories of losses and gains. In addition, from the 1970s, new churches, mostly charismatic and sometimes called House Churches, or loose federations like New Frontiers, began to grow. By 1998, these House Churches or new churches accounted for 200,000. New Frontiers, led by Terry Virgo, and the Vineyard Church, led by John and Eleanor Mumford, were some of these. But also, the Orthodox Church became one of the fastest growing denominations in the same period.

Remarkably, the Church of England had 29,000 clergy at the turn of the twentieth century (more than the total number of ministers across all denominations now) and some 17,000 parish churches. By 1979, there were 11,337 Anglican clergy. Now there are c. 7,000 stipendiary clergy and still 16,960 parish churches. Given that Dr Beeching recommended that a third of the rail track and 55 per cent of stations be closed, Anglican branch lines in rural locations proved doughty survivors. Despite a wave of church closures in the 1960s and 70s, there were still 16,247 Anglican churches and, in recent years, many new church plants (the term for new church communities) have begun in urban areas and have also been ecumenical projects. In 1979, there were 5.4 million adults in church; in 1998 that number had reduced to 3.7 million or 7.5 per cent of the population, of which some 900,000 were Anglican. By 2017, the number of Anglicans in church on Sunday was c. 720,000. A larger proportion of those Anglican worshippers are Evangelical, and in recent years London has bucked the trend of decline with an increasing number of worshippers, representing 20 per cent of all worshippers in England and Wales. Black churches and churches with strong overseas connections, like Hillsong, which is Australian, account in part for this rise.

For the Anglican Church, the 1970s were mixed in terms of outlook. The period resembles Dr Doolittle's pushmi-pullyu, an animal with two heads pulling in opposite directions. In 1977, two quite contrary events occurred. *The Myth of God Incarnate* was published, a series of essays edited by John Hick, which argued that in speaking of the incarnation, the New Testament was culturally conditioned. The underlying premise was that, for Christianity to be believed, it must be credible to the culture of the age. The Chalcedonian understanding of Christology (that Jesus was fully divine and fully human) was regarded as incomprehensible to modern people. Three of the contributors to the book were members of the Doctrine Commission of the Church of England. Don Cupitt, one of the most forceful contributors, published *Taking Leave of God* two years later. Some church leaders looked for an episcopal response, i.e. withdrawal of the licenses of those who were ordained, but no such response was forthcoming.

In the same year, a conference succeeding the Keele Conference of 1967 took place. It was called NEAC (National Evangelical Anglican Congress) and was once again masterminded by John Stott in Nottingham University. The theme was "Obeying Christ in a Changing World". About 2,000 delegates attended. Preparatory papers were made available, with contributions from Stott, Carey, Packer and Tony Thistleton, among others. Yet already the strain of keeping a more diverse Anglican Evangelicalism together was showing. Stott had approached NEAC with "much apprehension fearing the different emphases of our Evangelical coalition might lead to disarray".[15] Indeed, David Watson, an accomplished evangelist and leader in the Anglican Charismatic Movement, suggested provocatively that "the reformation was one of the greatest tragedies that ever happened to the Church".[16] He was pleading for the unity of the Church, but he set more than a few Protestant hares in the assembly running. Stott, who had recently come from a Conference of African Evangelicals (1976), the World Council of Churches Conference in Nairobi in 1975, and the Lausanne Conference on World Mission in 1974, once more pressed the case that mission should include proclamation *and* obedient, sacrificial service in the world.

At the Lausanne Conference, there were nearly 2,500 participants, many of great distinction, such as René Padilla, Samuel Escobar, Bishop Festo Kivengere (Uganda) and David Gitari (Kenya). The theme of the conference was "Let the Earth Hear His Voice"; once again the leading light was John Stott, and the funding came from the Billy Graham Association. In its concluding Covenant, emphasis was placed on proclaiming the biblical Christ as Saviour and Lord, combined with service and socio-political involvement. In a word, evangelism must accompany social and political involvement to alleviate need and further justice. The Lausanne Covenant defined mission anew for generations to come.

In 1974, after a long archiepiscopacy at York and then Canterbury, Michael Ramsey retired. By then he was exhausted, as most Archbishops of Canterbury become. In 1970, General Synod had been inaugurated by the Queen, and a younger man was needed to face the most contentious issue of the day—the ordination of women as priests—and prepare for another Lambeth Conference in 1978. Synod had already shown its mettle by rejecting the Anglican Methodist Union proposed in 1972. More successful had been the formation of the United Reformed Church in 1972, combining Presbyterians and Congregationalist churches in England and Wales. That church boasted Lesslie Newbigin as a leader, an inspiring and visionary thinker who was previously a bishop in the Church of South India, serving as its Moderator in 1978–9.

In the end, Donald Coggan, Archbishop of York, was appointed to Canterbury—a capable linguist and teacher of theology, and charming, but not given especially to listening. At sixty-five, he could only have five years at the helm, as there was now a compulsory retirement age of seventy. Coggan proposed an evangelistic campaign called "The Call to the Nation", based on something he had done in York, a "Call to the North". The campaign was ill-prepared and proved ineffective.

Coggan took forward the policy of reunion with Rome based on the ARCIC agreements on eucharist, ministry and ordination, but was rebuffed by Rome in 1977. The Lambeth Conference of 1978 was fruitful in producing many resolutions on human rights, women priests, prayer and the Holy Spirit, among other topics. At the end of the conference, Canon Michael Harper, with a group of "charismatic" bishops from across the Anglican Communion, founded SOMA (Sharing of Ministries Abroad)—a body to initiate cross-cultural missions to foster the work of the Spirit throughout the Communion. This was testimony to ways in which the unexpected (humanly speaking) and unplanned-for could spin off into effective ministry from the margins of a great gathering. SOMA was instrumental in encouraging renewal in African dioceses mostly and was given a distinctly prophetic edge, in difficult areas like the Congo and South Sudan, by a subsequent director, Don Brewin.

Coggan retired, and in 1979 a new female prime minister, Margaret Thatcher, took charge. The following year she appointed Robert Runcie, a decorated soldier, classicist and previously Bishop of St Albans and Principal of Cuddesdon Theological College, as Archbishop of Canterbury. It was to be an uneasy relationship.

1980s: Reversal, reaction and renewal

The 1980s in the West saw the arrival of a new conservatism. In fact, the Conservative party would govern Britain under Thatcher and Major for the next eighteen years. New leaders emerged across the world who were like Margaret Thatcher herself—John Paul II and Ronald Reagan, both of whom drew strength from earlier struggles to tackle present drift. Having struggled with communism as Bishop of Kraków in Poland, John Paul II now brought the same determination to deal with the self-indulgent West. For her part, Margaret Thatcher was determined to restore self-belief in the British nation and to turn around a failing economy.

In England, the political philosophy of Thatcherism soon came to be recognized. It was a philosophy through which the government sought to control inflation, the bane of previous governments, by controlling money supply and refusing to inject new funds into struggling industries. The squeeze on inflation brought rising unemployment, which soared to 3.3 million in 1982–3. There were violent riots in Brixton and Toxteth in 1981. Union power was restrained by legislation. Thatcher might have succumbed to economic woes as her predecessors had done, had not three things intervened to show her true mettle as a warrior-leader. They were a war, a strike and a terrorist attack, and they made her political brand. The war was the Falklands War (1983), probably the last war the UK will fight to defend an imperial asset across the world from an aggressive power, in this case the junta of Argentina. The strike was the Miners' Strike (1984–5) led by an avowed Marxist, Arthur Scargill, who pitted miners against government in a gruelling and, in the end, fatal strike for the industry. And the terrorist incident was the IRA attack on the Conservative Party Conference in October 1984, narrowly missing Margaret Thatcher, but killing or injuring several in the government and Tory Party.

Later, an equally unyielding foreign policy with Ronald Reagan towards the Soviet Union, and its new leadership under Gorbachev, brought about the collapse of the Soviet Bloc, the dismantling of the Berlin Wall, and the Warsaw Pact in 1989. A policy of initial engagement with the EU, in which Thatcher signed the Single European Act in 1986, morphed into a suspicion, expressed in her famous Bruges speech, that under Jacques Delors the EU would reimpose restrictive practices through its policies of political integration; and so began the mostly Conservative psycho-drama with Europe that persists today.

At home, privatization, the sale of council houses and a boom under Nigel Lawson, the Chancellor, brought great prosperity, but this only exacerbated the divide *between* the struggling inner cities and the de-industrialized North of England, Wales, *and* the South-East and London. By the end of the decade, boom had turned to bust and inflation returned. Lawson and Howe, the foreign secretary, fell out with Thatcher, and so was lit the final fuse that led to her fall in 1990.

For most of the premiership of Margaret Thatcher (1979–90), Robert Runcie was Archbishop (1980–90). On several of the big issues of the day, he appeared either critical of or out of step with Thatcher and her government. For a time, the Church of England was regarded as the official opposition to the government, given the Labour Party under Michael Foot was so ineffective and Thatcher's parliamentary majority was so large. And indeed, the SDP, led by David Owen, Roy Jenkins, Shirley Williams and Bill Rogers, had split from a divided Labour Party in 1981.

One issue of contention between church and government was the reaction of Runcie to social change, as evidenced by the Brixton and Toxteth riots. Writing to Home Secretary Willie Whitelaw in 1981, Runcie asked the government to listen more to community leaders, and in his Christmas sermon he criticized in passing "hearts that have become hardened in resentment", without mentioning any names.[17] The longer-term response to inner city fragility was the publication of the *Faith in the City* report in 1985.[18] Chaired by Sir Richard O'Brien and including David Sheppard, Bishop of Liverpool, and the black Bishop of Croydon, Wilfred Wood, the report sought to address how the mission of the Church might be advanced in Urban Priority Areas. Although criticized for being either Marxist (a Conservative reaction) or thin in its theology, its line, tersely stated, was not far removed from the Lausanne Covenant, which looked for a proclamation of the kingdom of God that took into account both social and political issues. The report iterated that "the personal dimension of the gospel is one that we must never lose sight of. Jesus was deeply concerned for the potential of every individual to become a true child of his Heavenly Father, and proclaimed the infinite worth of one sinner who repents."

The report went on to look at how the Church might organize itself and minister in areas of great need, before critiquing provision of housing, health, employment, community work, youth services, and law and order in Urban Priority Areas. It enabled the Church of England to rate all Urban Priority Parishes and, in time, to raise funds for grants to enable ministry in such places. It may not have been popular across the political spectrum, but the report was certainly ground-breaking, and gave new hope to communities seemingly left behind. For her part, Thatcher preferred the greater self-help approach found in the Jewish report on the inner-city riots called *From Doom to Hope*. In fact, the Chief Rabbi was more popular than the Archbishop, certainly with Thatcher and the Conservatives.

There were other areas in which Runcie was irksome to Thatcher. The Falklands War thanksgiving service held on 26 July 1983 at St Paul's Cathedral was thought by Thatcher insufficiently triumphalist in tone, and she disliked the fact that Runcie had equally remembered the Argentinian bereaved as well as British families. The Queen was more conciliatory in her reaction, writing through her private secretary that, "Her Majesty was full of admiration for the way in which you [Runcie] met this formidable challenge."[19]

The second area of tension was the effect of the Miners' Strike of 1984 on miners' families. Led by Arthur Scargill, who must bear much of the blame, the strike resembled a war of attrition. It was the most violent labour conflict in recent British history. The government wanted complete victory over Scargill, while the Church sought to represent the families and their poverty. The government won the battle. The coal industry more or less ended. Mining communities had the heart ripped out of them. The gruelling miners' strike and the subsequent boom in the City following the Big Bang (1986) and deregulation made for a more divided society, with many scars still to be healed. It seemed that the individualism of the financier had triumphed over the community around the pit. And one of Thatcher's abiding regrets was that new fortunes did not *then* lead to greater philanthropy.

If the Church of England was in part critical of Thatcher, it was also a house divided. Runcie was a leader of the liberal Catholic wing of the Anglican Church and several liberals were promoted to the episcopacy under him. Many were taken from his pupils at Cuddesdon Theological College, or had trained at Westcott House, Cambridge. No liberal was more famous than David Jenkins, made Bishop of Durham in July 1984. He was well known for his modernist views, which involved a denial of an actual or historical resurrection and of the virginal conception. On the other side, many of his clergy spoke of his compassionate concern as bishop. Two days after his consecration in York Minster, the building was struck by lightning, which started a very damaging fire. Many saw this as an act of God against Jenkins's heterodox views and consecration as bishop. However, the tide was turning against the more liberal position of the Sea of Faith movement and the liberalism of Runcie's rule. Emerging scholars, such as James Dunn, the Lightfoot Professor of Divinity in Durham, and particularly N. T. Wright, had a more confident approach to the record of scripture, and soon their writings, especially on Paul and the historical Jesus, gave new confidence to clergy and young academics in England.

The liberal elite of the 1960s was giving way to a new generation of theologians. However, the preface of Crockford's, a piece on the state of the Church of England written anonymously by Garry Bennett, an ordained academic at New College, Oxford, was very critical of Runcie. Bennett quoted the Labour politician and churchman Frank Field, saying that "the Archbishop is usually found nailing his colours to the fence".[20] A consequent press storm that sought to identify the author resulted in Bennett's tragic suicide. A few thousand miles away in Lebanon, the Archbishop's envoy, Terry Waite, caught up in the maelstrom of rescuing hostages from a Jihadist group in Beirut, was himself kidnapped. He was held for four years, most of them in solitary confinement. It was as if Runcie's archiepiscopacy was flimsily founded and accident prone. Runcie was to leave office just a few months after Thatcher. The warrior and her turbulent priest were replaced by a quite different combination in George Carey and John Major, London boys from the East End and Brixton respectively. Both left school young, at fifteen and sixteen respectively, although Major attended Rutlish Grammar School, from which he left early. Theirs would be an easier relationship.

During the 1980s, the Church of England, the Roman Catholic Church and many new churches experienced a renewal of faith. And in many ways, the seeds were sown for future mission and enterprise during these years. And in some ways, this reflected the sense of entrepreneurship at large in the country.

The Roman Catholic Church had as its leader John Paul II, no liberal reformer. The Pope's visit to England in 1983 in the midst of the Falklands War was a moment of renewal for the Roman Catholic Church *and the first such visit in history*. John Paul was pope for twenty-six years, from 1978 until 2005. And in England a Benedictine monk, Basil Hume, had been chosen as the leader of the English Catholics: quiet, deeply spiritual, pastoral, empathetic and much loved, he gave a very English lead to Catholics at a time of Catholic retrenchment. An example of his non-directive approach was the permission he gave to a Catholic priest, Bruce Kent, to lead the CND movement, which was opposed to the use of nuclear weapons.[21] What was for Hume a matter of personal vocation, and one way of achieving disarmament and peace, was considered politically toxic in 1983. Nor was Hume helped by the Papal Nuncio Bruno Heim, who referred to Kent in a letter to a Conservative MP (which was duly published) as a "useful idiot".[22] In fact, most churches were conflicted in their response to nuclear rearmament and American cruise missiles being sited at Greenham Common. Hume certainly inspired confidence in the Roman Catholic Church, even if, like many of this period, he did not recognize the destructiveness and reality of sexual abuse when he was Abbot of Ampleforth in the 1960s and 70s.

In the Church of England, renewal went on at various levels. There was renewal of the liturgy with the arrival of the *Alternative Service Book* (1980), and a new set of liturgies for communion, for morning and evening prayer, as well as for the occasional offices. They were a welcome addition to the Book of Common Prayer, but inevitably a point of controversy with traditionalists.

In the Evangelical wing of the Church, the Charismatic Movement took on new life in worship and evangelism. In 1982, visits from John Wimber of the Vineyard church in Anaheim, Los Angeles, to major charismatic churches in London—Holy Trinity Brompton, St Andrew's Chorleywood and St Michael-le-Belfry York—gave a significant boost to charismatic ministry. With a focus on healing and attendant gifts of words of knowledge and prophecy (see 1 Corinthians 12:7–11), Wimber substantially raised expectations, but in a relaxed Californian style not seen before. These visits built on events like Renewal Weeks held for clergy and leaders at St Michael-le-Belfry under David Watson. The results in England were a new style of ministry characterized by times of protracted worship followed by individual prayer (ministry), and in 1989 the beginnings of regular gatherings at New Wine, a summer Christian festival of teaching, praise, prayer and instruction. It was the Christian answer to Glastonbury. New Wine regularly attracts 35,000 attendees at its summer festival, and its youth offshoot, Soul Survivor (1993–2019), begun by Mike Pilavachi, attracted around 25,000 young people each year. Other Christian conventions continued, such as Spring Harvest at Skegness and Minehead, begun in 1979 with a focus on mission and teaching over several weeks around Easter, and the Keswick Convention in August. These conventions and festivals, together with several other events run by groups of churches, as well as youth missions run by Scripture Union and CPAS (Church Pastoral Aid Society), for the most part occur annually. All told they give regular encouragement, teaching and fellowship to large numbers of Christians from many denominations, and also opportunities for evangelism. And denomination seems to matter less and less to this group: it is more important what you receive than where you belong.

The healing ministry also enjoyed a resurgence in the Church as a whole. The healing ministry had been present from the turn of the twentieth century with the Guild of Health, the Order of St Luke, the Guild of St Raphael and the London Healing Mission or, as it was known from the 1990s, the Christian Healing Mission. In the Anglican Church, from the 1970s Bishop Morris Maddocks advocated the healing ministry in both a sacramental and liturgical setting, writing very helpfully on it. His winsome presence allayed fear and encouraged faith. He founded the Acorn Christian Healing Trust, taken forward later by Russ Parker, who extended its range of work into "listening" and reconciliation. Throughout the country centres of therapeutic care have sprung up, enabling counselling and prayer. Cathedrals and churches now have healing services firmly in their ministry.

Further renewal for evangelism was provided by the spread of the Alpha course in the 1980s. The days of very large and costly rallies held in football stadiums, such as those led by Billy Graham, were coming to an end. Something more personal and conversational was needed in a more "word-resistant age". In 1979, the Alpha course was initiated by Charles and Tricia Marnham in their curate's flat in Church House, Brompton, following a parish mission led by John Collins to that church. It was the acorn from which the Alpha course grew, and it was given great encouragement by Sandy Millar, the successor to John Collins as Vicar of Holy Trinity Brompton, and by Bishop Richard Chartres, who galvanised church growth in the London diocese through his very effective Capital Plan, cutting out dead wood and beginning new congregations. Alpha was developed into a ten-week course with its main parameters fixed by John Irvine, later Dean of Coventry Cathedral, and then by Nicky Gumbel in 1990, who turned it into a video-/DVD-based course organized around discussion. Soon it was to go world-wide. Other courses on similar lines, but with differing emphases, were developed, such as Emmaus and Christianity Explored, and likewise used in small groups—a new form of dialogue evangelism had been developed that could be used by any church for evangelism and instruction. It was a modern form of catechesis and was also widely used by the Roman Catholic Church.

A further act of fundamental reform occurred at the end of the decade with the ordination of women to the priesthood of the Church of England. The issue had been boiling for some years. The secular world had taken a lead in appointing a female prime minister. In 1975, the Sex Discrimination Act was passed, followed by the appointment of the Equal Opportunities Commission. Women figured at the forefront of medicine, academia, law and the arts. In the Church of England, a woman could not proceed beyond deacon. Feminism had grown in strength since the publication of *The Female Eunuch* by Germaine Greer in 1970. In 1988, Nigel Lawson saw to it that a wife's tax was no longer the responsibility of her husband. In 1991, the new Archbishop, George Carey, a supporter of women's ordination to the priesthood, found that the issue was at the top of his in-tray. Women's ordination was opposed by some Evangelicals on scriptural grounds, by some Anglo-Catholics on grounds of scripture and tradition, and by some churchmen on the grounds that it should be a collective decision by the universal Church, given it was opposed by the Roman Catholic and Orthodox churches.

Nevertheless, the General Synod voted in favour of women's ordination on 11 November 1992, with substantial majorities in the three houses of bishops, clergy and laity.[23] Generous provision was made for those who in conscience could *not* continue as clergy in the Church, with some being received by Rome. There was a backlash from conservative elements in the Church and society, but equally there was great rejoicing. Parishes were allowed to opt out of having a female incumbent, and supervision of such parishes and clergy was given to "flying bishops", themselves opposed to the ordination of women. The Anglo-Catholic wing of the Church founded Forward in Faith in 1992 to encourage parishes and clergy in their tradition: around 400 parishes are currently involved. Meanwhile, at the time of writing (2020), around 28 per cent of stipendiary clergy are female, according to Church of England ministry statistics.

The 1990s saw the Church grow in confidence, if not in numbers; although overall numbers still declined, there were many shoots of life and almost a third of churches were growing. New patterns of ministry had been laid down, and differences over the ordination of women were accepted as the existence of two integrities. There was a setback to ecumenism between the Anglican and Roman Catholic churches, with Cardinal Ratzinger (the future Pope Benedict XVI) saying in 1998 that "supporters of women priests were no longer in full communion with the Catholic church".[24] Ecumenical ambitions were further curtailed. The overriding purpose of the churches now was not how close they could grow institutionally, but how they could engage in joint mission, or mission from their own integrities. As numbers declined further and the gulf between the secular world and the Church widened, how was this mission to be conducted? There were big questions about engaging with a new culture, about doing church differently, and about methods of evangelism.

By the mid-1990s, John Major's government was in decline, in part the effect of the by then fifteen years of Conservative government. A war in the Gulf had been successfully fought against Saddam Hussein, reclaiming Kuwait from his invasion. As shown in the revolt of a large minority of Conservative MPs against the Maastricht Treaty of 1992, European policy was a source of deep division, even though Major gained significant opt-outs. Major's desire to take public services "Back to Basics"[25], which he described as coming "from his innermost personal beliefs", was overrun by ministerial scandals, with the result that "back to basics" was weaponized against him by the press. The economy had taken a battering in 1992 over Black Wednesday, when the pound had to leave the European Exchange Rate Mechanism, but was recovering under new inflation control through interest rates.

When the election came in 1997, Major's government was swept from office by a political tsunami, and Tony Blair and New Labour took power. Blair's government kept many of the economic policies of his predecessor. He began a process of devolution for Scotland and Wales, intervened to restore justice in several foreign conflicts, brought the Troubles in Northern Ireland to an end with the Good Friday Agreement of 1998, continued to work closely with Europe but did not join the eurozone, and, following 9/11, fatefully adopted President Bush's policies in the Middle East, in Afghanistan and Iraq. But by the 1990s, it seemed that the effect of the cultural changes in England of the previous twenty years had placed the Church on the margins of society.

CHAPTER 22

The End of Christendom?

By the turn of the millennium, many wondered if the Church and nation had parted company, and whether Christendom—as in the close relationship between Church and nation begun by Constantine in AD 312 and continued by European rulers for nearly seventeen hundred years—was coming to an end. It seemed so. In England, the monarchy, the state, and the ties between Parliament and the Established Church gave the appearance of that relationship continuing, but in reality, it was a legacy rather than the force it had been. In England, there were 26 million baptized Anglicans and 5 million baptized Roman Catholics, although between them less than 2 million attended church regularly. The fact that there were so many baptized adults was testimony to the residual strength of religion or Christian faith up to the mid-1960s. The truth is that many of the values still existed in England, but the culture, morality and attitudes to institutions had markedly changed.

Change of culture: Mind the gap

The gap between contemporary moral culture and the position of *traditional* church teaching is now very wide and this, in turn, has placed pressure on the churches to accommodate their stance to gain public support. In a recent survey, moral attitudes in 2019 were found to be significantly more liberal than in 1989. Far from faltering, the process of liberalization has been growing significantly. Only 13 per cent of adults questioned in 2019 were against homosexuality between consenting adults; in 1989, it had been 40 per cent. With regard to abortion, 18 per cent were against it in 2019, while in 1989, the figure had been 35 per cent. And more recently, gender reassignment has become more common. This trend is symptomatic of a wider issue over identity, and who and what defines sexual identity.

English culture had changed; morality has changed and is still changing. It is a plural culture rather than one that was monochrome. The high level of immigration over the previous sixty years has created new Hindu, Muslim and Buddhist communities. In more recent times, the sheer multiplicity of racial backgrounds in big cities—in some London boroughs a minority have English as their first language—means that churches need to conduct mission in new contexts.[1] Furthermore, the culture was changed by the advent of the internet and the almost prurient interest in the details of celebrities' lives, and indeed in anyone's life. This trend was exaggerated by social media, the foundation of Facebook in 2004, and other message-sharing forms that followed.

As Theodore Zeldin wrote, "What is unique about the present time is that humanity has never been so conscious of the primacy of its intimate concerns, nor expressed them so openly, in almost every part of the globe."[2]

The world-wide web, begun in 1991, brought blessings and curses, not least the pressure to live up to the images displayed of others, which created anxiety and low self-esteem, felt especially by young women. It would also bring the curses of hatred, abuse, bullying and self-harm. How to "police" the web so that we enjoy its benefits but not its curses remains a deep political and social issue. An anxious society, prone to depression, has only increased. The breakdown of communities through individualism, the result of increased prosperity, more solitary living and the break-up of primary relationships, has only weakened the bulwarks of resistance to self-doubt, and increased mental illness.[3] Institutions upon which we had come to rely were also shown not to be trustworthy.

Loss of trust

Many institutions, including the Church, have experienced the loss of trust, often brought about by particular events. Among these institutions are Parliament (the expenses scandal), the police (the murder of Stephen Lawrence and the Hillsborough disaster), the press (the Milly Dowler scandal), government (the Iraq War), political parties (the EU referendum), banking (the financial collapse of 2008), and local councils (Grenfell Tower). In some cases, church leaders like John Sentamu and James Jones, Bishop of Liverpool, were able to help the process of justice, following Stephen Lawrence's death and the Hillsborough disaster respectively. The Health Service, although proving so exemplary in dealing with

COVID-19, nonetheless has too frequently suffered from health scandals such as the Shrewsbury maternity scandal, Harold Shipman or infected blood. Nor has the Church been immune.

Most shaming of all, the Roman Catholic and Anglican churches, among others, were found to have abusers at the heart of their institutions, whether it be schools, churches, colleges, children's societies or missions. One Anglican bishop, Peter Ball, and many other clergy were imprisoned; some escaped justice and censure by death. Nor were the abusers readily reported or exposed; they were often protected by their institutions or by senior clergy seeking to diminish loss of reputation who put institution before the victims. The victims were not adequately supported or communicated with. Thus, the victims faced a double trial: abuse in the first instance and no redress or meaningful contact in the second. This state of affairs is borne out by publications like *Letters to a Broken Church*.[4] Perhaps it is time for the churches to move from being self-policed to having an independent body they fund collectively to oversee reporting, redress and communication with the victims. Justice cannot be the prisoner of reputational damage-limitation.

Such loss of belief has dealt huge blows to the willingness of people to trust the Church, or other institutions for that matter. Nor is it surprising that this breakdown of trust has only hastened our spiral into an anxious society with record levels of mental illness and depression. It is this anxiety and lack of trust, often driven by protection of vested interests, that has led to greater questioning of the most basic elements of our existence, namely our identities and gender relationships.

New challenges

At the time of his departure, George Carey thought the Anglican Church more settled and hopeful. He gave an optimistic account of the Church of England: church finances, which had suffered substantial loss in value, had been sorted out by the First Estates Commissioner, Sir Michael Colman; women had been ordained to the priesthood; Lambeth and the Church's administration had been reviewed by Lord Hurd in his report "To Lead and to Serve", which made for more effective administration; ecumenical relations had been strengthened by a good relationship with Cardinal Murphy-O'Connor; and the Lambeth Conference of 1998 had demonstrated the strength of the Anglican Communion.

More broadly, there were grounds for optimism across the churches in England, not least in London. Between 1998 and 2005, 34 per cent of churches in

England grew, which was more than the corresponding rate of growth of 21 per cent between 1989 and 1998. In London, where most of the Pentecostals are to be found (53 per cent), churches grew strongly and 57 per cent of all churchgoers were between the ages of twenty and twenty-nine. However, the other side of that statistic was that between 60 and 70 per cent of churches were declining over the country. The Church, despite initiatives like the Decade of Evangelism and the Springboard Project led by Canon Michael Green and Bishop Michael Marshall, continued to shrink. The years from 2002 would see greater tension in the Church, but also more causes for encouragement.

In 2002, Rowan Williams became Archbishop of Canterbury: a thinker, poet and theologian and the Lady Margaret Professor of Divinity at Oxford aged thirty-six. Although he had already expressed ambiguity on the issue of same-sex love in his lecture of 1989 entitled "The Body's Grace", Evangelicals like Alastair McGrath went on the record as saying, "Evangelicals will find him someone who understands their position and concerns, and will want to encourage them in their mission and ministry."

There would be two issues that would raise their head early in Williams's archiepiscopacy: war and homosexuality. In ecclesial terms, the latter was more incendiary than the former, while in terms of world peace the former would far outstrip the latter.

Williams knew at first hand the awful destruction of 9/11. He was visiting Manhattan at the time, and it was still a year before his appointment as archbishop. He showed courage and calm when it was still unclear whether he and his colleagues would survive.

In the build-up to the Iraq War of 2003, Rowan Williams and Cardinal Murphy-O'Connor made their reservations clear to Tony Blair's government. On 24 February, Williams met with an unyielding Blair in Downing Street. In Rome, three million people demonstrated against the war, and a letter asking for United Nations support and signed by all the bishops of the Church of England was handed to the government, but to no avail. Once the war had begun, Williams preferred silence to questioning a campaign already underway, and hence reducing morale among British forces. However, in England a different front had opened up over the appointment of a bishop living in a committed gay relationship.

Homosexuality and the Churches

The issue of homosexuality and the Church's response had become front and centre by the time of the millennium. In 1991, the House of Bishops had published *Issues in Human Sexuality*. In section 4 it dealt with "The Phenomenon of Homosexual Love" and in section 4.10, genital acts in homosexual relationships were proscribed, as only properly belonging to marriage between a man and a woman, thus upholding a General Synod motion of 1987. By 1994, Jack Spong, the American Bishop of New Jersey, was advocating gay relationships in the "Koinonia Statement", and saying that homosexuality—its practice, rather than its existence—was morally neutral. An Evangelical response started with the founding of the American Anglican Council in 1996. In London, OutRage!, led by Peter Tatchell, sought to out clergy suspected of being gay, in a disruptive and at times aggressive campaign. On Easter Day 1998, a protest was made in Canterbury Cathedral by a group led by Tatchell. They occupied the pulpit and had to be removed by the police. Clearly, the carefully crafted *Issues in Human Sexuality* was going to face further pressure.

The 1998 Lambeth Conference saw further tension on the subject, with a clear majority in favour of not altering the traditional position that the practice of homosexuality was wrong. A resolution, called 1.10, enshrined this principle. In the report on human sexuality submitted to the conference it was acknowledged, however, that different member churches espoused different teachings on the subject. Some advocated that "the church should accept and support or bless monogamous covenant relationships between homosexual people and that they be ordained", whilst the Ugandan Church reminded the conference that some Christian men were martyred in Uganda for refusing to enter into homosexual relationships with the King.[5] Whatever uneasy outcome there was on this issue, in Lambeth two things were clear: the Global South, in which far and away the greatest number of Anglicans lived, would not be silenced, and the issue of homosexuality was not going away.

With the advent of Rowan Williams, who was known to be supportive of loving and committed homosexual relationships, Richard Harries, Bishop of Oxford, proposed presenting Jeffrey John as the next Bishop of Reading, where he would function as a suffragan bishop in the Oxford diocese. John was known to be in a same-sex relationship, although he was living separately from his partner, as he had for a number of years. John was also an advocate of long-term same-sex partnerships, and had written about this in a booklet entitled *Permanent, Faithful, Stable*. With very little wider consultation, which was generally in keeping with how senior appointments were made, John's appointment was announced, followed by enormous reaction and opposition. A campaign against the appointment was quickly underway. The House of Bishops was split, with nine diocesans writing against the appointment on the grounds of John's heterodox views on sexuality and previously non-celibate relationship, about which he was unrepentant. Under immense pressure, Rowan Williams, who valued the unity of the Church more highly than the right to clerical office of an avowed homosexual, asked John to withdraw his acceptance in what must have been a deeply painful encounter. The result was relief in the orthodox camp, but deep and lasting disappointment in Williams himself on the part of the liberal wing of the Church and liberal opinion makers in the press.

What had been a storm in England would prove to be a far-reaching hurricane in the world-wide Anglican Communion when, on 2 November 2003, openly gay Gene Robinson was consecrated Bishop of New Hampshire in the presence of Frank Griswold, the Presiding Bishop of the Episcopal Church of the United States (ECUSA), and over forty other bishops. Such was the tension that Robinson wore a bullet-proof vest for the occasion. The action sent shock waves through the Anglican Communion and precipitated a split between the American Church and the Communion as a whole. ECUSA was accused of acting precipitately, heretically and without consultation.

A commission (the Lambeth Commission) was set up to look into what had happened and its effects. A report was issued in 2004 called the Windsor Report, which suggested a new Covenant for Provinces of the Communion to adhere to. The Covenant had a rocky path, however, as it was considered too prescriptive by the liberals, and too unenforceable and mealy-mouthed by the conservatives, especially in the matter of calling for repentance from ECUSA. The Covenant did not reach its final form until late 2009 and was never endorsed by all the provinces. It called for a moratorium on same-sex blessings and on the consecration of bishops in same-sex unions. Yet without strong implementation, with the forces of liberalism and conservatism opposed, it would never stick. For some its requirements went too far, for others not far enough.

In the end, some of the primates of the Global South took matters into their own hands, led by Peter Akinola of Nigeria, with support from the Bishop of Rwanda and others. When it came to responding to Williams's invitation to the Lambeth Conference of 2008, they made it clear that they would not come, citing the presence of ECUSA bishops who had attended the consecration of Robinson and who were therefore no longer orthodox in word or deed.[6]

Instead, an alternative conference, sponsored by the newly formed Global Anglican Future Conference (GAFCON), took place. Led now by Peter Jensen, Archbishop of Sydney, the conference met in Jerusalem before the Lambeth Conference, with over 1,000 attending, including 200 bishops. The Lambeth Conference went ahead and—given the circumstances—was surprisingly harmonious. An *indaba* process was used, based on a Zulu idea of consultation by elders without necessarily meeting a consensus. The *indaba* proved creative and in places cathartic. In one of his addresses, Williams made the point that welcoming delegates was not the same as agreeing with them or approving their teaching.

The combination of the debacle of Jeffery John and the schism produced by the ordination of Robinson had ongoing repercussions. A missionary branch of GAFCON was established called Anglican Mission in England, which has its own bishop, consecrated by the American Church in North America (ACNA). Some conservative Evangelical congregations in England now look to him for episcopal oversight. His consecration and ministry are not recognized by Lambeth, nor is the principle of anyone having oversight in an Anglican jurisdiction or diocese without legal episcopal standing.

In turn, in 2005 the Church of England's House of Bishops allowed persons living in same-sex civil partnerships, but who were celibate, to be eligible for ordination. Same-sex marriage, which came into being in 2014 in the UK, is not recognized by the Church of England. On the other hand, the Methodist Church and the Episcopal Church of Scotland and the Church in Wales have cleared the way for acceptance of same-sex marriages. The Baptist Union and all the more loosely connected independent churches retain the view that marriage can only be between a man and a woman.

Pressure on the churches in the public square

While the Anglican Church was struggling with the issue of homosexuality (and continues to do so) both in England and world-wide, other historic churches looked on with concern. The combination of ordaining women and then being riven by gay issues made the Roman Catholic and the Orthodox churches wary. When Williams met a failing-in-health John Paul II, it was made clear that differences over morals were as important as those over faith. John Paul II's lengthy and robust stewardship of the Catholic Church ended in 2005, and he was succeeded by Joseph Ratzinger, Pope Benedict XVI. A conservative theologically, and a theologian, Ratzinger faced the full effect of the sexual abuse scandal in

the Catholic Church and sought to deal with this awful and extensive reality
thoroughly. He also maintained that the inclination towards homosexuality itself
(not sexual activity) was a disorder; but there are signs now that Pope Francis
does not take the same view (from statements in October 2020). The Orthodox
Church, which had been growing quietly in England since the 1980s, was no less
concerned and, on a 2010 visit to Lambeth, Metropolitan Hilarion of Volokolamsk
voiced his concern that the Anglican Communion was in danger of "betraying
our common witness by departing from traditional Christian values and replacing
them with contemporary secular standards".[7]

In England, Basil Hume was succeeded by Cormac Murphy-O'Connor in 2000.
He was a cautious reformer, and a clear opponent of secularism, but one whose
pastoral gifts were tarnished by his failure to report Michael Hill, a paedophile
priest, during his time as Bishop of Brighton and Arundel. He was nonetheless a
steady hand on the tiller during years of strident secularism. Sexual abuse in the
Catholic Church, given opportunity by celibacy and secrecy, would continually
sully its pastoral and missional work.

Murphy-O'Connor was succeeded by Vincent Nichols in 2009. In 2010, and
during his time in office, Pope Benedict visited Britain. During that visit, John
Henry Newman was beatified, and in 2019 he would be canonized. The visit was a
success, and once again gave the Catholic Church high visibility in the nation and
encouraged a stalled ecumenism between Anglicans and Roman Catholics to get
going again. Only the year before, in 2009, the Congregation for the Doctrine of
Faith had sprung the Ordinariate of Our Lady of Walsingham on an unknowing
Vincent Nichols and Rowan Williams. The ordinariate was a way of receiving
Anglican priests, unnerved by the possibility of female bishops, into the Catholic
Church whilst retaining some of their Anglican heritage. Over nine hundred
Anglicans, including several bishops and clergy, entered the Roman Catholic
Church by this route. Rowan Williams's archiepiscopate was coming to an end.
His rule had been both rocky and revitalizing.

Williams instinctively saw both sides of a question and was drawn to the
marginalized and misunderstood. "He was also a loner endowed with self-
confidence that accompanies a willingness to shoulder a very large individual
burden."[8] It may have been this inner siding with the disadvantaged that made him
unwilling or unable to press a single line. He looked at what drove the terrorists
in his account of 9/11, *Writing in the Dust* (2002), and gave too much oxygen to
their motivation by crediting them with a sense of "powerlessness".[9] He wanted
Muslims to be judicially regulated in their own communities and suggested, to
enormous consternation, in a lecture at the Law Courts that some Sharia law be

incorporated into common law. When it came to legislation for women bishops, he sought to protect Catholic traditionalists, whilst at the same time welcoming the appointment of female bishops. There are those who argue that he made too many concessions.

In the end, he lost the legislation on the appointment of women bishops in Synod by a narrow margin in the House of Laity. It was a moment of great pain for him, as for many others. Such a *modus operandi* was crucifying for Williams, as he implied when talking about Thomas à Becket in a farewell documentary on BBC2 on New Year's Day 2013, entitled *Farewell to Canterbury*. Becket was murdered at the interface of church and state. Thankfully, Williams survived to enjoy a very fruitful "retirement", and books flowed from his pen that brought hope, insight and inspiration to thousands.

If the road travelled by Williams in the previous ten years was strewn with rocks, it was also a revitalizing journey, especially because of what it did for mission. For some time, the Church in England had been renewing its understanding of mission from the scriptures and from a study of changes in culture (e.g. in the brilliant works of Lesslie Newbigin: *Foolishness to the Greeks* and *The Gospel in a Pluralist Society*). We have already noted a far greater confidence in the message of the Gospel and the proclamation of the kingdom. Biblical scholars like Tom Wright, Richard Bauckham and Jimmy Dunn hastened the process. Publications such as Wright's *Resurrection of the Son of God* in 2003 gave new scope to the implications of Jesus's resurrection for all creation and humanity. Subsequent books by Wright built on this, not least in emphasizing the kingship of Christ rather than simply credal statements about his birth, death, resurrection and Parousia.[10] There were also new practitioners of mission working in inner London, such as Steve Chalke through Oasis and Patrick Regan through XLP. And new models of training ministers in non-residential ways were pioneered, particularly at St Mellitus College in London, led initially by Graham Tomlin, later Bishop of Kensington. There was fresh thinking about the disintegration of Christendom (e.g. Stuart Murray in his work of 2004, *Post Christendom*). Church leaders engaged more imaginatively through education, youth work and social care. CARE, under the able leadership of Lyndon and Celia Bowring, supported family life, marriage, and alerted the wider community to the moral effects of proposed legislation.

Amidst all this, in 2004 Lambeth published *Mission-Shaped Church*, produced by Graham Cray and his working group. Rowan Williams said in the introduction that, at its most basic, church is what happens when people encounter the resurrected Jesus and choose to sustain that experience together in community.

Here was permission given from the highest level, and swiftly endorsed by General Synod, to "do church" in new ways, in new places, in new styles, but with the same message at heart, only encultured differently in different communities. Theology was incarnational, catholic, imaginatively liturgical, and joyous—a signpost to the kingdom of God. It endorsed church planting of various kinds that had already been enacted, strategies that were pulled together in the work of George Lings, who distilled a methodology for church planting. *Mission-Shaped Church* envisaged the necessary support of episcopal mission orders to make such fresh expressions legal on the ground, which were forthcoming. This movement was part of a "mixed economy" (Williams's phrase) of doing and being church, both old and new. Along with Alpha and other evangelistic courses, a timely way of stimulating church growth had been provided which invigorated the Church and still does. In many ways, the principles announced in *Mission-Shaped Church* were good for all the churches in England. Indeed, the Methodists, represented by Graham Horsley, had helped to write the report.

Until 2020

Politically, the last ten years may have been the most tumultuous since the Second World War. The Iraq War was succeeded by the financial crash of 2008. The effects of this would affect government financial policy for ten years. The burden of austerity fell unevenly across the country, leaving many feeling left behind and overlooked. Globalization and distance from metropolitan centres were blamed for people in the North and Midlands being disregarded. Then, when the nation was given the chance to vote on its political destiny in the referendum of 2016, the people voted to leave the EU after an ill-tempered campaign in which one MP, Jo Cox, was murdered. Different parts of the United Kingdom voted in different ways, putting pressure on future unity. The exact nature of a new relationship or treaty with the EU is not yet known.

In many ways, the same issues faced the churches as before: climate change, homosexuality, the steady flow of cases of sexual abuse, the widening culture gap between society and church, issues around race and black lives, and a new confusion over sexual identity.

In 2013, the same year as Justin Welby's enthronement as Archbishop of Canterbury, Jorge Mario Bergoglio became Pope Francis, taking the name Francis in honour of Francis of Assisi, whose example of simplicity and love he sought to follow. Surprisingly, he was the first Pope Francis in history. The touchstones of Pope Francis's ministry are simplicity, humility, compassion, care of the poor and welcome. Although he followed Catholic moral teaching, he sought a more compassionate approach to those who had contravened morality and instated "a year of mercy" in 2015. He called a conference of bishops entitled "The Synod on the Family" that year. Although there was a new openness when it came to homosexuality, it was stated in the *Relatio Synodi* (the conclusion) that "there are absolutely no grounds for considering homosexual unions to be in any way similar or even remotely analogous to God's plans for marriage and families".[11] Pope Francis did hope that divorced people might receive communion and that couples would discuss their own responsibility for family planning, but even these proposals were tentative. The tone was welcoming of all, but the changes were modest and incremental. The tentative proposal that celibacy might no longer be a criterion for priesthood was swiftly shot down by the conservative parts of the Church and ruled out in February 2020. Women are still not eligible for the diaconate.

Pope Francis's first two encyclicals, *Evangelii Gaudium* and *Laudato Si'* ("Praise be to You") came in swift succession. *Evangelii Gaudium* ("The Joy of the Gospel") was published in 2013 and looked at the proclamation of the Gospel. It was certainly evangelistic. In its closing paragraphs we read, "We have a treasure of life and love which cannot deceive, and a message which cannot mislead or disappoint. It penetrates to the depths of our hearts, sustaining and ennobling us. It is a truth which is never out of date because it reaches that part of us which nothing else can reach."[12] Francis reminds us that "we were created for what the Gospel offers us: friendship with Jesus and love of our brothers and sisters".[13] In 2015, Pope Francis published *Laudato Si'* on the care of our environment or our earthly home. Francis turned to his namesake and reminded the reader "just how inseparable the bond is between concern for nature, justice for the poor, commitment to society and interior peace".[14] There was no mistaking the direction of his papacy.

The Roman Catholic Church in England welcomed this new note of compassion from the papacy, but some still yearned for certainty in a world of such moral flux. By 2011, the Roman Catholic Church had a slightly higher weekly church attendance than the Anglicans. Church of England congregations numbered 852,000 weekly, while there are 861,000 at the mass each week. Numbers had swollen from 2004 with many immigrant Poles coming to England. This made the Roman Catholic Church the largest single denomination in England, while independent churches together number more.

Nevertheless, the Catholic rate of decline is more rapid than in the Anglican Church. Most acute for the Catholic Church is recruitment to the priesthood, for it is predicted that by 2023 there will be only 1,500 priests under seventy. It is a huge reduction from the high-water mark of the mid-twentieth century.

In the same year as Francis's enthronement, though he eschewed all pomp, Justin Welby was enthroned as Archbishop of Canterbury. His route to this position could not have been more different from that of either his predecessor or the Pope, but in many ways Francis and Welby resembled each other, in emphases if not in background.

Welby exemplified the pattern of ministry laid down by Gregory the Great: contemplation leading to action. His route to Canterbury was fast and his future ministry would reflect his experiences along the way: a broken family affected by alcoholism, conversion at Cambridge, a business career as a financial director of a French oil company and the tragic loss of a beloved daughter. No previous archbishop had knowledge of the derivatives market, but after the financial crash of 2008, and when Bishop of Durham, he became a member of the Parliamentary Commission on Banking Standards and could speak with experience on financial matters.[15] Experience as a vicar and of church growth came at Southam, near Coventry, before he joined the team at Coventry Cathedral. It was a ministry of reconciliation exercised from Coventry that would take him to Iraq, Nigeria, Burundi and Kenya. Nigeria he already knew from his work as an oil executive. Risk and Reconciliation would soon become staples in his vocabulary.

The main tenets of Welby's spiritual formation were a deep appreciation of scripture, an experience of personal conversion, a profound commitment to evangelism and prayer. In 2006, he encountered a new Benedictine order, Chemin Neuf, founded in 1973 by Jesuit Laurent Fabre, and they were to oversee a prayer community in Lambeth.

The ministry of reconciliation took root during Welby's time at Coventry, where he discovered that if there was to be disagreement, it must honour the Gospel; and in it all the Lord's servants must be kindly to everyone (2 Timothy 2:24–5).

When taking up his role as archbishop, three goals were highlighted: prayer, evangelism and reconciliation. These were to shape his own and his staff's overriding concerns. Reconciliation was taken forward, for the most part, by Synod's belated agreement to women bishops in the Church of England. The legislation for female bishops was passed in Synod in 2014. And in 2015, the first female bishop, Rachel Treweek, was appointed: there are now five female diocesans (at the time of writing).

Nor was Welby slow in engaging with social grievances in Britain. This came not only from an innate interest in the political process, but also from a strong understanding of the notion of "the common good", and "human flourishing", in part a product of French social thought. To that end, and early on at Lambeth, he called out the pay-day lenders for charging exorbitant interest rates and promised a new commitment to credit unions. He extolled the work of food banks, whilst deploring their necessity in a Britain where too often people fall through the gaps, sometimes through the failure of Universal Credit. Cooperation by people of goodwill is a strong theme in his book *Reimagining Britain*, "indeed the common good—and all the values and practices it encompasses—is not something legislated or mandated, but is the sum of innumerable small and large actions by every participant in society".[16]

John Sentamu provided a complementary ministry as Archbishop of York (2005–20), with a natural affinity to the world-wide Church shared by Welby, an instinctive heart for mission, a prophetic edge to his ministry and a penchant for plain speaking in the Early Church *parrhesia* ("plain speaking") style. He had briefly been imprisoned in Uganda when he resisted Idi Amin when an advocate in the Ugandan Bar.

COVID-19

Then, in early 2020, the COVID-19 pandemic struck the UK. By late March, following the government lead, all churches were closed for worship. It was the first time since the papal interdict in the reign of King John that worship had ceased in the country's churches. While many churches took to broadcasting services on the internet, there was debate in the media about the necessity of closing the churches where prayer might have been said by the minister or priest and about the national presence of the Church and its leaders. How the ongoing nature of the virus will affect the Church, we cannot tell. The Lambeth Conference has been postponed for two years. The Church has been involved in food distribution and community contacting, as well as chaplaincy work in the hospitals and care of the bereaved. There are estimates that at least 25 per cent of the public have accessed its services, many more than is usual, and many people outside of church admit to praying.

Christendom (the fusion of church and state created by history) has not entirely passed, but it is passing—into a kind of twilight zone. The large numbers of people baptized in their childhood in the 1940s to 1970s (over 30 million) will decline, and the process is not being repeated. The Queen and her explicit and powerful

Christian faith, the great services of state, whether the royal marriages of the Cambridges or Sussexes or some other state occasion, all underline the Christian narrative of the nation. And the nation loves those occasions (mostly), but they are examples of televisual theatre, rather than an expression of beliefs that are widely practised. Nor is it a bad thing for Christendom to pass; it was the result of a fusion of imperial power and Christian confession in the person of the Emperor Constantine, and, in the end, it led to politically-motivated violence or pressure to uphold Christian (or not so Christian) doctrines and practices. But the Church will need to get used to a new way of being in the nation.

Undoubtedly the Church today is pared down, but like Gideon's army, is more observant, watchful and committed. Bits of the Church are declining, bits are increasing. It is as active as ever on the high street and in its many buildings. It is struggling to know how best to address a new culture: where to change, where to remain adamant. It is on the margins of society; some would say in a kind of exile. But it has the same mandate as ever (see Luke 4:16–20) and the same treasure at its heart—"the unsearchable riches of Christ" (see Ephesians 3:8–9). Christendom may be passing but the overarching message of the kingdom of God has never been more needed.

CHAPTER 23

The Characteristics of English Christianity

Eighteen hundred years of church history, set in the context of the nation's development, is a lot to encompass in a single volume, but now as we look back over that extended period, are there any discernible characteristics of the Church in England? For most of its history, England was made up of Britons, Celts (pushed to the margins by the Romans), Romans (not just Italians, but from all over the Empire), Anglo-Saxons, Vikings and then Normans. Over a thousand years they were melded into a nation. Other migrations would follow, not least Huguenots, Jews and the Irish. Then, from 1945 onwards, the next great wave of immigration followed: African-Caribbean, Asian, African, South American and European for the most part. We are a country of many peoples. In the past, the Christian faith as practised in this country—and as part of the four-nation union with Scotland, Wales and Northern Ireland—provided the glue, the values and the vision for our society. What were the characteristics of this faith practised by the Church, which at times was grievously divided by politics, such that war, death and enmity ruled when the Church had been called to peace and love? Over these 1800 years, what stands out amidst the all-too-human failings of a church called to be a signpost to the kingdom of God, but often in need instead of deep repentance and change?

Like Israel called to be a light to the nations in the Old Testament, the Church has too often failed in its calling and betrayed what it had been called to do. Yet amidst the gloom and sometimes deep darkness, there are still discernible characteristics of the English Church that shine through. Sometimes these characteristics shone in one part of the Church only to be extinguished (or attempts were made to do so) by another part; sometimes they illuminated the whole.

The English and the Word

Picture a few monks in the monastery of Monkwearmouth-Jarrow on the north-east coast of England, Northumberland, working in the *scriptorium* on the prized treasures of their community. Every day would be punctuated with prayer. Perhaps most days the Abbot Ceolfrith would call in to encourage the scribes. Three Bibles were in the making, being copied from another brought by the abbot from the dispersed library of Cassiodorus in Italy. Two thousand head of cattle were needed for their hides or vellum for these three prodigious books. When complete, they would weigh seventy-five pounds each. Only one would survive the raids of the Vikings and would turn up eventually at Amiata in Tuscany. It was there because it had been transported by land and sea from Monkwearmouth to the Lateran in Rome and given as a gift to Pope Gregory II in 716. It survives to this day in the Laurentian (Medici) Library in Florence as the oldest Latin Vulgate in the world, but came from the north-east of England. Other Bibles would follow or precede it in Canterbury, Winchester and Lindisfarne.

The English love words. In fact, their language of Anglo-Saxon would survive the accretions of many and spread throughout the world. It would incorporate into one language Latin, Greek, Viking and Norman-French. The language of the Western Christian world was Latin. In the East, in Byzantium, it was Greek. And no one loved using Latin in these early years more than the chronicler and biblical commentator, the Venerable Bede, who lived in the companion monasteries of Monkwearmouth-Jarrow, where Codex Amiatinus was produced. He was the first English historian and is considered the greatest scholar of the early medieval period. His commentaries spanned many books of the Bible: Genesis, 1 and 2 Samuel, Nehemiah, Ezra, Proverbs, the Song of Songs, Mark, Luke, Acts, and the Letters of St Paul. As he lay dying, he completed a commentary on John's Gospel. Many centuries later, Pope Francis used Bede's homily on the Call of Matthew as the basis for his Year of Mercy in 2015. And in the Middle Ages, what Bede began, others like Robert Grosseteste, Richard Rolle, Walter Hilton, Chaucer and Langland continued. By the fourteenth century, English replaced Latin and Norman-French as the language of national life, and it was into this language that the story of the Word made flesh would be increasingly rendered.

As spoken English outstripped Latin, the English needed their own text in their own language and Tyndale obliged while living on the continent. With a unique gift for English phrasing, he translated into that tongue most of the Bible. It was a monumental moment, both for English faith and the English language and culture. There had been translations before, notably by Anglo-Saxon monks, and John Wyclif and his associates in 1384, but here was a definitive translation (at least for the next 400 years) which would soon take centre stage. Tyndale and Coverdale's translations merged into the text known as the Great Bible. It was placed in every parish of England in 1539, with the first edition printed in Paris.

The extension of Bible translation and study was preaching, and the English, over time, became preachers. Initially, preaching in Northumberland occurred in small wooden churches or around a stone Celtic cross, and would take the form of a homily to a little-educated crowd. The illiteracy of clergy would for many years hamper preaching. Often the preachers came from monastic communities. The Franciscans were noted for their outdoor preaching, but by the latter part of the thirteenth century preaching had fallen into disrespect—at least as reflected in Chaucer's *Canterbury Tales*. It was too often taken up with fundraising and indulgences. It took John Wyclif and the Lollards to revive the discipline of preaching. The medieval Church was by then more sacramental and liturgical than verbal and instructional. In the sixteenth century, as Cranmer records, "the sweet grape of God's word was gathered in England. Then was God's word—for that is the sweet and pleasant grape 'that maketh glad the heart of man' (Psalm 104:15)—with great freedom preached, earnestly embraced, and with greedy hearts in all places received."[1] Preaching in Tudor England became a primary ministerial activity. The Puritans honed their skills through their "Prophesyings", so disliked by Elizabeth I. There is no doubt that, during the Commonwealth period, a plethora of preaching of all kinds emerged, from the Levellers to Richard Baxter. The eighteenth century would see great revivalist preachers criss-cross the country, notably John Wesley and George Whitfield. In the Church of England, homiletic skills were taught by Charles Spurgeon at Cambridge. Come the nineteenth century, no one was more celebrated as a preacher than the Baptist, Charles Haddon Spurgeon.

In twentieth-century England, there were the great Anglican preachers like William Temple, George Bell and Michael Ramsey, and the Free Church preachers: P. T. Forsyth, Donald Soper and Leslie Weatherhead. After the great "Crusade" preaching of Billy Graham came the carefully crafted sermons of parish clergy, such as John Stott, Dick Lucas and David Watson. They built their sermons around Bible exegesis, well-chosen illustrations and apt application to the lives of men and women, sometimes with deliberate evangelistic intent. It was a case of preaching with the Bible in one hand and a newspaper in the other, to make the biblical message clear and its appeal compelling. At this they excelled.

Equally, English theology came to be pre-eminently biblical and practical. It is true that the Oxford scholastics like Duns Scotus and William of Ockham in the fourteenth century carefully weighed the relationship of faith and reason, philosophy and revelation, and the universal and the individual, but what resonated more generally with the English was pastoral and apologetic theology. Perhaps it was this innate knowledge that prompted Alfred the Great to commission the translation of Gregory the Great's *Pastoral Rule*,[2] the most lucid exposition of pastoral care in the Latin West. Nor were the English the great systematizers of theology, unlike Lombard and his interminable *Sentences*, Aquinas and his *Summa Theologiae*, Calvin with his *Institutes of Religion*, or, much later, Karl Barth and his *Dogmatics*. The English frame of mind was more exegetical, discovering what the Bible says; more piecemeal, answering a specific question; and more pastoral, writing on how to pastor a congregation. Thus, the Puritans produced lengthy exegeses for the pilgrim, as in William Gurnall's work on the armour of God (Ephesians 6). Richard Baxter wrote *The Reformed Pastor* and *A Christian Directory*, which were more manuals on pastoral care than systematic methodologies. Bunyan gave the English an unforgettable description of a pilgrim's progress. Come the twentieth century, P. T. Forsyth, Austin Farrer, C. S. Lewis and J. R. R. Tolkien would furnish the English, and the world, with pithy and cogently expressed answers to the great questions of life, through well-argued apologetics like *The Problem of Pain* or through imaginative legends, such as the Narnia series or *The Lord of the Rings,* which had wide and lasting appeal.

If the English liked their faith expressed succinctly, they were nonetheless reflective. This surely gave rise to a strong contemplative and poetic tradition. While not set in the desert heat of Egypt, Syria or Palestine, such a tradition was found instead in the uplands, in nearby Wales and in the offshore islands of Lindisfarne and the Hebrides. The English mystics, who included Julian of Norwich, Margaret Kempe, the author of *The Cloud of Unknowing*, Richard Rolle and Walter Hilton and, much later, Evelyn Underhill, provided a significant strand in English spirituality. They were, for the most part, solitaries or hermits. If Julian restricted herself to a single room, Margaret Kempe's spiritual energy came from love of pilgrimage, and the others loved wide-open spaces. The Celtic tradition sought the sea and islands. They went offshore to be oft alone. Here they found God, the Trinity, saw illustrations of his power and goodness in nature, wrote for the benefit of the whole Church and prepared themselves for mission or dialogue: "Mother, give me a word" might just as well have been a question to Julian of Norwich as to a Christian in the Egyptian desert. Alongside them were the English poets: John Milton, William Cowper, John Donne, Gerard Manley Hopkins and T. S. Eliot. They bring us an extraordinary corpus of verse: reflecting on their faith, on creation, on their struggles—with blindness (Milton), with depression (Cowper and Hopkins), with emptiness (T. S. Eliot) and with death (John Donne)—and much else besides. That contemplative tradition continues anew today, whether at St Beuno's, where Hopkins spent three years and where Ignatian retreats are now frequently made, or on pilgrimage in England or beyond.

The English and their worship

All true reflection on the incarnation leads to worship in the name of the Father, Son and Holy Spirit. Worship is the overall offering of a life in sacrificial service to God (see Romans 12:1) but also, within that, the offering of a specific sacrifice of praise and *sometimes lament and silence* in the company of others. In all nations that worship is expressed in various combinations of architecture, liturgy, song, music, words and silence. It is in part culturally determined. Anyone who has travelled across England will know how much contrast there can be in worship. A person who has worshipped in a black-led church, or a village church in Somerset, or a city church crowded with young people, or a small community church in a struggling urban priority area knows how varied worship can be in England. Worship had several ingredients from the start, but the same point of origin, whether in the Roman Catacombs (where the dead were buried) or in a great soaring cathedral.

The second-century Roman governor Pliny wrote to Emperor Trajan explaining the nature of the worship of Christians in his province as follows: "They met regularly before dawn on a fixed day to chant verses alternately amongst themselves in honour of Christ as if to a god, and also to bind themselves by oath, not for any criminal purpose, but to abstain from theft, robbery, and adultery, to commit no breach of trust and not to deny a deposit when called upon to restore it. After this ceremony it had been their custom to disperse and reassemble later to take food of an ordinary, harmless kind."[3] Justin Martyr, writing his *First Apology* in c. AD 153 also gives us a very early account of the Eucharist.

The earliest Christian worship in England, whether in Canterbury or in Northumberland, followed a similar pattern: a reading from the scriptures, a homily or sermon, the celebration of the Eucharist, plain song, chanting or singing, and the exchange of the peace or holy kiss (see Justin Martyr's description). These were the ingredients of worship from earliest times, world-wide and in England.

In 705, the Anglo-Saxon King of Wessex, Ina, gave Aldhelm, Bishop of Sherborne, land to build a church at the foot of the Mendip Hills, on which were springs of life-giving water. It would become the site of Wells Cathedral (literally by the wells). As time went on, these buildings became more elaborate. The Normans replaced Saxon cathedrals with those of their own style, first Romanesque and then gothic. From Saxon times, parish churches were built; some like Brixworth in Northamptonshire and Earls Barton—where many of my Whitworth forbears are buried—survive to this day. The scale, grandeur, skill and decoration of these English cathedrals, abbeys, minsters and parish churches is unsurpassed. They were built to the glory of God over generations. They are not *museums* of faith, but *expressions* of faith, to be used as places of inspiration to faith in Christ. They may need to be adapted and reordered for today, but in these buildings and their churchyards, living connections with the worshipping communities of the past survive. In them, and indeed in all churches of all denominations and none, the scriptures are read and explained, and the Eucharist or Lord's Supper is celebrated.

Liturgy and sung worship form part of almost every church's life. Sometimes that liturgy will be formal and written down; other churches will pride themselves on having no liturgy, but will in fact have a more informal, but nonetheless habitual, liturgy to adhere to. By the time of Hippolytus of Rome in c. AD 220, there was a recognizable Eucharistic liturgy in the West, although Augustine of Canterbury appears to have used the new Gregorian Sacramentary. There was also evidence of a Gallican rite in a small Burgundian mission under Liudhard in Canterbury. The Irish Church, which was responsible for establishing the Iona community under St Columba (who then sent Aidan to Northumberland), also used a Roman rite, but with Irish variations. Further revision would come from Alcuin, who came from York and was Charlemagne's main religious adviser. Local variations developed within general norms, and in England the Sarum Rite gained increasing ascendancy during the time of the Norman Church. This, or variations of it, would remain the standard liturgy for the Eucharist in England until the Reformation. At that point, the English Church found in Archbishop Cranmer a talented and resourceful liturgist.

This movement in the liturgy from the Roman Catholic rite to the new rite of the Church of England, expressed in the holy communion service of the Prayer Book, was from *seeing* to *participating*. Hitherto, the high point of the liturgy had been the people seeing the actions of the mass; now with Cranmer it was understanding and participating. Cranmer had a remarkable facility for compressed and elegantly expressed theology, which is evident in morning and evening prayer, the occasional offices, and the collects.

In many ways, Cranmer represented the love of the English for simplicity, brevity and succinctness in worship, and it may be for that reason the Prayer Book lasted 400 years: from 1542, through the 1662 revision at the time of the Restoration, until the present day. Of course, there have been revisions since then—*The Alternative Service Book* (1980) and *Common Worship* (2000) notably—but in many ways these have simply built on what was achieved by Cranmer. While Non-Conformist churches that rarely held the Lord's Supper prided themselves on the minister's extempore praying and leading of worship, nonetheless they too were all for simplicity if not brevity, for extempore praying is often longer and more repetitive, and likewise unscripted preaching. Roman Catholic worship moved from Latin to English after the Second Vatican Council, and increasingly shared liturgical texts with other churches.

Alongside the liturgy, there was sung worship, and few have a richer diversity of hymns and spiritual songs than the English Church. Initially, sung worship came from monastic services: Benedict Biscop, the Abbot of Monkwearmouth-Jarrow, brought back a cantor from Rome to instruct the community in their singing of the Psalms. In Glastonbury Abbey, there are signs of medieval organs being used in worship, their liturgy being encouraged by Dunstan in the tenth century. Singing and music spread from the monasteries to the parishes. By the late Middle Ages, there was polyphonic singing (singing in parts) and the Chapel Royal, together with cathedral monastic communities, became major patrons of church music in the land. Thomas Tallis (1505–85) had begun to compose by 1532, and in turn trained William Byrd (1543–1623), his successor in the Chapel Royal of Elizabeth I. In the next century, Henry Purcell (1659–95) would become organist at Westminster Abbey and take choral music into the Baroque age. These composers have enduring power. Thomas Tallis's "If Ye Love Me" was sung in May 2018 at the wedding of Prince Harry and Meghan in St George's Chapel, Windsor, in all its perpendicular glory. English choral music would find its natural outlet in the choir schools of English cathedrals.

By the mid-nineteenth century, cathedrals were not yet on a sound financial footing, having exchanged lands they owned for a regular income from the Commissioners, although this was barely sufficient to cover their costs. But a combination of powerful deans and new ideas led to new nave services taking place in cathedrals in the 1870s, attracting thousands, and in the 1860s, cathedral choir schools were getting going. New hymn books were created, such as *Hymns Ancient and Modern* (1861), and Victorian hymn and anthem writers led by S. S. Wesley, John Stainer and J. B. Dykes wrote anthems and hymn tunes for a burgeoning hymnody. "Onward Christian Soldiers", "Abide with Me" and Newman's "Lead, Kindly Light" (Queen Victoria's favourite hymn) all focussed on the Christian's costly pilgrimage through doubt, sorrow and death—a typical Victorian theme.

If cathedral worship was finding its feet, and the Anglican parishes were getting new resources, the Non-Conformist churches had never had more hymns for their congregational singing. By the 1890s, the Salvation Army had begun to accompany its work and worship with a brass band, and hymn singing became a central part of its evangelism and outreach. The Methodists, who were practically founded with hymn singing, likewise thrived. No one would surpass the hymns of Charles Wesley that issued from the eighteenth-century revival and are now sung world-wide each week by millions.

Music reflects culture. At the turn of the twentieth century, great composers like Sir Edward Elgar and Sir Hubert Parry provided music and anthems for that *fin de siècle* period. Parry's "I was Glad" was a suitable successor to the majesty and drama of Handel's "Zadok the Priest". Written for the coronation of Edward VII, it had a similar timbre. Then, following two world wars, something more reflective and introspective was needed. Other composers came forward, influenced by Elgar and Parry, but schooled by Sir Charles Stanford (1852–1924). They were John Ireland, Ralph Vaughan Williams and Benjamin Britten. Ireland wrote the tune for the hymn "My Song is Love Unknown" in fifteen minutes on the back of a menu. It remains one of the great Passiontide hymns. Britten composed the "War Requiem". Composers of the late twentieth century are John Rutter (b. 1945) and John Tavener (1944–2013). The latter, a member of the Orthodox Church, composed a new setting for the Liturgy of St John Chrysostom and the former has written a whole series of carols and anthems that are already household pieces. Equally new hymn writers emerged, notably Timothy Dudley-Smith, who wrote a loved new setting of the Magnificat, "Tell Out, my Soul".

By the 1960s, a new musical tradition in England was burgeoning, inspired by popular music. Guitar, keyboard, drums and vocals comprised a band that was part of youth culture from the 1960s onwards. Soon, composers of songs and tunes were emerging in the churches using the same instruments, often linked to the Charismatic Movement, but not always. Graham Kendrick and Stuart Townend were early leaders and composers in this movement, and there have been many others since. Often leading a series of songs in a worship sequence, these new worship leaders create an attitude of openness to the sensing of God's presence. Many churches, like the Australian Hillsong Church, and others both inside and outside the main denominations, make this a fundamental characteristic of their worship.

What is clear from this survey is that there is an extraordinary range of church music and worship, hymns, songs, anthems and oratorios in English worship. The spectrum covers over a thousand years of church worship from the monastic plain song to modern guitar-led worship. All have the same aim of worshipping the Father, through the Son, in the power of the Spirit. Different people will respond in different ways to the styles and content of these forms of worship; they represent the inspiration of the Spirit, but none need be the exclusive preserve of selected sections of the Church.

Openness to the leading of the Spirit

Closely connected to worship, and often on the margins of English Christianity down the ages, was an openness to the Spirit and his leading of the Church. Oftentimes this was in contra-distinction to the institutionalizing of Christianity, whether through a rigid administrative or hierarchical system or through a body of teaching which was imposed by a structure, as in the Middle Ages with Scholasticism. This is symbolized by the Celtic choice of representing the Spirit not by a dove, but by a *wild goose*. Obviously, a goose was more likely to be seen off the shores of the North of England—migrating as they were in the buffeting wind from Siberia to England and back—than a peaceful dove. To Celtic spirituality the goose well represented the more untameable and powerful Spirit of God than any other bird.

In English church life, there have been people of prophetic spirit who have called the Church back to the essence of the freedom and radicalness of the Christian message. In earliest times, these would have been the Celtic saints like Aidan, Cuthbert and their Irish forbear Columba. They spoke from the margins to the centre, and indeed lived on the edge of society, frequently choosing islands as their base for community life. Others would follow their example, like St Guthlac in the fenland of Lincolnshire, at Market Deeping. Later, in the late Middle Ages, it was the mystics who set themselves to seek God at the margins of society or in solitude. In particular, Julian of Norwich and Richard Rolle sought the essence of the faith in prayer and testified to the love of God in Christ made manifest to them by the Spirit. They were sentinels and heralds on the edge of society. Their contemporary Margery Kempe, from King's Lynn, experienced the same love of God with copious tears, not so much in one place but on pilgrimage.

During the Commonwealth period, those who sought the Spirit's leading were to be found in the new Quaker movement as in the more politically focussed communities like the Levellers and the Diggers.

The same witness to the Spirit's power was manifested particularly by Wesley in his preaching and teaching. Although often emotionally unmoved himself, he witnessed, especially in the early years of his preaching ministry in England, manifest examples of the Spirit's presence in the lives of his listeners. He did not explicitly seek such manifestations, but they were the by-product of his preaching Christ to the people.

More recently, and resulting from the Pentecostal movement that began at the turn of the twentieth century in Los Angeles, the so-called Charismatic Movement has profoundly influenced the Church. It has inspired an expectation of healing; it has directed mission and has made the presence of God the touchstone of worship. Although always open to the dangers of self-indulgence, false expectations, manipulation and emotionalism, when purely led openness-to-the-Spirit brings vitality, true experience of God and a sense of the presence of Christ which is priceless. This fresh understanding of the Spirit's work included a renewed interest in retreats of all kinds, pilgrimage, and monastic communities. Such experience of God is not for the individual alone, but also to change society.

The English Church: Social care and justice

Like the rest of the medieval Church in Europe, the Church in England at its best sought to care for and engage with the social needs of the community. That is not to say that there was no corruption, simony or veniality.

The monastic communities in particular provided some elements of care, education and support for the communities of England. St Bartholomew's, the oldest hospital in England, was originally founded as a monastery in 1143 by a favourite courtier of Henry I. At the dissolution of the monasteries, it was taken over by the Corporation of London. Elsewhere, monastic communities were able to provide education, centres of scholarship and social support to their outlying communities. Franciscan houses at Oxford and Cambridge did much for the development of both universities in the thirteenth and fourteenth centuries. Although they had passed their peak by 1534, there is no doubting their contribution to society over the centuries.

Likewise, dioceses at their best provided some basic structure of care during the Black Death (1345–50), perhaps none more so than the Diocese of Norwich. It is estimated that Bishop Bateman, the founder of Trinity Hall Cambridge, stayed at his post as Bishop of Norwich throughout those years. The diocese lost some two thousand priests in all. During one year, to Lady Day 1350 (the Feast of the Annunciation celebrated annually on 25 March), 831 priests were lost to the plague and, amazingly, that number of ordinations followed to fill vacancies. Such sacrificial caring is remembered in Cambridge annually. And it has greater resonance as we experience a pandemic with all the support of modern medicine and economic intervention.

With the coming of the Reformation, social care was redirected by the Church of England. The laity were encouraged *not to remember* monastic orders, now suppressed, nor adorn parish churches with art, but rather use their wills to provide for the poor of the parish. Many parish-based charitable trusts were begun, administered by church wardens, and many of these were advertised in church porches across the land. The poor were now being looked after in parishes in accordance with the Poor Laws of Elizabeth I's government. The Victorians would later institutionalize this care in the form of workhouses, which often became centres of cruelty, abuse and dependency.

By the time of the Commonwealth (1650–60), social justice had taken a much more political bent (as we have seen). The Levellers recognized what we would call "human rights", sought greater equality for people, and were essentially biblically based "socialists". They represented a radical wing then present in the Non-Conformist churches that emerged during the Commonwealth, and which was still active well into the twentieth century.

The Evangelical Revival of the eighteenth century, chiefly inspired and organized by John Wesley, along with the Evangelical Revival in Anglicanism centred on the Clapham Sect, became the engine behind the abolition of the slave trade. By then England had been involved in the slave trade for over a century, with three million slaves transported to the sugar plantations of the West Indies and the American colonies under unspeakable conditions in English ships. Spearheaded by William Wilberforce in the House of Commons, the abolition of the slave trade was eventually achieved in 1807. Slavery was abolished in all British colonies in 1833. It was a campaign that emanated in large measure from the churches. The same tactics of stirring large-scale support from the public were used in the other great movement of the period, the campaign for electoral reform. In 1832, the first Great (Electoral) Reform Bill was passed, although in this case the bishops of the Church of England were almost uniformly against it.

The Church in the nineteenth century period produced many reformers, admittedly often alongside rather more socially complacent Anglican clergy, such as those depicted by George Eliot and Jane Austen in their novels. The Factory Acts and other Acts restricting child labour were largely the work of Lord Shaftesbury. Josephine Butler campaigned for women's health, and the dignified treatment of prostitutes. Florence Nightingale established the first schools of nursing at St Thomas's, following the Crimean War. The Church, both Anglican and Non-Conformist, was at the forefront of national primary school education.

Hannah More helped set up both Sunday schools and primary schools in the West Country. Elizabeth Fry, a Quaker, had an important role in prison reform after being horrified by conditions in Newgate Prison in London, and was supported in her work by Queen Victoria and Prime Minister Robert Peel.

Finally, during the twentieth century, a number of Christians had important roles in women's suffrage and the setting up of the welfare state. Emily Davison, a feminist and radical Christian, campaigned tirelessly for women's franchise, losing her own life in the process. R. H. Tawney was an influential Christian thinker behind the inception of the welfare state, although Sir William Beveridge, an agnostic and friend of Tawney, was its main visionary and administrator. Archbishop William Temple gave the Beveridge Report his unqualified support. In the second half of the century, Christians were involved in the beginning of youth services, hostels, credit unions, debt counselling, drug rehabilitation centres, counselling services, care centres, inner city support and welfare organizations. More recently, the Trussell Trust has been involved in starting over a thousand food banks in England, all begun from one food outlet in a home garage in Salisbury. The contribution the churches have made to the social welfare of England has been great. Although never perfect, it can be celebrated.

The English Church: Its independence and outreach

There is an interesting paradox in English Christianity that may well reflect national character: that is, the English Church shows signs on the one hand of residual independence, and on the other of centrifugal mission. If the former results in a tendency to be autonomous, the latter results in a desire to be outgoing. The former tendency appears to feed the latter.

Given the island mentality of England and its location at the extreme northern edge of the continent of Europe, the nation has a propensity to look out to sea, particularly following the Reformation, rather than across to the nations of Europe. Yet this too is a conflicted stance, since England inevitably found itself intervening with blood and treasure in the continent of Europe through most of the eighteenth century, at the start of the nineteenth century in the Napoleonic Wars, and then in the twentieth century in two world wars.

In fact, there never has been a century in which the interests of England were not caught up with the movement of power in Europe. Even at the height of the Empire, the value of trade with Europe outstripped trade with the rest of the world. We see this conflicted stance in politics at present, but we also see it in the history of the Church.

England was evangelized from two sources: Rome and the Celtic Church in Ireland, which was itself formed in part by French and southern European influences. At the Synod of Whitby in 664, the English Church decided to conform to the Roman Church with regard to the date for the celebration of Easter (and monastic tonsure), and for nearly nine hundred years it was part of the Western Catholic Church with its centre in Rome. Indeed, until 1538 there was only one church in England. The break with Rome was driven by political necessity: the remarriage of the King and his divorce from Catherine of Aragon. It was also underscored by that age-old sense of independence, now re-enforced by Protestant theology among many of the elite.

England had always shown itself reluctant to be ruled ecclesiastically by Rome, with kings like Henry II and bishops like Grosseteste both resisting papal appointments. Matthew Paris, the thirteenth-century chronicler, disliked the continental advisers, including several churchmen, that Henry III and his wife brought from France. Whether there would have been a break with Rome without the need for a divorce has always been a moot question. What is clear is that once the break was concluded and an attempt made to establish a new English Church, the cat was out of the bag. The cat in this instance was the spirit of independence and autonomy that was always just beneath the surface of religious conformity in England.

From the seventeenth century and the time of the Commonwealth, non-conformity emerged and would henceforward flourish, even in the face of strong opposition from the state from the Restoration onwards. Quakers, Presbyterians, Baptists and later Methodists of many shades, along with other smaller sects, developed and were soon, together, to become a sizeable proportion of all Christians in England.

When the culture in England changed once more in the 1970s, a plethora of new churches formed, many with Pentecostal connections or ties to particular ethnic backgrounds. While the traditional denominations—whether Anglican, Methodist or Roman Catholic—then experienced overall decline, these newer churches grew. And those parts of the traditional denominations that most resembled these other growing churches often also grew. In other words, while parts of the older denominations are declining, other parts are growing vigorously and surmounting a generational divide. One might say the new, more independent churches are refreshing and reskilling the older, less independent ones.

The energy that created independent and autonomous churches also began missions. The English Church always had a strong missionary focus from Anglo-Saxon times. St Boniface led a mission to the German tribes from c. AD 723 and became Germany's first archbishop; others, like Grimkell, who became Bishop of Trondheim, and Osmund of Ely, went to Scandinavia in the tenth century. Alcuin had been Charlemagne's chief adviser. In the early centuries, the English Church was a net receiver from continental Europe and Ireland of Christian teaching, practice and skills, and this would continue to be so in the early years of the Norman kingship, both Angevin and Plantagenet. By the time of the Tudors, English scholarship attracted Erasmus to the nation's shores and soon the English Church would become a missionary force under Elizabeth, and especially during the Commonwealth period. By the late eighteenth century, missionary societies would be formed by the Anglican and Non-Conformist churches. Mission would accompany the expansion of empire, as well as beyond it: in India, Canada, the American colonies, China, Japan and, later in the nineteenth century, in East and West Africa and the Pacific. Eventually, after Catholic emancipation in 1852, Roman Catholic missionary orders restarted from England, and there are now more than a thousand missionary orders in the UK.

Major missionary societies in England employ thousands of missionaries between them: World Horizons (170), USPG (124), WEC International (312), Wycliffe Bible Translators (255), Youth with a Mission (486), Operation Mobilization (366) and OMF (266). Catholic and monastic missions are also engaged in overseas outreach. Finally, relief and development agencies like CAFOD, Christian Aid, World Vision and Tear Fund account for considerable sums of money given through the churches to the two-thirds developing world. An independence of spirit and engagement with the wider world have certainly been characteristics of the English Church.

In brief, some of the main characteristics of English Christianity are devotion to the Bible, expression of that devotion in preaching, spiritual writing in a devotional and a pastoral manner, a poetic and a mystical expression of the faith. Among the English there is a love of architecture, music, song, drama and the visual arts as manifestation of faith in worship. There is also an openness to the Spirit connected at times to a radical challenge to the *status quo*. Often, English Christians oscillate between enthusiasm and scepticism, paradoxically exhibiting both traits as national characteristics. At their best, they cherish simplicity, prayerfulness and practical love. There is a desire to relate Christian faith to social needs and justice. There is a streak of independence as well as a desire to be adventurous, outgoing, missionary and educational. And in so far as any of this approximates to the ministry of Christ when he was on earth, then his feet have walked on English soil.

We have followed the history of the Church in England over nearly 1,800 years. If Tertullian and Origen were right, the first Christians were in England in the second half of the second century AD, which is only seventy years after the death of the oldest Apostle, St John. Yet it was not until after Constantine's Edict of Toleration, issued at Milan in 313, that the Church got underway in Britain. Bishops were sent to the Council of Arles in 314, which presupposes the existence of some mature Christian communities in England by then. After the withdrawal of the Roman legions in 410, Christians were scattered to outlying districts as pagan Anglo-Saxons settled in England. Their conversion, as we have seen, was due to missions originating from Ireland and from Rome. The English Church was fully incorporated into the Roman Catholic Church following the Synod of Whitby.

This state of affairs pertained until 1534 and the beginnings of the Reformation in England, but despite the establishment of the Church of England under the headship of the sovereign, the pressures on the Church to further divide increased. Religious violence grew as the Protestant Church of England sought to prevent the re-establishment of the Roman Catholic Church, and the Roman Catholic Church sought the military support of foreign powers. The climax of this conflict occurred around the time of the Spanish Armada and the Catholic missions to England.

Equally, from the Protestant side, the Church of England was too Roman in its ceremonies to be acceptable to more puritanical reformers. Splits began to occur, and by the time of the Civil War there were many sects. Despite force being used to proscribe Non-Conformity at the time of the Restoration of the Monarchy in 1660, Non-Conformism became part of the permanent landscape of the Church in England. Furthermore, many took their convictions to the New World, founding in time a new spiritual republic in America.

The eighteenth century saw a revival in Christian convictions through the preaching of John Wesley and others, and through the spread of Protestantism to the labouring and artisan classes in ways that had been lost during the Reformation, which had ended many church community customs and the social cohesion of the late medieval world. At the same time in the eighteenth century, Enlightenment rationalism was increasingly challenging Christian presuppositions about creation, the Trinity, and the divinity of Christ.

The nineteenth century would see the greatest revival of churchgoing since the medieval world and with it a desire for social reform, from the abolition of slavery to welfare and electoral reform in England. At the same time, English trade and arms, together with an English Bible and mission-minded men and women, made for a world-wide missionary movement from 1800.

The twentieth century saw the seeds of scepticism grow from new scientific understandings taken from *The Origin of Species*, from biblical criticism, and from the appearance of the atheistic philosophies of Marx, Bentham, Hume and Nietzsche. The effect of two world wars was to increase this scepticism and to distance the Church from society. The revolution in culture that took place in the 1960s and 70s magnified this distance in short order. The effect of this has been to reduce greatly the numbers of active Christians in England, although there are still large numbers of baptized, nominal members of traditional churches in the country, but this will decline further with the passing of the years. But those Christians who practise are, perhaps, more motivated than hitherto.

What of the future? Christians do not have crystal balls. They have hope, faith and confidence in Jesus Christ. What has become clear, even in overviewing this narrative, is that the Church is getting closer to that pre-Constantinian period when it was in an *exilic relationship* with society. It was then persecuted. Now it is marginalized in a land many of whose values it established. The legacy of Christendom is mixed: too often the story contains religious violence created by a very different worldview and abuses of power which, in recent years, have been rightly exposed. In the light of that, there can only be deep repentance, recognition of wrongdoing, restitution, wherever needed, and humility. But still what of the future?

Firstly, it is worth recalling how much the foundations of this nation's life and story are based upon Christian faith and principles. The Church gave impetus to education and medicine, from the monastic movement until the great Victorian reformers. It gave us models for business and care of the workforce from Cadbury's to Port Sunlight, from Colman's to Rowntree's—many businesses founded on Quaker and Dissenting principles. The ethos of public service, whether in the civil service or local government, was inspired by the idea that a government official is called a minister—a word taken from Christian vocabulary meaning "servant". The National Health Service and the welfare state came from the joint work of R. H. Tawney and a more agnostic Beveridge. Many of our greatest poets and authors were inspired by their Christian vision, whether Milton, Vaughan, Herbert, Eliot, C. S. Lewis or Tolkien.

I have been an Anglican minister for forty-five years, during which time there has been both numerical decline in church membership but also spiritual advance. (Even as I write in the midst of the COVID-19 pandemic, there is a recalibration of expectations and values going on in societies world-wide.) If that sounds like a paradox, it is. Although smaller in numbers, across the denominations the Church is now in many respects healthier. Growth will not come through an institutional fix—for there is widespread lack of trust in institutions—nor through large-scale preaching occasions as in the 1950s (or 1740s, for that matter). The culture is too word-resistant and essentially suspicious for any megaphone proclamation. Instead, it will be growth through "little colonies of heaven": that is, through working churches of honesty and faith where people can view genuine Christianity up close and personal. In the early centuries, it was the hope of the resurrection, a real and transforming experience of the Good Shepherd and care for the poor and broken that made those first "little colonies of heaven" so compelling.

At the centre of these "little colonies" there must be a celebration of faith in the Holy Trinity: Father, Son and Spirit; confidence in the power of the Cross to forgive and the power of the Resurrection to give hope. These "colonies of heaven" will have an otherworldly prayerfulness, opportunities to explore the meaning of the Christian faith in a setting of hospitality, ways of becoming fully human, a considered care of creation, a deep compassion and love for all people and a practical engagement with particular aspects of local communities. They will be therapeutic communities of healing and hope. People need to see to believe, to think that what they are seeing could be true, and then find out that it is.

We shall leave this history with the observations of a *thegn*, which we heard before, in the court of King Edwin when he heard the preaching of Paulinus in 625. For all our supposed advancement, the same issues confront a person today as then. Having heard Paulinus, Bede tells us that:

> Another of the king's chief men, approving of his [Paulinus's] wise words and exhortations, added thereafter: 'The present life of man upon earth, O king, seems to me, in comparison with that time which is unknown to us, like to the swift flight of a sparrow through the house wherein you sit at supper in winter, with your ealdormen and *thegns*, while the fire blazes in the midst, and the hall is warmed, but the wintry storms of rain or snow are raging abroad. The sparrow, flying in at one door and immediately out at another, whilst he is within, is safe from the wintry tempest; but after a short space of fair weather, he immediately vanishes out of your sight, passing from winter into winter again. So this life of man appears for a little while, but of what is to follow or what went before we know nothing at all. If, therefore, this new doctrine tells us something more certain, it seems justly to deserve to be followed.' The other elders and king's counsellors, by Divine prompting, spoke to the same effect.[4]

In recalling this story, Bede is echoing the famous statement at the beginning of the *Confessions* of St Augustine, written in 397: "You have made us for yourself, and our heart is restless until it rests in you."[5] As long as the Church in England issues the call of its master to the nation, made up as it is of so many parts, to come to *him*, take *his* yoke upon itself and find *rest for its soul* (Matthew 11:28, 29), then it need not fear the future. Not only that but we should recall that the Spirit of God often raises up people from the margins to renew and redirect the Church's life and mission. Perhaps the greatest of such people in our story are Bede, recording the life of the early Church in Britain on the *edge* of the North Sea in Northumbria, Tyndale, translating much of the Bible into English as an *exile* in Germany and Belgium (and being martyred for the cause), Wilberforce, pursuing with prayerful tenacity and oratorical gifts the abolition of the slave trade, Florence Nightingale, the "lady with the lamp" who in the strangeness of the Crimea inspired a nation and established nursing in our national life, Elizabeth Fry, personally conducting prison reform, and, in our own age, Cicely Saunders, spearheading the hospice movement which has had universal influence in the care of the dying. Each is an example of someone who changed the nation and the world through the exercise of their faith in Jesus Christ, and whose labours still form the values and essence of England.

APPENDIX I

Chronology of the English Church

The Conversion of England: The Romans and Anglo-Saxons

c. 190   Tertullian "Parts of Britain are conquered by Christ"—probably the South-West. Recorded in Tertullian's *Against the Jews*.

c. 305   The martyrdom of St Alban for hiding a priest.

306   Constantine proclaimed Emperor at York.

312   Battle of Milvian Bridge: Constantine defeats Maxentius, takes Rome. Constantine's vision of Christ and conversion.

313   Edict of Milan: religious toleration.

314   British bishops from York, London and Lincoln attend the Council of Arles.

410   Roman legions withdrawn from Britain.

c. 425   Patrick made missionary bishop for Ireland.

429   St Germanus in controversy with Pelagianism, see Bede *Ecc. Hist.* ch. XVII.

c. 500   Celtic monastery (from France) established at Tintagel.

c. 518   Early settlements of Saxons resisted by Celts: Battle of Badon, King Arthur defeats Saxons at Badon Hill. Saxons eventually push out the Celts from south-east England.

c. 550   Gildas, a Welsh monk, writes *The Ruin and Conquest of Britain*.

From the Anglo-Saxon Church to the Norman Conquest

521   Birth of St Columba at Gartan, Donegal, Ireland.

563   Mission to Picts, founding of Iona Monastery by Columba and twelve monks.

590–604   Pope Gregory I, "The Great", commissions the Mission to England.

597   Death of St Columba.
597   Arrival of St Augustine of Canterbury. Mission to Kent.
627   St Paulinus, sent by Gregory in 601, baptizes King Edwin of
       Northumbria.
633   Edwin defeated and killed by Cadwalla of the Britons, and Penda of
       Mercia.
634   Oswald brings Christianity back to Northumberland. Bishop Aidan
       (from Ireland and Iona) comes to Lindisfarne.
c. 650 Bishops Cedd and Chad, brothers from Northumbria, are sent to the
       Middle Angles and Mercia respectively.
664   Synod of Whitby accepts the Roman date for Easter and orientation of
       the Saxon Church to Rome.
668   Theodore appointed Archbishop of Canterbury, the forming of dioceses.
c. 675 St Etheldreda at Ely and St Hilda at Whitby.
687   St Cuthbert's death.
695   The Lindisfarne Gospels.
710   St Wilfrid's death.
716   Codex Amiatinus reaches Pope Gregory II from
       Monkwearmouth-Jarrow.
731   Bede completes the *Ecclesiastical History of the English People.*
757–96   Offa King of Mercia, Christian overlord of the Saxons.
775   Martyrdom of St Boniface.
782   Alcuin begins work for Charlemagne.
793   The Vikings sack Lindisfarne.
871   Alfred becomes King of Wessex.
878   Alfred's low point: hiding at Athelnay, Somerset.
878   Defeat of Vikings at Edington, Wiltshire: Baptism of Guthrum the Dane.
937   King Athelstan victory at Brunanburh against the Norse King Olaf of
       Dublin.
973   Edgar the Peaceful crowned in Bath Abbey by Dunstan.
1012   Martyrdom of St Alphege.
c. 1016   Wulfstan II Archbishop of York: *The Sermon of the Wolf to the English.*
1016   King Cnut reigns over Denmark, England and Norway. He conquered
       England.
1035   Death of Cnut.
1042–66   Edward the Confessor succeeds Harthacnut.
1066   Death of Edward the Confessor, January 1066.
1066   Duke William of Normandy defeats Harold Godwinson at Hastings.

From the Norman Conquest until the Tudors, Henry VII

1066   William crowned King of England, Westminster Abbey, Christmas Day.

1070   Lanfranc Archbishop of Canterbury.

1086   Domesday Book completed.

1093   Anselm Archbishop of Canterbury.

1093   Durham Cathedral started.

1095   27 November, Pope Urban II preaches the First Crusade.

1150   Lombard's *Sentences*; The textbook of Scholasticism (Paris).

1170   29 December, Martyrdom of Thomas à Becket.

1174   Rebuilding of Canterbury Cathedral, following a fire.

1209   Pope Innocent III gives permission to Francis to begin a new order: The Franciscans.

1214   Oxford University chartered.

1215   *Magna Carta* sealed by King John at Runnymede, 15 June. Drawn up by Archbishop Stephen Langton.

1220   Salisbury Cathedral begun.

1221   Dominicans reach England.

1224   Franciscans reach England.

1225–74   Thomas Aquinas: *Summa Theologica*, Paris, "The Angelic Doctor".

1235   Robert Grosseteste, Bishop of Lincoln: Lectures in Oxford.

c. 1240   Wells Cathedral: west front completed.

1245   Albert the Great teaching in Paris.

1269   Westminster Abbey rebuilt by Henry III.

1266–1308   Duns Scotus, "The Subtle Doctor", taught at Oxford.

1323   William of Ockham publishes his *Summa Logicae*.

1343   Richard Rolle, mystic, completes *The Fire of Love*.

1340–96   Walter Hilton: solitary mystic, wrote *Ladder of Perfection*.

1348–50   The Black Death: a third of the population dies.

1384   Edward III founds the Knights of the Garter.

1320–84   John Wyclif: writing against the corruption in the Church and translating the Bible into English. The Lollards.

1381   The Peasants' Revolt and Richard II.

1386   Geoffrey Chaucer begins *The Canterbury Tales*.

c. 1387   Julian of Norwich wrote *Revelations of Divine Love*: published in 1901.

1390   William Langland completes *Piers Plowman*.

1401   Statute for burning Lollards passed by Parliament.

1415   Henry V victory at Agincourt.

1441   Henry VI founds Eton College and King's College, Cambridge.
1483   Edward IV buried in St George's Chapel, Windsor.
1485   Richard III killed at Bosworth Field: Henry Tudor succeeds—Henry VII.

The Tudors

1509   Henry VIII comes to the throne.
1509   Henry VIII marries Catherine of Aragon: his brother's widow.
1512   Thomas Wolsey becomes Chief Minister of the Crown.
1516   Princess Mary born.
1521   Henry writes against Luther: *Assertio Septem Sacramentorum* ("Defence of the Seven Sacraments") and given the title *Fidei Defensor*.
1527   Henry petitions the Pope for an annulment of his marriage to Catherine.
1529   Wolsey fails to obtain a divorce/annulment; he swiftly falls from grace.
1530   Wolsey dies awaiting trial for treason: Sir Thomas More succeeds as Chancellor.
1531   Thomas Bilney martyred.
1533   Thomas Cranmer Archbishop of Canterbury.
1533   Henry marries Anne Boleyn: Princess Elizabeth born.
1529–36   English Reformation Parliament.
1534   Act of Supremacy (Henry VIII Head of the English Church); Treason Act: treasonable to question Henry's Supremacy. Annates (church dues) reserved to the English Crown.
1535   Execution of Thomas More.
1535   The Dissolution of the Monasteries: destruction of monastic libraries.
1536   Anne Boleyn executed.
1536   Henry VIII marries Jane Seymour.
1536   William Tyndale burnt in Belgium after capture in Antwerp.
1537   Birth of Prince Edward.
1537   Matthew's Bible authorized by the crown (mostly Tyndale's work).
1540   Execution of Thomas Cromwell.
1547   Death of Henry VIII: Edward VI—chantries suppressed.
1549   First Book of Common Prayer: Prayer Book Rebellion, Devon and Cornwall.
1552   Second Prayer Book.
1553   Death of Edward VI: succession of Queen Mary I.
1556   Burning of Latimer, Ridley and Archbishop Cranmer.

1558 Elizabeth I succeeds Mary.

1559 Acts of Supremacy and Uniformity passed: Book of Common Prayer revised and reissued.

1562 John Jewel's *Apologia* for the Church of England.

1563 John Foxe's *Book of Martyrs*: Thirty-Nine Articles of Religion—Archbishop Parker.

1570 Pope Pius V Bull dethroning Elizabeth I.

1572 Puritan *Admonition to the Parliament*.

1576 Archbishop Grindal refuses to suppress "Prophesyings", dies 1583.

1581 Execution of Edmund Campion.

1588 Defeat of the Spanish Armada.

1593 First four books of Richard Hooker's *Of the Laws of Ecclesiastical Polity*.

1603 Elizabeth I dies.

The Stuarts and the Commonwealth 1603–1714

1604 Hampton Court Conference: Commissioning of the Authorized Version of the Bible.

1605 The Gunpowder Plot: fresh hatred of Roman Catholics.

1607 Colonization of Virginia.

1611 Publication of the Authorized Version of the Bible.

1616 Death of William Shakespeare.

1617 Conversion experience of John Donne.

1620 *Mayflower* sets sail for Massachusetts.

1625 Charles I accedes to the throne.

1626 George Herbert associated with Little Gidding.

1633 William Laud, an Arminian, becomes Archbishop of Canterbury.

1642 English Civil War.

1645–70s Henry Vaughan and Thomas Traherne writing poetry.

1647 Cromwell suppresses the Levellers.

1649 Execution of Charles I.

1650 George Fox first called "Quaker".

1651 *Leviathan* by Thomas Hobbes.

1653 Oliver Cromwell becomes Lord Protector.

1656 Richard Baxter writes *The Reformed Pastor*.

1660 Restoration of Charles II.

1660 First meetings of the Royal Society.

1662 Act of Uniformity excludes Dissenters from the Church of England, Dissenting ministers imprisoned.
1664 First Conventicle begins persecution of Dissenters.
1667 *Paradise Lost* published by John Milton.
1675 Rebuilding of St Paul's under Sir Christopher Wren.
1678 The Popish Plot; John Bunyan publishes first part of *The Pilgrim's Progress*.
1681 William Penn chartered to fund Pennsylvania.
1685 Charles II dies, becoming a Roman Catholic on his deathbed.
1687 Isaac Newton publishes *Principia Mathematica*.
1688 The Glorious Revolution; Flight of James II; Accession of William III and Mary II.
1688 Bishops like Thomas Ken and others refuse to swear allegiance to William and Mary, called Non-Jurors.
1689 William defeats James II and Irish at the Battle of the Boyne.
1702 Queen Anne begins her reign, favouring High Churchmen.
1702 Occasional Conformity Bill aims at excluding Dissenters from public office.
1707 Act of Union between England and Scotland.

The Hanoverians

1704 Accession of the German-speaking George I: Whigs regain control.
1728 *A Serious Call to a Devout and Holy Life* by William Law.
1738 Conversion experience of John and Charles Wesley.
1739 George Whitfield begins open-air preaching.
1741 Handel composes *Messiah*.
1741 Richard Challoner becomes Vicar Apostolic (RC) of London district.
1760 Accession of George III.
1774 Founding of English Unitarianism by the scientist Joseph Priestley and Theophilus Lindsey.
1776 Declaration of Independence of the USA.
1779 Conversion experience of Charles Simeon.
1784 John Wesley ordains Methodist ministers to serve in America.
1784 Conversion experience of William Wilberforce.
1787 William Wilberforce takes on the cause of abolition of the slave trade.
1790 Edmund Burke's *Reflections on the Revolution in France*.

1793   William Carey sails to India.

1794   William Paley's *Evidences for Christianity*.

1799   Founding of the Church Missionary Society.

1801   Act of Union between Ireland and England; Irish MPs attend Westminster.

1807   Both Houses of Parliament vote to abolish the slave trade.

1811   National Society begins to found Church Schools.

1813   East India Company permits the appointment of missionaries and clergy.

1813   Elizabeth Fry begins her prison reform work.

1814   Missionaries begin work in New Zealand.

1818   Lord Liverpool's government votes funds for new churches: The Waterloo Churches in London.

1827   William Blake dies.

1828   Repeal of the Test and Corporation Acts against Dissenters.

1829   Catholic Emancipation.

1832   First Reform Act: opposed by bishops.

1833   Emancipation of Slaves.

1833   Beginning of the Oxford Movement; The Assize Sermon, John Keble.

1833   Jabez Bunting, President of the Methodist Conference.

1836   Sir Robert Peel establishes the Ecclesiastical Commissioners.

The Victorians

1837   Accession of Queen Victoria.

1838   F. D. Maurice publishes *The Kingdom of Christ*.

1841   Jerusalem bishopric founded.

1845   Start of the Irish Potato Famine.

1845   John Newman received into the Roman Catholic Church.

1847   Ten Hours Act, regulating factory working.

1848   Chartists demonstration in London.

1850   Restoration of the Roman Catholic hierarchy.

1851   Horace Mann's churchgoing census.

1854   Florence Nightingale in the Crimea.

1856   David Livingstone returns to England.

1857   The Indian Mutiny.

1859   *The Origin of Species* by Charles Darwin published.

1861   J. W. Colenso of Natal's *Commentary on Romans* published: questions eternal damnation and Old Testament history.

1863   Charles Haddon Spurgeon opens the Metropolitan Tabernacle.

1864   J. H. Newman publishes his *Apologia pro Vita Sua*.

1865   Henry Manning succeeds Nicholas Wiseman as RC Archbishop of Westminster.

1865   James Hudson Taylor founds China Inland Mission.

1867   First Lambeth Conference.

1868   Barnardo begins homes for orphans.

1869   Irish Disestablishment enacted.

1870   Papal infallibility enacted by the Vatican Council.

1870   Education Act establishes state schools.

1870   Death of Charles Dickens.

1873   David Livingstone dies in central Africa.

1875   Gerard Manley Hopkins writes *The Wreck of the Deutschland*.

1878   Salvation Army inaugurated by William Booth.

1885   Death of Lord Shaftesbury: 500 societies represented at his funeral.

1886   Josephine Butler secures the repeal of the Contagious Diseases Acts.

1889   *Lux Mundi* edited by Charles Gore.

1890   B. F. Westcott succeeds J. B. Lightfoot as Bishop of Durham.

1895   Cardinal Vaughan starts building Westminster Cathedral.

1896   Pope Leo XIII declares Anglican orders void.

1896   National Council of Free Churches formed.

1897   Queen Victoria's Diamond Jubilee.

1899   Boer War begins.

1901   Death of Queen Victoria.

The House of Windsor

1902   Education Act: State subsidises church schools.

1906   Liberal victory after ten years of Conservative government of Salisbury then Balfour (from 1902).

1909   Lloyd George's People's Budget, followed by two elections in 1910.

1910   Edinburgh World Missionary Conference.

1914   Outbreak of the Great War.

1917   Balfour Declaration promises a homeland for the Jews.

1919   Treaty of Versailles.

1924   First Labour government.

1926   The General Strike: Hierarchy of the Church of England mostly opposed.

1928   Cosmo Gordon Lang succeeds Randall Davidson as Archbishop of Canterbury: between them, archbishops for thirty-nine years (1903–42).

1929   Conversion experience of C. S. Lewis.

1931–40   National Government led by Ramsey MacDonald 1931–5, Baldwin 1935–7, Chamberlain 1937–40.

1942   Foundation of British Council of Churches.

1939–45   Second World War.

1940   Bombing of Coventry Cathedral.

1944   Butler Education Act with support of Archbishop William Temple.

1945   Clement Attlee PM: The foundation of the NHS and welfare state.

1948   SS *Windrush* docks in London from the Caribbean.

1950–6   C. S. Lewis publishes the Narnia series.

1951–74   Michael Ramsey, Archbishop of Canterbury.

1953   Coronation of Queen Elizabeth II.

1954   Billy Graham leads a Crusade at Haringey Stadium.

1963   Publication of *Honest to God* by Bishop John Robinson.

1964   Fountain Trust founded to encourage Charismatic Renewal.

1967   National Evangelical Conference at Keele led by John Stott.

1971   Festival of Light: Reaction to permissive society.

1979   Beginning of the Alpha course, Holy Trinity Brompton.

1982   Visit of Pope John Paul II to England.

1985   Publication of *Faith in the City* report.

1989   New Wine summer event begins, led by Bishop David Pytches.

1990s   The Decade of Evangelism.

1994   Ordination of women to the Church of England priesthood.

2004   Publication of the *Mission-Shaped Church* report.

2008   First GAFCON Conference in Jerusalem.

2014   Ordination of women to the episcopate in the Church of England.

2016   The UK votes to leave the European Union.

2020   COVID-19 pandemic national emergency.

Suggestions for Further Reading

Middle Ages

Bede, the Venerable, *Ecclesiastical History*, tr. Colgrave (Oxford University Press, 2008).

Dales, Douglas, *Light to The Isles* (James Clarke & Co, 2010).

Hunter Blair, Peter, *The World of Bede* (Cambridge University Press, 1990).

Julian of Norwich, *Revelations of Divine Love*, tr. Elizabeth Spearing (Penguin, 1998).

Southern, R. W., *Western Society and the Church in the Middle Ages* (Penguin, 1970).

Southern, R. W., *Saint Anselm: A Portrait in a Landscape* (Cambridge University Press, 1990).

Reformation

Daniel, David, *William Tyndale* (Yale University Press, 1994).

Duffy, Eamon, *The Stripping of the Altars* (Yale University Press, 2005).

Hill, Christopher, *God's Englishman: Oliver Cromwell and the English Revolution* (Weidenfeld & Nicolson, 1970).

MacCulloch, Diarmaid, *Thomas Cranmer* (Yale University Press, 1996).

MacCulloch, Diarmaid, *Reformation: Europe's House Divided* (Penguin, 2004).

Eighteenth to twentieth centuries

Chadwick, Owen, *The Victorian Church Vols I & II* (A & C Black, 1971 and 1972).

Colley, Linda, *Britons: Forging the Nation 1707–1737* (Yale University Press, 2012).

Duffy, Eamon, *John Henry Newman: A Very Brief History* (SPCK, 2019).

Hague, William, *William Wilberforce: The Life of the Great Anti-Slave Trade Campaigner* (Harper Perennial, 2008).

Hastings, Adrian, *A History of Christianity 1920–1985* (Collins, 1987).

Wesley, John, *Journals Vols I–V* (Everyman, Dent & Son, 1905).

A full bibliography of sources used may be found on the author's website, www.patrickwhitworth.co.uk.

Notes

Chapter 1

1   Suetonius, *Divus Claudius 25, The Twelve Caesars*, tr. Robert Graves and James Rives (London: Penguin Classics, 2007), p. 195; see also Acts 18:2.

2   J. R. H. Moorman, *A History of the Church in England* (London: A & C Black, 1973), p. 3.

3   Sam Moorhead and David Stuttard, *The Romans Who Shaped Britain* (London: Thames and Hudson, 2016), p. 20.

4   Caesar, *De Bello Gallico*, 4.20.

5   Caesar, *De Bello Gallico*, 4.24.

6   Cicero to Atticus 4:18, 5 July 54 BC, quoted in Moorhead and Stuttard, *The Romans Who Shaped Britain*, p. 35. Titus Pomponius Atticus was a wealthy man of letters, Cicero's closest friend and correspondent, a brother-in-law to Quintus Cicero, who was married to his sister, Pomponia. Wonderfully portrayed in Robert Harris's *Lustrum* (London: Arrow Books, 2009) and in the remaining volumes of the trilogy, *Imperium* and *Dictator*.

7   Bede, *Ecclesiastical History* (HE), tr. J. A. Giles, 1847 (London: Dent, 1965), p. 4.

8   David Mattingly, *An Imperial Possession: Britain in the Roman Empire* (London: Penguin, 2006), p. 35.

9   Cited in Barry Cunliffe, *Druids* (Oxford: Oxford University Press, 2010), p. 76.

10 Cunliffe, *Druids*, p. 82, quoting Tacitus's description of the presence of Druids in the Welsh tribal army.

11 Josephus, *Jewish War* III.4, cited by Moorhead and Stuttard, *The Romans Who Shaped Britain*, p. 57.

12 Dio 62,2, cited by Moorhead and Stuttard, *The Romans Who Shaped Britain*, p. 75; also, a large golden torch of the variety used by Britons was found in Snettisham, Norfolk.

13 See James Thomson's lyrics for "Rule, Britannia", written in 1740.

14 Tacitus 14.35, cited by Moorhead and Stuttard, *The Romans Who Shaped Britain*, p. 81.

[15] A. K. Bowman, *Life and Letters of the Roman Frontier*, p. 127, cited by Moorhead and Stuttard, *The Romans Who Shaped Britain*, p. 119.

[16] Peter Salway, *Roman Britain: A Very Short Introduction* (Oxford: Oxford University Press, 2015), p. 62.

[17] Cited by Mattingly, *An Imperial Possession*, p. 529, and Moorhead and Stuttard, *The Romans Who Shaped Britain*, p. 215; Jerome, *Chronicles* 371, p. 246c.

[18] David Potter, *Constantine the Emperor* (Oxford: Oxford University Press, 2013), p. 111.

[19] Timothy D. Barnes, *Constantine and Eusebius* (Boston, MA: Harvard University Press, 1981), p. 27.

[20] Optatus of Milevis App. 5 (Berlin: J. L. Maeir, 1987); cited by Potter, *Constantine the Emperor*, p. 201.

[21] Moorman, *A History of the Church in England*. I prefer Lincoln to Colchester as the place of the third bishopric, although Moorman prefers Colchester.

[22] Charles Thomas, *Christianity in Roman Britain to AD 500* (London: Batsford Press, 1981), p. 197.

[23] Gerald Bonner, *St Augustine of Hippo: Life and Controversies* (Norwich: Canterbury Press, 2002), p. 316.

[24] His main biographer is Georges de Plinval from Cherbourg in Normandy: *Pélage: ses écrits, sa vie et sa réforme* (Lausanne, 1943).

[25] Augustine, *Confessions*, Book X, xxxix, 40.

[26] Bonner, *Augustine of Hippo*, p. 321.

[27] Bonner, *Augustine of Hippo*, p. 325, citing Augustine, *De Diversis Questionibus* CSEL, xxiv A.

[28] Douglas Dales, *Light to the Isles* (London: James Clarke & Co., 2010), p. 30.

[29] Bede, *HE* Book 1.XVII, pp. 25ff.

[30] PG 51:594, cited by Thomas O'Loughlin, *St Patrick: The Man and His Works* (London: SPCK, 2014), p. 15.

[31] Patrick, *Confessio* 1, tr. O'Loughlin, *St Patrick*, p. 52.

[32] Patrick, *Confessio* 2, tr. O'Loughlin, *St Patrick*, p. 55.

[33] O'Loughlin, *St Patrick*, Patrick's "Address to the Soldiers", p. 103.

[34] There are two lives of Gildas: one written by an anonymous Bretton monk and the other by Caradoc of Llancarfan.

[35] Cited by Anthony Birley, *The People of Roman Britain* (Berkeley: University of California, 1980), p. 160.

[36] Mattingly, *An Imperial Possession*, p. 528.

Chapter 2

1   Bede, *HE*, Bk. I, ch. xiv, tr. J Stevens (London: Dent, 1965), p. 21.

2   F. M. Stenton, *Anglo-Saxon England* (Oxford: Oxford University Press, 1967), p. 5.

3   Gildas, *Ruin of Britain*, tr. H. Williams (Dodo Press), p. 24.

4   Bede, *HE*, p. 23.

5   Gildas, *Ruin of Britain*, p. 18.

6   James Campbell (ed.), *The Anglo-Saxons* (Harmondsworth: Penguin, 1991), p. 27.

7   Stenton, *Anglo-Saxon England*, p. 3.

8   Robin Fleming, *Britain after Rome* (London: Penguin, 2011), p. 45.

9   Henry Mayr-Harting, *The Coming of Christianity to Anglo-Saxon England* (Pittsburgh, PA: Pennsylvania State University Press, 1994), pp. 15–16.

10   *Beowulf*, tr. Seamus Heaney (London: Penguin, 1999), II, 1020–34, p. 33.

11   Mayr-Harting, *Coming of Christianity*, pp. 51ff; Peter Hunter Blair, *The World of Bede* (Cambridge: Cambridge University Press, 1990), p. 49; Stenton, *Anglo-Saxon England*, p. 32.

12   John Julius Norwich, *The Popes* (London: Chatto and Windus, 2011), p. 39.

13   Mayr-Harting, *Coming of Christianity*, p. 51.

14   *The Whitby Life of Gregory*, cited by Mayr-Harting, *Coming of Christianity*, p. 58.

15   Bede, *HE*, Bk. I, ch. xxvii.

16   Gregory's Letter, *GE VIII*, Vatican Papers, cited by Blair, *World of Bede*, p. 29.

17   Bede, *HE* 2.2, cited in Mayr-Harting, *Coming of Christianity*, p. 71.

18   Bede, *HE*, Bk. II, ch. vi, pp. 74–5.

19   Bede, *HE*, Bk. II, ch. xiii, p. 91.

20   Bede, *HE*, Bk. II, ch. xiii, p. 91.

21   Bede, *HE*, Bk II, ch. xiv, p. 92.

22   Bede, *HE*, Bk. III, ch. i, p. 104.

23   Charles Thomas, *Christianity in Roman Britain to AD 500*, p. 304, citing G. S. M. Walker, *Sancti Columbani Opera* (Dublin: Dublin Institute for Advanced Studies, 1957). My italics.

24   Adomnan of Iona, *Life of St Columba*, ed. and tr. Richard Sharpe (London: Penguin Classics, 1995), p. 9.

25   Bede, *HE*, Bk. III.

26   Adomnan of Iona, *Life of St Columba*, p. 109.

27   Bede, *HE*, Bk. III, ch. ii, p. 105.

28   Bede, *HE*, Bk. III, ch. iii, p. 106.

29   Bede, *HE*, Bk. III, ch. ix, p. 117.

30   Bede, *HE*, Bk. III, chs. xi–xiii, pp. 119–24.

31   Bede, *HE*, Bk. II, ch. viii, p. 115.

32   Bede, *HE*, Bk. III, ch. vii, pp. 112–13.

33   Bede, *HE*, Bk. III, ch. xix, pp. 132–3.

34   Bede, *HE*, Bk. III, ch. xxv, p. 146.

35   Bede, *HE*, Bk. III, chs. xxv, xxvi, pp. 146–54.

36   Bede, *HE*, Bk. III, ch. xxv, pp. 148–9.

37   Bede, *HE*, Bk. IV, ch. i, p. 162.

38   Bede, *HE*, Bk. IV, ch. xi, p. 164.

39   Bede, *HE*, Bk. IV, ch. v, p. 173.

40   See Eddius, *Life of Wilfrid*, in *The Age of Bede* (London: Penguin, 1998), p. 110.

41   Mayr-Harting, *Coming of Christianity*, p. 129.

42   Eddius, *Life of Wilfrid*, p. 119.

43   Eddius, *Life of Wilfrid*, p. 122.

44   Bede, *HE*, Bk. IV, ch. ii, p. 165.

45   Eddius, *Life of Wilfrid*, p. 124.

46   Bede, *HE*, Bk. IV ch. 25, p. 260.

47   Eddius, *Life of Wilfrid*, p. 144.

48   Bede, *HE*, Bk. IV, ch. xii, p. 184.

49   Bede, *HE*, Bk. IV, ch. xiii, p. 185.

50   Eddius, *Life of Wilfrid*, p. 157.

51   Bede, *Life of Cuthbert*, ch. 10, tr. D. H. Farmer (London: Penguin, 1998), p. 58.

52   Bede, *Life of Cuthbert*, ch. 17, p. 67.

53   Bede, *Life of Cuthbert*, ch. 17, p. 67.

54   Bede, *Life of Cuthbert*, ch. 26, p. 79.

55   Bede, *Life of Cuthbert*, ch. 32, p. 85.

56   Later to be the subject of corruption, see Bede, Bk IV, ch. xxv, p. 209.

57   Cuthbert's Letter on Bede's death in *Venerablis Bedae Opera Historica I*, ed. C. Plummer, pp. 142–4, cited by Mayr-Harting, *Coming of Christianity*, pp. 217–18.

58   PL vols 90–5 (Paris, 1861).

59   PEC 1843/4 (London).

60   Bede, "The Lives of the Abbots", in *Age of Bede*, p. 204.

61   The *Dream of the Rood* meant a "Dream of the Cross", with rood meaning rod or pole. It is a poem in which the Cross is personified, and thus recalls the Crucifixion.

62   Cited by Mayr-Harting, *Coming of Christianity*, p. 178.

63   *The Book of Cerne*, no. 17, ed. A. B. Kuypers (Cambridge: Cambridge University Press, 1902), cited by Mayr-Harting, *Coming of Christianity*, p. 184.

64   Mayr-Harting, *Coming of Christianity*, pp. 192–5.

65 This was c. 711 onwards. Moors is a generic term for North African Muslims who invaded and would remain in Spain, lastly in Grenada, until the start of the sixteenth century.

66 D. Edwards, *Christian England: Its Story to the Reformation* (London: Oxford University Press, 1980), pp. 83–4.

67 Bede, *HE*, Bk. III, ch. xxiv, p. 141.

68 Bede, *HE*, Bk. IV, ch. iii, p. 165.

69 Campbell, *Anglo Saxons*, ch. 4 by P. Wormald, p. 94.

70 Campbell, *Anglo-Saxons*, ch. 5; Patrick Wormald, *The Age of Offa and Alcuin* (London: Penguin, 1991), p. 101.

71 E.g. Robert Tombs, *The English and their History* (London: Penguin, 2014).

Chapter 3

1 See chronology of successive kings in Northumbria in James Campbell, *Anglo Saxons*, ch. 5; and Patrick Wormald, *Age of Offa and Alcuin*, p. 114.

2 Douglas Dales, *Alcuin: His Life and Legacy* (Cambridge: James Clarke, 2012), p. 65.

3 *Anglo-Saxon Chronicle* EHD, cited by John Blair in *The Anglo-Saxon Age: A Very Short Introduction* (London: Oxford University Press, 2000), p. 180.

4 Frank Stenton, *Anglo-Saxon England*, p. 205.

5 Chris Wickham, *The Inheritance of Rome: A History of Europe from 400–1000* (London: Penguin, 2009), p. 259.

6 Dales, *Alcuin*, pp. 58–60.

7 Julian D. Richards, *The Vikings: A Very Short Introduction* (Oxford: Oxford University Press, 2005), p. 2.

8 According to Asser, Berkshire takes its name from the box tree. See Asser, *Life of King Alfred*, tr. S. Keynes and M. Lapidge (London: Penguin, 2004), p. 67.

9 Of David, 1 Samuel 16:5–12 says: "He is the one".

10 Asser, *Life of King Alfred* 22, p. 75.

11 This work of c. 1395 is exhibited at the National Gallery, and shows Richard II being presented at a heavenly nativity by John the Baptist, St Edmund and Edward the Confessor.

12 Asser, *Life of King Alfred* 88, p. 99.

13 Asser, *Life of King Alfred* 88, p. 99.

14 Asser, *Life of King Alfred* 78, p. 93.

15 Asser, *Life of King Alfred* 74, p. 89.

16 Alfred's translation of Gregory's *Pastoral Care*, in Asser, *Life of King Alfred*, pp. 123–7.

17   "Laws of King Alfred" 42.7, in Asser, *The Life of King Alfred*, p. 169.

18   Campbell, *Anglo-Saxons*, p. 149.

19   Stenton, *Anglo-Saxon England*, p. 318.

20   Tom Holland, *Athelstan* (London: Penguin, 2016), p. 36.

21   Robert Tombs, *The English and Their History* (London: Penguin, 2014), p. 32.

22   Stenton, *Anglo-Saxon England*, p. 352.

23   Dales, *Dunstan*, citing *EHD* 234, p. 42.

24   Asser, *Life of King Alfred* 94–8, pp. 103–5.

25   Recorded in "source B", Dunstan's anonymous biographer, and published by Stubbs. *Memorials of St Dunstan* (London: Stubbs, 1874), p. 12f, cited by Dales, *Dunstan*, p. 19.

26   Dorothy Whitelock, ed., *EHD*, *Sermo lupi ad Anglos* 1014; *Cotton Nero Ai*, mss 240, p. 858.

27   Cited in "Aelfric's Life of Ethelwold", Whitelock, *EHD* 235.15, p. 835.

28   Cited in Whitelock, *EHD* 235/21/20/23, pp. 836–7.

29   "Ine's Laws", Whitelock, *EHD* 32, p. 365.

30   Source B, "Life of Dunstan", p. 49, cited by Dales, *Dunstan*, p. 59.

31   Source B, "Life of Dunstan", p. 49, cited by Dales, *Dunstan*, p. 59.

32   This prayer book was sold to the nation by the Duchess of Portland in 1753 for £10,000, a fraction of today's value.

33   Whitelock, *EHD*, ASC 1, p. 206.

34   There is some debate about the intensity of this anti-monastic movement: see Stenton, *Anglo-Saxon England*, p. 368, and Campbell, *The Anglo-Saxons*, p. 192.

35   Stenton, *Anglo-Saxon England*, p. 369.

36   E. V. Gordon, ed., *Battle of Maldon* (London: Methuen, 1960).

37   Stenton, *Anglo-Saxon England*, p. 373.

38   Galla Placidia married the Visigoth leader, Ataulf, and then the Western Emperor, Constantius III, and was regent for their son Valentinian III in his infancy.

39   Whitelock, *EHD*, ASC C, D, E, p. 228.

40   See Whitelock, *EHD*, ASC D, p. 229, for a full description of this great funeral in which Alphege's body was taken from Greenwich to Canterbury.

41   Whitelock, *EHD*, pp. 419–30, p. 431.

42   Whitelock, *EHD*, pp. 416–17.

43   Whitelock, *EHD*, p. 418.

44   Campbell, *Anglo-Saxons*, p. 214; Eric John, *The End of Anglo-Saxon England* (London: Penguin, 1991), ch. 9.

Chapter 4

1 Doris Mary Stenton, *English Society in the Early Middle Ages* (London: Pelican, 1951), p. 535.

2 Stenton, *English Society in the Early Middle Ages*, p. 484.

3 Judith Herrin, *Byzantium* (London: Penguin, 2007), pp. 226–7.

4 Richard Southern, citing *Nicholas II Letter to Lanfranc* PL 143 cols 1,349–50, in *Saint Anselm: A Portrait in a Landscape* (Cambridge: Cambridge University Press, 1990), pp. 20–1.

5 F. Barlow, ed., *Vita Edwardi Regis*, 2nd edn (Oxford: Oxford University Press, 1992).

6 For further discussion, see George Garnett, *The Norman Conquest: A Very Short Introduction* (Oxford: Oxford University Press, 2009), p. 33.

7 Tombs, *The English and Their History*, p. 41.

8 Morris, *William I*, p. 48, citing William of Poitiers, *Gesta Normannorum Ducum*, tr. R. H. C. Davis and M. Chibnall (Oxford: Oxford University Press, 1998), pp. 122–5.

9 ASC Worcester mss, p. 199, cited in Tombs, *The English and Their History*, p. 42.

10 Tombs, *The English and Their History*, p. 44.

11 William Shakespeare, *Richard II*, Act III, Scene II.

12 ASC "E" 1085.

13 Stenton, *English Society in the Early Middle Ages*, p. 614.

14 Garnett, *The Norman Conquest*, p. 11.

15 Letter of Pope Nicholas II, cited in Southern, *Saint Anselm*, p. 20.

16 Southern, *Saint Anselm*, p. 330.

17 Thorlac Turville-Petre, *England the Nation: Language, Literature and Identity 1290–1340* (Oxford: Oxford University Press, 2002), p. 92, cited in Tombs, *The English and Their History*, p. 53.

18 Moorman, *A History of the Church in England*, p. 62.

19 Southern, *Saint Anselm*, p. 312.

20 Southern, *Saint Anselm*, p. 79.

21 Southern, *Saint Anselm*, p. 143.

22 Southern, *Saint Anselm*, p. 144, citing *Epistle 4.i.4* (London, British Library MS Cotton Nero A vii 1092–1100).

23 Anselm, *The Prayers and Meditations of Saint Anselm*, tr. Benedicta Ward (London: Penguin, 1973), p. 98.

24 Southern, *Saint Anselm*, p. 271.

Chapter 5

1   Southern, *Saint Anselm*, pp. 292–3.

2   John Guy, *Thomas Becket* (London: Penguin, 2012), p. xxiii.

3   David Carpenter, *The Struggle for Mastery* (London: Penguin, 2004), p. 163.

4   *De Nugis Curialium* (Courtiers Trifle), tr. M. R. James (Oxford: Oxford University Press, 1983).

5   For a full list of the locations of Henry's Christmas Court, see Keith Feiling, *A History of England* (London: Macmillan, 1966), p. 127.

6   John of Salisbury, from *Materials for the History of Becket*, VI 72, cited in W. L. Warren, *Henry II* (New Haven and London: Yale University Press, 2000), p. 183.

7   Guy, *Thomas Becket*, p. 309.

8   Augustine, *Contra Faustum Manichaeum* 22.69–76.

9   Christopher Tyerman, *The Crusades: A Very Short Introduction* (Oxford: Oxford University Press, 2005), p. 68.

10   Steven Runciman, *A History of the Crusades*, Vol. I (London: Penguin, 1991), p. 77.

11   The *filioque* ("and *the Son*") clause is the clause added by the Western Church (Rome) to the Nicene Creed that the Spirit proceeds from the Father and the Son. This was objected to (and still is) by the Orthodox churches.

12   Carpenter, *The Struggle for Mastery*, p. 245.

13   William Shakespeare, *King John*, Act II, Scene II.

14   Magna Carta, from the Holt Magna Carta, cited by Nicholas Vincent, *Magna Carta: A Very Short Introduction* (London: Oxford University Press, 2012), p. 112.

15   Vincent, *Magna Carta*, p. 118.

16   Magna Carta 1215, as in J. C. Holt's edition of Magna Carta, 1992, cited in Vincent, *Magna Carta*, p. 122.

17   Vincent, *Magna Carta*, p. 83.

18   Holt, *Magna Carta*, cited by Vincent, *Magna Carta*, p. 111.

Chapter 6

1   Carpenter, *Struggle for Mastery*, p. 303.

2   Carpenter, *Struggle for Mastery*, p. 340.

3   Carpenter, *Struggle for Mastery*, p. 354.

4   Feiling, *History of England*, p. 168.

5   Feiling, *History of England*, p. 171.

6   Matthew Paris, *English History Vol. III*, tr. J. A. Giles (London: Bohn, 1854; 1923 Nabu Reprint), p. 349.

7   Tombs, *The English and Their History*, p. 76, citing *Song of Lewes, The English and their Rulers*, p. 259.

8   Neil B. McLynn, *Ambrose of Milan* (Berkeley: University of California, 1994), pp. 298–300.

9   John Chrysostom, *Oration against the Jews* 1, cited in Wendy Mayer and Pauline Allen, *John Chrysostom* (New York: Routledge, 2000), p. 151.

10 Tertullian, *An Answer to the Jews*, TANF Vol III, tr S. Thelwall, 1885 (repr. New York: Cosimo, 2007), p. 173.

11 Augustine, *Tractatus adversus Judaeos*, PL Vol. 42, pp. 51–64.

12 Carpenter, *Struggle for Mastery*, p. 249.

13 Jonathan Sumption, *Trial by Battle*, Vol. I of *The Hundred Years War* (London: Faber and Faber, 1990), p. 47.

14 Sumption, *Trial by Battle*, p. 43.

15 Sumption, *Trial by Battle*, p. 49, citing W. J. Whittaker, ed., *Mirror of Justices* (1895), p. 28.

16 Sumption, *Trial by Battle*, p. 51.

Chapter 7

1   Simon Schama, *At the Edge of the World: A History of Britain 300BC–1603* (London: BBC, 2000), p. 222.

2   Miri Rubin, *The Hollow Crown: A History of Britain in the Late Middle Ages* (London: Penguin, 2005), p. 57.

3   This wonderfully illuminated manuscript, made for Sir Geoffrey Luttrell (1276–1345), is in the British Library; likewise, the Macclesfield Psalter is in the Fitzwilliam Museum in Cambridge.

4   David Knowles, *Christian Monasticism* (McGraw-Hill, 1969), p. 34.

5   St Benedict, *The Rule of St Benedict*, ch. 2 (Collegeville, MN: Liturgical Press, 1982), p. 21.

6   Benedict, *Rule*, ch. 2, p. 23.

7   See also Esther de Waal, *Seeking God: The Way of St Benedict* (Norwich: Canterbury Press, 1984).

8   R. W. Southern, *Western Society and the Church in the Middle Ages* (London: Penguin, 1970), p. 228.

9   Southern, *Western Society and the Church in the Middle Ages*, p. 228.

[10]   Augustine, EP 211, PL 33, 958–68, cited in Southern, *Western Society and the Church in the Middle Ages*, p. 242.

[11]   Knowles, *Christian Monasticism*, p. 69.

[12]   Southern, *Western Society and the Church in the Middle Ages*, pp. 296–7.

[13]   Southern, *Western Society and the Church in the Middle Ages*, p. 291, citing *Oxford Deeds*, ed. H. E. Salter (Oxford: Oxford Historical Society 64, 1913), pp. 198–9.

[14]   The British Library Collection, Exhibition, Royal Mss 2A, xvii.

[15]   See Bede, *HE*, ch. xxvii, pp. 37–50; and Stenton, *Anglo-Saxon England*, pp. 106–7.

[16]   William of Malmesbury, *De antiquitate Glastonie Ecclesie*, 19, tr. John Scott (Woodbridge, Suffolk: Boydell Press, 1981).

[17]   *The Apostolic Fathers Vol II*, Loeb Classical Library 25 (Harvard Press, 2005), pp. 121ff.

[18]   Simon Jenkins, *England's Thousand Best Churches* (London: Penguin, 1999), p. 488.

[19]   Roy Strong, *A Little History of the English Country Church* (London: Vintage, 2008), p. 20.

[20]   Geoffrey Chaucer, *Canterbury Tales*, "Wife of Bath", tr. Peter Ackroyd (Penguin, 2009), p. 147.

[21]   Strong, *Little History of the English Country Church*, p. 24.

[22]   David L. Edwards, *Christian England*, Vol. I (Oxford: Oxford University Press, 1980), p. 156.

[23]   L. W. B. Brockless, *The University of Oxford* (Oxford: Oxford University Press, 2016), p. 3.

[24]   Peter Pagamenta (ed.), *The University of Cambridge: 800 Years* (London: Third Millennium Publishing, 2008), pp. 31–2.

Chapter 8

[1]   Philipp W. Rosemann, *The Story of a Great Medieval Book: Peter Lombard's Sentences* (Toronto: University of Toronto Press, 2007), p. 22.

[2]   Julia Annas, *Plato: A Very Short Introduction* (Oxford: Oxford University Press, 2003), p. 90.

[3]   Plato, *Theaetetus*, 150c–d.

[4]   *Timaeus*, 29d–30c, cited in Annas, *Plato*, p. 40.

[5]   Annas, *Plato*, p. 54.

[6]   Robin Lane Fox, *Augustine Conversions and Confessions* (London: Penguin Books, 2015), p. 398.

[7]   Jonathan Barnes, *Aristotle: A Very Short Introduction* (Oxford: Oxford University Press, 2000), p. 93.

8   Fergus Kerr, *Thomas Aquinas: A Very Short History* (Oxford: Oxford University Press, 2009), p. 104.

9   See the chronology of Anselm's life in R. W. Southern, *Saint Anselm: A Portrait in a Landscape* (Cambridge: Cambridge University Press, 1990), pp xxvii–iii.

10   See *St Anselm's Basic Writings*, tr. S. N. Deane (Chicago: Open Court Publishing, 1968), chs xvi–xlvii, pp. 64–111.

11   Southern, *Saint Anselm*, p. 127.

12   *St Anselm's Basic Writings*, "Proslogion", ch. III, p. 8.

13   Rosemann, *The Story of a Great Medieval Book*, p. 85, see British Library Royal 9.B.VI, fols 2r–24v.

14   James McEvoy, *Robert Grosseteste* (Oxford: Oxford University Press, 2000), p. 35.

15   L. W. B. Brockless, *The University of Oxford*.

16   Geoffrey Chaucer, "General Prologue", *Canterbury Tales* II, 293–6, cited in Brockless, *University of Oxford*, p. 42.

17   McEvoy, *Robert Grosseteste*, p. xi.

18   McEvoy, *Grosseteste*, p. 141.

19   McEvoy, *Grosseteste*, p. 135.

20   McEvoy, *Grosseteste*, p. 85.

21   Kerr, *Thomas Aquinas*, pp. 31–65.

22   Douglas Dales, *The Way Back to God: The Spiritual Theology of St Bonaventure* (London: James Clarke & Co., 2019), p. 174.

Chapter 9

1   Eamon Duffy's *Stripping of the Altars* (New Haven, CT: Yale University Press, 2005) is unparalleled as an insightful survey of these phenomena.

2   Duffy, *Stripping of the Altars*, p. 340, citing C. Horstmann (ed.), *Altenglische Legenden Neue Folge* (Heilbronn, 1881), p. 370.

3   Duffy, *Stripping of the Altars*, p. 344.

4   Duffy, *Stripping of the Altars*, p. 344, citing Thomas More's *Complete Works*, ed. T. M. C. Lawler and others (New Haven, CT: Yale University Press, 1981), pp. 377–8.

5   Duffy, *Stripping of the Altars*, p. 363, citing C. W. Forester, ed., *Wills II* (Lincoln Record Society, 1914), p. 89.

6   Duffy, *Stripping of the Altars*, p. 361.

7   Basil, *Letters 186-248*, tr. R. Deferrari, Loeb Classical Series, Vol. 243, No. CCXVII (Boston, MA: Harvard University Press, 2001), pp. 238ff.

8   Christopher M. Cullen, *Bonaventure* (Oxford: Oxford University Press, 2006), p. 175.

9   *The Book of Margery Kempe*, tr. Anthony Bale (Oxford: Oxford University Press, 2015), p. 45.

10 Geoffrey Chaucer, *The Canterbury Tales*, tr. Peter Ackroyd (London: Penguin, 2009), p. 22.

11 Strong, *Little History of the English Church*, p. 36.

12 *Book of Margery Kempe*, p. 185.

13 *Book of Margery Kempe*, p. 166.

14 Walter Hilton, *The Ladder of Perfection*, tr. Leo Shirley-Price (London: Penguin, 1988), p. 116.

15 Giovanni Boccaccio, *Life of Dante* (London: Hesperus Press, 2002), p. 49.

16 Duffy, *Stripping of the Altars*, p. 131.

17 Chaucer, *Canterbury Tales*, p. 181.

18 Chaucer, *Canterbury Tales*, p. 177.

19 Chaucer, *Canterbury Tales*, p. 191.

20 Chaucer, *Canterbury Tales*, p. 200.

21 Chaucer, *Canterbury Tales*, p. 201.

22 Chaucer, *Canterbury Tales*, p. 307.

23 Chaucer, *Canterbury Tales*, p. 17.

24 See Gregory Nyssen, *Life of Moses* (New York: HarperOne, 1978).

25 See Rowan Williams, *The Wound of Knowledge* (London: Darton, Longman & Todd, 1990).

26 *Book of Margery Kempe*, p. ix.

27 Richard Rolle, *The Fellowship of Angels*, tr. Henrietta Hick (Leominster: Gracewing, 2008), p. 7.

28 Rolle, *Fire of Love*, p. 26.

29 Rolle, *Fire of Love*, p. 119.

30 Rolle, *Fire of Love*, p. 119.

31 Hilton, *Ladder of Perfection*, p. 114.

32 Hilton, *Ladder of Perfection*, p. 116.

33 Hilton, *Ladder of Perfection*, p. 121.

34 Hilton, *Ladder of Perfection*, p. 121.

35 Hilton, *Ladder of Perfection*, p. 157.

36 Hilton, *Ladder of Perfection*, p. 34.

37 Julian of Norwich, *Revelations of Divine Life*, tr. Elizabeth Spearing (London: Penguin, 1998), ST, p. 5.

38 Julian, *Revelations of Divine Life*, p. 4.

39 Julian, *Revelations of Divine Life*, p. 6.

40 Julian, *Revelations of Divine Life*, p. 150, LT ch. 65.

41   Julian, *Revelations of Divine Life*, LT 4, p. 45.

42   Julian, *Revelations of Divine Life*, ST 4, p. 7.

43   Julian, *Revelations of Divine Life*, ST 5, p. 9.

44   Julian, *Revelations of Divine Life*, LT 32, p. 85.

45   Julian, *Revelations of Divine Life*, p. 83.

46   Julian, *Revelations of Divine Life*, LT 86, p. 179.

47   *Book of Margery Kempe*, p. 42.

48   *Book of Margery Kempe*, p. 42.

49   *Book of Margery Kempe*, pp. 25–6.

50   *Book of Margery Kempe*, p. 27.

51   *Book of Margery Kempe*, p. 58.

52   *Book of Margery Kempe*, p. 152.

53   *Book of Margery Kempe*, pp. 187–9.

54   *Book of Margery Kempe*, p. 189.

55   *Book of Margery Kempe*, p. 165.

56   *Cloud of Unknowing*, tr. A. Spearing (London: Penguin Classics, 2001), ch. 11, p. 43.

57   *Cloud of Unknowing*, ch. 26, p. 71.

Chapter 10

1   Laura Ashe, *Richard II*, Penguin Monarchs Series (London: Penguin, 2017), p. 40, citing *Knighton's Chronicle 1337–1396*, ed. and tr. G. H. Martin (Oxford: Oxford University Press, 1995), pp. 222–4.

2   Ashe, *Richard II*, p. 41.

3   Ashe, *Richard II*, p. 6.

4   Ashe, *Richard II*, p. 9, citing *Westminster Chronicle 1381–1394*, tr. L. C. Hector and Barbara Harvey (London: Clarendon Press, 1932), p. 139.

5   *Richard II*, Act III, Scene iii.

6   Rubin, *The Hollow Crown* (London: Penguin, 2005), p. 160.

7   *Henry IV Part II*, Act III, Scene i.

8   *Richard II*, Act III, Scene ii.

9   Stephen E. Lahey, *John Wyclif*, Great Medieval Thinkers Series (Oxford: Oxford University Press, 2009), p. 5.

10   Lahey, *John Wyclif*, p. 11.

11   Lahey, *John Wyclif*, p. 149.

12   G. W. H. Lampe (ed.), *The Cambridge History of the Bible, Vol. 2* (Cambridge: Cambridge University Press, 1976), p. 384.

13   Lampe, *Cambridge History of the Bible*, p. 388. John Julius Norwich, *The Popes* (London: Chatto and Windus, 2011), pp. 225–7.

14   Lahey, *John Wyclif*, p. 215.

15   *Henry IV Part I*, Act V, Scene iv.

16   Tombs, *The English and Their History*, p. 136.

17   Juliet Barker, *Agincourt* (New York: Little, Brown, 2006), p. 123.

18   *Henry V*, Act IV, Scene iii.

19   *Henry V*, Act V, Scene ii.

20   John Blacman, *Henry VI*, pp. 15–16, cited in James Ross, *Henry VI: A Good Simple and Innocent Man* (London: Penguin, 2016), p. 38.

21   Bertram Wolffe, *Henry VI* (New Haven, CT: Yale University Press, 1983), p. 55.

22   Alison Weir, *Lancaster and York: The Wars of the Roses* (London: Vintage, 2009), p. 222, citing *The Paston Letters and Papers 1422–1509*, ed. J. Gairdner (Edinburgh, 1910).

23   *Hamlet*, Act IV, Scene v.

24   Ross, *Henry VI*, p. 66, citing *Paston Letters II*, pp. 295–6, John Stodeley writing from London on 19 January 1454.

25   At Marston Moor in 1644 in the English Civil War, 40,000 troops took part with approximately 6,000 casualties.

26   Ross, *Henry VI*, p. 24, citing Blacman, *Henry VI*, p. 8.

27   A. J. Pollard, *Edward IV: The Summer King* (London: Penguin, 2016), p. 7.

28   Jenkins, *England's Thousand Best Churches*, p. xvii.

29   David Horspool, *Richard III: A Ruler and his Reputation* (London: Bloomsbury, 2015), p. 155.

30   Susan Bridgen, *New Worlds, Lost Worlds* (London: Penguin, 2000), p. 81.

Chapter 11

1   Sean Cunningham, *Henry VII* (London: Routledge, 2007), p. 105.

2   William Wordsworth, *The Prelude Bk 10*.

3   Alison Weir, *Henry VIII* (London: Vintage Books, 2008), p. 134.

4   J. J. Scarisbrick, *Henry VIII* (New Haven, CT: Yale University Press, 1997), p. 507.

5   Cited by Weir, *Henry VIII*, p. 134, citing PRO despatches from Sebastian Giustiniano entitled *Four Years at the Court of Henry VIII*, tr. L. Rawdon Brown (London, 1854).

6   Diarmaid MacCulloch, *Thomas Cranmer* (New Haven, CT: Yale University Press, 1996), p. 65.

7   Scarisbrick, *Henry VIII*, p. 217, citing *Hall's Chronicle* (1806 edn), pp. 754ff.

[8] Lyndal Roper, *Martin Luther: Renegade and Prophet* (London: The Bodley Head, 2016), p. 91.

[9] Scarisbrick, *Henry VIII*, p. 247, citing Styrpe, *Ecclesiastical Memorials* I, I, 172.

[10] Diarmaid MacCulloch, *Thomas Cromwell: A Life* (London: Allen Lane, Penguin Books, 2018), p. 219.

[11] Tracy Borman, *Thomas Cromwell* (London: Hodder, 2015), p. 22.

[12] Weir, *Henry VIII*, p. 347.

[13] Eric Ives, *The Life and Death of Anne Boleyn* (Oxford: Blackwell, 2005), p. 358.

[14] Ives, *Life and Death of Anne Boleyn*, p. 359.

[15] MacCulloch, *Cranmer*, p. 157, citing *Cranmer's Remains and Letters* (Cambridge: Parker Society, 1846).

[16] Peter Ackroyd, *The Life of Thomas More* (London: Vintage Books, 1999), p. 42.

[17] Eamon Duffy, *Reformation Divided* (Bloomsbury Continuum, 1917), p. 30.

[18] Duffy, *Reformation Divided*, p. 39.

[19] Ackroyd, *Life of Thomas More*, pp. 351-2.

[20] Ackroyd, *Life of Thomas More*, p. 369.

[21] David Daniel, *William Tyndale* (New Haven, CT: Yale University Press, 1994), p. 10.

[22] Daniel, *William Tyndale*, p. 191, citing Parker Society, *The Practice of Prelates* (1849), p. 337.

[23] Daniel, *William Tyndale*, p. 310.

[24] Daniel, *William Tyndale*, p. 290, citing Parker Society, *Expositions*, pp. 148-9.

[25] Daniel, *William Tyndale*, p. 379; James Frederic Mozley, *Tyndale* (London: SPCK, 1937), p. 335.

[26] Duffy, *Reformation Divided*, p. 387.

[27] Duffy, *Reformation Divided*, p. 405.

[28] Duffy, *Reformation Divided*, p. 422.

[29] Scarisbrick, *Henry VII*, p. 495.

[30] John Foxe, *Acts and Monuments*, ed. Josiah Pratt, 8 Vols, 1874, Vol. V. l689 (Thomas Cranmer).

Chapter 12

[1] Chris Skidmore, *Edward VI: The Lost King of England* (London: Weidenfeld and Nicolson, 2007), p. 51, citing BL Harleian MSS 5087, no. 34.

[2] Skidmore, *Edward VI*, p. 55, citing Agnes Strickland, *The Queens of England* Vol. II (London: George Bell and Son, 1901), p. 443.

[3] Skidmore, *Edward VI*, p. 61, citing *Works of Archbishop Cranmer Vol II*, ed. J. E. Cox (London: Parker Society, 1846), pp. 126–7.

[4] Duffy, *Stripping of the Altars*, p. 449, citing *The Remains of Thomas Cranmer* (Cambridge: Cambridge University Press, Parker Society, 1846), p. 141.

[5] Duffy, *Stripping of the Altars*, p. 462.

[6] MacCulloch, *Thomas Cranmer*, p. 328.

[7] Brian Cummings, *The Book of Common Prayer* (Oxford: Oxford University Press, 2018), p. 27 and p. 375.

[8] MacCulloch, *Thomas Cranmer*, p. 411, citing C. Whitaker (ed.), *Martin Bucer and the Book of Common Prayer* (London: Mayhew-McCrimmon, 1974), pp. 44–5.

[9] MacCulloch, *Thomas Cranmer*, p. 411.

[10] MacCulloch, *Thomas Cranmer*, p. 411.

[11] Diarmaid MacCulloch, *Tudor Church Militant* (Allen Lane, 2000), p. 101.

[12] Duffy, *Stripping of the Altars*, p. 502.

[13] David Loades, *Mary Tudor* (Stroud: Amberley Publishing, 2012), p. 57, citing Thomas Nearne, *Letters and Papers: Sylloge Epistolarum* (Oxford, 1716), p. x, 11137; MacCulloch, *Thomas Cromwell*, p. 350.

[14] John Edwards, *Mary I: The Daughter of Time* (London: Penguin Monarchs, 2017), pp. 23–5.

[15] John Foxe, *The Acts and Monuments* (London: 1583), pp. 1769–70.

[16] Foxe, *Acts and Monuments*, p. 1770.

[17] Diarmaid MacCulloch, *The Reformation: A History* (Penguin, 2003), p. 322.

[18] Duffy, *Stripping of the Altars*, p. 533.

[19] MacCulloch, *Thomas Cranmer*, p. 589.

[20] MacCulloch, *Thomas Cranmer*, p. 603.

[21] MacCulloch, *Thomas Cranmer*, p. 603.

Chapter 13

[1] Cited in David Starkey, *Elizabeth I* (London: Chatto and Windus, 2000), pp. 243–4.

[2] Helen Castor, *Elizabeth I: A Study in Insecurity* (London: Monarch Series, Penguin, 2018), p. 9.

[3] J. E. Neale, *Elizabeth I and her Parliaments* (London: Cape, 1953), p. 57, citing Strype, *Annals*, 1.i.154.

[4] Neale, *Elizabeth I and her Parliaments*, Vol. I, p. 395.

[5] Duffy, *Stripping of the Altars*, p. 565.

[6] Duffy, *Reformation Divided*, p. 134.

7   Duffy, *Reformation Divided*, p. 177, citing Martin's translation of the Rheims Bible.

8   Bridgen, *New World, Lost Worlds*, p. 328.

9   John Jewel, *The Apology of the Church of England* (USA: A Traffic Out Reprint, 2016), p. 8.

10 Calvin, *Institutes*, Book IV, ch. lxii, pp. 256–79, and surely Augustine of Hippo's argument.

11 Mark Kishlansky, *A Monarchy Transformed* (Penguin, 1997), p. 72.

12 Richard Hooker, *Of the Lawes of Ecclesiastical Politie*, pp. 394–5.

13 Neale, *Elizabeth I and her Parliaments*, Vol. II pp. 388ff.

14 Kishlansky, *A Monarchy Transformed*, p. 64.

Chapter 14

1   Kishlansky, *A Monarchy Transformed*, p. 67.

2   Donne, *Poetry and Prose*, p. 236.

3   David Edwards, *Christian England*, Vol. II (London: Collins, 1981–4; Fount, 1982–5), p. 245.

4   Bertrand Russell, *History of Western Philosophy* (London: Routledge, 2007), p. 504.

5   Hugh Trevor Roper, *Archbishop Laud* (Sheffield: Phoenix Press, 2000), p. 85.

6   Kishlansky, *A Monarchy Transformed*, p. 142.

7   Christopher Hill, *God's Englishman: Oliver Cromwell and the English Revolution* (London: Weidenfeld and Nicolson, 1970), p. 55.

8   Kishlansky, *A Monarchy Transformed*, p. 161.

9   Leanda de Lisle, *The White King* (London: Chatto and Windus, 2017), p. 262, citing *King Charles His Tryall*, 1649, p. 5.

10 De Lisle, *The White King*, p. 276.

11 De Lisle, *The White King*, p. 275.

12 Hill, *God's Englishman*, p. 109, citing *Leveller Manifestoes*, ed. D. M. Wolfe, p. 370 and p. 366.

13 Hill, *God's Englishman*, p. 136.

14 Hill, *God's Englishman*, p. 143.

Chapter 15

1   Vera Brittain, *In the Steps of John Bunyan* (London: Rich and Cowan, 1950), p. 202.

2   *School for Scandal* is the name of a Restoration comedy of 1777 by Richard Sheridan.

3   Kishlansky, *A Monarchy Transformed*, p. 255.

4   John Milton, *Complete Works of John Milton*, ed. Marjorie Nicholson (London: Bantam Classic, 1966), Sonnet XIX (1655), p. 198.

5   John Aubrey, *Brief Lives* (New York: Vintage, 2016), p. 202.

6   Rob Iliffe, *Newton* (Oxford: Oxford University Press, 2007), p. 8.

7   Iliffe, *Newton*, p. 33, and see Augustine of Hippo, *Confessions*, Book XXX, in which Augustine explores the nature of memory.

8   Iliffe, *Newton*, p. 99.

9   John Dunn, *Locke* (Oxford: Oxford University Press, 2003), p. 1.

10 Dunn, *Locke*, p. 95, citing *The Correspondence of John Locke*, ed. E. S. Beer, Vol. VI (Oxford: Clarendon Press, 1975), pp. 294–5.

11 Dunn, *Locke*, p. 87.

12 For the *Quo Warranto* procedure, see David Womersley, *James II: The Last Catholic King* (London: Penguin, 2015), p. 52.

13 That is, it was larger than William the Conqueror and Henry VII's invading armies.

14 Edward Gregg, *Queen Anne* (London: Routledge and Kegan Paul, 1980), p. 90.

15 Ophelia Field, *The Favourite* (Sceptre, 2003), p. 240, citing Arthur Maynwaring, *Four Letters to a Friend in North Britain—Upon Publishing the Trial of Dr Sacheverall* (London, 1710).

16 G. M. Trevelyan, *England Under Queen Anne, Vol. I: Blenheim* (London: Fontana, 1965), pp. 295–6.

Chapter 16

1   The Old Pretender was the son of James II and known as the Jacobite, from the Latin *Jacobus* for James.

2   Trevelyan, *England Under Queen Anne, Vol. I*, pp. 63–4, citing *Charter of a Low Churchman* (London, 1702), p. 26.

3   A clerical necktie or cravat.

4   Trevelyan, *England Under Queen Anne, Vol. I*, citing Dean Swift's *Country Parson*, p. 61.

5   B. W. Hill, *Sir Robert Walpole* (London: Hamish Hamilton, 1988), pp. 174–5.

6   Andrew Thompson, *George II* (New Haven, CT: Yale University Press, 2011), p. 74.

7   Romney Sedgwick, ed., *Lord Hervey's Journal, Vol. II* (London: The King's Printers, 1931), p. 457.

8   Stanley Ayling, *John Wesley* (HarperCollins, 1979), p. 24.

9   Ayling, *John Wesley*, p. 21.

10 John Wesley, *Journal of John Wesley*, Vol. I, p. 61.

11 Wesley, *Journal of John Wesley*, Vol. I, p. 74.

12 Wesley, *Journal of John Wesley*, Vol. I, p. 102.

13 John Pollock, *George Whitfield* (London: Hodder and Stoughton, 1972), p. 17.

14 Wesley, *Journal of John Wesley*, Vol. I, p. 207.

15 Wesley, *Journal of John Wesley*, Vol. I, p. 209.

16 Wesley, *Journals*, Vol. I, p. 233.

17 Edwards, *Christian England*, Vol. III, p. 69.

18 Wesley, *Journals*, Vol. I, p. 544.

19 Wesley, *Journals*, Vol. II, p. 219.

20 Stephen Tomkins, *John Wesley* (Lion Books, 2003), p. 170.

21 Wesley, *Journals*, Vol. IV, p. 133.

22 Wesley, *Journals*, Vol. IV, p. 322.

23 Ayling, *John Wesley*, p. 230.

24 Ayling, *John Wesley*, p. 231.

25 For example, "Amazing Grace" and "Glorious Things of Thee are Spoken" by John Newton (1725–1807); "Love Divine All Loves Excelling, Jesus the Name High Over All" by Charles Wesley (1707–88); "God Moves in a Mysterious Way" and "Oh! For a Closer Walk with God" by William Cowper (1731–1800); "As I survey the Wondrous Cross, Blessings Abound Where'er He Reigns" by Isaac Watts (1674–1748).

26 David Cecil, *The Stricken Deer* (London: Constable & Co, 1971), p. 32.

27 James King and Charles Ryskamp, eds, *Letters and Prose Writings of William Cowper*, Vol. II (Oxford: Oxford University Press, 1981), p. 469.

28 Jonathan Keates, *Handel: The Man and His Music* (Bournemouth: Pimlico, 2009), p. 6.

29 Keates, *Handel*, p. 280.

30 Paul Langford, *Eighteenth-Century Britain* (Oxford University Press, 2005), p. 69.

Chapter 17

1 Linda Colley, *Britons Forging the Nation 1707–1837* (Yale University Press, 1992), citing J. C. D. Clark, *English Society, 1688–1832* (New York: Cambridge University Press, 1985), p. 236.

2 Richard Holmes, *Coleridge Early Visions* (London: Hodder and Stoughton, 1990), p. 33.

3 William Doyle, *The French Revolution* (Oxford: Oxford University Press, 2001), p. 111.

4 Colley, *Britons Forging the Nation*, p. 304.

5 Colley, citing David Brion Davis, *The Problem of Slavery in an Age of Revolution* (Oxford: Oxford University Press, 1975), p. 239.

6 John Pollock, *William Wilberforce* (London: Constable & Co, 1977), p. 75.

7 Pollock, *William Wilberforce*, p. 77.

8 William Hague, *William Wilberforce* (Harper Perennial, 2008), p. 144, citing Pollock, *William Wilberforce*, p. 58.

9 Hague, *William Wilberforce*, p. 141.

10 Hague, *William Wilberforce*, p. 205.

11 Hague, *William Wilberforce*, p. 325.

12 Hague, *William Wilberforce*, p. 354.

13 Bernard Cornwall, *Waterloo* (London: Collins, 2015), p. 31.

14 Adam Zamoyski, *The Rites of Peace* (New York: Harper, 2008), citing M. H. Weil, *Les Dessous du Congres de Vienne*, Vol. 1 (Paris, 1917), p. 498.

15 Christopher Hibbert, *George III* (London: Viking, 1988), p. 404, footnote.

16 Elizabeth Longford, *Wellington: Pillar of State* (London: Weidenfeld & Nicolson, 1972), p. 69.

17 Colley, *Britons Forging the Nation*, p. 333, citing Edward Porritt, *The Unreformed House of Commons: Parliamentary Representation Before 1832*, Vol. II, 1963 edn, p. 468.

18 Eric J. Evans, *England Before the Reform Act: Politics and Society 1815–1832* (London: Longmans, 1990), p. 126.

19 Evans, *England Before the Reform Act*, p. 129.

20 David Cannadine, *Victorious Century: The United Kingdom, 1800–1906* (Penguin, 2018), p. 193.

21 W. A. Hay, *Lord Liverpool: A Political Life* (Woodbridge: Boydell & Brewer, 2018), p. 189, citing *Lord Brougham* (Woodbridge: The Boydell Press, 2018).

Chapter 18

1 Cannadine, *The Victorious Century*, p. 183.

2 Owen Chadwick, *The Victorian Church*, Vol. I (London: SCM Press, 1987), p. 133.

3 Chadwick, *Victorian Church*, Vol. I, p. 151.

4 Chadwick, *Victorian Church*, Vol. I, p. 143.

5 Chadwick, *Victorian Church*, Vol. I, p. 174.

6 Cannadine, *The Victorious Century*, p. 127.

7 Chadwick, *Victorian Church*, Vol. I, p. 43.

8 Henry Chadwick, "Newman's Significance for the Anglican Church", centenary essay in *Newman: A Man for Our Time*, ed. D. Brown (London: SPCK, 1990), p. 57.

9   John Cornwell, *Newman's Unquiet Grave* (New York: Continuum, 2011), p. 52.

10 Chadwick, "Newman's Significance for the Anglican Church", p. 58.

11 Chadwick, *Victorian Church*, Vol. I, p. 57, citing "Littleton's Diary" in *Three Diaries*, ed. A. Aspinall (London: Williams and Norgate, 1952), p. 301.

12 Chadwick, *Newman: A Man for Our Time*, p. 54.

13 Chadwick, *Newman: A Man for Our Time*, p. 169.

14 Chadwick, *Newman: A Man for Our Time*, p. 183.

15 Chadwick, *Newman: A Man for Our Time*, p. 185.

16 Chadwick, *Newman: A Man for Our Time*, p. 188.

17 Chadwick, *Newman: A Man for Our Time*, p. 207.

18 Douglas Hurd, *Robert Peel* (Manila, Philippines: Phoenix, 2007), pp. 50-1.

19 Hurd, *Robert Peel*, pp. 325-7.

20 Robert Blake, citing Disraeli's speech in the House of Commons in *Disraeli* (London: Methuen, 1969), pp. 178-9.

21 The Chartist movement had made electoral reform its principal objective by organizing great meetings and huge petitions.

22 Jane Ridley, *Victoria: Queen, Matriarch, Empress* (London: Penguin, 2015), p. 46, citing Queen Victoria's letter to her uncle Leopold of Belgium (QVL vol. 2, p. 318).

23 Chadwick, *Victorian Church*, Vol. I, p. 461.

24 Chadwick, *Victorian Church*, Vol. I, p. 364.

25 Chadwick, *Victorian Church*, Vol. I, p. 291.

26 Chadwick, *Victorian Church*, Vol. I, p. 375.

27 Arnold Dallimore, *Spurgeon* (Edinburgh: Banner of Truth, 1985), pp. 18-19.

28 Dispensationalism is a theory that God's work in humanity is spread over independent separate dispensations with their own characteristics.

29 Georgina Battiscombe, *Shaftesbury* (London: Constable & Co., 1974), p. 243.

30 Cecil Woodham-Smith, *Florence Nightingale* (London: Constable & Son, 1950), p. 32.

31 Herbert was the second son of the Earl of Pembroke of Wilton House and of a Russian mother, Catherine Vorontsov. He remained a close associate of Florence until his early death, partly from overwork.

Chapter 19

1   Ridley, *Victoria*, p. 63.

2   Robert Rhodes James, *Albert Prince Consort* (London: Hamish Hamilton, 1983), p. 273.

3   Roger Fulford (ed.), *Dearest Mama: The Private Correspondence of Queen Victoria and the Crown Princess of Prussia 1861–1864* (London: Evans Brothers, 1981), p. 29.

4   Jane Ridley, *Bertie: A Life of Edward VII* (London: Vintage, 2013), p. 158.

5   Charles Dickens, *A Tale of Two Cities* (London: Chapman & Hall, 1859).

6   Chadwick, *Victorian Church*, Vol. I, p. 495.

7   Chadwick, *Victorian Church*, Vol. II, p. 274.

8   Chadwick, *Victorian Church*, Vol. II, p. 10.

9   E. M. Goulburn, *Life of Burgon*, ii, 291, 404, cited by Chadwick, *Victorian Church*, Vol. II, p. 54.

10 Chadwick, *Victorian Church*, Vol. II, p. 55.

11 Chadwick, *Victorian Church*, Vol. II, p. 63.

12 Chadwick, *Victorian Church*, Vol. II, p. 106.

13 Eric J. Evans, *Parliamentary Reform c 1770–1918* (Longman Pearson, 2000), p. 132.

14 Richard Aldous, *The Lion and the Unicorn: Gladstone vs Disraeli* (London: Pimlico, 2007), pp. 263–5.

15 Niall Ferguson, *Empire: How Britain Made the Modern World* (London: Penguin, 2004), p. xxvii.

16 Ferguson, *Empire*, p. 122.

17 Ferguson, *Empire*, p. 154.

18 Ferguson, *Empire*, pp. 123–4.

19 Harold Lewis, *The Church Rambler* (1876), p. 316.

20 Chadwick, *Victorian Church*, Vol. II, p. 183, citing Walsham How, *Lighter Moments*, p. 37.

21 Chadwick, *Victorian Church*, Vol. II, p. 184.

22 Chadwick, *Victorian Church*, Vol. II, p. 224.

23 Chadwick, *Victorian Church*, Vol. I, p. 264.

24 See A. N. Wilson on Kingsley and his wedding night, *The Victorians* (London: Hutchinson, 2002), pp. 295–304, esp. p. 300.

25 Cornwell, *Newman's Unquiet Grave*, p. 167.

26 Lance Pierson, *Hopkins and Milton: 2018 Hopkins Society Annual Lecture* (Hopkins Society, 2019).

27 Ferguson, *Empire*, p. 251.

28 Whitworth family papers and the "Obituary of Colonel Hanford Flood" in the *Kilkenny Times*, 1921.

29 Ferguson, *Empire*, p. 267.

Chapter 20

1 Niall Ferguson, *Empire*, p. 380.
2 Peter Clarke, *Hope and Glory, Britain 1900–2000* (London: Penguin, 2004), pp. 56–9.
3 Adrian Hastings, *A History of English Christianity, 1920–1985* (London: Collins, 1986), p. 34.
4 Hastings, *A History of English Christianity*, pp. 36–40.
5 Hastings, *A History of English Christianity*, p. 60.
6 Hastings, *A History of English Christianity*, p. 75.
7 Hastings, *A History of English Christianity*, pp. 76–7.
8 Hastings, *A History of English Christianity*, p. 147, citing "English Ultramontanism and Christian Education", *The Clergy Review* (1977), pp. 266–78.
9 Hastings, *A History of English Christianity*, p. 155.
10 G. K. Chesterton, *Orthodoxy*, p. 53.
11 David Stevenson, *1914–1918: The History of the First World War* (London: Penguin, 2005), p. 41.
12 Margaret MacMillan, *The War that Ended the Peace* (London: Macmillan, 2014), p. 255, citing Stig Förster, "Facing 'People's War'", *Journal of Strategic Studies*, Vol. 10, no. 2 (1987), pp. 209–30.
13 MacMillan, *The War that Ended the Peace*, p. 593.
14 Georgina Howell, *Queen of the Desert* (London: Macmillan, 2006), p. 232.
15 Constance Babington Smith, *John Masefield* (Oxford: Oxford University Press, 1978), p. 125.
16 Whitworth family papers: "Correspondence of John Masefield with Miss Annie Hanford-Flood"; also C. Babington Smith, *John Masefield*, p. 12.
17 William Purcell, *Woodbine Willie* (London: Mowbrays, 1962), p. 131.
18 Robert Graves, *Goodbye to All That* (London: Penguin Classics, 2000), p. 164.
19 Siegfried Sassoon, *Diaries 1915–1918*, ed. Rupert Hart Davies (London: Faber & Faber, 1983), p. 107.
20 Graves, *Goodbye to All That*, p. 157.
21 George Orwell, *The Road to Wigan Pier* (London: Penguin Classics, 2001), p. 129.
22 Margaret MacMillan, *The Peacemakers* (London: John Murray, 2002), p. 421.
23 R. J. Q. Adams, *Balfour: The Last Grandee* (London: Thistle Publishing, 2013), p. 433.
24 MacMillan, *Peacemakers*, p. 470.
25 F. A. Iremonger, *William Temple* (London: Oxford University Press, 1948), pp. 387–427.
26 Martin Gilbert, *Churchill: A Life* (London: Heinemann, 1991), p. 475.
27 Hastings, *A History of English Christianity*, p. 188.

28 Hastings, *A History of English Christianity*, p. 189, citing George Scott, *The Roman Catholics* (1967), p. 85.

29 Owen Chadwick, *Hensley Henson: A Study in Friction between Church and State* (Oxford: Oxford University Press, 1984), p. 158.

30 Chadwick, *Hensley Henson*, p. 175.

31 Alister McGrath, *C. S. Lewis: A Life* (London: Hodder and Stoughton, 2013), p. 139, citing *Surprised by Joy*, p. 266.

32 A. J. Nicholls, *Weimar and the Rise of Hitler* (London: Macmillan, 1970), p. 176.

33 F. W. Fox, *Reinhold Niebuhr: A Biography* (San Francisco: Harper & Row, 1985), p. 91.

34 Hastings, *A History of English Christianity*, p. 293.

35 Hastings, *A History of English Christianity*, p. 297.

36 Michael Ramsey, *The Gospel and the Catholic Church* (Peabody, MA: Hendrickson, 2009), p. 7.

37 T. S. Eliot, *The Idea of a Christian Society* (London: Faber and Faber, 1939), p. 97.

38 Bernard Crick, *George Orwell: A Life* (New York: Secker and Warburg, 1980), p. 6 and p. 199.

39 Hastings, *A History of English Christianity*, p. 279.

40 Hastings, *A History of English Christianity*, p. 311.

41 Hastings, *A History of English Christianity*, p. 348.

42 Hastings, *A History of English Christianity*, p. 348.

43 John Butler, *The Red Dean*, citing "Letter to Cosmo Lang" (London: Scala Publishers, 2011), p. 72.

44 Eric Matexas, *Bonhoeffer: Pastor, Martyr, Prophet, Spy* (Nashville, TN: Thomas Nelson, 2010), p. 198.

45 Matexas, *Bonhoeffer*, p. 401.

46 Jack Colville, *The Fringes of Power: Downing Street Diaries 1939–1955* (London: Weidenfeld and Nicolson, 2011), p. 193.

47 Family papers of the Revd Tim Wood, West Woodhay, Smith's nephew.

48 Hastings, *A History of English Christianity*, p. 385, citing J. L. Wilson, "A Prisoner of the Japanese", *The Listener*, October 1946, pp. 555–6.

49 Hastings, *A History of English Christianity*, p. 384, citing M. Moynihan, ed., *People at War 1939–1945* (1973), p. 52.

50 Hastings, *A History of English Christianity*, p. 395.

Chapter 21

1   Peter Clarke, *Hope and Glory* (London: Penguin, 2004), p. 5, and Kenneth Harris, *Attlee* (London: Weidenfeld and Nicolson, 1982), pp. 3–5.

2   Roy Jenkins, *Churchill* (London: Macmillan, 2001), p. 843.

3   Evelyn Waugh, *Brideshead Revisited* (London: Penguin, 1945), pp. 176–7.

4   William Purcell, *Fisher of Lambeth* (London: Hodder and Stoughton, 1969), pp. 154–8.

5   Hastings, *A History of English Christianity*, p. 264.

6   Hastings, *A History of English Christianity*, p. 478.

7   Timothy Dudley Smith, *John Stott: A Global Ministry* (Downers Grove, IL: InterVarsity Press, 2001), p. 120.

8   Smith, *John Stott*, p. 127.

9   Michael Ramsey, *The Gospel and the Catholic Church*.

10 Smith, *John Stott*, p. 274.

11 Owen Chadwick, *Michael Ramsey: A Life* (London: SCM Press, 1998), pp. 228–30.

12 Chadwick, *Michael Ramsey*, pp. 257–8.

13 Chadwick, *Michael Ramsey*, p. 259.

14 Humphrey Carpenter, *Robert Runcie: The Reluctant Archbishop* (London: Hodder and Stoughton, 1996), p. 252.

15 Smith, *John Stott*, p. 160.

16 Smith, *John Stott*, p. 162.

17 Carpenter, *Runcie*, pp. 217–19.

18 *Faith in the City Report* (London: Church House Publishing, 1985).

19 Charles Moore, *Margaret Thatcher: The Authorized Biography, Vol. II* (Allen Lane, 2015), p. 258.

20 Carpenter, *Runcie*, p. 346.

21 Anthony Howard, *Basil Hume* (London: Hodder Headline, 2005), p. 145.

22 Howard, *Basil Hume*, p. 147.

23 Bishops: 39 for, 13 against; Clergy: 176:74 against; Laity 169:82 against. George Carey, *Know The Truth* (San Francisco: Harper Perennial, 2005), p. 144.

24 Rupert Shortt, *Rowan's Rule* (London: Hodder, 2014), p. 95, citing *Ad Tuendam Fidem*, John Paul II's Apostolic Letter of 1998, drafted by Ratzinger.

25 John Major, *John Major: The Autobiography* (London: HarperCollins, 2000), p. 387.

Chapter 22

[1] David Goodhart, *The Road to Anywhere* (Harmondsworth: Penguin, 2017), p. 136.

[2] Theodore Zeldin, *An Intimate History of Humanity* (Jerusalem: Minerva, 1994), p. 470.

[3] "The Thatcher Legacy", *Times*, Friday 23 November 1990, p. 17.

[4] Janet Fife and Gilo (eds), *Letters to a Broken Church* (London: Ekklesia, 2019).

[5] Lambeth Conference, 1998, Section I.1—Affirmation and Adoption of the United Nations Universal Declaration of Human Rights, <https://www.anglicancommunion.org/resources/document-library/lambeth-conference/1998/section-i-called-to-full-humanity/section-i10-human-sexuality>.

[6] Section 13 of the Jerusalem Declaration of 29 June 2008.

[7] Shortt, *Rowan's Rule*, p. 473.

[8] Shortt, *Rowan's Rule*, p. 413.

[9] Shortt, *Rowan's Rule*, p. 221.

[10] Tom Wright, *How God Became King: The Forgotten Story of the Gospels* (London: SPCK, 2012).

[11] <http://www.vatican.va/roman_curia/synod/documents/rc_synod_doc_20151026_relazione-finale-xiv-assemblea_en.html>.

[12] Pope Francis, *Evangelii Gaudium* (London: Catholic Truth Society, 2013), p. 126.

[13] Francis, *Evangelii Gaudium*, p. 126.

[14] Pope Francis, *Laudato Si'* (London: Catholic Truth Society, 2015), p. 11.

[15] Andrew Atherstone, *Archbishop Justin Welby: Risk-Taker and Reconciler* (London: Darton, Longman and Todd, 2014), p. 169.

[16] Justin Welby, *Reimagining Britain* (London: Bloomsbury Continuum, 2018), p. 236.

Chapter 23

[1] Thomas Cranmer, A *Confutation of Unwritten Verities*, ed. The Parker Society (Cambridge: Cambridge University Press, 1846), p. 9.

[2] Gregory the Great, *The Book of Pastoral Rule* (New York: SVSP, 2007).

[3] Betty Radice (ed.), *The Letters of the Younger Pliny* (London: Penguin, 1963).

[4] Bede, *Ecclesiastical History* (London: Dent Everyman, 1965), ch. XIII, p. 91.

[5] Augustine, *The Confessions of St Augustine*, tr. Henry Chadwick (Oxford: Oxford University Press, Classics, 2008), p. 3.

Index

EU GPSR Authorized Representative:

LOGOS EUROPE, 9 rue Nicolas Poussin, 17000 La Rochelle, France

contact@logoseurope.eu